The Competitive Economy:
Selected Readings

THE COMPETITIVE ECONOMY:
Selected Readings

edited by Yale Brozen

GENERAL LEARNING PRESS
250 James Street
Morristown, New Jersey 07960

Manufactured in the United States of America.

Published simultaneously in Canada.

Library of Congress
Catalog Card Number 74-76516
ISBN 0–382–18070–4

INTRODUCTION

The custom of treating the word "oligopoly" as a synonym for high concentration[1] in a market[2] has conditioned attitudes toward high concentration. The custom of treating the word "monopoly" as a synonym for a single seller also has had this effect, since oligopoly and monopoly are labels of opprobrium in many minds.

To economists, oligopoly usually means interdependent action among firms, resulting in tacit collusion equivalent to the explicit agreements made by cartels. Monopoly usually means the control over supply that occurs when a single seller's market cannot be entered by other suppliers. Yet suggestions have been made that antitrust law be amended to define highly concentrated markets as oligopolistic whether or not tacit or explicit agreement exists. The suggested amendments would have the government divide oligopolistic firms, defined as those with more than some specified percentage of some concentrated ("oligopolistic") market, into smaller firms.

The Hart Bill, currently before Congress, would break up large firms where four or fewer sell (the usual word is "control") more than 50 percent of the product sold in a market. The notion that such an addition to the antitrust arsenal should be enacted is an old one. It was proposed by Professor Henry Simons in the 1930s. It was reiterated in the Landis Committee (sponsored by the Twentieth Century Fund) report and recommendations. Many of the provisions in the Hart Bill or their equivalent appeared earlier as the "recommendations"[3] of Professors Donald Turner and Carl Kaysen in their book on antitrust policy (1959) and in the recommendations of the White House Antitrust Task Force (1969).

The attack on firms that are large (as made in former Attorney General John Mitchell's speech on that subject) or that have a large share of a market might be thought to spring from the general decline in regard for our institutions. But such attacks were even more vehement at the turn of the century. Between the turn of the century and the 1930s many economists were as denunciatory of competition as many now are of oligopoly. That fashion culminated in the National Industrial Recovery Act of the 1930s. It suspended the antitrust laws and made cartels compulsory. Now the question is, will the current fashion culminate in the passage of a Hart Bill?

Agreement that competition in markets is preferable to any alternative prevails more widely among economists now than at

---

[1] High concentration is variously defined as four firms with sometimes 50 percent, sometimes 60 percent, sometimes 70 percent, sometimes 80 percent or more of the business in a market.

[2] A market may be defined in terms of regional, national, or international extent and in terms of a single product or a group of products encompassing more or less close substitutes or a group of suppliers whose facilities can be readily used to supply each other's markets.

[3] Professor Kaysen, testifying in 1965 before the Subcommittee on Antitrust and Monopoly of the Senate Judiciary Committee, disavowed these "recommendations." He said, "Now, the context in which the proposal . . . was placed in this volume was a discussion of possible alternatives to or expansions of the Sherman Act. And let me say that we were writing in an academic or speculative fashion. We were not trying to draft a statute. . . ." (*Hearings on Economic Concentration*, Part 2, March 17, 1965, p. 554). Earlier in his testimony (p. 552P) Professor Kaysen said, ". . . if you want to look at a particular industry then you cannot answer the question of how competitive is that industry, merely by looking at the concentration figures." At a later point (p. 556), he argues that "it would be undesirable public policy . . . to accept the argument . . . that concentration itself gives rise to the presumption of illegality . . . it doesn't seem to me . . . that it is a good idea."

perhaps any previous time. But what, exactly, does competition mean? The first group of readings in this volume explores this question. The readings deal primarily with structural questions (for example, ease of entry and number of firms).

As many economists emphasize, conduct and performance must also be examined. If a market produces the *same* results as those associated with the rivalry of a large number of firms—that is, if price is pushed toward equality with long-run marginal cost —or *superior* results—that is, if long-run marginal cost is lowered more rapidly and price is lowered at least as rapidly—should we be concerned with the fact that firms may be few in number?[4]

Some of the readings point out that markets may be ideally competitive, in the conduct and performance sense, with only one or two firms in each market. In any case, there are large questions to be examined concerning the process by which disequilibrium is converted into or moves toward a long-run equilibrium. Do we prefer a large numbers structure that may attain a long-run competitive equilibrium, or a small numbers structure which, it is sometimes argued, moves the equilibrium position itself favorably at a more rapid pace than a many firm occupancy of the market would? Do large numbers of firms in a disequilibrium situation behave more competitively or any differently than small numbers? As Professor George Stigler has remarked, ". . . the possible paradoxes in applying

the theory of stationary economics to historical developments . . . clearly poses the problem of constructing a definition of competition which is suited to firms in a changing economy."[5]

Readings selected for Part II bear on the relationship between competition and concentration. First, how should we measure concentration? What does a number, and which number, tell us about which industries should be judged to be "concentrated"? Then, what are the consequences or correlates of concentration as measured in empirical studies? Finally, do increases in concentration come primarily from a drive to monopolize or oligopolize or is the market simply selecting more efficient organizations? Is high concentration, where it occurs, a consequence of competition with the efficient firms producing products preferred by consumers at the prices charged winning the market? Does attempting to prevent high concentration mean the stifling rather than the promotion of competition?

An aversion to concentration is usually founded on the belief that tacit, if not explicit, collusion is more likely to occur than in less concentrated markets. In Part III, a number of selections deal with the ease or difficulty of arriving at explicit, collusive agreements and the durability of these agreements. If explicit agreements are made with great difficulty and success is fleeting, tacit agreements may be viewed as unlikely and, certainly, impermanent.

On the other hand, even if tacit agreement is unlikely or unsuccessful, will not major firms in concentrated industries find predatory threats and actions impeding entry useful for protecting their positions? Turn of the century economists were not worried even by 100 percent concentration as long as potential entrants stood in the wings. They were worried that potential entrants would not come on stage at the appropriate time, however, for fear of predatory retaliation. The Federal Trade Commission —designed to prevent unfair or predatory

---

[4] Professor Clare Griffin, testifying in 1955 before the United States Senate Subcommittee on Antitrust and Monopoly of the Committee on the Judiciary, put the point in these words:

"I think we should recognize that the pattern of many small concerns in an industry may have the effect of keeping price close to cost and at any moment of time the resulting narrow profit margin may yield an advantage to the consumer. But in a longer view, more is to be gained by reducing cost or improving the product. Of course, both results are desirable, but if there is any merit in the theory of progress which I have described, it may be that the two are not always compatible." (*A Study of the Antitrust Laws, Senate Hearings,* Part I, June 9, 1955, p. 387).

[5] "Introduction," *Business Concentration and Price Policy* 7 (1955). Reprinted as selection 12 in this volume.

acts—was largely a product of those fears. The final group of articles in Part IV of this volume deals analytically and historically with various aspects of unfair competition.

In selecting material for this text, summary or critical pieces were preferred where available. They report previous work as well as examine some of these previous endeavors. Many classic pieces are omitted because of their availability in other collections and because of the compulsions of limited space. This anthology is intended to be complementary to those now available rather than competitive with them.

CONTENTS

I · THE REQUISITES OF COMPETITION

Part I–A · *Entry*

Concentration of business in the hands of a few firms was of little concern to late nineteenth and early twentieth-century economists, provided resources were mobile. Ease of entry and the availability of potential entrants was, to them, a sufficient guarantee of competitive performance. Consolidation of current supply in the hands of a few firms was even felt to be desirable. Consolidation would avoid wastes such as competitive advertising, duplicate sales forces, and cross-hauling. Aside from the elimination of these alleged wastes, there were the gains to be achieved from economies of scale.

Early decisions under the newly enacted Sherman Act reflected this view. The Justice Department lost its case against American Sugar Refining's acquisition of the E. C. Knight Company (and other sugar refiners) despite this placing 98 per cent of refining capacity east of the Rockies in American Sugar's hands. The decision rested largely on the fact that American had done nothing to impede (restrain) entry into interstate or international commerce. It had not required those selling their firms to agree not to re-enter the sugar refining business.

It might be argued that the court was borne out by experience in the industry. Sugar refining capacity outside of American's control grew to 28.7 per cent of the total by 1899. The growth of non-American capacity began as soon as it became known in 1892 that American was purchasing the four firms in Philadelphia and taking control of almost all the then existing capacity. Sugar refining margins were elevated in 1892 and 1893 to 25 and 40 per cent above the level in the year preceding the merger, but they fell back in 1894 almost to the 1891 level. Margins sank 12 per cent below the 1891 level by 1898 and 40 per cent below in 1899.

The opening reading, an excerpt from Professor Winston's 1924 piece on monopoly, expresses the early twentieth-century view of what makes the economy competitive and of the competitive quality of the American economy. Increased mobility (potential and actual entry) and lowered transportation costs had improved the competitiveness of the economy while it decreased the number of firms (although it increased the number actually or potentially operative in any small market segment).

The second selection argues that the immortal corporation serves to increase the supply of efficient entrepreneurial activity, as compared to a world of mortal businesses with life spans dependent on that of their founders and the capabilities of the descendants of founders. This large supply of entrepreneurship serves to force competitive performance if entry to any market is open. It concludes that the Antitrust Division should devote itself to demolishing barriers to entry, rather than concerning itself with deconcentrating industry or preventing concentration, if it wants competition to prevail as the organizing force in the economy. The selection warns, however, against accepting standard assertions that advertising or absolute cost advantages are barriers. It points to other barriers as the important competition preventing forces.

Professor Demsetz argues, in selection 3, that the absolute cost advantage of a "natural monopoly" does not give it the power to set monopoly prices if there are no barriers to bidding for business by firms not already resident in an industry. In selection 4, Professor Stigler suggests that the ability of oligopolists to extract any more than a competitive return depends upon "the conditions of entry of new firms and expansion of existing firms in an industry."

1. The Chimera of Monopoly

AMBROSE PARE WINSTON

Business Size and Monopoly

The opinion has come to prevail almost universally that the growth of large-scale industry within a half-century has marked the end of competition. Mr. and Mrs. Webb in their book on the *Decay of Capitalist Civilization* (dealing with the United States as well as England) have attributed the downfall of capitalism to a replacement of the competitive regime by monopoly. Mr. Eliot Jones in his *Trust Problem in the United States* concludes that it is impossible to "restore competition." This understanding of recent industrial history arises from a misinterpretation of one set of facts and an entire oversight of another group of processes which have given the industrial activity of our day an intensity of competition unknown to any earlier generation.

First, it should be understood that increased size in manufacturing organization is not the same thing as monopoly. The increase in size has resulted chiefly from improvements in transportation. When, one hundred years ago, it cost $249 to send a ton of iron from Philadelphia to Erie, the market for iron from any producing center was limited to a small radius. When a ton of iron can be sent from Pittsburgh to Vancouver for $18 the marketing radius is wide. The industrial unit was necessarily small when the market was narrow; it is large in an extensive marketing area. The change in size of factories and size of marketing areas does not mean a change in the number of producers within reach of the buyer. The twentieth-century consumer buys from a large factory selling across half a continent; his

nineteenth-century ancestor bought from a little shop or mill which sent its products across half a county.

A Local Situation

In the small gristmill a family had few mills to choose from and paid the same price (or toll) to everyone. The millers could readily agree on prices without interference by officers of the law. In my Illinois village we were confronted when we bought meat, not by a beef trust, but by an entire consolidation of the beef industry in one person, namely, Joe C. We bought our beef from him or went without. Later Charley D. came in—we dealt not with a Big Five and two hundred independents described in the Federal Trade Commission report, but with a Big Two. The rich man of the region in a neighboring town had his meat sent in from a distance. This doubled the cost. With that one exception and occasional purchases in the winter of frozen beef from farmers by the "quarter," not one family in that region ever found relief from the power of our Beef Trust.

Not only has the substitution of large for small producing units resulted in no weakening of competition; more than that, it is an obvious deduction, from facts known to all observers, even from the hackneyed commonplaces of recent industrial history, that, with and because of the growth of capitalism, competition has in our day become intense and swift and sure beyond all previous human experience.

What do we mean by competition? We ought to mean the ready movement of the factors of production—labor or productive instruments—toward those employments in which prices are exceptionally high and profits large. That is, competition is substan-

"The Chimera of Monopoly" by Ambrose Paré Winston first appeared in *The Atlantic Monthly* (1924) and was reprinted in *The Freeman* (Sept. 1960).

tially "mobility." Two things are necessary for this mobility: (a) knowledge, among persons outside of the high-priced employment, that it is profitable; (b) the possibility of increasing the use of capital and productive energy in employments whose superior attractiveness has become known. In both respects the tendency of recent industrial evolution has been toward making competition more prompt.

An even more striking factor in the situation before us is the fluidity, the mobility of productive forces, now that the craftsman has given way to the machine as the dominant factor in production. The skilled workman, having learned his trade, was immobile; he could not invade another craft and he had little fear of an invasion of his own field by unskilled men or by men of acquired ability unlike his own. Tasks like those which formerly required muscular strength and skill gained through long apprenticeship are now performed in a large and increasing percentage of cases by men of little strength and brief training. . . .

If labor is readily diverted from one employment to another by the allurement of profits, the other great factor in production is equally fluid. New capital—the current accumulation of surplus income—is unspecialized industrial protoplasm quickly turning in any direction, attracted by the hope of profit, creating new competing products with a promptness and certainty unknown in the age of handicraft.

The owners of investment capital and their advisers are looking incessantly for the most profitable opportunities for its employment. The earnings from oil, from steel, from the packing industry, from automobiles, from sugar, from commerce and shipping, flow into steel or automobiles or oil, or whatever gives greatest promise of high earnings. In the production of the chief staples, every sort of productive agency—labor, no longer specialized as in the past but adaptable to any use, and material of every kind—is at the disposal of any group of persons possessing the requisite number of dollars.

2. Competition, Efficiency, and Antitrust

YALE BROZEN

Economic theory tells that competition weeds out inefficiency. Competitive markets select those administrators of productive resources who employ the most efficient technology to produce the most efficacious (relatively most desired) products.[1] As a consequence of the competitive process, industry uses resources in the ways which maximize the flow of satisfactions to consumers.

If it happens that the most efficient producer operating at his most economic scale can supply the entire market, competition concentrates production in the hands of one firm. This the textbooks call "natural monopoly."[2] The courts may designate this as legal under the antitrust laws because the "monopoly" status was thrust upon the natural "monopolist." Reading some of the language of decisions of recent years, however, beginning with Judge Learned Hand's in the Alcoa case, I am dubious that a single seller could succeed in defending himself on these grounds unless he met certain tests.[3] If his product differed from that of his former competitors and was clearly superior enough in the eyes of all buyers that they willingly paid as high or higher price than that charged by other sellers, this defense might be accepted if his behavior has been pure. If he ever committed a sin, however, such as producing a special model of his product for a large buyer with whom he signed a requirements contract calling for the buyer to assign at least, let us say, three-quarters of his purchases to him before he invested in special tooling for the special model, he will be regarded as having unclean hands and be ruled guilty despite the superiority of his product. If he anticipated an expansion of the market and built capacity in time to supply the needs of his customers as their demand expanded, then su-

Reprinted by permission of *Journal of World Trade Law*, Volume 3, 1969.

Yale Brozen is Professor of Business Economics at the Graduate School of Business, University of Chicago.

This paper was delivered at the Business Economists' Conference, University of Chicago, 1 May 1969. The author is indebted to Betty Bock for her challenge to write this paper, to Joel Segall for the conversations which helped the author discard some of the obfuscations which encrust the field of industrial organization, and to Harold Demsetz for denting the stubbornness with which the author clings to his errors.

[1] A monopolist may be as efficient, as adaptive, and as innovative (Schumpeter argues more innovative, but he fails to consider the shelter provided by patents for investment in the development of new technology. Patents in many, perhaps most, instances provide as much opportunity to recoup and earn a return on such investment as a monopoly of a market.) as a competitive industry. However, he is as likely also to be a drone as a competitive firm. In that case, his protection from competition may keep him alive where a drone in a competitive market is less likely to survive and continue his maladministration.

[2] It is unfortunate that this term has been applied to a set of circumstances which may be far from monopoly in the sense that a single seller *controls* the market. If entry into a single seller's market is rapid when the price charged provides a more than compensatory return on the required investment, the single seller cannot control the price and cannot extract any more than the cost of capital as a return.

[3] Aaron Director and Edward H. Levi point out that Judge Hand distinguishes between a single seller status which has been "achieved" and one which has been "thrust upon" the firm. Although Alcoa tells us that, "the successful competitor having been urged to compete, must not be turned upon when he wins," any single seller status "achieved" by competing is illegal, judging by the outcome in Alcoa and the reasons given. As Director and Levi have pithily summarized this case: "Perhaps, then, the successful competitor can be turned upon when he wins because he has been told not to compete." "Law and the Future: Trade Regulation," *Northwestern Law Review*, Vol. 51 (1956), p. 286.

periority of a product and higher price than his former competitors would not preserve him from being ruled a transgressor.[4]

I am afraid that if a single seller succeeded in reaching this position with an inferior product for which he charged less, and enough less to offset its inferiority in the eyes of all buyers, our seller might be ruled as having engaged in predatory action despite this being the efficient way in which to use resources. Of course, if the other sellers he drives from the field by his greater efficiency and lower prices are larger companies engaged primarily in other markets, he would not be ruled in violation of the antitrust laws. In the latter case, he may be able to drive the other companies from the field legally. He may also collect triple damages from them. If they attempted to keep a toe hold in the market by reducing their

prices as he reduced his with his drive to larger volume and a more economical scale of operation, they are vulnerable.[5]

This is only one example of the conundrums that exist in our antitrust policy. These conundrums can be summarized in saying that the law as presently interpreted seems to say that firms should compete but should not win. Firms should be efficient enough to survive but, if more efficient, should not share the fruits of that greater efficiency with their customers. The relatively more efficient firms must not operate competitively; that is, they must not press the rate of output to the point where marginal cost approaches price if that rate of output is sufficient to supply most of the market, particularly if their efficiencies spring from the large scale provision of advertising. We have confused high concentration with monopoly and competitive activity by large firms with predatory behavior. We have taken descriptions of sufficient conditions for competition, such as a large number of firms, and confused them with necessary conditions.

If the U.S. Antitrust Division and the Federal Trade Commission are to permit the competition which will press efficiency in the economy to its optimum level, then they and the courts must learn what are the necessary conditions for competition. The leap beyond what is necessary to what is sufficient in some circumstances but not necessary is repressing competition when applied in inappropriate cases.[6] Unfortunately, although we economists are very sure of what are the sufficient conditions for competition to prevail, in some circumstances,

---

[4] Reading the Alcoa decision, a single seller who supplies the market less expensively than it would be supplied if the market were compelled to support two or more producing organizations cannot defend himself on the grounds that his status was "thrust" upon him if he *grew* to the scale of operation where he could realize the available economies of scale rather than inheriting his position by contraction of the market to where he was the only supplier left as a survivor from among a group of suppliers. Judge Hand tells us:

> "It was not inevitable that [Alcoa] should always anticipate increases in the demand for ingot and be prepared to supply them. Nothing compelled it to keep doubling and redoubling its capacity before others entered the field. It insists it never excluded competitors; but we can think of no more effective exclusion than progressively to embrace each new opportunity as it opened, and to face every newcomer with new capacity . . ."

Judge Hand felt that such growth is not natural or normal, but it is not at all clear what distinguishes this from natural or normal growth when there are economies of scale that can be attained by larger size, unless establishing a second plant is "unnatural" while enlarging an existing plant is natural. He does say:

> "A market may, for example, be so limited that it is impossible to produce at all and meet the cost of production except by a *plant* large enough to supply the whole demand" (emphasis supplied).

United States *v.* Aluminum Co. of America, 148 F. 2d 416 (2d Cir. 1945).

[5] W. Bowman, "Restraint of Trade by the Supreme Court: The Utah Pie Case," *Yale Law Journal,* November 1967.

[6] When the market can be more efficiently supplied by a single seller, the requirement that there be many sellers (one of the sufficient conditions when there are no economies of scale for a firm whose size approaches that of the market) means that an efficient seller dare *not compete* since this means he will win the market (he will "achieve" his status).

we are not at all sure of what are the necessary conditions in all circumstances.[7]

Open Entry Is the Necessary and Sufficient Condition to Maintain Competition

Professor Harold Demsetz has argued that a large number of producers is not a necessary condition for competition, although more than one bidder may be required.[8] He deals explicitly with the case where a single producer can be the most efficient supplier for a market because of economies of scale —the case that has been called "natural monopoly." He demonstrates that a competitive outcome can occur even in this situation if entry is not arbitrarily blocked.

Open entry is, it seems to me, a necessary condition if a competitive result is to prevail in a market.[9] With the abundant

---

[7] See George J. Stigler, *The Theory of Price*, third edition (New York: The Macmillan Company, 1966), p. 89.

[8] D. Demsetz, "Why Regulate Utilities?" *Journal of Law and Economics*, April 1968.

[9] In defining open entry, we may follow G. J. Stigler who says, "Free entry . . . may be defined as the condition that long-run costs of new firms if they enter the industry will be equal to those of firms already in the industry. This does not mean, as many infer, that a new firm can enter and immediately be as profitable as an established firm. We do not begrudge the new firm a decent interval in which to build its factory; we should be equally willing to concede a period during which production is put on a smooth-running schedule, trade connections are developed, labor is recruited and trained, and the like. These costs of building up a going business are legitimate investment expenses, and, unless historical changes take place in the market, they must be equal for both established and new firms." "Monopoly and Oligopoly by Merger," *The American Economic Review*, May 1950, p. 27. Although this definition is inadequate, it will do if we exclude from long-run costs the capitalized value of such legal privileges as being allowed to have a utility franchise, a tobacco acreage allotment or marketing certificate, a certificate of public convenience and necessity, or one or several of a limited number of taxicab or liquor store licenses or bank charters.

supply of entrepreneurs in the economy, I am willing to say that it is also a sufficient condition. The institutionalization of entrepreneurship in the American economy in the form of the immortal corporation, i.e., immortal as long as it is efficient, has accumulated a large fund of entrepreneurship. I am confident, therefore, that open entry is sufficient to enforce competitive behavior in most, if not all, circumstances.

If I am correct, the task of the Antitrust Division can be confined to the demolition of arbitrary (deliberately devised and imposed) barriers to entry and the prevention of the erection of such barriers. It need not confuse itself with such tasks as attempting to break up major firms in highly concentrated industries. It need not determine what is a market or an industry.[10] The courts would not have to listen to endless arguments as to whether a line of commerce or a market includes only domestically produced virgin aluminum, all virgin aluminum pig *used* in the United States whether produced at home or abroad, all virgin aluminum pig *sold* in the United States whether produced at home or abroad, all virgin aluminum plus secondary aluminum, all metals used for the purpose for which aluminum is used, all materials used for purposes for which aluminum is used, etc., or whether the shoe market consists of a neighborhood, a city, a metropolitan area, a state, a region, or a nation. If the Antitrust Division concentrated on the task of eliminating contrived impediments to entry, it would efficiently accomplish the twin goals

---

[10] The Merger Guidelines (U.S. Department of Justice, 30 May 1968) invites ridicule in its attempt to define markets, particularly in its discussion of the economic barriers ("significant transportation costs, lack of distribution facilities, customer inconvenience, or established consumer preference for existing products") which put a presumed boundary around a "commercially significant section of the country (even as small as a single community)" (p. 10). On the one hand, this seems to say that geography is illegal and on the other that no one can be expected to compete by making things more convenient or providing improved products and that those who have won markets in a locality by competing in this way have violated the law.

of insuring competitive behavior and maximizing efficiency in the economy. (To the extent that entrepreneurship is not a free good, the Division should, to avoid the diversion of entrepreneurship into unneeded areas, prosecute those who engage in collusive arrangements.)

The Barriers to Entry which are *NOT* Barriers

This answer sounds exceedingly simple, but the sophists in my profession have confused the meaning of "barrier to entry" to the point where I am sure that the Division would do ridiculous things in the name of removing impediments to entry. Even as enlightened a chief of Antitrust as Don Turner seems to have fallen for the notion that advertising is a barrier to entry. One of the widely used texts in industrial organization tells us that differentiation of product is a barrier to entry.[11] A basic text in price theory admirable for its paucity of errors informs us that, "Barriers to entry arise because of economies of scale." [12]

Limitations on advertising of the kind implied or suggested by those who believe

advertising is a barrier would erect a new block to entry rather than removing one. It would, in fact, create grandfather rights. It would become more expensive to inform prospective customers that a firm new to a given market is prepared to supply them. It would raise the cost of letting the world know that a better mouse trap has been built. It would force firms to invest more heavily in a dealer network or in a distribution system if they were limited in their advertising outlays, thus raising the long-run cost curves of prospective entrants. It would become more expensive to build volume quickly to a level which would achieve the major part of the available economies of scale. Efficiency would fall because firms would be forced to resort to the inefficient substitutes for advertising they avoid when this method of selling and promotion is open.[13]

Attacks on product differentiation by the Antitrust Division or the Federal Trade Commission also could result in blocking entry; the conclusion of the staff of the Cabinet Committee on Price Stability that "product differentiation protects established firms . . . from potential competitors" [14] to the contrary notwithstanding. A new entrant can usually insinuate itself more easily into the market if its product is not identical with those offered by established firms. Why should buyers switch to a new supplier unless its product serves their tastes more efficiently than those already available? "Product differentiation . . . is often a means of competition that serves the public, providing minimum assurances of quality and catering to a real consumer desire for product improvement or variation." [15]

It may be argued that a market may be

---

[11] J. S. Bain, *Industrial Organization* (New York: John Wiley & Sons, 1968), p. 255.

[12] G. J. Stigler, *The Theory of Price,* op. cit., p. 220. Stigler apparently retracts this statement in *The Organization of Industry* (Richard D. Irwin, Inc., 1968) where he says, "Some economists will say that economies of scale are a barrier to entry, meaning that such economies explain why no additional firms enter. It would be equally possible to say that inadequate demand is a barrier to entry. If we define a barrier as a differentially higher cost of new firms, there is no barrier . . ." p. 67. He should add that the view economies of scale are a barrier to entry would also mean that it is equally possible to say that an equilibrium amount of capacity in industry in purely competitive, long run equilibrium is a barrier to entry. No firm with standard technology would find it worthwhile entering such an industry anymore than it finds it worthwhile entering an industry where the economies of scale and limited size of the market have resulted in a single firm occupying the market with a price equal to the average cost required to supply the market at that price.

[13] See L. Telser, "Some Aspects of the Economics of Advertising," *Journal of Business,* April 1968; "Advertising and Competition," *Journal of Political Economy,* December, 1964.

[14] *Studies by the Staff of the Cabinet Committee on Price Stability* (Washington Government Printing Office, 1969), p. 42.

[15] A. E. Kahn, "Standards for Antitrust Policy," *Harvard Law Review,* 1953, p. 36.

more competitive—more open to entry—with product differentiation than without it because of its effect on buyer behavior. Buyers dissatisfied with a product from a current supplier will more readily engage in a search for an alternative supplier if there are no legal barriers to the offering of alternative varieties. If only a standardized product is allowed, search is less likely to be fruitful and less likely to be undertaken. Someone entering the market as a new supplier, then, will be less likely to find buyers seeking him and he will find it necessary to invest more heavily in seeking buyers.

I do not want to belabor you with elaborations of the errors of these notions concerning barriers to entry, but only to indicate that even with the Antitrust Division focusing on the task of removing artificial impediments, there will be thickets of sophistry to clear away if the Division is to do a proper job of promoting competition. That sophistry can lead to ridiculous attacks by the Division was certainly demonstrated in one case in which the Division maintained that it needed certain accounting and budgetary data from the defendant in order to prove that he was the low cost producer. The Division's theory was that being a low cost producer conveyed monopoly power by making it possible for the defendant to sell at lower prices than its competitors and thereby drive them from the field.[16] Being a low cost producer and *not* using such efficiency to pre-empt the market would seem to me to be more akin to undesirable monopolistic behavior than pre-empting the market by maintaining prices at levels such that no inefficient producer would find the market an attractive one in which to remain resident or to enter. Efficiency is hardly an arbitrary or artificial barrier to entry.[17]

What Barriers to Entry are Barriers?

If free entry is the (or only a) necessary condition for the maintenance of the competition which maximizes efficiency, then I would suggest that the Division should be devoting itself to attacking controls on entry. It should be destroying contrived impediments to entry. It should enter those cases where, for example, the Interstate Commerce Commission denies certificates to those who would enter, let us say, the trucking industry. When the CAB denies entry to firms seeking to move into the scheduled air transportation industry, the Division should intervene on behalf of the petitioner. When someone seeks a charter from the Comptroller of the Currency or from state banking authorities to enter the banking business and is arbitrarily denied, the Division should come to the assistance of the applicant. When the Massachusetts Pharmacy Board refuses permission to a pharmacist to open a drug store, presumably because an adequate number already operate in the area, the Division should leap to attack this artificial barrier. When the Minnesota Pharmacy Board denies any non-pharmacist the right to start a drug store and hire a pharmacist, there is a barrier to entry that is certainly arbitrary and the Division should train its legal artillery on the barricade. When New York, Chicago, San Francisco, and all major cities other than Washington refuse to issue taxi cab licenses to those who willingly satisfy all requirements for the provision of trained, licensed chauffeurs and safe equipment, with appropriate amounts and types of insurance, the Division could certainly ride to the rescue of the patrons of this fenced in market. When the Post Office harasses those who would compete with it and shuts them out of the postal market on the authority of a law which makes it illegal for anyone but the

---

[16] Affidavit of A. I. Jacobs, 5 November 1962, p. 8, Civil Action 15816, U.S. Dist. Court for the Eastern District of Michigan.

[17] Nevertheless, "the Federal Trade Commission and the Supreme Court have held that the advantages to be derived from increased efficiency after an acquisition might operate as a barrier

to entry by third companies into the acquired company's markets and, therefore, might substantially lessen competition in violation of Clayton 7." Betty Bock, *Mergers and Markets: Studies in Business Economics*, No. 100, p. 140.

U.S. Post Office to use a householder's mail box or to carry written messages, the Division should recommend the repeal of such arbitrary barriers. When the Division attacks the New York Stock Exchange, it should concentrate on the practices and rules of the exchange which impede entry to the stock brokerage business, such as limitations on the business member firms are allowed to do with non-member firms or the services they are allowed to perform for non-member firms. Increased ease of entry will do more to generate an efficient set of commission rates than an attack only on the agreement to set rates.

The Division should also be devoting attention to the attempts to erect new barriers to entry. When tariffs are proposed on products which compete with those produced by highly concentrated industries, the Division should attack those rather than concentration. When the Livestock Carriers Division of the Common Carrier Conference-Irregular Route pushes for regulation of truckers carrying livestock and persuades Senator Cotton to introduce legislation calling for regulation, the Division should be prepared to offer opposition. When bills are offered prohibiting banks from entering the computer service market, the Division should be as eager to maintain this source of potential entrants to an industry as it is when it attacks joint ventures and acquisitions.

What is Entry

The latter activity by the Division raises some interesting questions as to the meaning of entry and of "arbitrary barriers to entry." It would appear that the Antitrust Division itself has become an arbitrary barrier to entry.

The Division seems to define entry as the appearance of a new name in the list of those competing for the custom of a given set of customers. If the new name is simply a replacement of an old name because an acquisition has occurred, the Division regards this as no improvement in the com-

petitive situation and quite probably a degradation of competition because a name has been removed from the list of potential entrants.

To an economist, expansion of capacity either by *de novo* entrants or by established companies is entry in the meaningful sense of moving resources (capital and manpower) into the use in question. Monopoly in an economically functional sense means a situation where an industry fails to add resources when justified and called for by the demand and cost situation.[18] If customers are willing to pay more for the additional product than the cost of using resources to produce more, and if these resources are not moved into the industry in question, then monopoly prevails and inefficiency is a consequence. Economists define monopoly as a situation which results in conduct and performance causing an inefficient allocation of resources.[19] (Failure of resources which can be better utilized in alternative applications to withdraw from an industry is simply the other side of the same coin.)

The Antitrust Division as a Barrier to Entry

If a potential entrant into an industry chooses to enter by acquisition of an established firm, it will have to offer a price which is worth more to the sellers than retaining ownership of the firm. Presumably, it will offer such a price if it believes that it can manage the acquired assets more efficiently than they are being managed. Alternatively, it finds it cheaper to enter the industry in this way than by building new

---

[18] Judge Hand should have praised Alcoa for behaving competitively when it expanded capacity and mill margins declined instead of castigating it for monopolizing by facing "every newcomer with new capacity."

[19] See G. J. Stigler, *The Theory of Price* (New York: Macmillan Co., 1952). Revised edition, p. 213. Also, J. McGee, "Some Economic Issues in Robinson-Patman Land," *Law and Contemporary Problems*, Summer 1965, pp. 531–2.

assets, and it believes the industry worth entering at this cost. If the former is the situation, and the Division blocks the acquisition, it is blocking a probable improvement in efficiency. If the latter is the case, the blockage of the acquisition may block the entry of the firm since more expensive methods of entry may mean that it will not be worth entering at the higher cost.

In both cases, the blockage of entry by acquisition to a firm that might be a potential entrant is likely to block the expansion of capacity which is true entry. In the former case, an improvement in efficiency, if it materializes, will lower long-run marginal cost and lead to expansion beyond what otherwise would have occurred. In the latter case, where a potential entrant finds acquisition the cheapest method of entry, the would-be entrant evidently sees opportunities for expansion and profit not recognized by the resident firm. It is for this reason it is willing to offer a price exceeding the value of the firm to its present owners.

Where a potential entrant sees an opportunity in an industry—perhaps an opportunity to offer a new product or apply a new technique—it may prefer acquisition of an established firm with a producing organization or established dealer body in order to move the new product into the market or apply its new technique quickly. If it must struggle to build a viable producing and marketing organization from zero at the same time that it is trying to develop and establish an innovation, it may find the speed with which it can move its innovation into use hampered. The consequent slower growth may make the pay-off too small and too distant to make the investment in product or technique development and acceptance worth the cost. Established competitors will have a longer time in which to develop competitive new products and thus prevent the large sales which would have made entry worth the cost. It appears to be a rule of thumb that an organization growing more rapidly than approximately 10 per cent a year (measured by asset growth) finds itself faced with problems which in-

crease costs markedly.[20] This limits the rate of entry (expansion of capacity) and confines the *de novo* entrant with an innovation to a much lower rate of entry than if he enters via an acquisition.

Preventing acquisitions in new markets or new industries by major firms because they might be potential entrants *de novo* may *reduce* the number of *de novo* entrants rather than increasing them, Antitrust Division expectations to the contrary notwithstanding. Barring minor firms from selling their assets to leading firms already established in the field and to leading firms outside their field who may be interested in the field will limit their marketability. *De novo* entrance into a field by new firms will be reduced by this lack of marketability.[21] The incentive for entrepreneurs to establish firms will be reduced and it will be more difficult to obtain financial resources. Reduced marketability of minor firms increases the risks to those who might provide financial resources for the establishment of such firms as well as reducing prospective returns to the entrepreneurs involved.

---

[20] G. J. Stigler found that the fifteen industries with the largest relative increase in number of firms (1948–56) had an asset growth rate of 17 per cent per year and a growth rate in number of firms of 9 per cent per year. The industries with the smallest relative increase in number of firms had an asset growth rate of 4·5 per cent and the number of firms declined by 4 per cent per year. *Capital and Rates of Return in Manufacturing* (Princeton: Princeton University Press, 1963), p. 32. Interpolating, this argues that an asset growth rate of 8 per cent per year can be readily accommodated by internal growth of resident firms in an industry without costs and prices rising to the level which requires and attracts new firms to minimize the cost of expansion.

[21] ". . . to forbid mergers that would or might produce substantial efficiencies would narrow substantially the category of acceptable mergers, thereby drastically weakening the market for capital assets and seriously depreciating the price entrepreneurs could get for their businesses when they wish to liquidate. Such a policy . . . might have adverse effects on entry and growth of small business . . ." Donald Turner, "Conglomerate Mergers and Section 7 of the Clayton Act," *Harvard Law Review*, May, 1965, p. 1326.

For no apparent reason which can be justified by economic analysis the Antitrust Division and the Federal Trade Commission take a dim view of vertical acquisitions. They do have a (non-) theory of foreclosure —a set of words without an analytic base.[22] Rather than barring the entry of a firm into the industry of its suppliers or customers via acquisition, the Division and Commission should permit such entry for all the reasons described above plus three additional reasons. First, there is a possibility that transaction costs will be reduced.[23] Second, where a bilateral monopoly situation prevails, merger will frequently improve efficiency, increase the use of resources which were barred from the two industries, and increase output. The two industries will move closer to a competitive equilibrium. In no case will efficiency and the use of resources in the two industries decrease, moving the industries further from a competitive equilibrium.[24] Third, even where a monopolist acquires customers in order to practice price discrimination which it formerly was unable to practice for fear of leakage from low price to high price customers, the resulting discrimination will almost always result in a greater use of resources and greater output from the monopolist, thus moving it closer to the competitive equilibrium.[25] Vertical integration is not automatically anticompetitive and should not be treated as if it were. It does not extend monopoly power outside the field of the monopolist.

With open entry, we can be less fearful of horizontal acquisitions. This is the one variety of acquisition where the acquiring firm may find the acquired firm worth more to it than to the seller for reasons other than those which are likely to result in greater efficiency and more entry, or perhaps saving in taxes (if we consider saving taxes as an instance which cannot be classified under the efficiency-entry classifications). If entry is slow for reasons other than arbitrary barriers, or arbitrary barriers are not completely removed, then a case can be made for preventing the growth of undue concentration *via* the acquisition route. Open entry will not, then, be a sufficient condition to prevent monopoly or undetected collusion in the short run and, with arbitrary barriers remaining, it cannot prevail and prevent long run monopoly.

A Comment on Conglomerates

The current *furor* over conglomerates apparently may lead to legislation limiting the ability of multi-industry companies to move into new fields. If this occurs, it will block the openness of entry which, I believe, is the one condition necessary to enforce competition. It will reduce the list of potential entrants. The Antitrust Division should be alert to such a possibility and be prepared to recommend against inappropriate legislation.

To the extent that conglomerates improve efficiency in the use of resources currently applied in a field by acquiring those which are poorly managed, the antitrust authorities should approve. If conglomerates remove resources from fields where they are used less efficaciously than they can be used

---

[22] Foreclosure could have an effect, if it has any, only when there is high concentration and difficult entry in at least one of the two industries. Absent this condition, no entrant at either or both levels will be impeded by foreclosure. Even with monopoly at one level, it would be irrational for a monopolist to refuse to buy supplies from more efficient suppliers or to sell product to more efficient distributors than his own. He would hurt his own profits doing this.

[23] R. H. Coase, "The Nature of the Firm," *Economica*, New Series, Vol. IV (1937), pp. 386–405.

[24] G. J. Stigler, *The Theory of Price*, third edition (New York: The Macmillan Company, 1966), pp. 207–8.

[25] "The final result of effective price descrimination might be a total output that falls not far short of the competitive level. Thus monopoly that cannot discriminate may lead to a more serious misallocation of resources than one that can." L. Telser, "Abusive Trade Practices: An Economic Analysis," *Law and Contemporary Problems*, XXX, No. 3 (Summer 1965), 504.

in alternative applications, and move them into these applications, they should be applauded. These activities make markets more competitive and move industries more rapidly toward a long-run competitive equilibrium than might otherwise occur.

To the extent that conglomerates are saving corporate taxes by converting dividends into interest payments and find it profitable to operate with higher leverage because stockholders find it less costly for the corporations they own to undertake leveraging activity for them than to engage in these transactions themselves, given their risk preferences, they are simply doing for such stockholders what the acquired companies could and should be doing themselves for their stockholders. These activities do not require the conglomerate form. They do require the kind of entrepreneurship which is scarce enough that it finds it profitable to do this in company after company. To the extent that antitrust laws bar doing this in company after company in the same industry, these entrepreneurs do it in companies in various industries and become conglomerates as a consequence.

As entrepreneurship of this kind is imitated and spreads, financial structures of single industry companies will be reshaped by issuing debt to obtain the funds to make tender offers for their own stock if the risks involved do not make this unprofitable. With high leverage and most earnings paid as interest, the one industry corporation will not be attractive to the outside leveraging, tax-saving entrepreneur. If most one-industry corporations for which it is profitable to move in this direction move, this type of

conglomerate will cease to appear or to grow.

Conclusion

Open entry may be a sufficient condition for competition and enforcement of efficiency. The meaning of entry has been confused by considering only the appearance of a new contender in the market as entry and failing to consider that any expansion of capacity from whatever source is entry. Such expansion of capacity by a major firm has even been called a barrier to entry when it is anything but that in any economically meaningful sense.

To make our markets more competitive, the main thrust of antitrust activity should be in the direction of removing contrived barriers to entry. We must recognize that calling something such as advertising and product differentiation barriers does not make them such. The main barriers to entry are those imposed by regulatory commissions, tariffs, quotas, licensing requirements, and some of the activities of the antitrust authorities. They can at least cease these activities. Further, they can act as a "friend of the court" before agencies that are rejecting would-be entrants in many fields. Also, they should be recommending against proposed legislation which would erect more barriers and pressing for repeal of present legislative barriers. The return, in terms of the restoration of meaningful competition in the now protected areas, can be very large indeed, especially in the reinvigoration of the forces which guarantee efficiency and spur innovation.

3. Why Regulate Utilities? *

HAROLD DEMSETZ

Current economic doctrine offers to its students a basic relationship between the number of firms that produce for a given market and the degree to which competitive results will prevail. Stated explicitly or suggested implicitly is the doctrine that price and output can be expected to diverge to a greater extent from their competitive levels the fewer the firms that produce the product for the market. This relationship has provided the logic that motivates much of the research devoted to studying industrial concentration, and it has given considerable support to utility regulation.[1]

In this paper, I shall argue that the asserted relationship between market concentration and competition cannot be derived from existing theoretical considerations and that it is based largely on an incorrect understanding of the concept of competition or rivalry. The strongest application of the asserted relationship is in the area of utility regulation since, if we assume scale economies in production, it can be deduced that only one firm will produce the commodity. The logical validity or falsity of the asserted relationship should reveal itself most clearly in this case.

Although public utility regulation recently has been criticized because of its ineffectiveness or because of the undesirable indirect effects its produces,[2] the basic intellectual arguments for believing that truly effective regulation is desirable have not been challenged. Even those who are inclined to reject government regulation or ownership of public utilities because they believe these alternatives are more undesirable than private monopoly, implicitly accept the intellectual arguments that underlie regulation.[3]

The economic theory of natural monopoly is exceedingly brief and, we shall see, exceedingly unclear. Current doctrine is reflected in two recent statements of the theory. Samuelson writes:

> Under persisting decreasing costs for the firm, one or a few of them will so expand their q's as to become a significant part of the market for the industry's total Q. We would then end up (1) with a single mo-

Reprinted by permission of *The Journal of Law & Economics*, 11 J., 55 (1968), excerpt.

* The author is indebted to R. H. Coase, who was unconvinced by the natural monopoly argument long before this paper was written, and to George J. Stigler and Joel Segall for helpful comments and criticisms.

[1] Antitrust legislation and judicial decision, to the extent that they have been motivated by a concern for bigness and concentration, *per se,* have also benefited from the asserted relationship between monopoly power and industry structure.

[2] Cf., George J. Stigler and Claire Friedland, "What Can Regulators Regulate? The Case of Electricity," 5 *J. Law & Econ.* 1 (1962); H. Averch and L. Johnson, "The Firm under Regulatory Constraint," 52 *Am. Econ. Rev.* 1052 (1962); Armen Alchian and Reuben Kessel, "Competition, Monopoly, and the Pursuit of Pecuniary Gain," in *Aspects of Labor Economics* 157 (1962).

[3] Thus, Milton Friedman, while stating his preference for private monopoly over public monopoly or public regulation, writes:
> However, monopoly may also arise because it is technically efficient to have a single producer or enterprise. . . . When technical conditions make a monopoly the natural outcome of competitive market forces, there are only three alternatives that seem available: private monopoly, public monopoly, or public regulation.

Capitalism and Freedom 28 (1962).

15

nopolist who dominates the industry; (2) with a few large sellers who together dominate the industry . . . or (3) with some kind of imperfection of competition that, in either a stable way or in connection with a series of intermittent price wars, represents an important departure from the economist's model of "perfect" competition wherein no firm has any control over industry price.[4]

Alchian and Allen view the problem as follows:

> If a product is produced under cost conditions such that larger rates . . . [would] mean lower average cost per unit, . . . only one firm could survive; if there were two firms, one could expand to reduce costs and selling price and thereby eliminate the other. In view of the impossibility of more than one firm's being profitable, two is too many. But if there is only one, that incumbent firm may be able to set prices above free-entry costs for a long time. Either resources are wasted because too many are in the industry, or there is just one firm, which will be able to charge monopoly prices.[5]

At this point it will be useful to state explicitly the interpretation of natural monopoly used in this paper. If, because of production scale economies, it is less costly for one firm to produce a commodity in a given market than it is for two or more firms, then one firm will survive; if left unregulated, that firm will set price and output at monopoly levels; the price-output decision of that firm will be determined by profit maximizing behavior constrained only by the market demand for the commodity.

The theory of natural monopoly is deficient for it fails to reveal the logical steps that carry it from scale economies in production to monopoly price in the market place. To see this most clearly, let us consider the contracting process from its beginning.

Why must rivals share the market? Ri-

val sellers can offer to enter into contracts with buyers. In this bidding competition, the rival who offers buyers the most favorable terms will obtain their patronage; there is no clear or necessary reason for *bidding* rivals to share in the *production* of the goods and, therefore, there is no clear reason for competition in bidding to result in an increase in per-unit *production* costs.

Why must the unregulated market outcome be monopoly price? The competitiveness of the bidding process depends very much on such things as the number of bidders, but there is no clear or necessary reason for *production* scale economies to decrease the number of *bidders*. Let prospective buyers call for bids to service their demands. Scale economies in servicing their demands in no way imply that there will be one bidder only. There can be many bidders and the bid that wins will be the lowest. The existence of scale economies in the production of the service is irrelevant to a determination of the number of rival bidders. If the number of bidders is large or if, for other reasons, collusion among them is impractical, the contracted price can be very close to per-unit production cost.[6]

The determinants of competition in market negotiations differ from and should not be confused with the determinants of the number of firms from which production will issue after contractual negotiations have been completed. The theory of natural monopoly is clearly unclear. Economies of scale in production imply that the bids submitted will offer increasing quantities at lower per-unit costs, but production scale economies imply nothing obvious about how competitive these prices will be. If one bidder can do the job at less cost than two or more, because each would then have a smaller output rate, then the bidder with the lowest bid price for the entire job will

[4] Paul A. Samuelson, Economics 461 (6th rev. ed. 1964).

[5] Armen Alchian and William R. Allen, University Economics 412 (1st ed. 1964).

[6] I shall not consider in this paper the problem of marginal cost pricing and the various devices, such as multi-part tariffs, that can be used to approximate marginal cost pricing.

be awarded the contract, whether the good be cement, electricity, stamp vending machines, or whatever, but the lowest bid price need not be a monopoly price.[7]

The criticism made here of the theory of natural monopoly can be understood best by constructing an example that is free from irrelevant complications, such as durability of distributions systems, uncertainty, and irrational behavior, all of which may or may not justify the use of regulatory commissions but none of which is relevant to the theory of natural monopoly; for this theory depends on one belief only —price and output will be at monopoly levels if, due to scale economies, only one firm succeeds in producing the product.

Assume that owners of automobiles are required to own and display new license plates each year. The production of license plates is subject to scale economies.

The theory of natural monopoly asserts that under these conditions the owners of automobiles will purchase plates from one firm only and that firm, in the absence of regulation, will charge a monopoly price, a price that is constrained only by the demand for and the cost of producing license plates. The logic of the example does dictate that license plates will be purchased from one firm because this will allow that firm to offer the plates at a price based on the lowest possible per-unit cost. But why should that price be a monopoly price?

There can be many bidders for the annual contract. Each will submit a bid based on the assumption that if its bid is lowest it will sell to all residents; if it is not lowest it sells to none. Under these conditions there will exist enough independently acting bidders to assure that the winning price will differ insignificantly from the per-unit cost of producing license plates.

If only one firm submits the lowest price, the process ends, but if two or more firms submit the lowest price, one is selected according to some random selection device or one is allowed to sell or give his contracts to the other. There is no monopoly price although there may be rent to some factors if their supply is positively sloped. There is no regulation of firms in the industry. The price is determined in the bidding market. The only role played by the government or by a consumers' buying cooperative is some random device to select the winning bidder if more than one bidder bids the lowest price.

There are only two important assumptions: (1) The inputs required to enter production must be available to many potential bidders at prices determined in open markets. This lends credibility to numerous rival bids. (2) The cost of colluding by bidding rivals must be prohibitively high. The reader will recognize that these requirements are no different than those required to avoid monopoly price in any market, whether production in that market is or is not subject to scale economies.

Moreover, if we are willing to consider the possibility that collusion or merger of all potential bidding rivals is a reasonable prospect, then we must examine the other side of the coin. Why should collusion or merger of *buyers* be prohibitively costly if an infinite or large number of bidding rivals can collude successfully? If we allow buyers access to the same technology of collusion, the market will be characterized by bilateral negotiations between organized buyers and organized sellers. While the outcome of such negotiations is somewhat uncertain with respect to wealth distribution, there is no reason to expect inefficiency.

Just what is the supply elasticity of bidders and what are the costs of colluding are questions to be answered empirically since they cannot be deduced from produc-

---

[7] The competitive concept employed here is not new to economics although it has long been neglected. An early statement of the concept, which was known as "competition *for* the field" in distinction to "competition *within* the field" is given by Edwin Chadwick, Results of Different Principles of Legislation and Administration in Europe; of Competition for the Field, as compared with the Competition within the Field of Service, 22 *J. Royal Statistical Soc'y.* 381 (1859).

tion scale economies. There exists more than one firm in every public utility industry and many firms exist in some public utility industries. And this is true even though licensing restrictions have been severe; the assertion that the supply of potential *bidders* in any market would be very inelastic if licensing restrictions could be abolished would seem difficult to defend when producing competitors exist in nearby markets. The presence of active rivalry is clearly indicated in public utility history. In fact, producing competitors, not to mention unsuccessful bidders, were so plentiful that one begins to doubt that scale economies characterized the utility industry at the time when regulation replaced market competition. Complaints were common that the streets were too frequently in a state of disrepair for the purpose of accommodating competing companies. Behling writes:

> There is scarcely a city in the country that has not experienced competition in one or more of the utility industries. Six electric light companies were organized in the one year of 1887 in New York City. Forty-five electric light enterprises had the legal right to operate in Chicago in 1907. Prior to 1895, Duluth, Minnesota, was served by five electric lighting companies, and Scranton, Pennsylvania, had four in 1906. . . . During the latter part of the nineteenth century, competition was the usual situation in the gas industry in this country. Before 1884, six competing companies were operating in New York City. . . . Competition was common and especially persistent in the telephone industry. According to a special report of the Census in 1902, out of 1051 incorporated cities in the United States with a population of more than 4,000 persons, 1002 were provided with telephone facilities. The independent companies had a monopoly in 137 of the cities, the Bell interests had exclusive control over communication by telephone in 414 cities, while the remaining 451, almost half, were receiving duplicated service. Baltimore, Chicago, Cleveland, Columbus, Detroit, Kansas City, Minneapolis, Philadelphia, Pittsburgh, and St. Louis, among the larger cities, had at least two telephone services in 1905.[8]

It would seem that the number of potential bidding rivals and the cost of their colluding in the public utility industries are likely to be at least as great as in several other industries for which we find that unregulated markets work tolerably well.

The natural monopoly theory provides no logical basis for monopoly prices. The theory is illogical. Moreover, for the general case of public utility industries, there seems no clear evidence that the cost of colluding is significantly lower than it is for industries for which unregulated market competition seems to work. To the extent that utility regulation is based on the fear of monopoly price, *merely because one firm will serve each market,* it is not based on any deducible economic theorem.

The important point that needs stressing is that *we have no theory that allows us to deduce from the observable degree of concentration in a particular market whether or not price and output are competitive.* We have as yet no general theory of collusion and certainly not one that allows us to associate observed concentration in a particular market with successful collusion.[9]

It is possible to make some statements about collusion that reveal the nature of the forces at work. These statements are largely intuitive and cannot be pursued in detail here. But they may be useful in imparting to the reader a notion of what is meant by a theory of collusion. Let us suppose that there are no special costs to competing. That is, we assume that sellers do not need to keep track of the prices or other activities of their competitors. Secondly, assume that there are some costs of colluding that must be borne by members of a bidders' cartel. This condition is approximated least well where the government subsidizes the cost of colluding—for example, the U.S. Department of Agriculture. Finally, assume that there are no legal barriers to entry.

Under these conditions, new bidding

---

[8] Burton N. Behling, *Competition and Monopoly in Public Utility Industries* 19–20 (1938).

[9] However, see George J. Stigler, "A Theory of Oligopoly, 72 *J. Pol. Econ.* 44 (1964).

rivals will be paid to join the collusion. In return for joining they will receive a pro rata share of monopoly profits. As more rivals appear the pro rata share must fall. The cartel will continue paying new rivals to join until the pro rata share falls to the cost of colluding. That is, until the cartel members receive a competitive rate of return for remaining in the cartel. The next rival bidder can refuse to join the cartel; instead he can enter the market at a price below the cartel price (as can any present member of the cartel who chooses to break away). If there is some friction in the system, this rival will choose this course of action in preference to joining the cartel, for if he joins the cartel he receives a competitive rate of return; whereas if he competes outside the cartel by selling at a price below that of the cartel he receives an above-competitive rate of return for some short-run period. Under the assumed conditions the cartel must eventually fail and price and output can be competitive even though only a few firms actually produce the product. Moreover, the essential ingredient to its eventual failure is only that the private per-firm cost of colluding exceeds the private per-firm cost of competing.

Under what conditions will the cost of colluding exceed the cost of competing? How will these costs be affected by allowing coercive tactics? What about buyer cartels? What factors affect how long is "eventually"? Such questions remain to be answered by a theory of collusion. Until such questions are answered, public policy prescriptions must be suspect. A market in which many firms produce may be competitive or it may be collusive; the large number of firms merely reflects production scale diseconomies; large numbers do not necessarily reflect high or low collusion costs. A market in which few firms produce may be competitive or it may be collusive; the small number of firms merely reflects production scale economies; fewness does not necessarily reflect high or low collusion costs. Thus, an economist may view the many retailers who sell on "fair trade"

terms with suspicion and he may marvel at the ability of large numbers of workers to form effective unions, and, yet, he may look with admiration at the performance of the few firms who sell airplanes, cameras, or automobiles.

The subject of monopoly price is necessarily permeated with the subject of negotiating or contracting costs. A world in which negotiating costs are zero is a world in which no monopolistic inefficiencies will be present, simply because buyers and sellers both can profit from negotiations that result in a reduction and elimination of inefficiencies. In such a world it will be bargaining skills and not market structures that determine the distribution of wealth. If a monopolistic structure exists on one side of the market, the other side of the market will be organized to offset any power implied by the monopolistic structure. The organization of the other side of the market can be undertaken by members of that side or by rivals of the monopolistic structure that prevails on the first side. The co-existence of monopoly *power* and monopoly *structure* is possible only if the costs of negotiating are differentially positive, being lower for one set of sellers (or buyers) than it is for rival sellers (or buyers). If one set of sellers (or buyers) can organize those on the other side of the market more cheaply than can rivals, then price may be raised (or lowered) to the extent of the existing differential advantage in negotiating costs; this extent generally will be less than the simple monopoly price. In some cases the differential advantage in negotiating costs may be so great that price will settle at the monopoly (monopsony) level. This surely cannot be the general case, but the likelihood of it surely increases as the costs imposed on potential rivals increase; legally restricting entry is one way of raising the differential disadvantages to rivals; the economic meaning of restricting entry *is* increasing the cost of potential rivals of negotiating with and organizing buyers (or sellers).

The public policy question is which

groups of market participants, *if any*, are to receive governmentally sponsored advantages and disadvantages, not only in the subsidization or taxation of production but, also, in the creation of advantages or disadvantages in conducting negotiations.

At this juncture, it should be emphasized that I have argued not that regulatory commissions are undesirable, but that economic theory does not, at present, provide a justification for commissions insofar as they are based on the belief that observed concentration and monopoly price bear any necessary relationship.

4. Discussion of Papers on "Capitalism and Monopolistic Competition: I. The Theory of Oligopoly"

GEORGE J. STIGLER

The theory of oligopoly has usually been developed within a framework of three assumptions. The first is that the oligopolists are individually to maximize profits. The second is that monopoly yields maximum profits to the industry. The third is that the profit-maximizing oligopolists do not engage in complete collusion and act like a monopolist. The problem of oligopoly becomes: how can we limit the profit maximization of the oligopolists so that it does not lead to monopoly behavior?

The early writers placed easy but wholly arbitrary limits on the profit maximization of each oligopolist. Cournot, for example, had each oligopolist maximize profits subject to fixed outputs of other firms. In the course of time these arbitrary limits to profit maximization have been relaxed, and the oligopoly equilibrium (or the range of possible prices) has approached closer to monopoly equilibrium. The most recent and reasonable stopping point short of complete collusion is that proposed by Fellner, at this session briefly, and in his recent volume more elaborately. He finds pooling of profits necessary to complete maximization, and deems pooling impossible for reasons of long-run uncertainty of the relative strengths of firms and because of antitrust policy. Fellner's stopping point is also arbitrary and rests on too literal a view of pooling. It is possible to pool by dividing market areas, by dividing products, by asymmetrical patent royalties—by many devices of variable durability and detectability.

Of course any stopping point on the road to full collusion will necessarily be inconsistent with profit maximization; that is, the stopping point will be nonrational.

The inconsistency is assured by the formulation of the problem, which requires a rational explanation for an irrational policy.

There are in fact two serious objections to the conventional formulation in terms of how will firms A and B treat one another. One objection is that the formulation leads to arbitrary, nonrational answers, no one of which seems plausible to more than its sponsor and his close friends. The other objection is that we have very little evidence that A and B fail to treat each other with the utmost kindness.

Perhaps we should change our line of attack. One alternative formulation is: Why do firms A and B constitute the industry, and how long will they enjoy this position? That is, what are the conditions of entry of new firms and expansion of existing firms in an industry? I suggest that when attention is turned to this question, oligopoly behavior loses much of its arbitrariness and oligopoly price much of its indeterminacy. If the existing firms are there because of strong patents, we should expect full collusion, until recently carefully spelled out in the cross-licensing agreements. If the existing firms are there because of ownership of limited natural resources—a case more popular than important—we should expect a similar result. If the large firms are there by merger, the case I argued was most important; their policies are governed by the factors determining the rate of entry and expansion of rivals. This formulation does not completely eliminate the classical oligopoly problem, but it reduces it to a minor aspect of a more manageable problem.

I am encouraged that Bain is also giving entry and expansion of rivals an increasingly important role in oligopoly theory. His present position does not crowd mine, largely because he discusses long-run equi-

Reprinted by permission of the *American Economic Review*, volume 40, May 1950.

libria where I discuss a path to long-run equilibrium. I infer that in Bain's view, mergers that did not maintain their relative share of the industry's output represent unsuccessful attempts at monopoly, while in my view, had they maintained their relative positions they would not have obtained monopoly profits. An independent point on which I solicit examples and amplification is Bain's opinion that very easy entry into an industry will often make it unworkably competitive.

There is much instructive analysis in Scitovsky's paper, but I cannot (any longer) convince myself that consumer ignorance is a basic element of the oligopoly prob-lem. By his reading, we should expect only sporadic and minor quality improvements—and fairly frequent quality deterioration—in the oligopolistic industries. The evidence is all the other way: the main trend of quality change has been toward improvement, and it has been a strong and continuous trend. The basic limitation on consumer ignorance is producer knowledge. Until it can be shown that advertising has generally decreased cross-elasticities of demand or introduced economies of scale, in the theory of oligopoly I shall continue to be more impressed by the ignorance of economists than by the ignorance of consumers.

Part I–B · *Number of Firms*

Openness of entry as a determinant of the competitiveness of industry was the dominant theme of the first four selections. Demsetz indicated that even being a single firm in a market (even in the "natural monopoly" case) does not, with open entry into bidding, give control of supply and price and make the market monopolistic.

The following group of readings explicitly argues that a small number of firms may be just as competitive as a large number. Professor McGee reviews the many theories of oligopoly and duopoly. He points out that theoretically any outcome is possible, ranging from monopoly to competition, depending upon which *unprovable* assumptions one is willing to make with the common assumption that no entry occurs.

Professor McGee concludes his review of the theories concerning the effect of the number of firms on competition with a discussion of an antitrust policy question. Would antitrust dissolutions of firms in con-centrated industries improve conditions? Again almost any outcome is possible. With the dissolution of a large firm in a concentrated industry, the price of the product after dissolution may be higher, the same, or lower than the predissolution price. Given economies of scale, costs will be higher—a deadweight loss. Professor McGee's discussion covers static theories. It omits some dynamic considerations—such as the effect of more output concentrated in single firms on cost reduction through longer production runs and learning—which he discusses at another point in the book from which this selection was taken.

Professors Fama and Laffer show that two noncolluding firms per industry in a "many industry economy" are sufficient for producing perfect competition providing factors are mobile, indivisibilities are unimportant, entry is not barred, and information concerning returns is available. In selection 7, Professor Archibald and, in an addendum, Professor Webb argue that the number of firms in an industry is analytically irrelevant. Whether firms are few or many, what determines whether the market produces a competitive result depends upon the beliefs rivals hold concerning each others' policies.

In a forthcoming study of *The Market Concentration Doctrine,* Professor Demsetz suggests that heuristic devices used in economics have been confused with the reality of what is necessary for competition to prevail.

> The structural assumptions of the monopoly and competition models have been grasped as approximations of actual market structures because economic theory provides no general explanation of how monopoly power is acquired or how competition is avoided. What is called the theory of monopoly is an explanation of how market power will be exercised *once* obtained. In the absence of a theory of how monopoly power is acquired, there has been an irresistible inclination among economists to identify real world monopoly power with the structural postulate of the monopoly model—the one-firm industry. It is but a short step from this to the conviction that market concentration is an index of monopoly power.

> The monopoly model assumes a one-firm industry, and the competitive model a many-firm industry. But these assumptions are properly treated as thought facilitating devices and not as *descriptions* of real monopoly and competition. The single firm in monopoly theory is not to be understood as a description of the structure of a real monopoly but as a proxy for the statement that "for the purpose of the problem at hand, competitive behavior can be ignored." Competitive behavior can be unimportant even though there are many firms, such as in a smoothly working cartel or labor union. Similarly, the many-firm assumption of the competition model is to be thought of as a proxy for the statement that "for the purpose at hand, monopoly power can be ignored," rather than as a description of the structure of a competitive industry. The structure of the industry tells us more about cost conditions and the distribution of talent in an industry than it does about monopoly power.[1]

---

[1] Harold Demsetz, *The Market Concentration Doctrine* (Washington, D.C.: American Enterprise Institute for Public Policy Research, 1973).

5. "Competition" and the Number of Firms: Economic Theory

JOHN S. McGEE

Static resource allocation is said to be superior if all industries are purely competitive rather than if one is monopolistic and all others are purely competitive, at least if costs are not increased under competition. For such a static world, most American economists (though living in our real world) would surely approve programs to convert the monopoly industry into a purely competitive one. Even so, some would not approve unless the program to increase competition would cost less than the benefits it would bring. A presumably much smaller proportion might even ask whether the monopolist may not be so much more "deserving," or "cultured," than consumers in general as to justify the gains he gets at the cost of "larger" general allocative loss. This question may be eminently logical; but it is unanswerable.

Of course, not all or even most of the interesting antitrust problems are of the sort just discussed. In some of the most important ones the question is not whether many independent sellers will perform more "competitively" or "better" than one or very few sellers. Often the question is whether, say, five would perform "better" than, say, four; or, in general, whether a few more is "better" than a few, as Eugene Singer shows for specific antitrust cases.[1]

The purpose of this Chapter is to discover what, if anything, economic theory has contributed to that question, and to appraise it on its own ground.

Theories of Duopoly and Oligopoly

So far as dissolution and merger policy go, the basic problem concerns modest changes in the number of sellers when that number is relatively small. The only part of traditional economic theory that seems to be relevant is, therefore, the theory of oligopoly, of which duoply is a special case. And in spite of strongly held opinions about the effects of small changes in the number of sellers, the formal theory turns out to be rather ambiguous. And oddly enough, the strongest support for trust-busting turns out to come either from antique theories in which few now profess any confidence, or from very recent theoretical formulations that were developed long after present opinion crystallized.

The first task is, then, to indicate some of the hypotheses generated in the theories, and partially to trace their development over time.

Classical Theories Concerning Numbers

Cournot. Cournot's theory is relevant, since it is concerned, for a narrow range of assumptions, with what happens as the number of sellers changes.[2]

It was the first systematic formulation of oligopoly, and its hypotheses are still practically dominant. In its simplest form, the theory applies to homogeneous output

From *In Defense of Industrial Concentration* by John S. McGee. © 1971 Praeger Publishers Inc., New York. Excerpted and reprinted by permission.

[1] Eugene Singer, "The Concept of Relative Concentration in Antitrust Law," 52, *American Bar Association, Journal* No. 3 (March, 1966), pp. 246–250. For example, in *Continental Can* (1964), "the choice was not between unconcentrated or concentrated market structures, nor oligopoly or pure competition, but between two highly concentrated market structures." *Op. cit.,* p. 249.

[2] A. A. Cournot, *Researches into the Mathematical Principles of the Theory of Wealth* (1838). translated by Nathaniel T. Bacon (New York: Augustus M. Kelley, 1960), Chapter VII.

for which production costs are zero, and to a linear final demand curve. Cournot's initial assumptions about costs, demand linearity, and undifferentiated products are not crucial.[3] In Cournot's theory, as in all subsequent oligopoly theories of the "classical" persuasion, what *is* crucial is the treatment of rivals' response. Rival reaction is the essence of oligopoly, whereas it is absent from either simple monopoly or pure competition. This is extremely troublesome, for, as Hurwicz put it:

> There is no adequate solution of the problem of defining "rational economic behavior" on the part of an individual when the very rationality of his actions depends on the probable behavior of other individuals: in the case of oligopoly, other sellers. . . . Thus, the individual's "rational behavior" is determinate *if* the pattern of behavior of "others" can be assumed *a priori* known. But the behavior of "others" cannot be known *a priori* if the "others," too, are to behave rationally. Thus a logical impasse is reached.[4]

Detailed specification of rival reaction is what distinguishes the "classical" oligopoly theories—the dominance of which probably extends at least into the 1930s or 1940s—from their "modern" counterparts. The "classical" theories simply *postulate* one or another kind of rival *behavior* and *postulate* sellers' *assumptions* about their rivals' behavior. The "modern" theories assume a *goal*—whether it is maximizing joint profits or attaining the largest of the minimum profits likely to result from different

strategies—and infer or predict the sort and success of behavior sensibly directed to reach the goal. In principle, these are very different things.

Although Cournot recognized this difference, he specifically excluded collusion and merger from the oligopoly problem and set them aside in the simple monopoly category, which he analyzed separately. Dealing as he did with a homogeneous product sold in a perfect, centralized market, Cournot took output as the variable to be manipulated by each rival, since price will necessarily be the same for all sellers. Each seller, acting independently, seeks maximum profits. At any instant of time each rival knows his own cost function, the total commodity demand, his own and his rivals' output, and the market price. In short, he knows the "present" situation. But, except when at equilibrium, he is seriously wrong about one part of the future. He does not learn; he does not improve. In Cournot's system, each seller assumes that the sum of his rivals' output will not be altered because of changes in his own. For any given output rate of his rivals, any particular seller will take as his own that part of the industry demand curve not being satisfied by his rivals. As a consequence, equilibrium comes through equalizing the sum of output decisions independently made, with aggregate quantities demanded. At equilibrium, the market "clears" and no seller can unilaterally improve his position, given his view of the future.

Output and price are related in a straightforward way to the number of rivals. Thus, if the firms' cost functions are not changed by changes in the number of sellers, market price declines continuously as the number of sellers increases, tending to marginal cost in the limit. And the net effect on price can, furthermore, be easily shown for cases in which increasing the number of sellers raises the cost functions of each. All depends upon whether the cost effect outweighs the number effect.

Furthermore, for a given number of Cournot oligopolists, price will more closely

---

[3] William Fellner, *Competition Among the Few* (New York: Alfred A. Knopf, 1949), p. 69; Josef Hadar, "Stability of Oligopoly with Product Differentiation," *The Review of Economic Studies,* XXXIII (January 1966), 57–60; Dolbear, Lave, Bowman, Lieverman, Prescott, Rueter, and Sherman, "Collusion in Oligopoly: An Experiment on the Effect of Numbers and Information," *Quarterly Journal of Economics* (May 1968), pp. 240–259.

[4] Leonid Hurwicz, "The Theory of Economic Behavior," *American Economic Review,* XXXV (1945), 909–925; reprinted in G. J. Stigler and K. E. Boulding, *Readings in Price Theory* (Homewood, Ill.: Irwin, 1952), pp. 505–526.

approximate marginal cost as the market demand elasticity is higher. Thus, for even one seller, price will tend toward marginal cost (i.e., toward the purely competitive solution) as demand elasticity tends toward infinity. Thus, the allocation effect of even single-seller monopoly depends upon relatively poor total substitutability of other products. A "monopolist" of something for which demand elasticity is infinite has no monopoly power, and his price and output will be at the competitive level.

In general outline, these conclusions are so "sensible" that many economists would embrace them, especially if they were not attributed to Cournot. It is not clear whether this is because almost every economist has studied Cournot's conclusions, and many remember them, or that economists share his general view with respect to how the world really operates.

Whereas economists may embrace Cournot's general conclusions, most would probably deny their precision. For Cournot *is* precise. As Chamberlin's arithmetic explanation shows[5] for the simplest formulation, Cournot's logic makes monopoly output one half the purely competitive output; duopoly output two thirds; triopoly, three fourths; and so on. In short, going from monopoly to duopoly makes a big difference, whereas further increases in the number of sellers have progressively smaller and smaller effects. Reducing the number of sellers from, say, four to, say, three, would only lower output from 80% to 75% of the competitive level, *if* costs were not changed at all in the process. Recasting these additional conclusions in imprecise general form will further reveal the prevalence of Cournot-type conclusions among economists: Duopoly is very different from monopoly; other things equal, mergers are especially dangerous when sellers are very few and relatively innocuous when they are numerous; and practically competitive results emerge even when the number of sellers is not really very large. Cournot's conclusions could be couched and conceivably even tested in terms of Herfindahl indexes of concentration; for that index has a "numbers equivalent." Five firms of equal size would yield a Herfindahl index of .20; equal-share duopoly, an index of .50. If Herfindahl concentration values were perfectly related with "monopoly," equal values should yield the same outcomes even though the structures from which they were derived are different.[6] Plotted against its number equivalents, the Herfindahl index falls very rapidly as we move from pure monopoly to duopoly, then at a decreasing rate, since the product of index and number-equivalent is always 1. If Herfindahl indexes are related systematically and inversely to competitiveness, Cournot's predictions of the effects of an increased number of sellers would be confirmed in a general way. We will return to this comparative implication in the discussion of "modern" oligopoly theories.

Though Cournot did not do it, there is no logical reason why his behavioral assumptions cannot be applied to differentiated products. The problem then becomes enormously more varied and complicated, however.

Even if we want to believe completely in Cournot's model, for policy as well as theoretical purposes it is crucial to distinguish between an increase in the number of firms due to *entry* as opposed to *dissolution*. In this model, Cournot says little or nothing about either. The number of firms is simply given; it is not explained. And, given the cost functions he assumes, oligopoly simply will not endure: If costs do not change with the size or number of firms,

---

[5] E. H. Chamberlin, *The Theory of Monopolistic Competition* (6th ed.) (Cambridge, Mass.: Harvard University Press, 1948), pp. 32–34.

[6] The (full) Herfindahl index is computed by summing the squares of individual firm's market share expressed as a decimal fraction. The same index value could emerge for an industry with a very few large firms and a lot of very small ones, and from an industry of a smaller total number of identical intermediate sized firms. The equal-sized number equivalent is the reciprocal of the Herfindahl value: .2 = 1/5, or the value for an industry of five equal-sized firms.

any price higher than long-run marginal cost will attract entry. The explanation of permanent oligopoly thus must rest upon institutional restrictions or ownership of some absolutely fixed resource—as artesian wells in his examples. There can be more firms if there are more wells of given quality.

Nevertheless, under these assumptions, it may be legitimate to compare the outcomes for different numbers of firms by postulating something about entry. If there *are* more firms it is because fewer firms would produce prices higher than the relevant costs—which are not only equal among firms but unchanged by the number of firms. Entry would then occur. Hence, there would be a *natural* efficiency explanation for the number of firms.

Dissolution is a very different matter. It is an external force and unnatural force, which does not necessarily improve matters. The dissolution process *itself* has costs; and the cost functions and product varieties of individual firms may themselves be influenced by dissolutions of various kinds and degrees. These influences, which may be static and dynamic, are discussed later in greater detail.[7]

Bertrand and Edgeworth. After Cournot, Bertrand and Edgeworth also developed various oligopoly models. Perhaps the most famous of them also applied to homogeneous products, but explored the results of decision rules that differed from Cournot's. In general, they show that if each duopolist consistently assumes that his rival's present price will remain unchanged, it will pay each to undercut. Price will therefore be beaten down to the purely competitive level. One of Edgeworth's models has price oscillating indefinitely approximately between the limits of the simple monopoly and purely competitive prices; but this oscillation seems more the product of Edgeworth's peculiar formulation than of the general duopoly problem itself.[8] So far as their application to homogeneous products, these theories have simple implications with respect to the number of sellers. For, if we ignore effects upon costs and product varieties, it appears that increasing the number of sellers from one to two has a large effect; but further increases in the number of sellers would have virtually no effect. In their pure form, therefore, those theories surely afford little support for the assertion that "competitiveness" is more or less consistently related to numbers. At most, they predict that two sellers are enough for competitive performance.[9]

All of the models so far analyzed are based upon simple and "unrealistic" assumptions. The basic naiveté is, allegedly, that sellers adhere religiously to the incorrect assumption that their output (or prices) does not affect their rivals, even after experience shows that it is false. For many economists, this basic "unreality" has proved intolerable. Before passing to more complex classical models and to the more modern ones, it should be noted, however, that economists may have written off Cournot and Bertrand prematurely. For one thing, there continues to be intelligent methodological debate about the relevancy of realistic assumptions. According to the positiv-

---

[7] Suggestive analyses, for entry, but not dissolution, are William S. Vickrey, *Microstatics* (New York: Harcourt, Brace, and World, 1964), pp. 314–334; Harold Hotelling, "Stability in Competition," *The Economic Journal*, XXXIX (1929), 41–57, reprinted in Stigler and Boulding, *op. cit.*, pp. 467–84; Arthur Smithies, "Optimum Location in Spatial Competition," *Journal of Political Economy*, XLIX (1940), 423–439, reprinted in Stigler and Boulding, *op. cit.*, pp. 485–501; E. H. Chamberlin, *op. cit.*, pp. 100–104.

[8] There are various modern summaries of the Bertrand and Edgeworth models. For example, see Vickrey, *op. cit.*; Chamberlin, *op. cit.*; Cliff Lloyd, *Microeconomic Analysis* (Homewood, Ill.: Irwin, 1967), pp. 211–215; Stigler, *Essays in the History of Economics* (Chicago: University of Chicago Press, 1965), p. 248; George J. Stigler, "Perfect Competition, Historically Contemplated," *Journal of Political Economy*, LXV (February, 1957), 1–17; and Fellner, *op. cit.*, pp. 77–91. Fellner also discusses some implications of introducing product differentiation into the Bertrand framework, pp. 87–90.

[9] Compare Chamberlin, *op. cit.*, pp. 36–37.

its' view, predictive or, at least, explanatory power is the real test of a theory, and the realism of assumptions is irrelevant. On that view, the question becomes whether actual behavior under oligopoly with different numbers of rivals refutes or confirms the theory. To put it somewhat differently, do sellers act as they would *if* they adopted, say, Cournot decision rules? This is an empirical question, not a theological one. Baumol, for one, claims to find some favorable evidence from his own experience.[10] It seems true, however, that there has been little empirical testing; and the most becoming scientific posture is to reserve judgment till some returns are in.

Furthermore, as will be seen later, assumptions that look absurd within models that include instantaneous and correct transmission of price and output data may not seem so strange in other contexts.

Conjectural Variation Theories. Various economists attempted to broaden the Cournot–Bertrand models by explicitly including conjectures about rivals' responses. Bowley and Stackelberg are leading figures in this development.[11] Unlike the Cournot model, these variations make each seller aware that his rival will not remain inert, but *will* react; and specify his (often incorrect) appraisal of just how he will do so. For example, the total (expected) output change resulting from a change in one seller's output, is the *sum* of his own output change and the (expected) change in the rival's output that will occur in response to his own moves. These (expected) *induced* effects might just neatly offset, reinforce, or counterbalance his own direct effect,

with consequences that may differ significantly.

The appeal of these more complicated models presumably rests on two things. First, when each seller is an important part of the market for relatively close substitutes —i.e., when sellers are "few"—it is "plausible" to expect that each will recognize it, and will assume that rivals will react. Because they explicitly recognize that each seller assumes that rivals will react, these conjectural variation theories look more "realistic." Second, because a practically limitless number of symmetric and asymmetric assumed rival reactions can be made, these theories offer a rich variety of possible outcomes. These presumably include various "competitive" outcomes (one being warfare); quasi-competition—to essentially complete monopoly solutions; and indeterminacies of various sorts.

Unfortunately, the attractiveness of these complex classical models is quite superficial. On a logical level they are really subject to the same criticism that has, historically, been lavishly applied to Cournot: Why would sellers retain and act on even the most complex assumption about rival reactions once it is proved incorrect or less profitable than alternatives? And, on a practical or policy level, these theories are neither testable nor very useful. In the first place, what any particular version "predicts" will happen depends upon psychological expectation. It is impossible to reject such a prediction without quantifying undiscoverable private conjectures *and*, at the same time, proving that the results thereby "predicted" do not actually occur.[12] Second, since everything depends upon what sellers believe their rivals will do, by varying such beliefs, models of this kind can be made to generate practically any outcome. Even if costs do not vary among sellers, prices may be lower than under either pure competition or Cournot oligopoly; higher than Cournot predicts, but less than the simple monopoly level; precisely

[10] William J. Baumol, *Business Behavior, Value and Growth* (New York: Harcourt, Brace & World, 1959), p. 27.

[11] Bowley, *The Mathematical Groundwork of Economics* (New York: Augustus Kelley, 1924); Stackelberg, *Marketform and Gleichgewicht* (1934). The reliance here is upon discussions found in secondary sources: e.g., Fellner, *op. cit.*, Vickrey, *op. cit.* A compact summary is found in Kalman J. Cohen and Richard M. Cyert, *Theory of the Firm: Resource Allocation in a Market Economy* (New York: Prentice-Hall, 1965), pp. 236–239.

[12] The problem is comparable to testing the kinked demand curve hypothesis. Cliff Lloyd, *op. cit.*, pp. 216–217.

the same as under competition, simple monopoly, or Cournot oligopoly; may be indeterminate; and, perhaps, may be higher than the simple monopoly level. It therefore appears that, taken as a whole, these theories furnish no clear prescription for antitrust policy. With respect either to dissolution or mergers, everything depends upon the kinds of conjectures that are created or suppressed, and upon interactions among them. Even if costs were not affected, dissolution might raise, lower, or not affect prices, and the same is true of mergers.

Third, and crucial for the particular antitrust policy problem under consideration here, the theories do not tell us what changing the *number* of sellers will do. Stackelberg's bewildering array of possibilities is developed for duopoly, and he apparently made only unsystematic and gratuitous assertions about three or more sellers.[13] According to Fellner "there is a presumption that the addition of more firms increases the likelihood of Stackelberg disequilibrium." "Disequilibrium" in this sense is a euphemism for indeterminacy at best, or for the combative pursuit of incompatible objectives, which may lead to some kind of unlocated stalemate or warfare of undetermined character and duration. Since Stackelberg's theory predicts a high probability of "disequilibrium" even under duopoly, outcomes with more sellers may be even less determinate.

Finally, even if the theories are predicted unambiguously, there are other crucial problems in adapting them to real-world policy making. For example, they assume —but do not explain why—there is no entry; and they do not investigate the relationship between costs and the structure of industry.

Rightly or wrongly, believers in theories that predict indeterminate results need not adopt a hands-off policy position. Stackelberg himself found the high likelihood of duopoly impasse so distressing as to

justify comprehensive state control. On the other hand, anybody who believes in Stackelberg, admires rivalry, and believes that the social advantages of rivalry increase the more closely chaos is approached, might argue that any increase in the number of sellers is likely to be a good thing.

In important respects, applications of game theory to oligopoly are, paradoxically, both lineal descendants of and reactions against the classical theories. Game theories, by promising determinancy in complex cases, inspired much optimism.[14] Perhaps they deserve more study; but optimism about their usefulness has become much less intense with the passing years, and they will not be discussed further here.[15]

Qualified and Pure Joint Profit Maximization: Some "Modern" Theories

For the most part, the theories so far discussed discourage the notion that fewness of sellers—even two—will produce simple monopoly results. In more recent years, however, there has been some systematic theorizing—and much more assertion —to the effect that oligopoly is, essentially, monopoly. It is sometimes said that these modern theories are more "realistic," which may mean that their predictions are more often confirmed by industrial experience, or simply that their underlying assumptions look more plausible. Since there apparently has been no thorough analysis by oligopoly theorists of all of the industry studies and other anecdotal evidence, plausibility of assumptions is a more likely explanation.

[13] Fellner, *op. cit.*, pp. 102–103, and p. 115, note 19.

[14] Von Neumann and Morgenstern, *Theory of Games and Economic Behavior* (New York: Wiley, 1944); Martin Shubik, *Strategy and Market Structure: Competition, Oligopoly, and the Theory of Games* (New York: Wiley, 1959).

[15] Helpful introductions are found in Hurwicz's review, *op. cit.*, reprinted in Stigler and Boulding, *op. cit.*, pp. 505–526; and Vickrey, *op. cit.*, pp. 342–367. A critical and disappointed reaction is found in Carl Kaysen's review of Shubik's book, in *American Economic Review*, L (December, 1960), pp. 1039–1040.

In any case, the modern theories begin by recognizing that rivalry is expensive to participants (a notion that sets the stage for collusion theories); or that relatively large sellers are or will become aware of the direct and indirect consequences of what they do (a notion that sets the stage for joint profit maximization or near maximization without explicit collusion).

Chamberlin. Probably the two most popular and accessible sources of these doctrines are major works by Chamberlin and Fellner.[16] Though it is widely quoted and perhaps even more widely believed, Chamberlin's theory about numbers of sellers turns out to be at least two, and perhaps three, rather vague theories.

The first concerns a world of certainty, perfect knowledge, and given product varieties, and it seems to be the one most generally absorbed. Given perfect knowledge, and that each seller can have a significant impact upon the market, "If sellers have regard to their total influence upon price, the price will be the monopoly one."[17] And, "If the sellers are three or more, the results are the same, so long as each of them looks to his ultimate interest. There is no gradual descent to a purely competitive price with increase in numbers, as in Cournot's solution. The break comes when the individual's influence upon the price becomes so small that he neglects it."[18] Thus, it appears, only the most extreme atomism will break down the monopoly price. It is not clear why anybody who takes this theory seriously could ever conscientiously oppose mergers that stop short of single-firm monopoly, or propose dissolution that falls short of atomization. For, once numbers are relatively small, further reductions (or increases) would not appear to matter.

Chamberlin seems to say that atomism will produce competitive outcomes even when there is perfect knowledge and no uncertainty (he has a separate section on uncertainty). Whether this is a separate theory, it may not be consistent. With large numbers of firms, in Chamberlin's world each cuts price because he has "small" general market effects. All therefore cut. At this stage of his argument, Chamberlin apparently does not assume a significant time lag during which any single price cutter benefits because the others do not follow. With perfect knowledge and instantaneous reactions, and the same profit-maximizing rules that apply to oligopoly, it is not so clear that *anyone* will cut. For price cutting will hurt everybody, and will do so at once. This leaves to one side the important question of what level and kind of price is being cut: Numerous or not, firms do not cut a market-clearing competitive price.

Chamberlin seeks consistency by using a "disturbance" factor:

> No one seller will look upon himself as *causing* the dislodgement, since he secures his gains with comparatively little disturbance to any of his rivals. Under these circumstances there is no reason for him to withhold a shading of his price which is to his advantage, and which has no repercussions.[19]

The intrusion of "disturbance" into the argument may mean that sellers do not *recognize* the cause of sales loss and are therefore not "disturbed" by it; or that they have a higher pain threshhold; or that subjective costs of reacting are somehow higher than the value of sales lost. The first interpretation is inconsistent with the assumption of perfect knowledge.

In short, contrary to Chamberlin, it seems entirely possible that any atomism that does not produce *perfectly* elastic firm demand curves may not be enough to guarantee "competitive" outcomes. Imperfect knowledge or some "disturbance" coefficient may also be involved.[20]

---

[16] Chamberlin, *op. cit.*, pp. 46–51, 53–54; Fellner, *op. cit.*, passim.

[17] Chamberlin, *op. cit.*, p. 54.

[18] *Ibid.*, p. 48.

[19] *Ibid.*, p. 49.

[20] Compare George J. Stigler, *Essays in The History of Economics, op. cit.*, pp. 260–261.

Whether or not Chamberlin's large number theory is really a perfect knowledge theory, or even logically consistent with his other visions, he does attempt to treat uncertainty and market lags as a separate issue. His general conclusion is that uncertainty makes the outcomes indeterminate: Price may be at the monopoly level, competitive, or somewhere in between. At only one point is the number of firms treated as an explanatory variable, and then vaguely. As he put it,

> If numbers are fairly small, any one seller can be *certain* that his incursions upon the others by a price cut will be large enough to cause them to follow suit; and therefore no one will cut. If they are very large, he can be certain that his incursions will be such a negligible factor to each other seller that no one will "follow suit" (i.e., cut *because* he did); and therefore everyone will cut. But in between there is a range of doubt. . . . Between these limits the result is unpredictable.[21]

That is not too helpful, because "few" and "many" are undefined, or at best, are defined in terms of attitude rather than arithmetic; and because the really interesting dissolution and merger problems require information about what happens with *small changes* in the number of firms. In short, if small changes in the number of firms leaves the number still small, it apparently makes no difference. If we take Chamberlin literally, changes in number do not matter unless, for example, a clear "fewness" situation is pushed into the undefined intermediate number case in which anything may happen.

What does all of this imply for merger and dissolution policy? According to Chamberlin, in a world of perfect knowledge only extreme atomism will suffice to produce competitive results. Otherwise, the monopoly solution will emerge; and there seems to be no real room for improvement through antimerger or dissolution policy. In an uncertain world, however, results may lie at the monopoly or competition poles, or anywhere in between. This revelation, too,

affords little support for dissolution or merger policy: Results from fewness may be very "good" or even "perfect," without any policy; and, bad or good, it is quite unclear whether antitrust policy will have any effect, let alone whether it is likely to be "desirable." For somewhat obscure reasons, Chamberlin does assert that—even under uncertainty—*extremes* of concentration will tend to produce some sort of monopolistic results, while extreme atomism will tend to the competitive solution. But between the poles—i.e., for the sorts of situations for which dissolution is likely to be urged—anything can happen and small changes in concentration do not matter.

Chamberlin's doctrines therefore furnish no policy prescriptions. This is particularly strange, since much academic and judicial support for dissolution and merger policy seems to rest on the Chamberlinian notion that fewness is practically equivalent to monopoly. It would seem much more appropriate for antitrust fans to cite Cournot rather than Chamberlin. They almost never do.

All in all, Chamberlin says astoundingly little that is relevant to the number of firms as a central antitrust goal, which may reflect his emphasis on other market structures than oligopoly.

Fellner. On the other hand, Fellner devotes a whole book to oligopoly. So far as his contribution, Fellner offers us a qualitative theory of non-collusive, partially achieved joint profit maximization. In principle, maximum joint profits is a sensible goal, since it is theoretically possible to improve everyone's position by pursuing it.

Probably few real-world cartels have ever succeeded in joint maximization, and in Fellner's scheme, nonconspiratorial oligopoly will probably miss the goal still further. Some or all of the barriers to joint maximization that Fellner discusses are common to cartels and oligopolies: maneuvering with respect to profit division, which may prevent profit maximization; uncertainties and mistakes; cost and product differences that can be reconciled perfectly only with pooling, which is infeasible; dif-

---

[21] Chamberlin, *op. cit.*, pp. 52–53.

ferences in risk appraisal and risk-aversion; differences between the interests of shareholders and managers; infeasibility of perfectly coordinating the type and rate of innovation and other non-price variables; the fact or grisly prospect of periodic price warfare, for whatever reasons;[22] and so on.

In short, Fellner's oligopolies are very like cartels except in degree: "Coordination is likely to be tighter under explicit cartel agreements than under quasi-agreements. [But] the analytical framework suitable for the discussion of cartel problems is not fundamentally different from that developed in the preceding pages."[23]

Fellner's analysis is neither quantitative nor operational. For example, he never meaningfully defines fewness or differentiates degrees of it. Although he delivers an occasional dictum to the effect that larger numbers make perfect joint maximization even less likely, he never analyzes the problem of numbers at all.[24] Nevertheless, his Chapter XI, devoted to policy, bristles with recommendations to increase the number of sellers, presumably by dissolution. He asserts, without evidence or even explicit theoretical support, that increasing the number of sellers will increase competition in a static sense, and will increase technological progress over time[25] sufficiently to outweigh such static cost disadvantages as are likely to arise from increasing the number of sellers. These are powerful conclusions to be based neither on the theory he develops nor upon any empirical evidence at all.

Although Fellner does not link his policy recommendations to his theories, it may be possible to do so in a general way. In Fellner's scheme, it is *differences* among firms (and their managers) that cause departures from true joint-profit maximization. It might be argued, therefore, that variations among firms will rise with their numbers. But it is still not clear how *much* effect should be expected as numbers vary. Furthermore, as Fellner recognizes, raising the number of firms may raise costs.

Recent Theories: Cartel Instability

With the exception of Cournot, and theories based directly upon his work, the theories considered to this point are highly indefinite about the effects of small changes in the number of firms. Three recent theories resurrect the number of firms as a general explanatory variable for cartel instability: They are Stigler's, Warren Nutter's,[26] and Orr-MacAvoy's.[27] As we will see later, two other recent theories, those of Demsetz and Day, argue that numbers—at least in the usual sense—do not matter.[28]

Stigler. Stigler's theory is remarkable because it generates profound and wide-ranging economic hypotheses from purely

---

[22] For a theory of "warfare" see R. L. Bishop, "Duopoly: Collusion or Warfare," *American Economic Review* (December 1960), pp. 933–961.

[23] *Ibid.*, p. 230.

[24] Examples of his *dicta* appear at pp. 34–35, 102–103, 185, 189.

[25] For examples of his *dicta*, see *ibid.*, pp. 283, 286–288, 291–292, 294, 297–298, 310. But see also p. 306.

[26] Stigler, "A Theory of Oligopoly," *The Journal of Political Economy*, LXXII, 1 (February 1964), 44–61. An earlier paper furnishes valuable background methodology: Stigler, "Economics of Information," *Journal of Political Economy* (June 1961). See also the brief summary in Stigler, *The Theory of Price*, (3rd ed.) (New York: Macmillan, 1966), pp. 216–220; and Ronald I. McKinnon, "Stigler's Theory of Oligopoly: A Comment," *Journal of Political Economy*, LXXIV (June 1966), 281–285. Nutter's paper, "Oligopoly and the Competitive Process," is as yet unpublished. The draft I studied was dated June 14, 1966.

[27] Daniel Orr and Paul W. MacAvoy, "Price Strategies to Promote Cartel Stability," in Paul W. MacAvoy, *The Economic Effects of Regulation: The Trunk-Line Railroad Cartels and the ICC Before 1900* (Cambridge, Mass.: MIT Press, 1965), Appendix, pp. 205–218.

[28] Harold Demsetz, "Why Regulate Utilities?", *The Journal of Law & Economics*, XI (April 1968), pp. 55–65; Richard H. Day, "A Note on the Dynamics of Cost Competition within an Industry," *Oxford Economic Papers*, XX (November 1968), 369–373.

statistical laws and phenomena. It is a theory about information, and the major hypotheses are quantitative and, perhaps, testable. Indeed, Stigler even presents a few scraps of evidence. Like all manageable theories, it is abstract. Some may object that it is also biased, since it starts by accepting "the hypothesis that oligopolists wish to collude to maximize joint profits." [29] That this is as much a methodological convenience as a preconception about monopoly outcomes is, however, hinted in Stigler's fuller statement:

> A satisfactory theory of oligopoly cannot begin with assumptions concerning the way in which each firm views its interdependence with its rivals. If we adhere to the traditional theory of profit–maximizing enterprise, then *behavior is no longer something to be assumed but rather something to be deduced.* The firms in an industry will behave in such a way, given the demand–and–supply functions (including those of rivals), that their profits will be maximized.
>
> The combined profits of the entire set of firms in an industry are maximized when they act together as a monopolist. At least in the traditional formulation of the oligopoly problem in which there are no major uncertainties as to the profit–maximizing output and price at any time, this familiar conclusion seems inescapable. *Moreover, the result holds for any number of firms.*
>
> Our modification of this theory consists simply in presenting a systematic account of the factors governing the feasibility of collusion, which like most things in this world is not free.[30]

Whereas his argument is framed for collusion, Stigler does *not* assume or conclude that "fewness" of sellers guarantees the monopoly solution even *with* collusion; and it is only a modest further step to conclude that non-collusive oligopoly is even more likely to depart from monopoly. We will later see that Nutter's unpublished work attempts that step.

For a world of imperfect information

and knowledge, Stigler investigates how the incentive secretly to cut price will change with changes in the size and number of buyers, number of sellers, and the probability that customers who buy from a given seller in one period will do so in the next in the absence of price cutting. Although the value of each of these variables may have important economic explanations, Stigler does not investigate them.

Under collusion, when price exceeds marginal cost there is an incentive for any participant to shave prices so long as others do not. By definition, secret price cutting occurs when information is imperfect, and will be less attractive the more quickly or certainly it will be found out. If a seller has or tries to attract many small customers, for any given volume of sales increase, he will have to cut price to more customers than if they are large. And, as Stigler shows, the larger the number of buyers to whom cut prices are offered, the greater the probability that at least one rival will find out. As he puts it, "No one has yet invented a way to advertize price reductions which brings them to the attention of numerous customers but not to that of any rival." [31] For this reason, the number and size distribution of customers importantly influences the amount of secret price-cutting.

Given Stigler's assumptions, for a given volume of industry sales and number of customers, the larger the number of sellers the smaller is the absolute number, and proportion, served by any one seller. If there is not pooling of correct sales and price data by sellers, and if the cost of any seller's directly obtaining reliable price data is excessive, each seller can only infer what is going on by studying his own sales over time. By assumption, in the absence of price cutting there is still some random fluctuation in the number of customers served by a single seller per unit time. The number of customers served by any seller in one period is the sum of old customers who buy again, plus other sellers' customers who switch, less old customers who switch to

---

[29] Stigler, "A Theory of Oligopoly, *The Journal of Political Economy, op. cit.,* p. 44.

[30] *Ibid.,* my italics.

[31] *Ibid.,* p. 47.

other sellers.[32] Given a specific probability that customers in one period will repeat in the next—i.e., a "loyalty" probability—each seller expects his volume of business to fluctuate around some *average* volume even in the absence of "chiseling." By assuming that certain statistical principles are at work, it is possible to derive families of probability distributions that describe the chance variation of customers for different values of these parameters: the number of buyers and sellers, and the repeat purchase probability.

Since any seller may have below-average business because of chance variation or because someone else is chiseling, one problem is how and when to infer that price-cutting is going on. With incomplete information, a seller may draw two kinds of erroneous inferences: He can wrongly infer price-cutting, or he can wrongly infer that there is no price-cutting. Both errors have costs. Stigler does not attempt to specify the optimal decision rule, which among other things would require information about the costs and benefits of each rule. Under any reasonable decision rule, chance variation affords shelter behind which price cutters can hide. The degree to which they can do so influences their incentive to do so.

The incentive to cut price, which Stigler quantifies as the percentage increase in sales that a price cutter can get away with, thus depends upon (1) what decision rule is used to infer price cutting; (2) the number of buyers; (3) the number of sellers; and (4) the probability of repeat purchases if there is no price cutting. Stigler actually computes "incentive values" for price cutting in various circumstances. Suppose a seller infers price cutting if his sales fall below the mean expected sales value by more than one standard deviation, and if any single rival obtains a disproportionate share of the defecting customers. Then as Stigler's computations show:

(a) The gain in sales from any one rival by secret price-cutting is not very sensitive to the number of rivals, given the number of customers and the probability of repeat sales. The aggregate gain in sales of a firm from price–cutting—its total incentive to secret price-cutting—is the sum of the gains from each rival, and therefore increases roughly in proportion to the number of rivals.

(b) The incentive to secret price-cutting falls as the number of customers per seller increases—and falls roughly in inverse proportion to the square root of the number of buyers.

(c) The incentive to secret price-cutting rises as the probability of repeat purchases falls, but at a decreasing rate.[33]

With respect to point "(*a*)" however, an interpretive comment is necessary: There is of course *no* incentive to chisel when there is but a single seller; yet there is a significant incentive to chisel when there are only two; and there is a large increase in the incentive to chisel as we go from two to three sellers. Thus it is that some of the most important of Cournot's "predictions" are reinforced, for a world of imperfect information, by an analysis of quite different character.

Although one should be careful in evaluating the test, Stigler's predictions are confronted by a few data on newspaper and radio advertising rates, profitability among industries, and steel prices. Since it is directly relevant to the central problem of this book, the following observation should be noted:

> In general the [industry profitability] data suggest that there is no relationship between profitability and concentration if H [the Herfindahl index of concentration] is less than 0.250 or the share of the four largest firms is less than about 80 per cent. These data, like those on advertising rates, confirm our theory only in the sense that they support theories which assert that

[32] Stigler also considers customers entering the market for the first time. Since this complication is not essential, it is ignored here.

[33] Stigler, *op. cit.*, p. 51.

competition increases with number of firms.[34]

Stigler's theory predicts that, when information is poor, the incentive to chisel from a cartel price rises with the number of sellers. The central theory does not predict *how much* price effect a given small change in numbers will have; but the inference seems to be that, if the number of firms is high enough, it will not pay them to form a cartel. The two brief statistical investigations he made purport to show how price varied among markets containing different numbers of firms, given the unspecified conditions prevailing in the two special "industries" investigated. Stigler's data indicate that newspaper advertising rates were about 10.5% higher in towns having one evening newspaper than in those having two; and that on average, a 10% increase in the number of AM radio stations is accompanied by a .7% reduction in spot commercial rates. According to Stigler:

> Both studies suggest that the level of prices is not very responsive to the actual number of rivals. This is in keeping with expectations based upon our model, for that model argues that the number of buyers, the proportion of new buyers and the relative sizes of firms are as important as the number of rivals.[35]

---

[34] *Ibid.*, p. 57.

[35] *Ibid.*, p. 56.
Compare the experimental data revealed in a recent paper: Dolbear *et al.*, "Collusion in Oligopoly: An Experiment on the Effect of Numbers and Information," *op. cit.*, pp. 240–259. Unfortunately, the paper is troublesome in various respects. (1) The title is seriously misleading: The paper and the experiments underlying it have nothing to do with collusion, since the student participants did not collude. (2) This is "closed" oligopoly, with no regard to potential entry and no provision for actual entry. (3) As the authors recognize, the limited number of price choices probably biases the results. (4) Although the products *are* differentiated, product is not a variable, nor is the mode of production. (5) The *own* elasticity of demand for each firm is independent of the number of firms, but—apparently—the cross elasticities for all pairs of firms decline systematically with the number of firms. The implication is that, as the

Stigler's theory does not outline a sequential process through time. It is, rather, a statement of conditions that increase or decrease the incentive to cut price, specifically when there is collusion. Note that, by assumption, information is poor, product variety is fixed, entry is blocked, and costs are independent of the number of firms.

It must be remembered that Stigler's theory, like all others, was developed on the basis of specific assumptions; and it must be pointed out that the policy implications are somewhat ambiguous.

In Stigler's theory, products are, in effect, mildly differentiated; but they do not change. Product change is not a strategy. For many "oligopoly" industries, product change is in fact a vital part of the competitive process. And it is not clear how inferences about the number of firms would change for a world in which product change is important, and in which the costs and benefits of product change are themselves related systematically to the number of firms. Furthermore, Stigler's theory totally abstracts from entry.

So far as policy goes, in Stigler's theory the number of firms is only one of the ingredients that could be influenced by policy, and it is not certain that it is the best one to influence. For example, since, in Stigler's model, departures from the collusive solution arise from ignorance, it may be fruitful to tax information, as by prohibiting price-posting instead of requiring it. Changes in the laws with respect to price discrimination—to encourage chiseling—might be more helpful than attempting to alter the number of firms, especially

---

number of firms is increased, *each substitute* is now a correspondingly more remote substitute. (6) Costs are identical among firms and independent of industrial structure.

Whatever the results are worth, changing the number of firms had relatively small price effects. For "complete information," four firms produced 9% lower prices and 14% lower profits than two firms. For "incomplete information" four firms produced 7% lower prices and 9% lower profits than two firms; and 16 firms produced 12% lower prices and 20% lower profits than two firms.

since the latter may raise costs. Mergers of buyers would also seem to help, rather than hurt, "competition" among those who supply them. But, since sellers are also buyers, it is not obvious where the necessary trade-off leaves us. Furthermore, the evils of Stigler's oligopoly are really those of collusion. Particularly if costs are influenced by the number of firms (but in principle even if they are not), it can be argued that enforcement of laws against collusion make at least as much sense as policy that changes the number of firms.

Finally, at most, Stigler's theory says— for a particular set of assumptions—that in two otherwise comparable situations, the market with more sellers will tend to have lower prices than the one with fewer. It does *not* say that in the real world it is worthwhile to increase the number of sellers by dissolution or other artificial means. This is because policy has direct costs; and because product types, variety, and firms' cost may all be related to the number of firms.

Nutter. Nutter's tentative oligopoly theory is more "realistic" and more complex. Although it is now in unpublished preliminary form, it may be useful to summarize it very briefly.

In Nutter's model, prices are openly posted by each seller; but it costs something for buyers and sellers to discover what the prices are. The model is dynamic, and there is a discount rate for deferred gains and losses. An industry demand curve is specified. Buyers and sellers both monitor market prices. There are rules to decide whether to infer price cutting from sales lost. Unlike Stigler's model, Nutter's seeks to predict how *much* price will be cut. The model is extremely complicated, and the quantitative results are based on computer runs. According to Nutter:

As the broadest generalization we may say that, in order for price to be cut to any specific point relative to the monopoly level, the required number of firms will be smaller (a) the greater the competitive intensity of a community, (b) the greater the normal variability in daily sales in the

market at large, and (c) the lower the marginal costs of search for buyers relative to sellers. Put the other way round, the greater the number of firms, the more likely that price will be cut to some given level, other relevant factors the same. These considerations given their due, it may not be too rash to conclude that the monopoly price, once established, will rarely persist in an industry with more than one firm.

Nutter's theory is, thus, an extension of Stigler's. Taken together, they seem to argue that oligopoly is not simple monopoly, and that "competitiveness" tends to increase with the number of firms, at least if the larger number of firms is due to entry or has some other natural explanation.

Orr-MacAvoy. Some of the implications of MacAvoy's and Orr's model are similar to Stigler's and Nutter's. Under their "optimal" rule for a cartel's response to chiseling, they conclude that "the effectiveness of the cartel's strategy varies inversely with . . . the number of firms in the cartel. . . ."[37]

Entry Theories

Bain-Sylos-Modigliani. The version discussed here is Modigliani's.[38] The theory

---

[36] For Stigler's later views on oligopoly theory and facts, see Stigler, *The Theory of Price, op. cit.,* pp. 217, 219, 220. George J. Stigler, "The Economic Effects of the Antitrust Laws," *Journal of Law & Economics,* IX (October 1966), 225–237. (Compare J. T. Wenders, "Entry and Monopoly Pricing," *Journal of Political Economy,* LXXV, No. 5 (October 1967), 755–760.

[37] Daniel Orr and Paul W. MacAvoy, "Price Strategies to Promote Cartel Stability," *op. cit.,* p. 211.

[38] Joe Bain, "A Note on Pricing in Monopoly and Oligopoly," *American Economic Review,* XXXIX (1949), 448–464; *Barriers to New Competition* (Cambridge, Mass.: Harvard University Press, 1956); Franco Modigliani, "New Developments on the Oligopoly, Front," *Journal of Political Economy* (June 1958), pp. 215–232. Dale K. Osborne, "The Role of Entry in Oligopoly Theory," *Journal of Political Economy,* LXXII (August, 1964), 396–402; George J. Stigler, *The Organization of Industry* (Homewood, Ill.: Irwin, 1968), pp. 67–70; B. Peter Pashigian, "Limit Price and the Market Share

has been used both to explain how oligopoly can price so as to prevent entry, i.e., to forestall competition, and to show why potential competition lowers the oligopoly price, i.e., "works"! The theory does not explain the number of firms in the oligopoly, nor show how the effectiveness of the oligopoly would differ if it should have more or fewer firms.

The theory assumes that there are economies of firm size up to some point. Beyond this output rate, long-run average cost is flat. Even if the oligopolists and potential entrants have identical long-run curves, it may be possible to choose an oligopoly price and output rate such that profits are earned but no one will enter the industry. If potential entrants are convinced that the oligopoly will hold present output rate constant if they should enter, the entrants will be able to operate only on that part of the demand curve below the present oligopoly price. That is, entrants can expect price to fall, more drastically the larger is the optimum size of firm and the lower is the arc elasticity of industry demand. If the expected price after entry is lower than any value of average cost achievable by entrants, they will not enter. But this entry-limiting price *will*, according to the theory, be lower than if entry were not to be feared at all. Among others, Stigler, Pashigian, Osborne, and Wenders have criticized this theory severely.[39] Perhaps one additional comment needs to be made: If, beyond the minimum cost output, average cost is flat, why is there not pure monopoly everywhere? One firm could practice limit pricing from the very beginning. In short, why is there any oligopoly as opposed to single-firm monopoly? If we believe Modigliani, perhaps we should expect more pure monopoly and less "oligopoly" over the whole economy. That, however, is partly an empirical matter not settled here.

Demsetz. In a new tradition—based upon one long forgotten—Demsetz argues "that the asserted relationship between market concentration and competition cannot be derived from existing theoretical considerations and that it is based largely on an incorrect understanding of the concept of competition or rivalry." [40]

Even if, because of size economies, there is room in the market for only one efficient producer at a time, there can be rivalry to determine which firm that is. If this rivalry is expressed through product price, and if the average cost differences between the most efficient and next-most-efficient producers be small, price will in the limit approach average cost and profits will be at the competitive level. If only a single price is charged, this price will equal marginal cost precisely only if the product demand curve cuts long-run average cost precisely at its minimum point. Whether, in cases for which this is not true, price discrimination or "ideal" marginal-cost pricing regulation is still better is a question that involves cost and other welfare indicators. But Demsetz does make the case that the outcome, even under "natural monopoly," is likely to be comparable to average-cost pricing of the sort sought by regulation as we know it in the U.S. and that this outcome departs from the usual monopoly result assumed and approaches the competitive solution. The precise outcome depends upon information, costs of obtaining "bids," whether there is collusion, and costs of the prospective entrants, none of which is simply related to any given number of present producers.

Day. Richard Day develops a rigorous, abstract, model in which "Competitive equilibrium obtains even with a sole surviving low-cost producer." [41] Day's crucial assumptions seem to be that there is ignorance both of the industry demand curve

---

of the Leading Firm," *The Journal of Industrial Economics*, XVI (July 1968), 165–177; J. T. Wenders, "Entry and Monopoly Pricing," *Journal of Political Economy*, Vol. 75, no. 5 (October 1967), 755–760.

[39] See sources in fn 38.

[40] Harold Demsetz, "Why Regulate Utilities," *Journal of Law & Economics, op. cit.*

[41] Richard H. Day, "A Note on the Dynamics of Cost Competition within an Industry," *op. cit.*, pp. 369–373.

and of rivals' responses; that each seller takes current price as a datum and adjusts his own output to it; that there is a one-period lag between input and output; and that there is no borrowing. The competitive outcome results, quite independently of the number of sellers actually in the market at any given time. In a sense, through entry, he gets Edgeworth's results even though only one firm presently occupies the market.

By considering potential and actual entry squarely, Demsetz and Day redress a fatal weakness of the other oligopoly theories, in which entry is simply ignored.

In the Demsetz and Day theories, the number of actual sellers is neither here nor there. Entry, even in the limited sense of access to transactions, does matter. In both theories, competitive outcomes are approached with even one seller. So far as antitrust policy, both theories are consistent with punishing collusion and avoiding closed entry. Neither furnishes support for "trust-busting."

Thus there is still no coherent and consistent theory of oligopoly. There are many conflicting theories of oligopoly, and predicted behavior depends crucially upon the types of assumptions made.

It is true, for example, that one who wants to believe in the desirability of trust-busting can *assume* that there are no significant economies of firm size, and can choose theories—like Cournot's—to support his objective. But other choices yield other results, which is really the point. As a consequence, there is no single and no clear answer to the basic question. Depending upon which theory one chooses, increasing the number of firms may *increase* prices (even above the single firm monopoly level),[42] may lower prices, or may leave

prices unchanged. As one economist recently put it, *"We have no theory that allows us to deduce from the observable degree of concentration in a particular market whether or not price and output are competitive."* [43]

Nor does antitrust really offer us a choice between pure monopoly and pure competition. Most dissolution and merger cases involve the question of whether a few more firms in a "concentrated" industry would be "better" or more "competitive" than a few less. This question involves the analysis of "oligopoly"—in other words, markets of "few" sellers. At least since 1838 economists have approached the oligopoly problem by various routes, all of which have since been very heavily traveled by distinguished people. The same peak is still in view; but it has not yet been mapped, let alone scaled.[44]

---

[42] According to Machlup, for example, "There may be instances in which the risks of 'rocking the boat' are so high that oligopolists keep their prices *above* the price that would maximize their joint profits." Fritz Machlup, "Oligopoly and the Free Society," Vol. I, *Antitrust Laws and Economic Review* (July–August 1967), p. 18.

[43] Harold Demsetz, "Why Regulate Utilities?" *The Journal of Law and Economics, op. cit.,* pp. 59–60. Italics in the original.

[44] Anyone who believes that in spite of the variety of theoretic possibilities, there is general agreement about "concentration" and "oligopoly" should consult and compare the following sources: Morris A. Adelman, "Effective Competition and the Antitrust Laws," Harvard Law Review, LXI (September 1948), 1303; Joe Bain, "Price and Production Policies," in *A Survey of Contemporary Economics* (Homewood, Ill.: Irwin, 1948), pp. 159, 169, and "Conditions of Entry and the Emergence of Monopoly," in E. H. Chamberlin (ed.), *Monopoly and Competition and Their Regulation* (New York: St. Martins Press, 1954), p. 240; E. H. Chamberlin, "Product Heterogeneity and Public Policy," in R. B. Heflebower and G. W. Stocking (eds.), *Readings in Industrial Organization and Public Policy* (Homewood, Ill.: Irwin, 1965), pp. 237, 243; Clare E. Griffin, Testimony, June 9, 1955, Hearings Before Senate Subcommittee on Antitrust and Monopoly of the Committee on the Judiciary, 84th Cong., 1st Sess., Part I, "A Study of the Antitrust Laws," pp. 375–402, especially 383–385, 387, 389, 393, 395, 398–399; J. M. Clark, "Competition: Static Models and Dynamic Aspects," Heflebower and Stocking, *op. cit.,* pp. 246, 254, 255; Richard H. Leftwich, *The Price System and Resource Allocation* (3d ed.) (New York: Holt, Rinehart & Winston, 1965), p. 212; George W. Stocking, *Workable Competition and Antitrust Policy,* a

Theory, Costs, and Public Policy

The theories so far discussed compared the "competitiveness" of different outcomes on the usually implicit assumption that efficiency is independent of industrial structure. As we will now see, the efficiency question is important. It must ultimately be answered by facts rather than assumptions.

Efficiency has both static and dynamic aspects. Economists' standard two-dimensional diagrams, which compare "monopoly" and "competitive" prices and outputs, are barely adequate to treat static differences. They generally fail to settle dynamic questions. First, the static cost question. Reformers should recognize that forced changes in the number of firms may alter costs. If concentration arises because of economies of size (indeed, how else is

collection of essays (Nashville, Tenn.: Vanderbilt University Press, 1961), pp. 182, 272, 276–77, 368; R. B. Heflebower, "Monopoly and Competition in the United States of America," in E. H. Chamberlin, *Monopoly and Competition and Their Regulation, op. cit.*, p. 111; Paul M. Sweezy, "Demand Under Conditions of Oligopoly," Stigler and Boulding, *op. cit.*, pp. 404, 409; J. R. Hicks, "Annual Survey of Economic Theory: The Theory of Monopoly," in Stigler and Boulding, *op. cit.*, p. 374; William S. Vickrey, *op. cit.*, pp. 212–13, 367; Gideon Rosenbluth in *Business Concentration and Public Policy, op. cit.*, p. 57; Tibor Scitovsky, in *ibid.*, p. 112; Carl Kaysen in *ibid.*, p. 118; Shorey Peterson, "Antitrust and the Competitive Model," in Heflebower and Stocking, *op. cit.*, pp. 329, 331–332; Almarin Phillips, "Corporate Mergers, Industrial Concentration, and Public Policy," *Wharton Quarterly*, III, No. 2 (Winter 1968), 21–24; Edward Mason, "Market Power and Business Conduct: Some Comments," *American Economic Review* (May 1956), p. 480; Joel Dean, Testimony, *Economic Concentration,* Hearings Before the Subcommittee on Antitrust and Monopoly of the Committee on the Judiciary, U.S. Senate, 89th Congress, 1st Session, Part 4 (1965), p. 1697; John Blair, *ibid.*, part 2, p. 578; J. K. Galbraith, "Monopoly and the Concentration of Economic Power," in Howard S. Ellis (ed.), *A Survey of Contemporary Economics,* I (Homewood, Ill.: Irwin, 1948), pp. 102, 127; Jesse W. Markham, "Market Structure Business Conduct and Innovation," *American Economic Review*, LV (May 1965), 323–332.

the typical industrial oligopoly to be explained?), increasing the number of firms through public policy will raise costs. Even if, as in Cournot's world, more sellers will reduce the *spread* between marginal cost and price, more sellers might nevertheless hurt consumers, for costs are now higher. They may be enough higher that prices actually *rise*. Very few economists *qua economists* would applaud that result. It is all a question of whether the reduction, if any, of price *relative to* marginal cost is offset by losses in efficiency. It is therefore crucial to inquire into the magnitude of size economies and the amount of increased "competitiveness" reasonably to be expected from modest changes in the number of firms.

In a world like Cournot's there is a clear relationship between the number of firms and the *difference* between price and marginal cost. Even so, as in all other worlds, a rational antitrust policy must rest upon information about costs and demands. If Cournot is right, *approximately* "competitive" prices and outputs could be produced by relatively few firms, even if large firms were no more efficient than small ones. This could happen not only because, starting from one firm, small increases in the number of sellers would produce disproportionately large price and output affects. For a given number of sellers, price will more nearly approach the competitive norm as the elasticity of industry demand is higher; and the oligopoly industry in question may face a highly elastic industry demand.

In addition, if over a range larger firms have lower costs, an existing degree of oligopoly may more closely approximate an "ideal" outcome than will pure competition (or perhaps any other industrial organization). There are three major possibilities.

For clearer exposition—and with some violence to the strict logic, though none to the main point—let economies of size be reflected in the lower *level* of a constant cost function. In Figure 1 let D-D be the industry demand for a homogeneous product. LRMC, 0 is the minimum long-run marginal and average cost achievable. Assume that it obtains when the industry is "oligopolistic." Substantially higher or lower degrees of concentration would lead to higher costs. For example, let LRMC, C be the long-run marginal and average cost under a proposed dissolution scheme that brings price and marginal cost to practical equality. Let P_c be the resulting price, which will be called "competitive." Price under "oligopoly" may conceivably be equal to the "competitive" price, lower than the "competitive" price, or higher than the "competitive" price. Consider them in turn.

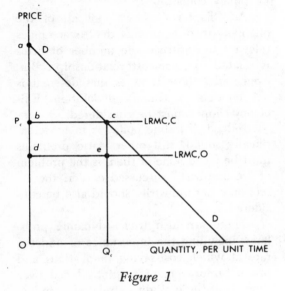

Figure 1

If the oligopoly price is *equal to P_c*, consumer surplus is *abc* for either oligopoly or competition.[45] There are zero profits under competition, but *bcde* profits under oligopoly. Consumers are equally well off, and producers are better off: The sum of profits and consumer surplus is greater under oligopoly than under competition. Unless the object of antitrust is simply to punish producers,[46] it is hard to defend the dissolution.

---

[45] Consumer surplus was defined on p. 13. As Stigler shows, given appropriate assumptions, consumer surplus is equal to that area under the demand curve and above the current price. G. J. Stigler, *The Theory of Price, op. cit.*, p. 80.

[46] Even so, the costs and spectator enjoyment from such punishment would have to be considered explicitly.

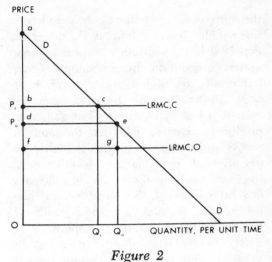

Figure 2

Figure 2 illustrates the possibility that oligopoly prices may be *lower* than the "competitive" price, because of cost-savings. "Competitive" price is P_c; oligopoly price is P_o. Under competition, consumer surplus is *abc*, and there are no profits. Under oligopoly, consumers are better off, and there are profits of *defg*. Since both consumers and producers are better off under oligopoly, it would be even harder to justify dissolution.

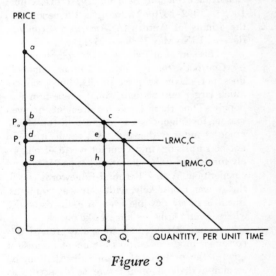

Figure 3

Figure 3 illustrates the possibility that prices may be higher under oligopoly, even though costs are lower.[47] By *assumption*,

---

[47] This is the so-called "mixed" or "trade-off" case to which Williamson directs his attention. Oliver E. Williamson, "Economies as an Antitrust De-

the sense of which will be considered later, price under "competition" is P_c; under oligopoly it is P_o. Consumer surplus is *larger* under competition, by an amount *bcdef*; but profits are higher under oligopoly by *bcgh*. Under oligopoly the area *bcde* cancels: It is lost by consumers but gained by producers. Hence, whether the sum of profits and consumer surplus is higher under oligopoly depends upon whether *degh*, the "net" profit *increase*, due to efficiency, is greater than *cef*, the "dead weight" allocation loss. In such a case a "trade-off" between efficiency and "monopoly" is required before establishing a case for dissolution. This is so even though price is *assumed* to be higher under oligopoly than competition.

For *closed* monopoly—in which entry is impossible—this type of trade-off may confront us, waiving dynamic complications. But antitrust seldom confronts closed monopoly or closed oligopoly. When entry *is* possible, there is little reason to assume that the oligopoly price will be greater than

that under "competition." If it were, entry would tend to occur. It *will* occur, at prices that are in the long run greater than P_c, if P_c is an atomistically competitive price: No single entrant will have significant price effects.[48] In short, Williamson's "trade-off" theory ignores entry. Even so, it does show that even if it lowered prices, dissolution is not necessarily economic. Thus, in the general case, Williamson's trade-off case is unlikely to persist in "open" oligopoly, which probably leaves us with the first two possibilities, and with Bork's and Bowman's major policy conclusions.[49]

As Chapter 5 shows, not all of the oligopoly theories predict that, over ranges relevant to antitrust, the number of firms is related to price-cost relationships. But, even under those theories that do, that is not enough to sanctify dissolution. Efficiency simply must be considered.

Indeed, if public policy is to be scientifically sound, still other static problems must be faced. One of them is the problem of "second-best," discussed earlier; the effect on other industries should also be considered.

There are also tricky dynamic problems, including the importance of and the rate at which cost-saving innovations and product-improvement are introduced over time. That these might be related to industrial structure would not be surprising, though relatively little is known about the relationship. For example, although W. Fellner argues, without evidence, that these dynamic improvements are favored by larger numbers of sellers, others take different positions. This problem is investigated in detail in Chapter 7.

---

fense," *American Economic Review* (March 1968), pp. 18–36; "Correction and Reply," *American Economic Review*, LVIII (December 1968), 1372–1376; "Allocative Efficiency and the Limits of Antitrust," *American Economic Review*, LIX (May 1969), 105–118.

This sort of analysis is neatly complemented by Cournot's theory, since Cournot oligopoly does not maximize joint profits, but produces much larger output than would single-firm monopoly. Thus there is no requirement, or even reason, for oligopolists to operate in the elastic range of industry demand. As a result, it would not be surprising, in a Cournot world, if oligopoly turned out to be allocatively superior to pure competition. With a Bertrand-Edgeworth world, this is even more likely, with as few as two firms. But it is surely possible even in Fellner's world, where several firms act almost like one.

Among other reasons, some may criticize this consumer-producer surplus argument because it ignores the problem of income distribution, by assuming that oligopolists are as deserving as consumers. This criticism will become more impressive when someone demonstrates that they are *less* deserving, and in what proportion.

---

[48] Compare the "limit pricing" hypothesis. Modigliani, *op. cit.*

[49] Robert H. Bork and Ward S. Bowman, "The Crisis in Antitrust," *Columbia Law Review* (March 1965), pp. 363–376; R. H. Bork, "The Goals of Antitrust Policy," *American Economic Review* (May 1967), pp. 242–253.

6. The Number of Firms and Competition

EUGENE F. FAMA AND ARTHUR B. LAFFER [*]

It is common economic doctrine that, strictly speaking, with less than an infinite number of firms in an industry, the demand curve facing any firm is negatively sloped. Moreover, the degree to which a firm faces a less than perfectly elastic demand curve is presumed to depend in part on the number of firms, with perfect competition arising in the limit as the number of firms approaches infinity. Since an infinite number of firms per industry is unrealistic, the assumption is made that as long as there are "many" firms, each acts "as if" there were an infinite number and this produces perfect competition. Firms, therefore, act as if they are price takers when in fact they are not.[1]

In this paper, we initially describe a partial equilibrium model—loosely called Cournovian, after Cournot—in which there is a positive relationship between the degree of competition and the number of firms in an industry. We then proceed to show that this relationship disappears in a general equilibrium model. In fact, the major result of the general equilibrium analysis is the fol-

lowing: under certain conditions, a general equilibrium with two or more noncolluding firms per industry is perfectly competitive.

I. The Cournot Model: Firms Mind Their p's But Not Their q's

Assume that there is an industry demand curve, $q = q(p)$, relating the quantity of the good demanded, q, to the price of the good, p, and that q has an inverse function, $p = f(q)$, which gives the price the market is willing to pay for q units of the good. It is assumed that both q and f are everywhere differentiable, and that the demand curve is negatively sloped, that is, $dq/dp < 0$.

If we also assume for simplicity that the costs to any firm, i, are only related to that firm's output, q_i, the firm's total profits, π_i, are

$$(1) \quad \pi_i = q_i p - \phi(q_i)$$
$$= q_i f \left[\sum_{j \neq 1} q_j + q_i \right] - \phi(q_i),$$

where $\phi(q_i)$ is the firm's cost function and $\sum_{j \neq i} q_j$ is the total output of the rest of the firms in this industry. Profit maximizing output for firm i occurs at a point where marginal revenue equals marginal cost

$$(2) \quad p + q_i f'(q) \left(1 + \frac{d \sum_{j \neq 1} q_j}{dq_i} \right) = \phi'(q_i)$$

In terms of equation (2), the degree of competitiveness of this industry depends on

$$d \sum_{j \neq i} q_j / dq_i$$

the output changes by all other firms that firm i anticipates will come in response to a one unit change in its output. For example, suppose that for any firm i,

$$d \sum_{j \neq i} q_j / dq_i = -1$$

so that a change in output by firm i is

Reprinted by permission of the *American Economic Review*, Volume 62, 1972.

[*] Professor and associate professor at the Graduate School of Business, University of Chicago, respectively. The paper has benefitted from the comments of Fischer Black, George Borts, Jacob Frenkel, John Gould, Michael Jensen, and Merton Miller. Financial support was provided by the National Science Foundation.

[1] A representative statement made by Armen Alchian and William Allen is the following:

We use the term "price takers' markets" to describe a class of markets where every supplier (and also every demander) provides so small a portion of the supply (or demand) that his output (or demand) has no significant effect on price; hence he "takes" the market price as if it were given by outside forces. [p. 106]

Similar and somewhat more detailed statements can be found in G. L. Bach, p. 370 and Paul A. Samuellson, p. 516.

anticipated to be precisely offset by changes on the part of other firms. In this case, even though the number of firms is finite, the industry is perfectly competitive: The individual firm's output decision literally has no effect on the market price of the good, and, from (2), profit maximizing output is where marginal cost is equal to price.

We eventually show that when there are two or more noncolluding firms in the industry, then under certain conditions a general equilibrium in fact implies the response function

$$d \sum_{j \neq i} q_j / dq_i = -1$$

so that the industry equilibrium is perfectly competitive. First, however, we consider the case, common in partial equilibrium treatments of firms and industry equilibrium, where other firms are not anticipated to change their output decisions in response to a change in the output decision of firm i— that is,

$$d \sum_{j \neq i} q_j / dq_i = 0$$

We find that the analysis of this case, which we call Cournovian, leads to relationships between the number of firms in an industry and the degree of competition like those described in the introduction.

When

$$d \sum_{j \neq i} q_j / dq_i = 0$$

equation (2) reduces to

(3) $$p = \phi'(q_i) - q_i f'(q)$$

In terms of elasticities, we get

(4) $$p = \phi'(q_i) + \frac{y_i}{\eta} p$$

were $\eta = -(dq/dp)(p/q)$ and $y_i = q_i/q$. Equation (4) in turn simplifies to

(5) $$p = \frac{\eta \phi'(q_i)}{(\eta - y_i)}$$

If all firms have the same technology and thus the same cost function, they make the same output decisions, and the share of any firm i in total output is $y_i = 1/n$, where n is the number of firms. Thus (5) can be rewritten

(6) $$p = \frac{n \eta \phi'(q_i)}{n \eta - 1}$$

Here the relationship between the number of firms and the degree of competition in the industry is clear. Other things equal, the larger n, the closer is price to marginal cost. Alternatively, in the Cournot model the firm's perceived elasticity of demand is $n\eta$. In the limit, that is, as $n \to \infty$, the firm's perceived elasticity is infinite, price is equal to marginal cost, and the industry is perfectly competitive.

From a general equilibrium viewpoint, the Cournot partial equilibrium assumption (that individually firms behave as if their price-output decisions have no effect on the output of other firms) can be criticized in that it places firms in the position of assuming that other firms do not behave optimally. And criticisms from the general equilibrium viewpoint are critical when their consideration would overturn the results of the partial equilibrium analysis. Such is the case here. We show now that under certain conditions the Cournovian relationship between the number of firms and the degree of competition in an industry disappears in a general equilibrium analysis.[2]

---

[2] In fact, even in the Cournot partial equilibrium model the conclusion that "numbers count" can disappear when there is a perturbation in the conditions of equilibrium. For example, suppose that there is a change in the industry's price elasticity of demand. This could result from a shift in the demand curve or from a change in slope. In such cases it is in the interests of firms to alter their prices. Since all firms start from the same position and have the same perceptions, they all change price by the same amount. But in the Cournot model firms assume that other firms do not change their output in response to a change in price; that is, each firm perceives the slope of its demand curve to be dq/dp, the slope of the industry demand curve. Thus each firm expects to experience the entire change in the industry quantity demanded implied by the price change. In fact, however, the change in the quantity demanded is divided evenly among all the firms. If each firm persists in assuming that other firms did not change their outputs, then observation of the effects of the price change leads each to adjust its estimate of the slope of the industry demand curve. If the adjustment is

II. The General Equilibrium Model

We are concerned with the usual static model in which tastes, endowments, technology, population, etc., are taken as given. The following conditions are also assumed to hold:

C1: Factors of production are infinitely divisible and fully and costlessly mobile across firms and industries. Moreover, either there are no factors that are used in only one industry, or such factors are owned by individuals and their services are sold to firms.

C2: Information about the returns earned by factors in different firms and industries is available costlessly to everybody, and factors act to maximize their returns.

C3: The same techniques of production are available to all firms in any given industry.

C4: The demand curve for the good produced by any industry is downward sloping with nonzero elasticity at all levels of output.

C5: At any given level of output, the curve showing the minimum marginal cost of industry output as a function of industry output has greater slope than the industry demand curve.

C6: Conditions of production are such that the rest of an industry can always use precisely the incremental quantities of factors of production demanded or released by a firm to offset precisely output changes by that firm.

Conditions C1 to C3 are standard. Conditions C4 and C5 are meant to rule out—and thus allow us to ignore—the types of "unusual" demand or cost conditions that could lead to problems with the stability of an industry equilibrium—problems that would only serve to confuse our arguments about the effects of the number of firms.[3,4] Finally, condition C6 has two major implications. First, strictly speaking, production functions must be characterized by constant returns to scale. Second, offsetting output changes by the rest of an industry in response to an output change by an individual firm must also precisely offset any externalities associated with the firm's new decision.

Given the maximizing behavior and

---

complete, firms now consider the slope of the industry demand curve to be $(1/n)dq/dp$ instead of dq/dp. Or equivalently, each perceives the elasticity of the industry demand curve to be $(1/n)\eta$. From equation (6), the new equilibrium price is

$$p = \frac{\eta \phi'(q_i)}{\eta - 1}$$

Comparing the above equation with equation (6), it is easy to see that the new price is precisely the price a pure monopolist would charge. And this result, which comes about without collusion, is independent of the actual number of firms in the industry.

Moreover, the result is much more general than the example of a shift in the industry demand curve. The Cournot equilibrium of equation (6) degenerates into the equivalent of a purely monopolistic industry equilibrium (irrespective of the number of firms in the industry) whenever (i) there is a shock that affects all firms in the industry in precisely the same way—for example, a common shift in cost curves—but (ii) in adjusting to the shock each firm persists in the Cournot assumption that other firms do not change their output decisions.

Finally, within the context of the Cournot partial equilibrium model, it is also possible to construct cases where there are shocks that affect firms differently, and where the result is that the industry goes from the Cournot equilibrium to a perfectly competitive equilibrium, irrespective of the number of firms in the industry. But rather than take this partial equilibrium path to perfect competition, we prefer to concentrate on the general equilibrium arguments that follow.

---

[3] If the industry is perfectly competitive, then C5 implies that at any given level of output, the industry supply curve has greater slope than the industry demand curve, so that equilibrium is unique. But C1–C6 are meant to be a minimum set of conditions that imply perfect competition, which in turn implies that the minimum marginal cost of industry output as a function of industry output is also the industry's supply curve. Thus, since the concern is with the minimum conditions that imply perfect competition, C5 is not stated directly in terms of supply curves.

[4] It is well to note that conditions C1–C5 are consistent with the Cournot model and are also commonly assumed in less specific analyses, like those referenced in the introduction, in which competition in an industry is assumed to depend on the existence of many firms, each producing only a small fraction of the industry output.

costless mobility of factors and technologies assumed in conditions C1–C3, under conditions C1–C6 a general equilibrium implies that returns to any factor are equal across all firms and industries.[5] We wish to show, however, that if there are two or more noncolluding firms in each industry, such a general equilibrium is also perfectly competitive in the sense that individual firms literally face perfectly elastic demand curves for their outputs. That is, when conditions C1–C6 hold, with two or more firms per industry the output decisions of a firm literally have no effect on prices.

To establish this result, suppose that, for whatever reason (perhaps simply to test the slope of its demand curve), a firm decides to disturb the general equilibrium by increasing its output. Without loss of generality, assume that there are no associated reactions from firms in other industries. Given the demand condition C4, if other firms in the changing industry initially did not lower their output, the per-unit price of the good produced by this industry would fall relative to prices of other goods. Given the industry cost condition C5, returns at least to some factors would then be lower in this industry than in others. Thus movement back to general equilibrium—that is, equality of returns across firms and industries—implies that other firms in the industry contract their output in response to an expansion by an individual firm.

Moreover, given the demand and cost conditions C4 and C5, and given the constant returns and offsetting externalities implied by condition C6, if other firms in the industry contract their output by an amount less than the individual firm expands, factor returns are still too low in this industry vis-à-vis others. On the other hand, given conditions C4 to C6 factor returns in the industry are too high vis-à-vis other industries if other firms in the industry contract their output by an amount more than the individual firm expands. Thus given the

maximizing behavior and costless mobility of factors assumed in conditions C1–C3, a return to the equality of returns implied by a general equilibrium requires that other firms in its industry respond by precisely offsetting any output increase by an individual firm.

Since analogous reasoning applies to output decreases, we can conclude that, given conditions C1 to C6, the ultimate general equilibrium response by other firms in an industry to a change in output by an individual firm is to offset precisely that output change; that is, in terms of (2),

$$d \sum_{j \neq i} q_j / dq_i = -1$$

so that price per unit of output is unaffected by the output decisions of individual firms. In short, as long as there are two or more noncolluding firms in each industry and conditions C1–C6 hold, then a general equilibrium implies that each firm is literally perfectly competitive in the sense that it faces a horizontal demand curve for its output.[6]

It is helpful to reexamine the roles of conditions C1–C6 in this result. First, the frictionless mobility and maximizing behavior of factors assumed in conditions C1–C3 are instrumental in the conclusion that in a general equilibrium factors are distributed across firms and industries in such a way that the returns to any factor are equal across all firms and industries. Then the "regularity" or "stability" conditions on demand and cost functions assumed in conditions C4 and C5 ensure that this general equilibrium principle of equal returns implies that the rest of an industry acts to offset the output changes of an individual firm. Finally, the constant returns and offsetting externalities implied by condition C6 then guarantee that the general equilibrium response of the industry is to offset precisely any output changes of a firm, which in turn,

[5] Thus if there are monopoly rents in the returns to any factor, then these monopoly rents must be equal across all firms and industries. The existence of such rents has no effect on the analysis.

[6] Note that this analysis *implies* that each firm is perfectly competitive, that is, faces horizontal supply curves in all factor markets, even though the industry as a whole may face upward sloping supply curves for factors.

of course, implies that the output decisions of a firm literally have no effect on prices.[7]

We emphasize that this analysis does not depend on any specific adjustment process by which other firms respond to output changes of an individual firm. Any adjustment process that converges to a general equilibrium—that is, equality of returns to any factor across all firms and industries—will do. And given conditions C1–C6, the general equilibrium is one in which individual firms are price takers.

Perhaps most objectionable in the conditions C1–C6 is the implication of C6 that production functions are characterized by constant returns to scale. With constant returns, though the output of the industry in a general equilibrium is determinate, the output or size of any individual firm is not. But except for some annoying "discontinuities," our analysis can also hold when there are nonconstant returns to scale—more specifically, when there is a finite optimal firm or plant size. Then we can only assume that condition C6 holds for output changes by individual firms that are multiples of the optimal firm or plant size. For such output changes, it is again true that price per unit of output is unaffected by the production decisions of individual firms. In other cases the general equilibrium response by other firms to a change in output by an individual

firm may be to offs
output change, th
sponse must be suf
profitable for another
enter or leave the indust

III. Summary

But even with the annoying discontinuities that arise when there is an optimal firm or plant size, the important general result still holds: When there are at least two noncolluding firms in an industry, there is no clear-cut relationship between the number of firms and the degree of competition. The absence of perfect competition must arise from violation of one or more of the conditions C1–C6—that is, it must arise from such things as indivisibilities, factor immobility, nonmaximizing behavior by factors, monopolistic access by individual firms to production techniques, and lack of information concerning the returns earned by given factors in different uses.

REFERENCES

A. A. Alchian and W. R. Allen, *University Economics*, Belmont 1967.

G. L. Bach, *Economics*, Englewood Cliffs 1963.

P. A. Samuelson, *Economics*, New York 1961.

---

[7] The offsetting output changes may come either from existing firms, including the possibility of exit, or from entry of new firms.

[8] One is, of course, hard pressed to reconcile the assumption of infinitely divisible factors with the existence of a finite optimal firm or plant size. But we do not wish to get into that issue here.

7. "Large" and "Small" Numbers
in the Theory of the Firm[*][1]

G. C. ARCHIBALD

The problem of group or industry equilibrium is commonly divided into a "large numbers" case and a "small numbers" case. The large numbers case is again subdivided into two: perfect competition and the large numbers case of Chamberlin. It is argued here that what matters to the analysis is not the (arithmetic) number of firms, but the beliefs about the policy of the rival(s) attributed to the individual firm. Number may be relevant as a test of the appropriateness of the beliefs attributed, but number itself is analytically irrelevant, and the distinction in terms of number alone is misleading. To illustrate this we shall consider first the analysis of Cournot and Chamberlin, and then the case of perfect competition. It will be shown that there is no *analytical* distinction between the Cournot solution in the case of two firms and the Chamberlin solution in the case of "many" firms because the same beliefs about the reaction of the rival(s), and hence the same behaviour, are attributed to the individual firm in each case. Not only the analytical tools but also *the equilibrium conditions* are identical. The argument is simply that, if the individual firm is assumed to believe that the price or output of its rival(s) remains constant, its behavior is independent of whether its rival is supposed to be one firm or many. We then go on to show that the distinction between a "large numbers" group and a

perfectly competitive group similarly depends, not on numbers, but on the beliefs attributed to the firms.

There is a subsidiary problem to clear up: the definition of a Chamberlin group in the large numbers case, which is well-known to be difficult if the product is differentiated. In the case of non-homogeneity, the concept of an "equal price change" is ambiguous, and so, therefore, is the "share-of-the-market" demand curve, the DD' of Chamberlin's analysis. Non-homogeneity also makes the concept of "equal costs" ambiguous or even meaningless. And non-homogeneity, of course, makes it difficult or even impossible, to mark off analytically the boundaries of the group. Hence, in order to make Chamberlin's analytical apparatus *work* in the large numbers case, and to obtain the tangency solution with the aid of the "share-of-the-market" and "particular" demand curves, it is necessary to assume a homogeneous product.[2] It is now also necessary to assume that firms adjust quantity rather than price. If this is not done, then in the large number case the demand for the product of each firm is infinitely elastic up to the total quantity which will be taken by the market at each price, and, for further individual price cutting, coincides with the total market demand curve. Thus in order to obtain the "share-of-the-market" and "particular" demand curves of Chamberlin, we must assume that the product is homogeneous, and that each firm adjusts quantity, accepting the new price, instead of quoting a new price itself.

Given, then, that these assumptions are necessary in order to make Chamberlin's

[*] Reprinted from *The Manchester School of Economics and Social Studies,* 1959, pp. 104–109 by permission of the author and publisher.

[1] The proposition discussed here appears rather obvious, and is mainly of scholastic interest. I discovered it while endeavouring to simplify the analysis for presentation in lectures, and offer it now merely because it does not appear to be generally known. I am indebted to Professor H. G. Johnson, Mr. K. Klappholz, and Dr. R. G. Lipsey for their comments and criticisms.

[2] The group we obtain is not the group assumed by Chamberlin; but it is the group we require for Chamberlin's analysis.

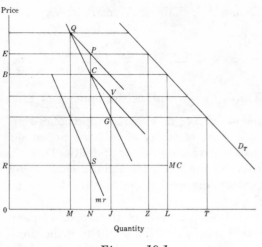

Figure 10.1

analysis of the "large numbers" case work, we can show that it does not differ from Cournot's analysis of the "small numbers" case. In the Cournot case, illustrated in Figure 10.1, we have two firms and a homogeneous product. We assume for simplicity a linear total market demand curve, D_T, and constant marginal costs, identical for each firm. If the two firms charge the same price, sales are equally divided between them.[3] Suppose that each firm is producing OM and that price is MQ. If both increase output by MN, total output increases to OL $(= 2ON)$, and the price that clears the market is OB. But each firm is to assume the output of the other constant at OM. If firm 'A' increases output to ON, it expects total output to be OZ $(= OM + ON)$, and price to be OE. Hence each expects to reach the position P, each increases output by MN, and each actually reaches the position C. Q, C, are, of course, points on the curve $\frac{1}{2}D_T$: QC is thus the "share-of-the-market" demand curve or DD', of Chamberlin. Q, P, are points on the curve $D_T - OM$, expected sales on the assumption that the other's output is constant: QP is thus the "particular" demand curve, or dd', of Chamberlin. And,

as in Chamberlin's analysis, dd' "slides down" DD': both firms increase output, hoping to reach P, and in fact reach C; through C there passes a dd' curve CV, so that both now expect to reach V, and in fact reach G on DD' with total output OT. If each firm endeavors to maximize profits on the assumption that rival's output is constant, each firm continues to increase output from any position such as Q or C so long as the marginal revenue to the dd' curve through that point exceeds marginal cost. Thus if, in Figure 10.1, marginal cost is constant at OR, and mr is the marginal revenue curve to CV, cutting mc in S at output ON, C is a position of equilibrium, obviously consistent with any level of (positive or negative) profits. This equilibrium is given by the cost curves, the "share-of-the-market" demand curve QCG, and the particular assumption about behavior. It is the short-run equilibrium of Chamberlin's group. In the long run we may alter QCG by changing the number of firms as easily in the case in which there are originally "two" as in the case in which there are originally "many." And, if we choose normal profits as a long-run equilibrium condition, we can obtain a tangency solution for *any* original number of firms.[4]

Thus there is no analytical difference between the Cournot duopoly case and Chamberlin's large numbers. The results are in both cases obtained by attributing to the individual firm the same belief about the behavior of the other(s), and so deriving the same policy, and the same equilibrium conditions. Given homogeneity, and the Cournot-Chamberlin assumption that each firm assumes the other(s) to be paralysed, the number of others makes no difference to the analysis.

We have been considering groups of firms producing a homogeneous product, and selling in a perfect market. An obvious question is how, if at all, a "large" group is to be distinguished from a perfectly com-

---

[3] If the product is homogeneous and the market perfect, demand is presumably divided between sellers at random. Analytical convenience requires that we assume the division of sales to be exactly fifty-fifty.

[4] There is the difficulty that, if the original number of firms is "small," DD' will move in "large" discontinuous jumps when their number alters.

petitive group. The answer once again depends, not upon members, but upon the beliefs attributed to the firms. We cannot, that is, proceed from a Cournot-Chamberlin group to perfect competition merely by increasing the number of firms. We shall now see how the assumptions must be changed to obtain perfect competition.

Consider the linear-demand duopoly case analysed above. If the market demand function is $p = a - nx$, the particular demand for the product of firm 'A' is $p = a - nx_a - nx_b$, which, when nx_b is assumed constant,[5] can be written $p = k - nx_a$. It is obviously immaterial what number of firms is deemed to contribute its output to k; and the slope of the particular demand curve is n whatever the size of k. Thus we cannot obtain the horizontal demand curve of perfect competition by altering the size of k or the number of firms sharing it. So long as the firm's particular demand curve is constructed by assuming the output of the rival's constant, and subtracting that constant from the market demand, the slope of the particular curve is necessarily that of the market curve. While the slope of the particular demand curve cannot be altered by changing numbers, however, its elasticity can be, and can be made to approach infinity. This apparent paradox is easily shown and easily resolved.[6] The elasticity of the market demand curve is

$$\eta = \frac{a - nx}{nx};$$

and the elasticity of 'A''s particular demand curve is

$$\eta_a = \frac{a - nx}{nx_a}.$$

Define 'A''s share of the market as $S_a = \frac{x_a}{x}$, and

$$\eta_a \cdot S_a = \frac{a - nx}{nx_a} \cdot \frac{x_a}{x} = \frac{a - nx}{nx} = \eta.$$

Thus $\eta_a = \frac{\eta}{S_a}$, and, as the number of firms increases, S_a ('A''s share) approaches zero, so η_a (the elasticity of 'A''s particular demand curve) approaches infinity. Thus we have, in the limit, the infinite elasticity of perfect competition, but not the horizontal slope.

The explanation of this apparent paradox is simply that the elasticity is the product of (the reciprocal of) the slope and the ratio of price to quantity, and that we can get it to infinity as easily by altering the latter as the former. When we change the number of firms without altering the construction of the particular demand curve, this is all we do: we move the curve bodily without altering its slope. In the limit the intercept of the curve with the vertical axis takes place at the price at which elasticity is measured, and elasticity is consequently infinity (if S_a is to approach zero without total output approaching infinity, 'A''s output must approach zero).

It follows, then, that so long as the group is selling a homogeneous product in a perfect market, no alteration in the size of the group alters the analysis. To obtain the horizontal demand curve of perfect competition we must drop the Cournot-Chamberlin assumption. We require instead the explicit assumption that the firm believes that changes in its output do not alter price. Between the limits of a single firm and an infinite number of firms, changes in number alone mark off no divisions or subdivisions for separate analysis.

Addendum[7]

In this note it will be argued that the theory

---

[5] We may complete the usual solution of the Cournot case as follows: assuming x_b to be a constant, total revenue for firm 'A' is $px_a = ax_a - nx_a^2 - nx_a x_b$, and expected marginal revenue is $a - 2nx_a - nx_b$, which may be put equal to marginal cost. Expected marginal revenue for firm 'B' is analogously $a - 2nx_b - nx_a$.

[6] On this point I am particularly indebted to Professor H. G. Johnson.

[7] The inclusion of this addendum follows an enjoyable correspondence with Professor Archibald and his generous suggestion that my points be summarized in this form rather than in footnotes to his reprinted article. I am grateful to Professor F. G. Davidson for helpful comments.

of duopoly presented in Archibald's Figure 10.1 is a variant of Cournot's, that in any case its exposition stands in need of correction at some points, and, finally, that Archibald's purpose could, perhaps, have been better served by comparing a price-variation version of duopoly with Chamberlin's large group. It should be stressed, however, that these observations in no way qualify Archibald's contention that "number itself is analytically irrelevant."

Identification of the Model. In Archibald's Figure 10.1 the firms are assumed to make their moves simultaneously. Thus, in the first period both increase their output by MN, and in the second period by NJ, and so on, in what appears as a Chamberlinian "slide." Simultaneous "plays" are also a feature of Chamberlin's dynamic adjustment process in his large group analysis. Cournot, however, assumed alternating moves, as is apparent in the adjustment process demonstrated in his "reaction curve" diagram.[8]

The assumption of simultaneous moves combined with the assumption of a homogeneous product makes it necessary to make a further assumption about the division of the market between the two firms in a situation where both set the same price and either could supply the whole market at that price. Archibald opts, reasonably enough, for equal shares. This combination of assumptions gives a starting point somewhere on the $QCG = \frac{1}{2}D_T$ curve in his diagram. The ex post position of each firm remains on this curve after each move. In contrast, in Cournot's model the firms produce different outputs in each period (except in equilibrium).

The Workings of the Model. In Archibald's model a downward price slide occurs; in Cournot's, a damped oscillation of price. In Archibald's model the (identical) outputs of the firms "slide" upward to the equilibrium level; in Cournot's the output of the firm having the first move will approach the

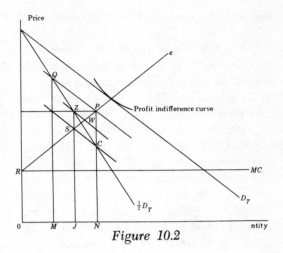

Figure 10.2

equilibrium level asymptotically from above, and that of the second firm asymptotically from below.[9] When the Archibald-Cournot model is correctly analysed, the Chamberlin-style price slide disappears here also. The simplest way of demonstrating this is to introduce into Archibald's diagram, here reconstructed as Figure 10.2, a set of isoprofit contours. Because of the assumption that marginal cost is constant, these will be rectangular hyperboles asymptotic to MC and the vertical axis and with origin R. The profit expansion path for the set of all straight-line "particular" demand curves with the slope of D_T is the ray R_e. This must be so if P is to be the maximum ex ante profit point on the particular demand curve QP. But if both firms, in trying to reach P, actually reach C, their next move must involve not an expansion of output and a slide down $\frac{1}{2}D_T$ but a *contraction* of output. For, from vantage point C, both firms see their ex ante profits maximized by the move to S. The effect of their identical reductions in output by JN is to shift their ex post position upward along $\frac{1}{2}D_T$ to Z, vertically above S. From Z the desired point for both firms is W, which involves an expansion of output, and so on. Equilibrium will be reached at the intersection of $\frac{1}{2}D_T$ and R_e. The dynamic adjustment process involves damped oscillations of firm and

---

[8] A. Cournot, *Researches into the Mathematical Principles of the Theory of Wealth,* translated from the original French by Nathaniel T. Bacon (1897).

[9] For a clear exposition of these properties of the Cournot model see Cliff Lloyd, *Microeconomic Analysis* (1967), p. 201 ff.

industry outputs, and also damped price oscillations.

An Alternative Approach. If we wish to compare Chamberlin's analysis with a theory of duopoly which *does* produce a "Chamberlinian slide," we can use Bertrand's price-variation version of Cournot.[10] In a situation where each firm sells the same product, and each sets his price on the assumption that his rival's price will not be changed in response to a change in his own, we can, with alternating moves, produce a competitive price war with each rival successively undercutting the other. With the further assumptions of simultaneous moves and 50/50 percentage market shares, we can

turn the process for each firm into an identical slide of a horizontal particular demand curve down a share-of-the-market demand curve. In each period each firm's actual sales will be given by the share-of-the-market demand curve.

To obtain Chamberlin's large group model from this simultaneous version of the Bertrand price-war model all we have to do is introduce product differentiation (which tilts the particular demand curve), relabel the share-of-the-market demand curve $\frac{1}{n}D_T$, where n is "large," and, for the tangency result, insert a U-shaped average cost curve. Clearly, if $n = 2$, no essential analytical features of Chamberlin's model are affected.

—L. Roy Webb

La Trobe University, Victoria, Australia
School of Social Sciences

---

[10] J. Bertrand, in a review of Cournot in *Journal des Savants*, 1883, p. 503. For a discussion of Bertrand-style "competitive bidding" see E. H. Chamberlin, *The Theory of Monopolistic Competition* (Cambridge, Mass., 1932 and later editions), chap. 3, section 3.

Part I–C • *Process*

In 1946, Professor Friedrich Hayek, in his Stafford Little lecture at Princeton University, argued that the theory of perfect competition is of little use as a guide to policy. His view was that the theory describes the conditions prevailing in equilibrium circumstances, but that it is uninformative about the process by which the economy moves toward an equilibrium. Policy must be concerned with how to achieve the competitive equilibrium and how to move the equilibrium position itself in ways that are desirable. Professor Hayek's view of the process was a forerunner of what we now call the economics of information, or the new microeconomics. He summarized his analysis in the following words:

> Competition is essentially a process of the formation of opinion: by spreading information, it creates that unity and coherence of the economic system which we presuppose when we think of it as one market.

It creates the views people have about what is best and cheapest, and it is because of it that people know at least as much about possibilities and opportunities as they in fact do. It is thus a process which involves a continuous change in the data and whose significance must therefore be completely missed by any theory which treats these data as constant.[1]

In selection 8, Professor Arrow echoes Professor Hayek, in a sense, when he says that "perfect competition can really prevail only at equilibrium." In disequilibrium, competitive markets display varieties of conduct normally associated with monopoly such as price discrimination (although sporadic rather than durable). It is lack of information which makes discrimination in competitive circumstances possible. Discrimination itself is the process by which

---

[1] Friedrich A. Hayek, "The Meaning of Competition," *Individualism and Economic Order* 106 (1948).

prices are moved from an old equilibrium level to a new position, the process by which information is spread and which causes prices to move more quickly to a new equilibrium than they would under a blanket prohibition of discrimination. Arrow introduces us to the problem that the price would never change in a market composed of price takers. Someone must "quote" a different price if, when in disequilibrium, the market is to move toward a competitive equilibrium.

Professor McNulty takes us a step further in the analysis of the competitive process. He argues that there are two varieties of competition—that which takes place in the market (determining price) and that which takes place in the firm (determining cost, quality, location, etc.). He broadens the concept of competition, taking it beyond the standard, static conception of given products produced with given techniques with given supplies of inputs. He reminds us of Adam Smith's aside about the competition of producers "who, in order to undersell one another, have recourse to new divisions of labour, and new improvements of art, which might never otherwise have been thought of." Competition, in the sense of a force, is a mover of equilibria, a dynamizer of the economy, doing those things which create disequilibria and in the static concept, result in monopoly (temporary).

But Schumpeter tells us, in selection 10, that the creative destruction by innovators which improves our economic lot would not occur if they could not achieve a monopoly (protected) status. The monopoly conveyed by being first with a new technique is protected, for a time, by the fact that competition materializes slowly because of "capital requirements or lack of experience" or even because of the use of means which "discourage or checkmate" would-be competitors. Schumpeter suggests that monopoly must be allowed innovators long enough to provide "the baits that lure capital on to untried trails."

With the Schumpeter selection, perhaps the circle has been closed. Instead of open entry, Schumpeter is asking for barriers to entry as a means of encouraging social progress. But that is a parody of Schumpeter. He is simply asking that entry be slow enough that an innovator can earn more innovating than not innovating—not that entry be barred. He is not even asking for as much as the patent system grants. Yet, episodes such as Bethlehem's introduction of the Grey beam under the price umbrella held by U.S. Steel [2] might be used to argue for the more than patent protection implied by Schumpeter in some passages as necessary.[3]

---

[2] U.S. Steel's pricing policy in the first decade of this century appears to have been a stabilization policy rather than an "umbrella" policy. Of course, its stable prices during a period of recession became an umbrella at such times (1904 and 1907–1908). On the other hand, in periods of growing demand, its stabilization policy apparently kept prices lower than they would otherwise have been. From 1901 through 1903, for example, it produced 64.7 percent of all steel ingot with 45 per cent of the capacity in the industry. Also, see Abraham Berglund, "The United States Steel Corporation and Price Stabilization," 38 *Quarterly Journal of Economics* 1 (1923) and Edward S. Meade, "The Price Policy of the United States Steel Corporation," 22 *Quarterly Journal of Economics* 452 (1908).

[3] Robert Hessen, "The Transformation of Bethlehem Steel, 1904–1909," 46 *Business History Review* 339 (1972).

8. Toward a Theory of Price Adjustment

KENNETH J. ARROW

The Role of Price Adjustment Equations in Economic Theory

In this essay, it is argued that there exists a logical gap in the usual formulations of the theory of the perfectly competitive economy, namely, that there is no place for a rational decision with respect to prices as there is with respect to quantities. A suggestion is made for filling this gap. The proposal implies that perfect competition can really prevail only at equilibrium. It is hoped that the line of development proposed will lead to a better understanding of the behavior of the economy in disequilibrium conditions.

In the traditional development of economic theory, the usual starting point is the construction for each individual (firm or household) of a pattern of reactions to events outside it (examples of elements of a reaction pattern: supply and demand curves, propensity to consume, liquidity preference, interindustrial movements of capital and labor in response to differential profit and wage rates). This point of view is explicit in the neoclassicists (Cournot, Jevons, Menger, and successors) and strongly implicit in the classicists (from Smith through Cairnes) in their discussion of the motivations of capitalists, workers, and landlords which lead to establishment of the equilibrium price levels for commodities, labor, and the use of land. The basic logic of Marx's system brings it, I believe, into the same category, although some writers have referred to his theories as being "class" economics rather than "individual" economics.[1] Although the dia-

lectical discussion of value in the opening sections of the first volume of *Capital*[2] lend some credence to this view, it is already clear in Marx's discussion of relative surplus value (Volume I, Part IV) that the introduction of new production processes is based on the profit-maximizing behavior of the individual entrepreneur;[3] and the role of the individual behavior reaction is basic in Marx's discussion of the equalization of profit rates in different industries in Volume III (especially Chapter X). In the opinion of most contemporary Marxist economists, such as Dobb [1945] and Sweezy [1942] and of sympathetic critics such as Lange [1934–35],[4] the value theory of Volume I is to be regarded only as a first approximation to that of Volume III, so that the latter must be regarded as the basic part of Marx's price theory.[5]

There remains one school which might be interpreted as objecting to the development of economics from the viewpoint of individual reaction patterns. These are the institutionalists, such as Veblen [1919], who attacked the behavior patterns hypothesized by contemporary economists for stressing the passive reacting character of individual behavior; but this argument

---

[1] See, e.g., Klein [April 1947, p. 118]: "Instead of studying the behavior of individuals, Marx studied the behavior of classes directly."

[2] K. Marx [1906]: Chap. I, and especially the discussion of surplus value in Chaps. VI, VII, VIII, and IX.

[3] See especially Vol. I, pp. 347–53.

[4] The same view has been expressed by at least one Soviet textbook, Lapidus and Ostrovityanov, *Outlines of Political Economy,* referred to by H. Smith in "Marx and the Trade Cycle" (6).

[5] An alternative interpretation sometimes adopted is that there is a basic contradiction between the two price theories. This position has been adopted by numerous critics of Marxism, following E. Böhm von Bawerk, *Karl Marx and the Close of His System* (7). The same view has been taken by the ultra-Marxist, Daniel de Leon, who rejected Volume III as Engels' misinterpretation.

seems partly a terminological question and partly an attack on the limited, excessively hedonistic expositions of the marginal utility theory current about 1900. Elsewhere both Veblen [1904] and Mitchell [1927] have emphasized the importance for the course of economic activity of the behavior of individuals, especially profit-making by firms.

In this individualistic framework, every relevant variable, except those classified as exogenous for the whole economic system, is the result of a decision on the part of some one individual unit of the economy. This paper considers the theoretical analysis of the decisions as to prices.

The standard development of the theory of behavior under competitive conditions has made both sides of any market take prices as given by some outside agency. Thus, for a single market,

$$(1) \qquad D = f(p), \; S = g(p)$$

where D is the demand for the commodity, S its supply, and p its price. The functions $f(p)$ and $g(p)$ represent the behavior of consumers and producers, respectively. But relation 1 constitutes only two equations in the three unknowns D, S, and p.

The theoretical structure is usually completed by adding the condition of equality of supply and demand,

$$(2) \qquad\qquad S = D.$$

What is the rationale of relation 2? In the usual treatise on economics, a great deal of attention is paid to the derivation of the functions entering into relation 1, but equation 2 is usually taken pretty much for granted. If we look further into the reasoning given by such writers as do not regard equation 2 as completely self-evident, it is clear that it is regarded as the limit of a trial-and-error process describable by an equation of the general type

$$(3) \qquad\qquad dp/dt = h(S - D)$$

where

$$(4) \qquad\qquad h' < 0, \; h(0) = 0.$$

(Here and below, primes denote differentiation, so that h' is the rate of change of the function h with respect to an increase in the excess supply.)

Relation 3 is, of course, the well-known "Law of Supply and Demand." It asserts that price rises when demand exceeds supply and falls in the contrary case. Equations 1 and 3 together define a dynamic process in which supply, demand, and price vary in a prescribed way over time. If the process is stable, these three magnitudes approach limits. At the limiting values, there can be no pressure for any of the variables to change. In view of equations 3 and 4, price will remain stationary if and only if equation 2 holds; but if price remains stationary, demand and supply will do so also, by relation 1. [See Samuelson [1947] and Arrow and Hurwicz [in pres].

The Law of Supply and Demand may be a useful basis for interpreting some empirical phenomena, particularly the course of prices in markets subject to rapid changes in supply or demand conditions, although in fact few such applications have been made; however, the Law is not on the same logical level as the hypotheses underlying equation 1. It is not explained whose decision it is to change prices in accordance with equation 3. Each individual participant in the economy is supposed to take prices as given and determine his choices as to purchases and sales accordingly; there is no one left over whose job it is to make a decision on price.[6]

Price Adjustment Under Monopoly

Before discussing the mechanics of price adjustment under competitive conditions, we may consider the determination of price under monopoly. Here, there is no question of the locus of price decisions. In the stand-

---

[6] This problem has not gone unnoticed in the literature; thus T. Scitovsky observes, "The difficulty lies in visualizing a price that everybody on both sides of the market regards as given and that is determined by the 'impersonal forces of the market'" [Scitovsky 1952, p. 16].

ard theory (essentially unchanged from Cournot's original presentation), the monopolist fixes his price and output to maximize $R(x) - C(x)$, where x is output, $R(x)$ the total revenue curve, and $C(x)$ the total cost curve. Price and output are related by the demand curve, and the firm's output will, therefore, always equal demand. This theory clearly presupposes that the monopolist knows the true demand curve confronting him.

Lange [1944] has sought to develop a theory of price adjustment for monopolies analogous to the Law of Supply and Demand under competition. Let $U(p)$ be the profit of the entrepreneur if he sets price p, assuming that the output has been fixed in accordance with the demand curve. Then Lange suggests

$$(5) \qquad dp/dt = F(U')$$

where

$$(6) \qquad F' > 0, F(0) = 0.$$

Rules 5 and 6 amount to saying that the entrepreneur varies his price in that direction which leads to an increased profit. The rules are of the type referred to in mathematics as gradient methods of maximization.

These rules have concealed in them implicit assumptions about the monopolist's knowledge of the demand curve facing him (I assume he has complete knowledge of his cost curve). Since Lange assumes that output equals sales, the monopolist must know the demand at the price chosen, and, to make equation 5 operationally meaningful, he must know the elasticity of demand at that price. On the other hand, the monopolist presumably does not know the entire demand curve, for otherwise he would jump immediately to the optimal position. Further, his knowledge must be changing over time. To see this, let p_o be the price set at some time t_o and p_1 the price at some later time t_1. Since the monopolist is increasing his profit by his successive trial prices, the profit $U(p_1)$ at time t_1 must be greater

than $U(p_o)$, the profit at time t_o. If, at time t_o, the monopolist had known the demand at price p_1, he would have known that p_o was not the point of maximum profit and would have chosen p_1 or, possibly, some price which yielded a still higher profit. Thus the value of demand at p_1 is knowledge which is available to the monopolist at time t_1 but not at time t_o.

Uncertainty, then, is a crucial consideration in the theory of monopolistic price adjustment. We cannot completely follow Lange in assuming that the monopolist never wets his toes in the cold waters of uncertainty as to the demand curve. It may be that, without knowing the exact value of demand at p_1, the monopolist knows that even under the worst possible conditions the profit will be greater than at p_o, where the demand is known. Indeed, it suffices that the expected profit corresponding to p_1 be sufficiently greater than the known profit at p_o to overcome the entrepreneur's distaste for the greater uncertainty. Hence we must admit the possibility of a discrepancy between output and demand for a monopolist. The discrepancy once observed has a twofold significance for price adjustment. On the one hand, it informs the monopolist of the extent to which he is in error and yields knowledge to estimate better his demand curve; on the other hand, the discrepancy alters his stock of inventories, which may in turn affect his cost situation in the next period.[7] The latter effect would, of course, not apply to cases where either no inventories can be accumulated, as with services, or where the carrying costs (including storage, depreciation, and foregone liquidity) are very high. It seems reasonable to conclude that price adjustment will be slower in the last-mentioned case than where inventories can be accumulated or decumulated more readily.

---

[7] If the total cost of producing x units is $C(x)$, the carrying cost is c per unit, and the amount carried forward is x_0, the cost associated with delivering x units in the next period is $C(x - x_0) + cx_0$. For low values of c, this cost will be less than $C(x)$, so that the cost curve for the next period has shifted downward.

Thus, if demand is higher than anticipated, the monopolist will, in general, raise his price because both his marginal cost and anticipated marginal revenue curves have shifted upwards, and conversely for demands lower than anticipated. If the true demand and cost curves remain unchanged in the process, the monopolist will gradually converge towards his optimal price-quantity position. If, however, the demand and cost curves are shifting over time in response to influences exogenous to the market under consideration, the monopolist's price adjustment relations become part of a general dynamic system which is not necessarily stable. I will not elaborate here a more complete model, which can become very complicated.[8]

Competitive Price Adjustment

The above sketch of monopolistic price adjustment theory has been introduced here not only for its own sake, but for the purpose of laying the foundations for a theory of price adjustment under competitive circumstances. As has been understood since the days of Cournot and emphasized in more recent times by Chamberlain and Joan Robinson, the competitive firm is a monopolist with a special environment.

Ordinarily, the firm acting under competitive conditions is pictured as a monopolist confronted with a perfectly elastic demand curve. More explicitly, it is assumed that there exists a price, which we may refer to as the market price, such that the firm can sell any output it desires at a price not exceeding the market price, but can sell nothing at a higher price.

Triffin [1940] has criticized this criterion of perfect elasticity of demand as a definition of pure competition, arguing that such a demand situation is itself a consequence of the fundamental technological and test factors involved. He defines perfect competition instead in terms of certain cross-elasticities of supply and demand as between different firms.

Indeed, suppose we have a situation which conforms in all the aspects of homogeneity of output and multiplicity of firms to the usual concept of perfect competition, but in which the aggregate supply forthcoming at the "market" price exceeds the demand at that price. Then the individual firm cannot sell all it wishes to at the market price; i.e., when supply and demand do not balance, even in an objectively competitive market, the individual firms are in the position of monopolists as far as the imperfect elasticity of demand for their products is concerned.

What is the meaning of market price in such a situation? We are always told by the textbooks that there is one price in a competitive market at a given time. But what determines this one price? The answer has been given clearly by Reder. Under conditions of disequilibrium, there is no reason that there should be a single market price, and we may very well expect that each firm will charge a different price [1947]. The law that there is only one price on a competitive market (Jevons' Law of Indifference) is derived on the basis of profit- or utility-maximizing behavior on the part of both sides of the market; but there is no reason for such behavior to lead to unique price except in equilibrium, or possibly under conditions of perfect knowledge.

Let us consider in somewhat more detail the case in which demand exceeds supply. Assume that no firm can increase supply in a very short period. Then any individual entrepreneur knows that he can raise the price, even if his competitors do not raise theirs, because they cannot satisfy any more of the demand than they do already. The entrepreneur is faced with a sloping demand curve and raises his price in accordance with the profit-maximizing tactics of a monopolist, as sketched in the previous section. If none of the other sellers do in fact raise their prices, the entrepreneur will gradually approach his point of

---

[8] Such models are closely related to those which have been developed in inventory theory over the last twelve years. See, for example, Arrow, Karlin, and Scarf [1958].

maximum profit, where the market will be cleared. But, under the conditions specified, it is equally to the profit of all other entrepreneurs to raise their prices also, although, if not subject to the same cost conditions, not necessarily by the same amount. The demand curve for the particular entrepreneur under consideration is thus shifting upward at the same time that he is exploring it. Thus supply will still not be in balance with demand, and the process continues.

It must also be stressed that the amount of uncertainty during this process is apt to be very considerable. Any estimate of the demand curve to a single entrepreneur involves a guess as to both the supply conditions and the prices of other sellers, as well as some idea of the demand curve to the industry as a whole. Under competitive conditions none of these is likely to be known very well. Thus the whole adjustment process is apt to be very irregular. Although the broad tendency will be for prices to rise when demand exceeds supply, there can easily be a considerable dispersion of prices among different sellers of the same commodity, as well as considerable variability over time in the rate of change of prices.

The uncertainty, in turn, puts a premium on information. Traditional economic theory stresses the sufficiency of the price system as a source of information for guiding economic behavior, and this is correct enough at equilibrium. But the monopolist in general has stricter informational requirements than the competitor, since he needs to know his whole demand curve, not merely a single price. In conditions of disequilibrium, the demand curve is shifting as a result of forces outside the private market of the monopolist, and a premium is placed on the acquisition of information from sources other than the prices and quantities of the firm's own sales.

So far, our detailed analysis has covered the case of a firm acting as a monopolist because demand exceeds supply for the industry of which the firm is a part. We have already seen that, in a market where supply exceeds demand, each firm can also be regarded as a monopolist, though for different reasons. By a parallel argument each buyer on a market with an inequality between supply and demand can be regarded as a monopsonist. The behavior of each firm as a buyer can be described in the same manner as that of the seller, and we forebear from detailed repetition.

However, this further remark requires some revision of our previous picture of the market. In disequilibrium, the market consists of a number of monopolists facing a number of monopsonists. The most general picture is that of a shifting set of bilateral monopolies. The range of indeterminacy in each bargaining situation is limited but not completely eliminated by the possibilities of other bargains. In general, though, it is reasonable to suppose that if the selling side of the market is much more concentrated than the buying side, the main force in changing prices will be the monopolistic behavior of the sellers. The buyers would find little possibility of exerting their individual monopsonistic powers because there are so many of them for each seller. Similarly, if the buying side of the market is the more concentrated, as in nonunionized labor markets, the dynamics will come from that side. It is perhaps for reasons such as these that the immediate location of price decisions is usually vested in the more concentrated side of the market, in sellers in the case of most commodities, in buyers in the case of unorganized labor. (In organized labor markets, bilateral monopoly prevails.) Thus the dynamics of prices may be affected by the structure of the market even in cases where there are sufficient numbers in the market to insure reasonably competitive behavior at equilibrium.

Implications for the Speed of Adjustment

The preceding shows, of course, that the difference between supply and demand is a major factor in explaining the movement of prices, so that the Law of Supply and Demand, as expressed in equations 3 and

4, can be thought of as a useful approximation. However, the "price" whose movements are explained by the Law must be thought of as the average price. The model presented in this paper has some implications for the speed of adjustment in different markets, as represented by the function h.

Consider, as before, the case where demand exceeds supply and sellers are led to behave as monopolists. The existence of this excess both for the particular seller under consideration and for his competitors enters into the determination of the seller's anticipated demand curve. Given this, he sets his price so as to equate anticipated marginal revenue (possibly discounted in some form for uncertainty) to marginal cost. The price increase will thus depend on the shape of the marginal cost curve. It will be greater if the marginal cost is rising sharply than if it is flat. In particular, then, the speed of adjustment will be greater during a period of full utilization of capacity than in a situation of excess capacity.

A second consideration affecting the speed of adjustment, already remarked in passing, is the possibility of accumulating and decumulating inventories. An accumulation of inventories is both a signal to revise downward the anticipated demand curve and a cause of a downward shift in the marginal cost curve in the next period. A decumulation of inventories has the opposite effects. Hence, price adjustment will be more rapid in industries where inventories play a significant role.

A third factor suggested by the preceding analysis is the degree of information available to the individual entrepreneur. Relative absence of information about the behavior of others in the market increases the degree of uncertainty. Even in the absence of an aversion to risk-bearing, the chances that the entrepreneur will misread the signals are greater than if more information were available; we would therefore expect on the average that the responsiveness of prices to supply–demand differences would be less in the absence of information. An aversion to risk-bearing would increase the entrepreneur's unwillingness to venture on price changes in the absence of information. We would expect, therefore, that well-organized exchanges would display the greatest degree of price flexibility.

One special case in which information would be expected to be relatively scarce is that where the products are poorly standardized. Then knowledge of prices and availabilities of supply for other firms will not have a clear meaning for a particular firm, since its product may not be a perfect substitute, and therefore an excess of demand over supply elsewhere in the market may not be due to an upward shift in demand for all products on the market but to a shift away from its product to that of its competitors.

The Competitiveness of the Economy

In any state of disequilibrium, i.e., any situation in which supply does not equal demand, it follows from the above model that the economy will show evidences of monopoly and monopsony. These evidences will be the more intense, the greater the disequilibrium. We can understand from this point of view the feeling of the businessman that, contrary to economic theory, sales are by no means unlimited at the current market price. The demand for advertising and other forms of nonprice competition thus makes more sense than under the model of perfect competition at all times.

The model casts some light on the much-discussed problem of administered prices.[9] It was brought out by Gardiner Means and others in the 1930's that the quoted prices of some commodities produced by industries in which there was a high degree of concentration tended to be rigid, that is, insensitive to inequalities of demand and supply. Against this point of view it has been objected that the prices

[9] See M. J. Bailey, "Administered Prices in the American Economy," pp. 89–106, and earlier references cited there [1958].

at which transactions actually take place differ from the quoted prices and are, for example, lower in conditions of excess capacity. Thus, the actual prices would be more nearly consistent with those of the competitive model. But it remains to be explained why the sellers resort to a fictitious price and secret undercutting instead of openly reducing prices. Explanations, such as Bailey's (18), which run in terms of informal social pressures within the industry, do not seem very satisfactory and, in any case, merely push the problem back one step.

If, however, it is accepted that an inequality of supply and demand leads to a condition of partial monopoly, then the most likely explanation for a divergence between quoted and actual prices is that it is a cloak for price discrimination. Not all buyers receive equal discounts, because they are not informed as to the prices actually paid. Such discrimination, if it can be shown to exist, would, of course, be incompatible with a purely competitive model.

The present model also suggests that the measurement of competitiveness by the concentration ratio has to be interpreted carefully. A degree of concentration which would be perfectly compatible with a reasonable degree of competition if the market were in equilibrium might easily fail to be so compatible in the event of serious inequality between supply and demand. There has been a position strongly held in recent years that the American economy is basically competitive, in that neither firms nor labor unions have, in fact, much control over prices, despite superficial appearances.[10] The present model suggests that the evidence, to the extent that it is valid, relates only to equilibrium and, therefore, to long-run situations. Such long-run competitiveness is not incompatible, on the present view, with considerable short-run monopoly powers in transitory situations.

The incomplete competitiveness of the economy under disequilibrium conditions implies a departure from the maximum of possible efficiency in the use of resources. To be sure, it does not necessarily follow that greater efficiency is necessarily achievable under feasible alternative rules. Any method of resource allocation requires a process for equating supply and demand (or some equivalent), and such a process may be in itself costly, though such costs are not considered in the usual formal analysis of welfare economics. Thus, a completely centralized system will incur high computational and informational costs. The monopolistic and monopsonistic misallocations implied by the model of the present paper may be thought of as costs alternative to those associated with centralization.

In particular, one would expect considerable departures from maximum efficiency in conditions of severe disequilibrium, such as inflations and depressions, despite Keynes's well-known remark to the contrary.[11] Under conditions of unemployment, the mobility of resources in response to price differences is seriously impaired. Thus, in a depression workers will not move from the farm to the city, despite considerable wage differences, because they are aware of the difficulty of getting a job; the individual worker faces a falling demand curve.

A Remark on Inflation

The above model casts some light on the concept of cost inflation. Such a doctrine requires that there be important elements of unregulated monopoly in the economy. There is at least some doubt that such elements are significant in the long run. However, the model of this paper suggests that in a certain sense all inflationary processes

---

[10] For firms, this view has been held by Stigler [1949]. Nutter [1899–1939], and Harberger [May 1954]. For trade unions, see Friedman [1951].

[11] "I see no reason to suppose that the existing system seriously misemploys the factors of production which are in use. . . . When 9,000,000 men are employed out of 10,000,000 willing and able to work, there is no evidence that the labor of the 9,000,000 men is misdirected" [1936].

are cost inflations in that it is the monopoly power resulting from excess demand which is their proximate cause. This may explain why acute observers differ so sharply in their evaluation of the same phenomenon. Those who see cost inflation may be looking at an immediate causal factor, while those who speak of demand inflation have their eye on a more ultimate stimulus.

In view of this, this paper would suggest caution in treating cost inflations by direct regulation.[12] They may be transitory phenomena which are necessary to achieve equilibrium, in which case regulation may simply lead to the replacement of overt by suppressed inflation.

REFERENCES

1. L. R. Klein, "Theories of Effective Demand and Employment," *Journal of Political Economy*, LV (April 1947), 108–31.

2. K. Marx, Capital. Charles H. Kerr, Chicago, 1906, Vol. I.

3. M. Dobb, Marx as an Economist. International Publishers, New York, 1945, pp. 19–20.

4. P. M. Sweezy, The Theory of Capitalist Development. Oxford, New York, 1942, Chap. VII.

5. O. Lange, "Marxian Economics and Modern Economic Theory," *Review of Economic Studies*, II (1934–35), 189–201; especially pp. 194, 195.

6. H. Smith, "Marx and the Trade Cycle," *Review of Economic Studies*, IV (June 1937), 197.

7. E. Böhm von Bawerk, Karl Marx and the Close of His System. Unwin, London, 1898.

8. T. Veblen, "Limitations of Marginal Utility" and "Professor Clark's Economics," reprinted in The Place of Science in Modern Civilization and Other Essays. Huebsch, New York, 1919, pp. 180–251.

9. T. Veblen, The Theory of Business Enterprise. Scribner's, New York, 1904.

10. W. C. Mitchell, Business Cycles: The Problem and Its Setting. National Bureau of Economic Research, New York, 1927, pp. 105–7.

11. P. A. Samuelson, Foundations of Economic Analysis. Harvard University Press, Cambridge, 1947, Chap. IX.

12. K. J. Arrow and L. Hurwicz, "On the Stability of the Competitive Equilibrium, I," *Econometrica* (to be published).

13. T. Scitovsky, Welfare and Competition. Allen and Unwin, London, 1952, p. 16.

14. O. Lange, Price Flexibility and Employment. Cowles Commission Monograph No. 8. Principia Press, Bloomington, Indiana, 1944, pp. 35–37, 107–9.

15. K. J. Arrow, S. Karlin, and H. Scarf, Studies in the Mathematical Theory of Inventory and Production. Stanford University Press, Stanford, California, 1958.

16. R. M. Triffin, Monopolistic Competition and General Equilibrium Theory. Harvard University Press, Cambridge, 1940, pp. 137–41.

17. M. W. Reder, Studies in the Theory of Welfare Economics. Columbia University Press, New York, 1947, pp. 126–51.

18. M. J. Bailey, "Administered Prices in the American Economy," in The Relationship of Prices to Economic Stability and Growth. Joint Economic Committee, U.S. Congress, Washington, D.C., 1958, pp. 89–106.

19. G. J. Stigler, Five Lectures on Economic Problems. Longmans, Green, New York, London, and Toronto, 1949. Lecture 5, pp. 44–65.

20. G. Warren Nutter, The Extent of Enterprise Monopoly in the United States, 1899–1939. University of Chicago Press, Chicago, 1951.

21. A. C. Harberger, "Monopoly and Resource Allocation," *American Economic Review*, XLIV, No. 2 (May 1954), 77–87.

22. M. Friedman, "Some Comments on the Significance of Labor Unions for Economic Policy," in D. M.

---

[12] See the proposals of Lerner [1958].

Wright (ed.), The Impact of the Union. Harcourt, Brace, New York, 1951, Chap. X, pp. 204–34.

23. J. M. Keynes, The General Theory of Employment, Interest and Money. Harcourt, Brace, New York, 1936, p. 379.

24. A. P. Lerner, "Inflationary Depression and the Regulation of Administered Prices," in The Relationship of Prices to Economic Stability and Growth. Joint Economic Committee, U.S. Congress, Washington, D.C., 1958, pp. 267–68.

9. Economic Theory and the Meaning of Competition*

PAUL J. McNULTY

There is probably no concept in all of economics that is at once more fundamental and pervasive, yet less satisfactorily developed, than the concept of competition. Although the hesitancy and inconsistency which has characterized the history of American competitive policy is doubtless partly due, as is often emphasized, to the fact that competition is, in our system, a political and social *desideratum* no less than an economic one, with some possible resulting conflict between these various values,[1] surely it is due also to the failure of economists adequately to define competition. Not the least among the many achievements of economic science has been the ability to erect a rigorous analytical system on the principle of competition—a principle so basic to economic reasoning that not even such powerful yet diverse critics of orthodox theory as Marx and Keynes could avoid relying upon it—without ever clearly specifying what, exactly, competition is. The purpose of this paper is to examine some of the factors which account for this curious development, and to indicate some specific inadequacies of the economic concept of competition both for analysis and for policy.

I

Probably the most general tendency concerning the meaning of competition in economic theory is to regard it as the opposite of monopoly. An unfortunate result of this way of thinking has been no little confusion concerning the relationship between economic efficiency and business behavior. There is a striking contrast in economic literature between the analytical rigor and precision of competition when it is described as a market structure, and the ambiguity surrounding the idea of competition whenever it is discussed in behavioral terms. Since, as Hayek has rightly noted, "the law cannot effectively prohibit states of affairs but only kinds of action," [2] a concept of economic competition, if it is to be significant for economic policy, ought to relate to patterns of business behavior such as might reasonably be associated with the verb "to compete." That was the case with the competition which Adam Smith made the central organizing principle of economic society in the *Wealth of Nations*, and with the competition whose effects Cournot, in the first formal statement of the idea of

Reprinted by permission of *The Quarterly Journal of Economics*, Volume 82 (1968).

* I am indebted to my colleague, Maurice Wilkinson, for a number of helpful suggestions and comments. Needless to say, I am solely responsible for the views expressed herein. I wish also to acknowledge the financial support provided by the faculty research fund of the Graduate School of Business, Columbia University.

[1] "It is possible, because of its indirect social or moral effect, to prefer a system of small producers, each dependent for his success upon his own skill and character, to one in which the great mass of those engaged must accept the direction of a few." *United States* v. *Aluminum Company of America*, 148 F. 2d 416 (1945). "Of course, some of the results of large integrated or chain operations are beneficial to consumers . . . But we cannot fail to recognize Congress' desire to promote competition through the protection of viable, small, locally owned businesses. Congress appreciated that occasional higher costs and prices might result from the maintenance of fragmented industries and markets. It resolves these competing considerations in favor of decentralization." *Brown Shoe Co.* v. *United States*, 370 U.S. 294 (962).

[2] F. A. Hayek, *The Constitution of Liberty* (Chicago: University of Chicago Press, 1960), p. 265.

"perfect" competition, could accurately claim to be "realized, in social economy, for a multitude of products, and, among them, for the most important products." [3] Whether it was seen as price undercutting by sellers, the bidding up of prices by buyers, or the entry of new firms into profitable industries, the fact is that competition entered economics as a concept which had empirical relevance and operational meaning in terms of contemporary business behavior. Yet on the question of whether such common current practices as advertising, product variation, price undercutting, or other forms of business activity do or do not constitute competition, modern economic theory offers the clarification that they are "monopolistically" competitive. While this is a useful way of illustrating the truth that most markets are in some degree both controlled and controlling, it is less useful as a guide in implementing a policy, such as our antitrust policy, which seeks at once to restrain monopoly and promote competition. It is too late in the history of economics, and it is surely not in any way here the purpose, to de-emphasize the truly monumental character of E. H. Chamberlin's great achievement a generation ago[4] in reconciling economic theory with the undeniable fact that much of the business world was really a mixture of competition and monopoly, as those concepts were then defined in economics, which fitted neither of those traditional economic models of business enterprise. But it is not, perhaps, too late to suggest that the traditional distinction between competition and monopoly was, in a fundamental sense, inappropriate to begin with; and that the merging of the concepts in a theory of monopolistic competition, while representing a profound improvement over the simplicity of the older classification, and giving microeconomics a new vitality almost

comparable to that which Keynes was at the same time bringing to employment theory, has, nonetheless, allowed us to avoid defining a concept of competition, *as distinct from the concept of a competitive market*, which is at once relevant and adequate both for economic analysis and for economic policy.

Clearly, the failure to distinguish between the idea of competition and the idea of market structure is at the root of much of the ambiguity concerning the meaning of competition. As far as market structure, conceived of in terms of the paucity or plethora of sellers (buyers), is the appropriate focus of analysis, consistency would suggest relying on terms such as monopoly (sony), duopoly, triopoly, oligopoly, polypoly, and, perhaps, a newly-coined term ending in "poly," the prefix of which means an indefinitely large number.[5] Such a classification, although it would add to an already cumbersome body of technical jargon, would nonetheless retain for market taxonomy the analytical usefulness it currently possesses, while having the further advantage of eliminating much of the confusion that now exists between competition and monopoly. As it is, it is one of the great paradoxes of economic science that every *act* of competition on the part of a businessman is evidence, in economic theory, of some degree of monopoly power, while the concepts of monopoly and perfect competition have this important common feature: both are situations in which the possibility of any competitive behavior has been ruled out by definition.

That perfect competition is an ideal state, incapable of actual realization, is a familiar theme of economic literature. That for various reasons it would be less than altogether desirable, even if it were attainable, is also widely acknowledged. But that perfect competition is a state of affairs quite

[3] Augustin Cournot, *Researches into the Mathematical Principles of the Theory of Wealth*, trans. Nathaniel T. Bacon (New York: Macmillan, 1929), p. 90.

[4] Edward H. Chamberlin, *The Theory of Monopolistic Competition* (Cambridge, Mass.: Harvard University Press, 1956).

[5] Professor Machlup has employed a classification along these lines, adding the term "pliopoly" (more sellers) to cover the condition of free entry. Fritz Machlup, *The Economics of Sellers' Competition* (Baltimore: The Johns Hopkins Press, 1952), Chap. 4.

incompatible with the idea of any and all competition has been insufficiently emphasized. It is this last feature of perfect competition, and not, as is sometimes incorrectly claimed, its high level of abstraction or the "unreality" of its assumptions, which limits its usefulness, especially for economic policy. What needs more stress than it has generally received is not the inescapably abstract and "unreal" nature of theory but, rather, the fact that while all other forms of competition represent, in economic theory, an *admixture* of monopoly and competition, perfect competition itself means the *absence* of competition in quite as complete a sense, although for different reasons, as does pure monopoly. Monopoly is a market situation in which intraindustry competition has been defined away by identifying the firm as the industry. Perfect competition, on the other hand, is a market situation which, although itself the *result* of the free entry of a large number of formerly competing firms, has evolved or progressed to the point (of equilibrium) where no *further* competition within the industry is possible, or, in the words of A. A. Cournot, its intellectual parent, to the point where "the effects of competition have reached their limit."[6] It is for this reason that Frank Knight can correctly stress, as he often has, that perfect competition involves "no presumption of psychological competition, emulation, or rivalry,"[7] and can rightly assert that " 'atomism' is a better term for the idea."[8] Perfect competition, the only clearly and rigorously defined concept of competition to be found in the corpus of economic theory, which is free of all traces of business behavior associated with "monopolistic" elements, means simply the *existence* of an indefinitely large number of noncompeting firms. Economists have sometimes criticized American competitive policy for its not infrequently manifested tendency over the years to identify the maintenance of competition with the maintenance of competitors. But economic theory offers no clear guide for distinguishing between them. To the extent that we look to economics for an answer to the question "What are the advantages of competition over monopoly?", we ought also to be able to look to economics for an answer to the question "How may a business firm be expected to compete without monopolizing?" And the critical reader will search economic literature in vain for a clear answer to that question.

An analysis of the ambiguities and weaknesses of the competitive concept confirms the correctness of Schumpeter's assertion (despite the apparently widely held contemporary view to the contrary) that in economics "modern problems, methods and results cannot be fully understood without some knowledge of how economists have come to reason as they do."[9] In order fully to understand how our thinking on competition has come to be what it is, it is necessary, then, to examine briefly the emergence and evolution of the concept within the larger framework of the historical development of economic science.

II

Although competition, as we noted earlier, has usually been conceived of as being in general the opposite of monopoly, the conception has taken two basic, and fundamentally different, forms. On the one hand, it has been the "force" which, by equating prices and marginal costs, assures allocative efficiency in the use of resources. Competition in this sense is somewhat analogous to the force of gravitation in physical science; through competition, resources "gravitate" toward their most productive uses, and, through competition, price is "forced" to the lowest level which is sustainable over the long run. Thus viewed, competition assures order and stability in the economic world

---

[6] Cournot, *op. cit.*, p. 90.

[7] Frank H. Knight, "Immutable Law in Economics: Its Reality and Limitations," *American Economic Review,* XXXVI (May 1946), 102.

[8] *Loc. cit.*

[9] Joseph A. Schumpeter, *History of Economic Analysis* (New York: Oxford University Press, 1954), p. 6.

much as does gravitation in the physical world. But competition has also been conceived of in a second way, as a descriptive term characterizing a particular (idealized) situation. The concept of perfect competition, for example, to continue the comparison with physical science, is analogous not to the principle of gravitation but rather to the idea of a perfect vacuum; it is not an "ordering force" but rather an assumed "state of affairs"—one which, although an "unrealistic,"—indeed, too much unrealizable,—abstraction, is nonetheless a useful analytical device. That competition has been conceived of in these two quite different ways is of no small importance in explaining the ambiguity and confusion which has surrounded the concept.

It was the conception of competition as an ordering force which dominated classical economics. When Adam Smith spoke of competition, it was in connection with the forcing of market price to its "natural" level [1] or to the lowering of profits to a minimum.[2] It was not competition and monopoly per se, or as market models, which Adam Smith contrasted, but rather the level of prices resulting from the presence or absence of competition as a regulatory force.[3] Indeed, so unsystematic was any association between the idea of competition and that of market structure for Adam Smith that he applied the term to duopoly almost exactly as he did to a market in which a larger number of firms operated. If the capital sufficient to satisfy the demand for groceries in a particular town "is divided between two different grocers," he wrote, "their competition will tend to make both of them sell cheaper, than if it were in the hands of one only." [4] Although Smith and the classical

economists generally acknowledged that competition was more effective with a larger number than with a smaller number of competitors, competition was viewed as a price-determining force operating in, but not itself identified as, a market. On this, Ricardo was explicit:

> In speaking, then, of commodities, of their exchangeable value, and of the laws which regulate their relative prices, we mean always such commodities . . . on the production of which *competition operates* without restraint.[5]

And John Stuart Mill wrote:

> So far as rents, profits, wages, prices, are determined by competition, laws may be assigned for them. Assume competition to be their exclusive regulator and principles of broad generality and scientific precision may be laid down, according to which they will be regulated.[6]

The "perfection" of the concept of competition, that is, the emergence of the idea of competition as itself a market structure, was a distinguishing contribution of neoclassical economics. The groundwork for this development was laid by Cournot, whose interest was in specifying, as rigorously as possible, the *effects* of competition. According to him, the effects of competition had reached their limit when the output of each firm was "inappreciable" with respect to total industry output, and could be subtracted from the total output "without any appreciable variation resulting in the price of the commodity." [7] This implied a very large number of sellers, but Cournot was not much more explicit on the subject of market structure, and it was only with Jevons[8] and Edgeworth,[9] in the late nine-

---

[1] Adam Smith, *The Wealth of Nations* (New York: Modern Library, 1937), pp. 56, 57.

[2] *Ibid.*, p. 87.

[3] "The price of monopoly is upon every occasion the highest which can be got. The natural price, or the price of free competition, on the contrary, is the lowest which can be taken . . . for any considerable time together." *Ibid.*, p. 61.

[4] *Ibid.*, p. 342.

[5] David Ricardo, *The Principles of Political Economy and Taxation* (London: J. M. Dent, 1955), p. 6, emphasis added.

[6] John Stuart Mill, *Principles of Political Economy*, I (New York: D. Appleton, 1864), 306.

[7] *Op. cit.*, p. 90.

[8] W. Stanley Jevons, *The Theory of Political Economy* (4th ed.; London: Macmillan, 1911).

[9] F. Y. Edgeworth, *Mathematical Psychics* (London: C. Kegan Paul, 1881).

teenth century, that the actual wedding of the concepts of competition and the market was effected, leading ultimately, after refinements by J. B. Clark[1] and Frank Knight,[2] to the concept of perfect competition as we know it today.[3] As Stigler has rightly stressed, "the merging of the concepts of competition and the market was unfortunate, for each deserved a full and separate treatment."

> A market is an institution for the consummation of transactions. It performs this function efficiently when every buyer who will pay more than the minimum realized price for any class of commodities succeeds in buying the commodity, and every seller who will sell it for less than the maximum realized price succeeds in selling the commodity. . . . A market may be perfect and monopolistic or imperfect and competitive. Jevons' mixture of the two has been widely imitated by successors, of course, so that even today a market is commonly treated as a concept subsidiary to competition.[4]

Although we can agree that "the merging of the concepts of competition and the market was unfortunate," it is probably more accurate to say that competition has been conceived of as a concept subsidiary to that of the market rather than the other way around. In fact, Jevons' "mixture" of the concepts may be viewed as a development which was thoroughly in the tradition of, and, indeed, perhaps only a logical consequence of, the historical tendency on the part of economists to identify competition as entirely a phenomenon of exchange. For, if the classical economists did not, like their neoclasical successors, identify competition

with a *particular* market structure, they did nonetheless conceive of it as taking place exclusively *in* the various markets in which the business firm was operating. Competition, that is, was never related in any systematic way to the technique of production within, or to the organizational form of, the business firm itself. The concept has thus been divorced, since the earliest days of scientific economic analysis, from a major area or facet of economic activity.

Economic goods and services possess, broadly speaking, two characteristics: quality and price. In a free enterprise economy, moreover, there are two primary institutions through which resources are organized, transformed, and channeled for ultimate consumption as goods or services: the private business firm and the market. These institutions correspond to the two characteristics possessed by economic goods. Production, or the determination of physical form, or quality, takes place within the business firm; exchange, or the determination of economic value, or price, within the various markets in which the firm operates. However, although economic activity encompasses both production and exchange, the concept of competition has been generally associated only with the latter. The operations of the business firm, except for the exchange relationships associated with its purchase or sale of a factor, product, or service, have not traditionally come within the meaning of competition nor, indeed, have they been a part of economic theory generally. In economic analysis, one firm is seen as differing from another only with respect to the kind of product or factor market in which it buys or sells, and the economic system as a whole is seen not as a complex set of varied and changing institutions but, rather, the process of buying and selling is isolated as the critical element of economic activity and the economy is viewed as simply "a system of interrelated markets."[5] In short, as Allyn Young once put it, "for system's sake, the whole material equipment

---

[1] J. B. Clark, *The Distribution of Wealth* (New York: Macmillan, 1900).

[2] Frank H. Knight, *Risk, Uncertainty and Profit* (London: London School Of Economics and Political Science, Series of Reprints of Scarce Tracts, No. 16, 1933).

[3] George J. Stigler, "Perfect Competition, Historically Contemplated," *Journal of Political Economy*, LXV (Feb. 1957), 1–17.

[4] *Ibid.*, p. 6.

[5] Lloyd G. Reynolds, *The Structure of Labor Markets* (New York: Harper, 1951), p. 1.

of human living is recast in molds fashioned after the notions of catallactics." [6]

Both the dominance of exchange, and hence of price, in economic theory generally, and the limitation of the concept of competition specifically to the firm's external relationships in the market, relate to the way in which competition entered economics and came to occupy the position of primacy which it has held in the science ever since the work of Adam Smith. In one sense Smith was, and in another sense he was not, the great "prophet of competition" [7] that historians of the subject have often made him appear to be. Smith was a prophet of competition in that he did for the concept what no others before him did so effectively: he made it literally a general organizing principle of economic society and of economic analysis. No writer before Smith presented so effectively the conception of competition as a force which, operating in an atmosphere of "perfect liberty," would lead self-seeking individuals unconsciously to serve the general welfare. In a sense, Smith did for economics, through the principle of competition, precisely what he himself credited Newton with having done for physics and astronomy through the principle of gravity; "the discovery of an immense chain of the most important and sublime truths, all closely connected together, by one capital fact, of the reality of which we have daily experience." [8] But while Smith gave to competition an intellectual and ideological significance it had never had before, neither its specific economic meaning, nor its particular analytical function, was original with him. On the contrary, he incorporated into the *Wealth of Nations* a concept of competition already well developed in the economic literature of his time. That concept was a behavioral one, the essence of which was the effort of the individual seller to undersell, or the individual buyer to outbid, his rivals in the marketplace, and had earlier been employed and developed by a number of writers including Cantillon, Turgot, Hume, Steuart, and others, in their various efforts to explain how price was, in a free market, ultimately forced to a level which would just cover costs, that is, to the lowest level which would be sustainable over the long run.[9] Thus, although Smith played a major role in making the principle of competition quite literally the *sine qua non* of economic analysis, to the extent that Ricardo would later contemplate only cases in which "competition operates without restraint," [1] and John Stuart Mill would go on to assert that "only through the principle of competition has political economy any pretension to the character of science," [2] he contributed little, if anything, to its economic meaning.

Had the concept of competition in fact been, as is often implied, a major contribution of Adam Smith, or had he added significantly to its economic meaning, there is some reason, indeed, to suppose that economic theory would have produced at an early date a concept of competition not unlike that later called for by Schumpeter, that is, competition associated with internal industrial efficiency and with the development of "the new technology, the new source of supply, [and] the new type of organization." [3] For Smith after all, writing in the environment of the English industrial revolution, was eminently aware of the importance of dynamic changes in productive

---

[6] Allyn A. Young, "Some Limitations of the Value Concept," this *Journal*, XXV (May 1911), 424.

[7] John Maurice Clark, *Competition as a Dynamic Process* (Washington: The Brookings Institution, 1961), p. 24.

[8] Adam Smith, "The History of Astronomy," in *The Works of Adam Smith, LL.D.*, V, ed. Dugald Stewart (Aalen: Otto Zeller, 1963), pp. 189–90.

[9] Paul J. McNulty, "A Note on the History of Perfect Competition," *Journal of Political Economy*, LXXV (Aug. 1967), Part I, 395–99.

[1] Ricardo, *op. cit.*, p. 6.

[2] Mill, *op. cit.*, p. 306.

[3] Joseph A. Schumpeter, *Capitalism, Socialism and Democracy* (New York: Harper and Row, 1962), p. 84.

technique and industrial organization, which he somewhat loosely termed "the division of labor." It was precisely the productive and organizational relationships within the business enterprise and not, as with the physiocrats, the natural fertility of the soil, or, as with the mercantilists, exchange in the market per se, which was for Adam Smith the ultimate source of economic surplus and the essential basis of economic activity. But having opened the *Wealth of Nations* with an uncommonly strong tribute to the idea of division of labor and the associated productive efficiency to be found within the contemporary business firm, Smith curiously failed to relate productive technique to the concept of competition, the central organizing principle upon which, according to him, society could safely in most cases depend. At one point, it is true, he did speak of "the competition of producers who, in order to undersell one another, have recourse to new divisions of labour, and new improvements of art, which might never otherwise have been thought of." [4] But this was little more than a passing comment, and came only in Book V, well after his extended, but separate, discussions of competition and division of labor in Book I. Moreover, the "recourse to new divisions of labour and new improvements of art" were clearly subsidiary aspects of his concept of competition, the essence of which was the effort to undersell in the market by lowering price. As division of labor was limited by the extent of the market, so its analysis in terms of the organization of production within the business firm came to be circumscribed, even for Adam Smith, by the analysis of the firm's external market relationships. Not the essence of the industrial revolution—the changing mode of production—but rather, the mercantilists' overriding concern with price, continued, with Smith, to be the central theme of economic analysis. The division of labor came, with his successors, to be "given" as "the state of the arts," changes in which were ruled out through the use of the "pound of

ceteris paribus," and competition continued to be consistently viewed in terms of exchange relationships between existing and unchanging economic units.[5]

Although the classical economists thus viewed competition as exclusively a market process, the neoclassical development of the concept of perfect competition as itself a market structure nonetheless represented a sharp discontinuity in the development of social thought, for, although competition, according to the older view, took place exclusively within the market, the latter was always seen as allowing for individual initiative in buying and selling. That is, although the classical economists largely ignored the entrepreneurial function as far as it was concerned with operations within the business enterprise, their concept of competition was a disequilibrium one of market activity, with price a variable from the standpoint of the individual firm. Perfect

---

[4] *Op. cit.*, p. 706.

[5] This is not to suggest that the leading neoclassical economists were unaware of the dynamic aspects of competition. Their failure was in their inability to integrate these aspects systematically into their economic theory. J. B. Clark, for example, in *The Essentials of Economic Theory —as Applied to Modern Problems of Industry and Public Policy* (New York: Macmillan, 1915), a volume on economic dynamics which followed his static analysis of *The Distribution of Wealth,* and which made it clear that he was eminently aware of the significance of the changing mode of production, spoke of "the competition which is active enough to change the standard shape of society rapidly—that, for example, which spurs on mechanical invention" (p. 198), and of those situations in which "competition has reduced the establishments in one subgroup to a half dozen or less" (p. 201). But it was Clark's static analysis of perfect competition, and not his observations on economic change, or on the dynamic aspects of competition, which had a permanent effect on the development of economic theory. Marshall, too, took a quite realistic view of competition. But (and perhaps for that very reason) Marshall's impact on the development of the concept of competition, in contrast to his impact on economics generally, was minimal. Indeed, as Stigler has noted (*op. cit.*, p. 9), Marshall's "treatment of competition was much closer to Adam Smith's than to that of his contemporaries, . . . [and was] almost as informal and unsystematic."

competition, on the other hand, is an equilibrium situation in which price becomes a parameter from the standpoint of the individual firm and no market activity is possible. Thus the classical concept of competition as a guiding force, to which we earlier referred, is not only different from that of the neoclassical concept of competition as a state of affairs; the two are incompatible in a fundamental sense, reflecting precisely the difference between a condition of equilibrium and the behavioral pattern leading to it. As Hayek has rightly noted, the idea of perfect competition "throughout assumes that state of affairs already to exist which, according to the truer view of the older theory, the process of competition tends to bring about (or to approximate) . . . [and] if the state of affairs assumed by the theory of perfect competition ever existed, it would not only deprive of their scope all the activities which the verb 'to compete' describes but would make them virtually impossible." [6] Thus, the single activity which best characterized the meaning of competition in classical economics—price cutting by an individual firm in order to get rid of excess supplies—becomes the one activity impossible under perfect competition. And what for the classical economists was the single analytical function of the competitive process—the determination of market price—becomes, with perfect competition, the one thing unexplained and unaccounted for.[7] The perfection of competition thus drained the concept of all behavioral content, so that, using perfect competition as a standard, even price competition, the essence of the competitive process for Adam Smith, is imperfect or monopolistic. That perfect competition has come to be "a rigorously defined concept" [8] is not to be denied. But the result of that rigorous definition is that the verb "to compete" has no meaning in economic theory except in connection with activities which are also in some sense "monopolistic." Indeed, the perfectly competitive firm itself is but "a monopolist with a special environment." [9]

III

Some of the ambiguity concerning the relationship between the idea of perfect competition and business behavior might perhaps have been avoided if Cournot had not designated as "the hypothesis of unlimited competition" the very state of affairs which he had earlier characterized as that in which "the effects of competition have reached their limit." [1] But the classical, behavioral, "imperfect" concept of (price) competition itself possessed certain inherent weaknesses, which have persisted in economic theory to the present day. The remainder of this paper will be concerned with identifying what seem to be the most important of these, and with indicating their relevance for economic analysis and policy.

One fundamental deficiency of competition, as the concept has been employed in economic theory, is that it has never been related in a systematic way to costs of production. There has been a curious dichotomy in economic science in the assumption that self-interest alone will insure that the businessman will work optimally in the interests of society within the business enterprise, or in his *administration* of owned or hired resources and factors of production, while without the enterprise, in his *buying and selling* of factors or products in the market, either an "invisible hand" of competition, or a "visible hand" of public policy, is needed to insure efficiency. Although

[6] F. A. Hayek, *Individualism and Economic Order* (Chicago: University of Chicago Press, 1948), pp. 92, 96.

[7] As Arrow has pointed out, "there exists a logical gap in the usual formulation of the theory of the perfectly competitive economy, . . . [in that] there is no place for a rational decision with respect to prices as there is with respect to quantities." Kenneth J. Arrow, "Towards a Theory of Price Adjustment," in Moses Abramovitz and others, *The Allocation of Economic Resources* (Stanford, Calif.: Stanford University Press, 1959), p. 41.

[8] Stigler, *op. cit.*, p. 11.

[9] Arrow, *op. cit.*, p. 45.

[1] Cournot, *op. cit.*, pp. 90–91.

Adam Smith observed that monopoly "is a great enemy to good management, which can never be universally established but in consequence of that free and universal competition which forces everybody to have recourse to it for the sake of self-defence," [2] his successors failed systematically to relate competition to the search for cost reduction or to "good management" generally. On the contrary, the competitive and monopolistic firms of economic theory differ only with respect to the *demand* curves they face, and the single analytical function of competition has been to get price down to the level of marginal cost. "Under free competition," as Senior wrote, "cost of production is the regulator of price." [3] But the question remains: what is the regulator of cost? Economic theory stresses the optimality of the equation of price and marginal cost. There is nothing optimal in this equation, however, if marginal cost is higher than need be due to internal inefficiencies, and there is reason, indeed, to suppose that the latter is not infrequently the case. Chandler's research in the history of American business administration points up the significance of the search for cost-reducing methods *within the company itself* as one of the significant forces shaping the reorganization of American industry around the turn of the century. The 1901 Annual Report of the National Biscuit Company, for example, highlighted the company's dissatisfaction with its earlier policies of price competition and acquisition of competitors.

> The first meant a ruinous war of prices and a great loss of profits; the second, constantly increased capitalization. . . . We soon satisfied ourselves that within the company itself we must look for success. We turned our attention and bent our energies to improving the internal management of our business, to getting full benefit from purchasing our raw materials in large quantities, to economizing the expenses of manufacture, to systematizing and render-

ing more effective our selling department, and above all things and before all things to improving the quality of our goods and the conditions in which they should reach the customer. [4]

There is, of course, nothing in this list of undertakings which is inconsistent with the postulates of economic theory. On the contrary, the trouble is precisely that economic theory assumes the company should have been doing those things all along. To say that this company was not operating in a fully (or even moderately) competitive market is not to eliminate the problem. The fact is that there is no explanation even in the theory of the perfectly competitive firm for the minimization of costs; the latter is merely assumed. If all firms are equally inefficient in internal administration, a perfectly competitive equilibrium could involve a welfare loss not less significant than any which might result from market imperfections.

That there may currently be considerable room for increased efficiency within business enterprises is suggested by the evidence Leibenstein has summarized concerning the existence of what he calls "X-inefficiencies,"—those which, unlike "allocative inefficiencies," stem not from imperfections in the structure of the market but rather from the fact that "for a variety of reasons people and organizations normally work neither as hard nor as effectively as they could." [5] If economic efficiency is truly a goal of competitive policy, and if Leibenstein is correct that "in a great many instances the amount to be gained by increasing allocative efficiency is trivial, while the amount to be gained by increasing X-efficiency is frequently significant," [6] the desirability of a new dimension in American competitive policy no less than in the eco-

---

[2] *Op. cit.*, p. 147.

[3] Nassau W. Senior, *An Outline of the Science of Political Economy* (New York: Augustus M. Kelly, 1951), p. 102.

[4] Alfred D. Chandler, Jr., *Strategy and Structure* (Cambridge, Mass.: The Massachusetts Institute of Technology Press, 1962), p. 33.

[5] Harvey Leibenstein, "Allocative Efficiency vs. 'X-Efficiency,'" *American Economic Review*, LVI (June 1966), 413.

[6] *Ibid.*

nomic concept of competition—one which will relate to principles of managerial science as well as to those of market taxonomy —is apparent.

Another fundamental weakness of the competitive concept, and one not unrelated to the above discussion, has been its consistent failure to relate to economic growth. In this respect, competition seems never to have fully recovered from the influence of Ricardo, who, in a letter to Malthus, once wrote:

> Political Economy you think is an enquiry into the nature and causes of wealth—I think it should rather be called an enquiry into the laws which determine the division of the produce of industry amongst the classes who concur in its formation. . . . Every day I am more satisfied that the former enquiry is vain and delusive, and the latter only the true object of science.[7]

The analytical refinement of the concept of competition, from the work of Cournot to that of Frank Knight, is at one with this general point of view. Edgeworth's definition of a "perfect field of competition," for example, ran entirely in terms of contracting and recontracting over the division of an existing and unchanging quantity of economic resources.[8] Although economic theory is no longer coterminous with price theory, and although the question of allocative efficiency now seems, indeed, to be of less urgency and relevance than that of economic growth (the precise relationship between the two being, apparently, a matter of considerable uncertainty), the concept of competition has been only partially transformed from one of pure catallactics to one more closely related to the question of economic change. It is true that the beginnings of such a transformation are to be found in Chamberlin's reformulation, especially in his analysis of the product as a variable, his attention to sales effort, and in his general emphasis on commodities as "the most vola-

tile things in the economic system."[9] But the focus of the Chamberlinian analysis is still allocative efficiency, and much more needs to be done by way of systematically relating product and sales competition to economic change and growth. Moreover, Chamberlin's emphasis on variability of the product needs to be complemented by an increased emphasis on the variability of the form of the business firm itself and of the conditions under which commodities are produced and distributed—the latter being, perhaps, hardly less "volatile" than commodities themselves, and undoubtedly of no less significance for the overall growth process.

It was precisely during the years when the concept of competition was being analytically refined by becoming more and more closely identified with the atomistic market at the hands of Jevons, Edgeworth, J. B. Clark, and Knight,[1] that the industrial structures of the advanced economies of the world were taking shape, largely through changes in organizational forms which had little to do with price competition except in terms of the search for ways to avoid it. The analysis of these changes— indeed, the whole question of economic growth—was by that time largely becoming the province of the newly emerging discipline of economic history, which has necessarily had to give a broader meaning to competition than that traditionally associated with economic theory. The theorist cannot, for example, view the transformation of (say) the meat-packing industry in the United States during those years as a "competitive" development, for it was a movement which resulted in a market structure dominated by a "Big Four" or "Big Five"— results exactly opposite to those specified by Cournot. The historian, on the other hand, can—indeed, must—view this development as an adaptive response on the part of Armour, Morris, Cudahy, and Schwarzchild and Sulzberger, who, faced with

---

[7] *Works and Correspondence,* Vol. 8, ed. Piero Sraffa (Cambridge, England: Cambridge University Press, 1958), p. 278.

[8] *Op. cit.,* pp. 17–19.

[9] *Towards a More General Theory of Value* (New York: Oxford University Press, 1957), p. 114.

[1] Stigler, *op. cit.*

the innovations in production and marketing introduced by Gustavus Swift, "had to build similarly integrated organizations" if they were "to compete effectively." [2] It is well known that the essence of industrialization and economic growth is a changing production function and the development of new products, techniques, and forms of business organization. What has been lacking is any systematic effort to relate these changes to the concept of competition. The separation of so central a concept of economic theory from much of the analysis of our most pressing economic problem is unfortunate. Clearly, the time has come to incorporate into *the mainstream of economic theory* (as distinct from monographs on "new" or "workable" competition recurrently emerging in the specialized literature of industrial organization) a concept of competition closer to that occasionally suggested by Adam Smith and strongly advocated by Schumpeter—competition associated with new "divisions of labor" within the business firm and in the industrial structure generally, and one that is more closely allied with concepts of "internal, especially technological, efficiency." [3] It is unfortunate that Schumpeter's defense of monopoly and big business has tended to overshadow his insights into the competitive process, insights which extended beyond those of even Chamberlin because they included an appreciation of the importance of changing methods of production and forms of industrial organization. Although Schumpeter was probably wrong, as recent evidence suggests,[4] in his assertion that "the large scale establishment . . . has come to be the most powerful engine of progress and in particular of the long run expansion of total output," [5] he seems less likely to be mistaken in his insistence that, at least from the standpoint of economic growth, "it is not . . . [price] competition which counts but the competition from the new commodity, the new technology, the new source of supply, the new type of organization . . . competition which commands a decisive cost or quality advantage and which strikes not at the margin of the profits and the outputs of the existing firms but at their foundations and their very lives." [6]

Finally, a persistent weakness of the concept of competition has been the tendency of economists to minimize, ignore, or deny, its externally interdependent nature, that is, the extent to which the competition of one economic unit tends to affect the economic position of others, and thus, the overall industrial structure. Despite the etymology of the verb (literally, "to seek together"), to compete, in economic theory, has generally meant to act independently. "The meaning of 'competition,'" Frank Knight has written, is simply that the competing units "are numerous and act independently." [7] Even the literature of the so-called "new" or "workable" competition reflects the influence of this way of thinking.[8] This emphasis on independence has meant a close conceptual connection between competition, on the one hand, and both economic rationality and economic freedom, on the other. Thus Henry Moore, in his classic categorization of the various meanings given to competition in economic theory concluded that "the essential meaning of the term" is that "every economic factor

---

[2] Chandler, *op. cit.*, p. 26.

[3] Schumpeter, *op. cit.*, p. 106.

[4] F. M. Scherer, "Firm Size, Market Structure, Opportunity, and the Output of Patented Inventions," *American Economic Review*, LV (Part I, Dec. 1965), 1097–1125.

[5] Schumpeter, *op. cit.*, p. 106.

[6] *Ibid.*, p. 84.

[7] "Immutable Laws in Economics," *op. cit.*, p. 102.

[8] In his last major work, J. M. Clark shifted his emphasis from "workable" to "effective" competition, and then went on to say: "For the competition to be effective, *the crucial thing seems to be that prices be independently* made under conditions that give some competitors an incentive to aggressive action that others will have to meet, whenever prices are materially above the minimum necessary supply prices at which the industry would supply the amounts demanded of the various grades and types of products it produces." *Competition as a Dynamic Process, op. cit.*, p. 18, emphasis added.

seeks and obtains a maximum net income," [9] and Knight, on another occasion, wrote: "What competition actually means is simply the freedom of the individual to 'deal' with any and all other individuals and to select the best terms as judged by himself, among those offered." [1]

The trouble with this view is that it fails to specify *how* the competing units act, either in terms of securing a "maximum net income" or in "dealing" with "any and all other individuals." Moreover, it ascribes to the competing unit altogether too passive a pattern of behavior. Rather than merely "selecting" the best terms among those offered, a competitor may well choose to try to twist the terms of trade to his own advantage. In this respect, as Morris Copeland has rightly noted, "competition frequently means discrimination."

> In fact a competitor that gets ahead in an industry may do so in substantial part by developing business connections, i.e., arrangements that give him preferential treatment in terms of financing, in terms of purchase, in access to market information, in the award of private contracts, even preferential treatment in the administration of a public office. [2]

Implicit in Professor Copeland's view of competition is the realistic notion that some competitors may be better *able* to compete than others. Such a difference in competitive ability would allow for differential growth and profit rates among the firms within an industry—variables to which the Jevonian "Law of Indifference" need not, apparently, apply even in an otherwise conceptually perfect market. Moreover, competition which involves the active effort to improve the terms on which one trades, rather than the merely passive selection of the best terms available, may well be, in fact, competition for a position of monopoly power—a not unrealistic view of the actual competitive process in the light of our industrial history. To compete for monopoly power is not, of course, necessarily to realize it. But to the extent that the result, not to say the purpose, of economic competition is a changed environent in which that competition proceeds, the case is strengthened for distinguishing between, rather than identifying, the idea of competition and that of market structure.

IV

A promising, if not yet altogether satisfying, new dimension has been suggested for microeconomics in recent years in the various efforts to develop a "behavioral theory of the firm," in which analysis would go beyond that of the traditional determinate equilibrium toward which the business firm is assumed to be perfectly adapting in a world of no uncertainty, to include also "at least some description of the processes and mechanisms through which the adaptation takes place." [3] The reformulation and expansion of the concept of competition would appear to be an important, if yet underemphasized, part of that general task. To the degree that that effort is successful, it seems reasonable to predict that the idea of the market and that of competition may increasingly come to be separately identified, and competition itself may be, once again, what it was at the hands of Adam Smith: a disequilibrium, behavioral concept which is meaningful and relevant in terms of the contemporary pattern of economic life.

---

[9] Henry L. Moore, "Paradoxes of Competition," this *Journal*, XX (Feb. 1906), 213.

[1] "The Meaning of Freedom," *Ethics*, LII (Oct. 1941), 103.

[2] M. A. Copeland, "Institutionalism and Welfare Economics," *American Economic Review*, XLVIII (Mar. 1958), 13.

[3] H. A. Simon, "Theories of Decision-Making in Economics," *American Economic Review*, XLIX (June 1959), 256.

10. The Process of Creative Destruction

JOSEPH A. SCHUMPETER

The theories of monopolistic and oligopolistic competition and their popular variants may in two ways be made to serve the view that capitalist reality is unfavorable to maximum performance in production. One may hold that it always has been so and that all along output has been expanding in spite of the secular sabotage perpetrated by the managing bourgeoisie. Advocates of this proposition would have to produce evidence to the effect that the observed rate of increase can be accounted for by a sequence of favorable circumstances unconnected with the mechanism of private enterprise and strong enough to overcome the latter's resistance. However, those who espouse this variant at least avoid the trouble about historical fact that the advocates of the alternative proposition have to face. This avers that capitalist reality once tended to favor maximum productive performance, or at all events productive performance so considerable as to constitute a major element in any serious appraisal of the system; but that the later spread of monopolist structures, killing competition, has by now reversed that tendency.

First, this involves the creation of an entirely imaginary golden age of perfect competition that at some time somehow metamorphosed itself into the monopolistic age, whereas it is quite clear that perfect competition has at no time been more of a reality than it is at present. Secondly, it is necessary to point out that the rate of increase in output did not decrease from the nineties from which, I suppose, the prevalence of the largest-size concerns, at least in manufacturing industry, would have to be dated; that there is nothing in the behavior of the time series of total output to suggest a "break in trend"; and, most important of all, that the modern standard of life of the masses evolved during the period of relatively unfettered "big business." If we list the items that enter the modern workman's budget and from 1899 on observe the course of their prices not in terms of money but in terms of the hours of labor that will buy them—i.e., each year's money prices divided by each year's hourly wage rates—we cannot fail to be struck by the rate of the advance which, considering the spectacular improvement in qualities, seems to have been greater and not smaller than it ever was before. If we economists were given less to wishful thinking and more to the observation of facts, doubts would immediately arise as to the realistic virtues of a theory that would have led us to expect a very different result. Nor is this all. As soon as we go into details and inquire into the individual items in which progress was most conspicuous, the trail leads not to the doors of those firms that work under conditions of comparatively free competition but precisely to the doors of the large concerns—which, as in the case of agricultural machinery, also account for much of the progress in the competitive sector—and a shocking suspicion dawns upon us that big business may have had more to do with creating that standard of life than with keeping it down.

The essential point to grasp is that in dealing with capitalism we are dealing with an evolutionary process. It may seem strange that anyone can fail to see so obvious a fact which moreover was long ago emphasized by Karl Marx. Yet that fragmentary analysis which yields the bulk of our propositions about the functioning of modern capitalism persistently neglects it. Let us restate the point and see how it bears upon our problem.

Capitalism, then, is by nature a form or method of economic change, and not only never is but never can be stationary. And this evolutionary character of the capitalist process is not merely due to the fact that economic life goes on in a social and natural environment which changes and by its change alters the data of economic action; this fact is important and these changes (wars, revolutions and so on) often condition industrial change, but they are not its prime movers. Nor is this evolutionary character due to a quasi-automatic increase in population and capital or to the vagaries of monetary systems of which exactly the same thing holds true. The fundamental impulse that sets and keeps the capitalist engine in motion comes from the new consumers' goods, the new methods of production or transportation, the new markets, the new forms of industrial organization that capitalist enterprise creates.

The contents of the laborer's budget, say from 1760 to 1940, did not simply grow on unchanging lines but they underwent a process of qualitative change. Similarly, the history of the productive apparatus of a typical farm, from the beginnings of the rationalization of crop rotation, plowing and fattening to the mechanized thing of today—linking up with elevators and railroads—is a history of revolutions. So is the history of the productive apparatus of the iron and steel industry from the charcoal furnace to our own type of furnace, or the history of the apparatus of power production from the overshot water wheel to the modern power plant, or the history of transportation from the mailcoach to the airplane. The opening up of new markets, foreign or domestic, and the organizational development from the craft shop and factory to such concerns as U.S. Steel illustrate the same process of industrial mutation—if I may use that biological term—that incessantly revolutionizes the economic structure *from within*, incessantly destroying the old one, incessantly creating a new one.

This process of Creative Destruction is the essential fact about capitalism. It is what capitalism consists in and what every capitalist concern has got to live in. This fact bears upon our problem in two ways.

First, since we are dealing with a process whose every element takes considerable time in revealing its true features and ultimate effects, there is no point in appraising the performance of that process *ex visu* of a given point of time; we must judge its performance over time, as it unfolds through decades or centuries. A system—any system, economic or other—that at *every* given point of time fully utilizes its possibilities to the best advantage may yet in the long run be inferior to a system that does so at *no* given point of time, because the latter's failure to do so may be a condition for the level or speed of long-run performance.

Second, since we are dealing with an organic process, analysis of what happens in any particular part of it—say, in an individual concern or industry—may indeed clarify details of mechanism but is inconclusive beyond that. Every piece of business strategy acquires its true significance only against the background of that process and within the situation created by it. It must be seen in its role in the perennial gale of creative destruction; it cannot be understood irrespective of it or, in fact, on the hypothesis that there is a perennial lull.

But economists who, *ex visu* of a point of time, look for example at the behavior of an oligopolist industry—an industry which consists of a few big firms—and observe the well-known moves and countermoves within it that seem to aim at nothing but high prices and restrictions of output are making precisely that hypothesis. They accept the data of the momentary situation as if there were no past or future to it and think that they have understood what there is to understand if they interpret the behavior of those firms by means of the principle of maximizing profits with reference to those data. The usual theorist's paper and the usual government commission's report practically never try to see that behavior, on the one hand, as a result of a piece of past history and, on the other hand, as an attempt to deal with a situation that is sure to change presently—as an attempt by those firms to keep on their feet, on ground that is slipping away from under them. In other words, the problem that is usually being visualized is how capitalism administers existing structures, whereas the relevant problem is how it creates and destroys them. As long as this is not recognized, the investigator does a meaningless job. As soon as it is recognized, his outlook on capitalist practice and its social results changes considerably.

The first thing to go is the traditional conception of the *modus operandi* of competition. Economists are at long last emerging from the stage in which price competition was all they saw. As soon as quality competition and sales effort are admitted into the sacred precincts of theory, the price variable is ousted from its dominant position. However, it is still competition within a rigid pattern of invariant conditions, methods of production and forms of industrial organization in particular, that practically monopolizes attention. But in capitalist reality, as distinguished from its textbook picture, it is not that kind of competition which counts but the competition from the new commodity, the new technology, the new source of supply, the new type of organization (the largest-scale unit of control for instance)—competition which commands a decisive cost or quality advantage and which strikes not at the margins of the profits and the outputs of the existing firms but at their foundations and their very lives. This kind of competition is as much more effective than the other as a bombardment is in comparison with forcing a door, and so much more important that it becomes a matter of comparative indifference whether competition in the ordinary sense functions more or less promptly; the powerful level that in the long run expands output and brings down prices is in any case made of other stuff.

It is hardly necessary to point out that competition of the kind we now have in

mind acts not only when in being but also when it is merely an ever-present threat. It disciplines before it attacks. The businessman feels himself to be in a competitive situation even if he is alone in his field or if, though not alone, he holds a position such that investigating government experts fail to see any effective competition between him and any other firms in the same or a neighboring field and in consequence conclude that his talk, under examination, about his competitive sorrows is all make-believe. In many cases, though not in all, this will in the long run enforce behavior very similar to the perfectly competitive pattern.

Many theorists take the opposite view which is best conveyed by an example. Let us assume that there is a certain number of retailers in a neighborhood who try to improve their relative position by service and "atmosphere" but avoid price competition and stick to methods to the local tradition—a picture of stagnating routine. As others drift into the trade, that quasi-equilibrium is indeed upset, but in a manner that does not benefit their customers. The economic space around each of the shops having been narrowed, their owners will no longer be able to make a living and they will try to mend the case by raising prices in tacit agreement. This will further reduce their sales and so, by successive pyramiding, a situation will evolve in which increasing potential supply will be attended by increasing instead of decreasing prices and by decreasing instead of increasing sales.

Such cases do occur, and it is right and proper to work them out. But as the practical instances usually given show, they are fringe-end cases to be found mainly in the sectors furthest removed from all that is most characteristic of capitalist activity. Moreover, they are transient by nature. In the case of retail trade the competition that matters arises not from additional shops of the same type, but from the department store, the chain store, the mail-order house and the supermarket which are bound to destroy those pyramids sooner or later. Now a theoretical construction which neglects this essential element of the case neglects all that is most typically capitalist about it; even if correct in logic as well as in fact, it is like *Hamlet* without the Danish prince.

Monopolistic Practices

We have seen that, both as a fact and as a threat, the impact of new things—new technologies for instance—on the existing structure of an industry considerably reduces the long-run scope and importance of practices that aim, through restricting output, at conserving established positions and at maximizing the profits accruing from them. We must now recognize the further fact that restrictive practices of this kind, as far as they are effective, acquire a new significance in the perennial gale of creative destruction, a significance which they would not have in a stationary state or in a state of slow and balanced growth. In either of these cases restrictive strategy would produce no result other than an increase in profits at the expense of buyers except that, in the case of balanced advance, it might still prove to be the easiest and most effective way of collecting the means by which to finance additional investment. But in the process of creative destruction, restrictive practices may do much to steady the ship and to alleviate temporary difficulties.

Practically any investment entails, as a necessary complement of entreprenurial action, certain safeguarding activities such as insuring or hedging. Long-range investing under rapidly changing conditions, especially under conditions that change or may change at any moment under the impact of new commodities and technologies, is like shooting at a target that is not only indistinct but moving—and moving jerkily at that. Hence it becomes necessary to resort to such protecting devices as patents or temporary secrecy of processes or, in some cases, long-period contracts secured in advance. But these protecting devices which most economists accept as normal elements of rational management are only special cases of a larger class comprising many others which most economists condemn although they do not differ fundamentally from the recognized ones.

If, for instance, a war risk is insurable, nobody objects to a firm's collecting the cost of the insurance from the buyers of its products. But that risk is no less an element in long-run costs, if there are no facilities for insuring against it, in which case a price strategy aiming at the same end will seem to involve unnecessary restriction and to be productive of excess profits. Similarly, if a patent cannot be secured or would not, if secured, effectively protect, other means may have to be used in order to justify the investment. Among them are a price policy that will make it possible to write off more quickly than would otherwise be rational, or additional investment in order to provide excess capacity to be used only for aggression or defense. Again, if long-period contracts cannot be entered into in advance, other means may have to be devised in order to tie prospective customers to the investing firm.

In analyzing such business strategy *ex visu* of a given point of time, the investigating economist or government agent sees price policies that seem to him predatory and restrictions of output that seem to him synonymous with loss of opportunities to produce. He does not see that restrictions of this type are, in the conditions of the perennial gale, incidents, often unavoidable incidents, of a long-run process of expansion which they protect rather than impede. There is no more paradox in this than there is in saying that motorcars are traveling faster than they otherwise would *because* they are provided with brakes.

This stands out most clearly in the case of those sectors of the economy which at any time happen to embody the impact of new things and methods on the existing industrial structure. The best way of getting a vivid and realistic idea of industrial strategy is indeed to visualize the behavior of new concerns or industries that introduce new commodities or processes (such as the aluminum industry) or else reorganize a part or the whole of an industry (such as, for instance, the old Standard Oil Company).

As we have seen, such concerns are aggressors by nature and wield the really effective weapon of competition. Their intrusion can only in the rarest of cases fail to improve total output in quantity or quality, both through the new method itself—even if at no time used to full advantage—and through the pressure it exerts on the preexisting firms. But these aggressors are so circumstanced as to require, for purposes of attack and defense, also pieces of armor other than price and quality of their product which, moreover, must be strategically manipulated all along so that at any point of time they seem to be doing nothing but restricting their output and keeping prices high.

On the one hand, largest-scale plans could in many cases not materialize at all if it were not known from the outset that competition will be discouraged by heavy capital requirements or lack of experience, or that means are available to discourage or checkmate it so as to gain the time and space for further developments. Even the conquest of financial control over competing concerns in otherwise unassailable positions or the securing of advantages that run counter to the public's sense of fair play—railroad rebates—move, as far as long-run effects on total output alone are envisaged, into a different light; they *may* be methods for removing obstacles that the institution of private property puts in the path of progress. In a socialist society that time and space would be no less necessary. They would have to be secured by order of the central authority.

On the other hand, enterprise would in most cases be impossible if it were not known from the outset that exceptionally favorable situations are likely to arise which if exploited by price, quality and quantity manipulation will produce profits adequate to tide over exceptionally unfavorable situations provided these are similarly managed. Again this requires strategy that in the short run is often restrictive. In the

majority of successful cases this strategy just manages to serve its purpose. In some cases, however, it is so successful as to yield profits far above what is necessary in order to induce the corresponding investment. These cases then provide the baits that lure capital on to untried trails. Their presence explains in part how it is possible for so large a section of the capitalist world to work for nothing: in the midst of the prosperous twenties just about half of the business corporations in the United States were run at a loss, at zero profits, or at profits which, if they had been foreseen, would have been inadequate to call forth the effort and expenditure involved.

Our argument, however, extends beyond the cases of new concerns, methods and industries. Old concerns and established industries, whether or not directly attacked, still live in the perennial gale. Situations emerge in the process of creative destruction in which many firms may have to perish that nevertheless would be able to live on vigorously and usefully if they could weather a particular storm. Short of such general crises or depressions, sectional situations arise in which the rapid change of data that is characteristic of that process so disorganizes an industry for the time being as to inflict functionless losses and to create avoidable unemployment. Finally, there is certainly no point in trying to conserve obsolescent industries indefinitely; but there is point in trying to avoid their coming down with a crash and in attempting to turn a rout, which may become a center of cumulative depressive effects, into orderly retreat. Correspondingly there is, in the case of industries that have sown their wild oats but are still gaining and not losing ground, such a thing as orderly advance.

All this is of course nothing but the tritest common sense. But it is being overlooked with a persistence so stubborn as sometimes to raise the question of sincerity. And it follows that, within the process of creative destruction, all the realities of which theorists are in the habit of relegating to books and courses on business cycles, there is another side to industrial self-organization than that which these theorists are contemplating. "Restraints of trade" of the cartel type as well as those which merely consist in tacit understandings about price competition may be effective remedies under conditions of depression. As far as they are, they may in the end produce not only steadier but also greater expansion of total output than could be secured by an entirely uncontrolled onward rush that cannot fail to be studded with catastrophes. Nor can it be argued that these catastrophes occur in any case. We know what has happened in each historical case. We have a very imperfect idea of what might have happened, considering the tremendous pace of the process, if such pegs had been entirely absent.

Even as now extended, however, our argument does not cover all cases of restrictive or regulating strategy, many of which no doubt have that injurious effect on the long-run development of output which is uncritically attributed to all of them. And even in the cases our argument does cover, the net effect is a question of the circumstances and of the way in which and the degree to which industry regulates itself in each individual case. It is certainly as conceivable that an all-pervading cartel system might sabotage all progress as it is that it might realize, with smaller social and private costs, all that perfect competition is supposed to realize. This is why our argument does not amount to a case against state regulation. It does show that there is no general case for indiscriminate "trust-busting" or for the prosecution of everything that qualifies as a restraint of trade. Rational as distinguished from vindictive regulation by public authority turns out to be an extremely delicate problem which not every government agency, particularly when in full cry against big business, can be trusted to solve. But our argument, framed to refute a prevalent *theory* and the inferences drawn therefrom about the relation between modern capitalism and the development of total output, only yields another *theory*, i.e., another outlook on facts and another principle by which to interpret them. For our purpose that is enough. For the rest, the facts themselves have the floor.

II · ARE CONCENTRATED
INDUSTRIES OLIGOPOLIES?

Part II–A · *Overview*

In the opening selection, Professor Fred Weston points out that both the courts and the defense in antitrust suits (at least, in merger cases) implicitly accept the notion that those activities that increase concentration above some critical level are anticompetitive and, practically speaking, *per se* violations of the antitrust laws. Defense arguments tend to revolve around attempts to enlarge what is defined as the market in which the share of business is measured. Occasionally, the defense argues that the economies resulting from a merger are a social good. In the Brown Shoe case, however, the Supreme Court felt this would make life difficult for competitors, and the merger was ordered dissolved for this reason.

Professor Weston summarizes some recent research which, he says, "establishes that concentration has had favorable effects on the economy." Examining recent studies dealing with causes of concentration[1] and with price and profit correlates, it appears that those industries are concentrated in which technological and economic factors dictate such a structure and that concentration is not "higher than it need be for efficiency." He concludes that the equating of high concentration with shared monopoly "is without foundation in fact or in the reality of market behavior."

In his "Introduction" to a set of studies on business concentration and price policy (selection 12), Professor Stigler raises questions concerning the definition of industries

---

[1] Professor Weston omits Stephen Hymer and Peter Pashigian, "Firm Size and Rate of Growth," 70 *Journal of Political Economy* 556 (1962) which develops evidence consistant with the thesis that "unit costs decrease with size," at least in the range of experience (1000 largest manufacturing companies, 1946–1955) used in their analysis.

for the purposes of structural study: how long is the long run in which short run monopoly disappears (a question partially answered in his later study of *Capital and Rates of Return in Manufacturing Industries*) and what is an appropriate measure of industry structure? Professor Stigler even questions the use of the neoclassical theory of competition and monopoly, developed with stationary economy assumptions, in historical circumstances with "frequently unpredictable changes in consumer demands and productive techniques and resources."

Professor Stigler also suggests that industry structure may largely be a consequence of economies (or lack of economies) of scale. "All comprehensive definitions of economies of scale ultimately imply that firms with the lower costs prosper relative to other sizes of firms, and it is desirable to recognize this explicitly by defining the most efficient size as that which grows relative to other sizes."

In selection 13, Sanford Rose dissects census concentration figures, both aggregate and market, discussing their deficiencies and their significance. Aggregate concentration is dismissed as being economically meaningless. Census manufacturing concentration ratios may be combined in various ways to measure the trend in market concentration. Unfortunately, changes in industry definitions make it difficult to construct a representative sample usable over a meaningful time span, aside from the fact that the years in which the business census happens to have been taken are not exactly comparable. In addition, the concentration figures are deficient in several aspects ranging from "specialization" and "coverage" problems to lack of allowance for import market shares. If we do not have meaningful concentration figures comparable over time, it is difficult to determine whether concentration is a disappearing or growing "problem." In any case, is concentration a "problem"?

11. Implications of Recent Research for the Structural Approach to Oligopoly

J. FRED WESTON

Introduction

While Section 2 of the Sherman Act has not been applied in major cases in recent years, it has been an active threat as manifested by proposals for deconcentration. On July 24, 1972 Senator Philip A. Hart announced the introduction of a bill to create an Industrial Reorganization Commission with power to "dismantle corporate giants." [1] If Section 2 has been slumbering, it may be an awakening giant.

The main basis for the attack on oligopoly has been the structural approach to industrial economics. The structural theory states that high concentration or oligopoly can be equated with collusion and shared monopoly. The structural theory holds that there are presumptions of adverse competitive effects from high concentration. Thus the structural approach to oligopoly would create a Section 2 of far-reaching impact.

Some recent research findings have important implications for the structural approach to oligopoly. After summarizing the what, why and wherefores of the structural approach, this paper will describe some of the new research findings in the areas of (1) causes of concentration, (2) concentration and profits, and (3) concentration and prices. Some implications of this new evidence will then be sketched. This new evidence establishes that concentration has had favorable effects on the economy, not adverse.

The Basis for the Structural Theory. The structural approach to oligopoly holds that when concentration, variously measured, exceeds some number, the effects on competition will be adverse. [2] This view stems from the economic theory of the idealized atomistic market model in which there are so many sellers and buyers in an industry that each one is too small for its individual behavior to have a perceptible effect on industry price or output. Much empirical research beginning during the 1950's and continuing through the 1960's yielded results that appeared to be consistent with this theoretical model. [3]

The structural theory was embraced in a stream of Supreme Court decisions from the *Philadelphia Bank* case[4] (1963) through *Von's Shopping Bag*[5] (1966). In most cases, however, no defense was made to the assumption of the structural theory that concentration, *per se,* is anticompetitive. The

---

Reprinted by permission of the *Antitrust Law Journal,* Volume 41, 1972.

[1] S 3832 "Industrial Reorganization Act".

[2] Adams, Walter, *The Case for Structural Tests,* Public Policy Toward Mergers, J. F. Weston and S. Peltzman, Eds., (Goodyear Publishing Co., 1969); Blair, John M., Economic Concentration: Structure, Behavior and Public Policy, (Harcourt Brace Jovanovich, 1972); Mueller, Willard F., *Industrial Structure and Competition Policy,* Studies by the Staff of the Cabinet Committee on Price Stability, Washington, 39–50 (1969).

[3] Shepherd, W. G., *Elements of Market-Structure,* LIV Review of Economics and Statistics, 25–37 (Feb. 1972); Shepherd, W. G., *Elements of Market-Structure: An Inter-Industry Analysis,* XXXVIII Southern Economic Journal, 531–537 (April 1972); Weiss, L. W., *Quantitative Studies of Industrial Organizations,* Frontiers of Quantitative Economics, edited by Michael D. Intriligator, (Amsterdam: North-Holland Publishing Co., 1971).

[4] 374 U.S. 321 (1963).

[5] 384 U.S. 270 (1966).

defense primarily was on market definition to attempt to prove that concentration was not high. The acme of the structural approach was expressed in the Department of Justice merger guidelines announced on May 30, 1968 [6] and in the FTC's complaint in the *Cereal* case issued on April 26, 1972 [7] that oligopoly can be equated to shared monopoly. As the structural theory moved to a pinnacle of dominance in public policy applications, some defects in that body of doctrine have become increasingly evident. As empirical research has continued, new findings are having a feedback impact on the structural theory, requiring a reassessment.

The Causes of Concentration. One basis for assessing the structural theory which equates oligopoly to shared monopoly is to analyze the causes of concentration. This goes to the issue of whether concentration results from fundamental forces producing economic benefits or whether concentration reflects distortion of normal economic processes.

We are indebted to Professor Joe Bain for another set of pioneering measurements with important implications. In his book *International Differences in Industrial Structure*,[8] Professor Bain presents data which show that (1) concentration ratios for the same industries are generally higher in foreign countries than in the United States, (2) that the industries in which concentration is high are generally the same industries as those in which concentration is high in the United States, (3) the industries that are not concentrated in foreign countries are generally the same as those which are not concentrated in the United States.

These results suggest that it is not motivations that determine whether or not an industry is concentrated but rather more fundamental underlying technological and economic factors. Further evidence is that commissions in the European Economic Community are fostering mergers in a number of industries for rationalization of production to achieve greater economies. This suggests an economic basis for large size and casts doubt on Bain's earlier studies[9] that concentration is much greater than necessary for efficiency or plant economies of scale in the United States. Another study, by Lars Engwall [10], of various Eastern European countries including the U.S.S.R. finds concentration to be higher than in the United States.[11] Centralized planning, of course, could be combined with decentralized production to any degree that efficiency dictates, the higher degree of concentration observed is further evidence that large scale operations yield production economies.

In the United States, recent analysis re-emphasizes the finding that underlying factors such as capital intensity are statistically significant in explaining differential concentration between industries.[12] Further corroboration is provided by the fact that six of some 150 three-digit industries account for 40% of total manufacturing assets.[13] That these six industries should represent almost

---

[6] 1 Trade Reg. Rep. ¶ 4430.

[7] 3 Trade Reg. Rep. ¶ 19, 898 (1972).

[8] Bain, Joe S., International Differences in Industrial Structure, (Yale University Press, 1966).

[9] Bain, J. S., *Economies of Scale, Concentration, and the Condition of Entry in 20 Industries,* 44 American Economic Review, 15–39 (Mar. 1954); Bain, J. S., Barriers to New Competition, (Harvard University Press, 1956).

[10] Engwall, Lars, *Industrial Concentration in Different Economic Systems,* ms.

[11] John M. Blair in (n. 2, *supra*) attributes inefficiency problems in the U.S.S.R. and Yugoslavia to ubiquitous oligopoly. For a more balanced view, see Adizes, Ichak, Industrial Democracy: Yugoslav Style, (New York: The Free Press, 1971).

[12] Ornstein, S. I., R. E. Shrieves, M. D. Intriligator and J. F. Weston, *Determinants of Market Structure,* Southern Economic Journal (Ap. 1973).

[13] The industries are (1) Industrial Chemicals (281), (2) Blast Furnaces & Basic Steel Products (331), (3) Motor Vehicles & Equipment (371), (4) Primary Nonferrous Metals (333), (5) Petroleum Refining (291), (6) Aircraft & Parts (372). Senator Hart's list of seven industries for "priority attention" include the first 4

half of the manufacturing economy cannot be explained by mergers, desire for market power, etc., but rather reflects basic technological and economic factors. These six industries also account for 53 of the largest 100 firms in the economy. Furthermore, the value added per plant in these six industries is $8.4 million, compared with the average value added per plant in all manufacturing industries of under $800 thousand—further evidence of large capital investment as a basic cause of high concentration. These data also demonstrate the practical impossibility of achieving atomistic structures in concentrated industries. Adding two or three firms by breaking up the largest would not basically change the oligopolistic structure of an industry. The underlying theory of deconcentration and the actions it proposes are internally inconsistent.

Furthermore, our understanding of the important role of the technology of management in the performance of business firms is increasing. The inability of respondents to Professor Bain's survey of the early 1950's to explain the nature or importance of managerial economies of scale or multi-plant economies is giving way to new findings also.[14] The logic and sources of managerial and multi-product, multi-plant returns of scale have been formulated.[15] A basis is now provided for repeating Bain's

study of the early 1950's, using these new theoretical concepts as a guide to survey questionnaires and interviews.[16] Furthermore, there is evidence that continuity of management organization is an important factor in the efficiency of large firms.[17] A further implication is that there would be important losses in managerial efficiencies from a deconcentration program.

Thus, in summary, recent evidence runs against the view that concentration in the United States is higher than it need be for efficiency. It suggests that differences in concentration among industries are explained by underlying factors, the most important of which are fundamental economies of scale in manufacturing or management.

Studies of the Relation Between Concentration and Profit. If concentration is due primarily to technological and economic forces rather than motivations for market power, the next issue is the performance consequences of the resulting oligopolistic structure of many industries. The economic research on performance has proceeded within the narrow confines of the atomistic market model upon which the structural theory is based. Symptomatic of the restrictive influence of the underlying model is the preoccupation with concentration and profit studies as purported indicators of performance. In these studies, the possibility that higher profits might result from greater efficiency was set aside. In Bain's 1951 article,[18] he suggested the criti-

listed plus the computer industry, energy, and electrical machinery and equipment; Weston, J. Fred, *Business Power Over Markets and Consumers—The Facts*, Chapter 20, Contemporary Challenges in the Business-Society Relationship, George A. Steiner, ed., Printing and Publication Department, UCLA, 1972.

[14] Bain, J. S., Barriers to New Competition, n. 9, *supra.*

[15] Weston, J. Fred, *Changing Environments and New Concepts of Firms and Markets*, New Technologies, Competition, and Antitrust, National Industrial Conference Board, March 5, 1970; Weston, J. Fred. *Discussion*, American Economic Review Proceedings, 125–127 (May 1971); Williamson, Oliver E., Corporate Control and Business Behavior, (Prentice-Hall, Inc., 1970); Williamson, Oliver E., *The Vertical Integration of Production: Market Failure Considerations*, American Economic Review Proceedings, 112–123 (May 1971).

[16] If managerial economies were the *sole* explanation of concentration, it would have to bear the burden of explaining why it is important in some industries, but not in others. More work needs to be done in this area. My present hypothesis is that the importance of managerial factors interacts with plant scale economies, potentials for multi-plant economies, and activities requiring the use of specialist or staff expertise in managing complex research, manufacturing, distributional, promotion, etc., requirements.

[17] *See,* n. 16, *supra.*

[18] Bain, J. S., *Relation of Profit Rate to Industry Concentration: American Manufacturing.* 65 Quarterly Journal of Economics, 293–324 (August 1951).

cal point of concentration as 70% or more. The industries in the group with concentration of 70% or more had higher average profits than the industries grouped in the less than 70% concentration category. Even in Bain's data, however, a group of industries with concentration less than 20% could be found that had higher average profits than the over 70% concentration group. It was only by grouping these into the broad under-70% category that their higher profit rates could be submerged.

This was only one of a number of findings in the Bain article and Bain himself presented his results generally with a large number of qualifications. However, a number of other studies published subsequent to Bain's article appeared to support his findings. Increased importance was attached to these results. It was argued that if high concentration is associated with high profits, evidence of collusion and/or monopoly power in concentrated industries is provided.

In recent years new studies have substantially altered the box score in the concentration and profit relationship studies. Yale Brozen has examined various aspects of the original Bain thesis in a series of publications.[19] He began by attempting to update the Bain sample of 20 industries for the late 1960's. However, this was very difficult to do because of the changing nature of the industries and the fact that many of the firms in those industries had disappeared. The typewriter industry, which was one of the highly concentrated industries in Bain's sample of 30 industries, provides a good illustration. My own examination of the data of the typewriter industry established that the only years in which the typewriter industry had higher than average profits were in the two four-year periods, 1936–39 and 1946–49, which Bain

studied.[20] None of the four traditional typewriter companies which had over 90% of industry sales from the early 1920's to the early 1950's exist as separate companies today. As a part of larger firms, in recent years these four traditional typewriter companies combined had less than 20% of relevant, important typewriter markets. A firm not in the industry in the 1920's has the largest market share.

This highlights the underlying dynamism of the U.S. economy revealed by the Brozen data. He found that industries with the greatest profits at the time of Bain's study at some earlier period, expanded at a higher rate in subsequent periods, and their profits trended downward toward the average of profits in all manufacturing industries. Those industries with the lower profits in an earlier period expanded at a lower rate and their profits trended upward toward the average for all manufacturing industries. This is very powerful evidence that competitive processes were in fact operating in these industries. Even if it were argued that high profits are associated with temporary monopoly power, this is quite different from the public policy implications usually stressed. The dynamic elements of our economic system provide its own self-corrective. High profit industries trend down toward the average; low profit industries trend up toward the average. Intervention is not required.

Indeed, when Brozen expanded Bain's original list of 42 industries and included some additional firms from each industry, no relation between concentration and profits was found. Other studies reinforce the implications of Professor Brozen's highly significant findings. In a forthcoming article in the *Journal of Business*,[21] Professor Ornstein applies a multiple regression analysis

[19] Brozen, Yale, *Bain's Concentration and Rates of Return Revisited,* 14 The Journal of Law and Economics, 351–369, (Oct. 1971); Brozen, Yale, *An Ivory Tower (Chicago) View of Advertising,* ms. of presentation before the AAA Eastern Annual Conference, New York. June 5, 1972.

[20] These were the years embraced for all of the companies in the Bain study. One readily notes that these were not "normal" years coming just before and after World War II.

[21] Ornstein, Stanley, I., *A Multiregression Analysis of the Concentration and Profits Relation.* Journal of Business, (Oct. 1972).

to the investigation of concentration and profits. The logic of his study is that the link between the structural theory and the concentration-profit relation has never been established. Factors other than concentration could explain the association between concentration and profit in simple correlation studies. Ornstein found that profit rates are statistically related to economies of scale in production and to growth rates of both the industry and firms, but not to concentration.

As a variant of this approach, another study[22] introduces in the relationship between concentration and profits, measures of risk derived from recent developments in the theory of finance. These measures apparently serve as a proxy for the more risky activities characteristically engaged in by large firms such as a higher fixed capital intensity, research and development efforts, advertising, etc., because no net relationship between concentration and profit was found to remain.

In a paper forthcoming in the *Journal of Law and Economics*,[23] Professor Demsetz subjects the shared monopoly argument to another statistical test. If collusion or shared monopoly takes place in concentrated industries, it should produce high profit rates for the smaller firms in the industry as well as for the larger firms. Indeed the traditional oligopoly theory upon which the shared monopoly argument is based, predicts that the umbrella held by the large firms will provide even higher profit rates for the smaller firms. The facts, however, are the reverse of the shared monopoly theory. The larger firms have higher profit rates than the smaller firms in concentrated industries. This finding is consistent with the conclusion that the larger firms are more efficient for a number of possible reasons ranging from good luck to the cumulative effects of a capable management team

built up and developed over a period of years.

A variant of the concentration and profits analysis was developed by then Professor Michael Mann in introducing barriers to entry as another explanatory variable in the relationship.[24] However, in later studies Stephen Rhoades, employing a multiple regression analysis, demonstates that the net influence of barriers to entry does not have a statistically significant influence on rates of return after the influence of the concentration variables has been accounted for.[25] This issue is still being debated on a statistical level [26], but the argument highlights the ambiguity of the barriers to entry concept. The most quoted statement of the sources of barriers to entry were the four identified by Professor Bain: (1) lower costs, (2) economies of scale, (3) advertising, (4) and patents.[27] We can set aside the fourth as determined by government policy. The first, having a lower cost curve throughout its length, is a matter of efficiency. To call this a barrier to entry is like saying that athletes who are able to run the mile in under four minutes or pole vault over 18 feet have imposed barriers against those unable to do so. Are the peculiar connotations of "barriers" appropriately applied to firms that have lower costs, that is, because they are more efficient? The same argument applies to lower costs achieved through scale of operations. Lower costs and efficiencies would appear to be fundamental economic virtues. The arguments with re-

[22] Weston, J. Fred and Baese, Jerome, *The Effect of Risk on the Concentration-Profit Relation*, ms.

[23] Demsetz, Harold, *A Size Distribution Analysis of Profits*, Journal of Law and Economics, forthcoming.

[24] Mann, H. Michael, *Seller Concentration, Barriers to Entry, and Rates of Return in Thirty Industries, 1950–1960*, 48 The Review of Economics and Statistics, 296–308. (August 1966).

[25] Rhoades, Stephen A., *Concentration, Barriers, and Rates of Return: A Note*, Journal of Industrial Economics, November 1970. Of course, the remaining concentration-profits relation is subject to the infirmities described above.

[26] Mann, H. Michael. *The Interaction of Barriers and Concentration: A Reply*. 19 The Journal of Industrial Economics, 291–293, (July 1971).

[27] Bain, J. S., Barriers to New Competition, n. 9, *supra*.

gard to advertising represent an entire body of literature unto themselves, beyond the scope of this presentation.[28]

Hence, regardless of how the statistics on barriers relate to increased concentration, economic logic compels the conclusion that unless the ambiguity of the barriers to entry concept can be reduced, it can provide little guidance for economic analysis or public policy decisions.

Concentration and Prices. The unfortunate experience with inflation in the United States since 1966 has highlighted another area of economic performance, the relation between concentration and prices.

Many statements refer to large firms as a primary cause of inflation. The evidence is contrary to this assertion. The facts are that there is an inverse relation between the degree of concentration and the extent of price changes: the more concentrated the industry, the smaller the price change; the less concentrated the industry, the larger the price change.[29] The statistical studies of the relation between concentration and prices by Professor L. Weiss sought to determine the net effect of concentration on prices by adjusting for the cost increases of labor and materials.[30] Professor Weiss found a negative or no relation between concentration and price changes except for the period 1953–1959. In my judgment, if he had adjusted for changes in capital costs during this period his results for 1953–1959 would have agreed with his findings for the periods 1953–1957, 1959–1963, 1963–1968, and 1967–1969.[31]

A very comprehensive study of the same subject in the Western European countries was published in a book entitled *Effects of Industrial Concentration: A Cross-Section Analysis for the Common Market.*[32] Therein it stated:

> Concerning the first, a certain literature —which is in contradiction with standard economic theory—suggests that more concentrated industries are responsible for what has been called "administrative inflation": during the upswings of the business cycle, more concentrated industries would use their monopolistic power to increase selling prices more than would be justified by increases in demand or costs. Our analysis of Belgian, Dutch and French wholesale prices over the period 1958–65 shows very clearly that this was not the case. Over this period, more concentrated industries behaved exactly like less concentrated industries. (at pp. 172–173.)

The facts simply controvert the assertion so often repeated that it has attained the stature of a widely-believed myth that inflation is caused by the price-raising activities of large firms. The facts are just the reverse.

Implications of the Recent Research. The evidence accumulating is diametrically opposed to the structural theory. Competitive processes are observed in industries described as oligopolies. The dimensions of competition are much more diverse than the price and output adjustments emphasized in the atomistic market model of pure and perfect competition. The model of dynamic competition includes consideration of differences in product quality, changes in

---

[28] Important new research findings have appeared in the Journal of Business and the Journal of Law and Economics reflecting new doctoral dissertation research as well as monographs by faculty members. It would appear that important threads of intellectual revisionism are taking place in the advertising literature as well, *cf.* note 19, *supra.*

[29] Weston, J. Fred, *Appraising Price and Pay Controls,* Presentation to Public Hearings of U.S. Price Commission, San Francisco, California, April 6, 1972, revised June 8, 1972.

[30] Weiss, L. W., *Business Pricing Policies and Inflation Reconsidered,* 74 Journal of Political Economy, 177–187, (April 1966).

[31] Weiss, L. W., *The Role of Concentration in Recent Inflation,* appendix to statement of Richard W. McLaren before the Joint Economics Committee July 10, 1970.

[32] Phlips, Louis, Effects of Industrial Concentration: A Cross-Section Analysis for the Common Market, Amsterdam, North-Holland Publishing Company, 1971, with the collaboration of M. Biart J. C. Dos Santos, A. Gilot, and J. P. Loiseau.

relative product quality, changes in performance capabilities of products, research and development efforts to increase market share over the long term, etc.[33]

An important conceptual distinction has been made by Ewald T. Grether.[34] The data compilations upon which the structural theory has rested have been based on groupings such as those developed in the Bureau of the Census' Standard Industrial Classification (SIC) which accords heavy emphasis to physical characteristics of products and the production methods used in producing them, not economic markets. Concentration ratios for some SIC categories may have little relevance to economic markets, such as SIC 2327, separate trousers —and incidentally, the sexist Census segregates women's slacks into SIC 2339, a "not elsewhere classified" category, which includes in addition such items as aprons, rufflings, hoovers, and dickeys.[35] And even when the SIC category comes close to a relevant economic market, the concentration ratio conveys nothing on the economic processes taking place in that market.

A recent paper sets forth aspects of how competitive processes take place in concentrated markets.[36] The planning and control activities of business firms represent efforts for making adjustments to external economic and general market conditions as well to the strategies and efforts of rival firms. The use of standard costing and the targeting of prices, market positions and market shares, sales volume as well as other cost revenue and investment elements are practices common to small and large firms alike.

There is a vast difference between the assumptions of the atomistic market model and actual behavior. In the real world, adjustments to change are not automatic or instantaneous and these adjustment processes are of the greatest theoretical and practical interest. The atomistic theory assumes that all firms are equally able in choosing methods of production, selection among inputs and achieving what is referred to as the best "production function." In the real world these decisions make the difference between efficient and inefficient firms. In the real world discretionary behavior takes place in business firms with regard to important elements that are assumed away in the atomistic theory. Thus, analyses which are supposed to be absent in atomistic firms are, in fact, the heart of decision-making and discretionary choices in small firms as well as large. The small farmer exercises discretion in the selection of crops and the appropriate mixes of capital equipment, labor and fertilizer. The small retailer must choose among different locations, different groups of products and different strategies between price, volume, advertising, personal service, etc. I refer to the small farmer and small retailer because these are presumed to be the archetype of atomistic firms in the textbook theory of pure and perfect competition.

The thrust of the accumulating evidence is that the development of concentrated industries or oligopolies is a result of competition and an expression of competitive processes. We see the competitive forces operating from both directions. In some industries in which a dominant firm with more than 50% market share, and in some instances close to 100% market share, had resulted mainly from mergers at the turn of the century, underlying competitive forces (with the help of divestiture decrees in two industries and a saluatory antitrust climate as well) moved the industries to a larger number of firms with changing market shares over a period of years. The decline in the market share of the dominant firm took place without divestiture in other industries, *e.g.*, agricultural implements,

[33] Again, I will eschew treating the role of advertising. Much of the new literature emphasizes the role of advertising as an aspect of competitive efforts and competitive behavior.

[34] Grether, Ewald T., *Industrial Organization: Past History and Future Problems*, LX American Economic Review, 83–99, (May 1970).

[35] Acknowledgment to Dr. Betty Bock.

[36] Weston, J. Fred, *Pricing Behavior of Large Firms*, X Western Economic Journal, 1–18 (Mar. 1972).

cans, meat packing, steel, leather, sugar refining, etc.

From the other direction, industries which formally were characterized by a large number of firms have been replaced by oligopolies. This, again, was a result of competitive processes which weeded out a large number of firms either through the bankruptcy or merger route.[37]

Indeed, in a long-term perspective it is clear that the reduction from hundreds of firms in an industry over a period of decades is a result of the operation of competitive forces. In the operation of these competitive forces in this long perspective, merger activity may be seen as a superior alternative to bankruptcy. It is a superior alternative to bankruptcy in preserving some organization values and the use of executives, workers and plant and equipment in more productive use than would have been achieved if the firm had been broken up and sold off at auctions through the bankruptcy courts with executive talent and workers dispersed to other firms and perhaps other industries.

As a consequence of these processes, assumptions of the atomistic model upon which the structural theory depends, are not appropriate for some industries or markets. For such industries it would not be possible for a large number of sellers and buyers as required by the atomistic model to exist in competitive and efficient markets. For many important industries or markets, technological, managerial and economic realities make the existence of large numbers of sellers or buyers impossible and irrelevant as a standard in any sense and provide no basis for *presumptions* about the conduct and performance of such industries. With the many dimensions of products and decision-making, it is not possible *a priori* to predict whether a market

with 5, 10 or 100 sellers or buyers would be more competitive than a market with 2 sellers or buyers.[38]

Conclusions. All of this shows that the structural approach to oligopoly which equates it with shared monopoly is without foundation in fact or in the reality of market behavior. Empirical evidence is consistent with the theory of dynamic competition by large firms in concentrated markets.[39] Price increases have been smaller in concentrated industries. It is precisely the factors that explain concentration that explain their moderation in price increases. It is the greater capital intensity, it is the greater research and development activities, it is the continued pressures of large firm rivalry, efforts to attract consumer spending to their products by price reductions, that explain why firms in concentrated industries succeed in offsetting the general inflation to some degree. Instead of the general myth that some people are seeking to perpetrate that the present inflation is due to oligopoly which is equated to shared monopoly, the facts are the opposite. Concentration reflects and creates economic efficiency, which moderates the inflationary pressures rather than causing them.

Industries described as oligopolies are subject to the same competitive market pressures for cost reduction, price reduction, product improvement of the kind that atomistic industries were supposed to have produced. The atomistic model upon which the structural theory is based is a useful abstract for some purposes. However, it is misleading as a guide for industrial economic theory and policy.

---

[38] Posner, Richard A., *Oligopoly and the Antitrust Laws: A Suggested Approach*, 21 Stan. L. Rev., 1562–1606 (1969).

[39] McGee, John S., In Defense of Industrial Concentration, (Praeger Publishers, 1971); *see* n. 36, *supra*.

---

[37] Cohen, Kalman J. and Cyert, Richard M., Theory of the Firm: Resource Allocation in a Market Economy, (Prentice-Hall, Inc., 1965).

12. Introduction to *Business Concentration and Price Policy*

GEORGE J. STIGLER

One task that economists have long taken seriously is that of explaining what determines the behavior of an industry. Under what conditions do prices fall (or rise) with expansion of output? How does the industry change its methods of production in response to changes in prices of inputs? When will customers be classified and each class asked to pay a different price? Will relatively large profits lead to an increase in the number of firms and, if so, how rapidly? Such questions—to which many economists would like to add less-studied questions such as: How does industry structure affect the rate of technological advance?—are at the center of modern economic analysis.

When one turns to the empirical investigation of such questions, he must at the outset determine what industries are. (Most empirical studies have dealt almost exclusively with manufacturing industries, and we shall follow this regrettable tradition here.) Almost invariably the empirical workers have accepted, perhaps with minor modifications such as Rosenbluth applies to the Canadian data, the practices of the census officials who compile the data. They cannot be blamed: the task of appraising the relevance of census classifications to questions of industrial organization is so vast that it would swallow up any more specific investigation the economist had in mind.

Moreover, it is not obvious that the census classification is inappropriate to our interests, which here center in questions of competition and monopoly. Conklin and Goldstein summarize the principles of the present classification. These principles rest fundamentally upon similarity of products or production processes of establishments (plants) which are to be combined into one industry. Particular attention is paid to supply conditions, and "the industry generally represents a group of close competitors, producing close substitute commodities." Homogeneity is sought: most of the products attributed to the industry must be accounted for by the establishments in the industry, and most of the products of the establishments in the industry must fall into the industry defined by its major products. The fact that in the application of such rules to specific industries, census bureaus are influenced by opinions of businessmen, demands of other government agencies, etc., insures that the classifications are not insulated from business experience and public policy.

Yet the rules are intrinsically ambiguous. Economists have written acres on the problem of defining the closeness of substitute products, and no doubt problems of equal complexity are encountered in estimating the similarity of production processes. The influence of business attitudes and public policy is also not an unmixed blessing, for the classifications that are germane to taxation, labor problems, tariffs, and the like are not necessarily suitable to the analysis of problems of competition and monopoly.

Price theory has certain direct implications for this problem of defining industries that have not received adequate recognition in official practice, and they deserve at least brief comment here. An industry should embrace the maximum geographical area and the maximum variety of productive activities in which there is strong long-run substitution. If buyers can shift on a large scale from product or area B to A,

Reprinted by permission of the National Bureau of Economic Research, Inc. from *Business Concentration and Price Policy*, A Conference of the Universities—National Bureau Committee for Economic Research, copyright 1955, pp. 3–14.

then the two should be combined. If producers can shift on a large scale from B to A, again they should be combined.

Economists usually state this in an alternative form: All products or enterprises with large long-run cross-elasticities of either supply or demand should be combined into a single industry. In this form it is perhaps forbidding to the statistical worker, for generally cross-elasticities are calculated from empirical equations relating quantity supplied or demanded of one commodity to a host of prices, and we do not have—and cannot in the reasonable future expect to get—enough of these equations to base a general census upon them. But much more feasible methods of detecting substitution exist. If establishments making wooden office furniture in one year shift in considerable numbers within a year or two to making metal office furniture, this is conclusive evidence of high supply substitution—and can be measured with information now collected but not published. If numerous buyers of cardboard shipping containers in one year are found to be buyers of wooden or burlap containers soon thereafter, this is conclusive evidence of high demand substitution —and can be measured with the type of information now collected.

One important application of the rule of high substitution is to international trade. If a commodity is on either an export or an import basis, its concentration should usually be measured for a market larger than the domestic area. If the commodity is on an export basis, foreign buyers have alternative sources of supply, which must be included in the "industry"; if it is on an import basis, domestic buyers have alternative domestic supply sources, which again should be combined with the foreign supply. In either case it is necessary to take account of the industry structure abroad, but this extension of the area of work of the Bureau of the Census may not be objectionable to its staff.[1]

Once supplied with the frequency distribution of firms by size within properly defined industries, how shall we measure concentration? The large-scale statistical studies have so far employed measures that are directly formed by the disclosure rules of censuses. Despite Rosenbluth's welcome assurance that it does not seem to matter whether we take the proportion of the industry's output coming from the largest three, four, or other small number of firms or the number of firms required to account for, say, three-quarters of the industry's output, we can be certain of one defect in the calculation of these measures. It lies in the time period.

One of Marshall's greatest contributions to economics was to show that calendar time units are seldom a proper basis for measuring economic forces and to elaborate a schema of short- and long-run periods which were defined in terms of the forces which dominate them. The classification was especially relevant to competitive industries because long-run forces can usually be assumed to be negligible in the short run. Under monopoly, however, long-run forces may be decisive even in the short run because the monopolist reaps a large share or all of the future effects of his current policies. A good concentration measure (like a good industry concept) should relate to the long run. This has always been recognized implicity; no one has ever said that concentration rises in late afternoon as eastern factories close down.

The long run is defined in terms of the period necessary for specified changes to take place, and two such changes or forces seem specially significant in studies of monopoly. One is on the demand side: How long a time is required for buyers to move along their long-run demand curves? If buyers can make fairly complete adjustments to prices only by such time-consuming procedures as moving their plants

---

[1] The problem of the market area is greatly complicated if tariffs or quotas permit price discrimination between domestic and foreign markets, except in the extreme case when the two markets are completely independent and must be treated separately.

or radically modifying them, this period may be of several years' duration. The second force is on the supply side: How long a time is required for outsiders to detect large profits and to enter the industry? Normally I would expect this period to be at least as short as the demand period (although this conjecture has hardly any empirical basis) if no conventional barriers to entry, such as patents and raw material control, exist. Clearly calendar length of the long run may vary widely among industries.

Since the long-run forces may require a fairly long period of calendar time to work themselves out, one might infer that concentration measures should be calculated for periods of, say, five years. But against this must be put the consideration that the long run does not always completely dominate the short run: it may be sensible, for example, to behave monopolistically for a few years and then to lose one's monopolistic position. It is one of the tasks of empirical research to determine the relative roles of these arguments,[2] and I should think that we ought to have concentration measures calculated for three, five, and possibly even ten years, as well as for the inevitable one year.

The other question remains: Which parameters of the frequency distribution of firm sizes are relevant to the behavior of the industry? The relative output of a small number of firms, which is now used, is surely one relevant parameter, although most of the proof for this assertion still lies in the formal theory of oligopoly and not in empirical studies. Until we get the empirical studies, we are not likely to progress far in the refinement of concentration measures. It is easy enough to introduce additional parameters whose relevance to the behavior of the industry can be plausibly argued: for example, I would expect to find also that the absolute number of

firms and the degree of instability in the shares of the largest firms from year to year were important in influencing the industry's behavior. But plausibility is at least as much an effect of skillful argument as an evidence of probability of truth in an area as complicated and unexplored as oligopoly, and there is little point in multiplying such parameters at the present time.

Scitovsky properly emphasizes the fact that our interest in concentration is not restricted to its effects on the allocation of resources among firms—the traditional focus of the theory of monopoly. We are also interested in the effects of concentration on the distribution of income, the distribution of political power, the efficiency with which resources are used within the firm, etc. Wholly different measures of concentration may be called for in the empirical study of these other facets of the monopoly problem. The relationship of monopoly to the distribution of income, for example, surely involves the absolute sizes of firms and the distribution of ownership of monopolies. Important as these other problems are, however, one may still argue that the traditional focus on the power of the firm in the market is basic, for if this power is absent all the other problems vanish (as monopoly problems).

Miller examines an important deficiency in the traditional theory of monopoly, from which the concentration studies stem. The neoclassical theory of competition and monopoly was developed with two paramount objectives: to provide a clear and consistent theory of economic behavior, and to be analytically manageable. Both of these objectives were met fairly well by defining competition in terms of a stationary economy—one in which consumers' tastes, production techniques, and productive resources were stable through time. The resulting theory is immensely useful in a wide range of economic problems; but it is not directly applicable to problems raised by economic development —the rapid growth, and frequently unpredictable changes, in consumer demands

---

[2] From the viewpoint of social policy, short-run monopolies are of course much less important, and—with present durations of antitrust court actions—almost beyond control.

and productive techniques and resources.

Schumpeter has sketched with great brilliance the possible paradoxes in applying the theory of stationary economies to historical developments.[3] The argument is weighty and clearly poses the problem of constructing a definition of competition which is suited to firms in a changing economy. Schumpeter's "solution," which was to label as monopoly all departures from perfect competition in a stationary society, is not useful. Real progress in this area seems also to demand that incisive empirical work for which economists so monotonously beg. But I suspect that when our knowledge of economic growth has increased, we shall not be called upon to reverse all the conclusions reached by stationary analysis.

Let us put aside these and other possible complications and return to the concentration of industry. Industries vary greatly in their concentration, and we naturally seek to learn why. Three papers in this volume deal with important forces affecting concentration: the economies of scale, mergers, and taxation.

Since Cournot's time it has been recognized that at most only a few firms can usually survive in an industry in which the average cost of production of a firm declines as its size increases, and even today this is the popular explanation for concentration. Smith has summarized recent work on this subject, including the interesting efforts to estimate the costs of firms of different sizes from technological relationships between inputs and outputs. This latter type of approach has many attractions, especially in studies of the social (in contrast to private) economies of scale. But it also has two major defects. One defect is generally recognized: the method cannot be extended to selling, recruiting labor, financing, etc. Another defect is not always recognized: the economist is "solving" the problem of measuring economies of scale by turning it over to someone else, and yet it is fundamentally an economic problem.

Smith shows how difficult the problems of measurement are, even though he does not emphasize the point (the valuation of inputs) that I find most troublesome. Difficulty is not an adequate reason for abandoning a problem, but I think there are some positive reasons for determining economies of scale from changes in concentration over time rather than using economies to explain concentration. That is, those firm-sizes whose outputs are growing relative to the industry may be interpreted as having the lowest (private) costs. All comprehensive definitions of economies of scale ultimately imply that firms with the lowest costs prosper relative to other sizes of firms, and it is desirable to recognize this explicitly by defining the most efficient size as that which grows relative to other sizes. This interpretation does not inhibit research on the factors that lead to concentration, for one may still investigate the influence of plant size, of advertising, of the nature of the product, etc. In fact, I would consider it a merit of the reformulation that it divides a vast and complex problem into a series of more specific and manageable problems.

The merger of firms within an industry (putting aside "vertical" mergers) has been a major force in changing the firm structure of many industries. Mergers provide an interesting problem in measurement because of the peculiar basis for recording them: mergers leading to large firms, and acquisitions of all sizes of firms by firms that are already large, constitute the elements of newsworthiness which leads the financial press—and thus the historians of mergers—to record them. Absolute size, moreover, is commonly the test of "large" firms, although size relative to the industry is more relevant to questions of industrial structure. Because large firms are necessarily relatively few in number, perhaps on the order of one merger in a hundred is recorded, and the proportion no doubt varies through time and among industries. The available historical series on mergers, given by Markham, are thus

---

[3] Joseph A. Schumpeter, *Capitalism, Socialism, and Democracy* (Harper, 1942), Chaps. VI–IX.

sketchy to an extreme: long periods (before 1887, 1904–1918) have not been studied; size of firms has not been studied, or always recorded, for the variable points of truncation in reporting; horizontal and other mergers have not been distinguished; the industrial composition, when reported at all, is very crude; etc.

Much of the uncertainty over the causes and effects of mergers is attributable to this lack of information. For example, some economists believe that the improvements in transportation in the decades after the Civil War were an important factor in bringing mergers—chiefly because the expansion of market areas increased competition. Simple tests of the hypothesis are easy to devise: mergers should have come earlier in commodities whose production was geographically localized and in products (like ships and jewelry) for which transportation costs were relatively unimportant. We cannot, with our present empirical material, apply such tests.[4] A systematic recompilation of the historical record would be a vast task, but it would be labor well spent.[5]

Fifty years ago only one class of taxes was ever mentioned in studies of industrial organization: tariffs, "the mother of the trusts." Now taxes insist upon intruding into every branch of economic analysis, and in a variety of forms and with a labyrinth of technical details sufficient to discourage casual generalization. Lintner and Butters' survey of the effects of income and estate taxes reveals the possibility that many significant influences on the industrial structure now flow from these taxes,

and the same can be said of certain excises, payroll taxes, etc. Students of public finance may not welcome this new facet of their work: it is hard enough to devise a tax that will raise substantial revenue, be allocated equitably, counteract cyclical fluctuations, encourage efficiency and innovation, and keep the party in power, without adding a due regard for the preservation of competition.

One feature of the taxes Lintner and Butters discuss is that their effects appear to be related usually to the absolute rather than to the relative size of firm. The effects of these taxes upon concentration would therefore appear to be more powerful in industries in which the relatively large firms are large in absolute size, for then substantial absolute growth is required of new rivals before they can offer important competition (and it is absolute growth that taxes may retard). With this in mind it is interesting to compare changes between 1935 and 1947 in concentration in manufacturing industries classified by the absolute sizes of the largest firms. It would be preferable to measure size by assets in this connection, but value added is the most relevant measure available. The results of this tabulation are given in the accompanying table. The decline in concentration was substantial in industries where the largest firms are absolutely small, but no decline occurred at the opposite end of the scale. Taxation may have been one of the significant influences in this pattern of change.

In the essays of Adelman and Edwards we leave the subject of horizontal concentration and explore other aspects of industrial structure. Adelman estimates by several procedures the quantitative extent of vertical integration in different firms and industries. We customarily view vertical integration as a technological problem: if a firm or plant produces an input it previously purchased, we say it has become more fully integrated. One difficulty with this approach is that it is applicable only if technology is stable. The National Bureau of Economic Research recently turned over publication of its books to the Prince-

---

[4] One basis for my belief that this particular explanation of mergers will not be found useful is that England had a wave of mergers at approximately the same time, although its regions became close-knit considerably before ours.

[5] When it is undertaken, particular attention should be paid to the timing of the several steps in mergers. The period between the initiation of negotiations and the formal merger or acquisition may be variable but substantial—indeed this is one reason, I believe, why the time series show considerable erratic short-run fluctuation.

Table 1 • Concentration Ratios in Manufacturing Industries, 1935 and 1947, Classified by Average Value Added in the Four Largest Firms, 1935

Value Added per Firm in Four Largest Firms, 1935	Number of Industries	Per Cent of Value of Product Produced by Four Largest Firms (concentration ratio)	
		1935	1947
Under $250,000	7	36.5	29.5
$250,000– 500,000	13	42.0	39.8
500,000– 750,000	14	41.7	37.7
750,000– 1,000,000	10	36.4	33.8
1,000,000– 2,500,000	37	43.4	42.3
2,500,000– 5,000,000	23	43.1	41.1
5,000,000–10,000,000	16	52.6	51.0
10,000,000–25,000,000	7	63.8	66.3
25,000,000 and over	4	70.7	70.7
Total	131		

Source: *The Structure of the American Economy*, National Resources Committee, 1939; *Concentration of Industry Report*, Dept. of Commerce, 1949.

ton University Press, so we may say that it is now less vertically integrated. But if its researches should be televised—I have been informed of no such plan—no degree of program preparation corresponds to publication, so the change in vertical integration is indeterminable.

A quantitative measure of vertical integration comparable among industries must be monetary in nature, and the most common such measure is the ratio of value added (roughly, receipts minus purchases of materials) to value of product. This measure pertains only to intra-establishment integration when it is calculated from census data, and even then is subject to two serious ambiguities. The first is that when a plant produces a variety of products, with different ratios of value added to value, the extent of vertical integration varies with the composition of output, even if production processes do not change. The second ambiguity is that census industries frequently contain plants engaged in successive operations—motor vehicles is an extreme example—so the value of product contains much duplication.

Rather than enter into the problem of dealing with value-added data, we shall be content to notice that occasionally the Census of Manufactures reports information that is directly relevant to the extent of

vertical integration. In each census, for example, there are reported the quantities of some commodities made and consumed in the same establishment and the quantities made for sale. Sample figures may be reproduced:

Year	Production of Sulfuric Acid, 50° Baumé, tons	Percent Made and Consumed in Same Establishment
1909	2,764,455	46.5
1919	5,552,581	40.0
1929	8,491,114	31.5
1939	7,711,487	33.2

It might be possible to make a general analysis of vertical integration by recasting census data in this form.

One may argue—as I would—that the fundamental basis of power of the conglomerate firm that Edwards describes is monopoly in the conventional sense. Some of the phenomena he describes are illustrations of well-known theoretical propositions, such as that individual monopolists of goods complementary in demand will make smaller aggregate profits if they act independently than will a single monopolist who takes account of the interrelationships in demand. Again, many aspects of the large, diversified firm's activities seem explicable if there are substantial difficulties in accumulating large amounts of equity capital; the capital market for small firms is possibly a strategic factor in a vast array of industrial practices.

But whatever its basis, the conglomerate firm poses new problems also. When large firms are cooperating in relatively concentrated industries, will they not also tend to cooperate in other industries where concentration is so low that normally competitive behavior would have been expected? Conversely, if the firms that are large in one industry are medium-sized or small in other industries, may not their differences in activity raise substantial difficulties in arriving at agreements in any one of the industries? We need to know which of the infinitely many possible constellations of related concentration in several industries are of empirical significance and to analyze their workings in detail.

Price behavior is so important an aspect of industrial behavior that apology is required, not that the conference had several essays in this area, but that there could not have been more. Still, the full-cost principle, price rigidity, and price discrimination are all sufficiently important, so the conference planning committee cannot be accused of gross neglect. I shall restrict my remaining comments to a problem on which all of these papers touch: How can one measure the relationship of price behavior to the structure of an industry and, in particular, to its concentration?

The output of a competitive industry is such that price equals long-run marginal cost. It is therefore natural to measure, or possibly even to define, the departure of an industry's price from the competitive level by the ratio of price to long-run marginal cost. Useful as this ratio is in the analysis of individual industries, there is unfortunately no known method of making tolerably comparable estimates for many industries so that one might correlate this measure with concentration data. For such broad surveys one is forced to employ a substitute measure.

The temporal rigidity of prices, with respect to either frequency or amplitude, has been the most popular substitute measure, and the vast literature on its use is discussed by Ruggles. For a time, price rigidity was hopefully taken as good evidence of noncompetitive behavior, but both economic theory and statistical studies have greatly weakened the confidence in this evidence. Monopolies may charge flexible prices in their own interests, and competitive industries may have periods of stable supply and demand conditions. The statistical work has shown little correlation between rigidity and concentration, but this work has been plagued by problems of data. Price data and production data are usually collected by different agencies, so that one must use (quoted) prices that are uncertain samples of the industry's real price structure or values of output which are influenced by changes in the composition of output.[6] Extreme price rigidity is inconsistent with competition, but beyond this the association is at best weak.

Since persistent and systematic price discrimination is also invariably associated with noncompetitive behavior of an industry, one might look to this area for measures. Yet price discrimination takes on a considerable variety of forms—geographical, product class, customer class, etc.—as the reader of Machlup's essay will be persuaded. (Machlup is apparently more optimistic than I on the possibility of also disentangling the motives which lead to price discrimination.) Some of the forms of price discrimination deserve study as possible bases for measures of noncompetitive behavior; in particular, the comparison of domestic and export prices might be feasible for a considerable number of industries.

The full-cost principle, in the only one of its numerous versions that I shall con-

---

[6] Census value-of-product figures are possibly seriously biased because two components of output —interplant transfers and inventory additions— are often valued at cost.

sider, states that prices are set equal to average variable cost plus a stable markup per unit of output. If this hypothesis is correct, we have a new measure of noncompetitive behavior because no competitive industry can adhere to such a formula in the face of large fluctuations in output. But if this theory is correct, then the conventional theory of imperfect competition, which makes demand a factor in price determination, is incorrect, and this dispute must first be settled. The settlement—presumably by a recourse to empirical tests—is difficult for two reasons. One is that the full-cost theory has many versions in addition to that stated above, as Heflebower shows, and its sponsors also differ considerably among themselves on the factors governing the markup on variable costs. The other difficulty is that both the conventional theory and the full-cost theories generally agree on the most easily tested predictions: the general correspondence between movements of price and costs, the similar movements of profits and output, etc. They differ qualitatively only in that the conventional theory affirms, and the full-cost theories deny, that short-run changes in demand will affect selling price even though prices of inputs do not change.[7] It is to be hoped that proponents of the full-cost theories will soon test its ability to predict price movements as compared with the conventional theory.

These various measures of price behavior do not of course constitute a complete listing.[8] The available measures, however, are usually either difficult to quantify or ambiguous in interpretation, and much work remains to be done here. Progress in the measurement of price behavior as an index of performance will in turn contribute greatly to improvements in the measurement and interpretation of concentration, for our interest in concentration is centered in its effects on the behavior of industries.

---

[7] Certain less prominent differences also exist. For example, on the conventional theory a monopolist is less concerned over the effect of current price on future demand if the commodity is perishable, whereas the full-cost theories make no such distinction.

[8] In addition to the popular measure, the ratio of price to average cost (or profitability), interesting experiments have been made with differences among firms in the level, and time and direction of change, of prices.

13. Bigness Is a Numbers Game

SANFORD ROSE

Is economic power in the U.S. getting more concentrated? A lot of people say so, but the current alarm is largely based on wobbly statistics that give off a hazy message.

Anxiety about concentration of economic power in the U.S. runs in cycles. The Thirties and early Forties were a nervous period. Roosevelt denounced the "economic royalists" and Gardiner C. Means said there was a good chance that the top 200 non-financial corporations would account for 70 per cent of "industrial activity" by 1950 and almost all by the early 1970s.

During a considerable span of years after the war, bigness no longer seemed menacing. Means's prediction for 1950 turned out to be conspicuously wrong. Many economists came to identify size with efficiency—often uncritically, but at times with persuasive evidence.

By the mid-Sixties, however, people were back to biting their nails over the concentration threat. Popular attention focused on the upsurge in mergers. The number of mergers in the manufacturing and mining sector of the economy more than quadrupled from 1958 to 1968. Last year, says the government, there were about 4,000 corporate marriages in the U.S.

Such statistics can panic even sober men. Recently, Attorney General John N. Mitchell, hardly a William Jennings Bryan populist, was moved to utter portentous words: "We do not want our middle-sized and smaller cities to be merely branch-store communities, nor do we want our average consumers to be second-class economic citizens." In Mitchell's rhetoric, this is exactly

what's going to happen if the nation's manufacturing and financial assets "continue to be concentrated in the hands of fewer and fewer people."

Such evidence as Mitchell had for his warnings came from studies carried out for the Cabinet Committee on Price Stability under the direction of Willard F. Mueller, who had taken a leave from his post as chief economist of the Federal Trade Commission. (He recently left government service to return to the University of Wisconsin.) The thrust of these studies can be summed up in two propositions: (1) The top 200 manufacturing corporations have substantially increased their share of total manufacturing assets within the past twenty years. (2) The leading companies in a large number of consumer-goods industries dominate those industries to a far greater extent than they did when the first postwar Census of Manufactures was conducted in 1947.

These conclusions have stirred rumblings in and out of Congress and produced disquiet within the business community itself. But while the government's case looks formidable at first glance, on closer analysis it proves less than convincing. In fact, some statistical sleight-of-hand is involved. The share of total manufacturing assets held by the top 200 companies may be increasing, but probably not nearly as much as the government suggests. And what seems like a dramatic rise in sales concentration within a major category of consumer-goods industries vanishes almost entirely when the rather primitive statistical techniques used in the government studies are set aside in favor of methods that are more sophisticated, though quite commonly employed by economists.

But more important, there are serious questions as to what the various sets of numbers published by the U.S. Government imply for public policy. As one economist said to a corporation lawyer inquiring about the accuracy of the official figures on concentration: "You are asking the wrong question. The central issue is not accuracy but relevance. The figures are suspect. But right or wrong, they are not especially significant."

The Two Faces of Concentration

Economists use the term "concentration" in two quite distinct senses. One of them, the kind Mitchell has been talking about, might be called megacorp concentration. It focuses on the ratio of the sales or assets of the top 50, 100, 200, or 500 manufacturing companies to those of the entire manufacturing sector. The other kind is market concentration. This is usually measured by the percentage of total sales accounted for by the top four companies within an industry —an "industry" being whatever the government defines as such. At the most recent official count, in 1966, the number of industries came to 417.

The two measures are logically separate. Market concentration can be increasing in every industry while megacorp concentration is decreasing, provided industries in which relatively small companies do most of the business are growing at a much faster pace than those dominated by giants. Conversely, megacorp concentration can be increasing while concentration in every industry is decreasing, provided the largest companies are diversifying into many new industries. To take an extreme example, if the 200 largest companies kept growing until they accounted for all the manufacturing in the country, and if each diversified to such an extent that all were equally represented in every market, then none of the top 200 companies would account for more than 0.5 per cent of sales in any industry. The megacorps would be monstrously big, but none of them would have any great amount of market power.

It is market power that economists are primarily concerned with. Power in the marketplace is usually defined as the ability of a group of sellers to raise prices, restrict

output, and limit innovation. The extent of market power is largely, though not exclusively, determined by market structure. Generally speaking, the larger the share of an industry's sales accounted for by, say, the top four firms, the greater the opportunity and incentive to control prices and restrict output. In contrast, in "atomistic" markets, where there are a great many competitors, price-fixing agreements are both impractical and unenforceable. The more decision-making units there are, the harder it is to work out an agreement and, subsequently, to enforce it by collective action— e.g., price wars—against defectors.

It is often said that if the market share of the Big Four comes to 50 per cent or more the industry is to be considered oligopolistic. But this formula, or any similar formula, tells us too little about market structure. Actual market behavior partly depends, for example, on the relationship between the first and the next three companies. If the top company has 30 per cent of the market while the next three more or less equally divide the remaining 20 per cent, a follow-the-leader pattern is a strong possibility. If each of the four companies has 12.5 per cent, the competition among them is likely to be far more intense.

Yet there are no official published data on the degree of market-share asymmetry among the top four companies in most industries. An old law forbids the Bureau of the Census, which collects this data, from revealing either the names of the top four or their market shares. Indeed, if there is some danger that the publication of the four-company ratio will shed light on the shares of individual companies, the Census simply omits it. In this respect, Japan is more advanced than the U.S. The Japanese publish complete data on the market shares of the top ten companies in many industries.

Phantom Leaders

Under the Census classification system, all shipments from a plant, of whatever nature, are allocated to the industry in which the plant is primarily engaged. Thus if a plant produces $400,000 of product X, $300,000 of product Y, and another $300,000 of product Z, the entire $1 million is assigned to industry X. This can lead to some ludicrous results. Oil companies, for example, account for nearly 70 per cent of U.S. production of lubricants and greases, but all this production is included in the oil industry (code 2911). There is, however, a separate "lubricating oils and greases" industry (code 2992), composed of companies whose plants primarily produce lubricants and greases. It does not take much imagination to see that any concentration ratio in industry 2992 is worthless because total industry shipments cover only one-third of the country's output of these products. In fact it is possible that none of the industry leaders of record—the four largest producers classified in 2992—are among the actual leaders in production of lubricants and greases.

To help users of concentration ratios determine the seriousness of this type of problem, Census publishes both a "primary product specialization ratio" and a "coverage ratio" for nearly every industry. Specialization ratios measure the extent to which plants classified as belonging to a particular industry concentrate on what are regarded as primary products of that industry. During 1963, for example, 88 per cent of the shipments of plants in the chewing-gum industry consisted of gum and 12 per cent of other products. The chewing-gum specialization ratio was therefore .88.

Coverage ratios measure the extent to which shipments of the primary product of a given industry are made by plants classified in that industry. In 1963, again, 96 per cent of all chewing gum made in the U.S. was shipped by plants in the chewing-gum industry. The industry's coverage ratio was thus .96.

Clearly, unless the specialization and coverage ratios are quite high, the nominal concentration ratio for an industry provides an untrustworthy measure of the actual concentration. Many economists believe that skepticism is justified unless the ratios for the industry remain at or above 85 per cent. Yet in more than one-fourth of the industries included in the latest government report on market concentration, coverage and specialization ratios did not measure up to that standard.

Coverage and specialization ratios are published only on an industry basis; there are no available ratios for the top four companies within an industry. If the plants of these four happen to be more diversified than the industry average, the concentration ratio will be exaggerated. For example, if an industry's total shipments are valued at $100 million and the share of the top four is $50 million, the industry concentration ratio is 50 per cent. But if the plants of the top four are only 60 per cent specialized in the primary product of that industry, while those of the smaller companies are 80 per cent specialized, the leaders will actually account for only 43 per cent of total sales of that product. Similarly if the top four are *less* diversified than the industry average, the concentration ratio will be understated—that is, the leaders will be a bigger force in the market than the figures show.

Only One Way to Grow

Government officials feel that the effect of this factor is purely random—that the top four are just as likely to be below as to be above the industry average in diversification. This is only a supposition, however, and there are considerations that suggest otherwise. Large companies are more likely than small ones to run multiproduct operations. Fearful of running afoul of antitrust if they expand their market shares, big companies often find that the only way to grow is to move into other product lines. And in some cases companies do this by turning out secondary products in plants they already own. As the Bureau of the Census says in its 1963 report: "In many industries there are some large plants with a product mix such that the value of secondary products is as large as, or larger than, the value of primary products."

A possibly more serious upward bias stems from the statistical treatment of exports and imports. Imports are excluded from the Census data, but no attempt is made to exclude production that is sold abroad. In some markets, failure to include imports can exaggerate concentration by understating the total production available to domestic consumers. An extreme example is the newsprint industry. Since so much newsprint comes from Canada, a concentration ratio based on the share of U.S. production accounted for by the top four companies is just a curiosity. The failure to exclude exports may also exaggerate concentration when the share of foreign business accounted for by the top companies in an industry is proportionately greater than that of the smaller companies. That is very likely to be the case.

A Dish of Shepherd's Pie

Some scholars, however, maintain that the biases tending to exaggerate concentration are more than matched by those running the other way. Among the best known is William G. Shepherd of the University of Michigan. Shepherd points out that when an industry definition encompasses many noncompeting products, the concentration ratio for that industry may be biased downward. For example, toilet preparations is a catch-all industry that takes in many noncompeting subindustries; e.g., toothpaste and hair dyes. In such a case, a moderate industry concentration ratio is quite compatible with higher concentration in some of the subindustries.

Shepherd broke down about half of the more than 400 Census industries into what he believes are economically sensible groupings. He also combined industries where the definitions are underinclusive and therefore tend to bias the concentration ratios in an upward direction. Finally Shepherd adjusted concentration ratios to take account of local and regional monopolies. The newspaper industry, for example, has a four-company concentration ratio of only 14 per cent; but local ratios are much higher since there are a great many cities with only one or two newspapers. Together, these adjustments make quite a difference. Without them, average concentration works out to 39 per cent for the industries and the year (1966) Shepherd studied. With his adjustments, the figure rises to 60.3 per cent. But Shepherd's conclusion, while dramatic, is by no means universally accepted by other experts.

Shepherd is primarily concerned with the level rather than the trend of market concentration, but most analysts are more interested in whether it is going up, down, or nowhere. A high but declining level of average concentration may be less worrisome than a lower but rising level. In analyzing concentration trends, ideally, one should compare only similar points on the business cycle—recession with recession or boom with boom. Concentration generally rises during recessions as the weaker companies, which are usually also the smaller ones, retrench or go under. During boom periods, on the other hand, concentration tends to decline. Hence any comparison starting from 1937, a recession year, would tend to understate an upward trend. But a comparison starting from 1947, a buoyant year, would tend to overstate an upward trend. And 1947 happens to be a favorite starting point for studies of concentration trends because that was the year of the first complete postwar Census of Manufactures. By the same token, 1963 is a favorite terminal point because that was the year of the latest complete published Census of Manufactures. Since the economy was a bit soft in 1963, the frequently cited 1947–63 comparisons have some inherent upward bias.

In another respect 1947 is a bad year to start any comparison of trend: it was the terminus of a period of catch-up from the war years. Since a seller's market prevailed, small companies participated in the economy to a greater than normal extent. Concentration could thus be expected to rise after 1947 until more typical market conditions returned.

The government's analysis of average concentration trends was done for the Cabinet Committee on Price Stability. According to this study, which covered 213 industries, average concentration shows only a slight increase—from 41.2 per cent in 1947 to 41.4 percent in 1963 and 41.9 per cent in 1966 (a year for which there are preliminary Census figures). But this near stability, the report argues, masks an underlying trend. In producer goods, market concentration declined, from 45.1 per cent in 1947 to 43.3 in 1963 and 43.4 in 1966. In consumer goods, however, it increased, from 34.8 per cent in 1947 to 38.2 in 1963 and 39.6 in 1966.

The government report contends that the trend is particularly alarming in one important category of consumer industries, those labeled "highly differentiated." A highly differentiated industry is one in which consumers actively discriminate among different brands of the same product —cigarettes, razor blades, and autos are notable examples. The Cabinet committee study identifies seventeen highly differentiated consumer industries. Concentration in these seventeen, it says, leaped from 48.2 per cent in 1947 to 59 per cent in 1963 (and moved up to 60.2 per cent in 1966).

Absent Industries

Two notable facts about the government study should be borne in mind by anyone who undertakes to draw conclusions from it. One is that the figures are completely unweighted: all industry concentration ratios are simply added up and divided by the number of industries. In effect, each industry is treated as if it were just as important as any other. Since some industries are clearly more important than others, many authorities in this field compute average concentration ratios by weighting each industry—most often according to its sales or its value added (sales minus cost of materials).

The difference between simple average concentration and weighted average concentration can be quite decisive. If petroleum refining and explosives were the only two industries in the economy, average con-

centration in all manufacturing for 1963 would have been 53 per cent (34 per cent in oil and 72 per cent in explosives). But since oil is about sixty times as important an industry as explosives, average weighted concentration would have come to only about 35 per cent.

The other notable fact is that the 213 industries the government study covers are unrepresentative of the U.S. economy's manufacturing sector. The 213, just over half the official number of manufacturing industries, accounted for only about half of all manufacturing sales in 1963. The principal reason for leaving out the other manufacturing industries in the economy was that their products had changed too drastically to permit comparisons between 1947 and 1963. By definition, the government's 213 industries (those comparable over the 1947–63 span) belong to the older, more stable sectors of the economy. Oil, steel, autos, and beer are represented, but not electronic measuring instruments, industrial controls, television, or many U.S. chemical products.

Still another consideration limiting the validity of the government figures is that many of the industries in the sample, particularly those in consumer durables, may be in the late stages of the product life cycle. J. Fred Weston, professor of business economics at U.C.L.A., argues that products of many industries go through four stages: introduction, growth, maturity, and decline. In the first stage, before the product has achieved acceptance, sales increase at about 1 to 2 per cent a year. During the growth phase, with acceptance won, sales rise at an annual rate of 7 to 10 per cent. After the initial demand has been met, maturity sets in; the growth rate slows to 3 to 7 per cent, with replacement accounting for most of the sales. In the period of decline, substitute products come along, and sales growth slips back to 1 or 2 per cent.

During the introduction and growth phases, notes Weston, profit margins rise steeply, attracting additional capacity. This capacity usually comes on stream near the end of the growth stage and continues to increase in response to past profits, even though sales growth is moderating. Unfavorable capacity-sales relationships develop and profit margins dip. If that happens, smaller companies usually get out one way or another. In other words, concentration increases.

That need not be the pattern, however. By introducing new or remodeled products, or at least new brands, at fast enough rates, producers of goods subject to product life cycles can keep sales growth and profit margins from deteriorating. Small companies can then survive, and concentration may show no tendency to increase. But these innovative industries are likely to be omitted from the government sample because their product lines changed so much over the 1947–63 period.

Down the Up Staircase

It would not be surprising then, if there was some tendency toward increasing concentration in consumer goods, as the government claims. Even so, the government case keeps bumping into inconsiderate facts. Take those "highly differentiated" consumer industries where concentration is supposed to be rampant. Upon examination, it turns out that the apparent increase in concentration from 1947 to 1963 is mostly attributable to a single industry, autos and parts. And in that industry, nearly 80 per cent of the increase in concentration took place between 1947 and 1954. During this period General Motors raised its market share from 42 to 51 per cent, while Ford's climbed from 21 to 31 per cent. Some name-plates—Hudson, Kaiser, and others—disappeared. After this postwar shake-out, market shares tended to stabilize. From 1954 to 1963 there was a scant four-percentage-point rise in the automobile industry's concentration ratio, and this is of doubtful significance because the exclusion of imports, which increased sharply during this period, understates the number of vehicles available to U.S. consumers and thus exaggerates the market dominance of the leading companies.

Eugene Singer, a consultant who is scheduled to deliver a paper on concentration before the American Economic Association meeting in December, recalculated government figures for "highly differentiated" industries, leaving out autos. He left out autos because usable sales data are unavailable, and he wanted to arrive at a figure for weighted average concentration, using each industry's sales for weighting. Within the "motor vehicles and parts" industry the output of many plants is input for other plants, so there is a lot of double counting in the industry-wide sales figures. For the same reason, Singer omitted "wines and brandy" (too small to affect the result anyway). Finally, Singer excluded greeting cards on the grounds that it is not really highly differentiated at all—consumers generally know the name of only one manufacturer, Hallmark, and are quite unlikely to go from store to store until they find a Hallmark card. Calculating the weighted average change in concentration for the remaining fourteen industries, Singer found a flat trend—48 per cent in 1947 and 48 per cent in 1963. Concentration increased in eleven of the fourteen from 1947 to 1963, but with weighting by sales, the increases are offset by declines in the other three industries—cigarettes, liquor, and drugs.

On closer examination, moreover, it appears that the increases in concentration in some of those eleven industries could well have had the paradoxial effect of reducing concentration. In the beer industry, concentration has grown because national companies have been moving into what were previously local markets, and what shows up as a rise in concentration on a national basis may actually represent a decrease in concentration, and an increase in the range of choice, at the local or consumer level.

Household laundry equipment, another of the eleven, provides an instance of a highly differentiated industry whose large increase in concentration—thirty-eight percentage points from 1947 to 1963—may be completely misleading. In the first place this is an industry in which a product has gradually replaced a service. There is no solid information on the level of concentration in the laundry-service industry, but it is conceivable that in many areas it was highly concentrated. If so, the growth of the laundry-equipment industry could have reduced the degree of effective concentration in the economy at the same time as it increased the level of concentration in the manufacturing sector.

Like household laundry equipment, many of the consumer-durables industries have interacted with the service sector in intricate ways. Concentration in these industries is typically associated with high advertising expenditure. While advertising expanded volume and altered relative market shares, it also tended to undermine the traditional explaining and demonstrating functions of the retailer. Since national advertising in effect presold the product, discount houses, operating with far smaller forces, could flourish. Competition at the retail level increased, retail margins were trimmed, and prices to the final consumer either fell or rose more slowly than they might have. Increasing concentration at the manufacturing level in effect reduced concentration at the retail level.

The Yardstick Makes a Difference

While market concentration is the more interesting to the economist, megacorp concentration is the more interesting to the politician, so it was predictable that a major part of the government's study would be given over to an analysis of the megacorps. By 1967, according to the report, the 100 giants had collected close to half of all assets in the manufacturing sector. In nineteen years they had increased their share of total manufacturing assets from 40.1 per cent to 47.6, and the top 200 had increased theirs from 48.1 per cent to 58.7.

A sizable part of this asset growth occurred from 1948 to 1955—in the case of the 200, more than two-fifths of their total relative increase. Part of this rise was predictable for some of the same reasons that an increase in market concentration was to be anticipated. When the economy began

to settle back into more normal economic patterns following the hectic readjustment period of 1945–47, large companies inevitably increased their relative market shares in a number of industries. Since many of these industries also bulked quite large in the total economy, the ratio of assets held by the giants was bound to increase.

A more important contributing factor might be called the industry-growth component. If a particular industry is growing at a faster pace than the rest of the economy, its leaders may work their way into the circle of manufacturing giants, whether or not they increase their relative share in their own industry. Indeed, there may be a *decrease* in market power, as measured by the industry concentration ratio, but an increase in the share of the giants, as measured by the ratio of the 200 to the rest of the manufacturing economy.

Although the government's study doesn't say so, Willard Mueller, who directed it, admits that most of the increase in megacorp concentration in the 1947–54 period can be ascribed to this industry-growth factor. The big debate is over what has happened since 1954. According to the government's study, about three-fifths of the growth in the asset share of the top 200 over the span 1948–67 occurred after 1954. When the trend in megacorp concentration is measured on a value-added basis, however, very nearly the reverse pattern of relative growth turns up. The top 200's share of total value added in manufacturing increased from 30 per cent in 1947 to 42 per cent in 1966; but about three-fifths of this increase occurred prior to the middle 1950's.

An Enormous Potential for Distortion

It is not difficult to see why this discrepancy arises. Value added is a comparatively pure measure; it is the difference between the value of shipments and the cost of materials for each U.S. manufacturing plant. Value-added data, accordingly, cover only domestic manufacturing. Asset data, in contrast, constitute a hodgepodge. Foreign assets and domestic assets employed in nonmanufacturing activities are lumped together with assets employed in domestic manufacturing—so long as these appear on the consolidated balance sheet of a company that is classified as a manufacturer.

The potential for distortion is enormous. Since 1958 there has been a dramatic upsurge in foreign direct investment. In fact, overseas outlays have increased more rapidly than domestic investment during this period. And the big companies are the chief acquirers of foreign assets. Since it fails to deflate asset figures for foreign investment, the government's reckoning of relative asset growth necessarily exaggerates both the level and the trend of megacorp dominance in domestic manufacturing.

A similar type of bias may result from the failure to exclude the domestic *nonmanufacturing* assets of manufacturing companies. In the past several years large manufacturing companies have been diversifying into businesses such as leasing, transportation, hotels, and, particularly, finance companies. For example, Avco recently bought Seaboard Finance. Avco includes Seaboard in its consolidated statement, so all of Seaboard's assets are part of the manufacturing sector, although that company does no manufacturing at all. There is a lack of hard data, but many economists believe that companies within the top 200 are diversifying into nonmanufacturing areas to a far greater extent than are smaller manufacturing companies; if this is true, quite obviously the asset share of the top 200 will be overstated.

It is conceivable that this bias might be offset if some of the top 200 companies so diversified into nonmanufacturing assets that they ceased to be classified as manufacturers. But this seems to be occurring less frequently than is the reverse situation —i.e., a large service, mining, or utility company picking up enough manufacturing assets to be reclassified as a manufacturer. Examples are hard to come by because membership in the top 200 corporations by asset size is not public information. The FTC, which collects the data on a comprehensive basis, will not disclose the names.

But in the last two years only two of the top 200 companies among the FORTUNE 500 —ranked, to be sure, by sales, rather than assets—went from manufacturing into nonmanufacturing. They were Foremost Dairies and Container Corp. Four much larger companies went the other way: Consolidated Foods, Occidental Petroleum, Northwest Industries, and International Utilities. If International Utilities, for example, has also worked its way into the FTC's top 200, it has carried roughly $360 million of utility assets, $45 million of mining assets, $185 million in transportation assets, $30 million in communication assets, and about $90 million in miscellaneous portfolio investments into the so-called manufacturing sector.

It Takes Only Mild Flutterings

While the government's asset figures appear to be exaggerated, there is still evidence of increasing megacorp dominance in the manufacturing sector. Even on a value-added basis the share of the top 200 has risen. From 1963 to 1966, to be sure, the rise was only one percentage point, and there was no increase whatever in the value-added share of the top 50 and top 100 companies during this period. But it takes only very mild flutterings in the numbers to concern those who are disposed to be concerned.

From a somewhat more rational point of view, it is far from easy to pinpoint the significance of any rising trend in megacorp concentration. Measurements of it say little or nothing at all about market power. This type of power is, by definition, exercised in individual industries or markets and is measured, albeit imperfectly, by the respective industry concentration ratios, which show no particular trend.

A number of analysts link megacorp concentration to market power on what is sometimes called the "cross-subsidization" theory. A major thesis is that large diversified companies can get their subsidiaries to slash prices, compensating for their temporary earnings shortfall from other areas of the business. After rivals are either wiped out or forced to retrench, the argument runs, the subsidiary of the large company can dominate the market. Such practices have never been proved, however, nor do they seem sensible business policy. They would be profitable only in industries where barriers to entry by new firms are high. If entry barriers are low, new competitors will come in as soon as the subsidiary starts to jack up its prices. Entry barriers are indeed high in many industries, but, if anything, the trend toward increased megacorp concentration, especially through conglomerate mergers, is reducing them. Huge corporations now have few qualms about crossing industry lines. And these companies have the economic muscle to invest enough capital or purchase enough advertising to secure a reasonably strong position in the market. A megacorp is unlikely to see any profit in predatory behavior if it has to contend with the possibility that, just when predatory behavior is about to pay off, other megacorps will jump into the market.

Less Size, More Dynamism

While megacorp concentration is only tenuously related to market power, some people feel that corporate bigness is closely associated with political power—the larger the corporation, the more open the congressional ear. But to whose voice will legislators listen? If measures of megacorp concentration are indeed rough indicators of potential political power, they suggest that those who formerly had the biggest say may be losing influence. While the ratio of the assets held by the top 200 or 500 to total manufacturing assets may be increasing, the position of the top ten, twenty-five, or fifty companies within the top 500 is eroding. In 1954 the ten largest companies by asset size on the FORTUNE list had 27.4 per cent of the total assets of the FORTUNE 500. By 1968 the top ten held only 24.3 per cent. The twenty-five largest had 41.9 per cent of the assets in 1954 and 38.8 per cent in 1968. And the share of the fifty largest

fell from 54.6 per cent to 52.2 per cent during the same period. If this pattern means anything at all, it is that power within the manufacturing sector is becoming more diffused, passing from the older, more stable companies—whose growth has been impeded by antimerger legislation and, in some cases, by managerial lethargy—to companies with less size and more dynamism.

In a broader sense, the apparent increase in megacorp dominance may not really indicate any increase in political power at all. Business may be becoming a weaker force within the whole constellation of forces that bear on government. Certainly the relative power of the young, the aged, and the poor has been rising. The business community has not been able to stop—if indeed it tried to—the trend toward increasingly ambitious and expensive social-welfare legislation. Nor has big business, for all its power, been successful in preventing enactment of tough antimerger legislation. Whether the data on megacorp dominance suggest the need for additional legislation to curb business power is highly doubtful.

Indeed, it is doubtful whether any clear directives for policy are conveyed by the concentration statistics. Market concentration in manufacturing shows no tendency to rise. Megacorp concentration has been increasing, but the rise is less dramatic than the government contends and, when viewed in relation to other trends in American life, less worrisome. Nearly twenty years ago Professor Morris Adelman of M.I.T. summarized the concentration debate in six short sentences, and with only minor modifications Adelman's conclusions can still serve. He wrote: "(1) The American economy is highly concentrated. (2) Concentration is highly uneven. (3) The extent of concentration shows no tendency to grow, and it may possibly be declining. Any tendency either way, if it does exist, must be at the pace of a glacial drift."

"What are the implications for public policy? Strictly speaking, none."

Part II–B · *Profits*

Profits, measured as a rate of return on total investment in a firm, are an index to relative efficiency in the firm's employment of its capital if it operates under competitive circumstances. If we take all the firms in an industry, some of which are more efficient and some less efficient, assume that there is a normal dispersion of entrepreneurial talents in the firms composing the industry, and be sure we include the firms disappearing through failure, the average return should tell us something about how attractive that industry is for additional investment, provided allowance is made for risks which may repel investors and for accounting distortions resulting from conventions which cause accountants regularly to expense some varieties of capital outlays required to enter and operate efficiently in an industry.

If an industry is relatively attractive and capacity fails to expand and depress the return to where it has no greater at-tractiveness than other industries, econo-mists would argue that there must be bar-riers to *de novo* entry. In addition, firms within the industry must be failing to ex-pand and must be behaving in non-com-petitive fashion—perhaps tacitly or explic-itly colluding to restrict capacity and output to maintain returns above competitive levels. On this basis studies showing a posi-tive correspondence between concentration and rates of return have been accepted as evidence that collusive behavior and bar-riers to entry must be characteristic of con-centrated industries on the average, al-though not necessarily true in any single concentrated industry.

The first selection in this section argues that a correlation between concentration and profitability is not sufficient for the establishment of oligopolistic behavior. As-suming profitability has been correctly measured, the correlation may be a coinci-dence resulting from disequilibrium conditions being correlated with concentration. If it is coincidental disequilibrium rather than oligopoly behavior and entry barriers which causes higher returns at some given time in concentrated industries, then rates of return should converge over time (to the extent that risk and the differential impact of accounting conventions are not the cause of dispersion in rates of return). The selection examines a number of samples of industries for which a correlation between concentration and rates of return has been found. It follows them through time and finds that the correlation deteriorates with the passage of time, indicating that barriers to entry into concentrated industries are not strong or that the members of concentrated industries behave competitively, expanding when the return is attractive.

The next selection examines the experience of thirty-five combinations of five or more firms which occurred around the turn of the century during the infamous "trust" era. The sample of combinations used is biased inasmuch as those picked had to be successful enough to have lasted for at least ten years to be included. Since a large number of combinations failed or had to be reorganized because they could not otherwise remain solvent, the sample of consolidations used probably overstates the average success of the mergers occurring in this period.

If merging a major share of the capacity in an industry enables the then concentrated industries, or their leading firms, to behave oligopolistically or monopolistically, earnings in these firms should have been enhanced by the concentration of capacity. Professor Dewing finds that, contrary to popular impression, the average combination was less profitable than the predecessor firms before they were merged. Entry could not be or was not blocked in the typical American market. The attempt at oligopolization or monopolization of markets did not turn out to be the royal road

to riches. Although the antitrust authorities did not intervene in any of these combinations in the period examined, the market worked competitively despite the extreme levels of concentration resulting from these consolidations.

In selection 16, the question is raised as to why any correlation between concentration and profitability was found in studies such as the one by Professor Bain, the first in a series appearing since 1950. In this instance, the correlation appears to be a happenstance resulting from the particular forty-two industries composing the Bain sample. An enlarged sample of industries, including all those used by Bain, does not show the relationship he found.

The last selection in this section reviews and summarizes the series of studies referred to above. The main omission in this review is a discussion of the aggregation problems and biases involved when concentration ratios of four digit industries are averaged to obtain three or two digit concentration ratios for use in correlations with the available three and two digit profit data. The larger the number of four digit industries within any three digit or two digit group, the less likely it is that the average concentration ratio means what it is supposed to mean. The latter problem is discussed by Professor Stanley Boyle in an important article which could not be included here for lack of space. In an experiment computing average concentration ratios for four digit industries from five digit data, Boyle found that, "In almost half of the instances [214 industries] the difference [between the true concentration ratio and the ratio computed as an average] was 50 per cent or more." [1]

---

[1] "The Average Concentration Ratio: An Inappropriate Measure of Industry Structure," 81 *Journal of Political Economy* at 420 (1973).

14. The Antitrust Task Force
Deconcentration Recommendation[*]

YALE BROZEN

In 1968, the Task Force on Antitrust Policy headed by Dean Phil C. Neal delivered a report to the White House recommending new legislation supplementing present antitrust statutes. The report included a proposed draft of a Concentrated Industries Act. Its purpose "would be to give enforcement authorities a clear mandate to use established techniques of divestiture to reduce concentration. . . ."[1]

The act would define any market amounting to $500,000,000 or more in which any four or fewer firms' market share exceeds 70 per cent to be an "oligopoly industry." Any firm whose market share exceeds 15 per cent in such an industry would be designated an "oligopoly firm." Such firms, then, could, under the proposed act, be subjected to proceedings in equity for the reduction of concentration. Decrees could be entered requiring steps to be taken to achieve "a reduction of concentration such that the market share of each oligopoly firm in such oligopoly industry does not exceed 12 per cent."[2]

The recommendation rested on the suspicion that, "In an oligopoly market—one in which there is a small number of dominant sellers, each with a large market share —each must consider the effect of his output on the total market and the probable reaction of the other sellers to his decisions;

the results of their combined decisions may approximate the profit-maximizing decisions of a monopolist."[3]

The evidence offered by the Task Force for this suspicion was stated as follows:

The adverse effects of persistent concentration on output and price find some confirmation in various studies that have been made of return on capital in major industries. These studies have found a close association between high levels of concentration and persistently high rates of return on capital, particularly in those industries in which the largest four firms account for more than 60% of sales. High profit rates in individual firms or even in particular industries are of course consistent with competition. They may reflect innovation, exceptional efficiency, or growth in demand outrunning the expansion in supply. Above-average profits in a particular industry signal the need and provide the incentive for additional resources and expanded output in the industry, which in due time should return profits to a normal level. It is the persistence of high profits over extended time periods and over whole industries rather than in individual firms that suggest artificial restraints on output and the absence of fully effective competition. The correlation of evidence of this kind with very high levels of concentration appears to be significant.[4]

The Task Force does not give any specific reference to studies showing a "close association between high levels of concentration and persistently high rates of return."[5] Professor Donald Turner, who evi-

---

Reprinted from The Journal of Law and Economics, Volume XIII (2), October, 1970, Copyright 1970, The University of Chicago.

[*] The author is indebted to James C. Ellert for his contributions in assembling and analyzing data.

[1] White House Task Force on Antitrust Policy, Report 1 (in Trade Reg. Rep., supp. to no. 415, May 26, 1969).

[2] Id. at app. A, A-1.

[3] Id. at I-4–5.

[4] Id. at I-8–9.

[5] The evidence relied upon probably consists of some or all of the following tests of the statistical correlation between accounting rates of return on book values and concentration ratios,

dently agrees with the Task Force recommendation, stating that, "In my opinion, any costs of applying divestiture remedies to . . . highly concentrated industries would be far outweighed by the gains," refers to studies by Bain. These, to him, suggest "a correlation between seller concentration and excess profits beyond what would appear to be accounted for by special

circumstances like windfalls or rewards to innovation." [6]

The Bain Study

The evidence offered by Professor Bain in his pioneering study consists of the relationship between 1935 eight firm concentration ratios in forty-two industries and weighted average accounting rates of return on book net worth in three or more companies in each industry over the years 1936–1940 (Table 1, columns a, b, c, d).[7] He did not use all the 340 industries for which concentration ratios were calculated because he did not have data on at least three companies in some industries,[8] because of the regional character of other industries, or because he felt that the available concentration ratios were made meaningless by the inclusion of firms producing several nonsubstitute products or because the firms specialized by products.

For his forty-two industries, Bain found a correlation coefficient of 0.28 (reported as 0.33 in his 1951 article) between rates of return and concentration. He concluded that the relationship was not linear, since the coefficient was very low (implying that variation in concentration ratios could account for only 8 per cent of the variation in rates of return if the relationship were accepted as statistically significant). However, dividing his industries into the most and least concentrated halves (the dividing line fell at a 70 per cent eight firm concentration ratio), he found a significant difference between the rates of return in the two groups. The most concentrated half of his industries showed an 11.8 per cent average accounting rate of return and the least con-

---

although none shows a *close* association. Joe S. Bain, Relation of Profit Rate to Industry Concentration: American Manufacturing, 1936–1940, 65 Q. J. Econ. 293 (1951); Norman R. Collins & Lee E. Preston, Concentration and Price-Cost Margins in Food Manufacturing Industries, 14 J. Ind. Econ. 226 (1966); Victor R. Fuchs, Integration, Concentration, and Profits in Manufacturing Industries, 75 Q. J. Econ. 278 (1961); Robert W. Kilpatrick, The Choice Among Alternative Measures of Industrial Concentration, 49 Rev. of Econ. & Stat. 258 (1967); Harold M. Levinson, Postwar Movement of Prices and Wages in Manufacturing Industries, (Joint Economic Committee, Study Paper No. 21, 1960); H. Michael Mann, Seller Concentration, Barriers to Entry, and Rates of Return in Thirty Industries, 1950–1960, 48 Rev. Econ. & Stat. 296 (1966); Richard A. Miller, Marginal Concentration Ratios and Industrial Profit Rates: Some Empirical Results of Oligopoly Behavior, 34 Southern Econ. J. 259 (1967); Howard J. Sherman, Introduction to the Economics of Growth, Unemployment and Inflation, Ch. 8 (First published as Macrodynamic Economics, 1964); George J. Stigler, A Theory of Oligopoly, 72 J. Pol. Econ. 44 (1964); Leonard Winchell Weiss, Average Concentration Ratios and Industrial Performance, 11 J. Ind. Econ. 237 (1963).

Only Bain, Collins and Preston, Mann, and Stigler used four digit industries. The other studies used profits in two and three digit industries with averages of four digit industry concentration ratios. The Collins and Preston study did not use return on investment as a measure of profitability, using price-cost margins instead with cost defined to omit some expenditures such as those on advertising with an allowance for capital requirements by using gross book value to output ratios as an independent variable.

None of the studies examined the question of the *persistence* of high and low profits. All of them used essentially the same body of data, that is, data taken from the same time period, the 1950's, with the exception of Bain whose data were taken from the last half of the 1930's.

---

[6] Donald F. Turner, The Scope of Antitrust and Other Economic Regulatory Policies, 82 Harv. L. Rev. 1207, 1215 (1969). Turner also refers to the Collins and Preston studies.

[7] Joe S. Bain, *supra* note 5, at 312, tab. I.

[8] He had profit and concentration data on 149 industries, *id.* at 314.

Table 1 • **Concentration Ratios and 1936–1940, 1953–1957 Average Profit Rates for a Sample of 42 Industries**

Census Number	Industry Designation (Abbreviated)	Proportion of Value Product Supplied by First Eight Firms in 1935	Industry Average Profit Rate After Income Taxes[a]	
			1936–1940	1953–1957
a	*b*	*c*	*d*	*e*
222	Linoleum	100.0	9.0	8.3
1652	Cigarettes	99.4	14.4	11.5
1314	Typewriters and Parts	99.3	15.8	5.1
108	Chewing Gum	97.3	16.9	15.9
113	Corn Syrup, Sugar, Oil and Starch	95.0	9.3	11.8
1408	Motor Vehicles	94.2	16.3	17.6
803	Rubber Tires and Tubes	90.4	8.2	12.5
629	Rayon and Allied Products	90.2	12.1	8.0
1301	Agricultural Implements	87.7	9.1	7.7
1022	Gypsum Products	86.4	10.1	15.6
1123	Tin Cans and Other Tinware	85.6	9.1	10.2
1636	Photographic Apparatus & Materials	84.9	12.9	16.1
1647	Tobacco, Chewing and Smoking	84.3	11.7	10.2
1405	Cars, Railroad	84.0	2.8	9.4
1201	Aluminum Products	83.7	9.7	14.7
631	Soap	83.1	15.2	11.8
1634	Pens, Fountain, etc.	82.8	12.3	10.0
1218	Smelting and Refining Zinc	82.2	4.7	7.2
1315	Washing Machines	79.7	14.0	16.5
1401	Aircraft and Parts	72.8	20.8	18.6
133	Liquors, Distilled	71.4	14.2	6.4
1638	Roofing	68.2	7.4	10.8
201	Carpets and Rugs	68.2	4.7	4.2
1112	Steel Works and Rolling Mills	63.8	4.9	12.2
123	Meat Packing	63.5	3.6	5.5
1102	Cast Iron Pipe	63.0	8.6	12.0
705	Petroleum Refining	58.9	6.8	13.4
1126	Wire	54.0	7.5	14.1
115	Flavoring Extracts	54.0	1.8	13.1
1608	Cigars	50.7	6.9	7.4
1104	Doors and Shutters, Metal	49.0	18.3	11.0
1325	Printer's Machinery	47.4	2.2	9.8
1002	Cement	44.7	5.4	16.6
116	Flour	37.0	7.6	8.6
907	Leather	34.3	0.8	8.7
1117	Screw Machine Products	32.9	8.2	10.4
904	Boots and Shoes	30.8	7.5	10.9
105	Canned Fruits and Vegetables	30.4	7.4	8.4
209	Rayon Manufactures	27.1	8.4	7.9
408	Paper Goods	23.7	12.4	13.8
112	Confectionery	19.9	17.0	11.7
311	Lumber and Timber Products	7.6	9.1	11.7

Sources: Columns a, b, c and d from Joe S. Bain *supra* note 5, at 312, Tab. I. Column e from Report of the Federal Trade Commission on Rates of Return for Identical Companies in Selected Manufacturing Industries (1940, 1947–1960); Standard and Poor's Compustat Tapes, Moody's Industrial Manual, 1952–1958.
[a] Net profit after income taxes as a percentage of net worth.

centrated half a 7.5 per cent return (Table 2).[9]

Bain felt that any conclusion from the evidence was subject to a number of reservations. These ranged from the differences between accounting and economic rates of return and the variations in differences between the economic rate of return and equilibrium rates in various industries to the representativeness of his sample of industries and of firms. He pointed out that among the thirty-four industries excluded because he had data from fewer than three firms, the relationship between concentration and accounting rates of return was the *reverse* of that found in the forty-two industries he used. "Averages of industry profit rates above and below the 70 per cent concentration line in these thirty-four industries were 9.1 and 10.5 per cent respectively." [10] Bain was much more cau-

tious in his conclusions concerning the significance of the relationship between accounting rates of return and concentration than the Task Force or Professor Turner.

Bain also warned that his hypothesis "refers to profit results which should occur in long run equilibrium" while the measurement of profits in any given time period includes "profit differences . . . which are explicable . . . as windfalls [unanticipated shifts in demand or costs] and not by our hypothesis." [11] It should, then, be illuminating to analyze the accounting profit experience of his industries at some later point in time. To the extent that above and below average accounting rates of return are not the result of systematic biases such as the failure to capitalize some investment outlays (research expenditures and training costs, for example) or of explicit or implicit collusion in highly concentrated industries, we would expect above and below average rates to move toward the average. As the Task Force indicated, "It is the persistence of high profits over ex-

[9] Bain reported the rates as 12.1% and 6.9% in his paper and subsequently corrected the original report. Corrigendum, 65 Q. J. of Econ. 602 (1951).

[10] Joe S. Bain, *supra* note 5, at 315, n. 8.

[11] *Id.* at 309.

Table 2 • **Average of Industry Average Profit Rates Within Concentration Deciles, 1936–1940 and 1953–1957, for 42 Selected Industries**

Concentration Range Per cent of Value Product Supplied by Eight Firms (1935)	Number of Industries	Average of Industry Average Profit Rates[a]	
a	b	1936–1940 c	1953–1957 d
90–100	8	12.7%	11.3%
80–89.9	10	9.8	11.3
70–79.9	3	16.3	13.8
60–69.9	5	5.8	8.9
50–59.9	4	5.8	12.0
40–49.9	3	8.6	12.5
30–39.9	5	6.3	9.3
20–29.9	2	10.4	10.9
10–19.9	1	17.0	11.7
0–9.9	1	9.1	11.7
0–100	42	9.6	11.1
70–100	21	11.8	11.7
0–70	21	7.5	10.6
Difference		4.4	1.1

Sources: Columns a, b, and c (above the line) from Joe S. Bain, *supra* note 5, at 313, tab. II, as corrected in Corrigendum, *supra* note 9. Column d (above the line) from Table 1.

[a] Average of net profits after income taxes as percentage of net worth.

tended time periods . . . that suggest artificial restrains on output and the absence of fully effective competition." [12]

If the above average rates of return Bain found to be typical in the most concentrated half of his forty-two industries do not move toward the average, *persisting* at their high level despite the passage of time and the apparent attractiveness of the rate of return, then they must be examined for the occurrence of relatively greater bias and for whether they represent a necessary premium for relatively greater risk or other factors repelling investors. In the absence of such factors, and in the absence of data indicating a continuing relatively more favorable movement of the long run equilibrium position of these industries, the rates may then be regarded as equilibrium rates evidencing collusion combined with barriers to entry. In the absence of remedies which can remove the barriers to entry, deconcentration may be the only remedy available for attempting to obtain competitive performance.

The Task Force paid little attention to the question of whether it would be preferable to act on barriers to entry as a method of obtaining competitive performance, although such barriers are a necessary condition for the maintenance of collusively determined rates of return in excess of competitive levels.[13] It concluded that deconcentration would result in competitive performance, assuming that concentration

results in non-competitive performance, without examining the question of whether the barriers to entry which made explicit or implicit collusion effective would still insulate the industries acted upon from competitive forces.

Returning to the question of whether the above average accounting rates of return found by Bain in his more concentrated industries were equilibrium rates, Table 1 shows Bain's forty-two industries, the accounting rates of return he computed for 1936–1940, and accounting rates of return for 1953–1957 (the first five year postwar period in which the aberrations introduced by the disequilibrium resulting from the shift in the structure of demand from military to civilian dominated markets or by the Korean episode were no longer strong). In the most concentrated half of Bain's list of forty-two industries, twelve "earned" above average (1953–1957 average) rates of return in the period he examined. Nine "earned" below average rates. We would expect rates in most above average return industries to decline, if this was a disequilibrium situation, accounting rates of return are not differentially biased, and differentials in risks do not cause most of the above average rates. Most did. They declined despite the above average concentration level. Of the twelve above average return concentrated industries, rates declined in nine and rose in three. We would also expect most below average return industries to rise, if this was a disequilibrium situation. Most did. Of the nine below average return industries, rates rose in seven and declined in two.

In the least concentrated half of Bain's list, three industries "earned" above average returns. Eighteen "earned" below average. We would expect most above average return industries to decline, if this was a disequilibrium situation. Most did. They declined in almost the same proportion as the above average industries in the most concentrated half of the list. Of the three above average, rates of return declined in two and rose in one. We would also expect most below average industries to rise, if this was

---

[12] White House Task Force on Antitrust Policy, *supra* note 1, at II-8.

[13] ". . . a few dominant firms may, in the long run, earn higher rates of return on the owners' investment than the opportunity cost of equity capital. . . . The word 'may' indicates that seller concentration is a necessary, but not sufficient condition. . . . [I]f entry is relatively easy, the oligopolists may set a price close to the competitive level. . . ." H. Michael Mann, *supra* note 5, at 296.

"An inquiry into a firm's monopoly power . . . must concern itself with the conditions of entry into its markets." Irvin M. Grossack, Towards an Integration of Static and Dynamic Measures of Industry Concentration, 47 Rev. Econ. & Stat. 301 (1965).

a disequilibrium situation. Most did. Of the below average industries, rates of return rose in sixteen (and declined in two) despite their low concentration.

We do not expect the accounting profit rate of every industry to move toward the average since, as Bain pointed out, "there are numerous sources of deviation of individual accounting profit rates from their theoretical long-run tendency. These are of sufficient weight that we should judge it quite improbable that the major hypothesis, even if true, would be verified by every pair of individual firms or industries."[14] For this reason, the use of profit rates of groups of industries is preferable. Bain groups his industries by concentration decile, stating as his reason the foregoing and,

> So far as firms or industries compared experienced different average price levels as of the date of acquisition of fixed and other amortizable assets, their relative accounting profit rates will of course give a distorted picture of their relative theoretical profit rates, to which our hypothesis refers. However, for relatively large groups of firms and industries, we may suppose that on the average the price change effects on accounting profit rates will be similar, and that for such groups the sort of potential aberrations referred to will 'average out,' with any true net relation of theoretical rates surviving in group averages.[15]

Bain's industry groups and their average accounting rates of return for 1936–1940 and for 1953–1957 are shown in Table 2. If high concentration coupled with barriers to entry accounted for the above average rates of return in 1936–1940 in the more than 70 per cent (eight firm ratio) concentrated industries and the inability to move resources into these more profitable industries accounted for the below average rates of return in the less than 70 per cent concentrated industries, then there should be little or no movement expected toward the average rate of return between 1936–1940 and 1953–1957.

---

[14] Joe S. Bain, *supra* note 5, at 309.

[15] *Id.* at 308.

The two groups of industries which showed above average accounting rates of return in 1936–1940 out of the three more than 70 per cent concentrated groups both moved toward the average. The 90–100 per cent concentrated group dropped from 12.7 to 11.3 per cent and the 70 to 79.9 per cent concentrated group dropped from 16.3 to 13.8 per cent. The one above average return industry in the less than 70 per cent concentrated groups (10 to 19.9 per cent) also dropped toward the average, from 17.0 to 11.7 per cent.

All the below average return industry groups in 1936–1940 moved up between 1936–1940 and 1953–1957. There seems to be no evidence of barriers to movement of resources into the higher return uses nor any manifestation of a persistently high return in the above 70 per cent concentration group. The gap between the more and less than 70 per cent concentrated industries closed from a 4.4 percentage point gap in 1936–1940 to a 1.1 percentage point gap in 1953–1957, a statistically insignificant difference between the two groups.

Of course, it may be argued that a decline in concentration may have been the cause of the decline in the high rates of return in the highly concentrated group with the consequence that explicit or implicit collusion became more difficult. However, if a decline in concentration occurred without antitrust intervention, and there was intervention in only two of the twenty-one more concentrated industries (one of the above average return more concentrated industries), then a deconcentration act does not seem to be required. The market will do the deconcentrating.

What we find is that the nine above average return concentrated industries whose return declined had no decrease or an increase in concentration in five cases. Concentration ratios declined in four. Whether or not concentration declined, and whether or not the industries were more or less concentrated, most above average return industries suffered a decline in their accounting rates of return.

Bain hinted strongly that the difference

between accounting rates of return in the more and less concentrated industries in his forty-two industry sample was a statistical artifact. He pointed out that his 335 firm sample was heavily weighted with large firms and that their rates of return may not have been representative of the differences in rates of return among industries. In his less concentrated industries, he found little difference between the rates of return of large firms and the few small firms in his sample. The rates he found for the less concentrated industries were, then, probably representative of those industries despite the dominance of large firms in his sample. In the more concentrated industries, however, the large firm rates of return were higher than the small firm rates.

Since large firms earned higher rates of return than small firms in the more concentrated industries, the rates of the larger firms in more concentrated industries were not representative of these industries. To the extent that small firms were underrepresented in the sample employed, the rates of return in the more concentrated industries were overstated relative to the rates in the less concentrated industries where large firms were more representative for their industries. The higher rates found for the more concentrated industries were, at least to some extent, then, a consequence of bias in the sample of firms (and of probable bias in the selection of industries, as Bain indicated, because of thirty-four industries dropped which were represented by less than three firms).

Bain found a dichotomous rather than a linear relationship between concentration and accounting profits in his sample. The lack of linearity, it may be argued, may be a result of the fact that the possibilities of collusion diminish linearly but approach zero once the concentration level drops to the 70 to 80 per cent range. Within and below this range, rates of return may be randomly distributed with respect to concentration since the probability of successful collusion is the same at all concentration levels in the range below 80 per cent.

Using four firm concentration ratios, the correlations of profit rates and concentration approach statistically significant levels for the group whose ratios exceed 60 per cent (82.2 per cent was the cut off at the eight firm concentration level). The coefficient of determination for all forty-two industries is a not-significant 8 per cent while that for the seventeen industries which are more than 60 per cent concentrated is 40 per cent. This suggests that four firm concentration levels in excess of 75 to 80 per cent may possibly present opportunities for workable collusion if we can accept Bain's industry and firm sample as representative and his rates of return as equilibrium rates.

However, the same seventeen industries show a coefficient of determination of only 16 per cent between their 1954 concentration ratios and 1953–1957 rates of return and 9 per cent between their 1963 concentration ratios and their 1962–1966 rates of return (Table 3). This deterioration strongly suggests that the rates of return observed by Bain in his concentrated in-

Table 3 • **Coefficient of Determination (r^2) Bain's 42 Industries and 17 More Than 60% Concentrated Industries among the 42**

	42 Industries			17 Industries		
	C_{35}	C_{54}	C_{63}	C_{35}	C_{54}	C_{63}
ROE						
(1936–1940)	0.08 (1.86)			0.40 (3.14)		
(1953–1957)	0.01 (0.69)	0.03 (1.02)		0.18 (1.83)	0.16 (1.70)	
(1962–1966)	0.05 (1.39)	0.07 (1.77)	0.14 (2.54)	0.11 (1.37)	0.01 (0.44)	0.09 (1.25)

ROE is accounting rate of return on book equity.
Rate of return figures are the unweighted means of industry annual rates. Annual rates are a weighted average of return on average equity in each year.
C_{35}, C_{54}, and C_{63} are four firm concentration ratios in 1935, 1954, and 1963.
Figures in parentheses are t-values.

Table 4 • Coefficient of Determination (r^2) (Stigler's 17 Industries) Concentration and Rate of Return

		C_{54}	C_{63}
Stigler ROE	(1936–1957)	0.28 (2.43)	
Brozen ROE	(1953–1957)	0.35 (2.84)	
Brozen ROE	(1962–1966)	0.01 (0.39)	0.17 (1.73)

ROE is accounting rate of return on book equity.
C_{54} and C_{63} are four firm concentration ratios in 1954 and 1963.
Figures in parentheses are t-values.

dustries were not at equilibrium levels and were not an appropriate test of his hypothesis. The evidence offered by Bain is neither strong enough in its original form to support a policy of deconcentration nor does it stand up to the test of time and the later evidence generated by the passage of time.

A Stigler Study

A more recent test of the oligopoly-collusion thesis has been made by Professor George Stigler.[16] Using seventeen industries with four firm concentration levels in excess of 60 per cent, he found a coefficient of rank correlation between 1954 concentration and 1953–1957 accounting rates of return on book net worth of 0.507 (coefficient of determination from a linear correlation equals 28 per cent).[17] This is a somewhat weaker relationship than that found for 1936–1940 in the above 60 per cent concentrated seventeen industries in the Bain sample. Stigler very cautiously concluded from his data "that there is no relationship between profitability and concentration if . . . the share of the four largest firms is less than about 80 per cent." [18]

Again, whether or not the correlation

means that the more than 80% concentrated industries are suffering "artificial restraints on output and the absence of fully effective competition" [19] depends upon whether the accounting rates of return relate to each other in the same way as economic rates of return in the seventeen industries and whether or not the industries are in equilibrium. Leaving aside any question as to the meaning of accounting rates of return, what happened to the above average returns in the more concentrated industries with the passage of time? Do they persist at their high levels as equilibrium rates would or do they move toward the average accounting rate of return?

The coefficient of determination in Stigler's sample of industries deteriorates from 35 per cent for 1953–1957 to a statistically non-significant 17 per cent for 1962–1966 rates of return and 1963 concentration (Table 4) and only 1 per cent for 1962–1966 returns and 1954 concentration. Out of the eight industries comprising the most concentrated half of Stigler's list (more than 83 per cent concentrated), seven industries had above average rates of return (Table 5). Of these seven, rates of return

---

[16] George J. Stigler, *supra* note 5, at 57.

[17] *Id.* at 58, tab. 8. Using my rate of return figures, the coefficient of determination becomes 35%, a somewhat stronger relationship than that found by Stigler, but still weaker than that for Bain's seventeen more than 60% concentrated industries in 1936–1940.

[18] *Id.* at 57. It is interesting to trace the evolution in Stigler's thinking about the critical concentration level dividing monopolized (or oligop-

olistic) and competitive industries. In his Industrial Organization and Economic Progress in The State of the Social Sciences 276 (L. D. White, ed., 1956), he uses the level of concentration as his measure of monopoly. The industries whose concentration level is 44.8% or higher are classed as monopolies, *id.* at 277. In Capital and Rates of Return in Manufacturing Industries 57, n.4, and 67 (1963), he classes 50 to 60% concentrated industries as "ambiguous" and the more than 60% concentrated industries as "concentrated."

[19] White House Task Force on Antitrust Policy, *supra* note 1, at II-8.

Table 5 • Trend in Profitability (1953–1957 to 1962–1966) of Stigler Selected Industries

Industry	Concentration Ratio 1954	Average Rate of Return on Net Worth		
		Stigler 1953–1957	Brozen 1953–1957	1962–1966
Sulfur mining	98	23.85 (4)	25.5 (4)	11.3 (3)
Automobiles	98	20.26 (3)	19.2 (3)	19.6 (3)
Primary aluminum	98	13.46 (4)	16.9 (3)	8.5 (3)
Flat glass	90	16.17 (3)	16.5 (3)	10.7 (3)
Gypsum products	90	20.26 (2)	15.6 (2)	9.4 (2)
Floor covering, hard surface	87	7.59 (3)	8.3 (3)	12.9 (3)
Chewing gum	86	17.06 (2)	17.7 (2)	13.9 (1)
Industrial gases	84	11.53 (3)	11.7 (3)	11.0 (3)
Cigarettes	83	11.18 (5)	11.5 (5)	13.7 (5)
Typewriters	83	5.39 (3)	5.1 (3)	7.6 (2)
Metal cans	80	13.90 (4)	10.2 (5)	9.9 (3)
Rubber tires	79	14.02 (9)	12.6 (13)	9.9 (11)
Rayon fiber	76	6.62 (4)	8.0 (4)	11.8 (2)
Corn wet milling	75	11.55 (3)	11.8 (4)	14.2 (4)
Carbon black	73	9.97 (2)	10.5 (2)	6.5 (1)
Domestic laundry equipment	68	17.76 (2)	18.1 (2)	19.7 (2)
Distilled liquors	64	7.55 (6)	6.4 (12)	7.2 (12)

Sources: George J. Stigler, *supra* note 5, at 58, tab. 7; Report of the Federal Trade Commission, Rates of
   Return for Identical Companies in Selected Manufacturing Industries (1940, 1947–1960); Standard and
   Poor's Compustat Tapes, 1966, 1968; Moody's Industrial Manual, 1952–1958. Figure in parentheses is
   number of companies used in computing rate of return.
Note: Brozen return figures are a simple average of the weighted return for each year (return computed on
   average equity). Stigler figures are a weighted average of return on end of year equity.

declined in six. In the one industry in the
most concentrated half of Stigler's list
which had a below average rate, the rate of
return rose. Most of Stigler's more concentrated industries behave as if their accounting rates in 1953–1957 were not equilibrium
rates. His correlation, therefore, is not relevant evidence for support of the Task
Force's recommendation.[20]

The Mann Study

Another study using the relationship between four digit industry concentration ratios and accounting rates of return was
done by Professor H. M. Mann.[21] His work
for the postwar period appears to confirm
Bain's finding in the prewar period. His
twenty-one more than 70 per cent concentrated (eight firm) industries show an average return of 13.3 per cent and his nine less

than 70 per cent concentrated industries
show an average return of 9.0 per cent for
1950–1960. The difference in accounting
rates of return in the two groups is the
same as that found by Bain. However, the
sample of firms Mann uses suffers from the
same deficiencies as Bain's sample. Also, his
industry sample is small in the below 70
per cent range.[22]

In a later paper, Mann presented 1950–
1966 data for nineteen of his twenty-one
more than 70 per cent concentrated industries.[23] These data enable us to examine the
movement of accounting rates of return. Inasmuch as a decline in the rate occurred in
fifteen out of his nineteen industries between 1950–1960 and 1961–1966, although
no decline occurred in accounting rates of

---

[20] Stigler warned that this with the other "bits of
   evidence" he offered "do not constitute strong
   support" for the theory of oligopoly, *supra* note
   5, at 59.

[21] H. Michael Mann, *supra* note 5.

[22] Adding just two industries, 3561 (pump and
   compressors) and 3471 (lighting fixtures) which
   are 40% and 23% concentrated (eight firm),
   raises the below 70% concentrated rate of return
   average to that of the above 70% concentrated
   group.

[23] H. Michael Mann, A Note on Barriers to Entry
   and Long Run Profitability, 14 Antitrust Bull.
   845 (1969).

return on equity in all manufacturing (Table 6), it appears that the rates used by Mann were not equilibrium rates. Mann's data in his first article, which appeared to support the Task Force position on the need for antitrust action on concentrated industries, turns out to be inadequate evidence for this position when examined after the passage of time. The rate of return of 13.6 per cent for 1950–1960 in the nineteen concentrated industries, which was 2.5 percentage points above the average of all manufacturing, drops to 10.4 per cent for 1961–1966, which is 0.8 percentage points below the average of all manufacturing in the latter period. Fifteen out of nineteen highly concentrated industries show a decline in rate of return between 1950–1960 and 1961–1966.

Bain and Mann concur in believing that ". . . seller concentration alone is not an adequate indicator of the probable incidence of . . . monopolistic output restriction." [24] They both suggest that high barriers to entry are necessary along with high seller concentration to enable an industry to price at levels approaching the monopoly price. They therefore classify highly concentrated industries in three groups according to their judgment of the height of barriers to entry.

---

[24] Joe S. Bain, Barriers to New Competition 201 (1956), cited in H. Michael Mann, *supra* note 5, at 296.

Table 6 • **Movement of Average Accounting Rates of Return on Net Worth for Nineteen Concentrated Industries Selected by Mann 1950–1960 to 1961–1966**

	1950–1960[a]		*1961–1966*[b]	
Very high barriers				
Nickel	18.9%		16.4%	
Sulfur	21.6		10.3	
Ethical drugs	17.9		16.5	
Flat glass	18.8		12.0	
Automobiles	15.5		16.1	
Chewing gum	15.3		14.2	
Cigarettes	11.6		12.5	
Liquor	9.0		7.3	
Mean (8 industries)		16.1%		13.1%
Substantial barriers				
Soap	13.3		13.3	
Cement	15.7		8.6	
Biscuits	11.4		10.0	
Copper	11.5		9.8	
Steel	10.8		7.7	
Farm machinery & tractors	8.8		7.7	
Shoe machinery	7.4		4.8	
Mean (7 industries)		11.3		8.9
Moderate-to-low barriers				
Gypsum products	14.4		9.3	
Glass containers	13.3		11.0	
Tires & tubes	13.2		9.8	
Metal containers	9.9		9.9	
Mean (4 industries)		12.7		10.0
Mean (19 industries)	13.6		10.4	
All mfg. corporations[c]	11.1		11.2	

Sources:
[a] H. Michael Mann, *supra* note 5, at 229, tab. 2.
[b] Computed from data in H. Michael Mann, *supra* note 21, at 847–48, tab. 1, and his 1950–1960 data, *supra* note 5, at 229, tab. 2.
[c] 1969 Econ. Rep. of the President 310.

Both Bain and Mann find that highly concentrated industries with high barriers to entry exhibit higher accounting rates of return on book net worth than highly concentrated industries with lower barriers to entry. Mann found a 16.1 per cent average rate for the 1950–1960 period in the highly concentrated high barriers group in contrast to 11.3 per cent and 12.7 per cent rates in the lower barrier classes (Table 6).[25]

Even when only the "high barriers" group among the highly concentrated industries is examined, the same behavior of rates of return over time is exhibited as in the unclassified sample of concentrated industries used by Bain and by Stigler. Out of seven above average return industries in the eight placed in the highly concentrated-high barriers group by Mann, five decline between 1950–1960 and 1961–1966. The mean rate of return for the whole group declines from 16.1 per cent to 13.1 per cent between the two periods (Table 6).

Conclusion

Both Bain and Stigler warn of the weakness of the evidence they offer for the thesis that collusion is more likely to occur in highly concentrated industries.[26] Also, in review-ing the "substantial number of investiga-tions that have been made of the relation-ship between concentration and rates of return," Stigler points out that the ". . . re-lationship . . . is usually weak; not more than one half, and often less than one-fifth, of the variance of rates of return among in-dustries is accounted for by difference in concentration." He also finds it ". . . dis-quieting . . . that profitability is better correlated with crude industry measures (food) than with more sharply defined in-dustries (canned fruits and vegetables)." [27]

We have chosen for review those stud-ies that use sharply defined industries in re-lating profitability and concentration. Since the Task Force and Professor Turner lean on the studies that "have found a close as-sociation between high levels of concentra-tion and persistently high rates of return on capital" for their deconcentration recom-mendations,[28] we thought it important that these studies be extended beyond their original time frame to see whether the "high" rates of return persist in the indus-tries with "high levels of concentration." Such an examination discloses a lack of per-sistence of "high" rates of return in highly concentrated industries and denies the as-serted basis for the deconcentration recom-mendation.

---

[25] Table 6 includes the industries used in both Mann's 1966 study and his 1969 study. In the larger sample of firms and industries used only in his 1966 study, the rate of return he found in the very high barriers group is 16.4% in con-trast to 11.1% and 11.9% in the lower barriers group. H. Michael Mann, *supra* note 5, at 300.

[26] In an analysis of the relationship between the number of price fixing cases with criminal pen-alties and industry concentration, James M. Clabault & John F. Burton, Jr., Sherman Act In-dictments, 1955–1965: A Legal Economic Analysis 130, Tab. 3 (1966), find that 94% of the 1955–1965 cases occurred in the 85% of in-dustries with a less than 60% four firm concen-tration level. Detected explicit collusion does not seem to occur with a disproportionate fre-quency in the highly concentrated industries.

[27] George J. Stigler The Organization of Industry 145–46 (1968).

[28] The evidence relied on by Turner and the Task Force does not show a "close association," as Stigler points out in the citation above. Also, as Peter Pashigian points out, "The available em-pirical evidence is contradictory and hardly one-sided." Limit Price and the Market Share of the Leading Firm, 16 J. Ind. Econ. 176 (1968).

15. A Statistical Test of the Success of Consolidations

ARTHUR S. DEWING

Statements concerning the advantages or disadvantages of large scale enterprises brought about through combination—the so-called "trusts"—are ordinarily based on certain theoretical assumptions. These *a priori* assumptions have emphasized the various economies and various wastes which are alleged to accompany consolidation. No attempt, however, has been made to apply specific and definable tests to a sufficiently large collection of actual cases to justify generalizations possessing empirical value.[1] To do this is the purpose of the present study. The consolidations here under review were for the most part organized before 1903. A period of at least ten years elapsed, therefore, between their organization and the economic disturbances caused by the Great War. The period affords ample opportunity to judge of the ultimate success or failure of the trusts, since in that time they should have been able to prove the economic advantages of consolidation.

The specific problem whether or not large combinations of units of production are successful is divisible into two parts: the definition of success and its specific application to the trusts. In order that our study may have an objective standard we must establish some clearly describable criterion of success; and we must be able to apply it to a sufficiently large group of trusts to give the results at least some semblance of inductive value.

The term success when applied to a business may mean a variety of things. A successful business may be one which is conducted so economically that the commodities it deals in reach the ultimate consumer at a low price relative to the competitive cost of production. It may be one that endures through a long period of time. It may be one that grows in mere size without reference to the relative yield to invested capital or to business ability. And finally it may mean—in fact usually does—a business that yields a relatively large profit to the managers. In the end all these usages are reducible to the last. A business cannot long produce or distribute commodities to the consumers at a relatively low price unless it yields a profit to its managers; it cannot long endure unless the activities of a manager are stimulated by liberal profits; it cannot increase in mere size unless the profit is sufficient to encourage the continuous investment of capital. It is difficult, however, to determine that amount of true profit or of return on invested capital which marks the line between success and failure. Both profit and success are relative terms. But they are relative to what?

In this study three separate standards of relative profit or relative success are used. I shall assume that an industrial combination, in order to be called successful, should yield a larger net profit than the sum of the net profits of the component elements that entered the combination. This is our first criterion. A second assumption will be that the combination should yield a net profit at least approximately equal to what its proponents, including its bankers, owners, and promoters, estimated that it

---

Reprinted by permission of the *Quarterly Journal of Economics,* Volume 31, pp. 84–101, 1921–22.

[1] A preliminary study of this kind, using fewer corporations and less critical methods, was undertaken by me in another connection. See my Financial Policy of Corporations, vol. iii, p. 221.

would yield. And lastly it must be assumed that the average net earnings over a considerable period of time—say ten years—should show a conspicuous increase over the net earnings prior to the combination and during its first year. In other words, there must be a sustained increase. The application of these tests to industrial combinations in general is not as simple as their mere formulation. Something of a more or less arbitrary procedure has to be adopted, involving certain further assumptions. These will be explained in detail as we proceed.

A random selection of thirty-five industrial combinations was chosen which met the following six conditions. In order to qualify for the group the combination must (1) have been in existence at least ten years before 1914, (2) must have been formed as a combination of at least five separate, independent and competing plants, (3) must have a national rather than a mere sectional or local significance, (4) must have published financial reports in which at least some degree of confidence can be placed, (5) must have available published or accessible reports covering the earnings of the separate plants prior to their consolidation and the estimates of earnings made at the time the combination was effected. Lastly, the group as a whole must represent a wide diversity of industries.

A period of ten years was selected as sufficient to enable the "trust" to develop its weaknesses and its strengths; and cases were omitted from the tabulation when this period extended beyond 1914, since extraordinary profits or extraordinary losses due to the Great War might vitiate the calculation. Again, every effort was made to exclude from consideration all corporations not industrial combinations, strictly speaking. This was done by refusing to consider a business organization as an industrial consolidation unless it represented, at the time of its organization, at least five separate and relatively independent units, all previously competitors of each other. This

eliminated from consideration large businesses arising from internal growth, with now and then a sporadic addition from the outside, and those businesses arising from the union of only two or three relatively large units. Such combinations should be considered business expansions rather than industrial consolidations. All purely local combinations having only a local market for their products and only a narrow and restricted market for their securities were left out of account. Furthermore, in order to be included in the group a corporation must have available reliable published reports, covering a period of ten years. These reports must be of such character that the annual earning statements can be reduced to something like a uniform basis.[2] Even with the published reports available it was difficult to standardize the accounts; the necessary assumptions and interpretations will be described under the appropriate headings. Lastly, considerable effort was made to obtain a wide distribution of corporations, in order to ensure representation of many different industries. Aside from the purpose to secure such a wide distribution no effort whatever was made to include corporations known to be either successful or unsuccessful—either those which have attained an investment standing or those which became bankrupt. It will be observed that the list includes some consolidations, like the United States Envelope Company, which have been conspicuous in their able management and their steadily maintained success, and some others, like the American Window Glass Company, which have been equally conspicuous failures. The majority of the corporations, however, are those reported to have attained a modicum of success.

In preparing the tables the most diffi-

---

[2] The American Window Glass Company—of which more will be said from time to time—is included notwithstanding the fact that its published reports are inadequate for our purpose. It was included in order that there should be at least one combination allied to the building trades.

cult problem was that of reducing the statements of the different corporations to a uniform basis. It was, in fact, the problem of establishing a uniform system for the accounting of net profits. Owing to the meager data ordinarily furnished by the different corporations, especially those obviously unsuccessful, results were obtainable only by using a large amount of guessing. The statements of the previous earnings were, almost invariably, taken from the published reports of accountants, chosen in the majority of cases by the bankers who underwrote the original security issues at the time of promotion. All estimates or predictions of earnings were, except in the cases explained in footnotes, taken from published statements issued by the bankers or the promoters at the time of promotion. Where more than one prediction was made, the lowest and least extravagant statement was used. A few instances were found of estimates of earnings so extravagant and unreasonable that one is reminded of Johnson's phrase about wealth beyond the dreams of avarice. Such cases were disregarded altogether, even though they illustrate the extravagant expectations nurtured by some of the trust promotors. And the fact that the most extravagant predictions were often made in connection with consolidations which later proved utter failures, while not pertinent to the present study, is yet suggestive of the prevailing conception of profits expected through industrial consolidation. The earnings of the first year, as was true of the earnings for the later years, represent the net earnings after taxes and depreciation but before the payment of any interest or dividends. It was generally difficult and sometimes impossible to determine whether or not the company had charged its published net earnings with a reserve for depreciation. When no information of this character was available, the benefit of the doubt was given to the company; that is, it was assumed that the company made proper depreciation charges. In fact, in all cases of uncertainty in the computation of the net earnings the more liberal interpretation was adopted, so that the company was placed in the most advantageous light. The calculation of the average earnings for the first ten years presented no serious problem, except when the date of the beginning of the fiscal year was changed. In such cases the full twelve-month period was computed by a species of dead reckoning. Attention is called to the detailed descriptive notes, indicating the sources of figures and the method of compilation in cases involving some uncertainty. Where there is no reference the figures are taken directly from the annual reports of the corporation.

Table I gives the primary material on which all the others are based. Deductions from it will be discussed, in connection with the subsequent tables, under three headings: (1) the previous earnings of the separate plants before consolidation in comparison with the earnings after consolidation; (2) the estimated earnings at the time of consolidation in comparison with the earnings after consolidation; and (3) the earnings during the first year in comparison with the earnings during a period of years.

The figures in the tables that follow (Tables II to V) are in the nature of index numbers, being ratios expressed on a basis of 100 between the different figures for each of the thirty-five corporations. The medians of each group of thirty-five were computed from these ratios. Certain ratios could not be determined as real integers, because one of the terms was a negative quantity. Other ratios at the extremes of the arrays were very large. For these reasons an inclusive arithmetical average of the entire group of thirty-five ratios would be meaningless. Accordingly averages were computed of the twenty-one ratios lying between and including the quartiles. Owing to the relatively close dispersion in most cases on either side of the median these averages are perhaps more significant than the medians themselves. The closeness with which they approximate the medians should be noted in estimating the statistical value of the general conclusions.

Table 1 • **Fundamental Data**

Name	Date incorpo- rated	Bonds issued at incorporation	Preferred stock	Preferred stock dividend	Fixed charges
1 U.S. Leather	1893	$6,000,000	$62,282,300	8 c[1]	$360,000
2 Am. Matting	1897	none	2,500,000	7 c	none
3 Am. Linseed	1898	none	16,750,000	7 n	none
4 U. S. Envelope	1898	2,000,000	3,750,000	7 c	120,000
5 Inter. Paper	1898	8,699,000	20,530,700	7 c	521,940
6 Am. Agri. Chem.	1899	none	17,000,000	6 c	none
7 Am. Beet Sugar	1899	none	4,000,000	6 n	none
8 Am. Car and Foundry	1899	none	30,000,000	7 n	none
9 Am. Cement	1899	930,000	none	none	46,500
10 Am. Chicle	1899	none	3,000,000	6 c	none
11 Am. Hide and Leather	1899	8,445,000	13,000,000	7 c	506,700
12 Am. Pneu. Tube Service	1899	none	5,000,000	6 n	none
13 Am. Window Glass	1899	none	4,000,000	7 c	none
14 Am. Woolen	1899	none	16,000,000	7 c	none
15 Am. Writing Paper	1899	17,000,000	12,500,000	7 c	850,000
16 Inter. Steam Pump	1899	none	8,850,000	6 c	none
17 Natl. Enam. and Stamp	1899	none	7,375,000	7 c	none
18 Natl. Salt	1899	none	5,000,000	7 c	none
19 N. E. Cotton Yarn	1899	5,591,000	5,000,000	7 c	279,553
20 Pittsburgh Coal	1899	none	32,000,000	7 c	none
21 Pressed Steel Car	1899	none	12,500,000	7 c	none
22 Republic Iron and Steel	1899	none	25,000,000	7 c	none
23 Rubber Goods Mfg.	1899	none	6,196,000	7 c	none
24 Sloss-Sheffield	1899	3,835,000	6,700,000	7 n	202,575
25 Univ. Bag and Paper	1899	none	11,000,000	7 c	none
26 Crucible Steel	1900	none	25,000,000	7 c	none
27 Standard Milling	1900	5,750,000	6,900,000	6 n	287,500
28 Allis Chalmers	1901	none	25,000,000	7 c	none
29 Am. Locomotive	1901	none	25,000,000	7 c	none
30 Quaker Oats	1901	1,600,000	7,500,000	6 c	80,000
31 U. S. Steel	1901	304,000,000	425,000,000	7 c	15,200,000
32 Harbison Walker Refractories	1902	3,500,000	8,000,000	6 c	175,000
33 Natl. Candy	1902	none	2,200,000	7 c	none
34 Inter. Merc. Marine	1902	68,000,000	54,600,000	6 n	3,140,000
35 United Box Board and Paper	1902	3,873,000	14,948,900	7 c	197,380

[1] Under table of preferred stock dividend "c" denotes cumulative dividends and "n" denotes noncumulative dividends.

Table 1 • **Fundamental Data** (*continued*)

Contingent charges (preferred dividends)	Previous earnings	Estimated earnings	Fixed and contingent charges	First year	Tenth year	Average ten years
$4,982,184	$4,800,000[1a]	$4,900,000[1b]	$5,342,584	$1,340,494[1c]	$4,784,997	$3,753,839[1d]
175,000	1,300,000[2a]	2,300,000[2b]	175,000	225,000[2c]	−157,503	393,117[2d]
1,172,500	1,094,374[3a]	1,800,000[3b]	1,172,000	−1,083,858[3c]	166,538	113,200[3d]
262,500	428,848[4a]	828,848[4b]	382,500	457,523	573,557	497,375
1,437,149	4,100,000[5a]	5,600,000[5b]	1,959,089	2,845,035	1,635,918	2,393,172
1,020,000	1,419,879[6a]	2,040,000[6b]	1,200,000	1,615,594[6c]	2,394,498	1,680,238
240,000	428,057[7a]	1,248,000[7b]	240,000	240,359[7c]	1,470,611	612,313
2,100,000	2,900,000[8a]	4,000,000[8b]	2,100,000	4,915,671[8c]	2,895,831	5,050,963
none	323,000[9a]	350,000[9b]	46,500	250,619[9c]	152,352	278,480
180,000	560,000[10a]	540,000[10b]	180,000	688,510[10c]	1,530,000	1,199,896
910,000	1,585,748[11a]	2,750,000[11b]	1,416,700	926,582[11c]	2,085,996	1,024,938[11d]
300,000	281,449[12a]	381,449[12b]	300,000	288,616	144,959	162,316
280,000	1,466,182[13a]	2,500,000[13b]	280,000	373,357	−556,718[13d]	−13,638[13d]
1,120,000	2,593,000[14a]	3,000,000[14b]	1,120,000	3,287,006	4,179,522	2,808,783
875,000	1,250,620[15a]	2,200,000[15b]	1,725,000	837,997[15c]	1,410,841	1,172,863
531,000	1,317,791[16a]	2,500,000[16b]	531,000	1,813,907	1,447,653	1,671,440
516,250	1,073,000[17a]	1,589,250[17b]	516,250	1,442,589[17c]	924,596	1,198,555
350,000	450,000[18a]	600,000[18b]	350,000	478,145	547,198	680,336
350,000	1,106,197[19a]	1,600,000[19b]	629,550	1,086,500[19c]	355,602	721,595[19d]
2,240,000	4,078,274[20a]	5,414,089[20b]	2,240,000	3,181,568[20c]	1,822,557	3,388,080
875,000	1,500,000[21a]	3,000,000[21b]	875,000	2,237,000	155,478	1,875,849
2,750,000	2,679,000[22a]	3,445,000[22b]	1,750,000	3,643,729	1,629,346	2,013,055
433,762	1,177,228[23a]	1,200,000[23b]	433,762	629,821[23c]	2,369,972	1,076,308
469,000	1,355,000[24a]	2,380,000[24b]	671,575	1,100,424[24c]	1,336,947	1,237,965
770,000	1,226,000[25a]	1,562,000[25b]	770,000	1,494,169	956,920	964,540
1,750,000	4,000,000[26a]	4,000,000[26b]	1,750,000	3,250,429[26c]	3,523,402	1,876,704
345,000	922,873[27a]	1,172,873[27b]	632,500	605,948[27c]	766,737	660,006
1,750,000	1,137,500[28a]	3,290,000[28b]	1,750,000	1,442,260	−18,600[28d]	707,945
1,750,000	3,000,000[29a]	3,600,000[29b]	1,750,000	3,107,177	4,122,870	4,446,091
450,000	639,248[30a]	2,000,000[30b]	530,000	540,745	1,780,095	1,052,579
29,750,000	108,000,000[31a]	100,000,000[31b]	44,950,000	98,551,542[31c]	107,830,000[31d]	92,931,854[31d]
480,000	806,572[32a]	1,116,000[32b]	655,000	1,036,489[32c]	1,325,549	1,401,543
154,000	335,000[33a]	465,277[33b]	154,000	175,655[33c]	168,255	247,556
3,276,000	6,107,675[34a]	16,100,000[34b]	6,416,000	4,000,522[34d]	3,941,747[34d]	3,439,514[34d]
1,046,423	1,667,000[35a]	1,872,000[35b]	1,243,803	279,710[35c]	182,874	282,282

Notes for Table 1

[1a] Prospectus of company. See Dewing, A. S., *Corporate Promotions and Reorganizations*, p. 21.

[1b] This is one of the three cases in which the estimate of earnings was not obtained from printed sources. One of the tanners stated in conversation that the "net saving would be at least $300,000, which would result in increased profits." On this basis the estimated earnings were obtained by adding the "previous earnings" to $100,000. Unquestionably the tanners believed that the profits would be vastly larger. They planned numerous "economies," and laid great stress in their conversations with bankers upon the increased earnings following the suspension of competition. The figure used here is, therefore, very much less than that confidently expected by the promotors. See also ibid., p. 21.

[1c] This represents the first full year. 60 *Commercial and Financial Chronicle* 391. (The references to this periodical will be abbreviated hereafter, Chron.)

[1d] In computing the average, the published earnings for the first 20 months were reduced to a 12-month basis. This gave the constructive earnings of the first year as $472,053. This reconstruction was necessitated by the change in the corporation's fiscal year. See table of earnings, Dewing, *Corporate Promotions and Organizations*, p. 22, footnote 3.

[2a] Average of the preceding five years, 65 Chron. 619.

[2b] Ibid.

[2c] Dewing, *Corporate Promotions and Reorganizations*, p. 294, footnote 1.

[2d] Earnings for third year, adjusted owing to change in fiscal year.

[3a] Average of preceding four years, 67 Chron. 1206.

[3b] Estimate of "$1,800,000 to $2,000,000." Ibid.

(Notes for Table 1, con't)

[3c] Computed by adding five-twelfths of the profits of 1900 to the deficit for the 7 months of 1899 during which company operated.

[3d] From 1902 to 1909 the company published no reports. The probable profits have been constructed from the surplus as at the beginning and end of the period, with adjustments for capital expenditures during the intervening period.

[4a] 66 Chron. 1003.

[4b] Ibid.

[5a] 67 Chron. 177.

[5b] 13 U. S. Ind. Com. of 1901, 409.

[6a] Average preceding five years, 68 Chron. 974.

[6b] This is the second of the three cases in which the estimate of earnings is not obtained from printed sources. It is based on two statements, both agreeing that the company would be able to earn at least 6 per cent on its common stock. One of these statements was made by a prominent manufacturer to a small independent who was asked to enter the consolidation. One other was made to a banker by a man close to the promotion.

[6c] Adjusted to 12 months from published statement of 14 months.

[7a] Average preceding two years, 68 Chron. 280.

[7b] Ibid.

[7c] Adjusted to 12 months from published statement of 21 months.

[8a] 68 Chron. 1029.

[8b] 68 Chron. 280.

[8c] Adjusted to 12 months from published statement of 14 months.

[9a] 69 Chron. 1249.

[9b] Ibid.

[9c] Adjusted to 12 months from published statement of 16 months.

[10a] 68 Chron. 1021.

[10b] Ibid.

[10c] From published statements the earnings for the first period of 13 months were constructed. This figure was then adjusted to a 12-month basis.

[11a] 70 Chron. 77.

[11b] 69 Chron. 646. More extravagant estimates were made by the promotor. One Thomas J. Ryan, in Shoe and Leather Reporter, May 18, 1899, estimated "economies of consolidation" at $4,000,000; in ibid., May 24, 1899, $5,3000,000 to $6,9000,000 or "7% on the preferred and from 8% to 12% on the common stock."

[11c] Adjusted to 12 months from published statement of 9 months.

[11d] The sinking fund on the bonds was deducted, as was not done in other cases, from the net earnings because the management and its auditors specifically state that the sinking fund on the bonds was a charge in lieu of depreciation.

[12a] Given at $300,000 in 68 Chron. 1130. Figure stated above taken from banker's circular, at time of promotion.

[12b] Banker's circular at time of promotion.

[13a] Average for preceding three years, 69 Chron. 745.

[13b] 69 Chron. 745.

[13d] The company published no reports from 1902 to 1909, due probably to the excessive losses it was enduring. On September 1, 1902, the report showed an apparent surplus of $819,862. On September 1, 1909, the report showed an apparent deficit of $3,067,165. The above average is based on the assumption that the net loss of $3,897,027 during the intervening seven years can be prorated—$556,718 average loss per year.

[14a] 68 Chron. 472.

[14b] This is the third of the three cases in which the estimate of earnings is not obtained from printed sources. The bankers who were interested in the underwriting of the securities were assured by the mill operators that the company would earn "6% on its common stock" and would probably do better. This estimate is, therefore, computed as the preferred dividend of 7 per cent together with a common dividend of 6 per cent.

[15a] Average for the preceding ten years, 69 Chron. 128.

[15b] 69 Chron. 128.

[15c] Adjusted to 12 months from published statement of 17 months.

[16a] 1900 Moody 617.

[16b] 68 Chron. 723.

[17a] 68 Chron. 187.

[17b] Ibid.

[17c] Adjusted to 12 months from published statement of 11 months.

[18a] 68 Chron. 524.

[18b] Ibid.

[19a] 69 Chron. 81; Dewing, Corporate Promotions and Organizations, p. 316.

[19b] Ibid.

[19c] Adjusted to 12 months from published statement of $11\frac{1}{2}$ months.

[19d] Computed from successive published balance sheets. Sinking fund on bonds deducted from net earnings as company considered such charges were made in lieu of depreciation.

[20a] 69 Chron. 442.

[20b] Ibid.

[20c] Adjusted to 12 months from published statement of 16 months.

[21a] 68 Chron. 131.

[21b] Ibid.

[22a] 68 Chron. 674.

[22b] Ibid

[23a] 68 Chron. 872.

[23b] Ibid.

(Notes for Table 1, con't)

[23c] Adjusted to 12 months from published earnings of 11 months.

[24a] 69 Chron. 286.

[24b] 8 Ind. Com. Rep. of 1901, 55.

[24c] 72 Chron. 774.

[25a] 68 Chron. 333.

[25b] Ibid.

[26a] 73 Chron. 841.

[26b] 71 Chron. 32. "Confidently expected earnings will be largely increased." This was the current report in the Pittsburgh district. One rumor stated that the earnings would be "twice as great." Nevertheless, in the absence of direct evidence for a larger estimate, the estimated earnings were considered the same as the previous earnings.

[26c] Adjusted to 12 months from published earnings of 13 months.

[27a] 68 Chron. 929.

[27b] Ibid.

[27c] 75 Chron. 1252. Reference inexact "12 to 14 mos." Computed on average of 13 months and reduced to 12 months basis.

[28a] 72 Chron. 874.

[28b] 72 Chron. 937.

[28d] Boston News Bureau, October 12, 1911—after allowing for depreciation.

[29a] 72 Chron. 1036.

[29b] Boston News Bureau, November 14, 1901.

[30a] 68 Chron. 329.

[30b] Ibid.

[31a] Wilgus, United States Steel Corp., p. 33.

[31b] 72 Chron. 441.

[31c] Adjusted to 12 months from published earnings of 9 months.

[31d] The computation of the United States Steel Corporation's "net earnings" has always presented considerable difficulties owing to the management's avowed purpose of charging capital betterments to earnings. Wall Street has interpreted this policy as "squeezing out the water." Expedient though it may be from the standpoint of business, it is disconcerting to the statistician, especially in an inquiry like the present, where uniformity in methods of accounting is a prerequisite to the value of any of the conclusions. In this study the net earnings of the United States Steel Corporation were computed as the sum of: surplus for the year, sinking fund on subsidiary and parent bonds and interest of United States Steel Company bonds, expenditures made for additional property, preferred and common stock dividends.

[32a] 74 Chron. 1359.

[32b] Ibid.

[32c] Adjusted to 12 months from published earnings of 15 months.

[33a] Average of three years, 75 Chron. 983.

[33b] Estimate computed from estimated capacity (75 Chron. 983) reduced to current basis of profit.

[33c] Adjusted to 12 months from published earnings of 15 months.

[34a] 76 Chron. 975. In 79 Chron. 157, it is stated that the average for the preceding 5 years, before depreciation, was $6,519,017. Also, by dead reckoning, the estimated earnings would appear to be $9,500,000, provided tonnage of 1903 had been in service.

[34b] Ripley, W. Z., Trusts, Pools, and Corporations, p. 107.

[34d] These are based on the published earnings. Later the management admitted that the depreciation reserves had been inadequate and charged off a lump sum from the excessive earnings of the Great War. An attempt was made in another connection to determine the earnings more accurately by prorating the depreciation. The largest published earnings, however, were used here so as to give the corporation the benefit of a possible doubt. See Dewing, Financial Policy of Corporations, vol. 4, p. 49.

[35a] Average of preceding three years, 75 Chron. 247.

[35b] 75 Chron. 1044.

[35c] Adjusted to 12 months from published earnings of 5 months 6 days.

Table 2 • Earnings of the Separate Plants Before Consolidation Compared with Earnings after Consolidation

Table 3 • Promotors' Estimates of Earnings Compared with Previous and Later Earnings

	Previous to estimated earnings	Previous to sum of fixed and contingent	Previous to first year	Previous to tenth year	Previous to ten year average	Estimated to previous	Estimated to sum of fixed and contingent	Estimated to first year	Estimated to tenth year	Estimated to ten year average
1	98.0	90.0	large	100.3	128.0	102.1	91.6	large	102.4	132.4
2	56.5	743.1	577.5	large	330.8	177.0	1314.0	1022.2	large	585.0
3	60.8	93.3	large	658.0	966.0	164.5	153.3	large	108.2	1589.0
4	51.7	111.8	93.9	74.9	86.2	193.2	216.5	181.1	144.5	166.7
5	73.3	209.3	144.1	250.9	171.5	136.6	285.9	196.8	342.5	234.1
6	69.6	118.2	87.8	59.3	84.5	143.7	170.0	126.3	85.2	121.5
7	34.3	178.4	178.6	29.1	70.0	291.0	520.0	519.6	84.8	203.9
8	72.6	138.1	58.9	100.1	58.5	137.9	190.5	82.4	138.1	79.2
9	92.3	69.0	128.8	212.2	115.9	108.6	752.9	139.6	229.8	125.6
10	105.7	311.0	81.4	36.6	46.7	96.5	300.0	78.4	35.3	45.0
11	57.7	112.0	171.2	75.9	154.8	173.5	194.1	297.0	131.8	268.5
12	73.8	93.7	98.0	194.2	173.1	135.6	127.2	132.1	263.2	235.0
13	58.7	523.6	393.1	large	large	171.0	893.5	669.1	large	large
14	86.4	231.2	78.9	62.0	92.4	115.7	267.9	91.3	71.7	107.1
15	56.9	72.5	149.5	88.7	106.6	175.9	127.5	262.9	155.9	188.7
16	52.7	248.0	72.6	91.1	78.7	190.0	471.6	137.8	172.9	149.5
17	67.5	208.1	74.4	116.2	89.6	148.0	307.5	110.1	172.0	132.5
18	75.0	128.6	93.1	82.2	66.1	133.5	171.5	125.6	109.6	88.3
19	69.1	176.0	101.8	311.8	153.5	144.7	254.2	147.2	451.1	222.0
20	75.3	182.0	128.1	223.9	120.4	132.9	241.9	170.2	297.6	159.9
21	50.0	171.3	67.1	9.6	79.8	200.0	343.0	134.4	1930.5	160.1
22	74.8	147.5	70.7	158.3	128.1	128.7	197.1	94.6	211.7	171.2
23	98.3	272.0	187.1	49.7	109.3	102.1	277.0	190.8	50.7	111.5
24	56.9	201.9	123.1	101.3	109.5	175.5	354.5	216.3	178.1	192.5
25	78.5	159.3	82.2	129.5	128.5	127.5	202.9	104.5	165.2	162.1
26	100.0	228.5	123.0	113.4	213.0	100.0	228.3	123.0	113.5	213.2
27	78.6	146.1	152.2	120.4	139.6	127.2	185.4	193.5	152.9	177.7
28	34.6	64.9	78.8	large	160.6	289.0	188.1	227.9	large	464.9
29	83.3	171.6	96.5	72.8	67.5	120.0	205.9	115.8	87.3	81.0
30	32.0	120.8	118.2	35.9	60.8	312.9	377.6	370.0	112.2	189.9
31	108.0	240.3	109.6	100.1	116.2	92.6	222.5	102.9	92.7	107.8
32	72.7	123.0	77.8	60.8	57.5	138.5	170.5	108.6	84.2	79.8
33	72.0	218.5	191.0	199.1	135.4	138.9	302.2	265.2	277.0	188.4
34	37.9	95.3	152.6	154.9	177.1	263.9	251.1	402.7	408.0	467.0
35	89.0	134.1	596.0	912.5	588.5	112.4	150.3	669.2	102.3	662.0
Median	72.6	171.3	118.2	101.3	116.2	138.5	228.3	147.2	165.2	171.2
Average between quartiles	70.1	166.8	118.5	122.4	118.5	145.0	239.4	186.1	189.2	174.8

Table 4 • Comparison of the Sums of the Fixed and Contingent Charges, with the Previous, the Estimated and the Later Earnings

Table 5. Comparison of the Earnings of the First Year with the Previous Estimated and Later Earnings

	Sum of fixed and contingent to previous	Sum of fixed and contingent to estimated	Sum of fixed and contingent to first year	Sum of fixed and contingent to tenth year	Sum of fixed and contingent to ten year average	First year to previous earnings	First year to estimated earnings	First year to sum of fixed and contingent charges	First year to tenth-year earnings	First year to ten-year average
1	111.2	109.0	large	111.6	142.4	small	small	smal.	small	small
2	13.5	7.6	77.7	large	44.5	16.3	9.8	128.5	large	57.2
3	107.1	65.2	none	732.5	1039.0	small	small	small	small	small
4	89.8	46.4	84.3	67.2	77.3	106.9	55.2	119.5	79.8	92.0
5	47.8	35.0	68.8	119.7	83.9	69.5	50.8	145.2	174.1	119.0
6	84.8	58.9	74.6	50.3	71.6	113.9	79.2	134.7	67.5	96.2
7	56.0	19.2	99.9	16.3	39.2	56.2	19.3	100.3	16.4	39.4
8	72.4	52.5	42.7	72.5	41.5	169.6	122.9	234.2	169.8	97.5
9	14.4	13.3	18.6	30.5	16.7	77.7	71.7	539.0	164.6	90.0
10	32.1	33.3	26.1	11.8	15.0	121.9	127.4	382.5	45.0	57.4
11	89.2	51.5	152.9	68.7	138.3	58.4	33.7	65.4	44.4	90.4
12	106.6	78.7	104.7	207.1	184.7	102.6	75.5	96.3	199.2	177.9
13	19.1	11.2	75.1	large	large	25.5	14.9	133.5	small	small
14	43.2	37.3	34.1	26.8	39.9	126.9	109.6	298.8	78.7	117.1
15	138.0	78.3	205.9	122,1	147.1	67.1	38.1	48.6	59.4	71.4
16	40.3	21.2	29.3	36.7	31.8	137.7	72.6	361.1	125.4	108.5
17	48.0	32.4	35.7	55.8	43.1	134.3	90.8	279.8	156.2	120.4
18	77.8	58.3	73.2	64.0	51.4	106.2	79.7	136.6	87.5	70.3
19	56.8	39.4	57.9	177.3	87.3	98.4	68.0	172.9	306.5	150.7
20	54.8	41.3	70.3	122.8	66.1	78.0	58.8	142.0	174.6	93.9
21	58.3	29.2	39.1	563.0	46.7	149.0	74.5	255.7	1437.0	119.1
22	65.3	50.8	48.0	107.4	86.9	136.2	105.8	207.4	22.9	181.2
23	36.8	36.1	68.9	18.3	40.3	53.4	52.5	145.0	26.6	58.4
24	45.5	25.9	56.0	50.3	54.3	81.3	46.3	164.1	82.3	89.0
25	62.8	49.2	51.5	80.5	79.8	121.8	95.7	194.1	156.2	155.0
26	43.8	43.8	53.8	49.7	93.2	81.3	81.3	185.9	92.2	173.5
27	68.5	53.9	104.4	82.5	95.8	65.8	51.7	95.8	79.1	91.9
28	153.9	53.2	121.1	large	247.1	126.8	43.8	82.4	large	203.8
29	58.3	48.6	56.3	42.4	39.4	103.6	86.3	177.7	75.3	69.9
30	82.9	26.5	98.1	29.6	50.3	84.7	27.1	102.2	30.4	51.5
31	41.6	45.0	45.7	41.7	48.4	91.1	98.6	219.1	91.3	106.1
32	81.3	58.7	63.2	49.4	46.7	128.6	92.8	158.3	78.2	73.9
33	45.9	33.1	87.7	91.5	62.2	52.4	37.8	114.0	104.5	71.0
34	105.0	39.9	160.4	162.8	186.5	65.6	24.8	62.4	101.5	116.5
35	74.6	66.3	444.0	690.0	439.2	16.7	14.9	22.4	152.2	98.7
Median	58.3	43.8	70.3	72.5	71.6	84.7	58.8	142.0	91.3	91.9
Average between quartiles	62.7	43.4	72.3	72.1	90.1	89.4	60.7	145.1	107.8	89.6

I. Previous Earnings before Consolidation Compared with the Actual Earnings Realized

From Table 2 it will be observed that the aggregate earnings of the separate competing establishments prior to consolidation were seven-tenths of the earnings estimated to follow consolidation. Roughly, the promotors of the consolidations believed that the mere act of combination would increase the earnings by about a half. But in actual results the earnings before the consolidation were nearly a fifth *greater* (18%) than the earnings of the first year after consolidation. (See also Table 5.) The promotors expected the earnings to be a half greater than the aggregate of the competing plants; instead they were about a fifth less. Nor were the sustained earnings an improvement, for the earnings before the consolidation were between a fifth and a sixth greater than the average for the ten years following the consolidation. In brief, the earnings of the separate plants before consolidation were greater than the earnings of the same plants after consolidation.

II. Estimated Earnings at Time of Consolidation Compared with the Actual Earnings Realized (See Tables 3 and 4)

The estimated probable earnings made by the promotors at the time the trusts were organized can be reached by two lines of evidence—the prophecies of the promotors themselves and the patterns according to which they cut the financial plans of the embryo corporations. The former we can consider the direct line of evidence, the latter the indirect line.

When we compare the estimates of the promotors covering the earnings of the new corporations with the earnings actually realized, some striking results are apparent. See Table 3.

So confident were the promotors and bankers of the success of the trusts that they estimated the earnings resulting from consolidation to be a little over a third greater than the earnings of the separate plants before consolidation. On the basis of this estimate they considered themselves safe in making the sum of the fixed charges on the bonds and the dividends on the preferred stock to be less than a half of the estimated earnings. This conservative procedure would have worked well in practice, provided the actual earnings following consolidation had even approximated the estimates made by the promotors. But they did not. The estimated earnings were half again as large as the actual earnings of the first year after the union, and nearly twice as great (175%) as the average earnings during the ten-year period following consolidation. The divergence between the estimates and the actual results is even more apparent when we observe that in only four out of the thirty-five cases did the earnings during the year following consolidation equal or exceed the estimates made by the promotors; and in only five cases—one-seventh of the total—did the average earnings for the ten-year period following consolidation equal or exceed the estimates made by the promotors and bankers at the time the trust was organized.

This conclusion is indirectly shown by the relative load of fixed charges and contingent preferred stock dividends placed upon the trusts at the time of consolidation. It is a well known and thoroughly established principle of financial practice that the fixed interest charges and contingent preferred stock dividends of industrial or manufacturing corporations should not be more than half the net earnings, after reasonable, but not extraordinary, allowances have been made for depreciation and obsolescence. In the case of these industrial combinations it amounted to nearly three-fourths of the net earnings of the first year and the tenth year, and nine-tenths (90% average between quartiles) of the average earnings of the ten-year period after consolidation. See Table 4.

III. Comparison of the Earnings of Industrial Consolidations Immediately After Consolidation with Later Earnings

The ratios given in Table 5 are intended to compare the earnings of each industrial consolidation during the first full year of its existence with the earnings before consolidation and with the earnings after the trust has been fully established.

The later earnings, however, should be subject to some adjustment. In almost every case new capital was invested by the managers of the consolidation in betterments and improved equipment, not properly chargeable to depreciation and reasonable obsolescence. In some cases, like the acquisition of the Tennessee Coal and Iron Company by the United States Steel or of the Guggenheim plants by the International Steam Pump, whole units were added to the aggregate of property already owned by the trust at the time of its organization. The betterments and the new plants added materially to the net earnings of the combination, or should have done so provided the promise of increased earnings through enlarged scale of production was fulfilled. Strict accounting would require that the average net earnings for the ten-year period and the net earnings for the tenth year should be reduced by amounts corresponding to the presumptive earnings of the added capital before these earnings were compared with the earlier earnings. How-ever, such adjustments to the reported net earnings because of actual additions to property would be very difficult to make and controversial at best. Accordingly no such adjustments were made, so that the figures for the ten-year average and of the tenth-year earnings are greater than those of the groups of plants entering the consolidation or contributing to the earnings of the first year.

The representative earnings of consolidation during the first year were less, by about a tenth, than the average earnings during the ten-year period. The ten-year period began, in twenty cases out of the thirty-five, in 1900; it included, therefore, quite as many years of marked business activity as of marked business depression. The earnings of the first year after consolidation were greater—by a little less than a tenth (7%)—than the earnings of the tenth year. In other words, after sufficient time had elapsed to permit the consolidation to perfect its organization, to reconstruct its plants and to effect all the anticipated economies of combination and large-scale production, and after considerable sums of new money had been invested in betterments and new plants, the earnings gradually diminished until they were no more, perhaps a little less, than during the first year of consolidation. And the first-year earnings, as has been shown already, were less than the earnings of the separate plants before consolidation.

16. Concentration and Profits: Does Concentration Matter?

YALE BROZEN

In the post-World War II period, the economics profession made a 180° turn from its pre-Great Depression position in its view of concentration. In the late nineteenth and early twentieth century, the prevailing view seems to have been that even with only a few firms in an industry, price competition would be persistent and collusion difficult. There was little concern with any probability of successful collusion (shared monopoly or oligopoly) in industries where four firms had, say, 70 per cent or more of an industry's capacity or sales. Three or four firms was felt to be sufficient for competitive behavior.[1] What concern was expressed was in terms of "trusts" combining most of an industry's capacity under a single management.

Even where more than 70 per cent of an industry's capacity had been combined to form a *single* firm, no fear was felt by many economists that a monopoly result would ensue.[2] (Some expressed approval of such combinations in terms of the economies that would be realized.)[3] J. B. Clark, for example, pointed to the power of potential competition to produce the same competitive result as a larger number of firms or non-colluding behavior of a few saying

> Let any combination of producers raise the prices beyond a certain limit, and it will encounter this difficulty. The new mills that will spring into existence will break down prices; and the fear of these new mills, without their actual coming, is often enough to keep prices from rising to an extortionate height. The mill that has never been built is already a power in the market: for it will surely be built under certain conditions, the effect of this certainty is to keep prices down.[4]

Even Professor Jones, who believed in the necessity of active government intervention to break up trusts because they would seek to maintain unfairly high prices, provides evidence of the failure of the trusts to accomplish their objective. He lists a number which failed financially and were voluntarily dissolved. In addition, he mentions others which were unable to keep the dominant position required to maintain consumers, rather than that of the producers. Has every consumer a choice of efficient and independent producers to buy from? If so, there is no monopoly, even if one combination should control three quarters of the output." J. B. Clark and J. M. Clark, *The Control of Trusts* 184-5 (1912).

This article will appear in a forthcoming issue of *The Antitrust Bulletin*, Volume XIX (1974). © 1974 by Federal Legal Publications, Inc. 95 Morton Street, New York, N.Y.

[1] Eliot Jones, for example, remarks that, "In 1904 there were some seventy-five independent refiners all told. . . . Had the total independent output been concentrated in a few large refineries, competition with the Standard Oil Company would have been much more vigorous and successful." *The Trust Problem in the United States* 59 (1929). George Stigler has pointed out that, "When the Sherman Act . . . was passed in 1890, most economists and most non-economists believed that an industry with a modest number of firms could be tolerably competitive." "The Changing Problem of Oligopoly," Proceedings of the Mont Pelerin Society 3 (1966).

[2] "The key to the situation is the position of the

[3] H. R. Seager, *Introduction to Economics* 150 (1905); C. J. Bullock, *Introduction to the Study of Economics* 178 (1908); F. W. Taussig, *Principles of Economics* i, 53–55 (1915); E. R. A. Seligman, *Principles of Economics* 345 (1921).

[4] J. B. Clark, *The Control of Trusts* 13 (1901).

prices above the competitive level when they attempted to do so.[5]

Professor A. S. Dewing undertook an empirical analysis to determine whether or not any advantages accrued to "large scale enterprises brought about through combination—the so-called 'trusts'"[6] Choosing "a random selection of thirty-five industrial combinations" where "at least five separate, independent and competing plants" were merged, he examined profits of the independent companies in the year preceding consolidation. These he compared with the profits in the year following consolidation, in the tenth year following consolidation, and average profits in the ten years following. He found no evidence showing, on the average, that combinations of 40 to 95 per cent of an industry's capacity produced any enhancement of profits either through economies of scale or combination or through monopoly.

> Roughly, the promoters of the consolidations believed that the mere act of combination would increase the earnings by about a half. But in actual results the earnings before the consolidation were nearly a fifth *greater* (18%) than the earnings of the first year after consolidation. The promoters expected the earnings to be a half greater than the aggregate of the competing plants; instead they were about a sixth less. Nor were the sustained earnings an improvement, for the earnings before the consolidation were between a fifth and a sixth greater than the average for the ten years following the consolidation. In brief, the earnings of the separate plants before consolidation were greater than the earnings of the same plants after consolidation.[7]

As late as the 1930's, after the discussion of administered (rigid) prices in con-

centrated industries had begun, Professor Henry Simons said

> I am, indeed, not much distressed about private monopoly power. . . . Serious exploitation could be prevented by suppression of lawless violence. . . . The ways of competition are devious, and its vengeance—government intervention apart—will generally be adequate and admirable.[8]

In the post World War II era, in contrast to this earlier view, "most practitioners assumed that successful (tacit or explicit) collusion [among oligopolists] would approach joint maximization and that the ability to collude increases with concentration."[9] A major exception to this post World War II view appeared in a book by Paul MacAvoy, describing competition among the few in transportation "between the Mississippi River Valley and the East Coast."[10]

Discussing the observed behavior of these few firms, MacAvoy found that collusion was not effective despite being *explicitly* agreed upon among them. He observes that ". . . there seems to have been persistent 'cheating' on the rates set in conference, so that the level of rates declined markedly as one agreement after another broke down."[11] He goes on to point out that collusively determined rates became the actual rates only after governmental support was provided in 1887 under the Act to Regulate Interstate Commerce. As he says, "The effect of regulation seems to have

---

[5] Eliot Jones, *op. cit.* 538–540.

[6] A. S. Dewing, "A Statistical Test of the Success of Consolidations," 36 *Quarterly Journal of Economics* 84 (1921–22).

[7] *Id.* 90–91. Inasmuch as no failures were included in the thirty-five consolidations examined since only those with a ten year history of earnings were included in the sample, the decline in earnings is underestimated.

---

[8] Henry C. Simons, "The Requisites of Free Competition," 26 *American Economic Review,* Supplement 68 (1936). Simons spoke out strongly against concentration largely to offset the drive in government and the press at that time to force independent firms into cartels (as under NRA) and combinations. *Id.* 72.

[9] Leonard Weiss, "Quantitative Studies in Industrial Organization," in *Frontiers of Quantitative Economics* at 363, ed. M. D. Intriligator (1971).

[10] Paul W. MacAvoy, *The Economic Effects of Regulation* v (1965).

[11] *Id.* v.

been to establish the cartel rates as the actual rates." [12]

The question, "Why did economists' views shift from the earlier outlook to the opposite view characteristic of the post war period?", may well be raised. The answer appears to be that the data relating concentration and profits first provided by Bain and later by other students in industrial or-ganization convinced economists they had been wrong. The ground work for accept-ance had been laid by various discussions of administered pricing beginning in the thirties.[13]

This view that successful tacit or ex-plicit collusion was probable in concen-trated industries reached a culmination in the recommendation of the White House Antitrust Task Force that a deconcentration act be added to the antitrust arsenal.[14] The Task Force stated that there was some evi-dence for the view that underlay the recom-mendation, although it cited none. When the Staff Director of the Antitrust Task Force was asked for the evidence used, he referred to the articles by Bain, Mann, Stigler and others showing correlations be-tween concentration and profitability and to the price selected cost margin studies of Collins and Preston.[15]

The Task Force had stated that the evidence showed "a close association be-

tween high levels of concentration and per-sistently high rates of return." [16] None of the studies cited by the Staff Director, how-ever, had examined the *persistence* of high rates of return in concentrated industries. Each had provided a spot correlation show-ing a weak relationship between concentra-tion and accounting rates of return at a given time. None had looked at the profita-bility of the same industries at a later time to determine whether the above average rates of return in concentrated industries had persisted.

Since there was no evidence on persist-ence (or lack of persistence) of above aver-age ("high") rates of return in concentrated industries, I compiled data on accounting rates of return at a later time in the indus-tries used in the studies cited by the Task Force staff. For each of the samples of in-dustries used by Bain, Mann, and Stigler, rates of return in concentrated industries at a later time all turned out to be insignifi-cantly different from those in less concen-trated industries.[17]

The correlations between concentration and accounting profits, which were weak in the original studies, deteriorated to insig-nificance with the passage of time. In the seventeen Bain industries which were more than 60 per cent concentrated (four firm), the coefficient of determination dropped from 40 per cent for 1936–40 profitability on 1935 concentration ratios to a non-signifi-cant 16 per cent for 1953–57 profitability on 1954 concentration. It continued non-sig-nificant at 9 per cent for 1962–66 profita-bility on 1963 concentration. Similarly, Stigler's seventeen industries (eleven of which were in the Bain seventeen) showed a decline in the coefficient of determination from 34 per cent for 1953–57 profitability on 1954 concentration to a non-significant

---

[12] *Id.* v.

[13] *Industrial Prices and Their Relative Inflexibility,* Senate Document No. 13 (January 1935).

[14] White House Task Force on Antitrust Policy, Re-port 1 (in Trade Regulation Reports, supple-ment to no. 415, May 26, 1969) at I-8.

[15] Joe Bain, "Relation of Profit Rate to Industry Concentration: American Manufacturing, 1936–1940," 65 *Quarterly Journal of Economics* 293 (1951); H. Michael Mann, "Seller Concentra-tion, Barriers to Entry, and Rates of Return in Thirty Industries, 1950–1960," 48 *Review of Economics and Statistics* 296 (1966); George J. Stigler, "A Theory of Oligopoly," 72 *Journal of Political Economy* 44 (1964); Norman R. Collins and Lee Preston, *Concentration and Price-Cost Margins in Manufacturing Industries* (1968).

[16] White House Task Force on Antitrust Policy, Re-port 1 (in Trade Regulation Reports, supple-ment to no. 415, May 26, 1969) at I-8.

[17] Yale Brozen, "The Antitrust Task Force Decon-centration Recommendation," 13 *Journal of Law and Economics* 279 (1970).

seventeen per cent for 1962–66 profitability on 1963 concentration.[18]

The Task Force economists replied saying that the wrong industries had been selected.[19] They thoughtfully provided a list of the appropriate industries where concentration had been persistently high and said persistently high returns would be found in those industries. Examining rates of return for the industries they specified, it was found that rates of return were not even high (significantly above average), much less persistently high.[20]

There was still the puzzling fact that any correlation had been found between concentration and rates of return at any given time in some studies. Since there had been convergence on mean rates of return, it seemed that what had been found was a disequilibrium phenomenon. That is, concentrated industries happened to be earning above equilibrium rates of return which disappeared with the passage of time, as would occur under competitive circumstances. But why had a disproportionate number of concentrated industries been earning above equilibrium rates of return while a disproportionate number of less concentrated industries had been earning below equilibrium returns?

Since Bain had used only 42 out of 340 industries in the 1935 Census of Manufacturers to test for differences in rates of return between more and less concentrated industries, it was possible that his result was the consequence of the non-representativeness of his sample. Also, each of his industries was represented by only a few firms (three or more). Those he chose might have been non-representative of their industries.

In order to test whether Bain's 42 industries are representative, an enlarged sample of 98 industries (including Bain's 42) has been assembled (Appendix Tables 1 and 2). Industries for which less than three firms could be found were omitted (Appendix Tables 1A and 2A). In a few instances, rates of return computed by Bain have been recomputed using a larger number of firms (Appendix Table 3).

The results are strikingly opposed to those found in Bain's smaller sample. Where he found that the accounting profitability of concentrated industries was 4.4 percentage points *greater* than that of the less concentrated industries, the 98 industry sample shows profitability to be *less* (insignificantly) in the concentrated industries (Table 1). There is no greater proportion of concentrated industries at above equilibrium rates of return than of less concentrated industries (see Appendix). No disequilibrium explanation is needed to account for a higher average rate of return in concentrated industries. There is no higher average rate of return in concentrated industries.

There remain the Mann and Stigler findings using post World War II data to be explained. If competition is prevalent in concentrated industries, as is indicated by the convergence of rates of return on the average, why did Professors Mann and Stigler find a correlation at any given point in time between accounting profitability and concentration? Again, the non-representativeness of their small samples apparently accounts for their findings.

Professor James Ellert has examined the postwar data using larger samples of industries. He is unable to find a dichotomous relationship. Using 141 industries with 565 firms he finds no significant difference between more and less concentrated industries in any postwar period. What differences there are frequently have the wrong sign.[21]

---

[18] *Id.* at 287, 289.

[19] P. W. MacAvoy, J. W. McKie and L. Preston, "High and Stable Concentration Levels, Profitability, and Public Policy: A Response," 14 *Journal of Law and Economics* 493 (1971).

[20] Yale Brozen, "The Persistence of 'High Rates of Return' in High Stable Concentration Industries," 14 *Journal of Law and Economics* 501 (1971).

[21] James Ellert, "Industrial Concentration, Market Disequilibrium and the Convergence Pattern in Industry Rates of Return." Unpublished paper presented before the Industrial Organization Workshop, University of Chicago, January 27, 1972.

Table 1 • **Average of Industry Average Profit Rates Within Concentration Deciles**
(42 and 98 Industries)
1936–1940

Concentration Range Per cent of Value Product Supplied by Eight Firms (1935)	42 Industry Sample		98 Industries	
	Number of Industries	Average of Industry Profit Rates[a] 1936–1940	No. of Ind.	Profit rates[a] 1936–40
a	b	c	d	e
90–100	8	12.7%	14	10.0%
80–89.9	10	9.8	14	9.7
70–79.9	3	16.3	10	11.9
60–69.9	5	5.8	11	8.2
50–59.9	4	5.8	6	14.8
40–49.9	3	8.6	10	9.5
30–39.9	5	6.3	16	10.4
20–29.9	2	10.4	9	12.0
10–19.9	1	17.0	5	13.4
0–9.9	1	9.1	3	7.6
0–100	42	9.6	98	10.5
70–100	21	11.8	38	10.4
0–70	21	7.5	60	10.6
Difference		4.4		−0.2

Sources: Columns a, b, and c from Joe S. Bain, "Relation of Profit Rate to Industry Concentration: American Manufacturing, 1936–40," 65 Q. J. Econ. 313 (1951), as corrected in Corrigendum, 65 Q. J. Econ. 602 (1951). Columns d and e from Appendix Tables 1 and 2.
[a] Average of net profits after income taxes as percentage of net worth.

Professor Ellert also examined the high stable concentration group of industries. His findings agree with mine. That is, the rate of return in the high stable group is not high, much less persistently high.

A most interesting finding that emerged from a study of Bain's data was the relationship between rates of return in the Big 4 in the industries he selected for his book on Barriers to Competition[22] and other firms in those industries. Where the Big 4 showed higher accounting rates of return than smaller firms, they tended to grow more rapidly than their industries. Such behavior is that to be expected if the Big 4 behave competitively and we can take intra-industry comparisons of accounting rates of return seriously. Where the Big 4 showed lower accounting rates of return than smaller firms, they tended to grow less rap-

idly than their industries and concentration tended to decrease.[23]

This would seem to indicate that relatively high rates of return in manufacturing are manifestations of relative efficiency, if we can generalize from the inadequate sample of industries and firms provided by Bain. Resources flow from less efficient to more efficient firms. Manufacturing industry structure moves over time toward that dictated by an efficient allocation of resources. Persistent high concentration, where it is found, is a consequence of the economies of scale or the relative efficiency of specific managerial groups.[24] Mandatory

[22] J. S. Bain, Barriers to New Competition 195 (1956).

[23] Y. Brozen, "Concentration and Structural and Market Disequilibrium," 16 Antitrust Bulletin 241 (1971).

[24] Horizontal mergers of large groups of firms may overconcentrate an industry for efficient operation, as appears to have been the case in the turn of the century merger wave. However, such overconcentration appears to be a *temporary* phenomenon, judging by the experience of

deconcentration would cause a loss of efficiency with no gain in the competitiveness of the economy.[25]

Appendix

Bain's 42 Industry Sample and the 98 Industry Sample

Bain's sample contained fourteen concentrated industries (out of twenty-one) show-

these amalgamations. Of those merging a majority of the capacity in their industries, 40.4 per cent failed and 6.4 per cent went through voluntary financial reorganization. [Shaw Livermore "The Success of Industrial Mergers, 50 Quarterly Journal of Economics at 75 (1935–36).]

Of those which escaped this fate, most appear to have lost market share rather quickly. Of the few who lost market share slowly, some were broken up by dissolution decrees. However, even these were dropping in share before they were dissolved. American Tobacco, formed in 1890 with 91 per cent of the cigarette market, declined to 83.6 per cent in 1893. It acquired additional companies in 1894 and 1895 which brought it back to 85.6 per cent of the market, but then dropped to 80.9 per cent in 1896. Continued acquisitions brought it back to 93 per cent in 1899. This position faded rather quickly to 75.9 per cent in 1903. [U.S. Bureau of Corporations, *Report of the Commissioner on the Tobacco Industries* 329 (1909).] Similarly, Standard Oil's share of market declined from 88.15 per cent in 1899 to 83.38 per cent in 1904 to 67.10 per cent in 1909 despite acquisitions during this period [Ralph W. & Muriel E. Hidy, *Pioneering in Big Business* (1955) for data on Standard's crude runs to stills. *U.S. Census of Manufactures, 1919,* 757, cited in H. F. Williamson, R. L. Andreano, A. R. Daum, and G. C. Klose, *The American Petroleum Industry* 111 (1963) for data on U.S. crude runs to stills].

[25] Richard Posner indicates that limits on market share above which mandatory deconcentration would be applied would result in *less* competitive behavior. "The threat of dissolution may . . . have a serious disincentive effect. Firms may hold back from expanding sales to the point at which they would become subject to dissolution under the statute, even if they are more efficient than their competitors." "Oligopoly and the Antitrust Laws: A Suggested Approach." 21 *Stanford Law Review* 1562 (1969).

ing an accounting return greater than the sample average. The majority (67 per cent) of his concentrated industries were earning above equilibrium (sample average) rates of return (if we can assume that accounting biases did not differentially affect rates of return). The ninety-eight industry sample contains seventeen concentrated industries (out of thirty-eight) showing an accounting rate of return greater than the sample average (Appendix Table 1). In contrast to Bain's 67 per cent, only 45 per cent of the concentrated industries in the enlarged sample earned above equilibrium (sample average) rates of return. This is in the range we can expect by chance. It is the same proportion (43 per cent) as that found in the less concentrated portion of the ninety-eight industry sample (Appendix Table 2). In Bain's sample of less concentrated industries, only three (14 per cent) earned above sample average rates of return.

In the ninety-eight industry sample, there is not a disproportionate number of concentrated industries earning more than the sample average. Neither is there a disproportionate number of less concentrated industries earning less than the sample average. There are no differences to explain. The distribution is about as might be expected under competitive circumstances, confirming the finding that the behavior of rates of return in Bain's sample of industries over time indicates competitive circumstances in both concentrated and less concentrated industries.

Bain warned that his forty-two industry sample might not be representative. He discussed thirty-four industries he had excluded from his sample because data were available for only one or two firms in the thirty-four. He pointed out that, "Averages of industry profit rates above and below the 70 per cent concentration line in these thirty-four industries were 9.1 and 10.5 per cent respectively," [26] the reverse of the relationship in his forty-two industry sample.

In assembling the ninety-eight industry sample (in which no difference was found

[26] J. S. Bain, *supra* note 15, at 315, n. 8.

Appendix Table 1 • **Concentrated Industries***

Census No.[a]	Industry	Concentration ratio (1935)[b]		Profit rate (per cent of book net worth)[c] 1936–40
		4 firm	*8 firm*	
1406	Locomotives	D	D	1.7(3)
222	Linoleum	81.5	100.0	*8.4*(4, 5)
1215	Sm. & ref. copper	82.1	D	6.9(6)
1652	Cigarettes	89.7	99.4	14.4(7)
1314	Typewriters	(91.2)	99.3	*15.0*(4)
108	Chewing gum	92.0	97.3	16.9(3)
113	Corn prods.	79.2	95.0	*9.2*(4)
1408	Motor vehicles	87.3	94.2	16.3(17, 22)
1106	Firearms	81.9	92.4	9.0(4)
606	Carbon black	81.0	92.1	12.7(4)
312	Matches	70.3	91.3	4.8(4, 9)
803	Rubber tires	80.9	90.4	*8.0*(9, 11)
1312	Sewing mach.	78.9	90.4	7.2(3, 8)
629	Rayon	74.3	90.2	*9.0*(8, 9)
1301	Agricult. implem.	72.4	87.7	9.1(9, 10)
610	Compressed gases	79.2	87.0	13.9(4)
1022	Gypsum prods.	76.1	86.4	10.1(3)
120	Shortening, cook. & salad oil	69.0	85.9	6.0(3)
1123	Tin cans	80.8	85.6	9.1(4, 5)
636	Photo. app. & mat.	77.9	84.9	12.9(2, 4)
1647	Tobacco, ch. & sm.	63.5	84.3	11.7(4)
1405	Cars, Railroad	71.7	84.0	2.8(5)
1201	Aluminum prods.	76.0	83.7	9.7
631	Soap	73.5	83.1	*14.8*(4)
1634	Pens, Fountain, etc.	70.4	82.8	12.3(3)
1110	Blast furnace prods.	66.0	82.8	3.7(4)
106	Cereals	68.1	82.2	14.7(4)
1218	Sm. & ref. zinc.	64.0	82.2	4.7
1315	Washing machines, driers	56.0	79.7	*13.5*(6)
1001	Asbestos	63.1	78.4	8.5(3)
1407	Motor veh. parts	69.4	76.8	11.9(30)
1630	Pianos	51.1	75.8	3.6(5)
1021	Abrasives	67.4	74.3	24.9(4)
1401	Aircraft & parts	53.9	72.8	20.8(18, 31)
133	Liquors, dist.	51.2	71.4	14.2(8, 10)
1631	Optical goods	62.3	70.7	10.5(3)
129	Sugar, beet	68.8	89.4[d]	8.3(6)
131	Sugar ref., cane	69.6	88.3[d]	3.0(5, 6)

* See Appendix Table 2 for footnotes.

in rates of return between more and less concentrated industries), some industries have been excluded for the same reason Bain excluded some from his sample. In twenty-three industries, data could be found for only one or two firms. In the nine more than 70 per cent concentrated (eight firm) excluded industries, however, the ac- counting rate of return is *less* than that in the fourteen less concentrated industries (Appendix Tables 1A and 2A). The return in the concentrated group of excluded in- dustries is 10.6 per cent while that in the less concentrated industries is 11.4 per cent. The findings in the excluded group do *not* contradict the findings in the sample group.

Appendix Table 2 • Less Concentrated Industries

Census No.[a]	Industry	Concentration ratio (1935)[b]		Profit rate (per cent of book equity)[c] 1936–40
		4 firm	8 firm	
1638	Roofing	42.8	68.2	7.4(4)[e]
201	Carpets & rugs	51.1	68.2	4.7(3)
1213	Silverware	56.6	68.0	6.6(4)
1611	Dental equip.	51.5	67.7	7.6(3)
1410	Ship bldg.	44.8	64.7	10.8(3, 6)
1112	Steel-works & roll. mills	49.2	63.8	4.9(26, 30)
123	Meat packing	55.6	63.5	3.6(12, 13)
1102	Cast iron pipe	42.4	63.0	8.6
111	Condensed milk	44.6	62.7	10.2(3)
1008	Glass	44.9	61.0	14.3(7, 8)
618	Printing ink	49.0	60.9	11.8(3, 4)
1202	Clocks, watches	37.7	59.1	13.7(5)
705	Petroleum refining	38.2	58.9	6.8(33, 36)
1126	Wire drawn from pur. rods	40.2	54.0	7.5
115	Flavoring extracts	47.7	54.0	41.5(5, 7)
1303	Elect. mach., apparatus	44.1	52.3	12.3(28, 33)
1608	Cigars	38.5	50.7	6.9(8)
1104	Doors, & shutters, metal	33.3	49.0	18.3
1325	Printers' mach.	32.5	47.4	2.9(8)
1304	Engines, turb., w.w.	30.7	47.2	11.1(6, 8)
30	Sugar, cane (excl. ref.)	33.5	47.1	8.1(11, 14)
103	Cutting & edge tools	36.3	45.2	12.2(3)
1002	Cement	29.9	44.7	6.0(14)
1324	Cranes, dredging, excav. mach.	29.3	44.5	9.1(8)
626	Paints	32.3	41.8	7.9(11, 15)
614	Fertilizers	25.9	41.6	3.4(7, 8)
628	Perf. cosm. toil.	25.3	40.7	15.9(6, 8)
609	Cleaning & polish. prep.	28.0	39.9	20.7(3)
104	Canned fish	28.6	38.7	3.6(6, 7)
1319	Radio & phonograph	28.6	38.6	11.1(8, 14)
116	Flour & other grain mill prod.	29.4	37.0	7.6(3)
1127	Wirework	23.1	35.3	10.3(4, 5)
1309	Pumps	22.7	35.2	15.4(5, 6)
410	Pulp	22.7	34.5	14.2(2, 4)
907	Leather	22.5	34.3	2.1(8)
611	Drugs & medicines	23.4	33.5	21.6(12, 14)
1117	Screw mach. prod.	22.2	32.9	8.2(5, 8)
1322	Foundries	25.2	32.9	5.8(8, 9)
212	Wool & hair mfr.	24.2	32.9	1.8(7, 9)
1302	Cash reg. & other bus. mach.	21.3	31.4	14.1(4)
904	Boots & shoes	26.0	30.8	7.5(12, 14)
1318	Machine tool acc.	21.8	30.7	12.8(6)
105	Canned fruits & veg., etc.	22.7	30.4	7.5(9)
802	Rubber gds. (exc. tires, shoes)	19.2	28.5	11.5(3, 5)
209	Rayon mfrs.	18.5	27.1	8.4
1004	Clay prods. & nonclay refract.	19.3	26.6	3.7(12, 13)
102	Bread & bak. prods.	18.2	25.6	8.2(21, 22)
1648	Toys, playground equip.	16.6	25.6	17.1(3)
408	Paper goods, n.e.c.	14.2	23.7	12.4
1307	Machine tools	13.8	23.5	23.2(9, 11)
1121	Stoves & ranges & warm air f.	16.1	23.0	14.4(5, 6)
402	Boxes, paper	14.1	20.7	9.1(8, 9)
112	Confectionary	12.5	19.9	17.0(9)
134	Liquors, malt	11.8	17.7	15.2(31, 34)
1326	Machine shops	8.7	14.6	19.1(7, 9)

Appendix Table 2 • **Less Concentrated Industries** (*continued*)

Census No.[a]	Industry	Concentration ratio (1935)[b]		Profit rate (per cent of book equity)[c] 1936–40
		4 firm	8 firm	
203	Cotton mfrs.	8.4	14.4	3.2(45, 54)
101	Beverages nonalc.	8.7	13.2	12.5(6, 9)
309	Furniture	5.6	8.8	7.5(7)
207	Knit goods	5.3	8.5	6.2(23, 25)
311	Lumber & timber goods	4.7	7.6	9.1

[a] Census number is *underlined* for those industries added to the Bain sample.
[b] National Resources Committee, Structure of the American Economy 249–259 (1939).
[c] Joe S. Bain, "Relation of Profit Rate to Industry Concentration: American Manufacturing, 1936–1940," *Q. J. Econ.* 312 (1951); Securities and Exchange Commission, Survey of American Listed Corporations, Data on Profits and Operations, 1936–1942 (1944), Moody's Industrials, various issues.
Profit rate is *underlined* where it differs from that shown by Professor Bain. The difference occurs where a larger number of firms is used than that used by Professor Bain except for soap and typewriters. In the latter case, a weighted average of firm rates of return is substituted for the simple average used by Professor Bain. All other profit rates are weighted averages. Professor Bain's profit rate for the soap industry included cosmetics and toiletries firms. These were excluded for this computation.
Figure in parentheses is the number of firms used to compute profit rate. Number of firms is not shown where Bain's rate of return could not be replicated using his data source.
[d] Refined sugar industries (beet and cane) classified at the 70.5 per cent concentration level since they are competitive in their products and the leading eight refined cane sugar companies produced 70.5 per cent of all refined sugar. This may understate the concentration level since two of the leading refined beet sugar companies had larger sales than the fourth to eighth largest cane sugar refiners.
[e] The roofing industry rate of return based on three companies is 9.4 per cent. The fourth company evidently included by Bain had a 2.3 per cent return, reducing the industry return to 7.4 per cent. The fourth company (Certain-teed), however, was also the third largest firm in the gypsum industry (but was not used in calculating gypsum's rate of return). It would seem that it should be omitted in calculating roofing as well as having been omitted in calculating gypsum (or used in both places). We have, however, accepted Bain's figures for both these industries in the tabulation.

Appendix Table 1A • **Concentrated Industries**
(fewer than 3 firms)

		Conc. ratio (1935)		Profit rate 1936–40
		4 firm	8 firm	
1010	Graphite	86.4	100	13.3(1)
302	Billiard tables, b. alleys	D	D	11.4(1)
613	Explosives	82.0	93.1	10.2(2)
307	Cork products	76.9	90.2	6.1(1)
1206	Fire extinguishers	77.1	87.3	8.2(1)
1641	Soda fountains	74.0	80.4	18.9(1)
630	Salt	60.3	78.2	7.3(1, 2)
1629	Organs	57.0	77.5	9.3(2)
1311	Scales and balances	54.8	72.9	10.9(1)
	Average account profit rate on book equity			10.6

Appendix Table 2A • **Less Concentrated Industries**
(fewer than 3 firms)

122	Malt	44.6	65.5	19.1(2)
1128	Wrought pipe	47.4	64.8	2.9(1)
319	Wood preserving	50.5	60.2	18.7(1)
411	Wallpaper	41.4	58.9	2.1(1)
1310	Refrigerators	46.1	58.0	27.7(2)
1642	Sporting & athletic goods	36.0	47.2	−4.5(1)
306	Cooperage	25.9	40.5	13.3(1)
118	Ice Cream	32.7	37.7	6.0(1)
135	Liquors, vinous	26.8	37.6	10.7(2)
114	Feeds, prepared	23.0	34.3	14.6(2)
1624	Mattresses	25.8	31.2	15.7(1)
1606	Buttons	15.4	27.0	12.4(1)
1640	Signs & adv. novelties	9.2	14.7	13.2(2)
314	Planing mills	4.6	8.1	7.7(2)
	Average account profit rate on book equity			11.4

Appendix Table 3 • **Changes in 1936–40 Accounting Rates of Return**
From Those Shown by Bain

		Bain[a]	*New Rates*[b]
105	Canned fruits & veg.	7.4%(8, 9)	7.5%(9)
113	Corn products	9.3 (3)	9.2 (4)
115	Flavoring extracts & sirups	1.8	41.5 (5, 7)
222	Linoleum	9.0 (3)	8.4 (4, 5)
629	Rayon	12.1	9.0 (8, 9)
631	Soap	15.2 (8, 10)	14.8 (4)
803	Rubber tires	8.2	8.0 (9, 11)
907	Leather	0.8 (5)	2.1 (8)
1314	Typewriters	15.8 (4)	15.0 (4)
1315	Washing mach.	14.0	13.5 (6)
1325	Printers' machinery	2.2 (6)	2.9 (8)

[a] Joe S. Bain, *supra* Appendix Table 2, note c. Number of firms used by Bain shown in parentheses where it was possible to replicate from data in Securities and Exchange Commission, Survey of American Listed Corporations, Data on Profits and Operations, 1936–1942 (1944).
[b] See footnote c, Appendix Table 2.

17. Quantitative Studies of Industrial Organization

LEONARD W. WEISS

0. Introduction

In a famous article of 30 years ago E. S. Mason laid out the plan for systematic study of what was to become industrial organization (Mason 1939). He and his colleagues were to examine in depth a large enough number of industries with various structures to permit generalizations about relationships between the several leading elements of structure and performance. Over the next two decades the right and proper thing for a sincere young disciple was to thoroughly study some industry from the background of economic analysis. By the start of this decade, however, it seemed clear that the case study approach had yielded a great richness of special considerations, but had provided little basis for the hoped-for generalizations.

The alternative, to treat much of the rich detail as random noise, and to evaluate hypotheses by statistical tests of an inter-firm or inter-industry nature, also had a start in the late 1930's, but was long questioned. In a review of the TNEC Papers George Stigler (1942) concluded that, "It is doubtful whether the monopoly question will ever receive much illumination from large scale statistical investigations." Most of the profession seemed to agree. Industrial organization was one of the last fields of economics to be touched by the econometric revolution, and even now we use relatively unsophisticated tools.[1] Yet the fairly simple econometric techniques applied in the field over the last 10 or 15 years have yielded a set of generalizations that, to my mind, surpass in concreteness and certainty those attained by the preceding case studies. The statistical work in the field covers a range of topics much too broad for this paper. I will limit myself to the major structure-performance hypotheses.

1. Concentration and Profits

1.0. Bain and Stigler. The classic hypothesis of monopoly theory dealt with profits. The structure-profits relation was the first area of industrial organization to be systematically studied and has been by far the most thoroughly plowed field since. Although oligopoly theories could be constructed that would point in almost any direction, most practitioners assumed [2] that successful (tacit or explicit) collusion would approach joint maximization and that the ability to collude increases with concentration. Industries so unconcentrated that collusion was impossible were expected to yield only opportunity costs to all factors plus random deviations reflecting unanticipated changes in demand and/or cost. Profit rates were expected to increase with concentration as

Reprinted from *Frontiers of Quantitative Economics*, ed. *M.D. Intriligator* by permission *North-Holland Publishing Company*.

[1] To some extent our relatively simple methods may reflect the rudimentary preparation in econometrics received by many of us, but that was never true of all and is certainly not so of the younger men in the field today. I believe that a more basic explanation is that important con- tributions could be made with fairly simple techniques because of the character of our hypotheses and data. Most of our work led naturally to cross section rather than time series regressions, so we have been spared many of the pains of serial correlation and distributed lags. We have seldom been faced with the situation that seems common in time series work where a series of alternative and sometimes contradictory hypotheses all yield high R^2's.

[2] The assumptions of the concentration-profits model are often not spelled out. I am following Bain who was much more explicit than most of us (Bain 1951).

collusion became more successful until they reached a maximum attainable with given demand, cost, and entry conditions, again with short run profit differences due to un-anticipated changes in demand and/or cost.

A more complete model involves the determinants of that maximum profit level: the elasticity of demand, the pattern of long run marginal costs, and the conditions of entry. For lack of systematic data, we have almost all assumed that elasticity is unre-lated to other structural variables. A fair amount of evidence points to constant long run marginal costs over wide ranges of out-put in manufacturing (Johnston 1960, ch. 5) and this convenient condition has been generally assumed in cross section studies. Of course, Bain did explicitly include entry barriers in his model.

There have been at least thirty-two tests of some form of the classic profit-determi-nation hypothesis over the last 18 years, and the number seems to be accelerating if anything (Bain 1951, 1956; Schwartzman 1959; Levinson 1960; Fuchs 1961; Sato 1961; Minhas 1963; Stigler 1963, 1964; Weiss 1963; Sherman 1964, 1968; Mann 1966; Collins and Preston 1966, 1968, 1969; Food Marketing Commission 1966; Asch 1967; Kilpatrick 1967, 1968; Miller 1967; Hall and Weiss 1967; Comanor and Wilson 1968; George 1968; Kamerschen 1969; Kelly 1969; and, as yet unpublished theses or papers by Solomon 1967; Arnould 1968; Gambeles 1969; Telser 1969; Long 1970; and Imel 1970).

Bain was the first to formulate and test an operational concentration-profits hypoth-esis (Bain 1951). He carefully sorted rele-vant data that had been generated by the late New Deal (the 1935 concentration ra-tios tabulated by the National Resources Committee, 1939, and the 1936–40 profit data compiled by the SEC). He limited himself to 42 industries that corresponded to well-defined national markets for which at least three corporate series were avail-able. Within this sample he found a barely significant positive linear relation between eight firm concentration and a weighted in-dustry average of 5-year average rates of return on equity, but there appeared to be a highly significant positive difference be-tween industries with eight firm concentra-tion ratios above and below 70. He re-ported that the effect of concentration could not be explained by firm size, per-centage overhead, capital-output ratios, product durability, or type of buyer. These explanatory variables were apparently ex-amined one at a time. Of course he subse-quently (Bain 1956, ch. 7) went on to cross tabulate 1936–40 and 1948–51 profit rates against concentration and his estimates of barriers to entry and found a positive effect for both variables (see below).

Stigler, on the other hand, could find little or no statistical support for the tradi-tional hypothesis (Stigler 1963, ch. 4). He worked with income tax data for IRS minor industries using average four firm concen-tration ratios weighted by value added within these industries and assigning those with average concentration in excess of 60 to a group that he considered "concen-trated," these below 50 (or below 20 in industries that sell primarily on local or re-gional markets) to the "unconcentrated" category, and consigned the remainder to an "ambiguous" purgatory. The concen-trated industries showed higher average rates of return (on total investment) in 1938–41 and after 1948, but only in the periods 1951–53 and 1954–56 were these differences statistically significant. More-over, when he corrected for excessive en-trepreneurial withdrawals, he found no sig-nificant relation at all.

He felt he had found support for two related hypotheses, however—that profit rates would be more dispersed among con-centrated industries where high profits would attract less entry, and that inter-industry profit differences would persist longer in concentrated industries for the same reason. The former held up passably once allowance was made for entrepre-neurial withdrawals. The latter was tested by correlating current and lagged profit rates using various lags for all possible pairs of years within each concentration class. The correlation coefficients fell off much more rapidly in the unconcentrated class as the lag was increased. This result is most striking in 1938–47, but it is suspect because of the transition from depression and war in that period. The difference between the concentrated and unconcentrated classes in 1948–57 seems to be almost entirely explainable by differences in the number of degrees of freedom. In both classes the correlation falls to non-significance after 8 years.[3]

In general Stigler found ambiguity where others found a clear cut positive effect. Kilpatrick tried to rework Stigler's study (Kilpatrick 1968). He argued that Stigler's correction for entrepreneurial withdrawals had probably eliminated much of the effect of concentration on profits because of the correlations among concentration, firm size, and such withdrawals. He tried two alternatives, in one introducing the percentage of net worth assignable to small firms as an additional variable, and in the other, eliminating small firms from the study completely. The latter seems particularly well designed, both because it eliminates the effect of entrepreneurial withdrawals and because it drops the firms most likely to be suboptimal (or misclassified). The concentration-profits hypothesis does not refer to fringe firms. The results of Kilpatrick's reconstruction of Stigler was itself equivocal because he did not use precisely the same years as Stigler and because he did not find a very high correlation in 1950. However, his IRS data showed a clear cut positive relationship in 1956 and 1963.

Bain thought that Stigler's weak results were due to his having used weighted averages of uncorrected concentration ratios (Bain 1968, p. 451).[4] Averaging can distort

if the underlying relation is not linear, and the census concentration ratios are certainly not pure, but others have derived quite significant relationships of the expected sort using similar data (Sherman 1964, 1968; Kilpatrick 1968).

My guess is that the difference between Stigler and the rest of us is more a matter of timing than of technique. In a recent thesis, Gambeles (1969) correlated profit rates and concentration for FTC-SEC 2 digit industries on an annual basis and found significant positive correlations in 1949 and 1952–65, but virtually zero and even negative relationships in the years of open inflation or price controls: 1947–48, 1950–51 and now in 1965–67. The concentration-profits hypothesis apparently does not hold up well in such periods, and every period examined by Stigler except the last (1955–57) contained a preponderance of such years.[5]

1.1. Price-cost Margins. The collection by the census of gross book values of fixed capital in 1958 and from 1963 on has permitted studies at a 4-digit level, thus avoiding the weighted averages on which many studies have rested. The most comprehensive work along these lines has been that of Collins and Preston (1966, 1968, 1969). Their dependent variable was an approximation to

$$\left(\frac{\text{Price-Marginal Cost}}{\text{Price}} \right)$$

which they were at some pains to show "is most closely related to the theoretical prediction. . . ."[6] I am skeptical about this

---

[3] *Ibid.*, pp. 69–71.

[4] Bain also objects to the arbitrary cutoffs at concentration ratios of 50 and 60 though these translate fairly closely to the eight firm concentration ratio of 70 which he had invented. And he complains about Stigler's use of rates of return on assets rather than on equity, a point on which we agree (Hall and Weiss 1967, p. 321). Industries differ in their stability and growth rates and, therefore, in their ability to borrow.

Rates of return on assets are apt to reflect the latter in part. It is rates of return on equity which should be equalized in competitive industries in the long run.

[5] This may account for his different results from Bain's for the pre-war years. Bain used 1936–40 so that 45 of the 60 months covered were late depression. Stigler used 1938–41 so that 28 of his 48 months were during the first part of World War II.

[6] Collins and Preston 1968, pp. 13–4. This ratio would be a correct statement of optimal margin if entry were blockaded so that margin depended on demand elasticity, but blockaded

claim. The normal return to be equalized in unconcentrated industries would surely be a yield on capital, not sales, and the ability to successfully collude would increase yields above those available to all on competitive markets. Nevertheless, they do find that weighted average concentration ratios and weighted average capital-output ratios taken together "explain" a larger percentage of the variance in the profit-sales ratio than in the rates of return on equity or assets among SEC-FTC 2 digit industries.

The variable used in their regressions was not the profit-sales ratio, but "price-cost margins"—i.e. the difference between value of shipments and direct cost (labor and materials costs) as a percentage of shipments. The numerator in this variable is interpreted as "profits before taxes plus quasi-rents (depreciation)," but it contains a good deal more than that, most notably purchased services and central office expenses. Advertising is the most obvious of the purchased services. Central office expenses often include such items as research and development, sales, and general administrative expenses. In the 1969 article (though not the book) it also included non-wage labor costs. Advertising[7] seems to be

associated with large firms (Comanor and Wilson 1969), central office expenses probably are (Gort 1962, pp. 87–91), and one would expect the same fringe benefits. Margins should increase with concentration because of the relation of concentration and firm size, if for no other reason.

There is a good possibility that some net effect of concentration on profits is also detected, however. Telser (1969) attempted to allow for central office expenses by assigning those reported in *Enterprise Statistics* to 4-digit industries associated with an enterprise product class. He still found a significant positive effect of concentration on the remaining overhead even after controlling for payroll, inventory, and fixed capital. Payroll should pick up most of the fringe benefit costs, so the relation between concentration and overhead must reflect profits, taxes, depreciation, and purchased services such as advertising.

Collins and Preston regressed margins on concentration, capital-output ratios, and plant dispersion for 2-digit industries separately and for all industries taken together. The 2-digit regressions were mixed, yielding significant relationships about half the time. I have argued elsewhere (Weiss 1962) that 2-digit industries are particularly poor (and hardly random) samples of industries for tests of hypotheses in which changes in demand or cost are important, because they are fairly homogeneous with respect to concentration, perhaps reflecting related technologies, but are extremely heterogeneous with respect to change in output, perhaps reflecting intrasector competition. Within the 2-digit sectors we are apt to observe only a limited variance in concentration but a large variance in another important element in profits—changing demand or cost. The inevitable result is poorer fits, a point briefly acknowledged (Collins and Preston 1968, p. 96). A much closer fit was observed when the same in-

---

entry seems to be rare outside of regulated industries. I believe that conditions of entry rather than elasticity is the main determinant of optimal margin in most markets. The entry-inducing price yields a normal return on total investment (including entry costs) to the most likely entrant. The optimal price is a function of the entry-inducing price. It should yield a corresponding higher return on equity to insiders the higher the barriers to entry and the greater the insiders' ability to collude.

[7] Because of the inclusion of advertising in margins, one would expect higher gross margins for differentiated goods, and, if advertising increases with concentration (Mann et al. 1967), one would expect higher regression coefficients as as well. Preston's and Collin's concentration-margin relationships for consumers good industries were (Preston and Collins 1969):

High and moderately differentiated
$$M = 18.7 + 0.189CR.$$
Low differentiation $\quad M = 17.4 + 0.150CR.$

The difference in estimated margins (M) comes

---

to 1.26% when CR is zero, 3.21% when it is 50, and 5.16% when it is 100. These differences are in the same ballpark with the advertising-sales ratios for differentiated consumer goods.

dustries were combined. (The *t* ratio for concentration rose to 6.8 against an average of 1.8 in the sector regressions.) Spurious correlation could be a problem in these studies, since value of shipments is the denominator in the margin, the capital output ratios, and the concentration ratio. However, Telser avoided this problem and still found a significant effect (Telser 1969).

In their recent article (Collins and Preston 1969) they experimented with similar regressions for samples of industries where concentration was rising, stable or declining and where the margins of the largest four firms were high or low relative to the industry as a whole. Some plausible reasons are suggested for why margins should be high in consumer goods industries where concentration has risen or is stable, but further tests should be found for these seemingly after-the-fact hypotheses.

1.2. Firm Studies. Most past profit studies have used industries as observations, but current studies seem to use individual firms as observations instead. The industry make up of firms is estimated using directory data or interviews and weighted averages of appropriate industry variables are then assigned to the firms. In addition to the study that Marshall Hall and I published in 1967, I know of four theses (Solomon 1967; Arnould 1967; Kelly 1969; Imel 1970) that have taken a similar approach in at least some segments of manufacturing. The results have generally been conventional. Heteroskedasticity is a problem in these studies, since smaller firm size classes have a greater variance in profit experience than do large firms (Alexander 1949; Stekler 1964, Stigler 1963, p. 48), due, presumably, to less diversification. When Hall and I corrected for heteroskedasticity we detected a net positive effect of size on profit along with the expected effects of concentration, output growth, and leverage. Its effect was more strongly positive than that found in previous single-variable studies based on IRS asset size classes (Crum 1939; Alexander 1949; Stekler 1963; Stigler 1963). Some subsequent studies have shown equivocal results within individual 2-digit or IRS

minor industries (Marcus 1969; Kelly 1969), but these are not wholly inconsistent with our hypothesis.[8] We expected size to affect profits in broad, inter industry studies, since large firms have access to a wider range of industries than small and may be expected to invest in those industries with high prospective profits. On the other hand, our results may derive primarily from the peculiarities of the years studied, 1956–62, a relatively depressed period when the advantages of size and diversification might be most substantial.

1.3. The Low R^2's. The typical result of concentration-profits studies, especially those based on firms, has been a significant but fairly weak positive relationship. The weakness of the relationship has several sources. First, the data is poor. We measure the ability to collude very imperfectly with four firm concentration in 4-digit products, accounting profits are far from economic profits and contain a large random element due to the variety of accounting conventions in use, and the link between firm accounting and product data is inaccurate because of diversification. Our data are surely worse than the macro-aggregates used in estimating consumption or investment functions or the price, output, inventory, and input data available to agricultural or public utility economists. The resulting large random error element in our data biases the relationship toward zero.

Second, accounting procedures probably bias reported profit rates toward equality because large and profitable firms have the most to gain in tax avoidance and public relations by the understatement of profits, some corporate assets are revalued when they change hands or are written down if

---

[8] Samuels and Smyth (1968) found a negative relation between size and profits, but I believe this is due to a bias in their sample. It was drawn from Moody's which will contain almost all large firms but only publicly listed small firms. The more profitable small firms seem more likely to be listed, and as a result of the heteroskedasticity of profit rates with respect to size the most profitable small firms earn more than the average large firm.

profit prospects are low, and original cost asset valuation plus inflation leads to the relative overstatement of rates of return in slowly growing firms (which are usually relatively unprofitable).[9]

Third, much of the inter-industry and more of the inter-firm variance in profit rates reflects unexpected shifts in demand or cost or managerial errors in location, technique, product design or leverage. Some of these may be roughly allowed for by additional variables in multiple regressions, but never very precisely. Concentration is generally only a secondary reason for inter-industry or inter-firm profit differences, so R^2's are bound to be fairly low.[10]

Fourth, high prices may induce high costs, perhaps because they protect suboptimal, excess, or obsolete capacity, perhaps because of internal or union-induced incentives to pay high wages, or perhaps because of managerial preferences for certain expenses. The profit and margin studies probably miss some of the allocative effect of concentration as a result. In general, we can probably conclude that any relationships between profit and concentration, barriers, and/or output change that we observe are real and are probably badly underestimated.

1.4. Developing More Precise Parameters for Policy. Almost all of the 32 concentration-profits studies except Stigler's have

yielded significant positive relationships for years of prosperity or recession, though they have depended on a wide variety of data and methods.[11] I think that practically all observers are now convinced that there is something to the traditional hypothesis. This is a considerable accomplishment. Two decades ago Congress passed the antimerger act with little more than some merger statistics and economic theory to guide it. Nevertheless, I doubt that we need many more general concentration-profits studies.

What we *do* need still is a precise statement of what elements of concentration are important and over what range. This may seem humdrum, but it is highly practical. Life would be much easier at the Anti-Trust Division if we knew whether (a) there really is a critical level of concentration, (b) if it exists, whether concentration makes a difference above and/or below that level, and (c) how much difference is made by larger market shares for the third or sixth or ninth firms in the market. These questions arise continuously and I hope that sometime in the next few years we will at last have some fairly definite answers.

Profit rates, at least in stable prosperity or mild recession, have come to serve as a sort of thermometer to evaluate market power (Bain 1956; Weiss 1963; Comanor and Wilson 1967; Miller 1968; Preston and Collins 1969). This seems quite legitimate. Like the expansion of mercury in the thermometer, we have good theoretical reason to expect profits to increase with market power and have observed it many times. We should now use the established relationship to answer the practical questions.

Bain invented the critical concentration ratio. He found, on an after-the-fact basis, distinctly higher profit rates in industries where eight firm concentration exceeded 70 (1951). Several others adopted this cutoff or its four firm equivalent of 50 (Kaysen and Turner 1959, ch. 2; Schwartzman 1959;

---

[9] The accountants' practice of "expensing" intangibles may overstate or understate profit rates, but it is more likely to overstate, the more slowly intangible expenditures grow (Weiss 1969).

[10] The higher R^2's found in regressions using weighted averages for 2-digit industries probably reflect (a) the more accurate assignment of firms to 2- than to 4-digit industries, (b) the averaging out of random influences, and (c) the elimination of much of the effect of changing demand and cost. Two-digit industries are fairly homogeneous with respect to concentration but the variance of output change is almost as great within such industries as in manufacturing generally. Two-digit averages therefore retain much more of the underlying variance in concentration than in output change (Weiss 1963).

---

[11] The relationship became non-significant in (Comanor and Wilson 1967) when entry barriers were introduced, see p. 199.

Levenson 1960; Stigler 1963; Mann 1966; Comanor 1967; Kamerschen 1969), but only a few have tested it. Kilpatrick (1967) and Collins and Preston (1969) both attempted simple regressions with dummy variables for concentration greater than 50 and arrived at R^2's lower than those found for concentration as a continuous variable. Kilpatrick tried several alternative cutoffs as well. His R^2 reached a maximum when the critical value was 50 for profit rate level and when it was 75 for profit rate changes between 1949 and 1954 (p. 259) though the differences from other cutoffs were not significant. These tests do not seem conclusive for two reasons. Kilpatrick was comparing average profit rates and average concentration ratios for IRS minor industries. Even if a dichotomous relationship existed for realistic markets, it could tend to disappear when they were averaged. Collins and Preston use 4-digit industries and are less vulnerable on this point, but their profit variable is crude. Second, both studies ignore the possibility that slopes may differ substantially below and/or above the critical level. This could make a dichotomous subdivision consistent with a closer fit for a continuous than for a simple shift variable.[12]

The question of what level of concentration is important was also approached by Kilpatrick (1967) and by Miller (1967). Kilpatrick tried four firm, eight firm, and twenty firm concentration ratios as alternative variables and found he could "explain" a slightly larger percentage of the variance in 1950–57 average profit rates and of the change in profit rates between 1949 and 1954 with four firm than with eight firm concentration, and more with the eight firm than with the twenty firm concentration. Again the differences between the correlation coefficients were not significant. This seems to imply that the shares of the fifth through eighth firms and those of the ninth through twentieth firms add nothing to the determination of profit rates.

Miller (1967) resurrected [13] the "marginal concentration ratio" and found that with the four firm concentration given, the share of the fifth through eighth firms had a significant *negative* effect. He suggested a plausible interpretation—that an industry with four leaders and many small followers could collude more readily than one with eight leaders and many small followers. Preston and Collins (1969) have since pointed out that the marginal concentration ratio is a biased measure, since its value is constrained by $MCR \leq CR$ for $CR \leq 50$ and by $MCR \leq (100 - CR)$ for $CR \geq 50$. They attempted two makeshift alternative variables and found that the effect of marginal concentration was equivocal. One of their tabulations seems to show that marginal concentration has a positive effect, if anything, in the ranges where it is most constrained ($CR < 30$ and $CR > 70$) though it may have a negative effect where $30 \leq CR \leq 70$.

This range contains most of the important cases since few of us worry much about markets where $CR < 30$, and there just are not many markets where $CR > 70$.

I tried a rerun using Collins' and Preston's 1958 data (1968) and marginal concentration ratios from their sources. MCR had a non-significant negative effect on margins:

$$M = 15.17 + 0.125\,CR$$
$$ (1.55)\ \ (0.021)$$
$$ -0.058\,MCR - 0.015\,D$$
$$ (0.079) (0.014)$$
$$ + 0.013\,\frac{K}{VS}\qquad R^2 = 0.12$$
$$ (0.022)\phantom{\frac{K}{VS}}\ \ \mathrm{df} = 286 - 5 = 281,$$

where D is their dispersion index and K/VS is their capital-output ratio. The negative effect of MCR is enhanced when the range of CR is limited to $30 \leq CR \leq 70$:

$$M = 9.04 + 0.289\,CR$$
$$ (4.15)\ \ (0.068)$$
$$ -\,0.266\,MCR - 0.032\,D$$
$$ (0.127) (0.024)$$
$$ +\,0.060\,\frac{K}{VS}\qquad R^2 = 0.16$$
$$ (0.033)\,\frac{}{VS}\ \ \mathrm{df} = 117 - 5 = 112.$$

---

[12] Telser did distinguish industries where $CR \leq 25$, $25 < CR \leq 50$, and $CR > 50$ and found progressively steeper slopes (1969).

---

[13] As far as I can tell, Gort invented it (1963).

To eliminate the constraint completely, I substituted a variable V equal to MCR/CR when $CR \leq 50$ and to $MCR/(1 - CR)$ when $CR > 50$. V can range from zero to 100 just as CR can. It yields:

$$M = 13.85 + 0.121\,CR$$
$$\ (1.74)\ \ (0.021)$$
$$\ + 2.02\,V - 0.017\,D$$
$$\ \ (2.28)\ \ \ \ \ (0.014)$$
$$\ + 0.010\ \ K\ \ \ \ \ R^2 = 0.12$$
$$\ \ (0.022)\ \overline{VS}\ \ \ \ df = 286 - 5 = 281.$$

The main result from all this would seem to be that MCR has little effect one way or another.

There would be a clear cut policy implication of a negative coefficient for MCR —that the anti-trust authorities should *encourage* mergers among smaller firms. I do not feel that we know enough to give such advice until a more thorough exploration of this ground is done. Specifically, I would like to know if it makes any difference whether we are dealing with differentiated goods sold to consumers or standardized industrial materials. At the moment the most I can tell the Anti-Trust Division is that it does not look as if a merger among the smaller firms in a market would make a lot of difference so long as the four firm concentration ratio does not change. Even that is an enormous increase on what we could say on the subject 3 years ago.

Work on the parameters of the concentration-profits relationship has been woefully free of theory, with the one elegant and largely ignored exception of Stigler (1964). His proposition was that the success of oligopolistic collusion depends on the individual seller's ability to detect chiseling and that ultimately this depends on his ability to distinguish non-random sales losses. The implication, spelled out with mathematical precision, is that the ability to collude depends heavily on the number and relative size of sellers, falling off rapidly as firm sizes approach equality and as numbers rise. The concentration index directly derivable from his theoretical construct was the Herfindahl index rather than the conventional concentration ratio,[14] and he showed that for a group of 17 industries where concentration exceeded 63, profit rates were more closely related to this index than to four firm concentration.

If Stigler's hypothesis were supported, the implications for policy would be striking. It means that we should be very concerned about the shares of the top one or two firms and that the shares of any firm beyond about the fourth cannot make much difference.[15] Moreover, since the Herfindahl index increases with the square of the concentration ratio, if the degree of inequality is given,[16] it also implies that we should put most of our emphasis on mergers where the four firm concentration ratio exceeds 50. The familiar ring of these two

---

[14] The Herfindahl index seems also to be implied in the Cournot hypothesis (Long 1969 and Stigler 1968, ch. 4).

[15] If $K = X_n/X_{n-1}$, where X is market share and n is the rank of the firm in question, then the Herfindahl index is:

$$H = X_1^2(1 + K^2 + K^4\ldots) = X_1^2\,\frac{1}{1 - K^2},$$

and the value of H determined by the top t firms is:

$$V = X_1^2\,\frac{1 - K^{2 \cdot t}}{1 - K^2}.$$

The ratio of $V/H = (1 - K^{2 \cdot t})$. The share of the top two firms in the index ($t = 2$) is then 0.67 for $K = 0.7$, 0.94 for $K = 0.5$ and 0.99 for $K = 0.3$. The share of the top four firms is 0.94, 0.996 and 0.999994 for the same K's.

[16] Using the same notation as the previous footnote,

$$CR = X_1(1 + K + K^2 + K^3)$$
$$= \frac{1 - K^4}{1 - K}\,X_1 \text{ or } X_1 = \frac{1 - K}{1 - K^4}\,CR$$
$$H = X_1^2\,\frac{1}{1 - K^2}$$
$$= \left(\frac{1 - K}{1 - K^4}\,CR\right)^2\frac{1}{1 - K^2}$$
$$= \frac{1 - K}{(1 - K)(1 - K^4)^2}\,CR^2.$$

Since the ratio on the left is assumed a constant, H increases with CR^2 which, of course, ranges from 25 to 100 when CR goes from 50 to 100.

cutoff points suggests that Stigler might be right.

Some more general and sophisticated tests of the Herfindahl index are obviously in order. Although both Nelson's tabulation of 1954 Herfindahl indexes (1963) and Stigler's theory (1964) have been available for a half decade, no systematic tests of its effect have been attempted to my knowledge. I tried an unsophisticated test using Collins' and Preston's 1958 margins and Nelson's 1956 Herfindahl indexes for 34 industries where all data were available. The Herfindahl index yielded a lower R^2 (0.070) than CR did (0.082) and CR^2 did better than either (0.097). This does not support Stigler very well, but the evidence is at least as tenuous as his was.

Stigler also felt that the number and size of *buyers* was of crucial importance for the ability of insiders to collude (1964, pp. 47–8), large numbers of small buyers per seller making secret price concessions infeasible. Preston and Collins, in effect, tested this by running separate regressions for producer and consumer goods industries. They found a much sharper effect of concentration in the latter case ($\partial M / \partial CR = 0.033$ for producer goods and 0.199 for consumer goods where M is price cost margin). An alternative hypothesis, that it was product differentiation rather than numbers of buyers that control, did not show up well.

2. Conditions of Entry

2.0. Concentration, Barriers to Entry and Profits. It is customary to acknowledge that concentration is only one dimension of market structure, but the attempts to allow for barriers to entry have been few and usually rudimentary. Bain, himself, made qualitative judgments about the conditions of entry and concentration, and showed an apparently systematic effect of barriers (1956, pp. 199–201) on profits for 1936–40 and 1947–51. The second period is striking in view of the usually poor effect of concentration in "explaining" profits during open inflations. Michael Mann reproduced the experiment using profit rates for 1950–60 and mildly revised and expanded estimates of entry conditions, obtaining similar results (Mann 1966). Neither study attempted any statistical tests of the results.

In the basic model rising concentration increases the ability of industry members to cooperate and to approach the maximum profit rates permitted by entry conditions. Thus profits should rise more rapidly with concentration, the higher the barriers to entry, so that an appropriate model might be:

$$\frac{\Pi}{E} = a + b_1 B_I CR + b_2 B_{II} CR + b_3 B_{III} CR, \quad (1)$$

where B_I, B_{II}, and B_{III} are dummies with a value of 1 when barriers to entry are "low to moderate," "substantial" or "high" respectively. The intercept term presumably represents "normal profits." When Bain's and Mann's data were inserted into such a model, they yielded the expected results:

Bain 1936–40 $\dfrac{\Pi}{E} = 3.82 + 0.069CR \cdot B_I + 0.078CR \cdot B_{II} + 0.194CR \cdot B_{III}$
$\phantom{Bain 1936-40 \frac{\Pi}{E} = 3.82 + }(0.044)(0.034)\phantom{CR \cdot B_{II} + }(0.031)$
$R^2 = 0.78$ $df = 20 - 4 = 16.$

Bain 1947–51 $\dfrac{\Pi}{E} = 9.26 + 0.060CR \cdot B_I + 0.062CR \cdot B_{II} + 0.119CR \cdot B_{III}$
$\phantom{Bain 1947-51 \frac{\Pi}{E} = 9.26 + }(0.050)(0.039)\phantom{CR \cdot B_{II} + }(0.036)$
$R^2 = 0.47$ $df = 20 - 4 = 16.$

Mann 1950–60 $\dfrac{\Pi}{E} = 7.83 + 0.047CR \cdot B_I + 0.050CR \cdot B_{II} + 0.103CR \cdot B_{III}$
$\phantom{Mann 1950-60 \frac{\Pi}{E} = 7.83 + }(0.033)(0.027)\phantom{CR \cdot B_{II} + }(0.024)$
$R^2 = 0.51$ $df = 30 - 4 = 26.$

The results are roughly those that Bain had perceived but had not tested statistically. The effect of concentration seems to be about the same in industries with moderate and with substantial barriers to entry but a good deal greater where barriers are high.

2.1. Continuous Entry Variables. A few attempts have been made to introduce the various barriers as continuous, independent variables. If these can be measured, it may be possible to quantify the barriers to entry, permitting us to judge their relative importance and to add them up. A simple model might be:

$$\frac{\Pi}{E} = a + b_1 B_1 CR \ldots b_i B_i CR \ldots, \quad (2)$$

where B_i is a continuously measurable barrier such as optimal scale as a per cent of market size (MES/VS) or the capital requirement for optimal plants ($MES \cdot K/VS$). The coefficients in such a model would be hard to estimate because of multicollinearity, and they would reflect only crudely Bain's hypothesis that expected profits rise with barriers at an increasing rate. Moreover, it is overall barriers that counts, not any one barrier individually.

A logarithmic regression would preserve the multiplicative relation between concentration and barriers:

$$\frac{\Pi}{E} = kCR^a B_1^{b_1} \ldots B_i^{b_i} \ldots, \quad (3)$$

but it would not permit profits to rise at an increasing rate with barriers, and it would make the effect of each barrier depend on the levels of other barriers. A better model would be:

$$\frac{\Pi}{E} = KCR^a[b_1 B_1 + \ldots + b_i B_i \ldots]^c. \quad (4)$$

The value of c should exceed 1.0 if industries with low barriers charge entry-inducing prices while those with higher barriers charge entry-impeding prices as Bain surmises. This would be hard to estimate. One possibility would be to first estimate equation (2) and then use the resulting b_i's to define the bracketed aggregate entry barrier variable used in estimating equation (4).

To my knowledge, no one has ever pursued this approach, but Comanor and Wilson (1967) estimated equations of types (2) and (3) for a group of 41 IRS minor industries that produce primarily consumer goods. The major entry barriers seemed to be those associated with advertising and capital requirements, the latter depending

mainly on the auto industry. The scale barrier played a minor role, and concentration had a nonsignificant and sometimes negative effect. This was due in part to the close correlation between concentration and barriers as measured. Perhaps these are indistinguishable in consumer goods industries, or perhaps a more accurate estimate of the scale and capital barriers might be less closely related to concentration and would yield a different result.[17] I would be reluctant to reject the independent importance of concentration short of a more extensive investigation covering producer as well as consumer goods. A recent FTC study based on individual firm data in the food industries (Kelly 1969) yielded substantial positive effects for both concentration and advertising intensity.

A possible reason for the strong effect of advertising is the accounting treatment of advertising as current expense. To the extent that ads have lasting value, such accounting practice results in an understatement of both profits and equity. If advertising grows at a constant percentage rate, r, it can be shown that the rate of return on equity will be overstated if $\Pi/E > r/(1 + r)$ and vice versa (Telser 1969; Weiss 1969). I reworked Comanor and Wilson's results and found a significant positive effect of advertising intensity on profits even after correcting the profits and equity for previous ads and their depreciation (Weiss 1969). One reason was that r was high during the period covered so that profit rates were not greatly affected by the adjustment. This suggests that the barrier is real.

2.2. Vertical and Conglomerate Size. All studies reviewed to this point have tested some aspect of the classic concentration-barriers-profits hypothesis where empirical studies can now offer at least some guidance for policy, but current merger policy

---

[17] Their scale barrier is the average size of the plants accounting for half of shipments divided by total industry shipments. This has the same denominator as concentration and numerator which is correlated with the shipments of the four largest firms. They acknowledge this point (footnote 28, p. 345).

extends to some vertical, market and product extension, and pure conglomerate mergers as well. No one has presented tests of the vertical foreclosure, potential entry, and reciprocity theories that underlie many of these merger cases. Perhaps the size-profits studies can be thought of as partial tests of some aggregate economic power theory, though I interpreted a positive relationship as an index of the capital cost barrier (Hall and Weiss 1967). At any rate, the effect of size on profits is still far from established (Alexander 1949; Stigler 1963; Kelly 1969).

The one explicit attempt to test an aggregate concentration argument of which I know is in the new FTC conglomerate merger study (FTC 1969, Appendix, Table 4-4). They regressed the absolute change in 4-digit four firm concentration from 1947 through 1966 on the share of 4-digit industry value added accounted for by firms among the top 200 corporations in 1963. Their data consisted of all 55 industries for which such comparisons are possible, and they controlled for initial concentration, growth, and a high or moderate product differentiation dummy. The large firm variable had a significant positive effect. Since this variable had to be based on membership in the top 200 near the end of the period, increasing industry concentration might have played a role in putting a firm in that category. This possible bias seems remote, however. It is unlikely to account for all of the quite large observed effect

$$\frac{\partial \Delta CR}{\partial Pct200} = 0.191, \text{ } t\text{-ratio} = 2.44.$$

The aggregate economic power hypothesis seems to have been supported,[18] but we need a great deal more work on the subject.

[18] The FTC used the absolute change in concentration which would tend to be large in concentrated industries and might reasonably be deflated by initial concentration. I attempted a regression for a roughly random sample of 25 industries using $\frac{CR_{66} - CR_{54}}{CR_{54}}$ and the dependent variable and got results similar to theirs. For what it is worth, the same sample showed no relationship between top 200 participation and price-cost margins.

3. Competition and Labor Markets

3.0. The Monopoly Wage Hypothesis. An association between concentration and wage rates has been expected by many though such a relation does not derive easily from conventional theory of the firm. A few early tests using only simple correlations (Weiss 1963) wage changes (Garbarino 1950; Levinson 1960) and international comparisons (Schwartzman 1959) yielded unconvincing evidence. My own paper, or at least the data I developed for it, seems to have played a role here (Weiss 1966). I studied annual earnings and estimated average hourly earnings in four broad sex-occupation groupings and ten narrow groupings from the 1/1000 sample of the 1960 Census. When these were regressed on weighted averages of corrected concentration ratios and collective bargaining coverage, earnings seemed to be strongly affected by both variables in most occupations. The addition of other industry variables such as establishment size, employment growth, and various labor force characteristics did not alter this seriously, but when personal characteristics such as race, education, age, region, urban-rural residence, and family status were introduced, the effect of concentration disappeared. I doubt that this was due merely to inaccurate measurement of concentration. The effect of unionism, which was less well measured, held up for most production workers and showed values near those commonly found in the unionism-wage rate studies—6–8% for operatives and 8–15% for craftsmen (Lewis 1963, ch. V; but see Stafford 1968). I conclude that while concentrated industries pay higher wage rates, they also hire "superior" personnel whose incomes contain few monopoly rents. There were faults in this study which the subsequent work of Victor Fuchs avoided (Fuchs 1968, Ch. 6). If I were repeating it, I would now put primary emphasis on average hourly earnings. I would use a logarithmic form and would experiment with transformations of the concentration variable, but I doubt that these changes would change the basic results.

3.1. Labor Turnover. The main line of research in this area today seems to be converging on a study of quit rates. The three studies of which I am aware are those of Stoikov and Raimon (1968), Burton and Parker (1969), and Telser (1969). The first does not introduce market structure variables except for plant size (which has a non-significant, negative effect). They reject concentration as having no theoretical basis, but they show the expected negative effect of wage rates on quits in a relatively prosperous period. The second considers concentration relevant because of a greater possibility of slack, no-raiding agreements, and high quality of labor in concentrated industries. As it turned out, concentration had a significant, negative effect which held up in a variety of models with up to 13 additional variables including unionism and a variety of labor force and dynamic variables (layoffs, accessions, and wage changes). When wage levels were introduced, the effect of unionism largely disappeared but that of concentration was little affected. They concluded that unionism did not impede mobility, but that monopoly did. I would reverse this. Unionism raises wages above the opportunity cost of labor and in the process impedes mobility, but the high wages of concentrated industries are in line with the "quality" of labor hired. Important features of that high "quality" are age, race, sex, family status, and education, all of which are associated with stable employment. Masters, Burton and Parker, and I had all pointed to this aspect of a high "quality"—high wage policy (Masters 1969, pp. 342–3; Burton and Parker 1969, p. 206; and Weiss 1966b, p. 97).

Telser (1969) makes several points which may suggest some connection among concentration, wages and quit rates. He finds that various measures of payroll have significant positive effects on the difference between sales and direct costs after controlling for capital and concentration, which, he believes, reflects specific human capital—i.e., training that is specific to the firm involved. Where training costs are high, the firm should be willing to pay high wages to prevent labor turnover. Telser argues that concentration encourages investment in such forms because it reduces intra-industry mobility and permits the firm to capture much of the gain from even industry-specific human capital. This argument accounts for the otherwise mysterious concentration-quit rate relationship and suggests that the effect may be socially useful.

Yet another aspect of concentration and labor "quality" has come to light. Some have argued that monopolistic industries might take profits in such forms as "socially acceptable" staff (Alchian and Kessel 1960), which could mean racial discrimination. Shepherd found some basis for the assertion —in a simple regression the percentage of executive personnel that was Negro was systematically lower in concentrated than unconcentrated 2-digit industries if we ignore the telephone company (Shepherd 1969). Strauss (1970) found such a relationship for various well-paid occupations—managers, clerical workers, and craftsmen—in multiple regression analyses, though it was largely eliminated once he controlled for education-skill class. My guess is that race is at least partly a proxy for quality of education and that large firms in concentrated industries are buying a stable labor force once more, but there may be an element of managerial preference for whites present as well. One wonders to what extent Telser's specific human capital takes such forms.

3.2. Executive Compensation. An element of labor cost which most economists would probably expect to contain some profits is executive compensation. In small firms the manager and owner are often identical, and in large firms, the separation of ownership and control may provide leeway for officers to absorb some profits. No study attacks this directly, but Williamson produced some relevant results (1963a). His hypothesis was that managers would favor expenses that enter their utility functions. The most obvious is executive compensation. He expected and found a significant positive relation between the top executives' salaries and both concentration and Bain's entry barriers after allowing for general and selling expense as an index of administrative responsibility. The relation with market structure variables was somewhat closer than with profit rates in 1953 and 1961 and roughly similar in 1957. In his view, concentration and barriers show the profit rates available to the firm, some of which are appropriated by its executives. Reported profits would be less likely to determine executive prerequisites than the profit opportunities themselves. This concept is potentially important but it should be tested more thoroughly. The model was well specified (e.g., concentration and barriers were introduced multiplicatively) but he had only 26–30 observations and rather crude data. Executive compensation was limited to salary and bonus, and stockholder control was represented by the inside character of the board of directors. Extensive information on other forms of executive income and on stock diffusion is now available for more than 100 firms (Lewellen 1968; Larner 1966, 1968) and should be used.

The salary and bonus of the chief executive is itself a small portion of corporate profits, but the total cost involved may be large since salaries throughout the corporate hierarchy rise with those at the top of the pyramid.

The main effect of the labor and executive compensation studies is to reinforce the concentration—profits relationship. Some work in this area is useful as an offset to Harberger (1954), but I do not see much concrete policy application for it.

4. Other Expenses

4.0. Advertising. One of the most controversial expenses is advertising. It has been treated both as an element of product differentiation and hence, of structure, and as a type of performance. A tendency for concentration to result in heavy advertising is an old hypothesis. Dorfman and Steiner's model (1954) where the ratio of marginal net revenue to marginal selling cost is equated with elasticity, suggests that firms

in atomistic markets will find advertising less profitable. To this might be added Williamson's analysis of conditions in which it is profitable to advertise to increase entry barriers (Williamson 1963b). Telser (1962) makes the further point that if ads serve partly to enhance the demand for a generic product, then the profitability of advertising will rise with market share.

Another group of hypotheses suggests that heavy advertising causes high concentration. Firms that win strong consumer loyalties are apt to win large market shares in the bargain, and it is commonly supposed that the economies of scale in advertising are often large relative to economies in production.[19]

Both sets of hypotheses suggest a net positive relation between concentration and advertising intensity, but it has been hard to find. Telser (1964) worked with 44 IRS minor industries which sell primarily consumer goods, relating their advertising-sales ratios to weighted averages of four firm concentration in 3 census years and found a non-significant positive effect in each case.[20] He went on to show some evidence that brand market shares were less stable for heavily advertised products, but one wonders how valuable unstable market shares are as an element of performance. He pointed out that average concentration ratios may not reflect extreme values but claims that this does not bias his results since the dependent variable is averaged

---

[19] Comanor and Wilson (1969) tested this using 41 IRS minor industries that sell primarily consumer goods. They estimated minimum efficient firm size (*MEF*) by regressing profit rates on size in 29 industries where profits rise with size. Average advertising rates were relatively low in the other 12. They then attempted to "explain" the ratio of *MEF* to industry size in a cross-industry regression using estimated minimum efficient plant size (*MES*) and advertising intensity. A logarithmic interaction term provided the best (though quite weak) fit, suggesting that advertising increases *MEF* more when *MES* is low than when it is high.

[20] Doyle (1968) arrived at similar results with more detailed British data.

in a similar way. This is correct only if the underlying relationship is linear. Moreover, misdefinition of component markets makes no difference in computing average advertising but creates errors in average concentration. Precisely the same points can be made about an average concentration-profits relationship, however, and it usually does hold up. If there were a relationship present that Telser was unable to detect, it was probably due to an omitted variable, "differentiability" (Caves 1962, pp. 48–54), or, more precisely, the capability for differentiating the product via advertising. Casual observation suggests that this variable, while elusive and difficult to quantify, is large for a small number of products.

Mann et al. (1967) approached the same problem using firm data. They limited themselves to 14 4-digit industries for which data for two or more fairly specialized firms was available. They found a strong positive relationship between average firm advertising rate and concentration in each year covered. These results are also open to question, however, since their sample excluded drugs and toiletries, just the industries which combine high advertising rates with moderate 4-digit concentration ratios.

The expected relationship between concentration and promotion has not been confirmed. Perhaps it cannot be, but some improvements on the model could alter the picture. It is essentially a simultaneous equation problem, one hypothesis pointing to concentration as a determinant of advertising intensity along with product differentiability and the other, to advertising as a determinant of concentration along with the ratio of optimal scale relative to market size. An appropriate model might then be:

$$\frac{A}{S} = k(CR)^b \left(\frac{C}{S}\right)^c \tag{5}$$

$$CR = g\left(\frac{A}{S}\right)^h \left(\frac{MES}{S}\right)^i, \tag{6}$$

where A is advertising expenditures, S is sales, C is final consumption expenditures, and MES is the value of shipments of a plant of minimum efficient scale. A multi-

plicative form is used on the assumptions that the effect of concentration on advertising would be quite different for producer goods and that the effect of advertising on optimal scale is larger the smaller the optimal plant size is (Comanor and Wilson 1969). This simultaneous equation model is itself a simplification. In particular, concentration may well depend on a distributed lag series of advertising, as market share does in most intra-industry studies (Nerlove and Waugh 1961; Telser 1962; Palda 1964; Lambin 1969; Peles 1969). Introducing a distributed lag would result in a complex, dynamic model that would be difficult to estimate.

4.1. Other Costs. Market structure has been expected to affect costs in a variety of other ways as well. High prices associated with high concentration or product differentiation may attract or support excess capacity if barriers to entry are low and may prevent the elimination of excess or suboptimal capacity regardless of entry conditions. To my knowledge, no one has done any convincing empirical work on either hypothesis, presumably for lack of reliable data.

Then there is X-efficiency—the ability of firms to attain minimum costs for their given scales and techniques. Leibenstein's (1966) hypothesis does not directly deal with market structure, but he and Comanor have proposed that the ability or willingness of firms to attain minimum unit costs depends heavily on structure (Comanor and Leibenstein 1969). While this is plausible, no evidence has been presented to support it. I presume the correct test would depend on intra-industry differences in productivity or unit cost for many different industries, which could then be compared in a simple model of the sort:

Variance of Productivity $= a + bCR$.

The Bureau of the Census has the wherewithal to run such a regression; I do not know who else can. The effect of competition on cost is potentially important if it ever can be measured because it involves direct welfare losses due to excessive costs in addition to allocative losses.

5. Stability

The belief that industrial concentration contributes to economic instability is as old as the concentration ratio (National Resources Committee 1939). It has been resurrected in various forms as our experience with the cycle has changed. I wil! leave the role of price rigidity in the great depression to history (summarized in Ruggles 1955). The "administered inflation" hypothesis of the 1950's still seems to affect policy proposals, and it may well reappear once more in the 1970's. Less publicized but potentially as important is the unpredictable character of investment in oligopolistic industries.

5.0. Administered Inflation. Gardner Means, using his 30-year-old classification of industries into those with administered prices, "mixed," and market-determined prices testified in the late 1950's that industries with administered prices had played a minor role in the postwar inflation, but had been the primary element in what came to be known as the administered inflation of the 1950's (Means 1957, 1959).

George Stigler challenged the administered inflation hypothesis as illogical, because profit maximizing monopolists do not raise prices indefinitely. He cited evidence that BLS wholesale price indexes tend to understate price flexibility in concentrated industries and that those indexes rose no more in concentrated than other industries (Stigler 1962). DePodwin and Selden correlated BLS wholesale price relatives for 1959 based on 1953 with various concentration measures for 5-digit and again, 4-digit manufactured products where BLS and SIC definitions could be matched. When they worked with the entire range of manufactured products they found a mild positive effect of concentration on price change, but it was always weak and usually non-significant. Regressions within the larger 2-digit industries yielded seven negative and four positive relations—all but one non-significant again. They concluded that the administered inflation hypothesis could be rejected.

As in the Collins and Preston study discussed above, DePodwin's and Selden's 2-digit results should carry little weight because such samples minimize the variability in concentration while keeping a high variability in output change. The major problem with their study was their failure to allow for changes in cost and demand. I reworked their data for all their 4-digit industries that had comparable SIC definitions in 1953 and 1959, regressing price changes on changes in deflated shipments, unit materials cost, and unit labor cost as well as concentration (Weiss 1966b). Concentration then turned out to have a significant positive effect similar to that proposed by Means. In similar regressions for 1959–63, changes in output and unit material and labor costs had about the same coefficients as in the previous period, but concentration now had a non-significant negative effect. Taking the whole 1953–63 period together, concentration had about the same effect as in the 1950's, suggesting that there had been a once-and-for-all increase in BLS wholesale prices in concentrated industries relative to the less concentrated in the 1950's. This result would be consistent with profit maximization if the concentrated industries were not taking full advantage of their position at the end of the Korean War. Then the administered inflation would amount to a tendency for oligopoly prices to respond to inflationary pressures with a lag.[21] One problem with my administered price study, however, was that the dependent variable was used to deflate output, unit material cost, and unit labor cost. The coefficients of these variables may be biased upward and R^2 may be exaggerated if there were errors in these price relatives. This bias should not affect the main result, however, since the price change and concentration variables were derived independently.

5.1. Wage Rate Changes. The difficult wage change element of administered infla-

---

[21] W. J. Yordan had already shown that for 14 industries, the main effect of market structures on price was to produce relatively great lags between cost and price change (Yordan 1961).

tion is still unsettled. There is a long tradition in labor economics that wage rates rise faster in concentrated industries (summarized in Allen 1968, pp. 353–7). This barely makes sense as a continuous phenomenon, though it could apply in the 1950's if wage levels were initially less than optimal from the point of view of the affected unions.

Several studies have shown significant positive relationships between concentration and wage changes in the 1930's (Garbarino 1950), and the 1950's (Levinson 1960; Bowen 1960; Yordan 1961a; Weiss 1963, 1966b), though negative relationships appear to be common in 1923–29 (Lewis 1963, pp. 158–9) and 1940–47 (Weiss 1963; Lewis 1963, pp. 159–60). Lewis felt that the positive effect of concentration in the 1930's was due to its correlation with the growth in unionism. Bowen and Levinson also introduced employment growth, profit rates, and unionization in explaining wage changes at 2-digit levels for various short periods from 1947 through 1959. The net effect of concentration was ordinarily positive though there was some instability in the relationship due probably to colinearity among the profit, concentration, and unionism variables.

As with the administered prices, the tendency for wage rates to rise faster in concentrated sectors in the 1950's may have been a temporary phenomenon. Allen (1968) related wage changes to concentration on a 3- or 4-digit level on a year-to-year basis from 1949 on and found a non-significant effect in the Korean War Period (1949–51) and the early 1960's (1961–64). My guess is that in the recent inflation the relation will turn out to be negative again. Administered wages like administered prices seem to respond to changing market conditions with a lag. We can probably expect another period of moderate "administered inflation" in the early 1970's along with demands for more guideposts or even direct controls. The basic problem is simply that prices and wages are sticky in the monopolistic sectors.

I have excluded the enormous literature on the Phillips curve from this discussion.

Their results, which seem commonly to show an overall inflationary bias are consistent with only periodic and temporary administered inflations in concentrated sectors. Prices as a whole may rise persistently, but prices in monopolistic sectors only rise with the rest, on the average.

5.2. *Investment.* Scherer introduced another role for market structure in stability last year when he examined the effect of concentration on industrial investment. He found a few scraps of hypotheses on the subject in previous literature, some of which pointed to more stable and some to less stable investment in concentrated markets. Scherer's basic test consisted of a regression covering 80 4-digit industries for which investment series were available.[22] His dependent variable was the standard error of estimate around logarithmic trends of industry capital expenditures; and his explanatory variables were four firm concentration, variability of man-hours around its logarithmic trend, capital-value added ratio, industry size, and dummies for durables, consumer goods, and intermediate materials. The cross-industry regressions yielded a fairly large positive effect for concentration, but it was of only borderline significance. Although concentration is not closely correlated with any one of the other explanatory variables, the significance of its relationship to investment variability falls off rapidly as they are added. In interpreting this, he emphasized the common effects of industry size and concentration, feeling that they tend both to measure diversity of decision making. Finally he examined the residuals from investment functions for 13 2-digit industries estimated by Jorgenson and Stephenson (1967). The standard errors of estimate from these investment functions, expressed as ratios to mean investments, were regressed on

---

[22] His data was from the *Annual Surveys of Manufactures.* In industries where probability sampling is important, investment series from this source may be irregular merely because of periodic sample changes. Probability sampling is important in some unconcentrated but almost never in concentrated industries.

weighted average concentration. The errors were positively correlated with concentration,[23] perhaps supporting the contention that investment in concentrated industries is particularly unstable. Or perhaps, as he says, that the Jorgenson-Stephansen model is misspecified in concentrated industries.

Scherer's paper should eliminate any notions of concentration contributing to stability due to coordination of investment. On the other hand, the instability of investment within concentrated industries is probably not very serious since many such industries, taken together, contain many decision centers, even if any one does not.

Altogether, concentration seems to contribute to short term price and wage stability, though I doubt that this is a virtue, and may make investment somewhat less predictable.

6. Progressiveness

Technological progressiveness seems to be the most important area for industrial organization research for the future. Its main elements are research and development, innovation, and diffusion. The seminal work was that of Schumpeter (1942), who emphasized firm size and market power in explaining each of these, but more recent work has gone far beyond him.

---

[23] The relation to a simple weighted average of concentration ratios was stronger than for a set of weighted averages I had constructed in which I had attempted to correct for non-competing subproducts, inter-industry competition, and the regional character of the market (Weiss 1963). This could mean that my corrections merely introduced random noise. On the other hand, if the greater stability of investment in unconcentrated industries is due to diversity of decision-making rather than reduced monopoly power, then the uncorrected concentration ratios would be the superior measure. Diversity due to regional fragmentation of the market or non-competing sub-products should be just as successful in reducing the standard error of investment as is diversity due to competition within markets. This suggests that Scherer might be able to distinguish between the effects of concentration and diversity in his 4 digit data by using corrected and uncorrected concentration ratios.

6.0. Research and Size. There seems to be agreement that the benefits of basic research are unpredictable and inappropriate for most private enterprise. Only a broadly based monopolist would find such investment profitable. It happens that our most broadly based monopolist, the telephone company, *is* the leading business contributor to basic research.

Most empirical work has dealt with applied research and development where we have more degrees of freedom. Firm size is the favorite variable, presumably because it can be used within industries, thus finessing the problem of interindustry differences in technological opportunity. Most studies show strong positive effects of size on R and D employment or expenditures within broadly defined industries but weak, and often negative effects of size on R and D intensity (Worley 1961; Horowitz 1962; Hamberg 1962, reproduced in 1966, pp. 46–63; Mansfield 1962, reproduced in 1968, p. 39; Scherer 1965; Comanor 1967; Grabowski 1968). The positive effect of size is exaggerated in some broad-based studies because of the high proportion of large-firm research that is financed by government. On the other hand, the samples used in most of these studies contain biases against the size-R and D hypothesis, excluding small firms or, worse, including only those small firms with research staffs. There are other problems[24] in individual studies, but the consistent result is impressive.

---

[24] One problem deserves mention because it arises fairly commonly in industrial organization research and has received little attention. Both Mansfield (1962) and Grasbowski (1968) used pooled cross sections. I have used similar data (Hall and Weiss 1967), but it is quite tricky. It is apt to involve serial correlation because consecutive observations of the same firm are often more closely correlated with each other than with those of other firms. As a result, conventional *t*-ratios may exaggerate the significance of coefficients for slowly changing variables such as size or concentration. Mansfield's 150 observations obtained for 10 firms in 15 years were surely less distinct than 150 different firms, but we are likely to apply the same significance test to both sets of data.

These studies cover R and D inputs, which seem less significant from a public viewpoint than the output of new knowledge. Numbers of patents have sometimes been used as proxies for the latter, and small manufacturing firms (less than 5000 employees) play a larger role here, accounting for only 14% of R and D expenditures but around 40% of both manufacturing patents and sales (Scherer 1965, pp. 1104–5). The difference may reflect some bias in the propensity to patent (Schmookler 1966, pp. 32–5) but another element is the dependence of small firms on part time research done by managerial or sales staff (Schmookler 1959).

The most thorough patent numbers study was Scherer's (1965). He was able to "explain" a remarkably large percentage of inter-firm variance in patent numbers among 352 large industrials by regressing patents on firm size within 2- or 3-digit industries. Interindustry differences in the regression slopes were interpreted as differences in technological opportunity. Using these slopes, he then combined his observations into four fairly homogeneous groupings and tested a cubic sales-patents model and a quadratic R and D intensity-patent intensity model within each grouping. Diminishing returns to sales size and to the R and D personnel-sales ratio were evident over most of the observed range in most groupings. Diversification seemed to reduce patent output in technically progressive groupings, to increase it in the others and to have little overall effect. Altogether, Scherer seems to show that size adds even less to patent output than to R and D input, and that conglomerate bigness has a de minimus effect.

A major problem with patent numbers studies is the varying quality of patents involved.[25] Mansfield tried to avoid this by tracking down the most important inventions in chemicals, petroleum, and steel (Mansfield 1964, reproduced in 1968, pp. 40–2). He regressed the sum of these (weighted by the number of times they were mentioned by experts) on the firm's R and D expense, its R and D expense squared, and an R and D-size interaction. He imposed a zero intercept without giving any reason and he suppressed several non-significant coefficients—a dangerous practice when colinearity is as likely as it is here. But this is carping. The amazing thing is that he detected any relationship at all with only 10 observations in chemicals, 8 in petroleum, and 11 in steel.

Comanor's pharmaceutical industry study was based on more convincing data (Comanor 1965). He worked with 57 firms and could distinguish all new chemical entities, weighting them by their first two years' sales, a seemingly more objective basis for evaluating inventions. His model was unfortunately very complex:

$$\frac{N}{S} = f\left(\frac{R}{S}, \frac{R^2}{S}, S, R \cdot S, D\right), \qquad (7)$$

where N is the weighted sum of new chemical entities, S is sales, R is numbers of professional research personnel, and D is diversification within ethical drugs. After estimating the coefficients, he multiplied through by S in order to estimate the marginal product of R, so that:

$$N = f(S, R, R^2, S^2, R \cdot S^2, D \cdot S). \qquad (8)$$

The results were similar to Mansfield's chemical industry results: both show in-

---

[25] The propensity to patent appears to vary systematically over time (a downward trend), between individuals and corporations (higher for individuals) and among industries (Schmookler 1966, pp. 23–56). At least within the drug industry (Comanor and Scherer 1969) inter-firm variations in patent numbers seem to be signifi-

cantly correlated with the weighted sum of new products, but they are better correlated with total R and D staff, and the latter "explains" as much of the variance in new product as patents do. These results suggest that high R and D intensity is positively related to the propensity to patent. Moreover, patents correlate more closely with total R and D personnel than with professionals and more closely with all new products (including those already marketed in other dosages or combinations or under other brands) than with new chemical entities. All this suggest that patents reflect new R and D input better than significant R and D output.

creasing returns to research intensity[26] and a decline in the marginal product of R and D at any level of R and D as size grows. Rough calculations using Comanor's regressions suggest that dN/dS is also positive, but this is uncertain because no values are reported for D or for dR/dS, both of which are needed to find dN/dS.

6.1. Market Structures and R and D. Schumpeter emphasizes market power as well as size as determinants of progressiveness. Both Hamberg (1966, pp. 63–5) and Horowitz (1962) found significant positive effects of concentration on R and D expenditure at two digit levels using NSF and early post war surveys. Scherer (1965, pp. 1116–1121) identified the four leading firms in 48 narrower industries within his moderately or highly progressive groupings and regressed their 1954 patents appropriate to the industry involved on sales size, concentration, and chemical and electrical industry dummies. Concentration had a mild positive effect. In another test two years later (Scherer 1967) he used the numbers of scientific and engineering personnel by industry from the 1960 population census corrected for government-financed research and the percentage of such personnel in formal R and D activities. The ratio of this scientific and engineering personnel variable to total industry employment rose with both size and concentration. Most of the correlation between R and D intensity and concentration occurred within the sector that he had identified as "traditional," where there was little opportunity for progressiveness. Comanor (1967) found a similar result when he distinguished differentiated durables, where design competition is important, from material inputs and consumer non-durables. Concentration had a positive effect in the latter but no effect in the technologically more progressive differentiated durable goods industries.

Perhaps because I am a relative out-

sider in this area, I finish reading each of the size or concentration—R and D input or output studies with some skepticism, but, taken together, they are more convincing. Most studies show that within their range of observation, size adds little to research intensity and may actually detract from it in some industries. A common caveat is that a threshold size is probably required for many important types of R and D. Most studies are based mainly on firms from the top 500 industrials and are not well designed to detect that threshold (Markham 1965). The failure to detect the R and D size threshold is probably not very important for policy, however, since merger policy is normally oriented toward the leading firms in an industry. A strict policy at that level apparently cannot do much damage to privately financed R and D effort.

On the other hand, I draw the tentative verdict that concentration is positively related to R and D intensity. Perhaps, as some have suggested (Horowitz 1962; Phillips 1966; Comanor 1967; Scherer 1967) we have the line of causation at least partially reversed, with technological progressiveness contributing to concentration. If so, a simultaneous equation model along the line of the following seems in order:

$$\begin{cases} R/S = f(CR, \text{ Technological Opportunity}) \\ CR = f(R/S, MES/VS). \end{cases}$$

A logically superior alternative might be a dynamic system where concentration is dependent on distributed lags of R/S and is a partial determinant of current R/S, but such a model would be difficult to estimate.

Even if concentration has a significantly positive effect on R and D, it does not follow that oligopoly would increase productivity growth in presently unconcentrated industries. It seems common for process R and D to be centralized in equipment industries, so that many processing and consumer goods industries could be unconcentrated with little or no loss in inventive output.

Finally, there is the effect of diversification. I cannot find any good way to reconcile Grabowski's positive effect with

---

[26] The line of causation may be reversed here. Grabowski quite plausibly makes R and D intensity a function of patent productivity of the firm's scientific personnel (Grabowski 1968).

Comanor's negative effect and Scherer's roughly neutral effect.[27] At present, I judge that the issue is unsettled and a good candidate for more work, especially in view of its potential relevance to the conglomerate merger debate.

6.2. *Innovation.* Schumpeter put great emphasis on the innovation decision but data problems have virtually limited us to historical case studies and Mansfield's extensive and ingenious research. In his fundamental study Mansfield (1963; reproduced in 1968, Ch. 5) developed a list of major innovations in steel, petroleum and coal in 1919–38 and 1939–58 and found the first commercial user of each. The four largest firms had a larger share of total innovations than of capacity in petroleum and coal, but less than their share in steel. He also estimated the mean investment and asset size required to introduce each industry's innovations in each period, and developed a model where the four industry leaders' share of innovations depended on their size relative to other firms above the threshold and on the investment requirements relative to threshold size. The model was estimated using steel and petroleum process and product innovations in the two periods. It seemed to predict passably when later applied to the railroads. The analysis is impressive, but the empirical estimates based on five *possibly* independent degrees of freedom are inherently unconvincing.

He went on to regress numbers of innovations on the log of asset size in a cubic model for each type of innovation in each industry and period. The coefficients suggested diminishing returns to size after some

point for most products except coal. He had plenty of degrees of freedom this time, but the dependent variable was zero and size was apparently small in about 95% of the cases. His evidence of diminishing returns depended on the upper tail of the distribution where he again had only a few observations.

Mansfield's remarkable study was partially reconstructed by Williamson (1965), who used it to test the hypothesis that leading firms were more likely to innovate than small firms as concentration increased. He found that the ratio of the top four firms' share of innovations to their share of capacity declined as concentration increased with an almost perfect correlation ($R^2 = 0.985$). Adding Mansfield's later data on railroads would re-enforce this result if a national concentration ratio were used, but using regional concentration would reduce the correlation to non-significance. At any rate, the Schumpeterian hypothesis is not supported.

Between them, Mansfield and Williamson have wrung more results from the same 4 or 5 degrees of freedom than you commonly see in print. While in much of industrial organization research the theory has been weaker than the data, this case is at the opposite extreme. I should think that it would be possible to develop more lists of major innovations for maybe 20 industries and to identify the innovators so that at least some of the ingenious hypotheses in these papers could be properly tested. This enterprise would seem the natural subject for Ph.D. theses.

We have little more than hypotheses now, but it should be feasible to find enough data to test them. Until we do the correct statement is that we *probably* need not worry about the effect on innovation of merger policy within the range in which it operates.

6.3. *Diffusion.* The speed with which an industry adopts new techniques once they have been introduced is the final element of progressiveness. It is the crucial element in a competitive industry serviced by technologically progressive suppliers.

---

[27] In both Comanor and Grabowski (1965; and 1968) diversification is a determinant of R/S while in Scherer (1965) it is related to R. Comanor's data seem cleaner than Grabowski's. He has far more observations and his diversification variable is based on 40 classes of drugs instead of the nine 5-digit products used by Grabowski. Scherer's data were for one year rather than several, his diversification measure referred to four digit or broader classes and extended beyond the drug field. I can reconcile Scherer with either Grabowski or Comanor but not with both.

The classic study of diffusion was Griliches' work on hybrid corn (1957) in which he fit logistic curves to hybrid corn planting within states. The three parameters of the logistic, its origin, slope, and ceiling, then became dependent variables for further analysis. In a series of cross-state regressions he let the origin depend on variables likely to affect the initial entry of seed producers into a state and the initial adoption of the product by farmers. Similarly, the slope and the ceiling of the logistic curve depended on indexes of the profitability of the change in the various states. He concluded that corn growers had responded in a way that might be expected of rational profit-maximizers.

Mansfield adapted this model to the industrial sector. He decomposed diffusion into imitation, the initial adoption by a firm of a new technique, and intra-firm diffusion.

His imitation study (Mansfield 1961; reproduced in 1968, Ch. 7) traced the percentage of major firms adopting each of 12 innovations from four industries. He fit a logistic function to each imitation series, and made their slopes dependent on the size of the initial investment relative to assets per firm, the profitability of the new investment relative to industry expected profitability, and industry dummies. He then examined those industry dummies and felt that he saw the speed of imitation increasing with competitiveness. As usual, the model was brilliant and the fit was remarkable, but the second regression was based on 5 degrees of freedom, and the implicit regression of speed of imitation on competitiveness[28] may have had 2! We obviously need more observations, which should mean more Ph.D. theses.

Using similar data, he later showed (Mansfield 1963b, reproduced in 1968. Ch. 9) that individual large firms are, on the average, quicker to imitate than smaller firms, though he did not feel he had enough observations to answer the more basic question of whether the larger firms were quicker to imitate than groups of smaller firms with about the same number of investment decisions to make.

I wonder if the problem was all that difficult. He had almost 300 observations for 14 innovations. I should think that he could have grouped smaller firms to create combinations equal in size to the largest firm in each industry. Assuming each firm to be half the size of the next, he would have had 4 or 5 observations per innovation. He could have then regressed imitation delay on the average size of firm in a grouping, perhaps pooling innovations with dummies for each industry or even each innovation. He would have been able to say with unaccustomed certainty whether the speed of imitation was enhanced or delayed by having an industry of large firms.[29]

Finally, Mansfield studied intra-firm diffusion using the case of the diesel locomotive (1963c, reproduced in 1968, Ch. 9). He again fit logistic curves within each firm and was able to "explain" 69% of the inter-firm variance in the slope parameters using four plausible variables. The diesel locomotive, on the average, was diffused more slowly within larger firms. This size effect was non-significant where diffusion was measured in numbers of locomotives, but significant, though small, when measured in ton-miles hauled.

The upshot of the diffusion studies is that smaller firms and competitive industries do at least as well as large and oligopolistic firms in adopting new techniques once they have been introduced, but as usual, the evidence is based on a handful of instances. I would think that future work

---

[28] His two independent variables cast some light themselves. For any given innovation, imitation response would be slower, the greater the average expected rate of return in an industry. It will also be slower, the smaller the average assets of major firms. Competition affects both of these variables, so there may be some case for regressing the slope coefficients on concentration directly.

[29] In the one case for which data is given—dieselization (1968, p. 182)—a simple regression of group imitation lag on average firm size within the yields a significant tendency for large firms to delay longer ($R^2 = 0.62$ with $7 - 2 = 5$ degrees of freedom).

on this subject will often be easier if imitation and intra-firm diffusion are melded as they were in Griliches' study. Mansfield's distinction is conceptually useful, but the data probably will not allow it very often.

Altogether, the analysis of technological progressiveness has been more imaginative than that in much of the rest of industrial organization, but the data (except for patents) has been hard to come by, so the tests are often not convincing. Since I suspect the performance payoff from market structure could be great in this area, a high priority should be given to digging out enough data to make the conclusions credible.

7. Omissions

I have intentionally limited this paper to the market structure-performance relationship as probably the most critical for public policy. One element of performance—the social and political impact of the large or monopolistic firm—is omitted merely because statistically oriented economists have left it untouched, though it abounds in untested hypotheses. I have also left out the burgeoning studies of managerial motivation (Williamson 1963a; Larner 1968; Kamerschen 1968; Monsen et al. 1968). In addition I have largely ignored our spotty attempts to explain industry structure: (a) the still fairly blank field on economies of scale and of long production runs, (b) an occasional study of mergers that gets beyond the descriptive level, and (c) our enormous, intellectually elegant literature on the log normal distribution of firm sizes, the next important policy implication of which will be its first. I have also left out the industry studies completely—the annual, ever more precise, cost or production function for electric power (Johnston 1960, Ch. 4-1; Kimiya 1962; Nerlove 1963; Barzel 1964; Dhrymes and Kurz 1964; Ling 1964; Galatin 1968); Fisher's careful estimates of the elasticity of supply of oil and gas exploratory drilling (1964); MacAvoy's ingenious methods for detecting monopoly or competition in gas fields and ancient railroad documents (1964, 1965); Caves' study of air transport (1962); or Meyer et al.'s potentially revolutionary examination of rail and truck costs (1959). Such studies are of great importance—in regulated industries in particular—and their payoff may well exceed anything we can accomplish in the unregulated sector, merely because performance in the regulated sectors seems so unsatisfactory. Perhaps the right next step is back to the industry study, but this time with regression in hand.

REFERENCES

Alchian, A. and R. A. Kessel, 1960, Competition, monopoly, and the pursuit of money. In: Universities—National Bureau, *Aspects of Labor Economics*. Princeton, N.J., Princeton University Press, 70–81.

Alexander, S. S., 1949, The effect of size of manufacturing corporations on the distribution of the rate of return. *Review of Economics and Statistics* 31, No. 3 (August), 229–235.

Allen, B. T., 1968, Market concentration and wage increases: U.S. manufacturing, 1947–1964. *Industrial and Labor Relations Review* 21, No. 3 (April), 353–366.

Arnould, R. J., 1968, The effect of market and firm structure on the performance of food processing firms. Ph. D. Thesis, Iowa State Univ., Ames.

Asch, P., 1967, Industry structure and performance: some empirical evidence. *Review of Social Economy* 25, No. 2 (Sep.), 167–182.

Bain, J. S., 1951, Relation of profit rate to industry concentration: American manufacturing 1936–1940. *Quarterly Journal of Economics* 65, No. 3 (August), 293–324.

Bain, J. S., 1956, *Barriers to new competition*. Cambridge, Mass., Harvard University Press.

Bain, J. S., 1968, *Industrial Organization*, Second Edition, New York: John Wiley and Sons.

Barzel, Y., 1964, The production function and technical change in the steam power industry. *Journal of Political Economy* 72, No. 2 (April), 133–150.

Bowen, W. G., 1960, *Wage behavior in the post war period*. Princeton, N.J., Princeton University Press.

Burton, J. F., Jr. and J. E. Parker, 1969, Inter-industry variations in voluntary labor mobility. *Industrial and Labor Relations Review* 22, No. 2 (January), 199–216.

Cabinet Committee on Price Stability, 1969, *Studies by the staff*. Washington, Government Printing Office.

Caves, R., 1962, *Air transport and its regulators*. Cambridge, Mass., Harvard University Press.

Collins, N. H. and L. E. Preston, 1966, Concentration and price cost margins in food manufacturing industries. *Journal of Industrial Economics* 14, No. 3 (July), 226–42.

Collins, N. H. and L. E. Preston, 1968, *Concentration and price cost margins in manufacturing industries*. Berkeley, Calif., University of California Press.

Collins, N. H. and L. E. Preston, 1969, Price—cost margins and industry structure. *Review of Economics and Statistics* 51, No. 3 (August), 271–286.

Comanor, W. S., 1965, Research and technical change in the pharmaceutical industry. *The Review of Economics and Statistics* 47, No. 2 (May), 182–90.

Comanor, W. S., 1967, Market structure, product differentiation, and industrial research. *Quarterly Journal of Economics* 81, No. 4 (November), 639–657.

Comanor, W. S. and H. Leibenstein, 1969, Allocative efficiency, x-efficiency and the measurement of welfare loss. *Economica,* New Series 36, No. 143 (August), 304–309.

Comanor, W. S. and F. M. Scherer, 1969. Patent statistics as a measure of technical change. *Journal of Political Economy* 77, No. 3 (May/Je), 392–98.

Comanor, W. S. and T. A. Wilson, 1967, Advertising, market structure, and performance. *Review of Economics and Statistics* 49, No. 4 (November), 423–440.

Comanor, W. S. and T. A. Wilson, 1969, Advertising and the economics of scale. *American Economic Review* 59, No. 2 (May), 87–98.

Crum, W. L., 1939, *Corporate size and earning power*. Cambridge, Mass., Harvard University Press.

DePodwin, H. J. and R. T. Selden, 1963, Business pricing policies and inflation. *Journal of Political Economy* 71, No. 2 (April), 110–127.

Dhrymes, P. and M. Kurz, 1964, Technology and scale in electricity generation. *Econometrica* 32, No. 3 (July), 287–314.

Dorfman, R. and P. O. Steiner, 1954, Optimal advertising and optimal quality. *American Economic Review* 54, No. 5 (December), 826–836.

Doyle, A., 1968, Advertising expenditures and consumer demand. *Oxford Economic Papers,* New Series 20, No. 3 (November), 395–416.

Fisher, F. M., 1964, *Supply and costs in the U.S. petroleum industry*. Resources for the Future. Baltimore, Johns Hopkins Press.

Food Marketing Commission Technical Study No. 8, 1966. *The structure of food marketing*. Washington, Government Printing Office.

Fuchs, V. R., 1961, Integration, concentration and profits in manufacturing industries. *Quarterly Journal of Economics* 75, No. 2 (May), 278–290.

Fuchs, V. R., 1968, *The service economy*. New York, Columbia University Press.

Galatin, M., 1968, *Economies of scale and technological change in thermal power generation*. Amsterdam, North-Holland Publishing Company.

Gambeles, G., 1969, Structural determinants of profit performance in United States manufacturing industries, 1947–1967. Ph. D. thesis, University of Maryland.

Garbarino, J. W., 1950, A theory of interindustry wage variation. *Quarterly Journal of Economics* 64, No. 2 (May), 299–305.

George, K. D., 1968, Concentration, barriers to entry, and rates of return. *Review of Economics and Statistics* 50, No. 2 (May), 273–275.

Gort, M., 1962, *Diversification and integration in American industry*. Princeton, N.J., Princeton University Press.

Gort, M., 1963, Analysis of stability and change in market shares. *Journal of Political Economy* 71, No. 1 (February), 51–63.

Grabowski, H. G., 1968, The determinants of industrial research and development: a study of the chemical, drug and petroleum industries. *Journal of Political Economy* 76, No. 2 (March/April), 292–306.

Griliches, Z., Hybrid corn: an exploration in the economics of technological change. *Econometrica* 25, No. 4 (October), 501–522.

Hall, M. and L. Weiss, 1967, Firm size and profitability. *Review of Economics and Statistics* 49, No. 3 (August), 319–331.

Hamberg, D., 1966, *R and D, essays on the economics of research and development*. New York, Random House.

Harberger, A. C., 1954, Monopoly and resource allocation. *American Economic Review* 44, No. 2 (May), 77–97.

Horowitz, I., 1962, Firm size and research activity. *Southern Economic Journal* 28, No. 3 (January), 298–301.

Imel, B., 1970, Structure-profits relationships in the food processing sector. Ph. D. Thesis, Univ. of Wisconsin.

Johnston, J., 1960, *Statistical cost analysis*. New York, McGraw Hill.

Jorgenson, D. W. and J. A. Stephenson, 1967, The time structure of investment behavior in U.S. manufacturing, 1947–1960. *Review of Economics and Statistics* 49, No. 2 (February).

Kamerschen, D. R., 1969, The determination of profit rates in 'oligopolistic' industries. *Journal of Business* 42, No. 3 (July), 293–301.

Kaysen, L. and D. Turner, 1959, *Anti-trust economics*. Cambridge, Mass., Harvard University Press.

Kelly, W. (FTC), 1969, *Economic report on the influence of market structure on profit performance of food manufacturing firms*. A Federal Trade Commission economic report. Washington, Government Printing Office.

Kilpatrick, R. W., 1967, The choice among alternative measures of industrial concentration. *Review of Economics and Statistics* 44, No. 2 (May), 258–60.

Kilpatrick, R. W., 1968, Stigler on the relationship between industry profit rates and market concentration. *Journal of Political Economy* 76, No. 3 (May/June), 479–488.

Komiya, R., 1962, Technical progress and the production function in the United States steam power industry. *Review of Economics and Statistics* 44, No. 2 (May), 156–66.

Lambin, J. J., 1969, Measuring the profitability of advertising: an empirical study. *Journal of Industrial Economics* 17, No. 2 (April), 86–103.

Larner, R. J., 1966, Ownership and control in the 200 largest non-financial corporations, 1929 and 1963. *American Economic Review* 56, No. 4 (September), 777–87.

Larner, R. J., 1968, Separation of ownership and control and its implications for the behavior of the firm. Unpublished Ph. D. Thesis, University of Wisconsin.

Leibenstein, H., 1966, Allocative efficiency vs. x-efficiency. *American Economic Review* 56, No. 3 (June), 392–415.

Lerner, A., 1933, The concept of monopoly and the measurement of monopoly power. *Review of Economic Studies* 1, No. 3, 157–175.

Levinson, H. M., 1960, Post war movements in prices and wages in manufacturing industries. Joint Economic Committee, *Study of Income, Employment, and Prices*. Study Paper No. 21, Washington, Government Printing Office.

Lewis, H. G., 1963, *Unionism and relative wages in the United States.* Chicago, University of Chicago Press.

Lewellen, W. G., 1968, *Executive compensation in large industrial corporations.* National Bureau of Economic Research, New York, Columbia University Press.

Ling, S., 1964, *Economies of scale in the steam electric power generating industry.* Amsterdam, North-Holland Publishing Company.

Long, W., 1970, An econometric study of performance in American manufacturing. Ph. D. thesis, University of California.

MacAvoy, P. W., 1962, *Price formation in natural gas fields.* New Haven, Conn., Yale University Press.

MacAvoy, P. W., 1965, *The economic effects of regulation: the trunk line railroad cartels and the Interstate Commerce Commission before 1900.* Cambridge, Mass., The MIT Press.

Mann, H. M., 1966, Seller concentration, barriers to entry, and rates of return in thirty industries, 1950–1960. *Review of Economics and Statistics* 48, No. 3 (August), 296–307.

Mann, H. M., J. A. Hennings, and J. W. Meehan, Jr., 1967, Advertising and concentration: an empirical investigation. *Journal of Industrial Economics* 16, No. 1 (November), 34–45.

Mansfield, E., 1961, Technical change and the rate of imitation. *Econometrica* 29, No. 4 (October), 741–766.

Mansfield, E., 1963a, Intrafirm rates of diffusion of an innovation. *Review of Economics and Statistics* 45, No. 4 (November), 348–359.

Mansfield, E., 1963b, Size of firm, market structure, and innovation. *Journal of Political Economy* 71, No. 6 (December), 556–576.

Mansfield, E., 1963c, The speed of response of firms to new techniques. *Quarterly Journal of Economics* 77, No. 2 (May), 290–311.

Mansfield, E., 1964, Industrial research and development expenditures: determinants, prospects, and rela-

tion to size of firm and inventive output. *Journal of Political Economy* 72, No. 4 (August), 319–340.

Marcus, M., 1969, Profitability and size of firm. *Review of Economics and Statistics* 51, No. 1 (February), 104–107.

Markham, J. W., 1965, Market structure, business conduct and innovation. *American Economic Review* 55, No. 2 (May), 323–332.

Mason, E. S., 1939, Price and production policies of large scale enterprise. *American Economic Review* 29, No. 1 (March), 61–74.

Masters, S. H., 1969, An inter industry analysis of wage and plant size. *Review of Economics and Statistics* 51, No. 3 (August), 341–345.

Means, G., 1957, Before the senate judiciary, sub-committee on anti-trust and monopoly. *Hearings on Administered Prices,* Washington, Government Printing Office. Part I, 124–5. Part IX (do., 1959), 4746–58. Part X (do., 1959), 4897–4910.

Meyer, J. R., M. J. Peck, J. Stenason and C. Zwick, 1959, *The economics of competition in the transportation industries.* Cambridge, Mass., Harvard University Press.

Miller, R. A., 1967, Marginal concentration and industrial profit rates. *Southern Economic Journal* 24, No. 4 (October), 259–268.

Minhas, B. S., 1963, *An international comparison of factor cost and factor use.* Amsterdam, North-Holland Publishing Company, 82–84.

Monsen, R., J. S. Chiu, and D. E. Cooley, 1968, The effect of separation of ownership and control on the performance of the large firm. *Quarterly Journal of Economics* 82, No. 3 (August), 435–451.

National Resources Committee, 1939, *The structure of the American economy.* Part I: *Basic characteristics.* Washington, Government Printing Office.

Nelson, R. L., 1963, *Concentration in the manufacturing industries of the*

United States. New Haven, Conn., Yale University Press.

Nerlove, M., 1963, Returns to scale in electricity supply. *Measurement in economics—Studies in mathematical economics and econometrics in memory of Yehuda Grunfeld*. Stanford, Calif., Stanford University Press, 167–198.

Nerlove, M. and F. V. Waugh, 1961, Advertising without supply control. *Journal of Farm Economics* 43 (November).

Palda, K. S., 1964, *The measurement of cumulative advertising effects*. Ford Doctoral Dissertation Series. Englewood Cliffs, N.J., Prentice Hall.

Peles, Y., 1969, Rates of amortization of advertising expenditures. Unpublished Ph. D. thesis, Graduate School of Business, University of Chicago.

Phillips, A., 1966, Patents, potential competition, and technical progress. *American Economic Review* 56, No. 2 (May), 301–31.

Reder, M., 1962, Wage differentials, theory and measurement. In: Universities—National Bureau. *Aspects of Labor Economics*. Princeton, N.J., Princeton University Press, 285–286.

Ross, A. M. and W. Goldner, 1950, Forces affecting the interindustry wage structure. *Quarterly Journal of Economics* 64, No. 2 (May), 280–281.

Ruggles, R., 1955, The nature of price flexibility and the determinants of relative price changes in the economy. In: Universities—National Bureau, *Business Concentration and Price Policy*, Princeton, N.J., Princeton University Press, 441–495.

Sato, Kazuo, 1961, Price-cost structure and behavior of profit margins. *Yale Economic Essays* 1, No. 2 (Fall), 361–418.

Samuels, J. M. and D. J. Smyth, 1968, Profits, variability of profits, and firm size. *Economica* New Series 35, No. 138 (May), 127–149.

Scherer, F. M., 1965, Firm size, market structure, opportunity and the output of patented inventions. *American Economic Review* 55, No. 5, Part I (December), 1097–1125.

Scherer, F. M., 1967, Market structure and the employment of scientists and engineers. *American Economic Review* 57, No. 3 (June), 524–531.

Scherer, F. M., 1969, Market structure and the stability of investment. *American Economic Review* 59, No. 2 (May), 72–79.

Schmookler, J., 1959, Bigness, fewness, and research. *Journal of Political Economy* 67, No. 6 (December), 628–632.

Schmookler, J., 1966, *Invention and economic growth*. Cambridge, Mass., Harvard University Press.

Schumpeter, J., 1942, *Capitalism, socialism and democracy*. New York, Harper.

Schwartzman, D., 1959, The effect of monopoly on price. *Journal of Political Economy* 67, No. 4 (August), 352–62.

Segal, M., 1964, The relation between union wage impact and market structure. *Quarterly Journal of Economics*, 78 (February), 96–114.

Shepherd, W. G., 1969, Market power and racial discrimination in white collar employment. *Anti-Trust Bulletin* 14 (Spring), 141–161.

Sherman, H. J., 1964, *Macro-dynamic economics*. New York, Appleton-Century-Crofts, Ch. 8.

Sherman, H. J., 1968, *Profits in the United States*. Ithaca, Cornell Univ. Press, Ch. 3.

Solomon, B., 1967, Determinants of interfirm differences in profitability among the largest 500 U.S. industrial firms. Ph. D. thesis, University of California.

Stafford, F., 1968, Concentration and labor earnings: comment. *American Economic Review* 58 (March), 174–181 and my reply, 181–185.

Stekler, H. O., 1963, *Profitability and size of firm*. Berkeley, Calif., Institute of Business and Economic Research, University of California.

Stekler, H. O., 1964, The variability of profitability with size of firm 1947–1958. *Journal of the American Statistical Association* 59, No. 308 (December), 1183–1193.

Stigler, G., 1942, The extent and bases of monopoly. *American Economic Review* 32, No. 2, Part 2 (June), 1–22.

Stigler, G., 1950, Monopoly and oligopoly by merger. *American Economic Review* 40, No. 2 (May), 23–34.

Stigler, G., 1956, The statistics of monopoly and merger. *Journal of Political Economy* 64 (February), 33–40.

Stigler, G., 1962, Administered prices and oligopolistic inflation. *Journal of Business* 35, No. 1 (January), 235–251.

Stigler, G., 1963, *Capital and rates of return in manufacturing industries.* Princeton, N.J., Princeton University Press for NBER.

Stigler, G., 1964, A theory of oligopoly. *Journal of Political Economy* 72, No. 1 (February), 44–61.

Stigler, G., 1968, *The organization of industry.* Homewood, Ill., Irwin.

Stoikov, V. and R. L. Raimon, 1968, Determinants of differences in the quit rate among industries. *American Economic Review* 58, No. 5, Part I (December), 1283–1298.

Strauss, R. P., 1970, Discrimination against Negroes in the labor market. Ph. D. thesis, Univ. of Wisconsin.

Telser, L., 1962, Advertising and cigarettes. *Journal of Political Economy* 70, No. 5 (October) 471–499.

Telser, L., 1964, Advertising and competition. *Journal of Political Economy* 72, No. 6 (December), 537–562.

Telser, L., 1969, Some determinants of the returns to manufacturing industries. Report No. 6935. Center for Mathematical Studies in Business and Economics, University of Chicago. (Unpublished.)

Throop, A. W., 1968, The union–non-union wage differential and cost-push inflation. *American Economic Review* 58, No. 1 (March), 83–4.

Watson, D. and M. Holman, 1967, Concentration of patents from government financed research in industry. *Review of Economics and Statistics,* (August), 375–381.

Weiss, L. W., 1963, Average concentration ratios and industry performance. *Journal of Industrial Economics,* No. 3 (July), 247–252.

Weiss, L. W., 1966a, Concentration and labor earnings. *American Economic Review* 56, No. 1 (March), 95–117.

Weiss, L. W., 1966b, Business pricing policies and inflation reconsidered. *Journal of Political Economy* 74, No. 2 (April), 177–187.

Weiss, L. W., 1969, Advertising, profits and corporate taxes. *Review of Economics and Statistics* 51, No. 4 (November), 421–430.

Williamson, O. E., 1963a, Managerial discretion and business behavior. *American Economic Review* 52, No. 5 (December), 1032–1057.

Williamson, O. E., 1963b, Selling expense as a barrier to entry. *Quarterly Journal of Economics* 77, No. 1 (February), 112–128.

Williamson, O. E., 1965, Innovation and market structure. *Journal of Political Economy* 73, No. 1 (February), 67–73.

Worley, J. S., 1961, Industrial research and the new competition. *Journal of Political Economy* 59, No. 2 (April), 183–6.

Yordan, W. J., 1961a, Another look at monopoly and wages. *Canadian Journal of Economics and Political Science* 27, No. 3 (August), 372–9.

Yordan, W. J., 1961b, Industrial concentration and price flexibility in inflation: Price response rates in fourteen industries, 1947–1958. *Review of Economics and Statistics* 43, No. 3 (August), 287–294.

Part II–C · *Prices*

Concentrated industries have been charged with maintaining higher than competitive prices, price rigidity, causing inflation by raising prices, and causing recessions by failing to reduce prices in periods of declining demand. The contention that concentrated industries maintain higher prices than would less concentrated industries is, in part, based on the studies that found a correlation between profits and concentration. If profits are "high" in concentrated industries, then this must be, it is argued, because prices are high. That profits may be high because of temporary disequilibria (as shown in selection 14) or because of efficiencies flowing from concentration which both make profits high and prices low (as postulated in selection 5) tended to be disregarded.

On the latter point, Professor J. H. Landon found, in a study of the newspaper industry, that an increase in concentration may be more than offset by economies of scale in influencing the price of advertising.[1] Other things equal, an increase by 20 percentage points in a leading newspaper's percentage of total circulation in a metropolitan area increased the milline advertising rate by 22 cents, he found. However, other things do not, of course, remain equal. If, in a two newspaper town, a 400,000 copy newspaper merges with a 100,000 newspaper, not only would concentration increase, but also the circulation of the leading newspaper. If circulation increases to 500,000, the net effect of increased concentration and increased circulation is a reduction in the milline rate from \$3.58 to \$3.52.

Professor David Schwartzman attempted to measure directly the influence of concentration on prices by using Ca-

---

[1] J. H. Landon, "The Relation of Market Concentration to Advertising Rates: The Newspaper Industry," 16 *Antitrust Bulletin* 53 (1971).

nadian data in concentrated Canadian industries and U.S. data for the same industries which were not concentrated in the U.S. He concluded that concentrated industry prices were 8.3 percent higher than they would be if those industries were not concentrated, using a limited sample of industries available from a 1954 Canadian census.[2] Although this might be explained by the differences in scale of the two countries' industries, with scale economies accounting for the concentration found in Canada and lack of sufficient size to achieve full scale economies accounting for the higher prices in Canada, the data were, nevertheless, used to project welfare losses presumably occurring in the U.S. assuming that U.S. concentrated industries "raised" prices as much as Canadian concentrated industries.[3] Professor Joan Bodoff (selection 18), writing her dissertation under Professor Schwartzman, has found that larger samples, made possible by more recent Canadian censuses, do not show the price effects of concentration found by Professor Schwartzman.

Evidence appearing in selection 22, in the following section, shows "that the level of prices is not very responsive to the actual number of rivals. This is in keeping with the expectation . . . that the number of buyers, the proportion of new buyers, and the relative sizes of firms are as important as the number of rivals." It should be added that potential entry is also important as well as the economies of scale mentioned above.

The price rigidity charge made by Gardiner Means[4] was supported by a theoretical formulation rationalizing price rigidity produced by Professor Paul Sweezy in the form of the kinked demand curve.[5] Professor George Stigler refuted the latter logically and empirically in an often reprinted article.[6] The data used by Means have been shown to be inadequate for his purpose by Alfred C. Neal[7] and Professor Harry McAllister.[8] The final nail in the coffin in which the price rigidity thesis is now buried (at least, in terms of presently available data) was driven by Professors Stigler and Kindahl (selection 19) using transactions prices instead of the quoted prices used by the Bureau of Labor Statistics.

Professor Lester Telser (selection 20) points out "that prices of certain kinds of products tend to be stabilized . . . in order to gain narrower changes in rates of output." He, in effect, stands on its head the contention that rigid prices contribute to the deepening of recessions. He shows that stabilized prices for some goods contribute to economic stability. Further, the stabilization of prices depends not on concentration but on the character of the product and "can happen with perfect competition."

The last selection in this section reviews the data relating concentration and inflations and uses the most recent data available for testing the relationship in the period of the 1960's. Both positive and negative correlations are found, depending on the period examined. Evidently, there is no long run relationship between what Professor Weiss calls oligopoly (his synonym for concentrated industries) and inflation in the U.S.[9] Similar findings have been

---

[2] David Schwartzman, "The Effect of Monopoly on Price," 67 *Journal of Political Economy* 352 (1959).

[3] David Schwartzman, "The Burden of Monopoly," 68 *Journal of Political Economy* 627 (1960).

[4] *Industrial Prices and Their Relative Inflexibility*, Senate Document 13 (January 17, 1935), 74th Cong., 1st Sess. and National Resources Committee, *The Structure of the American Economy* (1939), Pt. 1.

[5] Paul Sweezy, "Demand Under Conditions of Oligopoly," 47 *Journal of Political Economy* 568 (1939).

[6] George J. Stigler, "The Kinky Oligopoly Demand Curve and Rigid Prices," 55 *Journal of Political Economy* 432 (1947).

[7] Alfred C. Neal, *Industrial Concentration and Price Inflexibility* (1942).

[8] Harry McAllister in *Government Price Statistics* (1961), Subcommittee on Economic Statistics of the Joint Economic Committee.

[9] Professor Fred Weston, testifying before the Subcommittee of the Committee on the Judiciary,

produced in an examination of European markets.[10]

U.S. Senate, March 29, 1973, summarized studies by Professors Leonard Weiss and Steven Lustgarten saying, ". . . only in the period 1954–58 was the net influence of concentration on price change significantly positive. In all other time segments the opposite was found.

The net relation between concentration and price change was negative. In other words, the higher the degree of concentration, the smaller the degree of price increase. . . . Thus the influence of concentration has been to moderate the degree of recent inflation . . ."

[10] Louis Phlips, *Effects of Industrial Concentration: A Cross-Section Analysis for the Common Market* (1971).

18. Monopoly and Price Revisited [*]

JOAN BODOFF

I

The theoretical literature in microeconomics agrees that in equilibrium monopoly price will exceed competitive price.[1] Empirical work has attempted to measure the extent of this price elevation and its burden with respect to resource allocation.[2]

The present paper represents a follow-up and elaboration of one approach to this question, that of Dr. David Schwartzman.[3]

The results do not support the expectation that price under monopoly conditions exceeds competitive price, neither in the immediate period nor in an intermediate run over a ten-year period. These findings are consistent with recent theory-based and empirical attacks on the assured efficiency of competition and on the dominance of adverse effects on the economy arising from concentration.[4]

[*] Excerpt from Joan Bodoff, *Monopoly and Price Revisited,* preliminary draft, Ph.D. dissertation, New School for Social Research (1973).

[1] See such basic textbooks as G. L. Bach, *Economics: An Introduction to Analysis and Policy,* Englewood Cliffs, N.J., Prentice-Hall, Second Ed., 1957; John F. Due and R. Clower, *Intermediate Economic Analysis,* Homewood, Ill., Irwin, 1966; Robert L. Heilbroner, *The Economic Problem,* Englewood Cliffs, N.J., Prentice-Hall, Third Ed., 1972; Lloyd G. Reynolds, *Economics,* Homewood, Ill., Irwin, Sixth Ed., 1964; F. M. Scherer, *Industrial Market Structure and Economic Performance,* Chicago, Rand McNally, 1970; Paul A. Samuelson, *Economics,* New York, McGraw-Hill, Eighth Ed., 1970.

[2] Estimates of the deadweight welfare loss due to monopoly have been provided by Arnold C. Harberger, "Monopoly and Resource Allocation," *American Economic Review,* Vol. 44, May 1954, pp. 77–97 and David Schwartzman, "The Burden of Monopoly," *Journal of Political Economy,* Vol. 68, December 1960, pp. 627–630.

Evidences of a positive relationship between industry concentration and profits have been found by Joe S. Bain, "Relation of Profit Rates to Industry Concentration," *Quarterly Journal of Economics,* Vol. 65, August 1951, pp. 293–324; Harold M. Levinson, *Postwar Movements of Prices and Wages in Manufacturing Industries,* Study Paper No. 21, Joint Economic Committee of the U.S. Congress, Washington, 1960; Victor Fuchs, "Integration, Concentration, and Profits in Manufacturing Industries," *Quarterly Journal of Economics,* Vol. 75, May 1961, pp. 278–291; Leonard W. Weiss, "Average Concentration Ratios and Industrial Performance," *Journal of Industrial Economics,* Vol. 11, July 1963, pp. 237–253; George J. Stigler, "A Theory of Oligopoly," *Journal of Political Economy,* Vol. 72, February 1964, pp. 44–61; Norman R. Collins and Lee E. Preston, "Concentration and Price Cost Margins in Food Manufacturing Industries," *Journal of Industrial Economics,* Vol. 14, July 1966, pp. 226–242; H. M. Mann, "Seller Concentration, Barriers to Entry, and Rate of Return in Thirty Industries, 1950–1960," *Review of Economics and Statistics,* Vol. 48, August 1966, pp. 296–307; William S. Comanor and Thomas A. Wilson, "Advertising, Market Structure and Performance," *Review of Economics and Statistics,* Vol. 49, November 1967, pp. 423–440.

Positive relationships between firm market share and profitability have been found by William G. Shepherd, "The Elements of Market Structure," *Review of Economics and Statistics,* Vol. 54, February 1972, pp. 25–37; Marshall Hall and Leonard Weiss, "Firm Size and Profitability," *Review of Economics and Statistics,* Vol. 49, August 1967, pp. 319–331; U.S. Federal Trade Commission, Bureau of Economics, W. Kelly, *Economic Report on the Influence of Market Structure on the Profit Performance of Food Manufacturing Companies,* Washington, 1969.

[3] David Schwartzman, "The Effect of Monopoly on Price," *Journal of Political Economy,* Vol. 67, August 1959, pp. 352–362; "The Burden of Monopoly," *op. cit.;* and "The Effect of Monopoly: A Correction," *Journal of Political Economy,* Vol. 69, October 1961, p. 494.

[4] Yale Brozen, "The Antitrust Task Force Decon-

Dr. Schwartzman's technique, discussed in several journal articles, consisted of comparing the ratios of value of shipments to direct costs (as proxies for the price-cost relationship) for Canadian and United States manufacturing industries, paired according to S. I. C. descriptions at the four-digit level. The primary sample consisted of matched industries "concentrated" in Canada and "unconcentrated" in the United States. Industries whose markets were regional rather than national were omitted. The dividing line of four-firm concentration at 50 percent of industry employment (or 59 percent of industry shipments) was suggested by Bain's finding, supported subsequently by Mann, that profit rates were dichotomously higher for firms operating in industries where the eight-firm concentration ratio exceeded 70 percent.[5] National differences in price-direct cost relationships, caused for example by differences in capital and transport costs and economies of scale, were eliminated by subtracting from the shipments-direct cost ratio found for the primary sample an "average" shipments-direct cost ratio for similar industries which were unconcentrated in both Canada and the U.S. In the light of the comparable cultural, consumption and production patterns prevailing in the two countries,[6] the selection of matched

industries and the allowance for systematic national price-cost differences leaves the monopoly effect on price to be residually observed.

Using mainly 1954 Census data and 1948 estimates of Canadian concentration levels,[7] Schwartzman found that monopolistic price exceeded competitive price by about 8.3 per cent, implying monopoly profits in manufacturing in the United States of $4.9 billion for 1954.[8] Extending these results for manufacturing to the aggregate economy led to an estimated welfare loss of several hundred million dollars, depending on the figure used for arc elasticity of demand, or approximately 0.1 per cent of national income for that year. This confirmed the magnitude of Harberger's earlier findings.[9]

The criticisms of Schwartzman's approach have centered on the smallness and unrepresentativeness of the sample, aggregation biases, the assumption concerning elasticity of demand,[10] the exclusion of

centration Recommendation," *Journal of Law and Economics,* October 1970, pp. 279–292 and "Bain's Concentration and Rates of Return Revisited," *Journal of Law and Economics,* October 1971, pp. 351–369; Stanley I. Ornstein, "Concentration and Profits," *Journal of Business,* Vol. 45, October 1972, pp. 519–541; David Schwartzman, "Competition and Efficiency: Comment," *Journal of Political Economy,* Vol. 81, May/June, 1973, pp. 756–764; Harold Demsetz, "A Size Distribution Analysis of Profits," *Journal of Law and Economics,* forthcoming. Also, George J. Stigler in *Capital and Rates of Return in Manufacturing Industries,* Princeton, N.J., Princeton Univ. Press for NBER, 1963, failed to find a significant relationship between profit rates and concentration once adjustment was made for excess entrepreneurial withdrawals in smaller firms.

[5] Bain, *op. cit.,* and Mann, *op. cit.*

[6] D. J. Daly, "Uses of International Price and Out-

put Data," pp. 108–109 in D. J. Daly, ed., *International Comparisons of Prices and Output,* New York, Columbia University Press for NBER, Studies in Income and Wealth, No. 37, 1972. Also, Gideon Rosenbluth, *Concentration in Canadian Manufacturing Industries,* Princeton, N. J., Princeton University Press for NBER, 1957, p. 85. Rosenbluth found that comparable industries are more highly concentrated in Canada than in the United States, a result of similar plant sizes and the relatively small Canadian market. D. J. Daly, B. A. Keys, and E. J. Spence, in *Scale and Specialization in Canadian Manufacturing,* Staff Study No. 22, Economic Council of Canada, Ottawa, 1968, pp. 18–20 find that while the average size of plant is often smaller in Canada than in the United States in the same industry, there seems to be greater diversity in plant size in the United States—numerous small plants and some very large plants.

[7] Rosenbluth, *op. cit.*

[8] Schwartzman, "The Effect of Monopoly: A Correction," *op. cit.*

[9] Harberger, *op. cit.*

[10] George J. Stigler, "The Statistics of Monopoly and Merger," *Journal of Political Economy,* Vol. 64, February 1956, pp. 33–40 criticizes Harberger's estimate, including his use of unitary

capacity-increasing effects resulting from the reduction of market power,[11] the omission from consideration of other inefficiencies (technical or general "X-inefficiency," trade barriers, occupational immobilities)[12] which serve to raise the economic cost of monopoly, and failure to extend the analysis to non-manufacturing sectors of the economy. All of the latter objections are beyond the scope of this paper and have been dealt with elsewhere.[13] The attempt to expand and evaluate the sample, to update data, and to observe trends over a period of years, for Schwartzman's sample as well as for the expanded sample, is described below.

II

The size and the composition of the Schwartzman sample were inhibited by the lack of concentration estimates for many Canadian industries, by the problems of treating industries selling in insulated regional and local markets, and by the difficulty of pairing manufacturing industries since the Canadian census was more highly aggregated than that of the United States.

Schwartzman's primary sample was both small and unrepresentative of the broad range of manufacturing activity. It consisted of 19 concentrated-unconcentrated pairs. Five were classified in the foods groups, four in textiles and clothing, and three in the miscellaneous category. About 11 percent of 1954 U.S. value added in manufacturing was represented in this group.

The largest single industry, Aircraft and Parts, accounted for almost one-half of the American value added in this primary sample. The four largest industries—Aircraft, Petroleum Refining, Cotton Yarn and Cloth, and Meat Slaughtering and Packing—accounted for 84 percent.

The control sample, subject to similar criticism, was composed of 27 industries representing 12½ per cent of U.S. value added in manufacturing. Six industries were in the foods group, five in clothing, five in textiles, and four in leather products.

The emphasis on foods and fabrics, coupled with the omission of industries in the tobacco, rubber, iron and steel products, non-ferrous metals, electrical apparatus, and printing and publishing groups and the near absence of industries in the chemicals and non-metallic minerals groups, makes the sample unrepresentative. Furthermore, fourteen of the nineteen industries constituting the concentrated-unconcentrated sample are smaller (based on Value Added) than the average Canadian manufacturing industry of 1954, most by considerable margins. The list of concentrated industries suggests that entry is not difficult, judged by the Bain criteria,[14] and that the number of firms in each is restricted primarily by the limited size of the market and/or by moderate pricing policies.[15] This suggests that the sample under-estimates the effect of monopolistic conditions on price, which would be revised upward by a more complete and representative group of industry pairs.

elasticity of demand. See also Ruth P. Mack, Comment in *American Economic Review*, Vol. 44, May 1954, pp. 88–92.

[11] William G. Shepherd, *Market Power and Economic Welfare*, New York, Random House, 1970, p. 197.

[12] Harvey Leibenstein, "Allocative Efficiency vs. X-Efficiency," *American Economic Review*, Vol. 56, June 1966, pp. 392–415.

[13] Dean Worcester, *Monopoly, Big Business, and Welfare in the Postwar United States*, Seattle, Univ. of Washington Press, 1967, pp. 214–229 and F. M. Scherer, *op. cit.*, pp. 402–411.

[14] Joe S. Bain, *Barriers to New Competition*, Cambridge, Mass., Harvard Univ. Press, 1956.

[15] Dale Osborne, in "The Role of Entry in Oligopoly Theory," *Journal of Political Economy*, Vol. 72, August 1964, pp. 396–402, suggests that the limit price theory is more relevant to concentration than to price in the long run: The long-run equilibrium price will be unaffected by short-run pricing strategies, as it depends on conditions of entry, long-run average cost, and long-run demand. But if firms practice restraint in pricing in the short run in an effort to deter entry, those firms will be larger in size and there will be fewer of them in the industry in the long run.

This a priori expectation was not fulfilled. The use of a broader sample eliminated the effect of monopoly on price in various census years examined, including 1958, the Census year closest to Schwartzman's 1954 results. The Schwartzman sample, however, continued to evidence a strong positive relationship between concentration and price-cost margins in 1967.

Tables 1 and 2 list the Concentrated (Canadian)-Unconcentrated (U.S.) industries, the Unconcentrated (Canadian)-Unconcentrated (U.S.) industries and the comparison ratios for 1954, the year used by Schwartzman, and 1967, the most recent Census year available. In both years the Canadian industries in the sample, both concentrated and unconcentrated, averaged about one-tenth the size of their U.S. counterparts. Data was not available for 1967 for three industries in the 1954 C-U group (Rice, Malt, Excelsior) and for two industries in the 1954 U-U group (Butter

and Cheese, Condensed Milk) because of changes in the Canadian reporting system or the incorporation of the product into a broader class. Results for 1954 are reported both including and excluding these industries; the latter figure is comparable to the 1967 data. In addition, 2 C-U industries became unconcentrated in Canada by 1967 (Pens and Pencils, Slaughtering and Meat Packing) and 2 U-U industries became concentrated in Canada (Flour, Leather Goods). Again, results are reported both including and excluding these industries in Tables 3 and 4 respectively. Although there is practically no change in the U-U averages when the industries with rising concentration are omitted, the exclusion from the C-U sample of those industries suffering declines in concentration resulted in higher $\frac{R \text{ Con}}{R \text{ Uncon}}$ ratios, up to 2.4 percentage points in some cases.

Schwartzman's results for 1954, and his

Table 1 • Concentrated-Unconcentrated Pairs, Schwartzman Sample

	1954		R Con. (C)	1967		R Con. (C)
Neither X nor M	*R Con. (Canada)*	*R Uncon. (U.S.)*	*R Uncon. (U.S.)*	*R Con. (Canada)*	*R Uncon. (U.S.)*	*R Uncon. (U.S.)*
Rice	133.0	119.9	110.9	n.a.	119.6	—
Malt	146.1	139.6	104.7	n.a.	120.0	—
Fur Dressing	180.5	159.1	113.5	154.4	151.2	102.1
Narrow Fabrics	143.9	131.6	109.4	144.1	134.8	106.9
Cement	200.6	194.5	103.1	231.5	202.5	114.5
Excelsior	129.5	138.9	93.2	n.a.	n.a.	—
Roofing Paper	162.2	132.2	122.7	146.2	137.6	106.2
Inks	189.8	158.3	119.9	161.2	148.6	108.5
Pens & Pencils	169.8	183.8	92.4	171.5	190.2	90.0
Umbrellas	145.1	133.6	108.6	148.3	116.1	127.8
Buttons	147.8	142.9	104.0	162.5	160.4	101.3
M-Competing						
Cotton Yarn & Cloth	119.2	112.6	105.8	121.7	127.3	95.6
Synthetic Textiles	151.5	119.7	126.5	137.4	124.2	110.6
Petroleum	144.0	112.8	127.7	118.0	125.2	94.3
X-Industries						
Macaroni	128.7	132.2	97.3	138.4	153.8	89.9
Slaughtering & Meat Packing	113.8	101.9	111.7	111.1	108.8	102.1
Aircraft & Parts	136.4	143.9	94.8	145.1	165.8	87.5
Abrasives	143.8	164.0	87.7	185.9	173.7	107.0
Vegetable Oils	112.6	111.3	101.2	110.4	110.2	100.2
Unweighted Average, 19 Industries			107.1			
Unweighted Average, 16 Industries[a]			107.9			102.8

[a] Excludes Rice, Malt, Excelsior: Canadian and/or American data n.a., 1967.

Table 2 • Unconcentrated-Unconcentrated Pairs, Schwartzman Sample

	1954		R (Can.) / R (U.S.)	1967		R (Can.) / R (U.S.)
	R (Can.)	R (U.S.)	R (Can.) / R (U.S.)	R (Can.)	R (U.S.)	R (Can.) / R (U.S.)
Fruits & Vegetables	135.0	130.8	103.2	140.3	143.9	47.5
Flour	111.9	114.2	98.2	115.7	119.2	97.1
Cocoa & Confectionery	140.7	131.0	107.5	151.9	152.7	99.4
Butter & Cheese	116.1	111.3	104.4	n.a.	109.4	—
Condensed Milk	121.9	166.3	73.3	n.a.	134.9	—
Fish	129.1	123.8	104.3	117.8	129.5	90.9
Woolen Fabrics	121.7	118.8	102.4	135.9	135.5	100.3
Woolen Yarn	119.8	116.1	103.2	129.4	125.7	102.9
Cotton & Jute Bags	110.2	114.1	96.6	119.6	126.9	94.3
Corsets	158.4	152.5	103.9	159.6	177.4	90.0
Canvas Products	135.8	137.8	98.6	135.7	140.8	96.4
Hosiery & Knit Goods	138.0	126.4	109.2	132.4	145.2	91.2
Men's Factory Clothing	130.5	125.7	103.8	129.4	161.5	80.1
Women's Factory Clothing	134.1	128.6	104.2	133.0	173.9	76.4
Fur Goods	126.6	121.9	103.9	128.7	128.2	100.4
Leather Goods	128.1	121.9	105.1	124.8	139.8	89.3
Leather Gloves	134.7	130.7	103.0	133.7	135.5	98.6
Misc. Leather Goods	138.1	137.5	100.4	139.2	149.0	93.4
Boots & Shoes	133.2	133.6	99.7	135.7	147.9	91.8
Paper Boxes & Bags	131.3	136.3	96.4	129.5	135.0	96.0
Plywood & Veneer	143.2	129.0	111.0	125.8	125.8	100.0
Boat Building	134.0	132.0	101.5	132.3	136.3	97.0
Furniture	136.0	138.3	98.3	139.6	149.2	93.6
Paints & Varnishes	162.3	156.5	103.7	165.5	160.9	102.9
Medicines & Pharmaceuticals	225.8	234.0	96.5	239.0	330.6	72.3
Ship building	138.3	133.4	103.6	129.6	134.4	96.4
Dyeing & Finishing Textiles	152.2	131.6	115.6	151.0	131.3	115.0
Unweighted Average, 27 industries			101.9			
Unweighted Average, 25 industries[a]			103.0			94.5
Unweighted Average, 23 industries[b]			103.1			94.6

[a] Excludes Butter & Cheese, Condensed Milk: Canadian data n.a., 1967.
[b] Excludes Flour and Leather Goods: Canadian industries became concentrated based on 1965 estimates.

various handling of industries affected by foreign trade, are repeated along with the modifications described above. In all 1954 to 1967 comparisons using the limited Schwartzman sample, subtracting the $\frac{\text{R Uncon}}{\text{R Uncon}}$ ratio from the $\frac{\text{R Con}}{\text{R Uncon}}$ ratio reveals a statistically significant effect of monopoly on price for this sample.

Several interesting features should be noted. Regardless of which data sets are chosen, the 1967 ratios are in all cases lower than the 1954 ratios, frequently by sizable amounts. Secondly, the HIGH and LOW ratios within each set, depending on the foreign trade effect, are uniformly reversed between 1954 and 1967. Finally, the average Canadian price-cost ratios for both the C-U and the U-U groups were virtually unchanged between 1954 and 1967, and in both years the average ratio for the C-U group was higher. In the case of the United States industries in the sample, all of which were unconcentrated, the average price-cost ratio rose between 1954 and 1967, particularly in the case of the U-U group.

Table 3 • **Concentration Categories as Measured in 1954**[16]

C-U	1954, 19 ind.	1954, 16 ind.[a]	1967, 16 ind.
1. Industries neither X nor M-Competing	107.5 (11 ind.)	109.2 (8 ind.)	−107.2 High
2. 1 + M-Competing	110.2 (14 ") High	112.1 (11 ") High	−105.3
3. 1 + X	104.7 (16 ") Low	105.1 (13 ") Low	−103.4
4. 1 + M + X (All industries)	107.1 (19 ")	107.9 (16 ")	−102.8 Low
U-U	**1954, 27 ind.**	**1954, 25 ind.[b]**	**1967, 25 ind.**
All industries	101.9	103.0	94.5

[a] Excludes Rice, Malt, Excelsior
[b] Excludes Butter and Cheese, Condensed Milk.

Table 4 • **Concentration Categories as Measured in 1967**[17]

C-U[c]	1954, 17 ind.	1954, 14 ind.[a]	1967, 14 ind.
1. Industries neither X nor M-Competing	109.0 (10 ind.)	111.6 (7 ind.)	−109.6 High
2. 1 + M-Competing	111.5 (13 ") High	114.1 (10 ") High	−106.8
3. 1 + X	105.1 (14 ") Low	105.7 (11 ") Low	−104.7
4. 1 + M + X (All industries)	107.7 (17 ")	108.7 (14 ")	−103.7 Low
U-U[d]	**1954, 25 ind.**	**1954, 23 ind.[b]**	**1967, 23 ind.**
All industries	101.9	103.1	94.6

[a] Excludes Rice, Malt, Excelsior.
[b] Excludes Butter and Cheese, Condensed Milk.
[c] Excludes Pens and Pencils, Slaughtering and Meat Packing.
[d] Excludes Flour, Leather Goods.

Wholesale prices for U.S. processed foods and leather-based industries rose more rapidly between 1958 and 1967 than wholesale prices for all commodities, and the wholesale prices of textile products and apparel also rose slightly:[18]

[16] Each number represents a ratio of ratios. For the C-U industries, the $\frac{R\ Con}{R\ Uncon}$ ratio is based on

$$\frac{\frac{P.Q}{AVC.Q}\ \text{Concentrated Canadian}}{\frac{P.Q}{AVC.Q}\ \text{Unconcentrated American}}\ \text{matched in-}$$

dustry. For the U-U industries, the $\frac{R\ Uncon}{R\ Uncon}$

ratio reported is based on $\dfrac{\dfrac{P.Q}{AVC.Q}\ \text{Unconcen-}}{\dfrac{P.Q}{AVC.Q}\ \text{Unconcen-}}$

trated Canadian matched industry. Thus, value trated American

of shipments in manufacturing (less resales) and total direct costs provide the required data.

[17] Canadian concentration categories were estimated by Rosenbluth for 1948, while American concentration figures were reported for 1954 by the Bureau of the Census. The later estimates were made for 1965 by the Canadian Department of Consumer and Corporate Affairs and for 1967 by the American Bureau of the Census. Present evidence indicates that concentration levels change very slowly and so concentration figures for the years reported are comparable. See Morris Adelman, "Monopoly and Concentration: Comparisons in Time and Space," in Richard E. Low, ed., *The Economics of Antitrust*, Englewood Cliffs, N.J., Prentice-Hall, 1968, pp. 43–59.

[18] U.S. Government, *Economic Report of the President*, Washington, January 1972, p. 250.

1958 *Wholesale Price Indexes (1967 = 100)*

All commodities	94.6
Processed foods and feeds	91.8
Hides, skins, leather, and related products	82.9
Textile products and apparel	97.0

The strong representation of these industries in the Schwartzman sample helps account for the rapid increase in the average $\frac{P}{AVC}$ ratios for U.S. industries. The final $\frac{R\ Con}{R\ Uncon}$ and $\frac{R\ Uncon}{R\ Uncon}$ ratios declined, then, because of the stable behavior of the Canadian industries represented in the sample and the rather wide shifts on the average for the American industries represented:

Table 5

16 Concentrated-Unconcentrated Industries

(C)	Canadian ratios only,	1954	149.4
		1967	149.2
(U)	U.S. ratios only,	1954	139.6
		1967	145.7

25 Unconcentrated-Unconcentrated Industries

(U)	Canadian ratios only,	1954	138.0
		1967	139.0
(U)	U.S. ratios only,	1954	134.3
		1967	149.4

While the *average* Canadian price-cost ratios were little changed between 1954 and 1967, the separate average for import-competing and exporting industries moved widely and in opposite directions. The U.S. price-cost ratios for both of those categories rose broadly:[19]

III

The expanded study reported here was suggested by the recently published work of Yale Brozen.[20] He re-examined the landmark studies of Bain, Mann and Stigler

---

[19] The same pattern occurs for the expanded sample reported below for the years 1958, 1963, and 1967.

[20] Brozen, *op. cit.*

Table 6

16 Concentrated-Unconcentrated Industries

		1954	1967
(C)	Canadian ratios only		
	All industries (16)	149.4	149.2
	Neither M nor X (8)	167.5	165.0
	M (3)	138.2	125.7
	X (5)	127.1	138.2
(U)	U.S. ratios only		
	All industries (16)	139.6	145.7
	Neither M nor X (8)	154.5	155.2
	M (3)	115.0	125.6
	X (5)	130.7	142.5

which found positive relationships between profits and concentration. Brozen's hypothesis was that *over time* the operation of the market would return above—and below—average profits toward the average, thus correcting temporary disequilibria without large-scale public intervention. In each case his hypothesis was confirmed, although the debate continues.

In the present international comparison, if monopoly prices were evident in any one year, perhaps they would be eroded over time due to competitive forces. Pursuing this argument depended upon the publication, for the first time under the auspices of the Canadian government, of data on concentration levels in manufacturing industries for 1965.[21] Figures for 154 homogeneous industries were published, including the percent of industry shipments accounted for by the largest 4, 8, 12, 20 and 50 enterprises and by the largest establishments, as well as the number of largest enterprises required to account for 80 percent of each industry's shipments. Concentration estimates for 18 of 34 regional industries were computed using weighted averages of regional shipments data. These weighted regional concentration figures were used when pairing with U.S. industries, and regional industries for which only national concentration figures were available were dropped from the sample. The U.S. data were also adjusted to reflect the

---

[21] Canadian Department of Consumer and Corporate Affairs, *Concentration in the Manufacturing Industries of Canada*, Ottawa, 1971.

higher levels of concentration realized in regional and local industries.[22]

Canadian industries in which exports and imports played a substantial role were identified in a 1970 report of the Economic Council of Canada,[23] permitting an examination of the effects of including or excluding them from the sample. Foreign trade is relatively more significant for the Canadian economy than the American, and Schwartzman argued that firms operating in international markets have restricted ability to determine prices independently. Other arguments may apply now, as a result of recent developments in Canadian foreign exchange, trade and tariff arrangements.

Comparable Canadian and U.S. four-digit manufacturing industries were selected based on the respective official Standard Industrial Classification descriptions with the further requirement that product comparability, as measured by value of shipments, exceed 90 percent.[24] The resulting pairing yielded 116 industries, including 123 Canadian and 231 American four-digit industries representing respectively 77 percent (based on 1965 Canadian data) and 68 percent (based on 1963 U.S. data) of value of shipments. The critical dividing line used was the four-firm value of shipments of 59 percent discussed above. A variant consisted of moving the critical level to 61 percent, based on regressing four-firm on eight-firm concentration ratios reported in the 1967 Census. The results were only minimally affected and are reported below. The year 1958 was used in-

stead of the year 1954 used by Schwartzman because of substantial revisions in both the Canadian and U.S. SIC codes between 1957 and 1960.

The final sample (which omitted some combined industries where concentration figures became ambiguous) consisted of 34 pairs of Concentrated (Canadian)-Unconcentrated (U.S.) industries and 65 pairs of Unconcentrated-Unconcentrated industries for 1967 and 1963. Every two-digit industry group listed in the U.S. SIC code for manufacturing is represented, with the exceptions of Tobacco and Rubber which are concentrated in both Canada and the United States. There were 33 C-U pairs and 63 U-U pairs for 1958, and later years can be made comparable by excluding from the averages those industries for which 1958 data is not available.

Using Schwartzman's method, the $\frac{\text{Price}}{\text{Average Variable Cost}}$ relationship was computed by relating shipments (less resales) to direct costs (wages of production workers, materials, fuel and purchased electricity).[25]

The extent to which the $\frac{P}{AVC}$ ratio in a concentrated industry exceeds that ratio for the same industry operating in an unconcentrated environment will reflect monopoly power, once national characteristics resulting in different $\frac{P}{AVC}$ levels have been accounted for. Here Schwartzman's adjustment is followed of subtracting the unweighted average of the $\frac{P}{AVC}$ ratios for the Unconcentrated (Canadian)-Unconcentrated (U.S.) pairs from the unweighted average of the $\frac{P}{AVC}$ ratios for the Concen-

[22] David Schwartzman and Joan Bodoff, "Concentration in Regional and Local Industries," *Southern Economic Journal*, Vol. 37, January 1971, pp. 343–348.

[23] Max D. Stewart, *Concentration in Canadian Manufacturing and Mining Industries*, Background Study to the Interim Report on Competition Policy, Economic Council of Canada, Ottawa, August 1970, Appendix List C.

[24] *Concentration in the Manufacturing Industries of Canada*, op. cit., lists of comparable industries compiled by the Dominion Bureau of Statistics, and correspondence with section chiefs.

[25] Data from Canadian Dominion Bureau of Statistics, *Manufacturing Industries of Canada*, Section A, Summary for Canada, Ottawa, 1958, 1963, and 1967, and U.S. Bureau of the Census, Department of Commerce, *Census of Manufactures*, Vol. III: Industry Statistics, Washington, 1958, 1963 and 1967.

Table 7 • 59% **Four-firm Concentration Ratio**

		1958	# ind.	1963	# ind.	1967	# ind.
C-U	1.	102.6	33	99.7	34	99.4	34
	2.	102.6	33	99.7	33[a]	99.0	33[a]
U-U	3.	101.3	63	99.4	65	97.8	65
	4.	101.3	63	99.5	63[b]	97.9	63[b]

Table 8 • 61% **Four-firm Concentration Ratio**[c]

		1958	# ind.	1963	# ind.	1967	# ind.
C-U	1.	102.5	32	99.4	33	99.2	33
	2.	102.5	31	99.3	31	98.8	31
U-U	3.	101.2	66	99.4	68	97.9	68
	4.	101.2	66	99.5	66	97.9	66

[a] Excludes Sugar Refineries: U.S. industry definitions for 1958 not comparable.
[b] Excludes Fish Products, Fruit and Vegetable Canners: U.S. industry definitions for 1958 not comparable.
[c] For Con-Uncon comparison, add Biscuits and Rubber Footwear and delete Narrow Fabrics, Metal Rolling, Casting and Extruding, nes, and Electrical Industrial Equipment. Add latter three industries to Uncon-Uncon.

trated (Canadian)—Unconcentrated (U.S.) pairs. Unweighted ratios are appropriate as the results should reflect the incidence of monopolistic pricing in both static and dynamic contexts, undistorted by changes in the structural composition of the manufacturing sector.

The study shows that in no case is the difference between the $\frac{R \, Con}{R \, Uncon}$ and

for each year regardless of continuity. The even-numbered lines consider the changes in the ratios for only those matched industries which qualify for inclusion in the sample throughout the ten-year period.

Schwartzman found that the average unweighted $\frac{R \, Con}{R \, Uncon}$ result varied depending on the treatment of industries affected by foreign trade:

Table 9 • **19 Concentrated-Unconcentrated Industries, Schwartzman Sample**

	1954	# of industries
1. Industries neither exporting nor import-competing:	107.5	11
2. Industries in (1) plus those import-competing:	110.2 High	14
3. Industries in (1) plus those exporting:	104.7 Low	16
4. Industries in (2) plus those exporting (All C-U industries):	107.1	19

$\frac{R \, Uncon}{R \, Uncon}$ ratios statistically significant by the normal criteria, although in every case the difference is positive.

The tables below present the various unweighted ratios in several ways: in Tables 7 and 8, the odd-numbered lines treat each Census year cross-sectionally, using the maximum number of paired industries

Schwartzman preferred to include industries whose shipments were competing with imported products. He interpreted the higher ratio resulting from the inclusion of such industries as reflecting the attractiveness of selling in markets protected by high tariff barriers. In the enlarged 1967 sample, the inclusion of import-competing industries results in a low $\frac{R \, Con}{R \, Uncon}$ ratio, and the

Table 10 • **33 Concentrated-Unconcentrated Industries, Expanded Sample**

	1967		# of industries
1. Industries neither exporting nor import-competing:	100.1		11
2. Industries in (1) plus those import-competing only:[a]	99.3	Low	22
3. Industries in (1) plus those exporting only:[a]	101.2	High	14
4. Industries in (2) plus those exporting only:[a]	100.0		25
5. All C-U industries:[a]	99.0	Low	33

[a] The data have been refined to indicate industries neither exporting nor importing (11), industries importing only (11), industries exporting only (3), and industries both exporting *and* importing along lines of specialization (8), Line 5 is the sum of all these categories.

inclusion of exporting industries results in the highest ratio—just the reverse of Schwartzman's result for 1954.

While all of the U.S. industries in the sample are defined as unconcentrated, the average price-cost ratios for the C-U set are above those for the U-U set for two of the three years tested. In addition, the rapid spurt in the U.S. U-U industries' margins between 1958 and 1967 is lacking in the more stable pattern of the U.S. C-U group. The main difference in industry composition between the two sets is the inclusion in the U-U group of a large number of industries in Knitting and Textiles

(15), in the lumber-based Wood, Furniture, Paper, and Publishing industries (12), and in Metal Fabricating (5). None of these basic groups is represented in the C-U classification.

Of the 33 C-U industries, nineteen are heavily affected by import competition. The $\frac{P}{AVC}$ ratios for the Canadian concentrated industries follows the patterns described above, with exporting industries experiencing improved price-cost relationships and import-competing industries suffering declines between the 1950's and 1967:

Table 12 • **33 Concentrated Canadian Industries**

	1958	1963	1967
1. Industries neither exporting nor import-competing (11 ind.)	153.1	153.3	149.2
2. Industries exporting only (3 ind.)	155.0	158.1	157.9
3. Industries import-competing only (11 ind.)	149.9	147.4	145.0
4. Industries importing and exporting (8 ind.)[a]	135.8	130.1	137.6
5. Lines 3 + 4 (19 ind.)	144.0	140.1	141.9

[a] The $\frac{P}{AVC}$ ratios in the Plastics and Synthetic Resins and the Dressed and Dyed Furs industries behaved erratically, each moving in widely opposite directions between 1958–1963 and 1963–1967.

Table 11

33 Concentrated-Unconcentrated Industries			
	1958	1963	1967
Canada (Con)	148.0	146.1	135.5
United States (Uncon)	144.7	145.8	146.4
63 Unconcentrated-Unconcentrated Industries			
	1958	1963	1967
Canada (Uncon)	143.1	142.9	142.5
United States (Uncon)	141.5	144.2	146.9

IV

What can we conclude at this juncture? 1. The Schwartzman finding that monopolistic production conditions were responsible for higher profit margins than were obtained in competitive industries was based on a narrow and biased sample for 1954. Enlargement of the sample, using Census definitions and data for 1958, does not yield such results.

But perhaps the 59% critical concentration level has been set too low. If it were raised, and if monopoly power increases with concentration, the average $\frac{P}{AVC}$ ratio for monopolistic industries might be greater than for competitive industries. However, from a policy standpoint fewer industries would be involved and there would be less room for corrective actions. Furthermore, there are no firm theoretical or empirical grounds for choosing any other concentration level as the critical boundary.[26]

Perhaps firms adopt some variant of the limit price policy and seek to forestall entry while earning satisfactory profits. If successful, this policy would reduce the observed price-cost ratio below its short-run profit maximizing point but would also prevent erosion over time. The raw data does not contradict this hypothesis.

Or perhaps four-firm concentration alone cannot satisfactorily explain profitability, but must be supplemented by a wide variety of structural and dynamic factors. Other writers have emphasized such elements as intra-marginal concentration, firm market share, absolute firm size, vertical integration, product diversification, advertising-sales ratio, capital intensity, market growth, economies of scale, managerial capabilities, capital structure, and accounting treatment of advertising and research and development expenditures.[27]

2. It was not possible to verify whether high price-cost margins are eroded over time since no significant effect of concentration on price-cost ratios was observed in any of the three years examined (1958, 1963 and 1967).

---

[26] Even on empirical grounds, there is disagreement as to the appropriate boundary. Bain noted a "break" in the average profit rate at eight-firm concentration of 70 per cent, but failed to account for the surprising fact that each of the industries in the sample with concentration below 30 per cent experienced higher profit rates than industries whose concentration ranged from 30 to 70 per cent. Kamerschen failed to find support for Bain's "threshold theory" in "The Determination of Profit Rates in Oligopolistic Industries," *Journal of Business*, Vol. 42, July 1969, pp. 293–301. Collins and Preston, however, found a continuous and curvilinear relationship between price-cost margins and concentration in 32 food manufacturing industries for 1958. Stigler concluded cautiously in "A Theory of Oligopoly" that "there is no relationship between profitability and concentration if . . . the share of the four largest firms is less than about 80%." But the Federal Trade Commission noted that firm profitability rose most sharply as four-firm concentration increased in the 40 to 60 per cent range.

[27] See, for example, William J. Baumol, *Business Behavior, Value and Growth*, New York, Macmillan, 1959, rev. ed., Harcourt Brace, 1967; Harry Bloch, "Advertising, Competition, and Market Performance," Ph.D. dissertation, University of Chicago, September 1971; Michael Gort, *Diversification and Integration in American Industry*, Princeton, N.J., Princeton Univ. Press, 1961; Richard A. Miller, "Marginal Concentration and Industry Profit Rates," *Southern Economic Journal*, Vol. 24, October 1967, pp. 259–268, as well as the articles by Bain, Collins and Preston, Comanor and Wilson, Demsetz, FTC, Fuchs, Hall and Weiss, Mann and Shepherd cited earlier.

APPENDIX A

Expanded Sample for 1958, 1963 and 1967, Four-Firm 59% Concentration Criteria

33 *Concentrated (Canadian)—Unconcentrated (U.S.) Industries:*

Neither Export nor Import (11):

Macaroni; Leather Tanneries; Iron and Steel Mills; Shipbuilding and Repair; Electrical Wire and Cable; Asbestos Products; Petroleum Refineries; Printing Inks; Buttons, Buckles and Fasteners; Typewriter Supplies.

Import-Competing (11):

Wineries; Cotton Yarn and Cloth; Narrow Fabrics; Carpets, Mats and Rugs; Linoleum and Coated Fabrics; Steel Pipe and Tubes; Electrical Equipment; Clocks and Watches; Ophthalmic Goods; Toys and Games; Musical Instruments and Sound Recordings.

Export (3):

Flour Mills; Distilleries; Copper and Alloy Rolling, Casting and Extruding.

Both Import-Competing and Export (8):

Vegetable Oil; Cordage and Twine; Aluminum Rolling, Casting and Extruding; Metal Rolling, Casting and Extruding, N.E.S.; Agricultural Implements; Abrasives; Plastics and Synthetic Resins; Fur Dressing and Dyeing.

63 *Unconcentrated (Canadian)—Unconcentrated (U.S.) Industries:*

Slaughtering and Meat Processors; Poultry Processors; Dairy Factories and Process Cheese; Feeds; Bakeries; Shoes; Leather and Fabric Gloves; Boot and Shoe Findings; Miscellaneous Leather Products; Wool Yarn and Cloth; Fibre Preparing Mills; Textile Dyeing and Finishing; Canvas Products; Cotton and Jute Bags; Hosiery Mills; Other Knitting Mills; Men's Suits and Overcoats; Men's Trousers; Men's Work Pants and Shirts and Other Clothing; Men's Fine Shirts; Men's Neckwear; Women's Coats, Suits, Skirts and Blouses; Women's Dresses; Women's Other Outerwear; Women's Lingerie; Children's Clothing; Fur Goods; Cap, Hats and Millinery; Foundation Garments; Sawmills and Shingle Mills; Veneer and Plywood Mills; Sash, Door and Other Millwork; Hardwood Flooring; Coffins and Caskets; Household Furniture; Office Furniture; Miscellaneous Furniture; Pulp and Paper Mills; Corrugated Boxes; Paper and Plastic Bags; Printing and Publishing; Platemaking, Typesetting and Trade Bindery; Iron Foundries; Boiler and Plate Works; Fabricated Structural Metal; Ornamental and Architectural Metal; Wire and Wire Products; Hardware, Tool and Cutlery; Commercial Refrigeration and Air Conditioning; Truck Body and Trailers; Boatbuilding and Repair; Household Radio and TV Receivers; Ready-mix Concrete and Concrete Products; Clay Products; Stone Products; Pharmaceuticals and Medicines; Paints and Varnishes; Toilet Preparations; Brooms, Brushes and Mops; Plastic Fabricators, N.E.S.; Sporting Goods; Signs and Displays; Fountain Pens and Pencils.

19. Introduction and Summary from
The Behavior of Industrial Prices

GEORGE J. STIGLER AND JAMES K. KINDAHL

The Setting

"When you cannot measure," Lord Kelvin tells us, "your knowledge is meager and unsatisfactory," to which Jacob Viner proposed the addition that even with measurement our knowledge would usually remain meager and unsatisfactory. The central task of this study is to determine what measurement has done for our knowledge of the behavior of industrial prices.

Our measurement problem is posed by the wholesale price index of the Bureau of Labor Statistics. This index of "wholesale" prices began publication in 1902 (extending retroactively back through 1890),[1] and has been maintained ever since on a continuous monthly basis, with frequent expansions of coverage. The primary purpose of the index was to measure changes in "the purchasing power of money," a function which gradually has been yielded up to the Consumer Price Index and the Implicit Price Deflator of the Gross National Product (although the latter index is of course based heavily upon the wholesale prices).

Other questions were later addressed to the wholesale price data, and of these one of the most interesting was: how do industrial prices respond to major fluctuations in business and price levels? The inquirer was Dr. Gardiner Means, and his famous answer was that large numbers of industrial prices were wholly unresponsive to cyclical fluctuations of markets. These prices were "administered" by large industrial enterprises and bore little resemblance to the volatile prices which are tossed about by supply and demand in traditional competitive markets such as the wheat pit. The contemporary interest in Means' findings, published in 1934, was much reinforced by his association of sticky price behavior with the economic malaise of the Great Depression.

The present study is primarily an independent examination of the behavior of industrial price indexes—the first moderately comprehensive "test" of the official wholesale price statistics since they were initiated two-thirds of a century ago. The word "test" is at least partially misleading because when the indexes of the Bureau of Labor Statistics and of our study (labeled NBER or NB) differ, it remains to be determined which is more correct. "Test" is also misleading when it implies that we employ the same procedures and sources of data as the BLS.

The Nature of Prices

The physical variety of products produced by most industries is substantial and for some industries it is essentially unlimited. Consider hot rolled carbon steel sheets, which are arbitrarily defined to be .23 inches or less in thickness if 12 to 48 inches wide, and .18 inches or less in thickness if over 48 inches wide. (Other dimensions are called bar, strip, or plate.) The buyer may choose among

1. Seven gauges of thickness
2. Ten classes of width
3. Four classes of length, if cut
4. Two classes of flatness
5. Two classes of squaring of ends
6. Six lot sizes
7. Three classes of oil treatment
8. Ten classes of carbon maximum
9. Seven classes of manganese maximum
10. Five classes of sulfur maximum
11. Three classes of silicon maximum
12. Seven classes of packaging

Reprinted by permission of the National Bureau of Economic Research, Inc. From *The Behavior of Industrial Prices* 3 (1970).

[1] "The Course of Wholesale Prices, 1890 to 1901," Bulletin of the Department of Labor, No. 39, March 1902.

And a dozen other dimensions of product variety! Many of the 135 million varieties implied by the twelve attributes have never been produced, one may reasonably conjecture, but the varieties produced in one year must be immense. Each class has its own price. This is one product category in steel.

Tier after tier of further differences may be piled upon the physical varieties. There are terms of credit, transportation charges, guarantees of performance, facilities for replacement, techniques of arbitration of conflicts, promptness of delivery in normal times and in crisis. To be told that the base price of hot rolled carbon steel sheets was $5.30 per 100 pounds on May 15, 1963, is rather an oversimplification of the price structure.

Faced by this indescribably numerous body of prices and terms, the Bureau of Labor Statistics chose to price a few well-defined, "typical" products and transactions. Necessarily these prices must usually be collected from sellers: every major steel producer will offer a typical product, but not one buyer of steel sheet in a hundred will continuously buy that typical product. One may certainly quarrel with the procedure of selecting typical products because it lacks a defensible basis in sampling theory, but that is not a quarrel we pursue (less out of magnanimity than due to our equal vulnerability to the charge!).

We proceed differently: we ask the co-operative buyer to tell us the price he has been paying for a particular kind of sheet he has bought over some period. Seldom will two buyers purchase identical physical products, to say nothing of the other terms of the transaction. We combine movements of these diverse prices into one index, whereas the BLS lets the well-defined product represent the class of product.

Two other details. First, the BLS will use an average of about three reporters per commodity, but with many based upon one or two reporters. We have a maximum of nearly 1,300 price reporters (many less in earlier years) for the seventy commodities, or an average of about seventeen reporters per price series at the time of best coverage. This heavier coverage reflects our distrust of the belief that there is only one price in a market at a given time (more on this topic later).

Second, we chose commodities (really classes of commodities as we have just said) which have figured prominently in the discussion of "administered prices." They include steel, nonferrous metals, basic chemicals, paper, petroleum products, and ethical drugs. By a universal consensus that rests upon intuition much more than upon evidence, everyone believes that it is easier to price over time a pound of steel than a typewriter or other more elaborate product—if for no other reason than that the more elaborate product changes more frequently and substantially. Our study is thus heavily biased toward widely used staple industrial materials, where quoted seller prices are widely believed to be most accurate. The commodities are listed in Table 3-2, pp. 24–25.

As a final element of this orientation, let us look at the transactions whose prices we seek. The buyer of copper ingots is usually a continuous buyer—he needs copper every month or quarter, and for many years. We have shifted our example from steel to copper because the price of copper changes often (although the BLS reports unbelievably few price changes—eleven in the seventy-two months of 1961–66). A buyer *could* go out each day and shop for the cheapest seller of copper, but he would be a profligate buyer—profligate in his expenditures on search, negotiation, testing of products, and all the other costs of creating and maintaining a trading relationship. So he commonly buys on contract, often at a fixed price which is his estimate of the average price over the contract period. (The contracts often allow for a renegotiation if the market "spot" price moves outside the range of expected fluctuation.) This is more economical than buying *de novo* each time, exactly as it is cheaper to rent an apartment for a year rather than by the week. We are not the first economists to be surprised at the economic sophistication of the market:

we must record our regret that we did not make a systematic study of the use and duration of contracts.

The BLS collects "spot" prices (whether those actually paid or not); we collect the contract prices. A large part of the short-run (within the year) differences between the two sets of price indexes come from the difference in type of prices sought.

We, as others, wish to turn necessities into virtues: the contract prices seem to us more appropriate to the measurement of the effects of prices upon both costs of buyers and receipts of sellers.

The Main Findings

Trend. Our price history covers ten years, and we begin with the obvious question: do the BLS and NB indexes differ in the broad sweep of their movement over the decade? This was originally a mechanical question —one normally seeks to separate the trend of time series—to which we received an unexpected answer. The trend of prices was essentially the same in the two groups of indexes during the first five years (through 1961), and this was exactly what we expected. But the BLS rose about .7 per cent a year relative to the NB index in the second period, and the literature of price indexes had not prepared us for this. The difference was too strong and general to admit the possibility that it was merely a sampling fluctuation.

The only plausible explanation we have produced for the tendency of quoted selling prices to lag in the downward movements that dominated the period is that there is an asymmetrical inertia in industrial price movements. Price quotations are not revised immediately when market conditions, and transaction prices, change: both the costs of changing prices and the desire to confirm the persistence of the price change dictate some delay. This delay operates more strongly against reductions in price quotations than against increases: inflation has made for a general upward drift of prices (so, on average, price increases are more likely to persist than price decreases). In addition, the policy of price "guidelines" and the possibility of more formal price controls in an age of international violence make it prudent for a businessman to be slow in authenticating price reductions and prompt in authenticating price increases. The data bear this view out: there is no systematic trend difference between BLS and NB price indexes when NB prices are stable or rising, but a most pronounced difference when NB prices are falling.

Cyclical Behavior. The main thrust of the doctrine of administered prices is that contractions in business lead to no systematic reduction of industrial prices, and, much more equivocally, expansions in business may only tardily lead to price increases. Whether because of a simple desire for stability, or more subtly because perhaps profits are better protected by stable prices, it has been argued that prices have at best only one-way flexibility, and that upward. The finding of Gardiner Means in his original study that numerous prices changed not at all, once, twice or a few times in a decade including the Great Depression was *the* sensational part of his study.

A great majority of economists have accepted this finding even though no explanation for this behavior of oligopolists commands general assent. Prices of concentrated industries—and most of our products are produced by industries that are so viewed—do not respond to reductions in demand, or so it is believed. We raise grave doubts of the validity of this belief.

Our period contains two short contractions, July 1957 to April 1958 and May 1960 to February 1961, according to the National Bureau chronology. It also contains one ordinary expansion, April 1958 to May 1960, and one of extraordinary length, February 1961 to the end of our period. This latter expansion is so long that it partakes of a trend, and so we distinguish the short, sharp expansion at the end of the period (say, November 1964 to November 1966— months dictated by our use of three-month averages) as a second expansion. Our decade clearly does not test the flexibility of prices in major depressions or major inflations, but we could not repair (or rather, damage) this characteristic of recent economic history.

Even the BLS price indexes are not especially cordial to this view of cyclical rigidity, and our price indexes are emphatic in their contradiction of it. We may tabulate the directions of price change including and excluding steel products (which are numerous in our sample and atypical in their price behavior) in the two contractions:

Price Changes	All Prices		Excluding Steel Products	
	BLS	NB	BLS	NB
Decreases	23	40	23	40
No change (−.05 to + .05% per month)	19	10	16	7
Increases	26	18	18	10

Similarly in the two expansions, we tabulate the results including and excluding steel products:

Price Changes	All Prices		Excluding Steel Products	
	BLS	NB	BLS	NB
Increases	36	37	36	36
No change (−.05 to + .05% per month)	20	14	18	13
Decreases	14	19	5	10

It is difficult to generalize these results because our collection of commodities is in no sense random; indeed it is purposely concentrated in the areas where "administered" prices are most often said to exist. Even with this bias, if such it be, toward price rigidity, we find a predominant tendency of prices to move in response to the movement of general business. As a summary figure, in the four cycles we find prices moving in the same direction as business 56 per cent of the time; remaining constant 17 per cent of the time; and moving perversely 27 per cent of the time.[2] Since there is no reason on earth or in space why all prices should move in the same direction, especially during relatively mild expansions and contractions, we find no evidence here to suggest that price rigidity or "administration" is a significant phenomenon.

Short-Run Fluctuations. The short-run movements of the BLS and NB indexes differ systematically in one respect: the NB index changes much more smoothly. The BLS indexes usually alternate between periods of little or no change and periods of large and fitful movement. We consider this difference to be favorable to our index. We share with Alfred Marshall the view that *natura non facit saltum.*

The correlation of changes in the two indexes is not very high (for example, $r = .32$ for simultaneous monthly movements), and neither series systematically leads the other. Yet the BLS prices should lead; spot prices should lead an average of contract prices of varying months of termination.

---

[2] If we first remove the trend, the corresponding percentages are 54 per cent of prices change with business, 34 per cent are constant, and 12 per cent move perversely.

20. When Are Prices More Stable Than Purchase Rates?

LESTER G. TELSER

1. Introduction

The doctrine of administered prices has gained widespread acceptance among economists and others as an explanation of the alleged pervasiveness of rigid prices. According to this doctrine the decline of competition is a necessary condition for control over prices. Indeed the very terms "administered prices" suggest this because under competition individual firms lack control over prices.

I shall contend that the evidence supposed to favor this doctrine has been misinterpreted. It is not that prices are actually rigid but rather that prices of certain kinds of products tend to be stabilized at the expense of wider fluctuations of purchase rates in order to gain narrower changes in rates of output. This can happen with perfect competition provided certain other conditions are satisfied and assuming that firms seek a maximum net return. Therefore, this phenomenon does not require abandonment of the competitive model which is fully capable of explaining the facts and in addition can give new implications capable of empirical testing.

Before presenting this explanation of the stability of prices relative to purchase rates, it is helpful to recall pertinent aspects of the administered prices doctrine, which has changed in order to explain facts inconsistent with the original version. Administered prices were born in the United States during the Great Depression when Gardiner Means claimed to have observed that in many industries prices stayed constant despite large decreases of demand. Data by industry taken from the ingredients of the

Wholesale Price Index seemed to show unbelievably long stretches of literally constant prices for some manufactured goods. In contrast, prices of agricultural products fell sharply while output remained close to pre-depression levels. Since farming seems more competitive than most manufacturing industries, it was natural to link the observed phenomena to the differences in the state of competition between these two sectors of the economy. This inspired more detailed study of various manufacturing industries to see whether there was a relation between the degree of price rigidity and the market power of the firms. The latter was measured by the market share of the four leading firms in the industry. Although Means claimed to find such a relation, several subsequent studies have failed to confirm his findings. Among these are DePodwin and Selden 1963, Weiss 1966, and Phlips 1969, the latter, however, using some data for certain western European countries.

During the inflationary period in the United States beginning in the early 1960's and accelerating toward the end of the decade, the doctrine of administered price regained popularity as several prominent economists used it to explain the rise in prices. However, this imposed some drastic changes on the doctrine. During depression, it was argued, firms are reluctant to lower prices and prefer to respond to lower demand by reducing output, and, ultimately, employment. In contrast, with rising demand firms are not equally reluctant to raise prices. Hence they use their market power to exploit the opportunity given by rising demand to raise prices. Stated so baldly I confess I find it hard to make sense of this doctrine and surely anyone would

Translated from *Revue d'Economie Politique* 1971, 81:273–301.

be reluctant to call it a theory. It is little more than a string of ad hoc assertions couched persuasively.

The difficulty with accepting this doctrine is that we are taught to derive explanations of firms' behavior from certain assumptions, viz. that firms pursue policies intended to be as profitable as possible. Hence it is hard to see why firms would want to respond differently to decreases than to increases in demand. Moreover, it is even harder to explain why firms would maintain rigid prices for as long a time as is claimed by the adherents of the administered prices doctrine.

Another explanation of price rigidity was put forward by Paul Sweezy in 1939, the kinky demand curve. It was criticized on both theoretical and empirical grounds by George J. Stigler in 1947. The Sweezy theory applies to oligopoly and assumes tacit collusion among the firms such that all firms will follow a price increase but none will follow a price decrease. As a result each firm faces a demand schedule with a kink at the current price. Hence changes in cost within certain limits do not result in price changes. However, this theory would presumably predict that changes in demand would result in price changes. Moreover, the theory is not derived from the hypothesis of profit maximization nor does it determine the initial price, i.e., the location of the kink. Hence even by starting from an arbitrary initial price where there is a kink, one could not predict the new equilibrium price corresponding to a new demand schedule. Finally, as Stigler points out, the empirical evidence refutes this theory.

One important byproduct of the administered prices doctrine has been a careful study of the accuracy of the price statistics. It is simply incredible that prices could actually stay constant, change so infrequently, as appears from the official statistics in the U.S. Wholesale Price Index. In a forthcoming National Bureau monograph, Stigler and Kindahl present the results of their inquiry into the accuracy of these statistics. They collect price data from the buyers instead of from the sellers as is done by the compilers of the Wholesale Price Index. This gives a picture of transactions prices which are most relevant to students as well as to buyers and sellers. The Stigler-Kindahl study shows that prices are much more flexible than is shown by the official figures. On the basis of this study hardly anyone would wish to make a serious empirical study of price stability using the official Wholesale Price Index statistics.

Despite these criticisms, a kernel of truth lies buried in the administered prices doctrine. It is not that prices are administered. Nor is it that prices stay constant over long periods. Rather it is that for some products prices are stable relative to rates of sale. This is the fact misinterpreted if not wholly ignored by the proponents of the administered prices doctrine.

If we are to discuss price and sales stability then we had better be clear about their meaning. Suppose there are time series available for prices and quantity sold per unit of time for a sample of products. Suppose also that neither variable displays a trend over the sample period. For every product in the sample calculate the mean and the standard deviation of both variables. The claim is that for products with certain characteristics the coefficient of variation of prices is smaller than the coefficient of variation of quantity sold. (The reader will doubtless recall that the coefficient of variation is the standard deviation divided by the mean.) The coefficient of variation is convenient for our purposes because it is independent of the units in which prices and quantities are measured but any other similar measure of relative stability would be acceptable.

If the data show trends then a more sophisticated measure of stability is necessary. One approach would transform the variables by using the first differences of the logs instead of the levels themselves. Thus the contention would be that the variance of the first differences of the logs of prices would be smaller than the variance of the first differences of the logs of quantities sold. This approach removes exponential trends. Other measures are required for other kinds of trend. In any case, the theory refers to the deviations of the variables from the trend and not to the levels of the variables themselves. This is the essential point.

The theory proposed herein to explain the conditions under which prices vary less than rates of sale postulates an industry cost of production subject to rising marginal costs in the short run, an industry cost of storage with the same property and a demand schedule subject to random shocks on average equal to zero.

2. The T-Period Competitive and Monopoly Equilibrium

For this theory it is necessary to distinguish between two kinds of products, those that are made to the customer's specifications and those that are standardized so that a class of customers can find them satisfactory. It is the holding of significant amounts of stocks of the final product that is essential for this theory. Producers of goods made to order do not hold much stocks of the final product in anticipation of sale at prices unknown in advance. However, producers of standardized products may do so under certain conditions. Producers of goods made to order may, however, hold stocks of the inputs instead of stocks of outputs. Producers of standardized goods typically hold stocks of both inputs and outputs.

Let us consider some examples of goods made to order. Electricity is such a good since it is very costly to store the final product, the current, in large amounts. Hence producers of electricity store the inputs, generating capacity, fuel, and labor, instead. They supply the product to their customers' specifications at terms that we can suppose are fixed in advance. In effect these terms are embodied in future contracts which set prices for various quantities of electricity over long time intervals. It often happens that the prices are regulated by state agencies but this is not essential to the argument. Electricity shares with many other goods made to order the characteristic that the terms of sale are agreed to in advance and there is a reason-

ably good forecast of the demand forthcoming at these prices.

Furniture, women's clothing, and steel are other examples of goods made to order. In these cases the buyers and sellers agree on the precise specifications of the product, the terms of sale, and the amounts bought before production begins. The producer assumes the risk of storing the inputs, the physical plant and equipment and the raw materials, but he does not bear the risk of holding stocks of the final product.

Whether or not a good is made to order depends on its method of production and the buyers' preferences. In the past, many, if not all, goods were made to order. Indeed it is a salient characteristic of modern economies that fewer goods are custom made and more are standardized and held in stock in the hope that customers will want to buy them at prices expected to be acceptable by their makers. Thus the manufacturers make goods for their inventory without the assurance that these goods can be sold at prices that will yield a normal rate of return. Since they could operate like producers of goods made to order, who do not assume these risks, we should explain their willingness to forego custom work. Nor is this all. The customers all have their individual needs and preferences. Hence at the same price they would surely prefer a good made to suit them to a standardized good. These considerations alone suggest that both buyers and sellers are worse off with standardized than with custom goods. Hence standard goods must have some compensating advantage. This is the savings in the cost of manufacture made possible by standardization. By making a large amount of the same item, the manufacturer can use more specialized and more efficient labor and machinery. Hence he can offer the good at a lower price which compensates the buyer for not getting exactly what he wants. This condition is necessary for standardization.

Some custom made goods are also produced in large lots for individual buyers. If so, these products therefore can be savings of large scale manufacture. Steel is a conspicuous example. However, other custom made goods are produced in small batches for individual buyers so that such economies are unlikely. In these cases the differences in individual requirements must be of sufficient importance so that they cannot be compensated by the savings of mass production.

The theory to follow applies to standardized goods for which it is optimal to hold stocks of the final product. In principle one can separate the stocks held by the customers from those held by their suppliers and study in detail the complicated implications from two sets of stock holders. Fortunately, we can avoid this tedious project because the main elements are present in a simple theory where all stocks of the finished product are held by the same entity, either the manufacturers, their customers, or a specialized intermediary who performs this and, possibly, other services. As a result we can employ a model with only three basic variables as follows:

z_t = manufacturers' rate of output during period t

v_t = customers' rate of consumption during period t

s_t = stocks at the end of period t.

All these variables are nonnegative and satisfy the accounting identity

$$s_t = s_{t-1} + z_t - v_t.$$

Although stocks are held for many reasons, we shall concentrate on only one. This is the reduction of total cost that can be obtained by stabilizing output rates through the use of stocks as a buffer. If a firm can maintain a constant rate of production then it can use that mode of production which is most efficient for this rate. Hence a firm can employ a technology such that the average cost is a minimum at the given output rate with respect to situations requiring more variable output rates. It is helpful to illustrate this argument with a diagram. Consider Figure 1. Suppose that the firm desires the best available technique for producing at an output rate OQ. This is

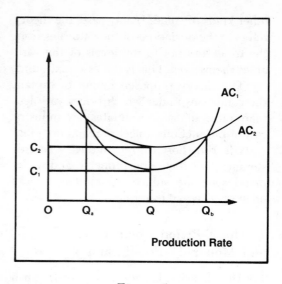

Figure 1

given by the average cost schedule AC_1 which has the least minimum in the class of available technologies such that all members of the class have the minimum average cost at an output rate OQ. However, AC_1 has higher average costs at output rates outside a certain range. Thus the flatter average cost curve, AC_2, which also has its minimum at OQ has a lower average cost than AC_1 for outputs greater than OQ_b or less than OQ_a. Hence the AC_2 average cost curve would be superior to the AC_1 average cost curve in a regime where output rates are often outside the range Q_aQ_b. In general there is a continuum of average cost schedules that all have their minima at the output rate OQ and that differ with respect to the degree of curvature at the minimum. The flatter the average cost around the minimum, the higher is the minimum.

AC_2 can be derived from AC_1 with an appropriate inventory policy. By holding stocks as a buffer, the firm can keep its output rate within the limits Q_aQ_b and thereby maintain the average cost of production close to the minimum AC_1 at the expense of larger storage costs. Thus AC_2 uses the same production method as AC_1 but with a larger inventory. The net result can lower the average cost as compared with a policy that makes production vary pari passu with consumption. Two conditions are sufficient for this result. First, demand is subject to unpredictable change, and, second, production is subject to more rapidly rising diseconomies of scale than is storage.

Although one can explicitly introduce the cost of changing output rates to show the advantage of stock holding, this is more easily accomplished with a proper hypothesis about the shape of the cost curve. A convex cost of production function can adequately represent the desired phenomenon. Formally, let

$$c = C(z)$$

denote the total cost of production as a function of the rate of output. If $C(z)$ is strictly convex, i.e., convex without being linear, then

$$C(\bar{z}) < (1/T) \, \Sigma_1^T \, C(z_t)$$

where

$$\bar{z} = (1/T) \, \Sigma_1^T \, z_t.$$

It is not hard to show that given the mean rate of output, $\bar{z}$, the more variable the output rate, the higher is the average cost.

Just as variable output rates are undesirable to the producers, so too variable consumption rates are undesirable to the customers. This follows for any negatively sloped demand function if the benefit to the customers is measured by consumer surplus. Let the demand function be defined as follows:

$$p = f(v)$$

where p is the price per unit of the good. The consumer surplus is defined by the function

$$F(v) = \int_0^v f(\alpha) \, d\alpha.$$

For any negatively sloped demand schedule $F(v)$ is concave. Hence

$$F(v) > (1/T) \, \Sigma_1^T \, F(v_t),$$
$$\bar{v} = (1/T) \, \Sigma \, v_t.$$

(From now on it is convenient to adopt the convention that whenever the limits of summation are omitted, they are understood to run from $t = 1$ to $t = T$.) It follows that, given the average rate of consump-

tion $\bar{v}$, the customer benefit is lower, the more variable the v_t's.

The purpose of measuring the consumer benefit with $F(v)$ is to study the competitive equilibrium as the solution of a minimum problem. This gives additional properties of the solution with simple methods. As we shall see, although stability benefits both producers and their customers, with both the competitive and the monopoly equilibrium stockholding tends to reduce both output and price variability at the expense of a more variable rate of consumption.

To derive the monopoly equilibrium as the solution of a minimum problem the customers' benefit is measured by total receipts, $vf(v)$ instead of $F(v)$ given above. Thus

$$M(v) = vf(v)$$

represents the customers' benefit under monopoly. Since concavity of F does not imply concavity of M, additional explicit assumptions are necessary about the form of M. To ensure the existence of a monopoly equilibrium it is convenient to assume that $M(v)$ like $F(v)$ is concave. However, one must exercise care in comparing monopoly with competition in the choice of the cost function. Since average output is smaller and average price higher with monopoly than with competition, the output where industry average cost is a minimum is smaller with monopoly than with competition. However, assume the shape of the marginal cost curves are the same and that the monopoly marginal cost is a parallel displacement to the left of the competition marginal cost schedule.

Storage costs contain two components, a cost incurred from the physical handling of the good and a financial cost proportional to the price of the product. The former includes the cost of the facilities required to keep the goods safely in a useable form and the latter is the interest cost of the investment in the inventory. If the inventory holder invests only his own capital in the stock and makes no direct outlays for interest payments, he nevertheless bears an interest cost due to foregone opportunities. Hence the interest cost is proportional to the value of the whole inventory. Denote the cost of storage function by

$$a = A(s).$$

It is assumed that storage costs are a convex and rising function of s.

If the demand schedule and the production cost schedule both remain constant over time, then, according to this model, there would be no reason to hold inventories. Hence it is necessary to introduce an exogenous set of shifts in either cost or demand to explain why firms would want to hold stocks. A convenient way to do this is to assume that the demand is subject to random change. Let the demand function now become

(1) $$p_t = f(v_t) + e_t$$

where e_t denotes the random variable which is assumed to have a mean value zero.

It is useful to sketch briefly the nature of the competitive equilibrium where the sequence of disturbances $\{e_t\}$ is known and

$$\bar{e} = (1/T) \Sigma e_t = 0.$$

The competitive equilibrium is the solution of a constrained minimum problem. Define the loss function as follows:

(2) $$H(z, s, v) = \Sigma [C(z_t) + A(s_t) - F(v_t) - e_t v_t].$$

This is the negative of the net consumer surplus. We now interpret C and A as the industry cost functions instead of as the individual firm cost functions.

The previous assumptions about the form of C, A and F imply that this loss function is strictly convex so that a minimum exists. The constraints are that the nonnegative values of z_t, s_t and v_t satisfy

(3) $$s_t = s_{t-1} + z_t - v_t,$$

an accounting identity, and

(4) $$s_0 = s_T > 0.$$

The latter constraint is imposed because under uncertainty with production subject to more rapidly rising marginal cost than

storage, it is optimal to begin with positive stocks. (4) implies

(5) $$\Sigma z_t = \Sigma v_t.$$

The competitive equilibrium is given by the necessary conditions for a constrained minimum as expressed by the Kuhn-Tucker conditions applied to the following Lagrangian function:

$$H(z, s, v) + \Sigma \lambda_t(s_t - s_{t-1} - z_t + v_t) + \mu \Sigma (z_t - v_t)$$

where λ_t and μ are the Lagrangian multipliers. The Kuhn-Tucker conditions imply that

(6) $$\frac{\partial C}{\partial z_t} \geqq \lambda_t - \mu$$

(7) $$\frac{\partial A}{\partial s_t} \geqq \lambda_{t+1} - \lambda_t, \quad t = 1, \ldots, T - 1$$

(8) $$f(v_t) + e_t \leqq \lambda_t - \mu.$$

Whenever the indicated control, z, s, or v is positive, these become equalities. The Kuhn-Tucker conditions also imply that

(9) $$\Sigma z_t \frac{\partial C}{\partial z_t} = \Sigma z_t(\lambda_t - \mu)$$

(10) $$\Sigma_1^{T-1} s_t \frac{\partial A}{\partial s_t} = \Sigma_1^{T-1} s_t(\lambda_{t+1} - \lambda_t)$$

(11) $$\Sigma v_t[f(v_t) + e_t] = \Sigma v_t(\lambda_t - \mu).$$

now

(12) $$\Sigma_1^{T-1} s_t(\lambda_{t+1} - \lambda_t) = \Sigma_1^T \lambda_t(s_t - s_{t-1}) + \lambda_T s_T - \lambda_1 s_0.$$

Summing (9)–(11) it follows that

$$\Sigma z_t \frac{\partial C}{\partial z_t} + \Sigma_1^{T-1} s_t \frac{\partial A}{\partial s_t} - \Sigma v_t[f(v_t) + e_t]$$
$$= \Sigma z_t(\lambda_t - \mu) + \Sigma \lambda_t(s_t - s_{t-1})$$
$$\qquad - \Sigma v_t(\lambda_t - \mu) + \lambda_T s_T - \lambda_1 s_0$$
$$= \Sigma \lambda_t(s_t - s_{t-1} + z_t - v_t)$$
$$\qquad\qquad + \lambda_T s_T - \lambda_1 s_0$$

(13) $$= \lambda_T s_T - \lambda_1 s_0,$$

which uses (12) in the second step and the accounting identity (3) in the next to the last step. It follows that with marginal cost pricing, the average net return in the industry is zero if on average $\lambda_T = \lambda_1$.

Let us now derive some of the stabilizing properties of the competitive equilibrium. To begin with let us assume that the following program is feasible:

$$s_0 = s_t = s_T$$
$$v_t = z_t > 0.$$

This simply means that it is possible to equilibrate supply and demand without changing the level of stocks. Hence

$$\left.\frac{\partial C}{\partial z_t}\right|_{z=v} = f(v_t) + e_t.$$

Of course, a feasible program is not necessarily optimal. In fact in this model it is not optimal to carry stocks from a period in which prices are high into one where prices are low. Starting from this feasible program, if $z_{t+1} > z_t$, then the convexity of C insures that

$$\frac{\partial C}{\partial z_{t+1}} > \frac{\partial C}{\partial z_t} \quad \text{and} \quad p_{t+1} > p_t.$$

With a gently rising marginal cost of storage, it would pay to lower z_{t+1} and raise z_t. This would lower p_{t+1} and raise p_t. Hence v_{t+1} must rise and v_t must fall. It follows that the change in output and the change in price is reduced at the expense of a larger change in the rate of consumption. Hence storage stabilizes the rate of output and the price in this case while increasing the variability of the consumption rate.

Now consider a situation in the feasible program where $z_t = v_t$ such that $z_{t+1} < z_t$. Hence

$$\frac{\partial C}{\partial z_{t+1}} < \frac{\partial C}{\partial z_t}$$

and $p_{t+1} < p_t$. Hence in the optimal program $s_t = 0$ because the marginal cost of storage is positive and it never pays to hold stocks with falling prices. Even so, the price and output is stabilized if $s_{t-1} > 0$ in the optimal program because some of the high demand in period t is satisfied out of stocks, allowing a smaller t period output as compared with the hand to mouth policy where $v_t = z_t$ in every period. However, if $s_{t-1} = 0$ in the optimal program then $v_t = z_t$ as in the hand to mouth program.

In general there is never less price and output stability in the optimal than in the hand to mouth program. Moreover, $\bar{e} = 0$

implies that there are some periods of positive stocks in the optimal program. Therefore, the optimal program stabilizes the price and the output at the expense of a less stable rate of consumption.

The monopoly equilibrium is more complicated than the competitive equilibrium because with a competitive storage industry the monopolist is subject to the additional constraint that the price rise in any period cannot exceed the marginal cost of storage. If this condition were not satisfied the monopoly could be undermined. Hence one must impose the constraint explicitly because the Lagrangian multipliers that guide the monopoly solution are marginal revenues not prices. Although the difference in marginal revenue for two adjacent periods does not exceed the marginal cost of storage, it does not necessarily follow that the same is true of the period to period price change. Hence to avoid anomalies assume that

$$(14) \quad p_{t+1} - p_t \leqq \frac{\partial A}{\partial s_t}, \quad t = 1, \ldots, T - 1.$$

There is a different measure of consumer benefit under monopoly, viz., $M(v_t)$, the total receipts, instead of $F(v_t)$, the consumer surplus. Denote the monopoly loss function by $G(z, s, v)$. It is defined as follows:

$$(15) \quad G(z, s, v)$$
$$= \Sigma \left[C(z_t) + A(s_t) - M(v_t) - e_t v_t \right],$$

which is a convex function given the hypothesis that $M(v_t)$ is concave. The monopoly equilibrium is the solution of the following problem:

$\min G(z, s, v)$ subject to (3), (4), (5) and (14).

Form the following Lagrangian function

$$G(z, s, v)$$
$$+ \Sigma \lambda_t [s_t - s_{t-1} + v_t - z_t] + \mu \Sigma [z_t - v_t]$$
$$+ \Sigma_1^{T-1} \sigma_t \left[\frac{\partial A}{\partial s_t} - p_{t+1} + p_t \right].$$

The Kuhn-Tucker conditions apply to this Lagrangian and give

$$(16) \quad \frac{\partial C}{\partial z_t} \geqq \lambda_t - \mu,$$

$$(17) \qquad \frac{\partial A}{\partial s_t} \geqq \lambda_{t+1} - \lambda_t - \sigma_t \frac{\partial^2 A}{\partial s_t{}^2},$$

$$(18) \quad e_t + \frac{\partial M}{\partial v_t} = f(v_t) + v_t \frac{\partial f}{\partial v_t} + e_t$$

$$\leqq \lambda_t - \mu + (\sigma_t - \sigma_{t-1}) \frac{\partial f}{\partial v_t}.$$

In addition the nonnegative Lagrangian multipliers σ_t satisfy

$$(19) \qquad \sigma_t \left[\frac{\partial A}{\partial s_t} - p_{t+1} + p_t \right] = 0.$$

Thus

$$p_{t+1} - p_t < \frac{\partial A}{\partial s_t} \quad \text{implies} \quad \sigma_t = 0$$

and

$$p_{t+1} - p_t = \frac{\partial A}{\partial s_t} \quad \text{implies} \quad \sigma_t \geqq 0.$$

Therefore, we may interpret the Lagrangian multiplier σ_t as the amount of stocks held by the customers of the monopolist in storage facilities of the competitive storage industry. This has interesting consequences. Thus assume that v_t and z_t are positive in every period so that (16) and (18) are equalities. Then rewrite (18) as follows:

$$(20) \quad f(v_t)$$

$$+ [v_t - (\sigma_t - \sigma_{t-1})] \frac{\partial f}{\partial v_t} + e_t = \frac{\partial C}{\partial z_t}.$$

Now $\sigma_t - \sigma_{t-1}$ is the change in the competitively held stocks while v_t is the t period consumption rate. Hence both are flows. The marginal revenue of the monopolist is reduced to the extent that his customers sustain some of their consumption by reducing their inventory. Hence the existence of the competitive storage industry raises the relevant demand elasticity facing the monopolist and reduces his power of extracting a monopoly return.

Nevertheless, like the competitive equilibrium, monopoly constrained by a competitive storage industry results in a more stable price and output and a more variable consumption rate than with a hand to mouth policy. Of course, the net revenue of a monopoly is positive even with a constant

long run average price. The Kuhn-Tucker conditions imply that

$$(21) \quad \Sigma\, v_t \left[f(v_t) + e_t \right.$$

$$\left. + (v_t - (\sigma_t - \sigma_{t-1})) \frac{\partial f}{\partial v_t} \right] - \Sigma\, z_t \frac{\partial C}{\partial z_t}$$

$$- \Sigma_1{}^{T-1} s_t \frac{\partial A}{\partial s_t} = \lambda_1 s_0 - \lambda_T s_T$$

$$+ \Sigma_1{}^{T-1} s_t \sigma_t \frac{\partial^2 A}{\partial s_t{}^2}.$$

Although storage makes prices and output more stable regardless of the competitive state of the industry, there remains the interesting question of determining whether monopoly results in greater stability than competition. The next section studies this topic for a two period model with uncertainty.

3. Storage in a Two Period Model with Uncertainty

The main purpose of this section is to throw some light on the question of whether monopoly with a competitive storage constraint results in more price and output stability than competition. We shall study this for a two period model by approximating the underlying functions up to second order terms. Work with a two period model is less restrictive than it may seem because the second period can represent the indefinite future. Hence one can quickly derive the essential features and can more readily understand the complications of a multi-period model with uncertainty.

First there is a preliminary problem. This is to show that with uncertainty and convex production and storage costs, it pays to hold stocks on average if production is subject to more rapidly rising marginal cost than is storage. In this section the additive disturbance affecting the demand schedule is a random variable with mean zero. We must determine under what conditions total costs are larger with $s_0 = 0$ than with $s_0 > 0$ regardless of the random shocks disturbing the demand.

Suppose $s_0 = 0$. There are two possibilities, a positive or a negative initial shock. First, assume that $e_1 > 0$ so that the first period demand schedule is higher than normal. Without stocks initially there is some market clearing price and a rate of demand v_1. Hence the total cost would be $C(v_1)$. Moreover, by hypothesis $v_1 > \bar{v}$ so that also $z_1 > \bar{z}$. We may assume that the second period demand equals the average value $\bar{v}$ giving a cost $C(\bar{v})$. Therefore, $s_0 = 0$ implies a total cost of

$$C(v_1) + C(\bar{v}).$$

However, provided $A(s)$ and $C(z)$ meet certain conditions, exactly the same demands can be satisfied with a lower total cost if $s_0 > 0$. Thus, with positive s_0, some of the first period demand can be satisfied from inventory and there would be a smaller required rise in current output than with a hand to mouth policy. With positive initial stocks we could have $z_1 < v_1$ with $s_0 = v_1 - z_1$. However, if it is optimal to begin with stocks then it is also optimal to end with them. Hence one would plan an output rate in the second period above the mean rate of consumption. Therefore,

$$z_1 = v_1 - (s_0 - s_1)$$
$$z_2 = \bar{v} + (s_2 - s_1) = \bar{v} + (s_0 - s_1)$$

if $s_0 = s_2$. Figure 2 shows that

$$C(z_1) + C(z_2) < C(v_1) + C(\bar{v}).$$

Therefore, $s_0 > 0$ can lower total cost while

satisfying the same demands as in a hand to mouth policy if

$$(1) \quad C(z_1) + C(z_2) + A(s_0) + A(s_1) < C(v_1) + C(\bar{v}).$$

This condition can be satisfied for positive stocks if the cost of production function is more convex than the cost of storage function which is equivalent to saying that marginal production cost rises more rapidly than marginal storage cost.

Next assume there is a negative initial shock, $e_1 < 0$. Hence $v_1 < \bar{v}$. In this case also it is cheaper to accumulate stocks in the first period in the expectation of selling them in the second period than to follow a hand to mouth policy. Moreover, by having $s_0 > 0$, the accumulation required in the first period is smaller and, simultaneously, there is a smaller change in output rates between the two periods. Therefore, in this case as well, $s_0 > 0$ allows a reduction of total cost. Figure 3 illustrates the advan-

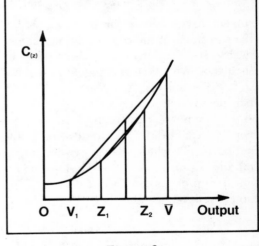

Figure 3

tage of a smoother output policy in the case where the current demand is below the long run average.

To ensure that the cost of storage function satisfies the necessary condition for a positive stock level in the optimal policy, assume that storage costs are a linear function of stocks so that

$$(2) \qquad A(s) = as$$

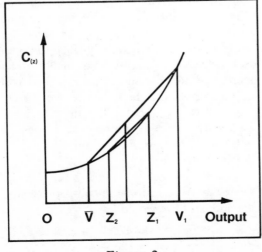

Figure 2

and that production costs are strictly convex.

According to the preceding argument, it is optimal to hold stocks on average. With linear storage costs, as_0 is the inventory contribution to overhead costs. To find the equilibrium value of the opening stocks one can minimize the expected loss with respect to initial stocks. Denote the probability function of the random disturbance in demand by $\phi(e)$. Under competition the expected loss function is

$$(3) \quad \Sigma_1^T \int [C(z_t) + A(s_t)$$
$$- F(v_t) - e_t v_t]\phi(e_t)\,de_t.$$

The optimal s_0 minimizes the expected loss (3) subject to the familiar constraints. Under monopoly where the stocks are held competitively, the opening stock is σ_0. Hence to find the optimal opening stock one would solve the problem

$$(4) \quad \min_{\sigma_0} \Sigma_1^T \int [C(z_t) + A(s_t)$$
$$- M(v_t) - e_t v_t]\phi(e_t)\,de_t$$

subject to the same constraints including the constraint of the competitive storage industry. It is harder to solve these problems than those with known exogenous demand shifts. Fortunately, one can obtain some pertinent results rather easily.

To compare the competitive and monopoly equilibria with storage for a two period model where the mean value of the random disturbance is zero, let us take a linear approximation to the demand function as follows:

$$(5) \qquad p = b_0 - b_1 v, \quad b_0, b_1 > 0$$

and a quadratic approximation to the production cost function,

$$(6) \quad C(z) = c_0 + c_1 z + c_2 z^2, \quad c_0, c_1, c_2 > 0.$$

A necessary condition for $s_1 > 0$ is that the first period demand is below normal. Hence it is convenient to assume that the first period disturbance is $-e$ and the second period disturbance is $+e$. In this way we can study the typical situation for a demand increase. Later we use the same approach for a demand decrease.

First, calculate the competitive equilibrium. If $s_0 = s_2$ then $\bar{v} = \bar{z}$. The short run supply curve is the marginal cost curve. If $b_0 > c_1$ and if the disturbance e is not too large then there will be positive consumption and production rates in both periods. Hence the equilibrium conditions are given as follows:

$$s_1 = z_1 - v_1 = v_2 - z_2$$
$$p_1 = MC_1 \quad (MC \text{ stands for marginal production cost})$$
$$p_2 = MC_2$$
$$p_2 - p_1 = a.$$

Routine calculations give the following equilibrium values:

$$z_1 = (b_0 - c_1)/(b_1 + 2c_2) - a/4c_2$$
$$z_2 = (b_0 - c_1)/(b_1 + 2c_2) + a/4c_2$$
$$v_1 = (b_0 - c_1)/(b_1 + 2c_2) - (2e - a)/2b_1$$
$$v_2 = (b_0 - c_1)/(b_1 + 2c_2) + (2e - a)/2b_1.$$

For the second period demand to exceed the first period demand, it is necessary and sufficient that

$$a < e/2.$$

There are certain interesting facts about these values. First, the equilibrium output rates are independent of the demand disturbances. Second, since

$$z_2 - z_1 = a/2c_2$$
$$v_2 - v_1 = (2e - a)/b_1,$$

both the change in the output rate and the change in the consumption rate are independent of c_1. This is important because c_1, which gives the intercept of the marginal cost curve, is typically not the same for competition as for monopoly since the optimal scale of operation will be smaller under monopoly and the short run marginal cost curve reflects this fact. Hence we do not have to worry about differences between monopoly and competition with respect to c_1 for studying period to period change with demand increases.

Under monopoly, ignoring for the moment the constraint of the competitive storage industry, we would have

$$z_2 - z_1 = a/2c_2$$
$$v_2 - v_1 = (2e - a)/2b_1$$
$$p_2 - p_1 = e + a/2.$$

However, the latter condition violates the constraint that

$$p_2 - p_1 \leq a$$

since

$$e/2 > a.$$

Although without the constraint of the competitive storage industry, monopoly would lead to a larger price change and a smaller change in the rate of consumption than with competition, this solution is unacceptable unless the monopoly can control the actions of its customers and prevent their use of the competitive storage industry. The correct solution for monopoly with the constraint of a competitive storage industry is exactly the same as for competition with respect to changes in the values of prices, consumption rates and production rates. Of course, the average level of consumption and production is higher with competition than with monopoly and the average price is lower. Hence given an unexpected increase in demand monopoly constrained by a competitive storage industry responds in the same ways as a competitive industry.

Let us now study a demand decrease. This means that the first period disturbance is $+e$ and the second period disturbance is $-e$. Under competition

$$v_1 = s_0 + z_1$$
$$v_2 = z_2 - s_0$$
$$z_2 - z_1 = 2(b_1 s_0 - e)/(2c_2 + b_1)$$
$$v_2 - v_1 = z_2 - z_1 - 2s_0$$
$$v_2 - v_1 = -2(e + 2c_2 s_0)/(2c_2 + b_1)$$
$$p_2 - p_1 = 2c_2(z_2 - z_1) < 0 < a.$$

To ensure positive prices in both periods, assume that s_0 is small enough so that

$$b_1 s_0 < e.$$

For monopoly constrained by a competitive storage industry, the pertinent conditions are given as follows:

$$\sigma_0 = v_1 - z_1$$
$$\sigma_2 = \sigma_0 = z_2 - v_2$$
$$v_2 - v_1 = -[e + (2c_2 - b_1)\sigma_0]/(b_1 + c_2)$$
$$z_2 - z_1 = (3b_1\sigma_0 - e)/(b_1 + c_2)$$
$$p_2 - p_1$$
$$= \{b_1[(2c_2 - b_1)\sigma_0 - e)] - 2c_2 e\}/(b_1 + c_2).$$

If $v_2 - v_1 < 0$ then also $p_2 - p_1 < 0$. Similarly, the output change is negative if σ_0 is not too large.

Assume that $\sigma_0 < s_0$ so that initially held stocks are at least as large with competition in production as with monopoly, a not implausible assumption since average output and consumption rates are lower with monopoly. It follows that the period to period change in consumption rates and prices are smaller in magnitude under monopoly subject to a competitive storage constraint than under competition if demand falls from the first to the second period. The effect on production rates is slightly more complicated.

Let $(z_2 - z_1)_m$ denote the output change under monopoly and $(z_2 - z_1)_c$ denote it under competition. Then

$$|z_2 - z_1|_c > |z_2 - z_1|_m$$

if and only if

$$(e - b_1 s_0)/(2c_2 + b_1)$$
$$> (e - 3b_1\sigma_0)/2(b_1 + c_2).$$

The latter inequality reduces to

$$e - 2(b_1 + c_2)s_0 > -3(2c_2 + b_1)\sigma_0.$$

Without some additional assumptions about the relation between stocks and average output rates nothing more can be concluded about whether output rates fall by a larger amount under competition than under monopoly. It is, however, reasonable to assume proportionality between stocks and average output rates (= average consumption. rates). This means that

$$\{s_0/[(b_1 - c_1)/(2c_2 + b_1)]\}$$
$$= \{\sigma_0/[(b_0 - c_1)/2(c_2 + b_1)]\}.$$

This assumption implies that

$$|z_2 - z_1|_m < |z_2 - z_1|_c.$$

We gain additional insight from the simple relations as follows:

$$(z_2 - z_1)_m = (v_2 - v_1)_m + 2\sigma_0$$
$$(z_2 - z_1)_c = (v_2 - v_1)_c + 2s_0.$$

Hence

$$(z_2 - z_1)_c < (z_2 - z_1)_m < 0$$

if and only if

$$(v_2 - v_1)_c + 2s_0 < (v_2 - v_1)_m + 2\sigma_0.$$

For the decrease in output under monopoly to be smaller in magnitude than under competition, it is, therefore, necessary that less stocks be held under monopoly constrained by a competitive storage industry than under competition.

In these exercises we assume the shocks are the same with competition as with monopoly although the average rate of consumption is smaller in the latter case. Hence the relative size of the shock is assumed to be larger in the case of monopoly. A fortiori the preceding conclusions hold if it is assumed that the relative size of the shocks are the same so that the absolute shock with monopoly is smaller than with competition.

The response of monopoly to random shocks of demand differs from the competitive response if demand unexpectedly falls but not if it rises unexpectedly. The changes in prices, output rates and rates of consumption are the same with monopoly in production constrained by a competitive storage industry as they are with competition in both production and storage. However the response to an unexpected fall in demand is smaller in magnitude with monopoly than with competition provided initial stocks are related to average consumption rates as shown above. In this case output rates, consumption rates and prices fall more with competition than with monopoly.

This analysis depends on the linear approximations to the underlying true functions. Hence the conclusions may not hold under all conditions and especially for certain kinds of nonlinear functions. Nevertheless regardless of the state of competition, there remains the general point that with storage there is more stability if firms and their customers do not commit persistent and avoidable errors.

4. Price Policies for Goods Made to Order

The preceding theory does not apply to nonstorable goods and, of these, goods made to order are the most important. Let us briefly look at the situation for these goods.

Assume a random shock affects the demand schedule. Initially this affects the purchase rate and the order backlog without necessarily changing the average price received by the suppliers. However, a change in the size of the order backlog with the same output rate does change the average cost to the buyer because there is a longer delay in filling orders. Hence we should see whether a stable or a variable price policy is more common in a competitive industry.

For goods made to order, a policy of stable prices goes with a policy of stable output rates, while a policy of variable prices accompanies a variable output rate policy. Since production costs are higher the more variable the output rate, it follows that firms which maintain a constant delivery time in the face of randomly varying purchase rates must charge a higher average price and must also have more variable prices. Those customers who wish speedier delivery during periods of active demand pay a higher price to cover the cost of the service they require. Otherwise, if the firm maintains a constant output rate and a constant price, it imposes the cost of a variable delivery time on its customers. Goods made to order are a complicated bundle of attributes of which the time to delivery is one. The price of a given product is a function of its composition including the time to delivery. The latter may not necessarily be the subject of explicit negotiation between the supplier and his customer. Given that product specifications vary from one order to the next, the average price is itself an ambiguous concept. Nor is it useful to define the price policy for goods of some standard type since time to delivery varies and represents an important aspect of a firm's policy. Whether or not the buyer and the seller negotiate explicitly on the time to delivery and adjust the price accordingly, depends on the costs and benefits to them of so doing, including the inconvenience of making this dimension of the product a subject of explicit negotiation. We would expect that where delivery time is important, there would be special charges for speedier delivery as a standard provision in the terms of sale. There is a substantive question of why there is a price list at all and we shall briefly consider some reasons in the concluding section.

5. Conclusions

Some topics related to the preceding analysis deserve our attention. Among these is the widespread use of price lists which is sometimes adduced as evidence in support of administered prices. However, price lists are compatible with competition and are easily explained in a competitive market. They are one way for the firms' managers to control the actions of their salesmen. Many firms make a variety of goods or make goods to order. Hence salesmen need to know what prices to quote for the available variety and for goods made up to customers' specifications. Experience has shown that written instructions to the salesmen in the form of price lists or catalogues avoid misunderstandings and give the managers an appropriate degree of control over their sales subordinates. Of course, it is necessary to change the written instructions from time to time. Piecemeal changes are adequate for small changes in underlying conditions and large ones for large changes. There are obvious costs of frequent revisions of instructions to salesmen. Hence under stable conditions disrupted only by small random change, price lists and catalogues are likely to remain in force for some time. In retrospect it sometimes appears that changes should have come sooner. But one must recognize the problem of distinguishing a change in the true underlying conditions from the normal day to day variations in orders. The problem is akin to quality control where one must discriminate between the normal vagaries of the output and a deterioration of the machinery.

This analysis implicitly assumes that sellers search for buyers, which is a common situation for many business goods where the individual buyers are relatively large. In retail markets it is normally the buyers who search for sellers. Here too we occasionally find stable retail prices and relatively small differences among the prices of the same good at different retailers. Possibly, this results from the cost of search. The average cost to the buyer of a good includes both the price per unit and an allowance for the time and trouble that it takes him to find something acceptable. Knowing that prices are stable over time and vary little among sellers reduces the optimal amount of buyer's search and therefore lowers the average cost per unit assuming the average retail price is unaffected by this phenomenon.

In both of these situations the buyers and sellers do not meet in one place. Either the seller delegates authority to his agents in writing in the form of price lists and instructs them to contact customers who are dispersed or the customers shop among the retailers. However, some products are traded on an organized exchange where the buyers and sellers or their agents meet face to face. In these markets price often changes from one transaction to the next. Moreover, the participants have more discretion and more authority to make terms. This is not sufficient to explain why there are such markets. One must also consider the nature of the goods. In the United States most of the goods traded on organized exchanges are agricultural products. For periods up to a year the output cannot be changed. Hence the price must adjust to random shocks affecting the demand schedule. Presumably, an organized market facilitates the price equilibrating mechanism when nature prevents output from bearing some of the brunt of adjustment. Certain metals such as copper, tin, silver and lead are also traded on organized exchanges. But without more knowledge about the conditions of production, storage and demand I hesitate to pronounce the existence of organized markets in these goods as further evidence in support of the theory.

The theory presented above applies to storable goods. For these goods we expect prices and output rates to be stabilized at the cost of a less stable rate of consumption by comparison with a hand to mouth policy where there are constant stocks of the final product. There is reason to believe that monopoly tends to have smaller decreases in price, consumption and output rates with demand decreases but to respond to unexpected demand increases in the same way as a competitive industry. The comparison of competition with monopoly poses some difficult problems. A critical assumption in this comparison is the competitive storage constraint on the monopolist. If the monopoly cannot control individual customer purchases so that buyers can obtain as much as they please at the monopoly price and if there is a competitive storage constraint then the price difference from one period to the next cannot exceed the marginal cost of storage.

Stocks have a convenience yield in this theory because they can reduce the total cost by allowing a more stable output policy. To represent the cost of variable output rates it is unnecessary to assume an explicit cost of changing the rates since the existence of such costs is a consequence of a convex production cost function. Moreover, for there to be positive stocks held on average it is sufficient that the marginal production cost rises more rapidly than the marginal storage cost, a condition satisfied by storage cost functions that are less convex than the production cost functions.

This theory has empirical implications. For those goods where stockholding is optimal there should be a more stable price and output rate and a less stable consumption rate than for other goods. In terms of the model the consumption rate corresponds to the purchase rate. Hence the pertinent classification of goods for the purpose of studying price stability is with respect to storability and not with respect to the competitive state of the industry.

However, the competitive state of the industry may affect the stability of the relevant variables as is shown in section 3. Given the storage incentive monopoly and competition respond in the same way to unexpected rises in demand but they respond differently to unexpected falls. Even so, the

difference between the output responses in the latter case depends on the relation between stocks and the average output rate. If stocks are proportional to the average output rate then given an unexpected fall in demand a monopolist would reduce his output by a smaller amount than would occur under competition. It follows that one should distinguish between unexpected demand falls and rises in an empirical study of how competition relates to price stability. Thus suppose one measures the state of competition by the four firm concentration ratio (share of the output accounted for by the four leading firms in the industry). If two firms differ significantly only with respect to the concentration ratio then they should exhibit a difference in the magnitude of price change only if there is an unexpected demand decrease and not for an unexpected demand increase. To verify this proposition requires considerable ingenuity. One would have to include the major factors that can explain difference in the behavior of the two industries other than the factors under explicit study.

It is also desirable to extend the analysis of section 3 to several periods in order to study differences in the response of competitive and monopolized industries to a wider variety of random factors affecting the level of demand. Only two patterns are considered in this section, the sequences $\{+e, -e\}$ and $\{-e, +e\}$. Although pertinent for studying the response at turning points recognized ex post, with a longer run of periods we might uncover other distinguishing aspects of monopoly.

I am especially grateful to George J. Stigler for his helpful comments and criticisms on an earlier draft. I have also benefited from comments of Jacques Dreze, Zvi Griliches and Agnar Sandmo. I assume sole responsibility for all errors and shortcomings.

REFERENCES

DePodwin, H. J. and R. T. Selden, 1963, Business Pricing Policies and Inflation. *Journal of Political Economy*, 81:110–27.

Dunlop, J. T., 1939, Price Flexibility and the 'Degree of Monopoly.' *Quarterly Journal of Economics,* 53:522–34.

Galbraith, J. K., 1967, *The New Industrial State.*

Kuhn, H. W. and A. W. Tucker, 1950, Nonlinear Programming. In *Proceedings of the Second Berkeley Symposium on Mathematical Statistics and Probability,* ed. J. Neyman, pp. 481–92. Berkeley, Calif.: University of California.

Means, Gardiner, 1935, *Industrial Prices and their Relative Inflexibility.* U.S. Senate Document 13, 74th Congress, 1st Session. Washington, D.C.: U.S. Govt. Printing Office.

Phlips, L., 1969, Business Pricing Policies and Inflation—Some Evidence from E.E.C. Countries. *Journal of Industrial Economics.* 18:1–14.

Stigler, G. J., 1939, Production and Distribution in the Short Run. *Journal of Political Economy.* 47:305–27.

———, 1968, *The Organization of Industry.* Homewood, Ill.: Irwin. Contains

———, 1947, The Kinky Oligopoly Demand Curve.

———, 1962, Administered Prices and Oligopolistic Inflation.

Stigler, G. J. and J. Kindahl, 1970, *The Behavior of Industrial Prices.* New York: National Bureau of Economic Research.

Sweezy, P., 1939, Demand Under Conditions of Oligopoly. *Journal of Political Economy.* 47:568–73.

Tucker, R. S., 1938, The Reasons for Price Rigidity. *American Economic Review.* 28:41–54.

Weiss, L. W., 1966, Business Pricing Policies and Inflation Reconsidered. *Journal of Political Economy.* 74:177–87.

21. The Role of Concentration in Recent Inflation

LEONARD W. WEISS

1. Background: The Inflation of the 1950s

Reexamination of the "administered inflation" of 1953–1958 seemed at first to show no significant relationship between price change and concentration,[1] but when changes in direct costs were allowed for, there turned out to be a significant tendency for prices to rise more, the greater the degree of industrial concentration.[2] A similar set of tests for the subsequent several years (1959–1963), however, showed no inflationary effect for concentration. These results were interpreted at the time to indicate that rising prices in concentrated industries during the 1950s were a temporary, delayed reaction to the inflations of World War II and the Korean War, during which periods the more concentrated industries had experienced relatively smaller price increases than the competitive sector.[3]

2. The Recent Inflationary Period

The role of concentrated industries in recent inflation has been examined following approximately the procedures used in the studies of the 1950s and early 1960s. Price data is now available for selected four-digit SIC industries from the Bureau of Labor Statistics for 43 industries for the years 1963–1969 and for 82 industries for 1967–1969.[4] Cost data are available for most of these industries from the Bureau of the Census through 1968.[5] The latest four-firm concentration ratios available are those reported for four-digit industries for 1966,[6] except for eight industries with regional or local markets, for which 1963 figures were used.[7] See Table 1.

The following variables were derived for each industry studied:

$$\frac{Pt}{Po} = \text{the ratio of the price index for year } t \text{ to price in year } o.$$

$$\frac{St}{So} = \text{the ratio of shipments in year } t \text{ to shipments in year } o.$$

$$\frac{Qt}{Qo} = \frac{St}{So} \bigg/ \frac{Pt}{Po} \quad \text{the ratio of shipments of industry in year } t \text{ deflated by } Pt \text{ to shipments in year } o \text{ deflated by } Po.$$

$$\frac{CMt}{CMo} = \text{the ratio of the cost of materials in year } t \text{ to cost of materials in year } o.$$

Reprinted from *The 1970 Midyear Review of the State of the Economy*, Hearings before the Joint Economic Committee, Congress of the United States, July 8, 9, and 10, 1970, pp. 115–121.

[1] H. J. DePodwin and R. T. Selden, "Business Pricing Policies and Inflation," *Journal of Political Economy*, April 1963.

[2] L. W. Weiss, "Business Pricing Policies and Inflation Reconsidered," *Journal of Political Economy*, April 1966, pp. 180–181.

[3] Ibid., pp. 183–186.

[4] BLS, *Wholesale Prices and Price Indexes*, Table 6, and *Monthly Labor Review*, August 1965.

[5] Bureau of the Census, *Censuses of Manufactures*, 1963 and 1967 and *Annual Surveys of Manufactures*, 1968. The 1967 Census and the 1968 Annual Survey data are from preliminary reports.

[6] Bureau of the Census, *Annual Survey of Manufactures*, 1966.

[7] Senate Judiciary Committee, *Concentration Ratios in Manufacturing Industry: 1963*, Tables 25 and 26. For the eight industries with regional or local markets, concentration ratios were obtained by taking weighted averages of either the divisions, states, or SMSAs (see Table 1).

$\dfrac{MHt}{MHo}$ = the ratio of production worker man-hours in year t to man-hours in year o.

$\dfrac{CLt}{CLo}$ = the ratio of total payroll in year t to that in year o.

$\dfrac{Wt}{Wo}$ = the ratio of total production worker payroll in year t to year o.

$\dfrac{CMt}{CMo} \Big/ \dfrac{Qt}{Qo}$ = the ratio of unit materials cost in year t to that in year o.

$\dfrac{CLt}{CLo} \Big/ \dfrac{Qt}{Qo}$ = the ratio of unit labor cost in year t to that in year o.

$\dfrac{Qt}{Qo} \Big/ \dfrac{MHt}{MHo}$ = the ratio of output per man-hour in year t to that in year o.

$\dfrac{Wt}{Wo} \Big/ \dfrac{MHt}{MHo}$ = the ratio of the wage rate in year t to that in year o.

$\dfrac{Ct}{Co}$ = four-firm concentration ratio in 1966.

Table 1

SIC Code	Industry	Four-Firm Concentration Ratio	P 68 P 63	P 68 P 67	P 69 P 68
3498	Fabricated pipe and fittings	13	1.210	1.074	1.093
2426	Hardwood dimension and flooring	15		1.063	1.093
2013	Sausages and other prepared meats	16		1.012	1.228
2015	Poultry dressing plants	17	1.048	1.055	1.127
2311	Men's and boys' suits and coats	17	1.185	1.061	1.121
3111	Leather tanning and finishing	19	1.103	1.018	1.068
2327	Men's and boys' separate trousers	20		1.021	1.040
3941	Games and toys	22		1.035	1.026
2033	Canned fruits and vegetables	24		1.053	1.004
3533	Oil field machinery	24	1.119	1.058	1.092
2321	Men's and boys' shirts and nightwear	25	1.083	1.025	1.067
3315	Steel wire and related products	26		1.014	1.070
3317	Steel pipe and tubes	26		1.020	1.067
2011	Meat packing plants	27		1.016	1.128
2381	Dress fabric and work gloves	27	1.116	1.041	1.075
2328	Men's and boys' work clothing	28	1.092	1.030	1.042
2521	Wood office furniture	30	1.204	1.036	1.088
2098	Macaroni and spaghetti	31		1.002	1.016
3271	Concrete block and brick	32 (S)	1.105	1.043	1.042
2036	Fresh or frozen packaged fish	33 (SMSA)	1.198	1.073	1.147
2254	Knit underwear mills	33		1.031	1.030
3259	Structural clay products n.e.c.	33	1.070	1.012	1.018
3316	Cold finishing of steel shapes	34		1.040	1.086
2091	Cottonseed oil mills	38	1.125	1.034	.913
2033	Malt	41		.971	1.000
2084	Wines, brandy, and brandy spirits	41	1.043	1.033	1.027
3255	Clay refractories	41	1.144	1.073	1.088
3493	Steel springs	41		1.022	1.045
2322	Men's and boys' underwear	42		1.027	1.044
3351	Copper rolling and drawing	43	1.423	1.071	1.223
2044	Rice milling	45	.959	1.030	.973
2069	Shortening and cooking oils	47	1.141	.981	1.083
3431	Metal sanitary ware	47	.989	1.018	1.074

Table 1 (*continued*)

SIC Code	Industry	Four-Firm Concentration Ratio	P 68 / P 63	P 68 / P 67	P 69 / P 68
2871–2	Fertilizers and mixing fertilizers	49 (D)	.978	.991	.858
3312	Blast furnaces and steel mills	49	1.064	1.024	1.072
3537	Industrial trucks and tractors	49	1.119	1.049	1.083
2061	Raw cane sugar	50		1.032	1.015
2515	Mattresses and bed springs	50 (D)		1.025	1.043
3576	Scales and balances	50	1.130	1.040	1.081
3339	Primary nonferrous metals, n.e.c.	51		1.143	1.102
3674	Semiconductors	51		.956	1.004
2911	Petroleum refining	52 (D)	1.021	.978	1.016
3273	Ready-mixed concrete	52	1.063	1.029	1.065
3519	Internal combustion engines, n.e.c.	52		1.035	1.061
3613	Switchgear and switchboard apparatus	52		1.032	1.027
2654	Sanitary food containers	53		1.010	.998
3496	Collapsible tubes	54	1.045	1.053	1.036
2833	Synthetic rubber	56	.942	.988	1.007
3261	Vitreous plumbing fixtures	56	1.126	1.027	1.065
3562	Ball and roller bearings	56		1.014	1.049
2092	Soybean oil mills	57		.960	1.020
3673	Electron tubes, transmitting	57		1.009	1.018
2121	Cigars	58	1.012	1.008	1.056
2052	Cookies and crackers	59		1.031	1.052
2131	Chewing and smoking tobacco	59	1.137	1.006	1.082
3221	Glass containers	59	1.123	1.072	1.075
3333	Primary zinc	60		.978	1.147
3263	Fine earthenware food utensils	61	1.126	1.042	1.060
3251	Brick and structured clay tile	62	1.107	1.038	1.060
2062	Cane sugar refining	63		1.021	1.063
3534	Elevators and moving stairways	63		1.024	1.075
2647	Sanitary paper products	64		.991	1.077
3612	Transformers	66		1.033	.945
2082	Malt liquors	67 (D)	1.044	1.015	1.026
2063	Beet sugar	68		1.024	1.037
3652	Phonograph records	71	1.108	1.044	1.031
2892	Explosives	72	1.014	1.013	1.029
3121	Industrial leather belting	72		1.097	1.072
3241	Cement, hydraulic	72 (S)	1.041	1.022	1.087
2271	Woven carpets and rugs	75		1.009	1.005
3262	Vitreous china food utensils	75	1.248	1.091	1.099
3635	Household vacuum cleaners	78		1.010	.987
3272	Concrete products, n.e.c.	79		1.005	1.026
3275	Gypsum	80	1.005	1.030	.990
2111	Cigarettes	81	1.106	1.022	1.080
2823	Cellulosic man-made fibers	85	1.010	1.003	1.004
2324	Organic fibers, non-cellulosic	85		.979	.999
2073	Chewing gum	88	.972	1.001	1.002
3692	Primary batteries, dry and wet	88	1.168	1.001	1.037
3672	Cathode ray picture tubes	89		.927	.926
3641	Electric lamps	93		1.038	.943
3671	Electron tubes, receiving type	95		1.050	1.144

(D):   Weighted average of geographic divisions.
(S):   Weighted average of states.
(SMSA): Weighted average of SMSAs.

The price ratios were regressed on concentration and on the control variables for 1963–1968 and 1967–1968, and on concentration alone for 1963–1968, 1967–1968, and 1968–1969. The results are shown in Table 2.

Table 2 • Regression and Correlation Coefficients Relating P_t/P_o to Indicated Independent Variables

R^2 and Degrees of Freedom	Year t	Year o	Constant	C_{66}	$\dfrac{Q_t}{Q_o}$	$\dfrac{CM_i}{CM_o} \Big/ \dfrac{Q_t}{Q_o}$	$\dfrac{CL_i}{CL_o} \Big/ \dfrac{Q_i}{Q_o}$	$\dfrac{Q_t}{Q_o} \Big/ \dfrac{MH_i}{MH_o}$	$\dfrac{W}{W_o} \Big/ \dfrac{MH_t}{MH_o}$
0.26...... 43−2=41	1968	1963	1.1510	−0.00113 (.00065)					
0.34...... 43−3=40	1968	1963	1.1648	−.00112 (.00064)	−0.00919 (.00651)				
0.79...... 43−6=37	1968	1963	.6508	−.00052 (.00046)	−.02553 (.00639)	0.51950 (.07735)	−0.05023 (.07713)		
0.79...... 43−7=36	1968	1963	.5639	−.00042 (.00047)	−.02535 (.00731)	.51459 (.07985)		0.02922 (.06201)	−0.00062 (.13983)
0.25...... 82−3=79	1968	1967	1.0449	−.00038 (.00017)					
0.25...... 82−4=78	1968	1967	1.0460	−.00038 (.00017)	−.00089 (.00272)				
0.51...... 82−6=76	1968	1967	.8282	−.00041 (.00016)	−.00087 (.00363)	.11910 (.03227)	.09670 (.05509)		
0.62...... 82−7=75	1968	1967	.9265	−.00037 (.00014)	.01169 (.00486)	.11746 (.02933)		−.08344 (.02135)	.07697 (.02232)
0.28...... 43−2=41	1969	1963	1.2602	−.00205 (.00109)					
0.34...... 82−2=80	1969	1967	1.1428	−.00128 (.00040)					
0.32...... 82−2=80	1969	1968	1.0943	−.00087 (.00029)					

Our studies show that concentration has a negative but statistically non-significant effect on price changes in the 1963–1968 period. But for periods after 1967, concentration has a statistically significant negative effect, whether or not unit costs and demand change are taken into account. This is quite different from the 1953–1958 period, when concentration had a positive effect, and from the 1959–1963 period, when it had no significant effect.

It would appear that concentration had a restraining effect on inflation up to 1968 and perhaps through 1969. Unlike the 1950s, the effect of concentration on price change holds up when wage and productivity change are substituted for unit labor costs.

Thus it appears that oligopoly had the effect of damping the inflation of the late 1960s. In light of the experience of the 1950s, the result may be another "administered inflation" in the early 1970s. It seems clear, however, that we should avoid drastic deflationary policies or direct controls aimed at "preventing" an inflation the causes of which have already occurred.

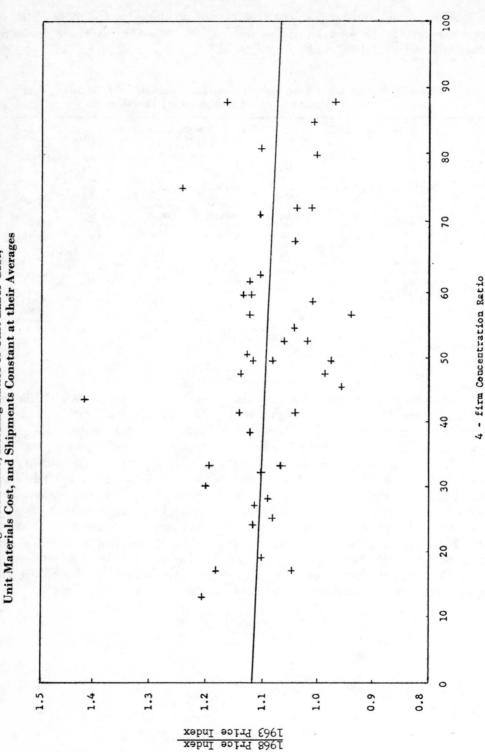

Concentration Ratio vs. Price Ratio
1968/1963
With Regression Line, Holding Ratios of Unit Labor Cost,
Unit Materials Cost, and Shipments Constant at their Averages

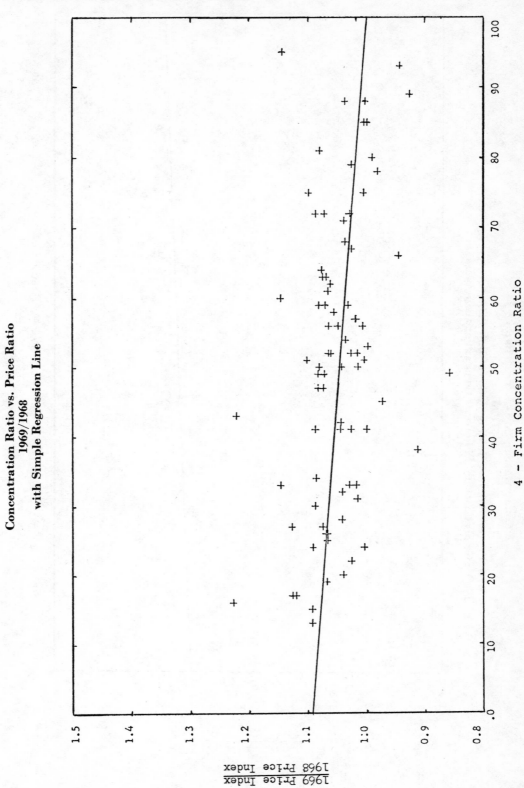

Concentration Ratio vs. Price Ratio
1969/1968
with Simple Regression Line

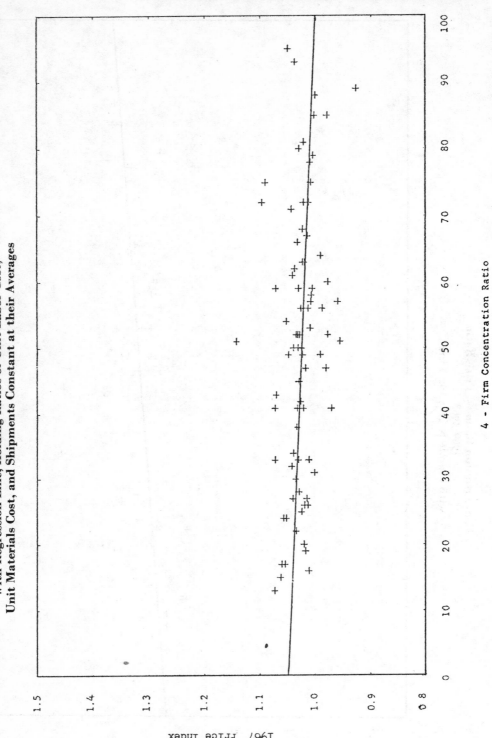

Concentration Ratio vs. Price Ratio
1968/1967
With Regression Line, Holding Ratios of Unit Labor Cost,
Unit Materials Cost, and Shipments Constant at their Averages

Part II–D · *Stability*

The tacit or explicit collusion of which dominant firms in concentrated industries are suspected should manifest itself, if true, in the form of stable market shares or at least stable shares of buyers. A collusive price cannot be maintained unless each of the conspirators restrains himself to some allotted share of the market. As Professor Stigler points out (in selection 22), "The literature of collusive agreements . . . is replete with instances of the collapse of conspiracies because of 'secret' price cutting" and "Fixing market shares is probably the most efficient of all methods of combating secret price reductions."

If a structural index such as a concentration ratio measures the likelihood of monopoly (collusive) behavior, stability of market shares and concentration should be correlated. If structure influences behavior, then we should find behavior manifesting itself in the greater stability of market shares in concentrated industries. Professors Hymer and Pashigian (in selection 23) find that, although "one might expect to find greater market share stability in the more concentrated industries, . . . the contrary appears true."

Professors Hymer and Pashigian point out that instability may prevent successful collusion as well as being a manifestation of its absence. ". . . incessant back-and-forth changes in market share and position might indicate that it was impossible to form any stable collusive understanding or agreement, since none of the oligopolists could count on the behavior either of himself or of his friendly rivals." This, of course, is what is shown elegantly in Professor Stigler's model of the incentives to secret price cutting.

Professor Neil Jacoby points out (in selection 24) that many influences operate to determine the stability of market shares. Low variance of market shares cannot be "taken *per se* as evidence of monopoly, and

213

high variance as proof of competition." However, taking into account influences such as rates of growth and of innovation, expected ranges in average annual changes in market share may be specified. Annual changes in market shares above or below these expected ranges indicate unusually active or passive competition. Professor Jacoby remarks on, for example, the unusually large annual changes in automobile market shares given the relatively slow growth in the industry during the observation period. This, in his view, indicates unusually vigorous competition.

22. A Theory of Oligopoly[1]

GEORGE J. STIGLER

No one has the right, and few the ability, to lure economists into reading another article on oligopoly theory without some advance indication of its alleged contribution. The present paper accepts the hypothesis that oligopolists wish to collude to maximize joint profits. It seeks to reconcile this wish with facts, such as that collusion is impossible for many firms and collusion is much more effective in some circumstances than in others. The reconciliation is found in the problem of policing a collusive agreement, which proves to be a problem in the theory of information. A considerable number of implications of the theory are discussed, and a modest amount of empirical evidence is presented.

I. The Task of Collusion

A satisfactory theory of oligopoly cannot begin with assumptions concerning the way in which each firm views its interdependence with its rivals. If we adhere to the traditional theory of profit-maximizing enterprises, then behavior is no longer something to be assumed but rather something to be deduced. The firms in an industry will behave in such a way, given the demand-and-supply functions (including those of rivals), that their profits will be maximized.

The combined profits of the entire set of firms in an industry are maximized when they act together as a monopolist. At least in the traditional formulation of the oligopoly problem, in which there are no major uncertainties as to the profit-maximizing output and price at any time, this

Reprinted from *Journal of Political Economy*, Vol. LXXII, No. 1 (February 1964) p. 44–61. By permission of the University of Chicago Press. Copyright 1964.

[1] I am indebted to Claire Friedland for the statistical work and to Harry Johnson for helpful criticisms.

familiar conclusion seems inescapable. Moreover, the result holds for any number of firms.

Our modification of this theory consists simply in presenting a systematic account of the factors governing the feasibility of collusion, which like most things in this world is not free. Before we do so, it is desirable to look somewhat critically at the concept of homogeneity of products, and what it implies for profit-maximizing. We shall show that collusion normally involves much more than "the" price.

Homogeneity is commonly defined in terms of identity of products or of (what is presumed to be equivalent) pairs of products between which the elasticity of substitution is infinite. On either definition it is the behavior of buyers that is decisive. Yet it should be obvious that products may be identical to any or every buyer while buyers may be quite different from the viewpoint of sellers.

This fact that every transaction involves two parties is something that economists do not easily forget. One would therefore expect a definition of homogeneity also to be two-sided: if the products are what sellers offer, and the purchase commitments are what the buyers offer, full homogeneity clearly involves infinite elasticities of substitution between both products and purchase commitments. In other words, two products are homogeneous to a buyer if he is indifferent between all combinations of x of one and (say) $20 - x$ of the other, at a common price. Two purchase commitments are homogeneous to a seller if he is indifferent between all combinations of y of one and (say) $20 - y$ of the other, at a common price. Full homogeneity is then defined as homogeneity both in products (sellers) and purchase commitments (buyers).

The heterogeneity of purchase commitments (buyers), however, is surely often at least as large as that of products within an industry, and sometimes vastly larger. There is the same sort of personal differentia of buyers as of sellers—ease in making sales, promptness of payment, penchant for returning goods, likelihood of buying again (or buying other products). In addition there are two differences among buyers which are pervasive and well recognized in economics:

1. The size of purchase, with large differences in costs of providing lots of different size.
2. The urgency of purchase, with possibly sufficient differences in elasticity of demand to invite price discrimination.

It is one thing to assert that no important market has homogeneous transactions, and quite another to measure the extent of the heterogeneity. In a regime of perfect knowledge, it would be possible to measure heterogeneity by the variance of prices in transactions; in a regime of imperfect knowledge, there will be dispersion of prices even with transaction homogeneity.[2]

The relevance of heterogeneity to collusion is this: It is part of the task of maximizing industry profits to employ a price structure that takes account of the larger differences in the costs of various classes of transactions. Even with a single, physically homogeneous product the profits will be reduced if differences among buyers are ignored. A simple illustration of this fact is given in the Appendix; disregard of differences among buyers proves to be equivalent to imposing an exicse tax upon them, but one which is not collected by the monopolist. A price structure of some complexity will usually be the goal of collusive oligopolists.

II. The Methods of Collusion

Collusion of firms can take many forms, of which the most comprehensive is outright merger. Often merger will be inappropriate, however, because of diseconomies of scale,[3] and at certain times and places it may be forbidden by law. Only less comprehensive is the cartel with a joint sales agency, which again has economic limitations—it is ill suited to custom work and creates serious administrative costs in achieving quality standards, cost reductions, product innovations, etc. In deference to American antitrust policy, we shall assume that the collusion takes the form of joint determination of outputs and prices by ostensibly independent firms, but we shall not take account of the effects of the legal prohibitions until later. Oligopoly existed before 1890, and has existed in countries that have never had an antitrust policy.

The colluding firms must agree upon the price structure appropriate to the transaction classes which they are prepared to recognize. A complete profit-maximizing price structure may have almost infinitely numerous price classes: the firms will have to decide upon the number of price classes in the light of the costs and returns from tailoring prices to the diversity of transactions. We have already indicated by hypothetical example (see Appendix) that there are net profits to be obtained by catering to differences in transactions. The level of collusive prices will also depend upon the conditions of entry into the industry as well as upon the elasticities of demand.

Let us assume that the collusion has been effected, and a price structure agreed upon. It is a well-established proposition that if any member of the agreement can secretly violate it, he will gain larger profits than by conforming to it.[4] It is, moreover,

---

[2] Unless one defines heterogeneity of transactions to include also differences in luck in finding low price sellers; see my "Economics of Information," *Journal of Political Economy*, June 1961.

[3] If the firms are multiproduct, with different product structures, the diseconomies of merger are not strictly those of scale (in any output) but of firm size measured either absolutely or in terms of variety of products.

[4] If price is above marginal cost, marginal revenue will be only slightly less than price (and hence

surely one of the axioms of human behavior that all agreements whose violation would be profitable to the violator must be enforced. The literature of collusive agreements, ranging from the pools of the 1880's to the electrical conspiracies of recent times, is replete with instances of the collapse of conspiracies because of "secret" price cutting. This literature is biased: conspiracies that are successful in avoiding an amount of price cutting which leads to collapse of the agreement are less likely to be reported or detected. But no conspiracy can neglect the problem of enforcement.

Enforcement consists basically of detecting significant deviations from the agreed-upon prices. Once detected, the deviations will tend to disappear because they are no longer secret and will be matched by fellow conspirators if they are not withdrawn. If the enforcement is weak, however—if price cutting is detected only slowly and incompletely—the conspiracy must recognize its weakness: it must set prices not much above the competitive level so the inducements to price cutting are small, or it must restrict the conspiracy to areas in which enforcement can be made efficient.

Fixing market shares is probably the most efficient of all methods of combating secret price reductions. No one can profit from price cutting if he is moving along the industry demand curve,[5] once a maximum profit price has been chosen. With inspection of output and an appropriate formula for redistribution of gains and losses from departures from quotas, the incentive to secret price cutting is eliminated. Unless inspection of output is costly or ineffective (as with services), this is the ideal method of enforcement, and is widely used by legal cartels. Unfortunately for oligopolists, it is usually an easy form of collusion to

detect, for it may require side payments among firms and it leaves indelible traces in the output records.

Almost as efficient a method of eliminating secret price cutting is to assign each buyer to a single seller. If this can be done for all buyers, short-run price cutting no longer has any purpose. Long-run price cutting will still be a serious possibility if the buyers are in competition: lower prices to one's own customers can then lead to an expansion of their share of their market, so the price cutter's long-run demand curve will be more elastic than that of the industry. Long-run price cutting is likely to be important, however, only where sellers are providing a major cost component to the buyer.

There are real difficulties of other sorts to the sellers in the assignment of buyers. In general the fortunes of the various sellers will differ greatly over time: one seller's customers may grow threefold, while another seller's customers shrink by half. If the customers have uncorrelated fluctuations in demand, the various sellers will experience large changes in relative outputs in the short run.[6] Where the turnover of buyers is large, the method is simply impracticable.

Nevertheless, the conditions appropriate to the assignment of customers will exist in certain industries, and in particular the geographical division of the market has often been employed. Since an allocation of buyers is an obvious and easily detectible violation of the Sherman Act, we may again infer that an efficient method of enforcing a price agreement is excluded by the antitrust laws. We therefore turn to other techniques of enforcement, but we shall find that the analysis returns to allocation of buyers.

In general the policing of a price agreement involves an audit of the transactions prices. In the absence or violation of anti-

---

above marginal cost) for price cuts by this one seller.

[5] More precisely, he is moving along a demand curve which is a fixed share of the industry demand, and hence has the same elasticity as the industry curve at every price.

[6] When the relative outputs of the firms change, the minimum cost condition of equal marginal costs for all sellers is likely to be violated. Hence industry profits are not maximized.

trust laws, actual inspection of the accounting records of sellers has been employed by some colluding groups, but even this inspection gives only limited assurance that the price agreement is adhered to.[7] Ultimately there is no substitute for obtaining the transaction prices from the buyers.

An oligopolist will not consider making secret price cuts to buyers whose purchases fall below a certain size relative to his aggregate sales. The ease with which price cutting is detected by rivals is decisive in this case. If p is the probability that some rival will hear of one such price reduction, $1 - (1 - p)^n$ is the probability that a rival will learn of at least one reduction if it is given to n customers. Even if p is as small as 0.01, when n equals 100 the probability of detection is .634, and when n equals 1000 it is .99996. No one has yet invented a way to advertise price reductions which brings them to the attention of numerous customers but not to that of any rival.[8]

It follows that oligopolistic collusion will often be effective against small buyers even when it is ineffective against large buyers. When the oligopolists sell to numerous small retailers, for example, they will adhere to the agreed-upon price, even though they are cutting prices to larger chain stores and industrial buyers. This is a first empirical implication of our theory. Let us henceforth exclude small buyers from consideration.

The detection of secret price cutting will of course be as difficult as interested people can make it. The price cutter will certainly protest his innocence, or, if this would tax credulity beyond its taxable capacity, blame a disobedient subordinate.

The price cut will often take the indirect form of modifying some nonprice dimension of the transaction. The customer may, and often will, divulge price reductions, in order to have them matched by others, but he will learn from experience if each disclosure is followed by the withdrawal of the lower price offer. Indeed the buyer will frequently fabricate wholly fictitious price offers to test the rivals. Policing the collusion sounds very much like the subtle and complex problem presented in a good detective story.

There is a difference: In our case the man who murders the collusive price will receive the bequest of patronage. The basic method of detection of a price cutter must be the fact that he is getting business he would otherwise not obtain. No promises of lower prices that fail to shift some business can be really effective—either the promised price is still too high or it is simply not believed.

Our definition of perfect collusion, indeed, must be that no buyer changes sellers voluntarily. There is no competitive price cutting if there are no shifts of buyers among sellers.

To this rule that price cutting must be inferred from shifts of buyers there is one partial exception, but that an important one. There is one type of buyer who usually reveals the price he pays, and does not accept secret benefices: the government. The system of sealed bids, publicly opened with full identification of each bidder's price and specifications, is the ideal instrument for the detection of price cutting. There exists no alternative method of secretly cutting prices (bribery of purchasing agents aside). Our second empirical prediction, then, is that collusion will always be more effective against buyers who report correctly and fully the prices tendered to them.[9]

---

[7] The literature and cases on "open-price associations" contain numerous references to the collection of prices from sellers (see Federal Trade Commission, *Open-Price Trade Associations* [Washington, 1929], and cases cited).

[8] This argument applies to size of buyer relative to the individual seller. One can also explain the absence of higgling in small transactions because of the costs of bargaining, but this latter argument turns on the absolute size of the typical transaction, not its size relative to the seller.

---

[9] The problem implicitly raised by these remarks is why all sales to the government are not at collusive prices. Part of the answer is that the government is usually not a sufficiently large buyer of a commodity to remunerate the costs of collusion.

It follows from the test of the absence of price competition by buyer loyalty—and this is our third major empirical prediction —that collusion is severely limited (under present assumptions excluding market sharing) when the significant buyers constantly change identity. There exist important markets in which the (substantial) buyers do change identity continuously, namely, in the construction industries. The building of a plant or an office building, for example, is an essentially nonrepetitive event, and rivals cannot determine whether the successful bidder has been a price cutter unless there is open bidding to specification.

The normal market, however, contains both stability and change. There may be a small rate of entry of new buyers. There will be some shifting of customers even in a regime of effective collusion, for a variety of minor reasons we can lump together as "random factors." There will often be some sharing of buyers by several sellers—a device commending itself to buyers to increase the difficulty of policing price agreements. We move then to the world of circumstantial evidence, or, as it is sometimes called, of probability.

III. The Conditions for Detecting Secret Price Reductions

We shall investigate the problem of detecting secret price cutting with a simplified model, in which all buyers and all sellers are initially of equal size. The number of buyers per seller—recalling that we exclude from consideration all buyers who take less than (say) 0.33 percent of a seller's output—will range from 300 down to perhaps 10 or 20 (since we wish to avoid the horrors of full bilateral oligopoly). A few of these buyers are new, but over moderate periods of time most are "old," although some of these old customers will shift among suppliers. A potential secret price cutter has then three groups of customers who would increase their patronage if given secret price cuts: the old customers of rivals; the old customers who would normally leave him; and new customers.

Most old buyers will deal regularly with one or a few sellers, in the absence of secret price cutting. There may be no secret price cutting because a collusive price is adhered to, or because only an essentially competitive price can be obtained. We shall show that the loyalty of customers is a crucial variable in determining which price is approached. We need to know the probability that an old customer will buy again from his regular supplier at the collusive price, in the absence of secret price cutting.

The buyer will set the economies of repetitive purchase (which include smaller transaction costs and less product testing) against the increased probability of secret price cutting that comes from shifting among suppliers. From the viewpoint of any one buyer, this gain will be larger the larger the number of sellers and the smaller the number of buyers, as we shall show below. The costs of shifting among suppliers will be smaller the more homogeneous the goods and the larger the purchases of the buyer (again an inverse function of his size). Let us label this probability of repeat purchases p. We shall indicate later how this probability could be determined in a more general approach.

The second component of sales of a firm will be its sales to new buyers and to the floating old customers of rivals. Here we assume that each seller is equally likely to make a sale, in the absence of price competition.

Let us proceed to the analysis. There are n_0 "old" buyers and n_n new customers, with $n_n = \lambda n_0$ and n_s sellers. A firm may look to three kinds of evidence on secret price cutting, and therefore by symmetry to three potential areas to practice secret price cutting.

1. *The behavior of its own old customers.* It has, on average, n_0/n_s such customers, and expects to sell to $m_1 = p n_0/n_s$ of them in a given round of transactions, in the absence of price cutting. The variance of this number of customers is

$$\sigma_1{}^2 = \frac{(1-p)p n_0}{n_s}.$$

The probability of the firm losing more old customers than

$$\frac{(1-p)n_0}{n_s} + k\sigma_1$$

is given by the probability of values greater than k. The expected number of these old customers who will shift to any one rival is, say,

$$m_2 = \frac{1}{n_s - 1}\left[\frac{(1-p)n_0}{n_s} + k\sigma_1\right],$$

with a variance

$$\sigma_2{}^2 = \frac{n_s - 2}{(n_s - 1)^2}\left[\frac{(1-p)n_0}{n_s} + k\sigma_1\right].$$

The probability that any rival will obtain more than $m_2 + r\sigma_2$ of these customers is determined by r. We could now choose those combinations of k and r that fix a level of probability for the loss of a given number of old customers to any one rival beyond which secret price cutting by this rival will be inferred. This is heavy arithmetic, however, so we proceed along a less elegant route.

Let us assume that the firm's critical value for the loss of old customers, beyond which it infers secret price cutting, is

$$\frac{(1-p)n_0}{n_s} + \sigma_1$$

$$= \frac{(1-p)n_0}{n_s}\left[1 + \sqrt{\left(\frac{p}{1-p}\frac{n_s}{n_0}\right)}\right]$$

$$= \frac{(1-p)n_0}{n_s}(1 + \theta),$$

that is, one standard deviation above the mean. Any one rival will on average attract

$$m_2 = \frac{1}{n_s - 1}\left[\frac{(1-p)n_0}{n_s} + \sigma_1\right]$$

of these customers, with a variance of

$$\sigma_2{}^2 = \frac{n_s - 2}{(n_s - 1)^2}\left[\frac{(1-p)n_0}{n_s} + \sigma_1\right].$$

Let the rival be suspected of price cutting if he obtains more than $(m_2 + \sigma_2)$ customers, that is, if the probability of any larger number is less than about 30 percent. The joint probability of losing one standard deviation more than the average number of

old customers and a rival obtaining one standard deviation more than his average share is about 10 percent. The average sales of a rival are n_0/n_s, ignoring new customers. The maximum number of buyers any seller can obtain from one rival without exciting suspicion, minus the number he will on average get without price cutting $([1 - p]n_0/n_s\ [n_s - 1])$, expressed as a ratio to his average sales, is

$$\frac{[\theta(1-p)n_0/(n_s - 1)n_s + \sigma_2]}{n_0/n_s}$$

This criterion is tabulated in Table 1.

The entries in Table 1 are measures of the maximum additional sales obtainable by secret price cutting (expressed as a percentage of average sales) from any one rival beyond which that rival will infer that the price cutting is taking place. Since the profitability of secret price cutting depends upon the amount of business one can obtain (as well as upon the excess of price over marginal cost), we may also view these numbers as the measures of the incentive to engage in secret price cutting. Three features of the tabulation are noteworthy:

a) The gain in sales from any one rival by secret price cutting is not very sensitive to the number of rivals, given the number of customers and the probability of repeat sales. The aggregate gain in sales of a firm from price cutting—its total incentive to secret price cutting—is the sum of the gains from each rival, and therefore increases roughly in proportion to the number of rivals.

b) The incentive to secret price cutting falls as the number of customers per seller increases—and falls roughly in inverse proportion to the square root of the number of buyers.

c) The incentive to secret price cutting rises as the probability of repeat purchases falls, but at a decreasing rate.

We have said that the gain to old buyers from shifting their patronage among sellers will be that it encourages secret

Table 1 • **Percentage Gains in Sales from Undetected Price Cutting by a Firm**

$$Criterion\ I: \frac{1}{(n_s - 1)}\left[\theta(1 - p) + \sqrt{\frac{n_s(n_s - 2)(1 - p)(1 + \theta)}{n_0}}\right]$$

$$\theta = \sqrt{\frac{p}{1 - p}\frac{n_s}{n_0}}$$

Probability of Repeat Sales (p)	Number of Buyers (n_0)	Number of Sellers					
		2	3	4	5	10	20
$p = 0.95$	20	6.9	11.3	11.3	11.4	11.8	12.7
	30	5.6	8.9	8.8	8.8	9.0	9.6
	40	4.9	7.5	7.4	7.4	7.5	7.9
	50	4.4	6.6	6.5	6.4	6.5	6.8
	100	3.1	4.4	4.3	4.3	4.2	4.4
	200	2.2	3.0	2.9	2.8	2.8	2.8
	400	1.5	2.1	2.0	1.9	1.8	1.8
$p = 0.90$	20	9.5	14.8	14.7	14.6	14.8	15.7
	30	7.8	11.7	11.5	11.4	11.4	12.0
	40	6.7	10.0	9.7	9.6	9.5	9.9
	50	6.0	8.8	8.6	8.4	8.3	8.6
	100	4.2	6.0	5.8	5.6	5.4	5.5
	200	3.0	4.1	3.9	3.8	3.6	3.6
	400	2.1	2.8	2.7	2.6	2.4	2.4
$p = 0.80$	20	12.6	19.3	18.9	18.7	18.6	19.4
	30	10.3	15.4	15.0	14.7	14.5	15.0
	40	8.9	13.1	12.7	12.5	12.2	12.5
	50	8.0	11.6	11.2	11.0	10.6	10.8
	100	5.7	8.0	7.7	7.4	7.1	7.1
	200	4.0	5.5	5.3	5.1	4.8	4.7
	400	2.8	3.8	3.6	3.5	3.2	3.2
$p = 0.70$	20	14.5	22.3	21.8	21.5	21.2	21.9
	30	11.8	17.8	17.3	17.0	16.6	16.9
	40	10.2	15.2	14.8	14.5	14.0	14.2
	50	9.2	13.5	13.1	12.8	12.3	12.4
	100	6.5	9.3	9.0	8.7	8.2	8.2
	200	4.6	6.5	6.2	6.0	5.6	5.5
	400	3.2	4.5	4.3	4.2	3.8	3.7

price cutting by making it more difficult to detect. Table 1 indicates that there are diminishing returns to increased shifting: The entries increase at a decreasing rate as p falls. In a fuller model we could introduce the costs of shifting among suppliers and determine p to maximize expected buyer gains. The larger the purchases of a buyer, when buyers are of unequal size, however, the greater is the prospect that his shifts will induce price cutting.

In addition it is clear that, when the number of sellers exceeds two, it is possible for two or more firms to pool informa-tion and thus to detect less extreme cases of price cutting. For example, at the given probability levels, the number of old customers that any one rival should be able to take from a firm was shown to be at most

$$(1 - p)\frac{n_0(1 + \theta)}{n_s - 1},$$

with variance

$$\frac{(n_s - 2)(1 - p)(1 + \theta)}{(n_s - 1)^2}n_0.$$

At the same probability level, the average number of old customers that one rival should be able to take from T firms is at most

$$\frac{T(1-p)n_0}{n_s - T}\left(1 + \frac{\theta}{\sqrt{T}}\right)$$

with the variance

$$\frac{(n_s - T - 1)}{(n_s - T)^2}(1-p)\left(1 + \frac{\theta}{\sqrt{T}}\right)n_0 T.$$

Each of these is smaller than the corresponding expression for one seller when expressed as a fraction of the customers lost by each of the firms pooling information.

There are, of course, limits to such pooling of information: not only does it become expensive as the number of firms increases, but also it produces less reliable information, since one of the members of the pool may himself be secretly cutting prices. Some numbers illustrative of the effect of pooling will be given at a later point.

2. *The attraction of old customers of other firms is a second source of evidence of price cutting.* If a given rival has not cut prices, he will on average lose $(1-p)$ (n_0/n_s) customers, with a variance of σ_1^2. The number of customers he will retain with secret price cutting cannot exceed a level at which the rivals suspect the price cutting. Any one rival will have little basis for judging whether he is getting a fair share of this firm's old customers, but they can pool their information and then in the aggregate

they will expect the firm to lose at least $(1-p)$ $(n_0/n_s) - 2\sigma_1$ customers, at the 5 percent probability level. Hence the secret price cutter can retain at most $2\sigma_1$ of his old customers (beyond his average number), which as a fraction of his average sales (ignoring new customers) is

$$\frac{2\sigma_1}{n_0/n_s} = 2\sqrt{\frac{(1-p)pn_s}{n_0}}.$$

This is tabulated as Table 2.

If the entries in Table 2 are compared with those in Table 1,[10] it is found that a price cutter is easier to detect by his gains at the expense of any one rival than by his unusual proportion of repeat sales. This second criterion will therefore seldom be useful.

---

[10] For example, take $p = .95$. The entry for 10 customers per seller is 13.8 in Table 2—this is the maximum percentage of average sales that can be obtained by price reductions to old customers. The corresponding entries in Table 1 are 6.9 (2 sellers, 20 buyers), 8.9 (3 and 30), 7.4 (4 and 40), 6.4 (5 and 50), 4.2 (10 and 100), etc. Multiplying each entry in Table 1 by $(n_s - 1)$, we get the maximum gain in sales (without detection) by attracting customers of rivals, and beyond 2 sellers the gains are larger by this latter route. Since Table 1 is based upon a 10 percent probability level, strict comparability requires that we use 1.6σ, instead of 2σ, in Table 2, which would reduce the entries by one-fifth.

Table 2 • **Old Customers That a Secret Price Cutter Can Retain, as a Percentage of Average Sales**

Criterion II: $2\sqrt{\dfrac{p(1-p)}{2}\dfrac{n_s}{n_0}}$

Probability That Old Customer Will Remain Loyal (p)	Number of Old Customers per Seller (n_0/n_s)			
	10	20	50	100
0.95	13.8	9.7	6.2	4.4
.90	19.0	13.4	8.5	6.0
.85	22.6	16.0	10.1	7.1
.80	25.3	17.9	11.3	8.0
.75	27.4	19.4	12.2	8.7
.70	29.0	20.5	13.0	9.2
.65	30.2	21.3	13.5	9.5
.60	31.0	21.9	13.9	9.8
.55	31.5	22.2	14.1	10.0
0.50	31.6	22.4	14.1	10.0

3. *The behavior of new customers is a third source of information on price cutting.* There are n_n new customers per period,[11] equal to λn_0. A firm expects, in the absence of price cutting, to sell to

$$m_3 = \frac{1}{n_s} \lambda n_0$$

of these customers, with a variance of

$$\sigma_3{}^2 = \left(1 - \frac{1}{n_s}\right) \frac{\lambda n_0}{n_s}.$$

[11] Unlike old customers, whose behavior is better studied in a round of transactions, the new customers are a flow whose magnitude depends much more crucially on the time period considered. The annual flow of new customers is here taken (relative to the number of old customers) as the unit.

If the rivals pool information (without pooling, this area could not be policed effectively), this firm cannot obtain more than $m_3 + 2\sigma_3$ customers without being deemed a price cutter, using again a 5 percent probability criterion. As a percentage of the firm's total sales, the maximum sales above the expected number in absence of price cutting are then

$$\frac{2\sigma_3}{n_0(1+\lambda)/n_s} = \frac{2}{1+\lambda} \sqrt{\frac{(n_s - 1)\lambda}{n_0}}.$$

We tabulate this criterion as Table 3.

Two aspects of the incentive to cut prices (or equivalently the difficulty of detecting price cuts) to new customers are apparent: the incentive increases rapidly

Table 3 • **Maximum Additional New Customers (as a Percentage of Average Sales) Obtainable by Secret Price Cutting**

Criterion III: $\dfrac{2}{1+\lambda} \sqrt{\dfrac{\lambda(n_s - 1)}{n_0}}$

Rate of Appearance of New Buyers (λ)	Number of Old Buyers (n_0)	Number of Sellers					
		2	3	4	5	10	20
1/100	20	4.4	6.3	7.7	8.9	13.3	19.3
	30	3.6	5.1	6.3	7.2	10.8	15.8
	40	3.1	4.4	5.4	6.3	9.4	13.6
	50	2.8	4.0	4.8	5.6	8.4	12.2
	100	2.0	2.8	3.4	4.0	5.9	8.6
	200	1.4	2.9	2.4	2.8	4.2	6.1
	400	1.0	1.4	1.7	2.0	3.0	4.3
1/10	20	12.9	18.2	22.3	25.7	38.6	56.0
	30	10.5	14.8	18.2	21.0	31.5	45.8
	40	9.1	12.9	15.8	18.2	27.3	39.6
	50	8.1	11.5	14.1	16.3	24.4	35.4
	100	5.8	8.1	10.0	11.5	17.2	25.1
	200	4.1	5.8	7.0	8.1	12.2	17.7
	400	2.9	4.1	5.0	5.8	8.6	12.5
1/5	20	16.7	23.6	28.9	33.3	50.0	72.6
	30	13.6	19.2	23.6	27.2	40.8	59.3
	40	11.8	16.7	20.4	23.6	35.4	51.4
	50	10.5	14.9	18.3	21.1	31.6	46.0
	100	7.4	10.5	12.9	14.9	22.4	32.5
	200	5.3	7.4	9.1	10.5	15.8	23.0
	400	3.7	5.3	6.4	7.4	11.2	16.2
1/4	20	17.9	25.3	31.0	35.8	53.7	78.0
	30	14.6	20.7	25.3	29.2	43.8	63.7
	40	12.6	17.9	21.9	25.3	38.0	55.1
	50	11.3	16.0	19.6	22.6	33.9	49.3
	100	8.0	11.3	13.9	16.0	24.0	34.9
	200	5.7	8.0	9.8	11.3	17.0	24.7
	400	4.0	5.7	6.9	8.0	12.0	17.4

with the number of sellers[12] and the incentive increases with the rate of entry of new customers. As usual the incentive falls as the absolute number of customers per seller rises. If the rate of entry of new buyers is 10 percent or more, price cutting to new customers allows larger sales increases without detection that can be obtained by attracting customers of rivals (compare Tables 1 and 3).

Of the considerable number of directions in which this model could be enlarged, two will be presented briefly.

The first is inequality in the size of firms. In effect this complication has already been introduced by the equivalent device

---

[12] And slowly with the number of sellers if customers per seller are held constant.

of pooling information. If we tabulate the effects of pooling of information by K firms, the results are equivalent to having a firm K times as large as the other firms. The number of old customers this large firm can lose to any one small rival (all of whom are equal in size) is given, in Table 4, as a percentage of the average number of old customers of the small firm; the column labeled $K = 1$ is of course the case analyzed in Table 1.

The effects of pooling on the detection of price cutting are best analyzed by comparing Table 4 with Table 1. If there are 100 customers and 10 firms (and $p = 0.9$), a single firm can increase sales by 5.4 percent by poaching on one rival, or about 50 percent against all rivals (Table 1).

If 9 firms combine, the maximum amount

Table 4 • **Percentage Gains in Sales from Undetected Price Cutting by a Small Firm**

$$Criterion\ IV: \quad \frac{1}{n_s - K}\left[\theta(1 - p)\sqrt{K} + \sqrt{\frac{n_s K(1 - p)(n_s - K - 1)(1 + \theta/\sqrt{K})}{n_0}}\,\right]$$

$$\theta = \sqrt{\frac{p}{1 - p}\frac{n_s}{n_0}}$$

Probability of Repeat Sales (p)	Number of Firms $(n_s - K + 1)$	Buyers per Small Seller (n_0/n_s)	Size of Large Firm (K)			
			1	2	5	9
$p = 0.9$	2	10	9.5	13.4	21.2	28.5
		30	5.5	7.7	12.2	16.4
		50	4.2	6.0	9.5	12.7
	3	10	11.7	15.8	23.9	31.4
		30	6.3	8.7	13.3	17.6
		50	4.8	6.6	10.2	13.5
	4	10	9.7	13.1	19.7	25.7
		30	5.2	7.1	10.9	14.4
		50	4.0	5.4	8.3	11.0
	10	10	5.4	7.2	10.7	14.0
		30	2.9	3.9	5.9	7.7
		50	2.2	2.9	4.5	5.9
$p = 0.8$	2	10	12.6	17.9	28.3	37.9
		30	7.3	10.3	16.3	21.9
		50	5.7	8.0	12.6	17.0
	3	10	15.4	21.0	32.1	42.3
		30	8.4	11.6	18.0	23.9
		50	6.4	8.9	13.8	18.4
	4	10	12.7	17.3	26.3	34.7
		30	6.9	9.5	14.7	19.5
		50	5.3	7.3	11.3	15.0
	10	10	7.1	9.5	14.4	18.9
		30	3.8	5.2	8.0	10.6
		50	2.9	4.0	6.1	8.1

the single firm can gain by secret price cutting is 28.9 percent (Table 4). With 20 firms and 200 customers, a single firm can gain 3.6 percent from each rival, or about 30 percent from 9 rivals; if these rivals merge, the corresponding figure falls to 14.0 percent. The pooling of information therefore reduces substantially the scope for secret price cutting.

This table exaggerates the effect of inequality of firm size because it fails to take account of the fact that the number of customers varies with firm size, or our argument that only customers above a certain size relative to the seller are a feasible group for secret price cutting. The small firm can find it attractive to cut prices to buyers which are not large enough to be potential customers by price cutting for the large seller.

The temporal pattern of buyers' behavior provides another kind of information: What is possibly due to random fluctuation in the short run cannot with equal probability be due to chance if repeated. Thus the maximum expected loss of old customers to a rival in one round of transactions is (at the 1σ level)

$$\frac{n_0}{(n_s - 1)n_s} (1 - p)(1 + \theta),$$

but for T consecutive periods the maximum expected loss is (over T periods)

$$\frac{T}{n_s - 1} (1 - p) \frac{n_0}{n_s} [1 + \theta\sqrt{T}],$$

with a variance of

$$\sigma_5{}^2 = \frac{(n_s - 2)}{(n_s - 1)^2} T(1 - p) \frac{n_0}{n_s} [1 + \theta\sqrt{T}].$$

This source of information is of minor efficacy in detecting price cutting unless the rounds of successive transactions are numerous—that is, unless buyers purchase (enter contracts) frequently.

Our approach has certain implications for the measurement of concentration, if we wish concentration to measure likelihood of effective collusion. In the case of new customers, for example, let the probability of attracting a customer be propor-

tional to the firm's share of industry output (s). Then the variance of the firm's share of sales to new customers will be $n_n s(1 - s)$, and the aggregate for the industry will be

$$C = n_n \sum_1^r s(1 - s)$$

for r firms. This expression equals $n_n(1 - H)$, where

$$H = \sum s^2$$

is the Herfindahl index of concentration. The same index holds, as an approximation, for potential price cutting to attract old customers.[13]

The foregoing analysis can be extended to nonprice variables, subject to two modifications. The first modification is that there be a definite joint profit-maximizing policy upon which the rivals can agree. Here we may expect to encounter a spectrum of possibilities, ranging from a clearly defined optimum policy (say, on favorable legislation) to a nebulous set of alternatives (say, directions of research).[14] Collusion is less

---

[13] A similar argument leads to a measure of concentration appropriate to potentional price cutting for old customers. Firm i will lose

$$(1 - p)n_0 s_i$$

old customers, and firm j will gain

$$(1 - p)n_0 \frac{s_i s_j}{1 - s_i}$$

of them, with a variance

$$(1 - p)n_0 \frac{s_i s_j}{1 - s_i} \left(1 - \frac{s_j}{1 - s_i}\right).$$

If we sum over all i ($\neq j$), we obtain the variance of firm j's sales to old customers of rivals

$$(1 - p)n_0 s_j (1 + H - 2s_j),$$

to an approximation, and summing over all j, we have the concentration measure,

$$(1 - p)n_0(1 - H).$$

The agreement of this measure with that for new customers is superficial: that for new customers implicitly assumes pooling of information and that for old customers does not.

[14] Of course, price itself usually falls somewhere in this range rather than at the pole. The traditional assumption of stationary conditions conceals this fact.

feasible, the less clear the basis on which it should proceed. The second modification is that the competitive moves of any one firm will differ widely among nonprice variables in their detectability by rivals. Some forms of nonprice competition will be easier to detect than price cutting because they leave visible traces (advertising, product quality, servicing, etc.) but some variants will be elusive (reciprocity in purchasing, patent licensing arrangements). The common belief that nonprice competition is more common than price competition is therefore not wholly in keeping with the present theory. Those forms that are suitable areas for collusion will have less competition; those which are not suitable will have more competition.

IV. Some Fragments of Evidence

Before we seek empirical evidence on our theory, it is useful to report two investigations of the influence of numbers of sellers on price. These investigations have an intrinsic interest because, so far as I know, no systematic analysis of the effect of numbers has hitherto been made.

The first investigation was of newspaper advertising rates, as a function of the number of evening newspapers in a city. Advertising rates on a milline basis are closely (and negatively) related to circulation, so a regression of rates on circulation was made for fifty-three cities in 1939. The residuals (in logarithmic form) from this regression equation are tabulated in Table 5. It will be observed that rates are 5 percent above the average in one-newspaper towns and 5 percent below the average in two-newspaper towns, and the towns with one evening paper but also an independent morning paper fall nearly midway between these points. Unfortunately there were too few cities with more than two evening newspapers to yield results for larger numbers of firms.

The second investigation is of spot commercial rates on AM radio stations in the four states of Ohio, Indiana, Michigan, and Illinois. The basic equation introduces, along with number of rivals, a series of other factors (power of station, population of the county in which the station is located, etc.). Unfortunately the number of stations is rather closely correlated with population ($r^2 = .796$ in the logarithms). The general result, shown in Table 6, is similar to that for newspapers: the elasticity of price with respect to numbers of rivals is quite small ($-.07$). Here the range of stations in a county was from 1 to 13.

Both studies suggest that the level of prices is not very responsive to the actual number of rivals. This is in keeping with the expectations based upon our model, for that model argues that the number of buyers, the proportion of new buyers, and the relative sizes of firms are as important as the number of rivals.

To turn to the present theory, the only test covering numerous industries so far de-

Table 5 • **Residuals from Regression of Advertising Rates on Circulation***

Number of Evening Papers	*n*	*Mean Residual (Logarithm)*	*Standard Deviation of Mean*
One	23	0.0211	0.0210
With morning paper	10	− .0174	.0324
Without morning paper	13	.0507	.0233
Two	30	−0.0213	0.0135

* The regression equation is

$$\log R = 5.194 - 1.688 \log c + .139 \, (\log c)^2,$$
$$(.620) \qquad\qquad (.063)$$

where R is the 5 M milline rate and c is circulation.
Source: American Association of Advertising Agencies, *Market and Newspaper Statistics*, Vol. VIIIa (1939).

Table 6 • **Regression of AM Spot Commercial Rates (26 Times) and Station Characteristics, 1961**
(*n* = 345)

Independent Variables*	Regression Coefficient	Standard Error
1. Logarithm of population of county, 1960	.238	0.026
2. Logarithm of kilowatt power of station	.206	.015
3. Dummy variables of period of broadcasting:		
a) Sunrise to sunset	−.114	.025
b) More than (*a*), less than 18 hours	−.086	.027
c) 18–21 hours	−.053	.028
4. Logarithm of number of stations in county	−.074	0.046
	R^2 = .743	

* Dependent variable: logarithm of average rate, May 1, 1961 (dollars).
Source: "Spot Radio Rates and Data," *Standard Rate and Data Service, Inc.*, Vol. XLIII, No. 5 (May 1961).

vised has been one based upon profitability. This necessarily rests upon company data, and it has led to the exclusion of a large number of industries for which the companies do not operate in a well-defined industry. For example, the larger steel and chemical firms operate in a series of markets in which their position ranges from monopolistic to competitive. We have required of each industry that the earnings of a sub-

stantial fraction of the companies in the industry (measured by output) be determined by the profitability of that industry's products, that is, that we have a fair share of the industry and the industry's product is the dominant product of the firms.

Three measures of profitability are given in Table 7: (1) the rate of return on all capital (including debt), (2) the rate of return on net worth (stockholders'

Table 7 • **Profitability and Concentration Data**

Industry*	Concentration (1954) Share of Top 4	H†	Average Rate of Return (1953–57) All Assets	Net Worth	Ratio of Market Value to Book Value (1953–57)
Sulfur mining (4)	98	0.407	19.03	23.85	3.02
Automobiles (3)	98	.369	11.71	20.26	2.30
Flat glass (3)	90	.296	11.79	16.17	2.22
Gypsum products (2)	90	.280	12.16	20.26	1.83
Primary aluminum (4)	98	.277	6.87	13.46	2.48
Metal cans (4)	80	.260	7.27	13.90	1.60
Chewing gum (2)	86	.254	13.50	17.06	2.46
Hard-surface floor coverings (3)	87	.233	6.56	7.59	0.98
Cigarettes (5)	83	.213	7.23	11.18	1.29
Industrial gases (3)	84	.202	8.25	11.53	1.33
Corn wet milling (3)	75	.201	9.17	11.55	1.48
Typewriters (3)	83	.198	3.55	5.39	0.84
Domestic laundry equipment (2)	68	.174	9.97	17.76	1.66
Rubber tires (9)	79	.171	7.86	14.02	1.70
Rayon fiber (4)	76	.169	5.64	6.62	0.84
Carbon black (2)	73	.152	8.29	9.97	1.40
Distilled liquors (6)	64	0.118	6.94	7.55	0.77

* The number of firms is given in parentheses after the industry title. Only those industries are included for which a substantial share (35 per cent or more) of the industry's sales is accounted for by the firms in the sample, and these firms derive their chief revenues (50 per cent or more) from the industry in question.
† *H* is Herfindahl index.

equity); (3) the ratio of market value to book value of the common stock.

In addition, two measures of concentration are presented: (1) the conventional measure, the share of output produced by the four leading firms; and (2) the Herfindahl index, H.

The various rank correlations are given

the expected positive relationship. In general the data suggest that there is no relationship between profitability and concentration if H is less than 0.250 or the share of the four largest firms is less than about 80 per cent. These data, like those on advertising rates, confirm our theory only in the sense that they support theories which

Table 8 • Rank Correlations of Measures of Profitability and Measures of Concentration

| Measure of Concentration | Measure of Profitability | | |
	Rate of Return on All Assets	Rate of Return on Net Worth	Ratio of Market Value to Book Value
Share of output produced by four largest firms	.322	.507	.642
Herfindahl index (H)	.524	.692	.730

Table 9 • Prices of Steel Products, 1939, and Industry Structure, 1938

| Product Class | Prices, 2d Quarter, 1939 (Percent) | | Herfindahl Index | Output in 1939 Relative to 1937 |
	Average Discount from List Price	Standard Deviation		
Hot-rolled sheets	8.3	7.3	0.0902	1.14
Merchant bars	1.2	4.5	.1517	0.84
Hot-rolled strip	8.5	8.3	.1069	0.56
Plates	2.6	4.8	.1740	0.85
Structural shapes	3.2	4.3	.3280	0.92
Cold-rolled strip	8.8	9.8	.0549	0.88
Cold-rolled sheets	5.8	5.0	.0963	1.14
Cold-finished bars	0.9	3.4	0.0964	0.83

Source: Prices: "Labor Department Examines Consumers' Prices of Steel Products," *Iron Age*, April 25, 1946; industry structure: 1938 capacity data from *Directory of Iron and Steel Works of the United States and Canada;* output: *Annual Statistical Report, American Iron and Steel Institute* (New York, 1938, 1942).

in Table 8. The various concentration measures, on the one hand, and the various measures of profitability, on the other hand, are tolerably well correlated.[15] All show

[15] The concentration measures have a rank correlation of .903. The profitability measures have the following rank correlations:

	Return on All Assets	Ratio of Market to Book Value
Return on net worth	.866	.872
Ratio of market to book value	.733	—

assert that competition increases with number of firms.

Our last evidence is a study of the prices paid by buyers of steel products in 1939, measured relative to the quoted prices (Table 9). The figure of 8.3 for hot-rolled sheets, for example, represents an average of 8.3 percent reduction from quoted prices, *paid by buyers*, with a standard deviation of 7.3 percent of quoted prices. The rate of price cutting is almost perfectly correlated with the standard deviation of transaction prices, as we should expect: the less perfect the market knowledge, the more extensive the price cutting.

In general, the less concentrated the industry structure (measured by the Herfindahl index), the larger were the price reductions. Although there were no extreme departures from this relationship, structural shapes and hot-rolled strip had prices somewhat lower than the average relationship, and cold-finished bars prices somewhat higher than expected, and the deviations are not accounted for by the level of demand (measured by 1939 sales relative to 1937 sales). The number of buyers could not be taken into account, but the BLS study states:

> The extent of price concessions shown by this study is probably understated because certain very large consumers in the automobile and container industries were excluded from the survey. This omission was at the request of the OPA which contemplated obtaining this information in connection with other studies. Since a small percentage of steel consumers, including these companies, accounts for a large percentage of steel purchased, prices paid by a relatively few large consumers have an important influence upon the entire steel price structure. Very large steel consumers get greater reductions from published prices than smaller consumers, often the result of competitive bidding by the mills for the large volume of steel involved. One very large steel consumer, a firm that purchased over 2 pct. of the total consumption of hot- and cold-rolled sheets in 1940, refused to give purchase prices. This firm wished to protect its suppliers, fearing that "certain transactions might be revealed which would break confidence" with the steel mills. However, this company did furnish percent changes of prices paid for several steel products which showed that for some products prices advanced markedly, and in one case, nearly 50 pct. The great price advances for this company in-

dicate that it was receiving much larger concessions than smaller buyers.[16]

These various bits of evidence are fairly favorable to the theory, but they do not constitute strong support. More powerful tests will be feasible when the electrical equipment triple-damage suits are tried.[17] The great merit of our theory, in fact, is that it has numerous testable hypotheses, unlike the immortal theories that have been traditional in this area.

Appendix

The importance of product heterogeneity for profit-maximizing behavior cannot well be established by an a priori argument. Nevertheless, the following simple exposition of the implications for profitability of disregarding heterogeneity may have some heuristic value. The analysis, it will be observed, is formally equivalent to that of the effects of an excise tax on a monopolist.

Assume that a monopolist makes men's suits, and that he makes only one size of suit. This is absurd behavior, but the picture of the sadistic monopolist who disregards consumer desires has often made fugitive appearances in the literature so the problem has some interest of its own. The demand curve of a consumer for suits that fit, $f(p)$, would now be reduced because he would have to incur some alteration cost a in order to wear the suit. His effective demand would therefore decline to $f(p + a)$. Assume further that the marginal cost of suits is constant (m), and that it would be the same if the monopolist were to make suits of various sizes.

The effect on profits of a uniform product—uniform is an especially appropriate word here—can be shown graphi-

---

[16] See "Labor Department Examines Consumers' Prices of Steel Products," *op. cit.*, p. 133.

[17] For example, it will be possible to test the prediction that prices will be higher and less dispersed in sales on public bids than in privately negotiated sales, and the prediction that price-cutting increases as the number of buyers diminishes.

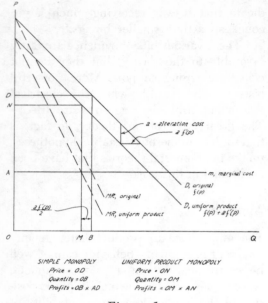

Figure 1

SIMPLE MONOPOLY   UNIFORM PRODUCT MONOPOLY
Price = OD   Price = ON
Quantity = OB   Quantity = OM
Profits = OB x AD   Profits = OM x AN

cally (Figure 1). The decrease is quantity sold, with a linear demand curve, is

$$MB = \tfrac{1}{2}af'(p).$$

The decrease in the price received by the monopolist is

$$DN = \frac{MB}{f'(p)} - a = -\frac{a}{2},$$

so if π is profit per unit, and q is output, the relative decline in total profit is approximately

$$\frac{\Delta\pi}{\pi} + \frac{\Delta q}{q},$$

or

$$\frac{MB}{OB} + \frac{ND}{AD}.$$

Since

$$OB = \frac{f(m)}{2}$$

$$AD = -\frac{p}{\eta},$$

where η is the elasticity of demand, the relative decline of profits with a uniform product is

$$\frac{af'(p)}{f(m)} + \frac{a\eta}{2p} = \frac{a\eta}{2p} + \frac{a\eta}{2p} = \frac{a\eta}{p}.$$

The loss from imposed uniformity is therefore proportional to the ratio of alteration costs to price.

Our example is sufficiently unrealistic to make any quantitative estimate uninteresting. In general one would expect an upper limit to the ratio a/p, because it becomes cheaper to resort to other goods (custom tailoring in our example), or to abandon the attempt to find appropriate goods. The loss of profits of the monopolist will be proportional to the average value of a/p, and this will be smaller, the smaller the variation in buyers' circumstances.

Still, monopolists are lucky if their long-run demand curves have an elasticity only as large as -5, and then even a ratio of a to p of $1/40$ will reduce their profits by 12 percent. The general conclusion I wish to draw is that a monopolist who does not cater to the diversities of his buyers' desires will suffer a substantial decline in his profits.

Addendum: Revisions

Roland McKinnon in a comment upon the foregoing article makes two improvements (*Journal of Political Economy*, June 1966).

The first improvement is to introduce a more powerful test by comparing (1) the loss of customers by firm X to a suspected price cutter Y, with (2) the gain of customers by X from Y. When these types of information are available, they greatly increase the power of the tests in detecting price cutting.

The second improvement is more basic: McKinnon uses the Neyman-Pearson theory to create more systematic criteria of price cutting. Type I errors (an unjust accusation that Y is a price cutter) and Type II errors (failure to detect price cutting) are explicitly introduced, to get more rational criteria than the arbitrary choices in the article.

The qualitative rules of the article (such as that the probability of price cutting increases with the number of rivals) continue to hold.

23. Turnover of Firms as a Measure of Market Behavior

STEPHEN HYMER AND PETER PASHIGIAN [*]

Firm turnover, that is, the change in rank among the leading firms, has had a long, if undistinguished, history as a measure of competition. To the best of our knowledge, it was first proposed by Rufus S. Tucker[1] in 1936 and later used by Edwin B. George.[2] In 1953 A. D. H. Kaplan and Alfred E. Kahn[3] revived interest in the measure and more recently it has been applied by Jules Joskow.[4] Recent work on the growth rate of firms by P. E. Hart and S. J. Prais,[5] and H. A. Simons and C. P. Bonini[6] has led them to encourage its use, not merely as a supplement to concentration ratios but as a replacement. The Kaplan and Kahn results were subject to a barrage of criticism. Stigler,[7] Markham[8] and Adelman[9] pointed out serious errors of fact and interpretation. But the usefulness of the turnover concept itself has not been questioned. The purpose of this article is to examine the turnover concept, to suggest that it is not very useful, and to propose another measure which is, in the authors' view, more defensible from the viewpoint of both economic and statistical theory.

Turnover Measures and the Size Distribution of Firms

It is convenient to begin with the work of Mr. Joskow. He has arrayed the largest 150 shoe-manufacturing firms as of 1950 and 1954 in order of size, and calculated the rank correlation coefficient. It is not difficult to show that this procedure has little meaning. According to the Census Bureau, the shoe industry ("footwear, except rubber") included 1,077 firms in 1947 and 970 firms in 1954. Sales were almost identical in the two years. In 1954, the largest four firms made 30 per cent of sales, the second four made 6 per cent, the next

Reprinted from *The Review of Economics and Statistics*, published by Harvard University. Copyright 1962 by the President and Fellows of Harvard College, Vol. XLIV, No. 1, February 1962.

[*] The article was written when the authors were graduate students in the Department of Economics at the Massachusetts Institute of Technology. They wish to express their appreciation to Professor M. A. Adelman for his important suggestions and criticisms. They are grateful for the generous financial support given to them by the Department.

[1] Rufus S. Tucker, "Increasing Concentration of Business Not Supported by Statistical Evidence," *The Annalist* (July 31, 1936), 149.

[2] Edwin B. George, "Is Big Business Getting Bigger?" *Dun's Review*, III (May 1939), 32.

[3] A. D. H. Kaplan, *Big Enterprise in a Competitive Society* (Washington, 1954), A. D. H. Kaplan and Alfred E. Kahn. "Big Business in a Competitive Society," *Fortune*, XLVII (February 1953).

[4] Jules Joskow, "Structural Indicia: Rank-Shift Analysis As a Supplement to Concentration Ratios," this *Review*, XLII (February 1960), 113–116.

[5] P. E. Hart and S. J. Prais, "The Analysis of Business Concentration," *Journal of the Royal Statistical Society*, CXIX (1956, Pt. 2), A119, 150–181.

[6] H. A. Simons and C. P. Bonini, "The Size Distribution of Business Firms," *American Economic Review*, XLVIII (September 1958), 607–617.

[7] George J. Stigler, "The Statistics of Monopoly and Merger," *Journal of Political Economy*, LXIV (February 1956), 33.

[8] Jesse W. Markham, Book Review of *Big Enterprise in a Competitive System* by A. D. H. Kaplan, *American Economic Review*, XLV (June 1955), 448.

[9] M. A. Adelman, "A Note on Corporate Concentration and Turnover," *American Economic Review*, XLIV (June 1954), 392.

12 made 9 per cent, and the remaining 950 firms made 55 per cent. In the three topmost groups, therefore, the average per cent of the industry per firm was respectively 7.50, 1.50, and 0.75. This is shown in Table 1, where we have estimated the average sales of the individual firms by assuming that the top firm and the bottom firm in any size group bear the same relation to the corresponding firms in the next lower size group as does the group average; and then interpolating linearly between the top and bottom within the group. Thus, since the average of the first four firms is five times the average of the second

Table 1 • **Estimated Market Shares of Firms in the Shoe Industry, 1954**

Rank	Per Cent of Sales	Average	Sales ($ in millions)	Average
1	10		178	
2	8		148	
3	7		118	
4	5		89	
1–4	30*	7.50*	534*	133.5*
5	2		36	
6	2		30	
7	1+		24	
8	1		18	
5–8	6*	1.50*	108*	27.0*
9	1.0		18	
10	1.0		17	
11	0.9		16	
12	0.9		16	
13	0.8		15	
14	0.8		14	
15	0.7		13	
16	0.7		12	
17	0.6		11	
18	0.6		11	
19	0.5		10	
20	0.5		9	
9–20	9.0*	0.75*	162*	13.5*
All others in sample				
21–150	30.0*	0.023*	534*	4.1*
All others				
151–970	25.0*	0.003*	985*	1.2*

Source: Report of the Subcommittee on Antitrust and Monopoly to the Committee on the Judiciary, U.S. Senate, 85th Cong., 1st Session (Washington, 1957), 81, code 3141. Cf. also 548, code 3141.

Note: The starred figures for percentages and sales are actual; all others are estimated. (Detail may not add to total because of rounding.)

four, we assume that the biggest shoe manufacturer is five times the size of the fifth biggest, and so on. (The reader may find it amusing to see how few degrees of freedom are left him, if he tries to make other estimates than ours for the shares of the leading companies, and how little room there is for differences of interpolation.)

For the first group, the average difference between successive ranks is around $30 million, and 27 per cent of the class average. For the second group, the average difference is $6 million, 22 per cent of the class average; for the third group, the average difference between any two adjoining firms is only $826 thousand, just over 6 per cent of the class average.

It is apparent, on the basis of the Census data, that the average difference, absolute or relative, between two firms of successive rank, shrinks rather drastically once we get away from the few at the top.

At the top of the industry, a difference of rank is large absolutely and relatively; some substantial force is needed to close the gap. But the great bulk (say seven-eighths) of the rank differences in Mr. Joskow's sample are trifling absolutely and relatively, and so are changes in rank. Chance alone would rarely wipe out a difference of $30-odd million dollars and 30 per cent in size; crossing of ranks among the largest firms represents some real market disturbance or change; but chance alone is incessantly wiping out and creating differences of $30-odd thousand and of a fraction of one per cent, so that even a great number of such rank changes signifies nothing.

In short, if we were to restrict the comparison to the largest firms, it would be defensible, but only as a rough measure, since the cut-off would be essentially arbitrary; to take in many more firms (though still a minority) does not get rid of the arbitrary element, but only imports a large number of irrelevant chance movements.

This example has been worth following through if it can be shown that it is a representative sample of industry structure; that is, that in many or most industries the size

Table 2 • Rank Correlation Coefficient for Two-Digit Industries by Quartile
and by Industry, 1946–1955

S.I.C. Number	Name of Industry	Number of Firms in Sample[a]	Average Size of Firm in 1946 ($ million)[b]	Industry Coeffi-cient	Quartile Coefficient[a]			
					1st	2nd	3rd	4th
20	Food	119	46.1	.928	.860	.420	.305	.432
21	Tobacco	12	127.6	.972				
22	Textile Mill Products	61	28.8	.910	.964	.588	.560	.064
23	Apparel	7	15.1	.964				
24	Lumber and Wood Products	16	24.9	.832				
25	Furniture and Fixtures	8	16.5	.833				
26	Paper	49	29.8	.803	.692	.455	−.440	.396
27	Printing and Publishing	25	26.2	.753				
28	Chemicals	74	57.0	.924	.817	.523	.560	.225
29	Petroleum	35	289.0	.725	.964	.929	.452	.467
30	Rubber	14	86.5	.851				
31	Leather	8	25.0	.738				
32	Stone, Clay and Glass	31	37.8	.946				
33	Primary Metals	76	106.5	.925	.973	.656	.434	.400
34	Fabricated Metals	51	28.1	.746	.873	.183	.373	−.103
35	Machinery (Except Electrical)	c	31.2	c	c	c	c	c
36	Electrical Machinery	46	51.0	.754	.909	−.321	.203	.745
37	Transportation	70	79.6	.856	.598	.374	.767	.188
38	Professional and Scientific	19	37.7	.902				

Source: Calculated from data in U.S. Federal Trade Commission, *Report of the Federal Trade Commission on Interlocking Directorates*, Appendix A (Washington, 1951), and Moody's Industrial Manual.
[a] Mergers and dissolutions excluded.
[b] Includes all firms on O.B.E. list.
[c] The coefficients are excluded for the machinery industry because of computational errors. The Miscellaneous and Ordinance industries have also been excluded, because of the heterogeneity of the former and the fewness of firms in the latter.

distribution is such that a Spearman co-efficient will reflect merely the accidental fact of number of firms and their initial size distribution. In connection with a study of firm growth rates, we have computed some data on the 1,000 largest manufac-turing firms in 1946, classified into 2-digit industries according to the Standard In-dustrial Classification. The rank correlation coefficient was computed for each industry and for each quartile within the industry. These data are presented in Table 2. These are, of course, the topmost sliver of all manufacturing firms (roughly one-fifth of one per cent), and their size distribution is approximately log normal. Hence, even in this group (corresponding to the largest two in Joskow's sample), the smaller firms are more closely bunched; *a fortiori*, smaller

firms would be even more bunched. The form of the distribution can be seen by comparing the average size of firm and the standard deviation of firm sizes by quar-tile. Two specific industries are shown in Table 3 for illustrative purposes.

Generally, the higher the standard de-viations of firm sizes in 1946, the lower the turnover of firms. It is obvious that the rank correlation coefficient is particularly sensitive to the size distribution of firms included in the sample, and it tends to fall, the greater the number of firms in-cluded in the sample, that is, the further down the ladder we go, even without our going far. If the distribution of firm sizes tends to approximate a log normal distri-bution or a normal, more generally, if there is any tendency to "bunch" absolutely and/

Table 3 • **Quartile Rank Correlation Coefficients, and Quartile Size Distribution of Firms, Food and Paper Industries, 1946–1955**
($ millions)

	Food			Paper		
Quartile	Average Asset Size of Firm (1946)	Standard Deviation of Firm Asset Size (1946)	Rank Correlation Coefficient	Average Asset Size of Firm (1946)	Standard Deviation of Firm Asset Size (1946)	Rank Correlation Coefficient
1st	126	88.4	.860	75	59.9	.692
2nd	32	6.0	.420	29	28.1	.455
3rd	17	3.1	.305	12	1.1	−.440
4th	10	1.6	.432	9	.8	.396

Source: Calculated from data in U.S. Federal Trade Commission, *Report of the Federal Trade Commission on Interlocking Directorates*, Appendix A (Washington, 1951), and Moody's Industrial Manual.

or relatively as we go down the scale, the rank correlation coefficient has no meaning.

This leads us to the question of what measures of rank change are supposed to show. Three possibilities suggest themselves. First, a high turnover rate may serve as an aid in calculating concentration ratios. It may indicate that the market or industry was too broadly or too narrowly defined. An industry with rather wild fluctuations, such that leading firms in one year drop to negligible "size" the next year, or disappear (and then perhaps return), is no industry or market at all; it has been too narrowly defined. For example, an industry defined as "all appliances selling for less than a certain price" might be completely falsified by even a slight change in price levels, and the erratic exits or drops in market share or position would be a symptom of an error in defining or using a statistical class; the industry had been truncated. A high and erratic turnover rate would pick out such a market immediately.[10] Second, in an industry which was defensible as the locus

of price- and production-determining forces, incessant back-and-forth changes in market share and position might indicate that it was impossible to form any stable collusive understanding or agreement, since none of the oligopolists could count on the behavior either of himself or of his friendly rivals. Third, an industry might show a gradual shift in one direction or another, rather than year-to-year reverses. This might be explained in more than one way. For example, it could be explained by the inroads of competitors under the price umbrella of a previously dominant firm, or by the decline in efficiency of a previously leading firm, and its displacement by more competent rivals.

In each such instance, a little reflection will show that the really significant phenomenon for understanding the market is not the change in the firms' rank, but the changes in their respective market shares. If so, these changes should be measured directly. The turnover measure in fact misses these changes, recording instead, events of little economic significance.

An example may help to make this more clear. Chart 1 shows the market shares of Ford and General Motors from 1924 to 1940. There were three changes in rank; one each in 1927, 1929, and 1931. A turn-

---

[10] It may also signal a market where the ratio not only should, but must, cover more than one year's output. For example, a concentration ratio for the shipbuilding industry, based upon the number of vessels delivered, may fluctuate wildly from year to year, with a very high rate of turnover. What this indicates is a market unusual both on the buying and selling side. The production period is so long that one year's deliveries are merely a haphazard sample of output and shares of output. As for the buyers, they are concerned with relatively small incre-

ments to their stock of capital, or capital (the shipping fleet), or replacements thereto, and if one yard is booked up, they wait their turn or go to another. Hence, the only meaningful concentration ratio based on output would be for several years.

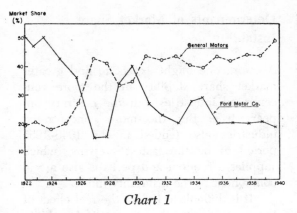

Market Share (%)

Chart 1

over measure would record no change for all years except these three. There is much more interest in a measure which would reveal the large changes in market shares from 1924 to 1927 and from 1931 to 1940,

when there were no changes in rank.

The following index was devised to meet the condition set forth above. For each firm we computed the change in its share of total industry assets from 1946 to 1955, and summed the absolute value of these changes.[11] This index directly measures changes in market shares. The more unstable are market shares, the higher the index. The value of the index in each two-digit industry is presented in Table 4.

[11] The formula for the instability index is

$$I = \sum_{i=1}^{n} \left[\frac{a_{t,i}}{\bar{A}_t} - \frac{a_{t-1,i}}{\bar{A}_{t-1}} \right]$$

where $n =$ the number of firms in each industry; $a_{t,i} =$ the asset size of the ith firm at time t; $\bar{A}_t =$ total industry assets at time t.

Table 4. • **A Comparison of the Instability Index and the Rank Correlation Coefficient, 1946-1955**

| | Industry | Instability Index[a] | | Rank Correlation Coefficient | Growth Rate (per cent) |
		Excluding Mergers and Dissolutions	Including Mergers and Dissolutions[b]		
20	Food	10.83	11.92	.928	60
21	Tobacco	9.06	9.64	.972	47
22	Textile	9.30	14.69	.910	72
23	Apparel	1.48	1.48	.964	74
24	Lumber and Wood Products	4.45	4.45	.832	117
25	Furniture and Fixtures	3.86	3.86	.833	142
26	Paper	9.63	12.03	.803	130
27	Printing	14.82	14.82	.753	94
28	Chemicals	17.42	21.16	.924	129
29	Petroleum	24.38	25.06	.725	134
30	Rubber	9.16	9.68	.851	94
31	Leather	5.69	8.20	.738	49
32	Stone, Clay and Glass	13.25	13.34	.946	121
33	Primary Metals	14.25	14.94	.925	109
34	Fabricated Metals	8.70	10.23	.746	117
35	Machinery (except Electrical)	12.71	14.65	[c]	107
36	Electrical Machinery	17.24	18.78	.754	166
37	Transportation	19.92	25.22	.856	171
38	Professional	17.19	25.43	.902	126

Source: Calculated from data in U.S. Federal Trade Commission, *Report of the Federal Trade Commission on Interlocking Directorates*, Appendix A (Washington, 1951), and Moody's Industrial Manual.

[a] The instability index is defined as

$$\sum_{i=1}^{n} \left[\frac{a_{t,i}}{\bar{A}_t} - \frac{a_{t-1,i}}{\bar{A}_{t-1}} \right] \quad \text{where } a_{t,i} = \text{the assets of the } i\text{th firm at time} = t$$
$$\bar{A}_t = \text{total industry assets at time} = t$$

[b] In the case of mergers, the merged firms were considered to be a single unit as of 1946. Alternative procedures would not seriously affect these results.

[c] The coefficient is excluded for the machinery industry because of computational error.

As the comparison in Table 4 shows, there is little relation between the turnover index and instability index and we would regard it as a fatal defect of the turnover measure that it shows nothing about changes in market shares.

The instability index can obviously be affected by the number of firms included in the sample, but it is not very sensitive to it. Small firms do not contribute greatly to the value of the index since they account for so small a share of the industry and since they tend to grow no faster on average than large firms. For example, in the paper industry, the contribution to the index by the 15 largest firms was 4.88; by the next 15 largest, 3.43; the third 15 largest, 2.39; and by the fourth 15 largest 1.33. If we had been able to obtain values for smaller firms, the index would have been increased, but not by very much. This is in contrast to measures of turnover where, as we have shown, adding more firms to the sample substantially increases its value.

The instability index weights a given percentage point increase in the market share of a small firm equally with the same percentage point increase in the market share of a large firm. This assumes that, other things being equal, a given percentage point change is the same whether occurring in a large firm's or small firm's market share, since there is the same increment or decrement to industry output. However, other things may not be considered equal.[12]

Determinants of Market Share Instability

A priori, one might expect to find greater market share stability in the more concentrated industries, but the contrary appears true. But the more concentrated industries also tended in the 1946-1955 period to be the fastest growing, which supplies a random and perhaps also a real component to the instability index.

It is difficult to isolate the real effect of the industry growth rate on the instability index because of inadequacies in the data. For example, the low value of the instability index for the apparel industry probably only reflects the fact that the apparel firms in our sample account for only 7 per cent of total assets in the apparel industry and not because the apparel industry grew at a slow rate.[13] In contrast, the higher value of the instability index for the electrical machinery industry must in part be because the electrical machinery firms in our sample account for 73 per cent of total industry assets, and not because the electrical machinery industry grew at a fast rate.

To help estimate these effects, a multiple regression analysis was completed. The value of the instability index was made a function of industry growth rate and of the share of industry assets accounted for by the firms in our sample. The correlation data are presented below:

---

could be measured by using the following weighting scheme:

$$I = \sum_{i=1}^{n} \left[\frac{a_{t,i}}{A_t} - \frac{a_{t-1,i}}{A_{t-1}} \right] \frac{a_{t-1,i}}{A_{t-1}}$$

i.e., weighting the absolute value of the change in market shares by the market share of the firm at the beginning of the period.

[13] The growth rate of an industry was defined as the percentage increase in total industry assets from the first quarter of 1947 to the fourth quarter of 1955. The data were obtained from Securities and Exchange Commission, *Quarterly Financial Report for Manufacturing Corporations* (Washington, D.C.).

[12] Alternative weighting schemes may then be considered. A small firm (a member of a fringe group of firms in an industry where there is a dominant oligopoly) often has greater freedom with respect to price, product, and investment policy than has one of the largest. Within limits, it can act without fear of retaliation or matching by the dominant firm. Therefore, it will be more difficult for a dominant firm to increase its market share by one percentage point than for the fringe firm. If the large firm actually does increase its market share by one per cent, it should therefore be weighted more than a one percentage point increase by a small firm. This

Coefficients of
Correlation with
Instability Index

Independent
Variables

	Industry Growth Rate	*Share of Industry Assets in Sample*
Simple correlation coefficient	.499ᵃ	.759ᵇ
Partial correlation coefficient	.460	.745ᵇ
Multiple correlation coefficient = .816ᵇ		

ᵃ Significant at the 5 per cent probability level.
ᵇ Significant at the 1 per cent probability level.

The correlation coefficients indicate that the share of industry assets accounted for by the firms in our sample is an important variable affecting the value of the instability index. These results would suggest that the industry growth rate is not a significant determinant of the instability index. However, a plot of the instability index against the share of industry assets shows that the combined share does not affect the instability index in those industries where a large bulk of industry assets is already included. Hence, we selected those industries where 50 per cent or more of total industry assets are accounted for by firms in our sample and regressed the industry growth rate against the instability index. The simple correlation coefficient is .724 and is significant at the 5 per cent probability level. Therefore, there is some reason to believe that the industry growth rate is a significant variable which determines the stability of market shares.

A final caution: the data in this paper have been used only to illustrate an analysis and a method, not for their substantive importance. The apparent correlation between the industry growth rate and the instability index is to some extent spurious, sometimes seriously so. It is often wrong to consider S.I.C. two-digit groups as industries. The literature is practically barren of principles or procedures which can be used to define industries and to classify firms. Perhaps the variability in the growth rates among the three-digit industries within each two-digit industry is directly related to the two-digit industry growth rate. The greater the two-digit growth rate, the greater is the expected variability among the component three-digit industry growth rates. Then, in the fast growing two-digit groups, a high instability index may merely register a shifting of industries within the two-digit group and not the pure industry growth rate effect on market share stability.[14] This must be studied group by group; but given adequate data, the instability index should be a help in analyzing it.

---

[14] The obvious way to correct for this is to study market share stability of three-digit industries. Generally, this is very difficult to do because (a) the sample of firms in each three-digit industry thins out very rapidly; (b) the problem of an industry definition still exists (which three-digit industries should be combined?); and (c) the lack of reliable industry asset data. With the use of unpublished Census data several of these problems could be overcome.

24. The Relative Stability of Market Shares: A Theory and Evidence from Several Industries[1]

NEIL H. JACOBY

This paper presents a tentative theory of temporal variation in the percentages of the market occupied by the largest firms in relatively concentrated industries. Data on annual changes in the market shares of firms in a number of such industries in the United States are presented and interpreted in the light of this theory.

I. Relative Stability of Market Shares as an Index of Competition

At least three structural characteristics of an industry are commonly held by economists to possess some evidential values in judging the effectiveness of competition. They are the number of firms in the industry, the relative concentration of output among the largest firms, and the relative stability of the proportions of the industry's market occupied by its largest members.[2] A consistently small number of firms, a consistently high concentration of industry output, and temporal invariance in the market shares of individual firms do not *per se* constitute proof of monopolistic behavior.

Yet if an industry exhibited these characteristics, especially in combination, it would be thought that there was an increased probability of collusion by its dominant members, or of a mutual recognition of their interdependence, resulting in an oligopolistic coordination of pricing and production policies adverse to the interest of consumers. Conversely, the presence of a large and increasing number of firms in an industry, a diminishing concentration ratio, and a high degree of variance in the market shares of the largest firms would tend to be regarded as presumptive evidence that competition was effective.

The existence of monopoly or effective competition in an industry cannot, of course, be determined solely by the application of structural criteria. It must be gauged directly by analyzing such aspects of industry behavior as the relation of prices to costs, the rapidity of response of prices to changes in supply-demand conditions, the rate of technological progress, and the normality of returns to investment in the long run. The structural features of an industry merely create the conditions for and raise the probability of certain patterns of behavior; they do not *per se* determine behavior. Yet, in a world in which solid evidence of industrial behavior is often hard to come by and is frequently ambiguous in meaning, knowledge of the structural dynamics of an industry is valuable.

Much attention has been given to the problems of measuring and interpreting data on the relative concentration of output, employment, or sales of industries. As a result of theoretical and methodological studies,[3] as well as of empirical studies by

---

Reprinted by permission of Basil Blackwell Publisher from *The Journal of Industrial Economics*, 12:2 March 1964.

[1] The basic analysis in this paper was developed more than a decade ago in connection with economic studies of the U.S. meat packing industry undertaken by the author as consultant to a number of its members. The analysis was reviewed and revised in the light of more recent work on the subject. The author thanks his colleagues, Professors J. F. Weston, Alfred Nicols and F. E. Norton for valuable comments on earlier drafts.

[2] See, for example, G. J. Stigler's Introduction to *Business Concentration and Price Policy* (Princeton: Princeton University Press, 1955), pp. 6–7.

[3] See, for example, Gideon Rosenbluth, 'Measures of Concentration' in *Business Concentration and*

the U.S. Federal Trade Commission and other agencies, there is now a general understanding of the technical conditions which produce industrial concentration, and information about the norms of concentration to be found in manufacturing industries.

Economists have devoted comparatively little attention to the theory and the measurement of temporal changes in the market occupancy ratios of the largest firms in industries, although this is regarded as a highly significant parameter by businessmen and may be a useful gauge of the vigor of competition.[4] Gort noted that the usefulness of industry concentration ratios depends primarily upon their accuracy as gauges of control of the industry's market by the few largest firms; that high concentration ratios may be found along with a considerable instability of the market shares of individual firms (e.g. the U.S. automobile manufacturing industry); and hence it is more significant to study changes in the market shares of the largest firms directly.[5]

Price Policy, op. cit., pp. 57–94, and the references cited and summarized therein; J. M. Blair, 'Statistical Measures of Concentration', *Bulletin of the Oxford Institute of Statistics,* Vol. XVIII (November 1956) 351–72; M. A. Adelman, 'The Measurement of Industrial Concentration', *Review of Economics and Statistics,* Vol. XXXIII (November 1951); S. J. Prais, 'The Statistical Conditions for a Change in Concentration', *Rev. of Econ. and Stat.* (August 1958); Leonard W. Weiss, 'Factors in Changing Concentration', *Rev. of Econ. and Stat.,* Vol. XLV, No. 1 (February 1963), p. 70; J. S. Bain, *Industrial Organization* (New York: John Wiley & Sons, 1959), pp. 124–33, has suggested specific standards for classifying manufacturing industries with respect to degree of concentration into 'very high', 'high', 'moderately high', 'moderately low' and 'low'.

[4] Business managers and investors watch changes in the market shares of large firms with intense interest. Other things being equal, a gain in the firm's share of its industry market is commonly regarded as evidence of managerial superiority; loss of market position is interpreted as a sign of managerial weakness.

[5] Michael Gort, 'Analysis of Stability and Change in Market Shares', *Journal of Political Economy,* Vol. LXXI, No. 1 (February 1963), p. 51.

Hymer and Pashigian also observed that the really significant measure of change in the structure of an industry's market is the annual change in firms' relative shares of the industry's market.[6]

Despite its considerable significance for public policy as well as business management, a general theory of temporal change in market occupancy of large firms has not been developed. Nor have adequate statistical analyses been made of annual variations in the market shares of firms in a large number of industries to test a theory. Consequently, low variance of market shares has sometimes been taken *per se* as evidence of monopoly, and high variance as proof of competition. It will subsequently be shown that the degree of variation to be expected *under effective competition* will differ widely from industry to industry as a result of differences in products, technologies, rates of growth of demand, and other determinants. Clearly, it is desirable to ascertain what inferences may be drawn regarding the vigor of competition in an industry from observation of a given degree of variation in the market shares of its largest firms; and what are the conditions under which invariance or small variance betokens the presence of overt or tacit collusion to 'share' a market.

II. Variation in the Market Shares of Major Buyers of Livestock at U.S. Terminal Markets

Scholarly interest in the variation of the market shares of large firms in concentrated industries apparently was first aroused during the 1930s in connection with purchases of livestock by the largest U.S. meat-packing firms at terminal markets. W. H. Nicholls studied empirically the annual variation in occupancy of five terminal markets for livestock by large meat-packing companies during the period 1931–37, and he also examined weekly variations in their propor-

[6] S. Hymer and P. Pashigian, 'Turnover of Firms as a Measure of Market Behavior', *Rev. of Econ. and Stat.,* Vol. XLIV, No. 1 (February 1962), p. 85.

tions of hog purchases.[7] In general, he concluded that short-term changes in the relative market positions of the major packers at the markets studied were 'small', and were evidence of 'imperfect competition'; but that they did not necessarily show the presence of—although they would be consistent with—a 'market-sharing' convention between the major packers at these markets and oligopsonistic behavior by them.

The complaint of the *U.S. v. Armour and Company* et al., was filed by the Department of Justice in 1948.[8] It charged that the four largest meat-packing firms were dominant buyers of livestock at certain public markets for livestock during the period 1934–45, that the proportions of their purchases relative to each other had not varied greatly through time, and that livestock prices had been depressed as a result of a 'concert of action' (legal synonym for collusive oligopsony) practiced by the defendant firms. The primary evidence adduced in the complaint to support the charges were figures said to reflect 'small' annual variations in the market occupancies of the four packing firms at terminal livestock markets. Later, the complaint was dismissed without a trial of the charges.

Profound changes in the whole structure of U.S. livestock marketing and meat packing during the past two decades have made the particular issue raised by Nicholls and the Antitrust Division irrelevant to present conditions.[9] Nevertheless, the inter-

pretation of the degree of variation in the market shares of livestock purchased by the four largest packers remains of lively theoretical interest, and forms a useful point of departure for the development of a theory of variation in market shares. How large a degree of variation in annual or weekly market shares would one *expect* to have found in a workably competitive livestock market,[10] given the particular conditions of demand and cost and their rate of change through time that prevailed in those markets? It is as reasonable to ask why the buying shares of the large packers on terminal markets varied *at all* as to inquire why they did not vary more! We proceed to develop a general theory of variation in market shares, using the example of livestock purchases by large packers on U.S. terminal markets during the pre-World War II era to illustrate and give concreteness to the discussion.

III. A Theoretical Model of Constant Market Shares with Effective Price Competition

It is useful to consider, first of all, the hypothetical conditions under which the purchase shares of a firm on a livestock—or any other—market *would have been constant through time,* assuming effective price competition among buyers. To do this, we posit a set of admittedly unrealistic assumptions which jointly define a theoretical model of the market. By constructing such

---

[7] See his 'Market-sharing in the Packing Industry', *Journal of Farm Economics,* Vol. 22 (February 1940), pp. 225–40. The substance of this article was later embodied in *Imperfect Competition within Agricultural Industries* (Ames: Iowa State College Press, 1941).

[8] U.S. District Court for the Northern District of Illinois. Civil Action No. 48 C 1351 filed September 15th, 1948. The case was dismissed in 1954 'without prejudice', so that there was no trial and decision on the merits of the charges.

[9] Even before 1948, and at an accelerated pace thereafter, the development of all-weather rural roads, refrigerated-truck transportation, and other factors produced sweeping changes in the operations of national meat-packing companies and in the technology, practices and patterns

of livestock buying. Today, terminal livestock markets have lost most of their historic economic functions, and the bulk of livestock is purchased directly from farmers and processed in 'inland' packing plants. The meat-packing industry has also undergone progressive deconcentration, and its individual firms have developed an amazing diversification of product lines.

[10] 'Workable competition' is essentially that kind of competition described by J. M. Clark, in which the share of the market attained by any one firm is a result of an active process of rivalry in an imperfect market of change and uncertainty, from which there is lacking any collusion or agreement among the several firms.

a model and examining its operation, one can direct attention to the particular factors that produce variance or invariance in market shares. Each assumption may then be examined for the degree of its conformance to reality. Thus, an estimate may be derived of the degree of variation in market shares to be expected in a market where competition is effective.

We construct such a model, with particular reference to meat-packing firms purchasing livestock at a terminal market, by making the following nine assumptions:

(1) *Two buyers.* At a public market for livestock, whose receipts consist of nothing but hogs of a uniform weight and grade, there are only two buyers, each a meat-packing firm operating a plant at the market for slaughtering hogs and processing pork products.

(2) *Fixed costs ignored.* Direct costs of livestock and of processing are so preponderant a fraction of total costs that fixed costs are disregarded, and the cost function which is to be considered will pertain only to direct costs.

(3) *Identical cost functions.* The sizes of the plants operated by the two packers, and their technologies of processing and selling, are identical so that their cost curves, showing the functional relations between output and total costs, are identical.

(4) *Identical demand functions.*[11] The products of the two packers, for any given amount of input, are identical in quantity, numbers, and proportions, are undifferentiated from the standpoint of buyers, and buyers are similarly distributed geographically about the two plants, so that the demand curves confronting each of the two packers are identical.

(5) *Single location of supply.* The two packers do not purchase hogs at any other place than at the public market in question, so that there is a single source of supply of raw material.

(6) *No uncertainty about receipts.* The daily receipts of hogs at the market fluctuate, but each packer possesses complete information about the amount of future receipts, and there is no uncertainty about them.

(7) *No uncertainty about demand.* The demand for pork products fluctuates daily, but each packer possesses complete information about future changes in demand, so that there is no uncertainty about demand for pork products.

(8) *Complete rationality and equal skill of management.* The managements of each of the two firms are completely rational and equally skillful in adjusting their buying policies and their bids to the present and impending daily receipts of hogs and to changing demands for pork products.

(9) *Active price competition.* The two packers compete aggressively on a basis of price bids for hogs received at the market as well as in the market for pork products. Each packer ignores the effect of his own bids upon those of his rival, formulates and makes his bids independently, and stands ready to purchase as many hogs as possible at a price which he estimates will enable him to maximize his net receipts or minimize his losses.[12]

Under these assumptions, it is easily demonstrated that the market occupancy of each of the two packers will be 50 per cent; and that the degree of variation in market shares, whether calculated on a daily, weekly, monthly, or annual basis, will be zero. This will be true irrespective of the number of hogs received at the market, or the relation of those receipts to the combined processing capacity of the two packing plants. Constant market occupancy follows from the principle that each packer will maximize his net receipts (or minimize his deficit) by purchasing, processing and selling pork products of that volume at

---

[11] Strictly speaking, the concept of a demand function is ambiguous in a case of duopsony, and it might be preferable to refer to a reaction function. However, the conventional practice has been followed here.

[12] Essentially, what is involved is 'circular competition', which means that the independent competitive behavior of one firm is circumscribed by its rival's reactions. Thus, this model of duopsony differs from some other classical models, although it arrives at similar results.

which his marginal receipts equal his marginal costs. As it has been assumed that both the marginal cost and the marginal revenue curves confronting each packer are identical, each will operate at his optimum position by purchasing the *same* number of hogs as his rival. If either packer attempted to buy more hogs than his rival, whatever the volume of daily receipts, he could do so only by deliberately assuming a financial loss, a course of action that is debarred by the assumption of rationality.

IV. The Relation of the Model to Reality

We may now examine each of the nine assumptions in the model, first, to show its particular bearing upon variance in market occupancy, and secondly, to estimate the extent of its departure from reality.

(1) *Two buyers.* If all of the other eight assumptions were maintained, removal of the assumption that only two packers purchased at the public market clearly would not affect the result. So long as marginal cost and demand curves were identical, fixed costs were ignored, there was only one source of supply, uncertainty about future changes in demand and cost was absent, and buying policies were rational and equally skillful for *all* packers buying at a public market, under aggressive price competition the market shares of each would be invariant whether their number were two, ten, or one hundred. Of course, the entry of a new firm would immediately produce a *pro rata* reduction in the occupancy of existing firms at the time it began operation; conversely, an exit would produce a *pro rata* increase in shares; but no further variation would occur thereafter.

In actuality, numerous small buyers of livestock competed at each terminal market in addition to several of the four large meat-packing firms. These buyers comprised the agents of regional and local meat-packing firms, speculators who bought not for slaughter but for resale on that market or elsewhere, and stock feeders who purchased lean cattle for fattening and subsequent resale. Although small buyers sometimes entered or withdrew from the market, they were not important factors.

Entries and exits of firms (measured by turnover ratios) are an important cause of variation in the market shares of firms in concentrated industries. Entrants usually bring new capital and management and often more advanced technology to the industry, and capture customers from established firms. Conversely, the customers of firms leaving an industry are the object of a competitive scramble among surviving enterprises, leading to changes in their market positions. Hence, the rate of turnover of firms in an industry is ordinarily an important determinant of variation in market shares. However, this factor appears to have played a minor role in the U.S. meat-packing industry between the two world wars.

(2) *Fixed costs ignored.* The effect of ignoring fixed costs in the theoretical model is to simplify the process of decision-making by each packer by making it necessary to take into account only the direct (and, by assumption, identical) costs of production and selling. In actuality, livestock-buying decisions were based upon estimates of the sales values of products processed from a given animal (based upon so-called 'cut out tests') the out-of-pocket costs of processing it, plus a standard *pro rata* of all overhead costs including depreciation, taxes, interest, and return on equity investment. Bid prices were thus normally based on estimated total unit costs, including a 'target' rate of return on investment, and estimated product selling prices. In the short run, a packer might have ignored fixed costs, equated marginal revenue and marginal cost, and raised his market share of livestock purchased by out-bidding his competitor. In the long run, however, the amounts of his bids for livestock were limited by the requirement of covering total costs, or else suffering the penalty of depleting financial resources to the point where he could not replace fixed assets, maintain his organization, and stay in business. If the two packers in the model had different fixed costs

per unit, or had identical fixed costs but adopted buying policies which took them into account to different degrees, this would be a cause of departure of their market occupancy ratios from 50–50. Also, temporal changes in these factors would produce changes in livestock purchase shares. In actuality, there were some differences in bid pricing policies among packers, as well as changes in the policies of a given packer through time.[13] The meat-packing industry, however, was one in which the ratio of direct costs, within the normal range of operations, was exceptionally high.[14]

The *range* of managerial discretion in making short-term product pricing or raw material buying pricing decisions varies directly with the ratio of fixed to total costs at normal volumes of operation. This range is much greater in such heavy capital-using industries as steel or automobiles than it is in meat packing. With the relatively narrow range of alternatives open to them in their day-to-day determination of livestock purchase prices, it was to be expected that independent decisions by each large meat-packing firm would produce a much closer similarity in the average prices bid for livestock, and correspondingly less variation in their market shares. The same point may be expressed by the statement that differences in the possible horizons of planning by managements of meat-packing firms were less dispersed than they were among steel or automobile-manufacturing firms. To generalize: instability of market shares is likely to increase with the ratio of fixed to total unit costs of production that is characteristic in an industry, other things being equal. However, because a firm must cover

its full costs in the long run in order to survive, this factor will be associated with short-term rather than long-term variation in market shares.

(3) *Identical cost functions.* It is obvious that the cost curves of different meat-packing plants operated at a given livestock market would remain identical only by accident. Nevertheless, there is much evidence to suggest that they may have moved along rather similar lines, in view of the relative stability of the producing and distributing technology of the meat-packing industry during the 'twenties and 'thirties. If the marginal cost curve of one of the packers in the theoretical model fell below that of the other as a result, say, of introducing some mechanical processing innovation, this would result in an equation of that packer's marginal revenues and marginal costs at a higher volume of purchases than before. *Ceteris paribus,* the market occupancy of this packer would increase above 50 per cent, and that of the other packer would fall below 50 per cent. However, once a new equilibrium had been reached, until some new factor appeared to differentiate their respective marginal costs, relative market occupancies would remain constant. Only differences among firms in the timing of technological changes, and not differences in costs at a given point of time, would produce variation in market shares. The comparative stability of production technology in U.S. meat packing during the pre-World War II era tended to make year-to-year changes in market occupancy of the larger firms rather small in comparison with such technically dynamic industries as electronics, aircraft, or chemicals.

Apart from differences in the timing of technological advances that produced divergences in the unit costs of *given* outputs, the cost functions of the two packers in the model might have diverged as a result of different *rates of plant expansion.* Assuming the existence of economies of scale and that fixed costs were taken into account, a relative enlargement of plant by one packer would lead him to bid higher than his rival to obtain a larger share of the livestock

---

[13] The standard cost-accounting procedures promulgated by the American Meat Packing Institute probably tended to produce similarity among the policies of different packing firms in this regard.

[14] Armour and Company, for example, reported sales of $1848 millions in 1949, direct costs of livestock and of plant payrolls of $1740 millions, and all other items of cost of $108 millions. Variable costs thus formed 94 per cent of total costs (*Annual Report to Stockholders, 1949*).

offered on the market. Differential rates of plant expansion, either through *de novo* investment or through acquisition of competitors' plants, appear to have been an important cause of variation in the market shares of firms in industries whose markets have expanded rapidly.[15] In the slowly growing U.S. market for livestock between the two world wars this factor does not appear to have had much effect, because there was comparatively little scope for variance among firms in estimates of growth in demand and therefore in investment schedules. Mergers and acquisitions by the large packers were relatively unimportant.

(4) *Identical demand curves.* The effect of removing this assumption may be analyzed along parallel lines to those of removing the assumption of identical cost curves. If, through some innovation in product design, product quality, packaging, advertising or sales promotion, one packer in the model experienced a rise of the demand curve for his products, this would result in an equation of his marginal revenues with his marginal costs at a larger volume of livestock purchases than before. His market occupancy would rise above 50 per cent; that of his rival would fall below 50 per cent. Again, the salient question concerns the relative dynamism of the market and of technological changes in the distribution of meat products. Although the nature of packing-house products and the technology of their distribution underwent a gradual evolution during the pre-World War II era, there were comparatively few startling innovations of major importance to which one may attribute frequent changes in occupancy of livestock markets

by individual firms. Measured by total annual livestock slaughter, the meat industry's market grew very sluggishly between the two world wars—a factor which tended to inhibit wide variations in market shares. One may contrast the meat-packing industry in this respect with such relatively dynamic industries as automobiles, frozen foods, or aluminum.

Divergences between the demand functions for the products of different firms in an industry are much more likely to arise from deliberate product differentiation than from differences in managerial estimates of changes in the amount and elasticity of demand for a standardized product. 'Favorable' product differentiation by one firm (i.e. product differentiation which significantly raises the demand schedule for its products relative to its cost schedule) is indeed a prolific source of variation in the market shares of firms in those industries within which product differentiation is an important basis of competition. The U.S. automobile industry, for example, has been marked by radical year-to-year shifts in the market shares of General Motors, Ford, and Chrysler, as a result of divergent design, styling, and engineering of products (see Fig. 2). In contrast, product differentiation played a very minor role in the U.S. meat-packing industry between the two world wars. Fresh meats came very near to being 'standard' products, consumer preferences for which were not much influenced by branding and advertising. This is another reason for expecting comparative stability in the livestock buying shares of the major packing firms.

(5) *Single source of raw material.* The effect of this assumption is to simplify the process of decision-making by each of the packers in the model, by eliminating the possibility of acquiring hogs elsewhere than from one terminal market. If the fact be admitted that each packer could obtain hogs directly from farmers or local commission men, another cause of variance in occupancy of terminal markets is clearly identified. 'Direct buying' steadily became a more important source of livestock for

---

[15] The world oil industry outside of the United States and Canada after World War II is an excellent example. Demand for petroleum products rose at the exceptionally rapid compound rate of 11 per cent per annum, on the average, between 1948 and 1962. Differential rates of investment by oil companies, resulting from divergent estimates of future growth of the market, produced substantial annual changes in market shares. See *Postwar Changes in the Foreign Oil Industry: A Study in Industrial Dynamics*, a forthcoming study by the author.

the national meat-packing firms after World War I. Whereas in 1930 the four largest firms bought only 28 per cent of their total purchases of all species of livestock directly, in 1948 they purchased 47 per cent directly, and in 1962 the preponderance of all live-stock was so purchased. This trend resulted from the efforts of the national packers to maintain their raw material sources in the face of rising competition from the so-called 'interior' (regional and local) pack-ers, coupled with vast improvements in roads and in refrigerated-truck transporta-tion. Direct buying from a variety of sources obviously increased the variation in occu-pancy of public markets by the large pack-ing firm because of changing differences in f.o.b. prices of livestock, changing trans-portation costs to packing plants, and changing proportions of total livestock ac-quisitions made at the terminal market. Thus, the secular phenomenon of increasing direct buying operated to increase the vari-ability in each firm's occupancy of public livestock markets.

The general point is that the total live-stock-buying market was segmented into sub-markets of different types and locations. Similarly, the total product sales market of an industry is usually the sum of a series of sub-markets, each of which pertains to a particular product-line, type-of-buyer, or geographical area. For obvious reasons the temporal instability of the market shares of the firm in each sub-market of its industry is likely to be greater than in the total mar-ket. One may assert the general rule that stability of market shares will rise with the degree of comprehensiveness of the market with respect to which the firm's position is measured.

(6) and (7) *Uncertainty.* Uncertainties regarding both future receipts of hogs at the market and future demand for pork products may be considered together for analytical purposes. The effect of ruling out uncertainties in the model is enormously to simplify for the two packers the task of deciding how many hogs to buy and how much to pay for them. If each packer had complete knowledge and used it rationally

with a skill equal to that shown by his competitor, the daily purchases that would be most profitable to each would be easily determined. Lacking such knowledge, there was a wide range of different possible es-timates of the situation, and two packers who brought independent judgments to bear upon the relevant factors would almost never arrive at *identical* buying quantities and average bid prices.

The value to the packer of hogs received at a terminal market on a particular day depended upon his estimate of the value of the products which could be produced from each hog. This, in turn, depended mainly upon what retail meat dealers would pay for pork products.[16]

Such prices depended upon the current demand of consumers and probable changes therein—a function of weather, consumer disposable income, prices of beef, lamb, veal and other substitutes for pork, and the amount of pork and other meats currently in the inventories of packers, wholesalers and retailers. In determining the quantity he should purchase and the average price he should pay per 100 lb. of hogs, each packer therefore had to make estimates of the preceding factors.

If one maintains all of the assumptions in the model except (6) and (7), and acknowledges that in reality each of the two packers was *uncertain* with regard to the values of these variables, it would be highly improbable that both packers would arrive at identical decisions regarding the average price they should pay for hogs. A difference in their estimates of any one of the numer-ous determinants would result in different average bids, and a difference in the num-bers and proportions of hogs purchased. Two conclusions become apparent: first, that *short-term* (day-to-day or week-to-week) variations in market occupancy would almost certainly result from uncer-tainty; secondly, that such variations would be compensatory in character. Errors in

---

[16] We ignore for the time being the value of hides, bristles, glands and other by-products of the slaughtered animal.

decisions of one day or week would probably be corrected by decisions producing opposite effects on the firm's market share during the following day or week. The principle of convergence of short-term market occupancy upon the longer term mean occupancy would apply.[17]

(8) *Equal rationality and skill of management.* The assumption in the model that both packers act with complete rationality and exercise equal skill in discovering and interpreting market information obviously has the effect of eliminating a potential cause of variation in market occupancy. However, it is unrealistic. Even though each packer possessed complete knowledge of future changes in demand and cost conditions, he would not at all times draw the correct deductions from that knowledge, or act upon it with necessary celerity. Large packing firms had hundreds of livestock buyers purchasing livestock at dozens of different locations daily. Their central offices functioned essentially as national centers of market intelligence. There was wide scope for errors or deficiencies in the market information emanating from these central offices, for delay and confusion in the communication of this information within the firm, and for variation in the ability of managers at each echelon to interpret such information. Changing differences among firms in managerial skill would produce long-term changes in market shares, because they would be reflected in relatively rising purchases and sales and higher profitability for firms with the higher levels of skill. However, the extent to which such differences in skill can persist in a stable fashion would be limited by the fact that consistently inferior management below some level would have to be replaced in the long run, if a firm were to survive. Superimposed upon any enduring differences in managerial skill are those short-term fluctuations in performance that are inevitable in any large business organization. Like variations in market shares traceable to uncertainties, these would be causes of short-term and compensatory shifts in market shares.

V. A Tentative Theory of Variation in Market Shares

The preceding analysis has brought into view the principal determinants of temporal variations in the firm's position in the market of its industry. It has shown that short-term (i.e. daily, weekly or monthly) changes are governed by a different set of factors than are long-term (i.e. annual or longer) changes.

(a) *Short-term Variation.* We posit tentatively that the degree of short-term variation in the shares of large firms in the markets of their respective industries can be written as an increasing function of the following variables:[18]

I. *Degree of short-term instability in demand* and in uncertainty about future changes therein (a function of nature of products, influence of weather, consumer buying habits, etc.).

II. *Degree of short-term instability in costs* and in uncertainty about future

---

[17] For simplicity, let us assume that the estimates by the two packers of all factors were identical, excepting those of future receipts at the market. Packer A estimated average receipts for the next three days at X, whereas packer B estimated them at *less* than X. Packer B therefore bid higher prices on the average, and acquired more hogs than packer A. The next day actual receipts proved to be *greater* than X, and additional market information resulted in an estimate that receipts for the balance of the week would be greater than originally anticipated. B's original estimate having erred by a larger margin than A's and his inventory of pork products having increased more by virtue of his larger purchases of the previous day, he would be likely to revise his bid for the current day downward *below* that of A. On the next day, A would be prepared to bid higher and would obtain a larger percentage of the hogs offered in the market. The market occupancy ratios of each of the two packers would change in opposite directions between the two days.

[18] The hypothesis could be formulated algebraically. In the present imperfect state of knowledge it is believed that nothing would be gained over a verbal formulation.

changes therein (a function of instability in raw material flows, instability of labor supply, etc.).

III. *Ratio of fixed to total unit costs* that is characteristic of the industry (a function mainly of capital intensiveness).

IV. *Ratio of value of stocks to value of annual output* that is characteristic of the industry (a function mainly of seasonality in demand and in production).

V. *Costs of holding stocks per month per dollar* (a function of perishability of product, temperature of storage, etc.).

All of the preceding factors combine to produce short-term variations among firms in the managerial decisions which affect the firm's rate of output or sale, and therefore its market share. Over a period of a year or more most of these short-term divergences in management decisions are likely to offset each other in their influence upon long-term variance in market shares. In comparison with the 'average' manufacturing industry, the U.S. meat-packing industry between the two world wars appears to have been characterized by relatively high values of all of the variables except III. Hence there would be expected an appreciable degree of short-term instability in the large firm's shares of both livestock-buying markets and meat-selling markets.

(*b*) *Long-term Variation.* Long-term variation in the market shares of large firms in concentrated industries is tentatively regarded as an increasing function of the following variables:

I. *Rate of turnover of firms* in the industry (ratio of entries plus exits per annum to total industry population, weighted by total assets involved).

II. *Dispersion of rates of investment among firms* (differences among firms in the ratios of annual capital expenditures to total assets, assumed to be positively correlated with rate of growth in the market of the industry).

III. *Rate of merger of firms* (ratio of total assets annually involved in mergers within the industry to total assets employed by the industry).

IV. *Dispersion of rates of innovation among firms* (assumed to be positively correlated with the industry's rate of technological change).

V. *Weighting of product differentiation as a competitive factor* (ratio of product design, styling, special tooling, advertising and selling costs per unit of product to total unit costs that is characteristic in the industry).

Long-term variations in market shares are obviously of more significance to anti-monopoly policy and business management than are short-term variations, because they are determined by forces that are more controllable. The technical and environmental conditions of an effectively competitive industry may produce *either* high variation of both types, low variation of both types, or high variation in one time-period and low variation in the other. Given the values of the determinants, the theory would enable one to predict the expected degrees of short-term and long-term stability in the market shares of large firms in any given industry.

In the case of the U.S. meat-packing industry before World War II, *a priori* considerations strongly suggest that the buying shares of large firms on terminal markets for livestock should have been relatively unstable in the short term and relatively stable in the long term under effective competition. Statistical analysis showed that this was, indeed, the case. The logical inference was that the behavior of the industry was consistent with effective competition. Had invariance or very small variance of market shares been found in the short term, an inference of non-competitive behavior would have been justified.

It is not possible to test the theory rigorously, because of insufficient knowledge of the values of the determinants in different industries. Only a beginning has been made in ascertaining for different industries the approximate rates of turnover of firms, distribution of firm investment and innovation rates, merger rates, and the relative roles of product differentiation.[19] A general knowledge of industrial technology and business practice may enable one, however, to judge the expected variation in the market shares of firms in different industries in terms of 'more' and 'less'. For example, one may predict upon a basis of general knowledge that the degree of the instability of the annual market shares of the largest firms in the automobile, aerospace, or television industries is greater than it is in, say, the flour-milling, cement, or metal-can industries. All of these industries are relatively concentrated; but they have had quite different rates of market growth and change in technology.

VI. Measuring Variation in Annual Market Shares

A concept and methodology is needed for measuring the mobility of enterprises within their industry which will readily permit of inter-industry comparisons as well as of inter-temporal comparisons within the same industry. The few empirical studies that have so far been made of this subject have employed a variety of data and statistical methods which render their results difficult to compare and interpret. One method has been to observe changes in the ranking of firms within an industry according to their size at each of two dates, and to calculate the relative frequency of changes in ranking.[20] However, such rank-shift analysis is of limited value, because trifling changes in the market positions of firms can produce shifts in rank; and very large changes in annual shares of the market may not produce any shift in rank if the firms were of widely disparate sizes at the beginning.

An *annual* measure of change in market shares is manifestly the best gauge of enterprise mobility, because it provides a 'snapshot' of industry structure at intervals sufficiently frequent to capture the essential facts of industrial dynamics without blurring the picture with short-term, transitory factors. However, reliable annual data on market shares are not readily available. Most studies have therefore compared market shares during years separated by long periods of time. Thus Gort correlated the market shares in 1947 and in 1954 of the largest firms in 205 U.S. manufacturing industries to find the degree to which shares in the latter year were dependent upon those in the earlier year. He found apparently high correlations.[21] He also found that stability in the firm's share of the industry market was strongly related to the concentration ratio for the four largest pro-

---

[19] Edwin Mansfield made a significant beginning at econometric study of this subject in his 'Entry, Gibrat's Law, Innovation, and the Growth of Firms', *American Economic Review*, Vol. III (December 1962), p. 1023. He found that the entry rate would increase by at least 60 per cent if an industry's profitability doubled, and would decrease by at least 7 per cent if its capital requirements doubled; that there were large deviations from the law of proportionate growth; that successful innovators grew about twice as rapidly as other comparable firms; and that the amount of mobility in an industry depended significantly upon its age and market structure. See also N. R. Collins and L. E. Preston, 'The Size Structure of the Largest Industrial Firms, 1909–1958', *American Economic Review*, Vol. LI, No. 5 (December 1961), for a good analysis of entry rates, exit rates, and mobility of the 100 largest U.S. industrial firms over a half-century. The authors found a decline in frequency of change in the identities and relative size positions of the giant firms, and a slight tendency for them to become more equal in size. However, they measured mobility by rank shifts rather than changes in market shares.

[20] For example, Joskow arrayed the 150 largest U.S. shoe-manufacturing firms in order of size (measured in annual sales) in 1950 and in 1954, and calculated the rank correlation coefficient between the two series. Jules Joskow, 'Structural Indicia: Rank-Shift Analysis as a Supplement to Concentration Ratios', *Rev. of Econ. and Stat.*, Vol. XLII (February 1960), pp. 113–16.

[21] Op. cit., p. 53. The coefficients for 152 of the industries were 0.85 or higher, for 111 industries 0.9 or higher, and for 74 industries at least 0.95.

ducers in each industry.[22] Gort attributed relative variation in market shares mainly to rates of growth in industry demand and rates of change in technology. However, his comparison of market shares in two years separated by a seven-year span removed from view the industrial dynamics of the intervening years.

Hymer and Pashigian measured changes between 1946 and 1955 in the market shares of the largest firms in eighteen major U.S. industries, using both the rank correlation coefficient and their own Instability Index.[23] The authors found that, while rank correlation coefficients were fairly high, suggesting considerable stability in market shares, there was little relation between them and the values of their Instability Index. They also found little relation between the Instability Index and the concentration ratio, but a strong positive relation between this index and the rate of growth of the industry—as one would expect on theoretical grounds. Again, their ten-year span of measurement left in darkness shifts in market positions of firms *within* the decade.

The present author studied changes in the *annual* purchase shares of the four largest U.S. meat-packing firms in terminal livestock markets during the nineteen-year period 1930–48 and compared them with changes in the annual shares of: (*a*) sales of new passenger automobiles by the three leading automobile manufacturers, (*b*) outputs of cigarettes by the four largest tobacco-manufacturing firms, (*c*) steel ingots produced by the six leading firms, and

(*d*) motor fuel sold in the Pacific states by the seven leading firms.

The particular industries were selected primarily because of the availability of data. For each large firm there was computed its mean market occupancy over the nineteen-year period, the standard deviation of its annual market shares from the mean, and the coefficient of variation in its market share (i.e. the standard deviation expressed as a percentage of the mean). In all industries market shares were measured in terms of annual physical output of the principal product group rather than in dollar sales or assets, which would have introduced extraneous factors into the determination of market shares.[24] The results appear in Table I, and Figs. 1–5 illustrating individual firms' market occupancies in the five industries covered.

The analysis indicates the magnitude of the *annual* change to be expected in the market share of the large firm in a relatively concentrated industry, although it would have to be applied to a much broader spectrum of industries over a longer period of time before a firm conclusion could be drawn. Apparently, coefficients of annual variation of market shares within a range of 7–15 per cent defined the range of expectation. The exceptional coefficients are subject to special explanation. Coefficients of higher value than this range were found only in three cases: in the automobile industry, where the battle between Ford and Chrysler during the 'thirties and 'forties produced coefficients of 23 per cent; in the cigarette industry, where the spectacular rise in the market share of Philip Morris (largely at the expense of other small firms rather than its larger competitors) produced a 49 per cent variation; and in the Pacific states' gasoline market, where the shares of General Petroleum and Texaco were also rather unstable, producing coefficients of 20 per cent and 18 per cent respectively.

What was the 'normal' change to be ex-

---

[22] The high annual variability of market shares of firms in the highly concentrated automobile-manufacturing industry does not conform to this generalization.

[23] Cf. Hymer and Pashigian, op. cit., pp. 82–7. This index was constructed simply by computing the number of percentage points of change in each firm's share of the industry market between the two years under comparison and summing the absolute values of these changes. Thus, the more unstable market shares, the higher the index.

---

[24] In the case of the meat-packing industry, the variable measured was input of the principal raw material—livestock.

Table I • **Mean Market Occupancy, Standard Deviation of Annual Market Shares from Mean, and Coefficient of Variation, for the Largest Firms in Five U.S. Manufacturing Industries, 1930–48**

Industry and Firm	Mean Market Occupancy (% of Industry)	Standard Deviation of Annual Shares	Coefficient of Variation (%)
Livestock slaughter			
Swift	20.0	1.86	9.3
Armour	16.4	1.32	8.0
Cudahy	5.8	0.49	8.4
Wilson	5.2	0.52	10.0
Total—four firms	47.4	3.79	8.0
Total—other firms	52.6	3.79	7.2
Passenger cars registered [1]			
General Motors	41.9	3.37	8.0
Ford	23.9	5.55	23.2
Chrysler	21.7	5.00	23.0
Total—three firms	87.5	3.49	4.0
Total—other firms	12.5	3.49	27.9
Cigarettes produced [2]			
American Tobacco	26.8	1.91	7.1
R. J. Reynolds	25.5	3.06	12.0
Liggett & Myers	21.2	1.62	7.6
Philip Morris	6.3	3.08	48.9
Total—four firms	79.9	5.42	6.8
Total—other firms	20.1	5.42	27.0
Tons of steel ingots produced			
U.S. Steel	34.8	2.39	6.9
Bethlehem Steel	13.9	1.45	10.4
Republic Steel	8.6	1.15	13.4
Jones and Laughlin	5.1	0.38	7.5
Youngstown	4.4	0.42	9.5
Inland	4.0	0.32	8.0
Total—six firms	70.9	2.64	3.7
Total—other firms	29.1	2.64	9.1
Motor fuel sold in the Pacific states			
Standard Oil	21.1	1.76	8.3
Shell Oil	13.4	1.29	9.6
Union Oil	10.5	0.75	7.1
General Petroleum	8.6	1.71	19.9
Richfield Oil	8.1	1.01	12.5
Tidewater Oil	8.1	0.68	8.4
Texaco	6.7	1.22	18.2
Total—seven firms	76.6	2.58	3.4
Total—other firms	23.4	2.58	11.0

Sources: U.S. Department of Agriculture, Standard and Poors, U.S. Iron and Steel Institute, *Petroleum World, Automotive Industries.*
[1] Omits years 1942–46, when no passenger cars were produced.
[2] Omits years 1930–33, for which data were unavailable.

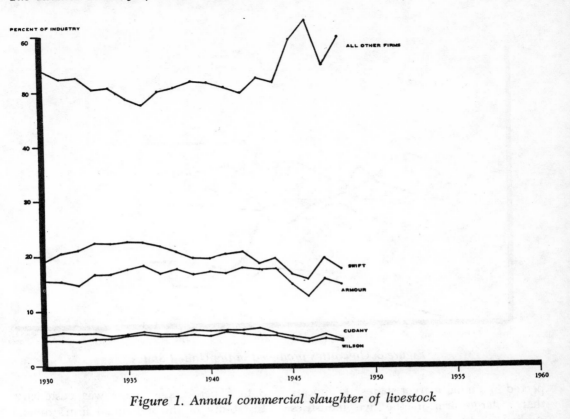

Figure 1. Annual commercial slaughter of livestock

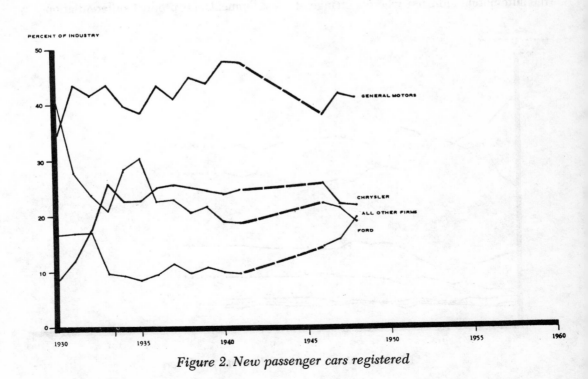

Figure 2. New passenger cars registered

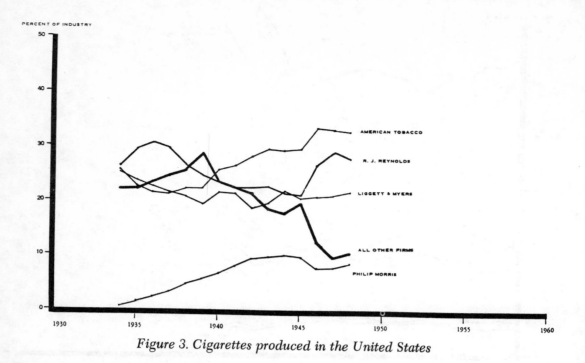

Figure 3. Cigarettes produced in the United States

pected in annual market shares? It appears that a large firm in the five industries studied could expect to have an annual change of 1 to 3 percentage points in its share of the industry market, excepting in the automobile industry, where a change of

3 to 6 percentage points was customary. Instability of the individual firm's annual market share was markedly higher in the U.S. automobile industry because of the dominant role played by technological development and product differentiation.

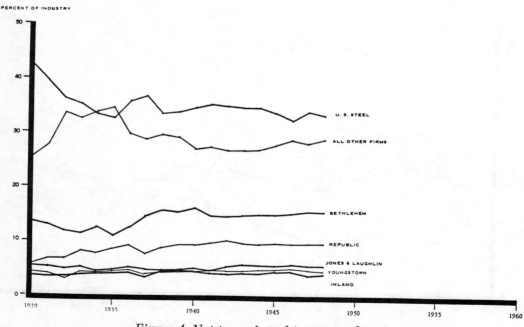

Figure 4. Net tons of steel ingots produced

PERCENT OF INDUSTRY

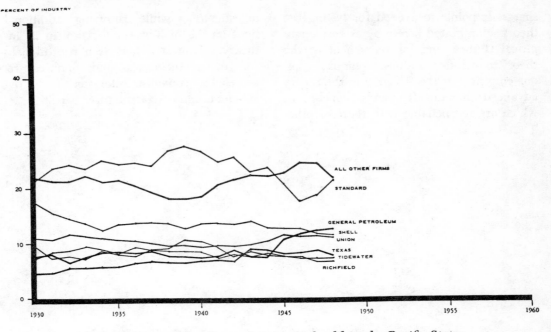

Figure 5. Tax-paid gallons of motor fuel sold in the Pacific States

The following figures show the secular growth of the markets of the five industries over the nineteen-year period:

	1930	1948	Change Amount	Percent
Commercial livestock slaughter (millions)	93.0	107.4	14.4	16
Passenger cars registered (thousands)	2626	3461	835	32
Cigarettes produced (billions)	125.6	387.0	261.4	208
Ingots of steel produced (millions of tons)	44.6	88.6	44.0	98
Motor fuel sold in Pacific states (millions of gallons)	1886	4527	2661	143

Evidently, the cigarette and Pacific motor fuel markets grew most rapidly, which probably accounted for the high annual variability in market shares of some members of these industries. The steel ingot output grew at a medium rate; and the industry had relatively small changes in annual market shares, except for Bethlehem and Youngstown. Annual market shares were generally more stable in livestock purchases than the other industries, presumably because of slow growth of the market, the relative inertia of technology, and lack of product differentiation; but they were not markedly stable. Indeed, the coefficient of variation in the annual market shares of Swift, the largest firm in the meat-packing industry, was *higher* than it was for the leading firm in any of the four other industries. Certainly, the evidence does not support a view that annual purchase shares in terminal livestock markets were so stable as to suggest a market-sharing agreement among the leading firms.

Table I reveals that each industry included some firms with relatively stable market shares, and others with relatively unstable market shares. This suggests that additional characteristics of the individual firm, such as relative profitability, may play a role in a theory of variation in market shares. It points to a need for testing the theory adumbrated herein by extensive empirical studies, and for refinement of the theory to include variables. So far as it goes, our empirical analysis bears out the theory advanced herein. It yields conclusions which are reconcilable with those of other investigators, while throwing additional light on the mobility of the firm in its industry. Manifestly, here is a fruitful field for further theoretical and empirical research by economists interested in the dynamics of industrial structure.

Part II–E · *Causes of Concentration*

At the turn of the century, horizontal mergers produced a large number of concentrated industries. Where those consolidations were efficient, they maintained their positions as leading firms although usually unable to keep as large a share of their markets as they obtained initially. Even before American Tobacco and Standard Oil were broken up under Sherman Act decrees, entry had eroded their preeminence. American Tobacco slipped from 93 percent of the cigarette market in 1899 to 76 percent in 1903. Standard Oil dropped from 88 percent of petroleum product production in 1899 to 67 percent in 1909. Similar fates were suffered by American Can, American Chicle, American Sugar Refining, United States Steel, etc.

Of the large number of amalgamations merging a majority of the capacity in their industries examined by Professor Shaw Livermore, 40.4 percent failed and 6.4 percent went through voluntary financial re-

organization.[1] The margin available to dominant firms was not sufficient to keep them alive if they were inefficient. Even when they were efficient, any attempt to obtain higher than competitive margins invited entry eroding their dominance rapidly. Where economies of scale beyond their current size were small or non-existent, their share of market fell as the market grew.

In selection 25, accounting rates of return in dominant firms and the balance of the industry are compared for a few industries. Where dominant firms earned more than others in their industries, evidently as a consequence of greater efficiency (perhaps from economies of scale, superior management, or sheer luck in selecting locations or technologies or in the timing of acquisi-

---

[1] Shaw Livermore, "The Success of Industrial Mergers," 50 *Quarterly Journal of Economics* 75 (1935–36).

tion of assets), they grew faster than their industries and their industries became more concentrated. This happened whether the initial position of their industries was or was not concentrated. Where leading firms earned less than other firms, evidently they were less efficient than other firms. They grew more slowly than their industries and concentration declined. "Concentrated industries are concentrated because that, apparently, is the efficient way to organize those industries."

Professor Harold Demsetz, in selection 26, examines rates of return in large and small firms in industries classified by the level of concentration. By finding the relationship among rates of return by size and how the relationship behaves with changing concentration, he provides a test of whether concentrated industries behave oligopolistically (collusively) and whether concentration is a consequence of greater efficiency in large firms. "A successful collusion is very likely to benefit the smaller firms, and this suggests that there should be a positive correlation between the rate of return earned by small firms and the degree to which the industry is concentrated [if high concentration is synonomous with oligopoly]. By the same token, if efficiency is associated with concentration, there should be a positive correlation between concentration and the difference between the rate of return earned by large firms and that earned by small firms."

Using IRS data, Professor Demsetz concludes that the data "fail to reveal the beneficial effects to small firms that we would expect from an association of collusion and industry concentration. The rate of return earned by firms in the smallest asset size does not increase with concentration. This seems to be true for the next two larger asset size classifications also. . . . The data do not seem to support the notion that concentration and collusion are closely related and, therefore, it is difficult to remain optimistic about the beneficial . . . effects of a deconcentration or anti-merger public policy. . . . [The data indicate that the largest] size firms in indus-

tries with concentration ratios greater than 50 percent produce at lower average cost." [2]

Selection 26, written by General Motors' staff in reply to a Congressional request, is a story of industrial heroism. In the face of railroad preference for steam power and nearly unanimous opinion in both the railroad and locomotive industries that the diesel was suitable only for special applications where pollution free or only slow speed, intermittent power was required, General Motors, under the leadership of Charles Kettering in its development effort, proved that diesel power could replace steam and generate enormous economies in rail operations. Essentially, General Motors became the leading company in the locomotive industry, displacing three previously dominant firms, by being first in the development of practicable diesel passenger and freight locomotives. It maintained its position in the face of challengers by constant improvement of its locomotives and by the use of a design and service philosophy that minimized maintenance inventories and maximized the opportunities for upgrading of locomotives in the process of normal maintenance and repair.

General Motors' continued leadership in locomotives may also have been a consequence of its greater experience and "learning." Selection 28 points out that a larger market share "leads to lower relative cost . . . because of the experience effect." The literature on what has become known as learning or progress curves is only infrequently employed in most industrial organization texts and courses. Yet, if we are to understand why many preeminent firms remain so, and are more profitable without

---

[2] W. G. Shepherd, "Elements of Market-Structure," 54 *Review of Economics and Statistics* 25 (1972), also finds a relationship between firm market shares, concentration, and rate of return which confirms Demsetz's conclusions. The influence of the market share of the leading firm on its rate of return is significantly positive while the influence of concentration is not. Since other members of the industry do not have high profits even when the leading firm in a concentrated industry does, it is lower costs

charging high prices, we must recognize the dynamics of the influence of experience on cost. If costs are inversely related to the serial number of the firm's product, and many studies indicate this to be the case,[3] then the firm with a history of the largest output will tend to be the lowest cost producer. This does not mean that there are indefinite economies of scale but rather, as Professor Demsetz indicates in selection 25, that the firm with the greatest experience will tend to have a lower, although positively sloped, marginal cost curve than other firms in its industry.

In the last selection in this section, increasing concentration in some industries is seen as a consequence of decline or very slow growth in output. Professor Stigler found, in his examination of *Capital and Rate of Return in Manufacturing Industries,* that in industries in which assets grew more slowly than 4 percent per year the number of firms tended to decline while in those with 7 per cent or more annual growth the number of firms tended to increase. Professors Ira and Ann Horowitz, examining brewing in the first decade and one half following World War II during which beer consumption increased by less than one per cent per year, present a detailed examination of an industry characterized simultaneously by stagnation and flux. As a consequence of the stagnation and a minimum efficient size larger than that of many firms, the number of firms in the industry declined. As a consequence of economies of scale, larger firms tended to grow and the industry to become more concentrated. These trends were the consequences of competition and could be expected to continue (as they have). Only a lack of com-

petitive behavior could have preserved the larger number of firms and lower concentration prevalent earlier.[4]

Studies dealing with the effects of government regulation on concentration are omitted from this section. Part VIII in Volume II will include some of the studies. Even there, space limitations force the omission of studies such as that by Professor David E. Kaun who finds that statutorily determined minimum wage rates have decreased the number of firms in several industries.[5] Also omitted is a study by Professor Lester Telser[6] which implies that some industries, where there is a high return to large investments per man in human capital, tend to become concentrated because only in this way can a return from the investment be obtained by those furnishing the required capital and undertaking the training programs. Weiss argues, in selection 17, that high concentration in these circumstances is socially useful. In addition to these omissions, nothing has been included on the effects of advertising on concentration. The advertising issue is dealt with in the selections included in Parts V and VI in Volume II. Some of the studies of the advertising-concentration relation-

---

[4] In selection 38, Part IV, Professor Kenneth Elzinga finds that the 1911 antitrust decree breaking up DuPont and ending attempts by the Gunpowder Trade Association to prevent competition was followed by a rapid decline in the number of powder firms and growth in concentration. When the government's complaint was brought in 1907, "There were approximately 53 independent explosive manufacturers . . ." The number declined to 27 in 1913 and "only nineteen in 1921." Elzinga also finds "that there were *more* new entrants during the trust's activities than after the relief decree . . ." (author's emphasis).

[5] "Minimum Wages, Factor Substitution and the Marginal Producer," 79 *Quarterly Journal of Economics* 478 (1965).

[6] *Some Determinants of the Return to Manufacturing Industries* (1969). Report No. 6935. Center for Mathematics in Business and Economics, University of Chicago.

---

that explain high profits in leading firms, not collusion.

[3] For example, A. Alchian "Reliability of Progress Curves in Airframe Production," 31 *Econometrica* 679 (1963); H. Asher, *Cost-Quantity Relationship in the Airframe Industry* (1956); and W. Z. Hirsch, "Firm Progress Ratios," 24 *Econometrica* 136 (1956).

ship are summarized by Weiss in selection 17.

Another omitted cause of concentration in this section is economies of scale. Space limitations precluded the inclusion of articles such as those by John Haldi and Professor David Whitcomb[7] and by Professor John McGee.[8]

[7] "Economies of Scale in Industrial Plant," 75 *Journal of Political Economy* 373 (1967).

[8] "Economies of Size in Auto Body Manufacture," *Journal of Law and Economics*, forthcoming.

25. Concentration and Structural and Market Disequilibria

YALE BROZEN

Professor Wenders[1] and I are both troubled by the positive relationship found between profitability and concentration. Studies by Professors Bain, Mann, and Stigler for four digit industries indicate this to be the case. We have sought explanations for this finding since there is no theory accounting for the phenomenon.[2] It has been assumed that collusion is less expensive in concentrated industries, but no theory predicts that there will be no entry into a profitable industry simply because it is concentrated and engaged in collusion. With open entry, collusion cannot enhance profitability.

It has been suggested that substantial barriers to entry account for the high profitability of concentrated industries, but there is no reason to presume that the height of barriers to entry is correlated with concentration. Examining the effective barriers to entry, such as those erected by governments, casual observation suggests that these barriers are negatively correlated with concentration. Agricultural restrictions, limitations on the capacity allowed to operate in the taxicab industry and on the mode of operation of taxicabs, prohibition of advertising of optometry products, restrictive licensing of pharmacists and prescription drug shops, difficulties in obtaining the certificates of public convenience and necessity required to enter interstate trucking, onerous requirements for bank charters, occupational licensure of barbers, plumbers, electricians, public accountants, lawyers, doctors, et cetera, are all associated with industries with low concentration.

All the studies of concentration and profitability have concentrated on manufacturing industries. They have neglected those industries with the most obvious and effective barriers to entry. Until these industries are studied, we cannot be sure what the actual consequences of effective barriers to entry are.

Concentration and Market Disequilibrium

In the meanwhile, both Professor Wenders and I have made some attempts to understand the Bain-Mann-Stigler findings. If the profitability of concentrated industries is a consequence of disequilibrium, why was a greater proportion of the concentrated than of less concentrated industries earning above equilibrium rates of return in 1936–40 in the Bain sample of industries, in 1950–60 in the Mann sample, and in 1953–57 in the Stigler sample? That the profitability of the concentrated industries was a disequilibrium phenomenon rather than a result of collusion and barriers to entry is demonstrated by the movement of the rates of return in the above average profit industries toward the average rate of return.[3] The question becomes, then, one of finding why disequilibrium more frequently produced above average returns in concentrated industries.

Both Professor Wenders and I have done unnecessary work. We both believed that there was a relationship between con-

Reprinted from the Summer 1971 issue of *The Antitrust Bulletin*, © 1971 by Federal Legal Publications, Inc. 95 Morton Street, New York, N.Y.

[1] John T. Wenders, "Profits and Antitrust Policy: The Question of Disequilibrium," 16 *The Antitrust Bulletin*, Summer 1971.

[2] Harold Demsetz, "Why Regulate Utilities," 11 *The Journal of Law and Economics* 55, April 1968.

[3] Yale Brozen, "The Antitrust Task Force Deconcentration Recommendation," 13 *Journal of Law and Economics* 279–292, October 1970.

centration and profitability that needed analysis. The phenomenon turns out to be non-existent. There is no relationship between profitability and concentration.

The forty-two industry sample used by Bain in analyzing 1936–40 data is non-representative. A larger sample of four digit industries selected by the Federal Trade Commission shows no relationship between profitability and concentration in either 1939 or 1940. Using Bain's dividing line to separate more and less concentrated industries—an eight firm concentration ratio of 70 per cent—twenty-two concentrated industries earned an average accounting rate of return of 9.58% and fifty-six unconcentrated industries earned 9.52% in 1939. In 1940, concentrated industries earned 11.76 per cent and unconcentrated industries earned 11.81 per cent.[4]

In the 1950–60 period covered by the Mann data, James Ellert,[5] using a 156 industry sample from the Standard & Poor compustat tapes, does not find the relationship found by Mann in his thirty industry sample. The thirty industry sample also is non-representative.

For 1951–55, Ellert found that the more than 70 per cent concentrated (eight firm) industries earned 12.25 per cent and that the unconcentrated industries earned 11.83 per cent. The difference is not significant. For 1956–60, the relationship reverses. The concentrated industries earned 11.52 per cent and the unconcentrated industries earned 11.74 per cent.

Ellert also examined the correlation between profitability and concentration for his entire sample and for portions of his sample stratified by concentration ratio. The correlations are all insignificantly different from zero or negative.

Professor Wenders examines the relationship between growth and profitability in the course of trying to find whether the

more profitable concentrated industries in the non-representative samples provided by Mann are more profitable because of higher growth rates. He finds "that concentrated industries (four-firm concentration ratio greater than 70%) grew at an average rate of 14.0% per year while unconcentrated industries grew at an average rate of 11.1% per year." Because of a correlation between growth and concentration, Wenders concludes that "disequilibrium, as measured by the rate of industry growth, could be responsible for part of the observed correlation between profits and concentration." But then he observes that, "The trouble with this explanation of why profits might be related to concentration is that there is no good *theoretical* reason why concentration and growth should be related in the way we have found."

Concentration and Structural Disequilibrium

Wenders' instinct is sound in believing this explanation to be inadequate. The industry growth rate measurements he relies on are those provided by K. D. George.[6] But George's data are for the growth rates of the leading firms used in Mann's sample, not for the industries occupied by these firms. In the concentrated industries these firms are frequently more profitable than the industries they represent. They probably grew faster than their industries. George found that the firms in concentrated industries which grew faster than 14 per cent per year had an average accounting rate of return of 15.2 per cent. Those which grew 8 to 14 per cent per year had an average return of 13.2 per cent while those which grew more slowly than 8 per cent per year had an average return of 10.5 per cent.[7]

One could suspect that the direction of causation is the reverse of that postulated by George and Wenders. Instead of high

[4] Yale Brozen, "Bain's Concentration and Rates of Return Revisited," 14 *Journal of Law and Economics*, October 1971.

[5] James Ellert, Concentration and Rates of Return, 1947–1969. Unpublished paper.

[6] K. D. George, "Concentration, Barriers to Entry and Rates of Return," 50 *Review of Economics and Statistics* 273–5, May 1968.

[7] *Id.* 274.

profits being attributable to rapid growth, rapid growth was the result of the attractiveness of the high rate of return earned by the more efficient firms. Behaving competitively, the high return firms bid resources away from the low return firms and probably expanded more rapidly than the industries of which they were a part.

The data provided by George tell us nothing about the growth rates of industries —only of some firms in these industries. Neither do the data tell us what the industry rates of return were. It may well be that the industries represented by high return firms had a lower industry rate of return and were in a structural disequilibrium. These industries may have been in the process of being restructured toward a more efficient use of resources.

A preliminary examination of the sample of firms chosen by Bain[8] to represent industries in his 1951 and 1956 studies[9] indicates this to be the case. Many of the concentrated industries used in these two studies were in the process of becoming more concentrated because large firms were more efficient (see Table 1). Using them to represent their industries overstated the average rates of return in their industries. Many of the unconcentrated industries used by Bain in his sample were in the process of becoming less concentrated because large firms were less efficient than smaller firms (see Table 1). Using only the rate of return in larger firms to represent these industries understated the average rate of return in unconcentrated industries.

Bain's finding that concentrated industries earned significantly more than unconcentrated industries seems to have been based on a sample of industries in which structural disequilibrium prevailed. In the sample selected by Bain for use in both his 1951 and 1956 studies, the structural disequilibria in his concentrated industries were such that rates of return in large firms were above the industry average. In his unconcentrated industries, the structural disequilibria were such that rates of return of the large firms were more frequently below industry rates of return than in the concentrated group (see Table 1).

That structural disequilibrium of the type specified above prevailed in the unconcentrated group of industries that Bain selected for his 1956 sample, as well as the opposite type prevailing in his concentrated group, is confirmed not only by the lower rates of return for the larger firms than for smaller firms in this group; it is also confirmed, as one would predict from this circumstance (other things remaining equal), by a shift in the structure of these industries. In the five unconcentrated industries where leading firms had lower rates of return, concentration ratios declined despite all the occurrences between the late thirties and 1947 which might have shifted the relative economies in the various size groups (Table 1). Concentration ratios also declined in each of the three concentrated industries where the leading four firms earned less than smaller firms.

Conclusion

Concentrated industries are concentrated because that, apparently, is the efficient way to organize those industries. Unconcentrated industries are unconcentrated because that, apparently, is the efficient way to organize them. Only among the concentrated industries in Bain's 1956 sample do we find larger firms earning more than smaller firms in the majority of cases. In the unconcentrated group, larger firms earn more than smaller firms in only two instances. To the extent that resources could be used more efficiently by increasing or decreasing concentration, these changes occurred in subsequent years.

Before accepting this conclusion, however, the sample of industries and firms

[8] The sample was drawn from Securities and Exchange Commission, *Survey of American Listed Corporations,* 1936–40.

[9] Joe S. Bain, "Relation of Profit Rate to Industry Concentration: American Manufacturing, 1936–1940," 65 *Quarterly Journal of Economics,* August 1951. J. S. Bain, *Barriers to New Competition* (1956).

Table 1 • **Rates of Return on Net Worth in Leading Firms and in a Larger Number of Firms (1936–40); Four Firm Concentration Ratios (1935, 1947)**

		Rates of Return[1]		Four Firm Concentration[2]	
	Industry	Leading Firms	Larger No. of Firms	1935	1947

Part I   Concentrated Industries

A. Leading firm rates of return in excess of larger number of firms

1652	Cigarettes	21.1% (4)	14.4%	89.7%	90.4%
629	Rayon	13.2 (2)	12.1	74.3	78.4
133	Liquor	15.2 (4)	14.2	47.7	74.6
1408	Motor vehicles	25.2 (4)	16.3	87.3**	N.A.
1022	Gypsum	11.2 (2)	10.1	76.1** ≠	84.6
1634	Fountain pens	17.5 (2)[3]	12.3	70.4** ≠	57.6

B. Leading firm rates of return below larger number of firms

803	Tires and tubes	7.8% (4)	8.2%	80.9	76.6
1123	Metal containers	9.3 (2)	9.1[4]	80.8	77.8
1301	Farm machinery	8.9 (4)	9.1	72.4*	49.8*
631	Soap	13.0 (2)	15.2[5]	75.5	79.0

Part II   Unconcentrated Industries

A. Leading firm rates of return in excess of larger number of firms

904	Shoes	8.1% (4)	7.5	26.0** ≠	27.9
105	Canned fr. & veg.	8.1 (4)[6]	7.4	23.1*	28.9

B. Leading firm rates of return below larger number of firms

123	Meat	3.0% (4)	3.6	52.5*	38.6*
1112	Steel	3.8 (4)	4.9	50.5*	47.5*
704	Petrol. ref.	6.6 (4)	6.8	38.2	37.3
1002	Cement	5.2 (4)	5.4	29.9	29.5
116	Flour	7.1 (2)	7.6	29.4	29.0

[1] Rates of return for leading firms are from J. S. Bain, *Barriers to New Competition* 195 (1956). Figures in parentheses are the numbers of firms used in computing rates of return. Rates for a larger number of firms are from J. S. Bain, "Relation of Profit Rate to Industry Concentration: American Manufacturing, 1936–1940," 65 *Quarterly Journal of Economics* 312 (August 1951).

[2] *Report of the Federal Trade Commission on Changes in Concentration in Manufacturing, 1935 to 1947 and 1950,* 138–147 (1954) except where marked with an asterisk or double asterisk. Figures marked * from G. S. Stigler, *Capital and Rates of Return in Manufacturing Industries,* 212–213 (1963). Figures marked ** from National Resources Committee, *Structure of the American Economy,* 265–269 (1939). The inequality sign indicates a change in industry definition which prevents direct comparison of the 1935 and 1947 concentration ratios. Industry 1634 definition was broadened which, in itself, would tend to reduce measured concentration. Industry 1022 and 904 definitions were narrowed which, in itself, would tend to raise measured concentration.

[3] In *Barriers to New Competition,* 195 (1956) this figure is given as 18.0%. Data on 193, however, average to 17.5%.

[4] The fifth largest company out of five companies listed in the industry earned 14.6% (1936–40).

[5] This figure given for the soap industry was evidently based on the SEC list of firms categorized in Toilet Preparations and Soap. The two soap firms in the SEC list had a 13.0% rate of return for 1936–40 (simple average). The seven toilet preparations firms had a 16.1% rate of return for 1936–40 (simple average) and concentration ratios of 25.3% (four firms) and 40.3% (eight firms) in 1935. The 15.2% figure is not for the same industry group as the 13.0% figure. They cannot be used to measure relative performance of larger and smaller firms in the soap industry.

[6] This figure is given as 3.2% in *Barriers to New Competition,* 195 (1956). Hunt Foods was one of the firms used in computing the 3.2% rate. In the SEC sample of firms in the food canning and preserving industry, it is seventh in size (excluding fish canners). If we take the fourth largest instead (Hawaiian Pineapple Co.), the rate of return in leading firms becomes 8.1% for 1936–40.

Note: The list of industries used is the twenty industry group used by Bain in *Barriers to New Competition.* The typewriter industry is omitted since the firm sample used to represent the industry in Bain's 1951 article is the same as the leading firm sample used in *Barriers to New Competition.* The copper refining industry is omitted since Bain does not give a rate of return for a larger group of firms in the 1951 article.

must be enlarged. The dangers inherent in the use of small samples are exemplified by work which supposedly established the existence of a relationship between concentration and profitability. The finding was a consequence of the use of small, unrepresentative samples of industries (together with the use only of a few firms—usually the larger ones—to represent each industry). In larger samples of industries with a larger number of firms to represent each industry the relationship is nonexistent. We can stop trying to explain the existence of the relationship since there is none.

26. Industry Structure, Market Rivalry, and Public Policy

HAROLD DEMSETZ

I. Introduction

Quantitative work in industrial organization has been directed mainly to the task of searching for monopoly even though a vast number of other interesting topics have been available to the student of economic organization. The motives for this preoccupation with monopoly are numerous, but important among them are the desire to be policy-relevant and the ease with which industrial concentration data can be secured. This paper takes a critical view of contemporary doctrine in this area and presents data which suggests that this doctrine offers a dangerous base upon which to build a public policy toward business.

II. Concentration Through Competition

Under the pressure of competitive rivalry, and in the apparent absence of effective barriers to entry, it would seem that the concentration of an industry's output in a few firms could only derive from their superiority in producing and marketing products or in the superiority of a structure of industry in which there are only a few firms. In a world in which information and resource mobility can be secured only at a cost, an industry will become more concentrated under competitive conditions only if a differential advantage in expanding output develops in some firms. Such expansion will increase the degree of concentration at the same time that it increases the rate of return that these firms earn. The cost advantage that gives rise to increased concentration may be reflected in scale economies or in downward shifts in positively sloped marginal cost curves, or it may be reflected in better products which satisfy demand at a lower cost. New efficiencies can, of course, arise in other ways. Some firms might discover ways of lowering cost that require that firms become smaller, so that spinoffs might be in order. In such cases, smaller firms will tend to earn relatively high rates of return. Which type of new efficiency arises most frequently is a question of fact.

Such profits need not be eliminated soon by competition. It may well be that superior competitive performance is unique to the firm, viewed as a team, and unobtainable to others except by purchasing the firm itself. In this case the return to superior performance is in the nature of a gain that is completely captured by the owner of the firm itself, not by its inputs.[1] Here, although the industry structure may change because the superior firm grows, the resulting increase in profit cannot easily serve to guide competitors to similar success. The firm may have established a reputation or goodwill that is difficult to separate from the firm itself and which should be carried at higher value on its books. Or it may be that the members of the employee team derive their higher productivity from the knowledge they possess about each other in the environment of the particular firm in which they work, a source of productivity that may be difficult to transfer piecemeal. It should be remembered that we are

---

[1] A detailed discussion of the implicit notion of team production that underlies these arguments can be found in Armen A. Alchian & Harold Demsetz, Production, Information Costs, and Economic Organization, 62 Amer. Econ. Rev. 777 (1972).

Reprinted from *The Journal of Law & Economics*, Volume XVI 1973, Copyright 1973, The University of Chicago.

discussing complex, large enterprises, many larger (and more productive) than entire nations. One such enterprise happens to "click" for some time while others do not. It may be very difficult for these firms to understand the reasons for this difference in performance or to know to which inputs to attribute the performance of the successful firm. It is not easy to ascertain just why G.M. and I.B.M. perform better than their competitors. The complexity of these organizations defies easy analysis, so that the inputs responsible for success may be undervalued by the market for some time. By the same token, inputs owned by complex, unsuccessful firms may be overvalued for some time. The success of firms will be reflected in higher returns and stock prices, not higher input prices, and lack of success will be recorded in lower returns and stock prices, not lower input prices.

Moreover, inputs are acquired at historic cost, but the use made of these inputs, including the managerial inputs, yields only uncertain outcomes. Because the outcomes of managerial decisions are surrounded by uncertainty and are specific to a particular firm at a particular point in its history, the acquisition cost of inputs may fail to reflect their value to the firm at some subsequent time. By the time their value to the firm is recognized, they are beyond acquisition by other firms at the same historic cost, and, in the interim, shareholders of the successful or lucky firm will have enjoyed higher profit rates. When nature cooperates to make such decisions correct, they can give rise to high accounting returns for several years or to a once for all capital gain if accountants could value *a priori* decisions that turn out to be correct *ex post*. During the period when such decisions determine the course of events, output will tend to be concentrated in those firms fortunate enough to have made the correct decisions.

None of this is necessarily monopolistic (although monopoly may play some role). Profit does not arise because the firm creates "artificial scarcity" through a reduction in its output. Nor does it arise because of

collusion. Superior performance can be attributed to the combination of great uncertainty plus luck or atypical insight by the management of a firm. It is not until the experiments are actually tried that we learn which succeed and which fail. By the time the results are in, it is the shareholder that has captured (some of) the value, positive or negative, of past decisions. Even though the profits that arise from a firm's activities may be eroded by competitive imitation, since information is costly to obtain and techniques are difficult to duplicate, the firm may enjoy growth and a superior rate of return for some time.

Superior ability also may be interpreted as a competitive basis for acquiring a measure of monopoly power. In a world in which information is costly and the future is uncertain, a firm that seizes an opportunity to better serve customers does so because it expects to enjoy some protection from rivals because of their ignorance of this opportunity or because of their inability to imitate quickly. One possible source of some monopoly power is superior entrepreneurship. Our patent, copyright, and trade mark laws explicitly provide as a reward for uncovering new methods (and for revealing these methods) legal protection against free imitation, and it may be true in some cases that an astute rival acquires the exclusive rights to some resource that *later* becomes valuable. There is no reason to suppose that competitive behavior never yields monopoly power, although in many cases such power may be exercised not by creating entry barriers, but through the natural frictions and ignorance that characterize any real economy. If rivals seek better ways to satisfy buyers or to produce a product, and if one or a few succeed in such endeavors, then the reward for their entrepreneurial efforts is likely to be some (short term) monopoly power and this may be associated with increased industrial concentration. To destroy such power when it arises may very well remove the incentive for progress. This is to be contrasted with a situation in which a high rate of return is obtained through a successful *collusion* to restrict output; here there is less danger to progress if the collusive agreement is penalized. Evidence presented below suggests that there are definite dangers of decreasing efficiency through the use of deconcentration or anti-merger policies.

III. Inefficiency Through Anti-Concentration Public Policy

The discussion in Part II noted that concentration may be brought about because a workable system of incentives implies that firms which better serve buyers will tend to grow relative to other firms. One way in which a firm could better serve buyers is by seizing opportunities to exploit scale economies, although if scale economies are the main cause of concentration, it is difficult to understand why there is no significant trend toward one-firm industries; the lack of such a trend seems to suggest that superiority results in lower but *positively* sloped cost curves in the relevant range of large firm operations. This would set limits to the size of even the successful firms. Successful firms thus would seem to be more closely related to the "superior land" of classical economic rent analysis than to the single firm of natural monopoly theory. Whether or not superiority is reflected in scale economies, deconcentration may have the total effect of promoting inefficiency even though it also may reduce some monopoly-caused inefficiencies.[2]

The classic portrayal of the inefficiency produced by concentration through the exercise of monopoly power is that of a group of firms cooperating to somehow restrict entry and prevent rivalrous price behavior. Successfully pursued, this policy results in a product price and rate of return in excess of that which would have prevailed in the absence of collusion. However, if all firms are able to produce at the same cost, then the rate of return to successfully colluding firms should be independent of the particular sizes adopted by these firms to achieve low cost production. One firm may require a small scale, and hence have a smaller investment, while another may require a large scale, and corresponding large investment. At any given collusive price, the absolute amounts of monopoly profits will be proportional to output, but capital investment also will be proportionate to output, so we can expect the rate of return to be invariant with respect to size of firm.

If one size of firm earns a higher rate of return than another size, given any collusive price, then there must exist differences in the cost of production which favor the firm that earns the higher rate of return. Alternatively, if there is no single price upon which the industry agrees, but, rather a range of prices, then one firm can earn a higher rate of return if it produces a superior product and sells it at a higher price without thereby incurring proportionately higher costs; here, also, the firm that earns the higher rate of return can be judged to be more efficient because it delivers more value per dollar of cost incurred.

A deconcentration or anti-merger policy is more likely to have benign results if small firms in concentrated industries earn the same or higher rates of return than large firms, for, then, deconcentration may reduce collusion,[3] if it is present, while simultaneously allocating larger shares of industry output to smaller firms which are no less efficient than larger firms. But if increased concentration has come about because of the superior efficiency of those firms that have become large, then a deconcentration policy, while it may reduce the ease of colluding, courts the danger of reducing efficiency either by the penalties that it places on innovative success or by the

---

[2] For a discussion of the social costs that might be incurred by deconcentration, especially in the context of scale economies, see John S. McGee, In Defense of Industrial Concentration 159 (1971).

[3] This statement is incorrect if a deconcentration or anti-merger policy causes firms to adopt socially less efficient methods of colluding than would be adopted in the absence of such a policy.

shift in output to smaller, higher cost firms that it brings about. This would seem to be a distinct possibility if large firms in concentrated industries earn higher rates of return than small firms.

The problem posed is how to organize data to shed light on the probability that deconcentration will promote inefficiency. Correlating industry rate of return with concentration will not be enlightening for this problem, for even if concentrated industries exhibit higher rates of return, it is difficult to determine whether it is efficiency or monopoly power that is at work. Similarly, large firms would tend to earn high profit rates in concentrated industries either because they are efficient or because they are colluding. However, partitioning industry data by size of firm does suggest that there exists a real danger from a deconcentration or anti-merger public policy, for the rates of return earned by small firms give no support to the doctrine relating collusion to concentration. A successful collusion is very likely to benefit the smaller firms, and this suggests that there should be a positive correlation between the rate of return earned by small firms and the degree to which the industry is concentrated. By the same token, if efficiency is associated with concentration, there should be a positive correlation between concentration and the difference between the rate of return earned by large firms and that earned by small firms; that is, large firms have become large because they are more efficient than other firms and are able to earn a higher rate of return than other firms.

Tables 1 and 2 show 1963 rates of return based on internal revenue data par-titioned by size of firm and industry concentration for 95 three digit industries. In these tables, C_{63} designates the four firm concentration ratio measured on industry sales, R_1, R_2, R_3, and R_4, respectively, measure accounting rates of return, (profit plus interest)/total assets, for firms with asset value less than $500,000, $500,000 to $5,000,000, $5,000,000 to $50,000,000 and over $50,0000,000. Table 1 is calculated by assigning equal weight to all industries. It is based, therefore, on the assumption that each industry, regardless of size, offers an equally good observational unit for comparing the efficiency and monopolistic aspects of industry structure. Table 2 presents the same basic data with accounting rates of return weighted by asset value. Hence, an industry with many assets owned by small firms receives a larger weight in calculating the small firm rate of return for a given interval of concentration ratios.

Both tables fail to reveal the beneficial effects to small firms that we would expect from an association of collusion and industry concentration. The rate of return earned by firms in the smallest asset size does not increase with concentration. This seems to be true for the next two larger asset size classifications also, although in Table 1 the 11.5 per cent earned by R_3 firms in industries with concentration ratios higher than 60 per cent offers some indication of a larger rate of return than in less concentrated industries.[4] The data

---

[4] Since firms are segregated by absolute size, for some industries the R_3 firms will be relatively large. A better test could be secured by contrasting the rates of return for the 1% largest and 10% smallest firms in each industry. But the data do not allow such a comparison.

Table 1 • **Rates of Return by Size and Concentration (Unweighted)**

C_{63}	Number of Industries	R_1	R_2	R_3	R_4	$\overline{R}$
10–20%	14	6.7%	9.0%	10.8%	10.3%	9.2%
20–30	22	4.5	9.1	9.7	10.4	8.4
30–40	24	5.2	8.7	9.9	11.0	8.7
40–50	21	5.8	9.0	9.5	9.0	8.3
50–60	11	6.7	9.8	10.5	13.4	10.1
over 60	3	5.3	10.1	11.5	23.1	12.5

Table 2 • **Rates of Return by Size and Concentration (Weighted by Assets)**

C_{63}	Number of Industries	R_1	R_2	R_3	R_4	$\bar{R}$
10–20%	14	7.3%	9.5%	10.6%	8.0%	8.8%
20–30	22	4.4	8.6	9.9	10.6	8.4
30–40	24	5.1	9.0	9.4	11.7	8.8
40–50	21	4.8	9.5	11.2	9.4	8.7
50–60	11	0.9	9.6	10.8	12.2	8.4
over 60	3	5.0	8.6	10.3	21.6	11.3

do not seem to support the notion that concentration and collusion are closely related, and, therefore, it is difficult to remain optimistic about the beneficial efficiency effects of a deconcentration or anti-merger public policy. On the contrary, the data suggest that such policies will reduce efficiency by impairing the survival of large firms in concentrated industries, for these firms do seem better able to produce at lower cost than their competitors.[5] Both tables indicate that R_4 size firms in industries with concentration ratios greater than 50 per cent produce at lower average cost.

Since a larger fraction of industry output is produced by larger firms in the more concentrated industries, these industries should exhibit higher rates of return than other industries. That this is so can be seen from the unweighted row averages given by column $\bar{R}$. Industries with $C_{63} > 50$ per cent seem to have earned higher rates of return than less concentrated industries. But this result, which is consistent with some earlier studies, may be attributed to the superior performance of the larger firms and not to collusive practices. Table 2 reveals this pattern even more clearly. Because the rates of return of smaller firms receive a larger weight (by total assets) in Table 2, industry rates of return are reduced even for concentrated industries in which large firms continue to perform well.

The general pattern of these data can be seen in Table 3. The results of regressing differences in profit rates on concentration ratios are shown in this table.

Table 3

$$R_4 - R_1 = -1.4 + .21^*C_{63} \qquad r^2 = .09$$
$$(.07)$$

$$R_4 - R_2 = -2.6 + .12^{**}C_{63} \qquad r^2 = .04$$
$$(.06)$$

$$R_4 - R_3 = -3.1 + .10^{**}C_{63} \qquad r^2 = .04$$
$$(.05)$$

*, ** significant at the 1% and 5% levels respectively. Standard errors are shown in parentheses.

These regressions reveal a significant positive relationship between concentration and differences in rates of return, especially when comparing the largest and smallest firms in an industry.[6] The three

---

[5] On the margin of output, however, these large firms need not have an advantage over small firms, just as fertile land has no advantage over poor land for producing marginal units. The failure of the large firms to become more dominant in these industries suggests the absence of such advantage.

[6] Three adjustments in procedure and in variables were undertaken to analyze certain problems in the data and the theory.

(1) It is believed by some of the profits of firms, and especially of small firms, is hidden in administrative wages. To check on the possibility that this phenomenon might have accounted for the data relationships shown above, the data were recalculated after adding back to profits all administrative salaries of firms in the R_1 asset size class. Although this increased very slightly the rates of return for this asset size class, as, of course, must be the case, no correlation between concentration and rate of return was produced. In fact, rates of return so calculated were virtually perfectly correlated with the rates of return shown above for this asset size.

(2) The asset sizes categories used to calculate the above data are uniform over all industries. Some industries, however, had no firms in the largest asset size category, and these were dropped from the sample. An alternative method was used to check on the impact of

regressions taken together indicate a non-linear, decreasing impact of concentration on relative rates of return as the size of the smaller firms is increased from R_1 to R_3.

The competitive view of industry structure suggests that rapid changes in concentration are brought about by changed

cost conditions and not by alternations in the height of entry barriers. Industries experiencing rapid increases in concentration should exhibit greater disparities between large and small rates of return because of the more significant cost differences which are the root cause of rapid alterations in industry structure. The monopoly view of concentration does not imply such a relationship, for if an industry is rapidly achieving workable collusive practices there is no reason to suppose that the difference between large and small firm profit rates should increase. At the time of writing, matching data on concentration were available for both 1963 and 1967. This time span is too short to reveal much variation in concentration ratios, and so we cannot be very confident about evidence gained by regressing differences in profit rates on changes in concentration ratios. However, the persistently positive coefficient of the variable $C_{67} - C_{63}$ in Table 4 is consistent with the competitive viewpoint, and must increase our doubts, however slightly, about the beneficial effects of an active deconcentration or anti-merger policy.

I have presented an explanation of industry structure and profitability based on competitive superiority. The problem faced by a deconcentration or anti-merger policy was posed on the basis of this explanation. Is there a danger that such a policy will produce more inefficiency than it eliminates? The date presented suggest that this danger should be taken seriously.

The author wishes to thank the Research Program in Competition and Public Policy at U.C.L.A. for assisting in the preparation of this article.

---

this procedure. For each industry, the largest asset size class was redefined so as to include some firms in every industry. The mechanics of the procedure was to categorize asset sizes more finely and choose the largest three size categories containing some observations for each industry. These were then counted as the larger firms in each industry, and the rate of return for these firms was then compared to those firms contained in the three smaller asset size categories containing some observations. The unweighted average difference between large firm rate of return, R_L, and small firm rate of return, R_s, compared with industry concentration is shown below. This table is consistent with the text tables.

C_{63}	$R_L - R_s$
0–20%	6.4%
20–30	9.4
30–40	7.0
40–50	7.0
50–60	12.8
over 60	14.0

(3) The efficiency argument suggests that for a given degree of industry concentration, measured by the four firm concentration ratio, the greater the difference between the sizes of the largest firms and the sizes of the smallest firms, the larger will be the disparity between R_4 and R_1. A linear regression of $R_4 - R_1$ on C_{63} and the average size of firms in the R_4 class yields a positive but not highly significant coefficient for the variable "average asset size of firms in the R_4 class." Also, there was a small reduction in the significance of the coefficient of C_{63}.

Table 4

$$R_4 - R_1 = 1.5 + .21{*}C_{63} + .21(C_{67} - C_{63}) \qquad r^2 = .09$$
$$ (.07) \qquad (.42)$$

$$R_4 - R_2 = -2.9 + .12{**}C_{63} + .37(C_{67} - C_{63}) \quad r^2 = .06$$
$$ (.06) \qquad (.28)$$

$$R_4 - R_3 = -3.4 + .10{**}C_{63} + .29(C_{67} - C_{63}) \quad r^2 = .05$$
$$ (.05) \qquad (.24)$$

*, **, respectively, 1% and 5% confidence levels.

27. The Locomotive Industry and General Motors

GENERAL MOTORS CORPORATION

I

General Motors' success in the locomotive business is solely the result of innovation and product superiority.

The record of General Motors' contributions in the locomotive business is, we believe, a classic story of our competitive system working at its best. Before General Motors entered, the locomotive business consisted principally of three companies (Alco, Baldwin & Lima) who were stubbornly wedded to steam. General Motors, in the face of almost universal initial skepticism, proceeded to develop and sell the diesel locomotive, whose superiority was so pronounced that it revolutionized the industry. In the face of healthy and continuing competition General Motors has maintained its front-running position with a record of innovation and continuing product improvement.

A. General Motors' Entry with a Revolutionary New Product

Innovations by General Motors literally created the modern diesel locomotive industry. Since the early 1920's the General Motors Research Laboratories, under the direction of Mr. Charles F. Kettering, had undertaken research studies to ascertain the potential of light-weight diesel engines as prime movers, without regard to specific application. The previously existing engines were both heavy and slow. The first prototype model of the new light-weight two-cycle diesel engine, which was to evolve into General Motors' first locomotive engine, was built in 1933 as a submarine engine. It weighed only around 20 pounds per horsepower, compared with 60 pounds

or more per horsepower for the lightest diesel engines of that era, and was also about one-third their size. For the first time in America, a commercially practical internal combustion engine of sufficiently high horsepower and sufficiently small size and weight was available for possible use in road locomotives.

The first contact with the railway industry, however, occurred purely by happenstance. In 1933 General Motors displayed two of its new 201 diesel engines at the Chicago World's Fair, where they were used to provide power for the Chevrolet exhibit. Ralph Budd, then President of the Burlington Railroad, saw these engines and sought them for a new streamlined train the Burlington was building. Although General Motors was reluctant to supply what was still an experimental and untried engine for such important railroad service, at Mr. Budd's urging it ultimately agreed to build a modified version (the 201-A) of the new engine for the train that later became famous as the Pioneer Zephyr.

Although there were many difficulties with the 201-A engine, it was the spectacular and highly publicized experience of the Zephyr and subsequent streamliners which demonstrated that the new diesel engine could make a contribution to railroad transportation and which led to General Motors' decision to enter the locomotive manufacturing field with the construction of a plant at LaGrange in 1935.

The entire period from the middle 1930's through World War II was a period in which the railroads carefully examined, studied, tested, and compared the performance of General Motors' new product in competition with steam locomotives. The question of diesel versus steam power was debated at almost every gathering of railroad personnel, and the controversy was

Reprinted with permission of General Motors Corporation.

abetted by the old-line locomotive builders, whose officials seemingly seized every available opportunity to make a speech or write an article "proving" that steam power was superior.

Indeed, the railroads first began purchasing General Motors locomotives only for use in unusual operating situations where steam could not do the job. For example, in early 1938 the Atlantic Coast Line, which competed with the Seaboard for the heavy winter railroad passenger traffic between Washington and the Florida resort area, announced a reduction of several hours in its operating schedule between Washington and Miami. Both railroads operated steam locomotives on that run, but because the Atlantic Coast Line had a shorter, straighter track and was placing the latest model Baldwin steam locomotives in that service, the Seaboard became concerned that it could not meet the reduction in the Atlantic Coast Line's schedule. Accordingly, when the Seaboard found that no steam locomotives were available which could do the job, almost as a last resort it ordered diesel locomotives from General Motors and placed them in service on its crack "Orange Blossom Special."

As it turned out, the competition between the Seaboard and the Atlantic Coast Line for the Miami passenger business attracted widespread attention in the railroad industry as a contest between diesel and steam power, pitting as it did the new General Motors diesel locomotive against the latest model steam locomotive. The diesel won hands down, for it not only enabled the Seaboard to meet the Atlantic Coast Line's faster schedule but in its first year of service the Seaboard attracted more passengers and realized more revenue than it ever had previously on the Miami run, mainly because of the new locomotive's on-time performance. As a postscript, the Atlantic Coast Line was as impressed by the performance of this new diesel locomotive as the Seaboard; shortly thereafter it stopped buying steam locomotives and began buying diesel locomotives.

Many other tests, studies and comparisons were made throughout this period. General Motors built demonstrator units which the railroads tested in actual service to see for themselves how General Motors locomotives performed relative to competing locomotives. General Motors made economic studies of the railroads' operations, to show that the economies which would be gained by operating General Motors locomotives more than justified their purchase. Frequently, these studies proved that General Motors locomotives would pay for themselves in a few years entirely out of the savings they produced.

Perhaps the most significant test of all occurred in 1939, when General Motors developed and built the first diesel freight locomotive ever produced. That locomotive, built as a demonstrator, became famous as the "No. 103" and is generally considered the most important locomotive ever built in America after the original steam locomotive. The No. 103 was developed for the express purpose of determining whether the diesel locomotive could compete with steam in freight service, which is the most important type of railroad service and which by 1939 was virtually the last stronghold of steam operations. If a diesel locomotive could compete with steam in freight service, then the way would be open to total dieselization of the railroads, which would yield enormous additional savings by completely eliminating the need for the expensive facilities necessary to support steam operations, including roundhouses, water towers, coal chutes, ashpits, turntables, etc.

When General Motors made the No. 103 available to the railroads for testing, it did so on the express condition that the locomotive would be tested in the most demanding and rigorous service available, so that both the railroads and General Motors would learn what the overall capability of the diesel locomotive was in such service. (Despite the "proofs" advanced by the old-line locomotive builders that the diesel was unsuitable to freight operations, no one really knew because it had never been tested in such service.) Such tests would not merely show whether the diesel locomotive could perform satisfactorily in freight service, they would yield data which would make it possible to measure the economic contribution, if any, which the diesel locomotive could make in such service.

The No. 103 was tested by about 20 major railroads, covering over 80,000 miles under every variation in operating conditions that could be found in some 35 different states. The tests proved dramatically and conclusively that General Motors' new diesel freight locomotive represented a significant economic advance over the steam freight locomotives offered by other companies.[1]

From about 1940 on, sales of General Motors' new locomotives began climbing rapidly as the savings which they could achieve became more and more apparent. And, except for the interruption occasioned by World War II, the railroads began dieselizing in earnest.[2]

In short, General Motors achieved a substantial position in the business by developing a revolutionary new product and then demonstrating to the railroads that this product could produce substantial savings for them. The railroads began purchasing from General Motors in appreciable volume only after they determined that its product was superior to what other companies had to offer.

B. Other Locomotive Manufacturers Regarded the Diesel Locomotive as a "Passing Fancy"

The loss of business by General Motors' competitors once the merits of General Motors' new diesel locomotives became known is not evidence that any anticompetitive influences were at work; it is evidence that the market was competitive, because the best product attracted most of the business. General Motors' competitors were penalized by their own failure to produce a competitive product, not by any control or market power of General Motors.[3]

When General Motors began developing and gaining experience with the diesel locomotive in the 1930's, Alco, Baldwin and Lima had all had a long history as producers of steam locomotives; both General Electric and Westinghouse had had considerable experience in building straight-electric locomotives; and all but Lima had experimented with diesels before General Motors' first diesel engine went into service on the Burlington Zephyr in 1934. The executives of those companies had been closely associated with the leaders of American railroads for many years; consequently, all of them were in an ideal position to analyze the railroads' motive power needs and to develop locomotives which would satisfy them. Moreover, all of those companies were large, well-established industrial concerns with ample facilities for designing and building any type of locomotive that the railroads desire. There

---

[1] Mr. Fred Gurley, former Santa Fe Chairman of the Board, testified on the initial General Motors diesel freight locomotive, introduced in 1939 as follows: "° ° ° here we had the ultimate. Here was an engine that in my judgment outperformed anything we had in the country. I just made up my mind to two things right now: That the day of the steam engine was history; that I owed a debt of gratitude to the fellows that made that all possible, and that was your company, my good fellow, General Motors." (Deposition testimony in the civil Electro-Motive case, p. 144)

[2] During the early part of the war General Motors was taken out of locomotive production entirely, to permit its entire production of diesel engines to be utilized in connection with the Navy's LST program.

Subsequently General Motors was permitted to resume production of freight locomotives only. The Government had allocated diesel switcher production to Alco and Baldwin exclusively and had suspended production of diesel passenger locomotives.

At various times during the war Alco and Baldwin were authorized to build diesel road locomotives, but were unable to do so because they had no suitable design ready.

[3] Mr. Kettering once testified, when questioned by Senator O'Mahoney regarding General Motors' large share of the diesel locomotive business, that General Motors' greatest competitive advantage was its competitors' belief "that we were crazy."

being no important patents involved, they had ready access to all of the latest technical developments, and most of the components necessary for a diesel electric locomotive were readily available to any interested company.[4] Yet, none of these companies promoted the use of diesel locomotives; indeed, most of them vigorously opposed it. A brief review of those companies' early diesel development activities and their subsequent attitude toward diesel power is sufficient to show why they lost their positions as the leaders in the American locomotive industry.

Alco had built diesel switching locomotives (in cooperation with General Electric and Ingersoll-Rand) as early as 1924 or 1925, and in the late 1920's built two experimental diesel road locomotives. In 1929, Alco acquired the McIntosh-Seymour Company which was then a leading builder of diesel engines. Alco used McIntosh-Seymour diesel engines to power its diesel switchers throughout the 1930's, to power a streamlined train in 1935 (the Rebel, on the GM&O), and also to power the few diesel passenger locomotives which Alco built before the war. But, according to Mr. Perry Egbert (former Alco President and Chairman of the Board), Alco did not even *begin* designing a new diesel engine specifically for a road locomotive until 1940, and Alco locomotives powered by that new engine were not available commercially until 1946.[5]

Baldwin, which had the largest locomotive plant in the world, had built two experimental diesel road locomotives in the late 1920's, and in 1931 it acquired a diesel engine manufacturer (De La Vergne). Baldwin built diesel switchers both before and during World War II, but did not market a diesel road locomotive until after the war. As late as November, 1945, Baldwin was still advertising steam locomotives, and it kept its steam locomotive building shops open until at least 1950. It dropped out of the locomotive business entirely around 1956. Its departure was no fault of General Motors; rather, according to its own officials:

"* * * the judgment of those of us who had been in the company back in the diesel period was that *General Motors had nothing to do with the Baldwin failure. It was our late start in the field and our inability to produce as good a competitive product.*"[6]

Lima Locomotive Works (later Lima-Hamilton), which had built no diesel locomotives at all prior to 1949 (and then built only diesel switchers), never deserted steam power as long as it remained in business as a separate company. Even after the war, Lima continued to promote steam power, and as late as 1949 was still advertising that in its belief there would continue to be a demand for steam locomotives "for a long, long time." In the following year, 1950, Lima-Hamilton merged with Baldwin, and ceased to exist as a separate company.

The straight-electric type of locomotive first built by *General Electric* and *Westinghouse* at the turn of the century is similar to the diesel electric locomotive (except that

---

[4] As early as the middle 1920's both General Electric and Westinghouse were manufacturing and selling all the components needed for the electric transmission system of a diesel electric locomotive, including traction motors, generators, and control apparatus.

[5] *Lukens Steel Co.* v. *American Locomotive Co.*, Civil Action No. 3596 (U.S.D.C., N.D.N.Y.), transcript of Egbert testimony, pp. 79–98 (1951). According to Mr. Egbert, Alco's initial reaction to General Motors' plan to build diesel road locomotives was that General Motors "would not be successful in the development of road line locomotives" (p. 86). Mr. Egbert also testified that, when events proved that prediction wrong and Alco brought out a diesel passenger locomotive which was "rated up to the hilt," Alco (and the railroads) found that "our maintenance costs were excessive, in compari-

son with the Electro-Motive locomotives which had a margin and which were designed especially for road service. And they gave us terrific competition to the extent that we were practically eliminated from the field productwise" (p. 91).

[6] Page 188 of deposition of Edward Hopkinson, Jr., former Chairman of Baldwin's Executive Committee (in *Evans* v. *Armour and Company, et al.*, 241 F. Supp. 705 (E.D. Pa. 1965)).

it obtains its electric power from an outside source), and both of those companies have been closely connected with diesel locomotive developments in this country.[7] General Electric collaborated with Alco and Ingersoll-Rand in building diesel switchers in the middle 1920's, and several of General Motors' early diesel locomotives were built at General Electric's Erie Works in 1934 and 1935. General Electric has built diesel electric locomotives for export since at least 1928, and for many years it has manufactured diesel locomotives in the low-horsepower ranges for a variety of domestic users, including some railroads. (Much later, in 1961, it came out with a new line of high-horsepower diesel electric road locomotives designed primarily for use on American railroads.)

In the late 1920's and early 1930's Westinghouse built several diesel electric locomotives, using diesel engines manufactured under license from the Beardmore Company of Scotland, and in 1935 Westinghouse furnished the diesel engines and electric transmission for a streamlined train operated by the New Haven. Shortly after that, however, Westinghouse discontinued its diesel locomotive activities, apparently in the belief that the diesel locomotive did not have a sufficiently attractive commercial future.

The diesel locomotive development efforts of all of those companies were limited by the view that the diesel locomotive was merely supplemental to the steam locomotive and was useful only in certain limited types of service, primarily switching. It is clear from their contemporary advertisements, as well as from speeches and papers by their executives, that those companies regarded the diesel road locomotive as a passing fancy which would never seriously challenge the dominance of steam, and that they considered General Motors' efforts to develop a diesel road locomotive to be sheer folly. None of them saw the diesel locomotive as the locomotive of the future.

C. The Diesel Locomotive Aided Competitors by Creating New Demand

The fact that the loss of market position suffered by the steam builders was due to normal rather than abnormal market forces is also proven by the fact that they, as well as Fairbanks, Morse,[8] found no barrier to producing diesel road locomotives once they decided to move in that direction after the war. In fact, General Motors facilitated such sales by others by creating the demand in the first place.

With the superiority of the diesel proved beyond any doubt by the end of the war or shortly thereafter, the railroads, following the dictates of economics, rushed to dieselize as fast as possible. Because General Motors had failed to gauge fully the extent of demand for its diesel locomotives, it lacked sufficient production capacity to fill that demand, and its share of sales declined as the railroads, again following the dictates of economics, purchased large quantities of diesel locomotives from its competitors. Even though the railroads regarded General Motors diesels as the best, any diesel was better than steam. During that period the railroads frequently purchased whichever make of diesel locomotive they could obtain first, in order to more quickly realize the economies of dieselization.

---

[7] Both General Electric and Westinghouse for many years were important suppliers of the major electrical components needed for the electric transmission system in diesel locomotives, including traction motors, generators, and control apparatus. General Electric had always supplied such equipment for Alco locomotives, and formerly supplied Fairbanks, Morse (and at one time General Motors) as well. Westinghouse built such equipment for Baldwin (and also at one time for General Motors).

[8] Fairbanks, Morse had manufactured marine diesel engines during the war. It never quite overcame the technical problems of conversion and fell aside when demand sharply declined in the 1950's.

D. Reasons for the Superiority of the Diesel Locomotive

The absolute superiority of diesel electric locomotives to steam locomotives is the key to the revolutionary changes which took place in the business. A simple illustration should serve to drive the point home.

In the 1920's over 60,000 steam locomotives were required by U.S. railroads to haul somewhat over 400 billion ton-miles of freight. By 1971 all but 13 of these steam locomotives had been replaced by only 27,000 diesels, even though total freight traffic had increased by about 85%. Thus each diesel was doing the work of about four of the steam locomotives which it replaced.

The main reasons for the superiority of diesel power are:

a. The diesel engine has a thermal efficiency more than three times that of the most modern steam engine.

b. The availability of an efficient diesel electric locomotive for useful work, when properly maintained, exceeds 95%, as compared to an availability of only 50% to 65% for a steam locomotive.

c. A diesel electric has much higher starting tractive effort than any steam locomotive, partly because all wheels are driving wheels and because its traction motors can exert full torque at zero speed.

d. The electrical system of a diesel electric can be used to stop or retard trains (dynamic braking), which is particularly important on downgrades. This allows greatly improved train handling and faster safe speeds, and also saves thousands of tons of iron brakeshoes for freight and passenger cars annually.

e. Because of mass production and parts standardization, repairs on a diesel electric are much more economical.

f. Diesel electrics are much more versatile, allowing more continuous use and eliminating the need for many special purpose locomotives.

g. Diesel electrics can run for long distances with only minor service. Moreover, unlike steam locomotives, a single type can be used in mountains or in prairies. Thus, a single train can travel coast-to-coast without a change.

In the early postwar period most knowledgeable men in the railroad field realized that steam locomotives were so inherently inferior to diesel locomotives as to constitute liabilities rather than assets to the owning railroads. In other words, steam locomotives were so expensive to operate relative to diesel locomotives that a railroad could not afford to operate them even if they were obtained free from the builder.

The displacement of steam locomotives by diesels yielded another benefit which was not fully appreciated at the time. Diesels are much cleaner. Studies of the Department of Health, Education and Welfare recently concluded that railroads accounted for less than 1% of emissions to the atmosphere.[9]

The initial revolutionary development of diesel electric locomotives had been completed by the early postwar period, and within another ten years the steam locomotives had largely disappeared. General Motors had created an entirely new industry.

E. Reasons for the Superiority of General Motors' Locomotives

General Motors achieved its initial success in the locomotive business by pioneering in the development of diesel power. It has continued to be successful because of the superiority of its product and its leadership in introducing innovations and improvements. A few indications of this leadership are discussed below.

1. Mass Production Technology. A modern diesel locomotive is a complex product, consisting of some 250,000 individual parts and components and requiring over 1,000,000 separate shop operations to make. Unless manufactured by modern

---

[9] HEW, *Nationwide Inventory of Air Pollutant Emissions 1968* (Aug. 1970).

mass production methods, utilizing tools, dies and fixtures, its first cost would be so high that its economic advantage would largely be lost. (The old-line locomotive manufacturers never tired of arguing that the first cost of the diesel locomotive was prohibitively high.)

General Motors was the first company successfully to apply mass production techniques to locomotives. Applying its know-how from the automobile industry, it developed new manufacturing methods and factory controls to fit the new product and, there being few tools then available in heavy industry which were suited to high precision manufacture, even designed and built its own tools.

While it may appear now that the application of mass production to this industry was an obvious step, there was a basic obstacle to its introduction in the 1930's. Mass production of course requires a standardized product. Yet the almost universal practice of the railroads in ordering steam locomotives was to specify a large number of individual variations, making it necessary to custom-build such locomotives by old-fashioned job shop methods. At first some railroads refused to accept the limitation that they order "off the shelf" locomotives, but in time they agreed that standardization was of great economic benefit. Today many railroad executives consider that standardization of locomotives was one of the most outstanding innovations that General Motors brought to the industry. No other builder of diesel locomotives adopted this philosophy until after World War II, and none ever applied it to the same extent that General Motors did.

2. *A Revolutionary Design Concept: Standardization and Upgrading of Locomotive Components.* Along with mass production and a standardized locomotive, General Motors introduced a basic locomotive design philosophy which has been one of the most far-reaching and significant cost-saving innovations in the history of heavy industry. Part of this philosophy is the "building block" concept, which involves the use of completely standardized and uniform components wherever possible in every locomotive in the line. Thus, in every General Motors locomotive engine—regardless of horsepower or number of cylinders—most of the important engine components have been interchangeable. Variations in horsepower from engine to engine have generally been accomplished simply by varying the number of standard cylinders (and standard cylinder components).

Other major components, such as electric traction motors, have also had exactly the same dimensions regardless of the size or type of locomotive on which mounted, so that a replacement traction motor in a railroad's spare parts inventory would fit any General Motors locomotive, regardless of size or type, from the smallest 600 h.p. switcher up to the largest road locomotive. Electric generators also were standardized to the several sizes necessary for the range of electrical output required in particular types of service.

Standardization of components not only has contributed greatly to General Motors' manufacturing efficiency (by reducing the amount of tooling needed), it has achieved important savings for the railroads by enabling them to carry less varied and hence smaller inventories of spare parts for their General Motors locomotives.

General Motors locomotive components have been standardized not only among the various models of locomotives being produced at any given time, but also among the different models produced through the years. Moreover, through the application of a revolutionary concept in engineering design, standardization has been retained *even though the components were continuously being improved.* This has been done by designing product improvements into components having the same physical configuration and exterior dimensions as the components they replace. For example, General Motors' curernt model electric traction motor has more than twice the horsepower of the 1939 model, but has precisely the same dimensions as, and is fully interchangeable with, that earlier model. This has also been true of crankshafts, cylinder heads and many other vital parts.

Thus locomotives built in 1939 could be repaired in 1972 with current production parts, and by the very process of repair older locomotives have constantly been upgraded and modernized through the replacement of worn out components with new, improved, longer-lasting, more powerful components. As a result, a General Motors locomotive built and sold ten years ago may, by the process of upgrading through repair, be intrinsically a better locomotive today than it was when new.

Moreover, even when a customer wants a new locomotive he can save a considerable amount of money by ordering what is called a "line replacement locomotive," which contains certain remanufactured parts and components. He trades in his old unit and certain salvable parts are removed. These parts are then remanufactured, modernized to current specifications and incorporated into a new unit.

3. *Ease of Maintenance and Repair.* General Motors' diesel engines have also been better designed than those of other locomotive builders from the standpoint of accessibility and ease of repair of vital moving parts. For example, removal of a power assembly (the cylinder head and liner, piston, connecting rod, and auxiliaries) from any General Motors locomotive engine is a relatively easy hand operation requiring no more than two men; however, on almost all models of competitive locomotive engines, a crane or chain hoist is required to effect the same repair because the pieces are far too heavy to be removed by hand.

The relative ease of repair of its locomotives has been an important factor in General Motors' success. In the early days of the diesel locomotive, when breakdowns were more frequent than now and replacement (or standby) locomotives were less apt to be available, General Motors service engineers often rode on the trains with the railroad service personnel, literally living with the locomotive around the clock. As a result of the ability to make vital engine repairs without the use of a crane or hoist,

it was possible, on a General Motors passenger locomotive equipped with two diesel engines, to make power assembly repairs on one engine while the other engine was pulling the train on its regularly scheduled run, without taking the locomotive out of service and without disrupting its schedule.[10] (One railroad repairman reported that it required exactly "42 miles" to change a piston on a General Motors locomotive engine on his assigned run.)

4. *Service.* Long before any other locomotive manufacturer even recognized the importance of providing such service, General Motors established after-sales service which has been outstanding in the locomotive industry. Under the guidance of the General Motors Institute, the first school in the industry was established at Flint (later at LaGrange) for the training of railroad personnel in diesel locomotive operation and maintenance. In addition to its permanent classroom at LaGrange, the school also outfitted railroad cars as traveling classrooms in order to bring instructions to the students. To date, some 35,000 railroad personnel have attended General Motors' locomotive training school at LaGrange and an additional 65,000 have been given on-site training in the traveling classrooms.

Recognizing the importance of having necessary repair parts for its locomotives readily available to the railroads, General Motors located parts warehouses or repair depots at 13 strategic locations throughout the country, so that needed parts would be within quick reach of every railroad operating General Motors locomotives. In order to further speed up the repair process, General Motors utilized a program of "unit exchange" on major locomotive components, whereby a railroad can exchange a worn or damaged component for a reconditioned component without waiting for repair of

---

[10] In order to change a cylinder liner on a Fairbanks, Morse locomotive, by contrast, it was necessary to lift a crankshaft which alone weighed more than 2000 pounds. The operation normally took the locomotive out of service for a day.

the damaged part; General Motors then re-
conditions the worn component, upgrades
it to current specifications and places it in
its stock, billing the railroad only for the
cost of the actual reconditioning involved.
The tremendously broad scope of General
Motors' unit exchange program, of course,
is feasible only because General Motors has
standardized so many of its major locomotive components.

By its efforts over the years, General
Motors has earned a reputation for providing prompt, reliable service to its customers and for "keeping its locomotives running" with a minimum of inconvenience
and expense to the railroad. In fact, in the
early years, railroads even called upon General Motors service engineers to help solve
problems on competitive locomotives.

5. *Continuity of Improvement.* Significant product improvements have been
made by General Motors in virtually every
important locomotive component over the
years. A typical example is piston ring life,
which has been increased from some 100,-
000 miles in 1945 to 400,000 to 500,000 miles
today. Life of the piston itself has also been
at least quadrupled during the same period.
One measure of the savings to customers
which improvements in component life have
produced is indicated by the fact that where
in 1945 about 7655 man-hours of railroad
labor were required to carry out each four-
year cycle of scheduled maintenance recom-
mended by General Motors for its then
current model freight locomotive, the comparable figure for a current GP-40 locomotive is 3425 hours. At current railroad labor
rates for locomotive maintenance, the saving in labor alone amounts to over $8,000
per year per locomotive.

F. Measuring the Superiority of General Motors Locomotives

The ultimate measure of how well General
Motors has succeeded in marketing the best
possible locomotives is, of course, how well
they perform in actual service. The evidence in that respect overwhelmingly establishes that General Motors locomotives

have proven superior to those of other
builders. This superiority can be measured
in cold, hard dollars and cents, and is
clearly apparent on the books and records
of almost every American railroad.

Although comparable models of almost
all makes of locomotives have about the
same initial price, locomotives are not fun-
gible commodities. The real price of a locomotive cannot be determined by reference only to its initial cost; more important
is the anticipated cost of operating and
maintaining it. Because a road locomotive
may be expected to operate in the neighborhood of 10,000 miles per month (2,000,-
000 miles or more during the course of its
normal useful life), it is obvious that even
slight differences in operating and maintenance costs between different makes of locomotives are of overwhelming importance
to railroads in their locomotive purchase
decisions. For example, a large railroad like
the Santa Fe operates its fleet of diesel road
locomotive units approximately 150,000,000
unit miles per year; thus on that railroad an
average saving of only 1¢ per unit mile in
costs of locomotive operation and maintenance would result in total savings of $1,-
500,000 per year.

Many railroads have compared their
costs of operating and maintaining General
Motors locomotives with their costs of operating and maintaining other makes of diesel locomotives. Over the years, on railroad
after railroad, the difference in operating
and maintenance costs between most models of General Motors locomotives and the
next best make of comparable diesel locomotive has not been just 1¢ per unit mile,
but rather has been in the neighborhood of
10¢ per mile or more. The more usual average saving of 10¢ per mile in operating and
maintenance costs on a single General Motors freight locomotive represents a saving
of approximately $200,000 over the useful
life of that locomotive—an amount approximating its initial cost.

It is small wonder that these railroads
(and others) have, on the basis of studies
such as these, awarded their locomotive
business to General Motors. Many railroads

even have asked General Motors to re-power competitive locomotives with General Motors diesel engines, and General Motors has performed such repowerings on virtually every type and make of competitive locomotive. General Motors has re-powered a total of 238 competitors' locomotives with General Motors engines, but to our knowledge there has never been a single instance of another locomotive builder repowering a General Motors locomotive.

At the time of the Government's anti-trust case the railroad executives who were responsible for the locomotive purchase decisions on almost every major railroad in the United States would have testified to a man that their purchases of General Motors locomotives were based on their superiority.[11] The fact that their purchases of General Motors locomotives depended solely on the merits is demonstrated by the way railroad purchases varied according to differing preferences for the various types of General Motors locomotives. The historical record shows that in the past railroads found General Motors' passenger locomotives to have the greatest superiority over competitors' passenger locomotives,[12] its freight locomotives to have the next most marked superiority, and its switcher locomotives third. The available data at the present time does not permit such comparisons, and they are less significant in any event because the three types are now more nearly interchangeable. But where there were significant differences, General Motors' position varied according to the degree of productive superiority, as might be expected in a competitive market.

In summary, the facts establish beyond

any reasonable doubt that General Motors' position in the business is the result of innovation and product superiority. Its contributions to the railroads of this country were characterized by Mr. James M. Symes (then President of the Pennsylvania Railroad) in a 1955 speech, as follows:

> The greatest single contribution to the economic and efficient operation of our railroads during my 40 years of association with the industry has been the development of the Diesel locomotive. We all know the important part General Motors has played in that development. Today they have 23 million horsepower operating on our railroads in more than 16,000 Diesel units, some of which have made between 2½ and 3½ million miles and are still on the road performing quite satisfactorily. I would guess that this development alone is saving the railroads a minimum of 500 million dollars a year—with initial investments being paid off in 3 to 4 years.

The 1956 staff report of the Anti-Monopoly Subcommittee of the Senate Judiciary Committee (then known as the O'Mahoney Committee) stated:

> "° ° ° The diesel locomotive revolutionized the railroad industry. General Motors can point to its entry into this field as an example of the operations of a progressive company at its best—entry into a new field, with a new product satisfying an economic need, and offering progressive reduction in the pricing of its product." (S. Rep. No. 1879, 84th Cong. 2d Sess. 35 (1956))

In September 1972, the railroading magazine *Trains* devoted an issue to Electro-Motive. In the lead article "The LaGrange Influence," the editor of the magazine summed up General Motors' contribution:

> The technology to replace steam was around even before GM was born, much less EMD—Dr. Diesel's engine, the dynamo, streetcar controls and motors, the works. And the principle of a self-contained electric went back even further—to Jean-Jacques Heilmann and his steam-electric *Fusée* of 1894. Conversely, it is a matter of record that while the little Elec-

---

[11] It is, perhaps, significant that the Alaska Railroad, which is Government-owned, has bought 100% of its road locomotives from General Motors.

[12] The greater reliability of General Motors locomotives was of special importance in passenger service where avoidance of breakdowns and delays was essential.

tro-Motive Company, minus GM parent-
age and headquartered in Cleveland, still
was selling put-put doodlebugs, diesel-
electric locomotives were switching box
cars in Jersey City and outpacing 4-8-2's
on intercity expresses between Montreal
and Toronto.

The moral is plain: commitment. Until General Motors, the diesel lacked a
totally committed sponsor. Until GM, the
diesel suffered from being dependent upon
suppliers and railroads with divided loyalties. GM alone was an outsider, free of
any investment in the factories and forges
and patents of steam or elecric power. GM
alone was young (1916), hence unen-
cumbered by tradition. GM alone was large
(of its automotive brethren, one may discount Chrysler as being not large enough
and Ford as entering a troubled period).
And GM alone was uninhibited, and already famous for its management structure, mechanical inventiveness, and promotional push. It is no coincidence that
the corporation which supplanted steam
simultaneously made Chevrolet No. 1.

*   *   *

It is reasonable even at a birthday
party to ask if the guest has been accorded an inappropriately large share of
the credit for railroad dieselization. Certainly the salesmen of Electro-Motive
would resent being called mere order takers. A review of the market evidence
would give Alco major credit for ridding
yards of 0-6-0's and 0-8-0's, pays homage
to GE for electrical gear, cites Fairbanks-
Morse for anticipating the high-horsepower
era, and otherwise concludes that La-
Grange never has enjoyed a monopoly on
imagination or inventiveness in the diesel
business.

Yet the question can be answered fairly
by asking other questions. Which firm
sold 7 out of each 10 of the diesels
that supplanted steam in America? What
other engine has equalled the 567 in power
increments, availability, and durability? If
a popularity poll of builders was conducted
among a cross section of chief mechanical
officers, locomotive engineers, train dis-
patchers, electricians, railroad presidents,
yardmasters, hostlers, security analysts,
and trainmasters, which builder would
win? What would be the state of the railroad art in 1972 if ground had not been
broken for a new factory in that farmland
along the Indiana Harbor Belt on the out-
skirts of LaGrange, Ill., on that blustery
March 27, 1935?

II

Competition in the locomotive business has been vigorous and productive.

General Motors locomotives have been
widely accepted by its railroad customers
and it currently accounts for about 75% of
the locomotives that are sold in the United
States. This does not mean, however, that
it had monopoly power in the locomotive
business. The nature of the product and the
market has thus far inevitably resulted in
a small number of producers, but at the
same time has resulted in extraordinary
pressures for continual product improvement.

The General Electric Company is a
strong existing competitor which is entirely
capable of capturing the lion's share of
the business if, for any reason, General
Motors' product ceases to be as attractive to
customers as it has been in the past. In addition, there are a number of substantial
companies, both domestic and foreign,
standing in the wings as potential entrants.
Finally, in the field of mass passenger transportation entirely new approaches and technologies are continually being explored, by
General Motors and by others, which may
have a dramatic impact on market conditions.

A. The Number of Competitors and the Nature of the Product

There is of course no particular magic number of sellers which is right for every product. The number to be expected depends
upon the level of demand and the nature of
the production process. In the case of locomotives domestic sales have been small in
recent years—averaging about 1200 units a
year. Moreover, locomotives are very large
complex products requiring substantial engineering skill and modern manufacturing
facilities. It is clear that, because of the
economies of standardized production, a
large number of U.S. producers would not
be expected.

For over half of a century two or three producers have always accounted for the vast bulk of all U.S. locomotive sales. This was true before General Motors had even thought of entering the locomotive market, when General Motors was in the process of entering the market, and during the period when General Motors was the largest locomotive supplier.

Thus, there never have been more than a small number of U.S. producers. However, such small numbers do not indicate that the largest supplier (currently General Motors) can in any way control the total supply—the prime requirement for the existence of monopoly.

General Motors is now opposed by the General Electric Company, a substantial business by any test.[13] General Electric produced its first diesel in 1961 and now has approximately one quarter of the business. General Motors' current share of sales is about the same as it was in 1955 when there were three other domestic suppliers.[14] These three companies have since withdrawn, but General Electric has demonstrated that it is entirely capable of expanding its business to make up the difference and it is unquestionably capable of expanding still further to supply the whole market if customer preferences dictate.

Moreover, the nature of the locomotive product is such that General Motors would feel substantial competitive pressure even if it were currently the only surviving domestic producer. In the first place, diesel electric locomotives are extremely durable capital goods. They are only bought in order to earn money for the purchasing railroad. Since railroads have not recently been a growth industry, almost all recent locomotive purchases have been for replacement purposes.

At the same time, however, locomotives are repairable—they can be maintained or rebuilt for extended periods of time. This means that a railroad rarely *must* purchase locomotives in any quantity, except to meet a growth in traffic. It can continue to use the locomotives already on hand until finally the point is reached where maintenance costs become prohibitive.

As a result, in order to make appreciable sales, the locomotive manufacturer must continually offer a better and better product for the money. Therefore, the manufacturer is competing as much against the existing stock of locomotives in use by railroads as against other locomotive manufacturers. In other words, a better product than your competitors' will avail you little unless that product is appreciably better than the locomotives already in use, including your own previous models.

In addition, U.S. locomotive producers compete for sales not only domestically but throughout the free world. Their success in making export sales is substantial, and this success indicates the basic healthiness of the U.S. locomotive industry. While foreign producers have not achieved any volume of sales in this country, sales are solicited and some have been made.[15] The relative failure here of foreign locomotive suppliers is due to the outstanding performance of the domestic producers (discussed previously), not because opportunities are closed.

Finally, the real possibilities of entirely new entry act as a continuing competitive discipline in the locomotive business. Patents are of no importance in the production

---

[13] Even if General Motors currently had all the business, it would not mean it had unlawfully monopolized. In *United States* v. *Grinnell Corp.*, 384 U.S. 563, 570–71 (1966), the Supreme Court stated that even "monopoly power" is not unlawful if it arose from "growth or development as a consequence of a superior product, business acumen, or historic accident." And Judge Learned Hand stated in *United States* v. *Aluminum Co. of America*, 148 F.2d 416, 430 (2d Cir. 1945): "The successful competitor, having been urged to compete, must not be turned upon when he wins."

[14] Alco, Baldwin and Fairbanks, Morse.

[15] Krauss-Maffei sold 21 diesel-hydraulic locomotives to the Southern Pacific and the Denver & Rio Grande during the 1960's.

of diesel electric locomotives and there are no limitations due to scarce resources. The necessary components are readily available to prospective entrants. For example, all items of electrical equipment (e.g., generators, traction motors and control apparatus) have been staple articles of commerce, sold to all comers, since at least the 1920's. In addition, engines and engine designs suitable for use in locomotives are available, as General Electric found when it wished to enter the market. Products of General Motors divisions supplying its locomotive manufacturing operation, Electro-Motive Division (EMD), such as bearings, gears, radiators, oil coolers, etc., are available, and in many instances have been regularly supplied to competing locomotive manufacturers.

Of significance from the standpoint of both entry and exit is the relatively unspecialized nature of much of the plant and machinery required for locomotive production. This means that the tangible capital required can be shifted out of locomotive production with relatively little loss, viz., Fairbanks, Morse, which continued in the same facilities to make diesel engines, generating sets and oil-field drilling equipment. And it means that any sizable manufacturing concern in the heavy equipment field can enter locomotive production with relative ease, viz., General Electric and Fairbanks, Morse.

Conclusive evidence as to the relative freedom of entry and exit is provided by the fact that both have occurred as economic conditions warranted. At the end of World War II there was a large pent-up general demand for locomotives of any sort, and a specific demand for diesel electric motive power to replace steam. In response to this demand, Fairbanks, Morse began producing diesel electric locomotives, Lima commenced building diesel electric switchers, and Baldwin increased the range of its offerings to include diesel electrics other than switchers.

As these unusual conditions disappeared, U.S. railroad locomotive orders de-

clined sharply from their peak of more than 3,500 units a year in 1950 and 1951 to less than 300 units a year in 1960 and 1961. In response to this drastic decline, Lima, Baldwin, and Fairbanks, Morse went out of the business—Lima by merger (with Baldwin) and the other two by conversion to other products.

At this point, expecting a rebound in demand to a level of approximately 1000 locomotives per year in the near future, General Electric entered as a supplier of diesel electrics for U.S. railroads. General Electric's expectations have been fulfilled —U.S. railroad orders for locomotives actually averaged approximately 1000 units a year for the 1962–1965 period and have averaged slightly over 1200 units per year since that time.

B. The Intensity of Rivalry and Its Effect on Performance

U.S. locomotive producers are now engaged in intense and active rivalry, although this was not always the case. During the steam era there was a well-known continuing series of relationships between particular railroads and locomotive suppliers. Railroads rarely changed locomotive suppliers —everyone apparently preferring the easy life to the competitive struggle.

With General Motors' entry as a substantial supplier, the traditional accounts went out the window. Other producers were forced to start competing, and the railroads learned that this competition was to their benefit. There are no longer any safe or traditional accounts. For example, although General Electric did not even enter the domestic diesel locomotive business until 1961, by the end of 1964 it was able to announce in its Annual Report that: "In the U.S. 18 major railroads are now operating General Electric high-horsepower mainline locomotives."

More important is the form this rivalry takes. In the days prior to General Motors' entry, the rivalry of producers was largely in attempting to utilize technical developments of the particular buying railroad. There were few meaningful improvements in the product or in its method of manufacture for a quarter of a century or more. Whether or not the locomotive producers were really trying, the market was stagnant.

In this context, General Motors' entry into the market resulted in a major change in emphasis. Technological changes in the product have been rapid—first the change from steam to diesel and then the rapid developments which increased the size and productivity of the diesel electrics.

This independent rivalry is well illustrated by the nature and timing of new features introduced by the locomotive producers. Size of the locomotive, for example, is of critical importance. A single large unit can haul freight faster and more cheaply than can two smaller units of the same aggregate horsepower, whether operated separately or as a single combined unit. Immediately after the war the largest single-engine diesels available were 1500 h.p. units. General Electric was the first to produce a successful 2500 h.p. unit in 1961; General Motors moved up to 2250 h.p. in 1962 and first reached a comparable 2500 h.p. unit in 1963. General Motors, on the other hand, was the first to offer locomotives capable of 3000 h.p. and 3600 h.p., only to see General Electric later expand into this range.[16]

Performance in the area of capacity has been matched by performance in the area of prices. During General Motors' early locomotive development period (through 1940) the savings it achieved as it reached higher volumes of production enabled it to make successive price reductions. Even in the early postwar period General Motors' diesel locomotives were selling at prices which had not increased substantially above those initially established in the 1930's. This

remarkable price performance was achieved despite a general increase in wholesale prices of more than 100% and in machinery prices of more than 50% (from 1939 to 1948), and despite an increase of more than 100% in EMD wage rates during the same period —from an average base rate of 75¢ per hour to $1.54 per hour.

Since the early postwar period, as everyone knows, there have also been substantial inflationary pressures. Starting in 1948, the general level of prices for machinery and motive products (BLS Wholesale Price Index) has increased more than 100%. During this same period, prices for diesel electric locomotives appear to have increased by approximately 60% for units of comparable horsepower (without taking into account technical improvement). If we were to take into account the relatively greater technical improvements, this contrast in price movements would be even greater.

The combined effect of progress in capacity and in pricing can be simply demonstrated. The 1500 h.p. GP-7 was brought out by General Motors in 1949 at $146,200 or $97.47 per horsepower. (Price per horsepower is a standard railroad measurement of value.) General Motors' current general purpose locomotive is the 3000 h.p. GP-40-2, selling at $243,000 or $81.00 per horsepower. Thus locomotives are now available to the railroads at a 16% lower cost per horsepower than in 1949. This remarkable result, after more than 20 years of continuously rising prices, is a demonstration of the effectiveness of competition.

This progress can be further dramatized by another comparison. In 1951, the highest unit production year in EMD history, 3,500,-000 horsepower was produced in 2400 locomotives. In 1966, only fifteen years later, the same 3,500,000 horsepower was produced for the railroads but with only half, or 1200 locomotives. It cost the railroads $80,000,000 less for this horsepower in 1966 than in 1951. At the same time, the railroads have been saving some 20 million dollars a year in reduced maintenance because of improvements in the engine and compo-

---

[16] Baldwin had a 3000 h.p. unit (Centipede) right after the war and Fairbanks, Morse a 2400 h.p. unit (Trainmaster) in 1950–1953, but the Centipede was a total failure and the Trainmasters were generally unsatisfactory to the railroads.

nents and, of course, reduction in locomotive units.

It is sometimes said that "concentrated" industries are non-competitive and cost the American consumer billions of dollars a year in excess prices. The record of the locomotive industry indicates, to the contrary, that outstanding performance for the consumer can occur in an industry with a small number of competitors.

C. New Developments in the Field of Passenger Transportation May Have an Impact on Competition in the Locomotive Business

The depressed conditions of railroad passenger systems have increasingly become a matter of popular concern and recently some critics have attempted to pin the blame on General Motors. They have suggested that General Motors has deliberately held back the development of superior and cheaper locomotives in order to benefit its automotive operations.

This criticism is, first of all, based on a profound misconception of the problem. It is true that rail passenger service is depressed, but the reasons have nothing to do with General Motors or its locomotives. A simple illustration should illustrate this point. According to the *Railroad Facts* yearbook, revenue ton miles of freight carried increased from 655 billion in 1947, right after the war, to 765 billion in 1970. During the same period of time revenue passenger miles decreased from 46 billion to 11 billion. Since freight locomotives and passenger locomotives are essentially similar, it is obvious that the precipitous decline in the volume of passenger traffic must be attributable to causes other than the locomotive. In fact, since the cost of locomotives is typically less than 10% of the cost of a railroad system as a whole, General Motors could give its locomotives away without having any appreciable impact on the volume of rail passengers carried.

It is necessary to recognize, then, that there is very little General Motors or any other locomotive manufacturer alone can do to reverse the trend away from passenger travel by rail.[17] At the same time, however, General Motors has repeatedly, if not always successfully, exerted its best efforts and spent its own money to develop more appealing modes of rail transportation.

Back in 1934 the experimental Burlington "Zephyr" initiated the era of streamline passenger trains. As we have seen, in the late 1930's the superiority of diesel power over steam was dramatically demonstrated in the competition between the Seaboard and the Atlantic Coast Line for the then lucrative Florida traffic. In 1945 General Motors pioneered in the development of "Astro-Dome" passenger cars. All of these cars were built to the General Motors design by outside companies and remained in service for more than 20 years. In 1955 and 1956 General Motors developed and extensively promoted the "Aerotrain", a lightweight passenger train. Despite its dramatic improvements in costs, comfort and convenience, however, this train was unable to stem the tide running against passenger service and only two complete trains were ever built.

General Motors has been experimenting with gas turbine engines for over 25 years. It is currently working on the development of electric locomotives and dual-powered rail cars (both gas turbine and external electric). We do not know today how successful these experiments will be, but significant efforts are being made. The Electro-Motive Division today has a staff of 35 engineers continually engaged in efforts to develop improved transportation systems.

Equally significant is the fact that other companies have also been continually engaged in research and development in this area. A recent issue of *Railway Age,* for example, features an article on a mass trans-

---

[17] To a considerable degree, of course, the declining popularity of rail transportation is attributable to the increasing availability, lower cost and attractiveness of air transportation for long runs and of personal transportation by automobile for short runs.

portation vehicle being developed by the Boeing Vertol Co. The same issue reports on developments by other domestic companies not now in the business such as Rohr, Budd, Pullman-Standard and by companies in France, Canada and Great Britain.

The ultimate outcome of these developments is still uncertain, but they demonstrate conclusively that competition is alive and vigorous. Perhaps out of this work will come another development as revolutionary as the diesel was over steam.

28. The Market Share Paradox

BRUCE D. HENDERSON AND STAFF

Market share is very valuable. It leads to lower relative cost and, therefore, higher profits. Unfortunately most efforts to improve market share depress profits, at least short term.

There are two principal reasons for a shift in market share between competitors. The most common is lack of capacity. The other reason is a willingness to lose share to maintain price.

Lack of capacity is a common occurrence. It must be. It is expensive to maintain unused capacity for very long. Even in the face of projected *industry* growth, it is not surprising that not all *individual* producers feel they can justify the incremental investment in added capacity. On the other hand, nothing is more obvious than the fact that your capacity limits your market share. If the market grows and your capacity does not, then whoever has the capacity takes the growth, and increases their share of the market—at your expense.

The decision to add capacity is a fateful one. Add too soon, and extra costs are incurred with no benefits. Add too late, and market share is lost. Added capacity means more than bricks and machines. It also means capable personnel in the proper proportions in the proper place. The lead time required is long. The decision must anticipate the need.

The competitive implications of all this are made more complex by the cost differentials among competitors. Simple arithmetic shows that the high cost producer must add capacity in direct proportion to the low cost firm, if relative market shares are to remain constant. But the high cost producer's return on the capacity investment is lower than that of the more efficient firm, because of the differential in profit margins.

The market share paradox is that, if the low cost firm would accept the high cost producer's return on assets, the low cost firm would preempt all market growth. And the resulting increase in his accumulated experience would further improve his costs and steadily increase the cost *differential* between the competitors thereafter. In short, *if the same investment criteria were used by all firms, then the low cost firm would always expand capacity first and other firms never would.*

All firms do *not* use the same investment criteria. The fact that market share is stable proves this. However, this also means that shares are unstable if there is vigorous competition.

The low cost producer can take market share, but only if he is willing to sacrifice near term profit. The high cost producer can obtain a significant return only because he is allowed to do so in order to maintain current prices.

The tradeoff is inviting. Since the low cost firm typically has the largest market share, his higher return expectations often lead him to sacrifice share to maintain near term margins. The loss of a modest amount of the market may seem far less costly short term than meeting a price concession of a minor competitor, or spreading the price reduction necessary to fill proposed new capacity over his entire sales volume.

Unfortunately, the tradeoff is cumulative. More and more share must be given up over time to maintain price. Costs are a function of market share because of the experience effect. Lost market share leads to loss of cost advantage. Eventually there is no way to maintain profitability.

The rate of growth is the critical variable in resolving the market share paradox and the tradeoff between share and near term profits.

— Without growth, it is virtually impossible to shift market share. No one can justify adding capacity. Neither can anyone afford to lose share at the price of idle capacity. Under such constraints, since prices will tend to be very stable, the appropriate strategy is to maximize profits within existing market shares.

— With only very little growth, a higher near term profit now may be worth considerably more than continued modest profit. Those who should hold share into the no-growth period are only those with enough share—and the resulting cost position—to anticipate satisfactory profits.

29. Firms in a Declining Market: The Brewing Case *

ANN R. HOROWITZ AND IRA HOROWITZ

Introduction

For many of us beer consumption conjures up rather pleasant thoughts and memories. While those of us who enjoy an occasional bottle or draught of beer have not exactly become extinct, we have, nonetheless, become a comparatively stagnant group whose number has not changed significantly in several years. For the majority of the brewers, therefore, contemplating past beer consumption is a far more pleasant undertaking than contemplating either present consumption levels, or the future prospects of the brewing industry.

Since the end of World War II, production in the brewing industry has increased by less than 10 per cent while the U.S. population has increased by more than 25 per cent. The result has been a decline in *per capita* consumption, the latter hovering around the 15 gallons per year mark in recent years as opposed to the 17–18 gallons that was the benchmark in the late forties.[1] Even if we confine our attention to *per*

capita consumption of the 21–60 age group where one might suspect that beer consumption would be most prevalent, we find a reduction between 1947 and 1961 from 25.1 to 23.2 gallons, the latter figure an increase from the low of 22.4 gallons in 1957.

The purpose of this paper is (1) to determine and analyze the factors that have led to the decline in *per capita* beer consumption, and the relative constancy of total beer consumption, and (2) to analyze and explain the impact which the declining popularity of beer has had on the structure of the brewing industry. A brief discussion of recent trends in the brewing industry is followed by an econometric analysis of the demand for beer, and an econometric analysis of the structure of the industry. The implication of these analyses conclude the paper.

Recent Trends in the Brewing Industry

Beer has been brewed in America in one form or another since the seventeenth century.[2] In 1914, the last year before many

Reprinted by permission of Basil Blackwell Publisher from "Firms in a Declining Market: The Brewing Case," in *Journal of Industrial Economics,* Volume 13:2 March 1965 (excerpt).

* Although discretion prevents us from commenting on when we first became interested in the brewing industry, it should be noted that portions of the paper are adopted from Mrs. Horowitz's M.A. thesis, *Economic Analysis of the Brewing Industry* (University of Kansas, 1960). We are grateful to the Indiana University Computing Center for making time available on the IBM 709, and to Mr. Ernie Wilhoit for computational and programming assistance.

[1] The data upon which this study is based were obtained from a variety of sources. Most of the data for individual firms came from such trade journals as *Modern Brewery Age, The Brewer's Digest, Brewer's Journal* and *Advertising Age.* Various issues of the *Brewer's Almanac* (New York: U.S. Brewers' Foundation) provided industry-wide data such as *per capita* consumption, total consumption, production and so forth. The U.S. Department of Commerce's *Business Statistics: 1961 Biennial Edition* (Washington, D.C.: Government Printing Office, 1961) provided additional cost data for costs other than labor costs. Because the data came from a variety of sources, and because we attempted to present the most recent figures available at the time of writing, the dates used in the descriptive portion of the paper vary to correspond to the available data. It should also be noted that we use the terms beer and malt beverages interchangeably.

[2] For a detailed history of the industry see Stanley

states adopted prohibition, there was a total of 1392 breweries in the United States. The majority of these breweries never did return to operations once the ban on beer had been lifted in 1933. There were only 331 breweries registered with Internal Revenue in June 1933, and while the figure rose to 756 by June 1934, brewing was never again to become as widespread as it had been prior to prohibition. Indeed, the brewing industry has never caught its second wind and has been in the throes of a decade-and-a-half long slump since the end of World War II. By 1947, the number of breweries was reduced to 485 and declined still further to 230 in 1961.

This post-war decline has occurred in states throughout the country. In 1947, the three states housing the majority of the breweries, Pennsylvania, Wisconsin and New York, had 62, 61 and 43 breweries, respectively; in 1961, these numbers had dropped to 26, 35 and 17. There were 38 states in which at least one brewery was located in 1947, while in 1961 breweries were located in only 32 of the Continental United States. Of these 32 states, 8 had 10 or more breweries, 7 had 6 to 8 breweries and 18 had 5 or less.

In 1962 there were 26 breweries producing over 1,000,000 barrels a year as opposed to only 14 in the 'over a million' club in 1947, with very few producing less than 10,000 barrels. When this fact is considered in conjunction with the earlier remarks on the fixed level of total consumption, it becomes quite obvious that the decline in the number of breweries has taken its greatest toll on the smaller breweries. The reasons for this will be discussed later in the paper.

The reduction in the total number of firms has also been accompanied by a shift in the companies occupying the top places in the industry. Only 8 of the top 15 companies in 1947 were still among the top 15 in 1961.[3] The newcomers were the so-called

'regional' brewers whose rapid rise can be dated from 1953. As opposed to the 'national' brewers who sell in nearly every state from a single, centrally located brewery with sales averaging between 3 and 6 million barrels a year, the regional brewers usually sold in a market consisting of 2 to 6 states, and often operated from a chain of small breweries strategically located to cut transportation costs. Prior to 1953, the latter would have sales of between 1.5 and 3 million barrels a year. A third classification would be the 'local' brewers who were confined to 1 plant serving a single metropolitan area, or, at most, a single state, with sales of 100,000 to 1,000,000 barrels. In addition to the difference in the scope of the marketing areas, the national beers would command a premium price. This price differential in favor of premium beers originally reflected the additional shipping cost of the nationally marketed beers, but as brand names became established, certain beers were able to maintain a price differential over the regional and local beers regardless of transportation costs.[4]

The rise of the regionals after 1953 can be traced to a prolonged strike in that year against the brewers in Milwaukee where the majority of the nationals are located. This strike resulted in higher wages and a subsequent increase in the price of the premium beers, which gave the regionals the opportunity to surge ahead.[5]

Baron, *Brewed in America* (Boston: Little, Brown and Company, 1962).

[3] The most striking example of a rapid rise by a newcomer to this select group is the Carling

Brewing Company which was 62nd in sales in 1949, the earliest year for which data are available, but 5th in 1961. The other newcomers are Theo. Hamm, Lucky Lager, Stroh, C. Schmidt, Adolph Coors, and Drewerys' Ltd.

[4] Of 113,305 comparisons made in 1953 and 1954 between Budweiser and all other regional or local beers selling in 78 major markets, 100,392 or 88.6 per cent, showed a 5 cent price differential on a 12 ounce bottle or can in favor of Budweiser. Over local beers only, Budweiser showed a 10 cent differential in 93.2 per cent of the comparisons (U.S. Federal Trade Commission, *In the Matter of Anheuser-Busch, Inc., Docket No. 6331: Initial Decision*, Oct. 23rd, 1956, p. 5).

[5] Today, regionals such as Carling, Hamm, Falstaff, and Stroh are marketed in the majority of the

With this increase in competition, both prospective and realized, the nationals took two steps to protect their positions. First of all, they began to decentralize their operations in order to cut their transportation costs to the level maintained by the regionals. Secondly, in an effort to protect their sales volume, Anheuser-Busch, Schlitz, and Pabst, the 'big three' of the nationals, each introduced a low price beer.[6]

The extent of the decentralization movement is seen by the fact that in 1955 the top 10 brewers operated only 10 plants in 7 states, while by 1961 the leading 10 companies operated 40 plants in 16 states.[7] Of the 4 companies marketing beer nationally, only Miller still operates from a single location.[8] Much of this decentralization has taken place by means of acquisitions or mergers. This eliminates the long delays involved when a company constructs its own brewery. Furthermore, the company acquires the brands of a competitor when it buys a brewery.[9] Still further, many of the larger brewers have diversified so as not to be entirely dependent upon their beer sales.[10]

states and have succeeded in pushing some of the former leaders aside in the top sales rankings. For example, in 1952 Falstaff was the only one of these 4 companies among the top 10 sellers of beer. By 1961, Falstaff was 4th in sales, Carling 5th and Hamm 7th, while Stroh, though not in the top 10, was 13th. Anheuser-Busch and Schlitz still led in sales along with Pabst. Ballantine, Schaefer, and Liebmann, all marketing primarily in the New York area suffered the brunt of the assault.

[6] Anheuser-Busch's first try in this line was a complete failure, apparently because the new beer, Busch Lager, was tied to the premium brand, Budweiser. In 1955 they introduced Busch Bavarian (essentially Busch Lager with a new name) with its own advertising campaign, delivery trucks, salesmen, etc. This low price beer enjoyed a rapid expansion. Between 1957 and 1958 it more than doubled its sales from 317,000 to 649,000 barrels and was selling slightly over 1,000,000 barrels in 15 states by 1959 ('Anheuser-Busch President Tells Holders Salary for First Time', *Wall Street Journal* (April 15th, 1960), p. 18).

With the additional competition stemming from the introduction of Busch Bavarian, Pabst and Schlitz were pressed to introduce a popular price brand. Each chose to expand the market of an established brand that had been selling in limited markets for several years. In 1956 Pabst broadened its distribution of Eastside Old Tap Lager, a beer popular in the Los Angeles area for 50 years. Schlitz, in turn, revived its Old Milwaukee brand which had been a big seller between 1934 and 1942. Neither had a very favorable reception. In fact, one of the reasons for Pabst's merger with the Blatz Brewing Company in 1958 was to add an already popular low price beer to its product line. Subsequently, Pabst changed the formula for its premium beer and reduced its price to the level of the low price brands.

Pabst also was one of the first nationals to begin operating from several locations. In 1948 it purchased the Los Angeles Brewing Company to become the first big brewer to move into the

California market area. California has since proved to be the choice of many brewers deciding to build or purchase additional breweries both because of the large and growing population of California and the West, and the savings on transportation that would be realized on shipments to this heretofore remote area. Among the companies eventually moving to the West were Anheuser-Busch, Schlitz, Liebmann, Falstaff, Hamm, and Goebel. Moves were made into the East by Anheuser-Busch, Schlitz, Hamm, Carling, and others.

[7] Pabst is prevented from operating the Blatz plant in Milwaukee pending the outcome of antitrust litigation growing out of a merger between these firms.

[8] Miller does own the Gettelman Brewery in Milwaukee, but markets this beer under separate label. In fact, beginning in 1960 Miller attempted to turn the fact that it produces beer under only one roof to its advantage, by stressing this fact in its advertising campaigns.

[9] As was almost predestined, the Federal Trade Commission and the Justice Department have become concerned over some of these mergers. Anheuser-Busch was ordered to dispose of its Regal holdings in Florida; Pabst is in the midst of a court battle in Wisconsin in an effort to retain its Blatz holdings; and Lucky Lager was ordered to dispose of the Fisher Brewing Co. of Utah.

[10] Pabst went into the soft beverage business in 1946 after it purchased the Hoffman Beverage Company. Moody's Industrials has listed some 16 products that are produced by Anheuser-Busch in addition to the customary by-products of the brewing process. These range from liquid

One important reason for the decentralization trend is that the brewers have been caught in a price-cost squeeze. The increased competition resulting from the inroads made by the regionals in marketing their low price beers occurred during a period of rapidly rising costs. Hence, brewers found themselves in a position of being in an industry with relatively constant total sales and increased competition from the top companies. This has prevented the brewers from raising prices in the face of higher costs for labor, bottles, cans, certain raw materials, freight, taxes, packaging, advertisement and management.

Between 1947 and 1960 production workers' wages, which currently account for about 25 per cent of the total cost of goods sold, rose slightly more than 2.7 per cent annually, or a total of 41.2 per cent. Between 1948 and 1961 average hourly earnings increased at an even greater rate, 5.6 per cent per year, or a total of 103.5 per cent. The increase in labour costs has been greater than in most other manufacturing industries. During the same period average hourly earnings in all food and all manufacturing industries were rising at annual rates of 5.0 and 4.4 per cent, respectively. The result is that the average hourly wage in brewing is 45.4 per cent higher than in all food, and 36.6 per cent higher than in all manufacturing industries.

In addition, the cost of metal containers increased 66.9 per cent between 1947 and 1957. Sugar, an important ingredient, increased in price by 14.5 per cent between 1948 and 1960. The price of grains used in brewing has fluctuated sharply over the years, but has been falling for most grains since 1948. Of the principal grains used in brewing, by 1960 barley was down 42 per cent, corn down 44 per cent, rye down 45 per cent and rice down 32 per cent.

Transportation costs have always been a problem to the industry because beer is a heavy, bulky commodity relative to its value. In addition, there has been the cost of returning empty bottles and barrels. The introduction of canned beer after Repeal eliminated this latter problem and was successful in reducing shipping costs because of the lighter weight and compactness of cans. Shipping costs average 40 per cent less for cans than for returnable bottles, including the costs of returning empties. However, the cost of beer in returnable bottles has remained lower than that of beer in cans because the bottles are used an average of twenty times instead of just once. In 1960, a case of 24 cans cost 99 cents while the same number of returnable bottles, due to frequent re-use, cost only 16 cents.[11]

Already plagued with the problems and expenses of shipping a heavy, bulky commodity, the brewers watched freight rates soar by 18 per cent between 1950 and 1957. The cost of shipping by intercity motor carriers also has risen sharply, by 27.6 per cent between 1950 and 1956.

The combination of federal and state taxes also has placed a heavy burden on the brewers. In many states the tax on beer increases its price by more than 100 per cent. These taxes have been steadily rising since Repeal with the Federal rate alone increasing 80 per cent since 1933. The many regulations imposed on the industry have a heavy impact on brewing costs because they require the brewers to maintain expensive legal and clerical facilities.

The growing need for large expenditures on merchandising and advertising in order for a firm to be successful also has an effect on costs. With the growth of the supermarkets the brewers have found it necessary to incur the additional expense of employing the services of designers so

sweetner to frozen and dried eggs and refrigerated cabinets. The entrance into other fields makes these brewers less susceptible to fluctuations in their beer sales than their non-diversified competitors.

[11] John J. Abele, 'Small No-Deposit Bottle for Beer Sparks Drive to Supplant Cans', *New York Times* (June 26th, 1960), p. 2F.

that they are insured of eye-catching packaging.

The squeeze exerted on the breweries by all of these rising costs while the price of the final product has remained relatively stable is indicated by the returns on net worth in brewing as compared to the returns in other manufacturing industries. In 1958, among 41 leading manufacturing industries, brewing ranks 36th with average net earnings of approximately 8 per cent of net assets and 3.25 per cent of net sales. This is substantially less than the average for all manufacturing which was 13 per cent of net assets and 6 per cent of net sales in 1958.

These facts do not make the industry of any less interest to the economist. Indeed, the industry presents an interesting picture of simultaneous stagnation and flux.

The Structure of the Brewing Industry

It has already been mentioned that one of the most interesting aspects in the postwar history of the brewing industry has been the rise to national prominence of what were heretofore strictly regional brewers. This has been accomplished through merger and plant acquisition, as well as through the construction of new plants to effect location, and the subsequent transportation, economies. We will now discuss the extent to which regional production patterns have changed over time, and at the same time draw some inferences regarding the minimum efficient size of plant in the industry.

In 1948 there were 38 states in which beer was brewed; by 1961 this figure was reduced to 32 states. One would expect that total beer production within a state would in some manner be dependent upon the number of breweries within the state. The relationship might not necessarily be linear, but it should, nonetheless, be present. Similarly, if transportation economies are to be effected, statewide production should be sensitive to changes in total consumption within the state. The extent to which

the latter two factors play a role in influencing production within a state will in part be dependent upon whether or not one of the so-called national brewers is located within the state. Inasmuch as they are satisfying the demands of a broader segment of the population, the national brewers should maintain higher production levels, and the states in which national brewers are located should account for greater production than other states to reflect this.

These hypotheses are summarized in the equation

$$O_{it} = D + d_1 B_{it} + d_2 C_{it} + d_3 N_{it} \quad (6)$$

where O_{it} represents production of beer in the ith state in year t, B_{it} represents the number of breweries in the ith state in year t, C_{it} represents total beer consumption in the ith state in year t, and N_{it} is a dummy variable which takes on the value of 1 or 0 depending upon whether there is, or is not, a national brewer located in the state in question. In order to illustrate the impact of the spread of the regional brewers into national markets, the dummy variable was assigned to only three states: Missouri, New Jersey and Wisconsin. This is consistent with the way in which the national brewers were distinguished prior to 1953. The results of performing this cross-section regression for the years 1948 through 1961 are shown in Table I.[12] States which had no breweries were omitted from the regression, and this accounts for the varying value of N, the number of observations. The value of R^2 for each of the regressions is in the neighborhood of .92 except for the regressions prior to 1952 when the R^2's are a bit higher. Of greater import is the fact that each of the regression coefficients is much greater than twice its standard error.

The return of the industry to regional production as opposed to centralized production is revealed quite well by the be-

---

[12] These regressions were also run with the variables in logarithms. This had the effect of reducing the R^2 values, but the statistical significance of the independent variables was unaltered.

Table I • Least Squares Estimates of Equation (6)

	D	d_1	d_2	d_3	R^2	N	$D + d_1 + d_3$
1948	−350.2017	72.5141 (14.1800)	.7263 (.0874)	4293.3797 (475.2923)	.9571	38	4015.6921
1949	−222.0824	95.5715 (11.8883)	.5160 (.0702)	5255.0535 (375.1015)	.9711	38	5128.5425
1950	−318.1174	86.8307 (17.6943)	.6225 (.0993)	5607.2623 (547.6604)	.9410	38	5375.9756
1951	−336.0848	111.4878 (21.8848)	.5249 (.1140)	5823.6736 (603.4057)	.9308	37	5599.0766
1952	−384.8088	109.9814 (24.3550)	.5735 (.1132)	6412.1260 (668.8658)	.9223	37	6137.2987
1953	−338.3274	90.3486 (24.5731)	.6772 (.1056)	6028.3040 (654.9488)	.9244	37	5780.3252
1954	−314.0678	90.6465 (24.8981)	.7703 (.1031)	5424.3788 (628.4226)	.9303	37	5200.9575
1955	−269.9698	115.7881 (28.0804)	.6675 (.1039)	4516.4877 (649.8700)	.9232	36	4362.3060
1956	−301.5396	107.6544 (30.8628)	.7298 (.1114)	4566.8604 (714.0804)	.9148	33	4372.9752
1957	−371.8106	135.5957 (31.8920)	.6905 (.1072)	4535.2757 (657.0898)	.9289	32	4299.0608
1958	−274.0173	152.1169 (32.0136)	.6024 (.1052)	4666.6470 (683.9353)	.9200	32	4534.7466
1959	−225.3562	112.7497 (32.2530)	.7131 (.0998)	4940.9930 (654.7437)	.9265	32	4828.2865
1960	−178.8778	110.2388 (39.5254)	.7299 (.1131)	5299.0573 (716.1261)	.9095	32	5230.4183
1961	−123.6718	110.3669 (34.5435)	.7032 (.0963)	5141.0695 (628.1187)	.9258	32	5127.7646

havior of d_2. The drop in the value of the d_2 estimate following the initial value of .73 in 1948 to a value of .52 in 1951 is indicative of a less sensitive response of local production to local consumption.[13] This coincides with the period when the national brewers were obtaining an increasing share of the market. As the trend towards merger and plant construction and acquisition begins, the d_2 coefficient begins to rise once more settling in the neighborhood of .70. The sole exception to this after 1952 is in 1958 when d_2 drops to .60. The reason for the fall in the 'response' coefficient is not readily apparent, although there was a brief shutdown in production in the

New York–New Jersey area during the summer because of a labor dispute. The varying trend in regional production is also revealed when one adds the D, d_1 and d_3 coefficients. The sum of these coefficients represents a base production in the states containing the national brewers, since N_{it} has a value of 1, and B_{it} is at least 1 in every case. This sum rises steadily from 1948 until 1952, after which it begins a downward trend which does not reverse itself until 1958. These cross-section results imply, then, a strengthening in the position of the national brewers until the early fifties, following which the growing regional producers attain increasing importance in the industry, with the nationals beginning on the comeback road at the beginning of the sixties.

It should also be noted that the value of the sum of D and d_1 represents the base production in those states which do not contain national brewers. The negative sign of the D's is not as troublesome as might first

---

[13] Dividing the nation into several broad regions such as New England, Southwest and so forth, it was thought that regional consumption might also influence state output. This was not the case. We suspect that the inherent difficulty here is that there is no simple and uniform way in which regional boundaries can be defined so as to reflect the potential influence of this factor.

appear to be the case since (1) the value of B_{it} cannot be less than 1 and (2) the value of C_{it} never actually falls below 250 in the states in which breweries are located. The fact that the sum of D and d_1 is also increasing (that is, becoming less negative) is a further reflection of the growing importance of local production.

The significance of the behavior of d_1 in these regressions should not be overlooked. With the exception of 1958, the strike year, d_1 consistently takes on a value within two standard errors of about 100; moreover, there are only three years when d_1 is farther than one standard error from 100. This coefficient provides information about the average decline in production that would result in the ith state with the removal of a single brewery in the state. Thus the value of the coefficient represents the average gain or loss in production resulting from the introduction or departure of the 'last' firm to join the industry, or the 'first' firm to depart from it. Presumably, this will be the marginal firm. Since d_1 regularly takes on the value of 100, one can deduce from this that the marginal producer in the brewing industry would account for approximately 100 thousand barrels of beer a year. In support of this conclusion is the fact that in 1947, when the leading 50 brewers in the industry accounted for 58.3 per cent of total sales, the 51st firm in the industry produced 358 thousand barrels of beer. In 1962, the leading 50 brewers accounted for 88.8 per cent of total sales. In the latter year, however, the 51st firm in the industry produced but 116 thousand barrels. It is true that many of the firms that have disappeared from the industry were among the larger producers of beer.[14] It is also true, nonetheless, that it has been the smaller brewer who has borne the brunt of the assault of the growing firms and fixed market. Our results imply that

the marginal producer will brew about 100 thousand barrels a year, and there is within these results the suggestion that 100 thousand barrels a year would be the minimum efficient size of a firm in the brewing industry.[15]

Table II presents concentration ratios and Gini coefficients for the leading 50 firms in the brewing industry for the years from 1947 to 1962 inclusive.[16] Ten coefficients are presented for each year giving the two concentration measures for the leading 50 firms taken in successive groups the addition of 5 firms at a time: that is, the two measures are calculated for the leading 5 firms, the leading 10 firms, the leading 15 firms and so forth. The concentration ratios necessarily increase as the number of included firms increases since the numerator increases with the denominator remaining fixed. Further, while there is no actual case in which the Gini coefficient falls as the number of firms increases, an increase in the Gini coefficient is not mandatory with the inclusion of successively smaller elements. It can be shown, however, that as the number of firms increases, there will be a tendency for the value of the Gini coefficient to increase.[17]

---

[14] As previously noted, this has occurred through both merger and acquisition. Thus Blatz and Piel Brothers, both among the leading 20 companies in the industry in 1957, were taken over by Pabst and Drewerys' respectively; however, their products are still on the market.

[15] The same conclusion on minimum efficient size or firm was reached in a *Business Week* article, 'New Ideas Shake up the Brewing Industry' (March 9th, 1957), p. 90.

[16] In certain years firms which undoubtedly belong in the top 50 do not appear because the data for these firms is not available, nor are estimates of their total sales.

[17] Where there are N and then $N+1$ firms included in the calculation of the Gini coefficient, where the ith firm's sales are denoted by x_i, the firms are listed in order of descending sales, and the arithmetic mean of their sales is given by U_1 and U'_1 for the Gini coefficient calculated for N firms and $N+1$ firms respectively, with the $N/1$ firm necessarily having smaller sales than any of the leading N firms, the ratio of the two Gini calculations will be given by

$$\frac{G'}{G}\left[\frac{\sum\limits_{i=1}^{N} i(N+1-i)(x_{i+1}-x_i)}{\sum\limits_{i=1}^{N-1} i(N-i)(x_{i+1}-x_i)}\frac{U_1}{U'_1}\right]\left(\frac{N}{N+1}\right)^2$$

Table II • Concentration Ratios and Gini Coefficients

Concentration Ratios

	1947	1948	1949	1950	1951	1952	1953	1954	1955	1956	1957	1958	1959	1960	1961	1962
1	19.03	21.42	22.94	23.35	25.05	26.59	25.37	24.88	24.97	25.48	26.04	28.47	31.50	32.63	33.32	35.40
2	28.22	30.79	32.30	35.07	37.18	38.04	38.11	38.33	40.46	41.62	42.19	45.18	49.94	51.40	52.87	54.97
3	34.11	37.07	39.08	41.89	44.71	45.74	46.38	47.15	50.06	51.41	52.28	54.98	60.56	62.28	64.18	66.80
4	39.24	42.53	45.26	47.13	50.25	51.44	52.95	53.88	56.09	57.22	59.17	61.64	68.34	69.90	71.96	74.44
5	43.34	46.84	49.65	51.44	54.61	55.74	57.91	59.09	61.02	62.03	64.68	66.66	73.75	75.25	77.46	79.74
6	47.01	50.59	53.17	55.26	58.40	59.47	62.22	63.46	65.00	66.14	69.28	70.83	78.42	80.03	81.90	83.67
7	50.33	54.12	56.57	58.66	61.79	62.60	65.83	66.75	67.78	68.83	73.13	73.28	81.84	83.30	84.51	85.77
8	53.34	57.27	59.80	61.67	64.47	65.31	68.82	69.11	69.15	70.32	75.88	74.94	84.13	85.34	86.08	87.17
9	56.05	60.10	62.64	64.25	66.63	67.31	71.29	70.75	69.95	71.23	77.88	75.98	85.41	86.65	87.12	88.10
10	58.28	62.79	65.15	66.41	68.15	68.75	73.15	71.56	70.51	71.92	79.06	76.71	86.30	87.63	87.92	88.79

Gini Coefficients

	1947	1948	1949	1950	1951	1952	1953	1954	1955	1956	1957	1958	1959	1960	1961	1962
1	.0757	.0857	.0963	.1196	.1293	.1431	.1555	.1223	.1139	.1239	.1377	.1172	.1254	.1160	.1020	.1081
2	.2164	.2467	.2542	.2214	.2346	.2700	.2342	.2050	.1653	.1564	.1663	.1817	.1910	.1949	.1806	.1958
3	.2822	.3018	.3014	.2974	.2980	.3167	.2855	.2607	.2368	.2340	.2362	.2601	.2670	.2693	.2601	.2681
4	.3040	.3202	.3098	.3385	.3406	.3527	.3153	.2984	.3019	.4064	.2912	.3177	.3152	.3225	.3172	.3300
5	.3262	.3412	.3380	.3647	.3712	.3834	.3457	.3299	.3419	.3489	.3285	.3603	.3605	.3689	.3652	.3803
6	.3394	.3559	.3638	.3806	.3911	.4038	.3655	.3542	.3733	.3778	.3546	.3908	.3898	.3963	.4007	.4222
7	.3487	.3629	.3759	.3923	.4051	.4218	.3845	.3827	.4090	.4154	.3802	.4334	.4215	.4304	.4455	.4718
8	.3566	.3702	.3823	.4026	.4234	.4374	.4037	.4145	.4565	.4600	.4098	.4739	.4567	.4689	.4896	.5152
9	.3644	.3777	.3901	.4147	.4430	.4587	.4229	.4518	.5009	.5021	.4404	.5130	.4961	.5066	.5293	.5539
10	.3774	.3826	.3992	.4287	.4676	.4834	.4457	.4869	.5393	.5379	.4757	.5479	.5317	.5397	.5629	.5868

The most notable aspect in the overall nature of the concentration ratios is that they increase fairly regularly over time regardless of the number of firms included in the calculation of the ratio. Thus, the leading 5 brewers increased their share of the market from 19.0 to 35.4 per cent between 1947 and 1962, the leading 10 brewers increased their share of the market from 28.2 to 55.0 per cent between 1947 and 1962, and so forth. The specific firms included in the calculation of the ratios are not necessarily the same, however, since shifts among the leaders (as well as the followers) were taking place during the 16 year period.[18] The trend towards increasing concentration within the industry as a whole is also revealed quite readily by the Gini coefficient calculated for the top 50 firms in the industry. The coefficient rises to .59 in 1962 from a level of .38 in 1947. Again, the only pronounced drop occurs in 1958.

Unlike the concentration ratios, however, for some groupings the Gini coefficients do not show a rising trend over the 1947 to 1962 period.[19] In fact, the behavior

---

Since $U_1 > U'_1$ and $\sum\limits_{i=1}^{N} i(N + 1 - i)(x_{i+1} - x_i)$
$$> \sum\limits_{i=1}^{N-1} i(N - i)(x_{i+1} - x_i)$$

the term in square brackets will necessarily be greater than 1. Therefore, the Gini coefficient for the expanded number of firms, G', will be greater than G whenever the $\left(\dfrac{N}{N + 1}\right)^2$ factor is relatively closer to 1 than the term in brackets. Since the deviation of this former term from 1 will be slight whenever N gets large, we can anticipate larger Gini coefficients for a greater number of included firms.

[18] Recall footnote 5.

[19] The Gini coefficient is simply a measure of dispersion somewhat akin to the standard deviation. Thus studying the trend of the Gini coefficient is not unlike comparing the ratio of standard deviations of market shares. Because not all data were available during the period, the latter approach was not possible. It is, however, the approach recently used by Michael Gort ('Analysis of Stability and Change in Market Shares', *Journal of Political Economy*, vol.

---

of these coefficients is in and of itself of the utmost interest. With respect to the leading 5 producers, the coefficient shows a mild increase over the period prior to dropping off towards the end of the period. Thus, since the values of the Gini coefficients are consistently close to zero, falling between .076 and .156, this means that the portion of the market controlled by the leading 5 producers has been distributed fairly equally among them, though less equally at the end of the period than at the beginning, and this has held true regardless of who the leading firms were. Furthermore, this quite equal distribution has been maintained even though the leading 5 firms were almost doubling their share of the total market. In partial contrast to this, the leading 10 firms in the industry show a less equal distribution of their larger market than is true of the top 5 firms, a result that should cause no great surprise. Nevertheless, the overall distribution of this market is maintained at a fairly constant level, which measured by the Gini coefficient, reveals a slightly more equal distribution by the end of the period than at the beginning. Once we pass beyond the leading 20 firms in the industry, the Gini coefficient no longer shows this tendency to remain stable over time; rather, it begins to increase and the increase becomes more pronounced as the number of included firms increases.

A most plausible interpretation of these results is realized when the time series of Gini coefficients and concentration ratios for each group of firms is correlated. With the concentration ratio as the independent variable, a negative correlation implies that an increase in the concentration ratio, or share of the market of the specific number of firms, results in a more equal distribution of that market among the firms; a zero correlation means that an increase in the

---

LXXI, no. 1 (Feb. 1963), pp. 52–63) and suggested by S. J. Prais ('The Statistical Conditions for a Change in Concentration', *Review of Economics and Statistics* vol. XL, no. 3 (Aug. 1958), pp. 268–72). While their approach might be somewhat more familiar, it was not possible to apply it in the present instance.

share of market controlled by that number of firms leaves the distribution of that market unaffected; and, a positive correlation means that as the share of the total market increases, the distribution of that market becomes less equally distributed among the firms accounting for that market.

Now, in an industry composed of many firms each of which is facing a perfectly elastic demand curve, an increase in total demand will, except for random deviations, be distributed in proportion to their original shares among these firms when each of the firms has constant and equal average costs; with some producers having cost advantages, these producers would obtain a larger share of the total increase in satisfied demand than would the remaining firms in the industry; and, when some firms in the industry are operating with cost disadvantages, the latter firms will account for a smaller portion of the increment in the increased total sales than will the remaining firms in the industry. While there are many firms in the brewing industry, the consumer does not have freedom of choice to purchase the product of any one of these firms. In addition, for many tastes, the products are not perfect substitutes. Within any given locality, however, the consumer does have his choice among several local and national beers. Furthermore, the fact that with few exceptions all of the brands within a particular class sell for the same price is indicative of the basic substitutability of the products, since the sellers are unwilling to invite the consequences of price increases that are not industry-wide. If, therefore, firms within the brewing industry have some degree of monopoly power, the extent to which this exists is likely to be quite limited, and we can assume that, within the relevant price range, the demand curves facing the individual firms are to some degree elastic, if not perfectly so. Thus the reactions of the brewing industry to a change in total demand should closely parallel those of the hypothetical industry discussed above.

It follows, therefore, that in an industry such as the brewing industry a positive cor-

relation coefficient between the Gini coefficient and concentration ratio implies that the bigger firms in the industry are operating at a point on their average cost curves so as to yield lower average costs than for the industry in general; a negative correlation coefficient implies that the bigger firms are operating at a point above this average; and, a zero correlation coefficient implies equal average costs. The 10 correlation coefficients between the Gini coefficients and the associated concentration ratios are presented in Table III.

Table III • **Simple Correlation Coefficients between the Gini Coefficients and Concentration Ratios**

No. of firms	V
5	.2159
10	−.5715
15	−.5969
20	.0035
25	.4747
30	.6763
35	.8399
40	.8688
45	.8550
50	.8427

The small, but positive correlation coefficient with respect to the leading 5 firms in the industry implies that the industry leaders have a slight cost advantage over the other firms comprising the top 5. The negative correlations for the top 10 and 15 firm concentration measures imply that the smaller producers among these top 10 and 15 benefit more, with respect to sales, than do the larger producers from an increase in the groups' market share. The implication, then, is that at least some of the 6th through 15th firms in the industry operate in the range of average costs below that for the first 15 firms as a whole. Of course, this analysis does not presume to pinpoint the lower cost firms in any precise way, but it would indicate that it is within the 6 to 15 firm range that one would find the lower cost firms. The fact that all of the 16th through 20th firms do not also operate with average cost advantages follows from the fact that there is a zero correlation co-efficient between the Gini coefficient and concentration ratio for the first 20 firms. Since the index of overall distribution of sales is basically unaffected by increases in the share of market going to these firms, the 16th through 20th firms in the industry must be undergoing a relative decline to balance off the relative gain of the 6th through 15th firms. Table IV also reveals that the remaining correlations are all positive and steadily increasing as the number of included firms increases, so that the remaining firms, below the top 20, do not benefit from increases in market share to the extent that the top 20 firms in the industry do. It appears, therefore, that the remaining firms in the industry operate on that portion of their cost curves such as to yield much higher average costs than for the top 50 as a group. To be more specific, the raw data reveal that the 20th firm in the industry generally produces in the neighborhod of 1,000,000 barrels of beer a year, and it has only been in the last few years that the 15th firm in the industry passed the 1,500,000 barrel a year mark. Until the 1960s, only the leading 2 producers were over the 5,000,000 barrel a year figure while one or more of the 3rd through the 8th firms produced over 3,000,000 barrels. The implication of this is that the lowest average cost range is somewhere above 1,000,000 barrels a year, probably closer to 1,500,000 barrels, and at or below 3,000,000 barrels. Higher average costs will arise at other levels, with firms once more enjoying economies at production levels in excess of 5,000,000 barrels. These results are with respect to firm, rather than plant size. We would conclude, therefore, that firms in the brewing industry face a U-shaped average cost curve with respect to firm size, except at high levels of firm size, when the cost curve would taper off, or perhaps begin to bend down again.[20]

Some possible explanations for this, and the implications for the future, will be discussed in the next section.

Explanations and Expectations

It scarcely comes as a surprise to come upon an industry in which the larger firms are the more efficient firms. In the brewing industry the greater efficiency of the larger breweries appears to have resulted from the many technological improvements incorporated in the brewing process in recent decades. Among the improvements introduced since Repeal were more power machinery, faster bottling operations, better refrigeration which provides exact control of temperature, improved laboratory techniques for checking all stages of the brewing process, and new devices to speed up the loading of trucks with the finished product. These improvements, some of which are a basic requirement in satisfying the consumer, are often too expensive for small breweries to incorporate in their plants. In addition, the larger firms marketing their product nationally have well-established distribution facilities which enable them to readily probe into any particular market of their own choosing. The lack of such a distribution system and the opportunity of obtaining one provided, from the point of view of the Blatz Brewing Company, one of the key motives for their merger with Pabst.

Although one might expect that there would be economies resulting from advertising, there does not appear to be a particularly strong case for this. For 1961 (and 1960) the figures on advertising cost per barrel of beer sold reveal that firms selling between 1.0 and 1.5 million barrels had a cost per barrel of $1.06 ($1.00); firms selling between 1.5 and 3.0 million barrels had a cost per barrel of $.71 ($.81); firms selling between 3.0 and 5.0 million barrels had a cost per barrel of $.84 ($1.00); and firms

---

[20] The same phenomena are observed in other countries. In particular, Great Britain experienced a sharp decline from 1400 breweries in 1930 to 835 in 1960, while more than 800 breweries

were either bought out or went bankrupt between 1930 and 1950 ('Pub Crowd Loses Thirst for Ale', *Business Week* (April 9th, 1960), p. 140).

selling over 5.0 million barrels had a cost per barrel of $1.35 ($1.58). The initial decline in advertising cost per barrel could simply be a result of increased sales with economies elsewhere in the firm; the rising cost per barrel figure for the largest firms implies that there are diseconomies of advertising expenditure beyond a certain point, and reinforces the argument that there must be economies resulting beyond the 5 million barrel mark or else the large advertising expense and sales level of the leaders could not be maintained.[21]

As several firms in the industry approach the 5 million barrel sales level, we anticipate that these firms, too, will once again achieve economies of large-scale production and distribution and that the competition within the industry will take a still heavier toll on the smaller firms. In particular, there are still some 40 out of the 148 companies in the brewing industry with production capacity of less than 100,000 barrels a year, the minimum efficient size of plant, and we can look for these firms to leave the industry in the near future. An additional 33 firms have production capacities of less than 200,000 barrels which, while greater than the minimum efficient size of plant, is well below the level necessary to achieve economies of scale. The future for these firms, too, would appear to be none too bright.

There are, however, some 23 (32) firms in the industry with production capacities in excess of 1.5 (1.0) million barrels a year, and 11 firms in the industry with capacities in the 1.5 to 3.0 million barrel range. Based on the results in the preceding section, these firms would seem to be in a position to strengthen their competitive standing, and it appears unlikely that concentration in the brewing industry, at least with regard to the leading 5 firms, will increase to any great extent in the near future, though we might anticipate that concentration for the leading 25 firms, say, will enjoy relatively appreciable gains.

It would seem, then, that the decline in the number of firms in the brewing industry which has occurred and, we believe, will continue to occur, is not at all a sign of a decrease in the need of any one firm to temper its market behavior to both the realized and potential actions of other firms in the industry. Rather, it signifies a stronger competitive position for a greater number of firms in an industry in which, through technological necessity, only the larger firms can survive. Further, the competitive nature of the industry and the failure of any individual firm or group of firms to establish anything resembling a pure monopoly position is revealed through consideration of the price behavior of firms in the industry. With the demand for beer being price inelastic, any monopolistic power could be exploited by collusive behavior or a price leader's pulling the price of beer up. Such does not appear to have been the case in the brewing industry where price increases have been few and far between. Rather, firms have maintained their traditional pricing structure, relying on such familiar competitive devices as either producing a product which people will find superior to the available alternatives, or trying to convince more people that the product is superior to the available alternatives.[22]

Whether or not the industry will ever 'get well' again is quite another matter.

---

[21] The Spearman Rank correlation between advertising expenditures and advertising cost per barrel of beer sold is .6861 and .6243 for the leading 22 firms in 1961 and 1960 respectively. The relatively high positive values indicate that there are no economies of advertising over the total range, though there might be economies at certain levels. It should also be noted that Schlitz and Budweiser spend more than double the amount of any other firm in the industry on advertising, which probably reflects a good deal of interfirm rivalry between these two alone since their sales are not correspondingly greater than those of the other large brewers.

---

[22] Selling beer in 11 ounce containers that do not appear to be much different from their 12 ounce mates is an approach used by some brewers on the West Coast to secure what is actually a price boost.

Tastes change, but there is probably an equal dosage of both hope and conviction in any statement to the effect that beer will regain its former popularity. Certainly, there is little evidence to support the claim. One can presume, however, that there will be a number of quite healthy firms getting healthier in this rather weak industry, and we really need not shed any tears either over the economic position of these firms, or over the state of competition in the brewing industry.

III · ARE PRICE CONSPIRACIES
EFFECTIVE?

Part III · *Are Price Conspiracies Effective?*

The Addyston Pipe Case began the establishment of the *per se* illegality of price conspiracies whether or not successful. What is interesting about this case, aside from the affirmation of common law precedents in this early Sherman Act case, is the lack of success of the conspiracy. Professor Armentano summarizes factual material (in selection 30) on the behavior of prices during the conspiracy period. He and his sources find competitive behavior despite the conspiracy.[1] After examining other cases, he concludes "(1) that the inherent market forces in a free market make most conspiracies completely unworkable, and (2) that a sampling of the most famous price-fixing antitrust cases . . . has revealed that they involved just such unworkable conspiracies."

The next, very short selection points out that the railroad rate conspiracies prevalent prior to 1887 were eroded by "persistent 'cheating' on the rates set in conference, so that the level of rates declined markedly as one agreement after another broke down." Governmental enforcement, provided by the Interstate Commerce Commission after its establishment in 1887, was required "to establish the cartel rates as the actual rates." Evidently, even *explicit* agreements among a *few* railroads were not effective in maintaining supracompetitive rates without governmental assistance.

Competition takes place in other dimensions besides price. Where there is a price floor set by a government agency, it can take place only in other dimensions. Professor George Eads, in his paper examining scheduling competition among air carriers, finds no tacit agreement occurring restricting the number of flights despite the great profitability of such agreement and the fewness of competitors on any given route.

---

[1] Also, see Ambrose Winston, *Judicial Economics* 21 (1957).

Even when the carriers were allowed to negotiate explicit arrangements to reduce flights in twenty-one "over-served" markets, meetings could not be arranged to discuss decreasing competition in eight of these markets. At least one carrier in each market refused to participate. In the remaining thirteen markets, agreement could not be reached in nine, despite meetings arranged explicitly for this purpose and the profitability of reaching agreement. "Agreement could only be reached on a formula for capacity reduction on four of these routes."

Professor Eads was not surprised by the difficulty of even negotiating, much less reaching, an agreement among the few competitors. He tells us that, "Experience with cartels leads us to believe that it would be extremely difficult to negotiate and even more difficult to enforce such voluntary agreements."

Professor F. M. Scherer comments (in selection 33) on the difficulties in establishing price fixing arrangements and the fragility of agreements. He summarizes studies of cartels in Denmark and in Germany which confirm *a priori* expectations of the sources of disagreement in trying to negotiate an understanding and the short-lived character of numerous price-fixing agreements. One of the factors making these agreements short-lived was new entry.

Under the Webb-Pomerene Act, U.S. firms are exempted from the Sherman Act when forming cartels for export purposes. Professor Dan Hamilton (in selection 34) follows the history of one of these export cartels in the oil industry. He finds that it was ineffectual in its attempt to control the export prices of gasoline and kerosene and "troubles were encountered from the start."

Professor Richard Zerbe, examining the history of the American Sugar Refining Company, finds that one of the motives for the formation of the trust was the ineffectiveness of an attempted price fixing agreement in 1882. Professor Zerbe also observes that growing concentration in sugar refining was accompanied by what was viewed by commentators as growing or excessive competition rather than a decline.

In the last selection in this group, Professor Richard Posner finds that oligopoly, meaning high concentration, may be "a necessary condition (in most cases) of successful price fixing . . . but . . . it is not a sufficient condition." He believes that the oligopolist is likely to set a competitive price if he "finds speculation about the probable reactions of his rivals . . . inconclusive; if he believes that new entry or the competition of substitute products will prevent him from obtaining appreciable monopoly profits; if he distrusts his competitors and fears that any higher price would be quickly eroded by cheaters . . ." He maintains that any attempt to set supracompetitive prices is likely to be unsuccessful because of cheating and points out that "few price-fixing conspiracies have come to light in which cheating was not rife and the benefits to the conspirators were enduring." He concludes "that oligopolists cannot be presumed always or often to change supracompetitive prices."

Following this discussion of the unlikelihood of tacit collusion in concentrated markets, Professor Posner suggests that if it does occur, it will have to be based on overt acts at least similar to unilateral contracts. Such overt acts will provide evidence sufficient for a court to act. He earlier indicated that tacit collusion is so unlikely that he can barely conceive its possibility in an extreme case such as "No more than three sellers selling a completely standardized product to a multitude of buyers (none large)," assuming static markets, similar size, and identical costs with no technological change. Even this he characterized as "speculation." Despite this skepticism concerning tacit collusion, his following discussion shifts to a readier acceptance of its possibility that does not seem consistent with the earlier discussion, although he reiterates his stand that "tacit collusion or noncompetitive pricing is not inherent in an oligopolistic market structure."

The readings in this group dwell primarily on the ineffectiveness and fragility of agreements not to compete, once made, and the difficulty of making explicit agreements. The last selection deals with the difficulty of arriving at a tacit agreement. This would certainly be expected if even explicit agreements are not readily made when the parties are bargaining face to face or even refuse to enter into such bargaining when given the opportunity to do so with antitrust immunity. If firms with few competitors refuse to bargain with their competitors, or cannot arrive at agreement when they do bargain, or do not stick to agreements made after bargaining, tacit agreements must be rare indeed. Durable tacit agreements can hardly be conceived to ever happen unless there is a large realm of unexamined experience which has never come to light that would tell us differently.

30. Price Fixing in Theory and Practice

D. T. ARMENTANO

The Theory of Price Fixing

The simple theory of price fixing suggests that an agreement by firms to restrict their output and raise the market prices of their product could be profitable, *under appropriate conditions*. Theoretically the firms would sell less, charge more, and reap the "monopoly" bonuses associated with collusion. Or, alternatively, the collusive agreement might bind the parties to submit noncompetitive bids at a public letting; somehow one of the firms would be selected to "get the job," and it would split the monopoly profits with the rest of the group. In some fashion, the firms involved would be taken out of direct price competition with each other—to their mutual benefit.

But what are these "appropriate conditions," and are they likely to occur? The widely-held presumption among economists for some time has been that price conspiracies would be common in the American business system without antitrust legislation. The intent of the following discussion is to challenge such a presumption and suggest, instead, that there are diverse economic factors which would tend at all times to limit the success, and hence the significance, of price-fixing agreements in a free market. It is to be assumed that the hypothetical firms under discussion here *want* to fix prices at more than competitive rates. What is being challenged is their collective ability to effectuate such a situation.[1]

Substitutes: The responsiveness of buyers to price changes (elasticity) is of crucial importance when considering the potential

Reprinted from *The Myths of Antitrust* by D. T. Armentano. Copyright 1972 by Arlington House Publishers, New Rochelle, New York, and used with permission.

[1] The following discussion is taken from my article, "The Inherent Weakness of Price Collusion," *The Freeman*, XX (January, 1970), 40–43.

effectiveness of price-fixing agreements. If, for example, the commodity to be price fixed has few good substitutes in the short run, an increase in its price may increase total revenues of the conspiracy and make price collusion financially rewarding. But if, as more often is the case, there is a plentiful array of goods that might be substituted for the commodity that is being price fixed, the higher fixed price may push marginal buyers to the cheaper substitutes, and thus lower total conspiracy revenues.

This consequence encourages firms to break the agreement to maintain a uniform price since the agreement does not, apparently, work in their interests. Certainly some firms will be *relatively* worse off with regard to substitute competition than others, and would be the first to feel the pinch of a revenue squeeze, and the first to consider a policy of selective price reductions. Thus, the threat of substitute competition may make price conspiracy difficult to form in the first place, or lead to competitive price reductions that break up the conspiracy.

Changes in Demand: A slight, even temporary reduction in demand for the price fixed commodity may break apart the price agreement; recession is the natural enemy of successful price collusion. A decrease in demand at fixed prices will curb sales, and the temptation to ease the decline with a price reduction will be strong, especially for the low-profit firms involved. Since all firms differ in financial strength, and in their willingness to "ride out" a demand decline, there must be such temptations and such pressures. When the relatively weaker firms cut prices in an attempt to increase or maintain sales, the formal price-fixing agreements tumble.

Output Agreements: Firms that agree to fix prices also agree to some marketing arrangement. Somehow, particular firms must be selected to "get" particular "jobs," or a particular percentage of industry output. This part of the conspiracy is crucial since it must produce proper revenues to all firms involved, else one or more of the conspirators will "chisel" prices to steal orders. However, these marketing arrangements are all but impossible to sustain for any extended period of time. Will the present market shares be maintained? And if they are maintained, how long will they last? What arrangements will exist for altering the status quo? Will a smaller firm attempt to cut the fixed price when it feels that its allotted share or territory is too restrictive, and no operational procedures for change exist? And what about *new* firms attracted to the market by the higher-than-competitive prices? By definition, they have no allotted outputs or selling instructions. Will they be content to just take a slice of the existing action? But which of the existing sellers in the conspiracy will give up sales to make room for the newcomer? The tendency of output restrictions is to frustrate all aggressive sellers and attract new producers, and thus to weaken and eventually break apart price-fixing agreements.

Costs: Assume a manufacturing firm A whose average production and selling costs per unit decline as output increases. As almost every businessman realizes, there are certain economies associated with larger outputs; spreading the overhead and purchasing supplies in larger quantities tend to lower average costs per unit of output, and make larger outputs cheaper to produce and sell than smaller outputs. The significant point for this discussion is that firms that *restrict* outputs as a part of a price conspiracy invariably raise their average costs per unit. Hence, profits will decline unless the extra revenue associated with the conspiracy exceeds the extra costs associated with the output restriction.

This important consideration must surely make firms hesitant to join such restrictive agreements. Smaller firms especially will be anxious to increase—not de-

crease—output, in order to enjoy the economies associated with larger scale output. To compete with the larger, more efficient firms in the future may make this output expansion mandatory. Price-fixing and output agreements are difficult to conclude when firms find it advantageous to increase, not decrease, their sales.

Imports: As long as international markets are free (and it is within our power to lower our quotas and tariffs to zero on all goods), a domestic price-fixing conspiracy appears limited by foreign competition. When foreign goods are price competitive, domestic price-fixing agreements are inherently unstable. A world-wide conspiracy is possible, but almost all such arrangements have existed and functioned successfully in the past with active *governmental* support.

Honesty and Trust: Honesty and trust between the firms involved in conspiracy is absolutely crucial to its successful operation. If one of the conspirators thinks, or is led to think, that anyone else is not living up to the price-output agreements (and they will have to police their own agreements), then price cutting is likely. And since it is hard to turn down old customers and their price requests, and difficult not to discount from book price when demand is flat, and since all firms know this, the *suspicion* of secret price concessions will always be strong. Furthermore, since firms don't trust each other in open competition, it is difficult to understand why they should suddenly trust each other in price conspiracy.

Buyer Power: It appears that some assumptions concerning the market "power" of the buyers is necessary before price collusion can be understood. The buyers must, obviously, have a relatively weak bargaining position *vis-à-vis* the selling conspiracy. If buyers are large firms that can threaten to make the price-fixed item or import it, or can use reciprocal agreements to the detriment of the price conspirators, then successful price conspiracy certainly becomes more difficult. It is hard to imagine firms such as Sears, DuPont, American Can, or any of America's industrial giants being the victim of price conspiracy in *their* purchasing markets.

Differentiated Products: Other things equal, one would expect price fixing to be more difficult in industries where the "products" being sold are highly differentiated. By definition, firms selling homogeneous products (e.g., cement) concentrate most of the competitiveness of their output in one bit of significant data: price/unit weight. A price fix on homogeneous products would, therefore, be relatively simple since the range of competitive variables is "managable." The greater the number of competitive variables or, correspondingly, the less important unit price becomes, the greater the difficulty that a simple *price* conspiracy could be arranged or could function in the interests of the parties involved. Consumer goods industries, with their usual emphasis on diversity and differentiation, would appear to be poor candidates for successful price collusion.

Transportation Costs: Local or regional price conspiracies would appear to be limited by transportation charges from areas where competition is still open. For example, to fix the price of septic tanks in area A, the area A septic tank sellers would have to take into account the fact that sellers in area B could begin to compete (and thus destroy the price conspiracy) when production costs plus transportation approached the price fix. Thus if the manufacturing costs of all the area sellers were roughly similar, the price fix in area A would be limited by the freight rates between themselves and the nearest competitive market. Put slightly differently, if transportation costs between markets were low relative to final price, a local price conspiracy would find it extremely difficult to increase and "fix" prices for any extended period of time.

Summary of Theoretical Factors. In summation, a price-fixing agreement would be unstable or unworkable when substitute competition is important, demand is falling, large producers are not party to the conspiracy, production quotas are to be agreed upon, larger outputs are cheaper per unit than smaller outputs, imports are an important part of market competition, mutual distrust and suspicion abound, buyers are in a position to bargain, products are widely differentiated, and where transportation costs are negligible between markets. Any of these factors might be enough to prevent successful price conspiracy. Since a great many markets, at one time or another, display these various conditions, it appears reasonable to assume that successful price collusion would be of minor proportions even without antitrust legislation. To test this conclusion, let us turn to an examination of some of the landmark price-fixing cases prosecuted under the Sherman Act, and attempt to discover what the "conspirators" were actually doing.

The Addyston Pipe Case (1899)

The Addyston Pipe Case[2] is an antitrust "landmark" for at least three different reasons. In the first place, it represents one of the few early victories for the Justice Department under the Sherman Act. Secondly, its successful prosecution may have been a factor in the significant structural changes that took place in American manufacturing during the 1895–1902 period.[3] Finally, the case is classic because it details vividly the difficulties of price collusion in a free and unstable market situation.

In 1896 the Justice Department brought suit in the Circuit Court for the Eastern District of Tennessee against six cast-iron pipe manufacturers: Addyston Pipe and Steel Company; Dennis Long and Company; Howard-Harrison Iron Company; Anniston Pipe and Foundry Company; South Pittsburgh Pipe Works, and the Chattanooga Foundry and Pipe Works. The firms were charged with rigging bid prices

---

[2] *Addyston Pipe and Steel Company* v. *United States*, 175 U.S. 211.

[3] Donald Dewey, *Monopoly in Economics and Law* (Chicago: Rand McNally and Company, 1959), pp. 53–55.

for cast-iron pipe to certain municipalities. Although the Circuit Court decision of 1898 argued that the "combination" only affected "manufacturing" and not interstate trade and commerce,[4] Circuit Court Judge Taft, on appeal, reversed the lower court decision on the grounds that such "associations" were *always* void at common law, and that there was "no question of reasonableness open to the courts with reference to such a contract."[5] Besides, Taft indicated, even if the reasonableness of the conspiracy were at issue, the facts in the case clearly demonstrated that the Addyston "group" was indeed charging unreasonable prices.[6]

On December 4, 1899, the Supreme Court agreed with Judge Taft's decision and reaffirmed the reversal of the appeals court. Justice Peckham, writing the majority opinion, simply quoted Taft's "analysis" of the unreasonableness of the Addyston group's prices and concluded that . . .

> The facts thus set forth [Taft's quoted decision] show conclusively that the effect of the combination was to enhance prices beyond a sum which was reasonable, and therefore the first objection above set forth need not be further noticed.[7]

In his history of the Addyston Pipe conspiracy, Almarin Phillips indicates that the object of the conspiracy was rather simple and logical.[8] The six firms involved were the major suppliers of cast-iron pipe in the Southern market area. Although there were many other cast-iron pipe producers in the rest of the country (particularly in the New Jersey area), transportation costs from the Eastern plants limited competition for jobs in the "safe" areas immediately surrounding the Southern manufacturers. The gen-

eral idea of the conspiracy was to end competition between the six firms for the local (reserved cities) jobs altogether, and to prearrange collusively a bid and a bidder for the public lettings in the "pay territory." Hopefully the internal reduction in price competition between the Southern firms—and the consequently higher prices—would increase group revenues and profits.

But there were difficulties with the scheme from the beginning. The major operational difficulty concerned the allocation of "pay territory" jobs. Which firms were to get them, and how were the final bid prices to be arrived at? The prearranged bid price in the pay territory certainly had to be below the delivered price of any (Northern) producer not a party to the conspiracy else the Southern group would get no business at all. Yet, at the same time, the price actually bid had to be close to the nonmember bid in order to realize a profit for the conspiracy.

In addition, the bid price had to be at least competitive with firms *in* the pay territory and not a party to the conspiracy. Judge Taft admitted that there were 170,500 tons of cast-iron pipe capacity in the pay territory associated with nonconspiracy firms.[9] Some of these nonconspiracy pay territory manufacturers were in Texas, Colorado, and Oregon; more important mills were in St. Louis, Columbus, in northern Ohio, and in Michigan.[10] Thus the prices worked out by the Addyston group would have to be tempered by potential competition from within and without the pay territory.

How, exactly, were the bid prices (and the bidder) determined? The solution to this problem was to allow secret bidding for pay territory jobs by conspiracy members. When a bid price was selected, the members were allowed to "bid a bonus" price per ton for the privilege of submitting that bid at the public letting and actually

---

[4] *United States* v. *Addyston Pipe and Steel Company*, 78 F. 712 (1897).

[5] 85 F. 293.

[6] *Ibid.*, pp. 293–295.

[7] 175 U.S. 238.

[8] Almarin Phillips, *Market Structure, Organization and Performance* (Cambridge, Mass.: Harvard University Press, 1962).

[9] The defendants capacity was estimated at 220,000 tons. See, 85 F. 291.

[10] *Ibid.*, p. 292.

doing the production. Other things equal, the firm with the lowest marginal production costs plus transportation could "bid" the largest bonuses and could get the jobs. Bidding bonuses introduced the necessary element of "competition," and allowed the conspiracy to allocate the appropriate jobs to the most efficient firms. Consequently, as should be obvious, the firm that bid the largest bonus and secured the job, derived little if any *additional* profit from the arrangement since the bonuses were paid to the group.

Was the attempt at price collusion successful? If the test of success is made to be a significant and sustained advance in the final price of cast-iron pipe sold by the Addyston group companies between 1893 and 1896, then clearly the collusion was far from successful. For example, the first preliminary attempts to advance prices and profits in 1893 and 1894 were admitted failures.[11] During this period, prices charged by the conspiracy members were actually lower (in some cases as much as 20 per cent lower) than they had been in the preconspiracy period. Amazingly, prices bid in some of the *reserved city* areas were significantly lower than prior to the conspiracy.

Although the Addyston group did agree on a "new plan" in late 1895, and although some bid prices did advance briefly, most bid prices by the middle of 1896 were as low *or lower* than in the previous periods. For example, in a statement by M. L. Holman, Water Commissioner of St. Louis, dated January 15, 1897, it is indicated that the contract price for cast-iron pipe per ton was $24.95 on April 12, 1892, $25.48 on July 26, 1892, $19.94 on August 7, 1894, $19.85 on March 26, 1895, $22.47 on September 17, 1895, $19.64 on July 28, 1896, and $19.94 on October 6, 1896.[12] These price movements are fairly typical of the patterns in other pay territory cities.

Were the prices charged by the conspiracy "fair and reasonable"? Almarin Phillips suggests that Judge Taft likely erred when he concluded that the prices charged by the conspiracy were unreasonable.[13] The rather incomplete cost-price information available suggests to Phillips that conspiracy prices in the period under consideration were frequently below average costs, and possibly even below average variable costs.[14] He speculates that a price of $20 per ton would have covered full costs including transportation if the mills had been operating close to capacity. Since they were operating well below capacity in 1896, Phillips concludes that the "charge that the general level of prices was exorbitant seems unjustified."[15]

The Record and Briefs in the Addyston Pipe case supply additional information concerning the "fairness" of the prices charged by the conspiracy during the period. Although Judge Taft summarily *dismissed* the fifty-odd affidavits from private contractors, gas and water companies, and public officials testifying to the reasonableness of the prices charged, nothing (for our purposes) could be more *relevant*. Affidavit after affidavit swore to the fact that the buyer was acquainted with all the firms that manufactured cast-iron pipe, with the past and present prices of pipe, and with the price of the basic raw material, pig iron. On that basis, all testified that the prices actually charged for pipe were fair and reasonable. The last paragraph from the affidavit of A. W. Walton dated December 30, 1896, is not atypical:

> The prices at which said pipe, and all other pipe, which aggregated large amounts have been purchased by me and furnished by the Addyston Pipe and Foundry Company and others are the lowest that could be obtained from any of the pipe works in the United States. From my knowledge and long experience, extending over a number of years past, re-

---

[11] Phillips, *op. cit.*, p. 108.

[12] *Addyston Pipe et al.* v. *United States*, 175 U.S. 211, *Transcript of Record*, Supreme Court of the United States, October Term, 1899, No. 51, pp. 196–197.

[13] Phillips, *op. cit.*, p. 111.

[14] *Ibid.*, p. 112.

[15] *Ibid.*

specting the cost of manufacturing cast-iron pipe, the loss entailed, and the capital required, I consider the prices at which said pipe was purchased as fair, reasonable and just. From my knowledge of such things I do not believe that the prices could reasonably have been less. The prices at which cast-iron pipe has sold since December, 1894, have been uniformly moderate, even low in a number of instances, much lower at all times that pipe could be purchased prior to that time.[16]

Now surely the sworn testimony of the supposed *victims* of the dastardly conspiracy (the buyers of cast-iron pipe) to the effect that they believed that they were *not being victimized* is important and relevant information. Yet almost all accounts of the Addyston case conveniently ignore this information.[17]

The probable reason for the inability of the conspiracy to increase and sustain high and unreasonable prices is not difficult to discover. Although many of the theoretical factors discussed earlier in this chapter would appear to favor successful price collusion, the one crucial nonfavorable factor was the level of demand. The period of the middle 1890s was one of extremely poor and unstable economic performance, even depression. In that context, it is doubtful that the number of bids for cast-iron pipe sought by contractors and municipalities would have been sufficient to sustain then-existing plant capacity without a severe reduction in market price. Further, idle capacity on the part of the nonconspiracy firms would have made them hungry for additional business at *any* price that covered out-of-pocket expenses. With the decrease in demand for pipe on the part of private contractors, and the uncertainty associated with the demand for pipe on the part of the municipalities, it is not surpris-

ing that prices could not even be maintained at 1892 preconspiracy levels, let alone pushed higher. *The general level of demand and the level of operating capacity of all pipe works (there were twenty-one firms operating in the United States) were, it appears, much more important influences on price than conspiracy.* Thus, in one of the landmark price fixing cases of all antitrust history, prices were not really fixed and monopoly profits were not obtained.

The Trenton Potteries Case (1927)

A. D. Neale, in his widely respected volume, *The Antitrust Laws of the U.S.A.*, declares that the Trenton Potteries case is the leading Supreme Court decision on price fixing.[18] And so it may well be. But few antitrust volumes—including Neale's own excellent survey—supply any substantial conduct-performance information that would allow the reader to determine what actually transpired during the alleged conspiracy, and during the very interesting proceedings at the trial court. The most general and repeated summaries of the Trenton Potteries case are legalistic. In this case, almost all accounts relate, Chief Justice Stone reaffirmed the Addyston Pipe precedent on price-fixing agreements, and stated that:

> Agreements which create such potential power may well be held to be in themselves unreasonable or unlawful restraints, without the necessity of minute inquiry whether a particular price is reasonable or unreasonable. . . .[19]

Thus price-fixing agreements were always *per se* illegal, and there was to be no "rule of reason" with regard to such conspiracies.

Such a legalistic approach, of course, leaves the most interesting *economic* questions unanswered—or even unasked. Did, for example, these so-called "price agreements" in the Trenton Potteries case ac-

---

[16] *Addyston Pipe et al.* v. *United States*, 175 U.S. 211, *Record and Briefs*, p. 195.

[17] The mention of the affidavits is omitted from Justice Peckham's opinion in the Addyston Pipe case as excerpted in Irwin M. Stelzer, *Selected Antitrust Cases: Landmark Decisions* (3rd ed.; Homewood, Ill.: Richard D. Irwin, 1966), p. 163.

[18] London: Cambridge University Press, 1970, p. 33.

[19] *United States* v. *Trenton Potteries Company et al.*, 273 U.S. 397.

tually accomplish "agreement," i.e., were the actual market prices for vitreous pottery bathroom and lavatory fixtures "uniform, arbitrary, and noncompetitive" as the federal grand jury indictment had charged? [20] It would be both informative and ironical, indeed, if in the "leading case on price fixing" it could be discovered that prices were *not* actually fixed and *not* uniform. Before we explore this and similar questions concerning the conduct-performance of the firms involved, a brief sketch of the industry and the supposed conspiracy is required.

At the time of the alleged illegal agreements, the pottery industry was regionally concentrated in New Jersey along the Delaware River. [21] Although there were pottery firms in Chicago, Kalamazoo, Evansville, and Wheeling, West Virginia, at least eight important firms (including Trenton Potteries and Thomas Maddock and Sons, the two largest firms) were located in Trenton, New Jersey. Also headquartered in Trenton was the Sanitary Potters Association, the trade organization to which at least 23 firms representing 82 per cent of the industry's 1922 output belonged.

The activities of the Sanitary Potters Association were varied—and eventually controversial. There is evidence to suggest that the association encouraged its members to adopt a more standardized approach to the design of certain bathroom fixtures, and that it strongly encouraged the use of a uniform system of cost accounting. It also kept records of the particular wholesalers (jobbers) to whom association members sold so-called "first line" class "A" material, and occasionally admonished its members for selling imperfect (class "B") fixtures in the home market. Its most controversial activity, however, involved the preparation and publication of an official industry "price list."

The price lists (there were six different lists for six different geographical areas of the country) were prepared from statistics of actual sale prices submitted monthly by the association members, [22] and from the recommendations of the Sanitary Potters "price list committee." The lists were then sent out to the member firms and, supposedly, served as the basis for *their* own price bulletins. In the individual firm price bulletin one might find the "list" price on a particularly styled wash bowl; in addition, the "discount" off that list price might also be indicated. Further, there were "surcharges" that might be added to actual order invoices on particular bathroom ware. If all firms in the same regional zone followed the *same* list price in their bulletins, and then applied the *same* discounts and the *same* surcharges to the *same* class "A" items, the final selling prices for these particular firms would have been identical.

In August, 1922, a federal grand jury returned an indictment against twenty-three vitreous pottery manufacturers, claiming that they had conspired through their trade association to "fix and exact non-competitive prices for the sale of said pottery," and that the firms had "refrained from engaging in competition with each other as to the prices of said pottery." [23] In addition, the indictment also charged that the defendants had illegally conspired to confine their sales of bathroom and lavatory fixtures to "legitimate jobbers." [24] The case was tried by Judge William C. Van Fleet, and on April 17, 1923 the jury returned a guilty verdict on both counts.

The convicted defendants appealed and on May 9, 1924, a Circuit Court of Appeals reversed the trial court decision on the basis of certain procedural errors in the conduct of the trial. Circuit Court Judge Hough (apparently speaking for Judges Rogers and Mayer, also) maintained that

---

[20] Phillips, *op. cit.*, p. 164.

[21] *Ibid.*, pp. 162–173.

[22] This practice was reportedly abandoned in 1920.

[23] 300 F. 551.

[24] It was the common practice of almost *all* manufacturers to market products exclusively through wholesalers. There was no evidence presented to indicate that any particular wholesaler had been discriminated against. See Phillips, *op. cit.*, p. 168.

"the learned court erred" when *it had re-fused to allow defense witnesses to testify as to the existence of competition between the indicted defendants,* and that it had erred when it instructed the jury that "if they found the defendants did conspire to restrain trade, as charged in the indictment, *then it was immaterial whether such agree-ments were ever actually carried out . . ."* (emphasis added).[25] Judge Hough argued that it "was essential for the prosecution to prove the absence of competition" and, thus, "incumbent upon the defense to show, if possible, the presence of actual competi-tion in respect of prices." [26] This was espe-cially important, Judge Hough observed, in view of the fact that none of the defendants lived in the district where the trial had been conducted (Southern District of New York), and that the federal indictment had not charged that the conspiracy was formed in that district.

> . . . consequently there was no juris-diction there to bring the indictment or there to try the case, unless it was shown that the jurisdiction was conferred by the commission of an overt act within the Southern District.
>
> The pleader understood this, for other-wise all the allegations concerning acts done in the Southern District in pursuance of the object of the conspiracy were mere surplusage. Why the United States was so anxious to institute and prosecute this case in the city of New York we do not know, but the frame of indictment compared with the undisputed facts show that New York was intentionally selected, and trial of these defendants in the Third Circuit, where most of them resided, was sedu-lously avoided. Such a choice as this car-ried with it the burden of proving some-thing done in the Southern district, i.e., an overt act—justifying the finding of the indictment. The peculiarity of this transplanted litigation was overlooked be-low, and *it was error, and very material error,* to instruct a New York jury in so many words that it was immaterial whether any effort had ever been made to carry out the conspiracy complained of.[27]

The essential question therefore, and the one totally ignored by the lower court, was: had the firms *successfully* conspired to fix arbitrary and uniform prices and, hence, "injure the public?"

Both the trial court record and the *United States Supreme Court Records & Briefs*[28] contain abundant evidence that selling prices during the period of the al-leged conspiracy were *not* fixed and *not* uniform, and that there was active compe-tition—active *price* competition—between the defendants. The many *buyers* of vitre-ous pottery, to the extent that they were *allowed* to testify, indicated that the de-fendants were in active price competition with each other, and that the bulletin prices were not actual selling prices. As one buyer recounted:

> . . . I received their bulletins . . . I did not make use of the bulletins except to put them in the waste basket, because I went around shopping and bought just as I found the market ripe to buy. My prices were not affected or controlled by these bulletin prices that I know of. . . .[29]

Although the government attorney repeat-edly objected—and Judge Van Fleet sus-tained almost all objections—to the intro-duction of defense testimony regarding whether actual competition existed in the market for the wares of the defendants, the official record of the case still contains con-clusive evidence that such price competi-tion did. The following excerpt is a sum-mary statement from respondents brief per-taining to price determination in the mar-ket; the trial record page references are in parentheses:

> During all of the period in question sales of sanitary pottery were made at prices below those announced in the cur-rent bulletins (R., p. 344, fols. 1030–1031; p. 375, fol. 1123; p. 397, fols. 1189–1191; p. 422, fol. 1264; p. 442, fols. 1324–1325;

---

[25] 300 F. 552.

[26] *Ibid.,* p. 555.

[27] *Ibid.,* p. 552 (Emphasis added).

[28] *United States* v. *Trenton Potteries Company et al.,* 273 U.S. 392, *Brief for Respondents, No. 27, United States Supreme Court Records & Briefs,* October Term, 1926.

[29] Phillips, *op. cit.,* p. 167.

p. 445, fol. 1335; p. 459, fol. 1375; p. 459, fol. 1376; p. 460, fol. 1378; p. 498, fol. 1453; p. 512, fol. 1535; p. 516, fol. 1547 and p. 521, fol. 1562). Some buyers never paid bulletin prices. (R., p. 424, fol. 1271) Others bought oftener below than at the bulletin prices. (R., p. 448, fol. 1342; p. 452, fol. 1356; p. 459, fol. 1375; p. 459, fol. 1376; p. 460, fol. 1378; p. 464, fol. 1391). The prices at which the various companies sold were usually different. (R., p. 528, fol. 1582) Sometimes the bulletin prices varied. (R., p. 450, fol. 1348; p. 459, fol. 1376). The prices charged by some of the companies were always lower than those of any of the others. (R., p. 381, fol. 1142). Some of the manufacturers regularly gave certain customers a stated reduction from their published prices. (R., p. 513, fol. 1539) Salesmen of defendant companies found themselves in competition as to price with those of other companies (R., p. 398, fols. 1193–1194), and manufacturers, if they wanted the business, met their competitors prices. (R., p. 471, fol. 1412). Buyers found manufacturers bidding against each other for their business (R., p. 422, fols. 1265–1266; p. 492, fol. 1475; p. 514, fol. 1541; p. 525, fols. 1573–1575) and reducing their prices to get orders (R., p. 439, fol. 1317; p. 446, fol. 1336; p. 450, fol. 1349). Some buyers obtained prices from several manufacturers at the same time and found that these prices differed (R., p. 436, fol. 1306; p. 438, fol. 1314; p. 440, fols. 1318–1319; p. 446, fol. 1336; p. 465, fol. 1393; p. 528, fol. 1582). Some of the buyers thought so little of price bulletins that they threw them away (R., p. 439, fol. 1316).[30]

Further, an analysis of the actual sales invoices of 21 of the 23 defendants between June 1, 1918, and July 31, 1922, showed that 26 per cent of the tanks sold by the defendants sold at bulletin prices, while 64 per cent sold below bulletin and 10 per cent above bulletin. Of the bathroom bowls invoiced, only 28 per cent sold at bulletin prices, while 68 per cent sold below bulletin and 4 per cent above bulletin.[31] And the differences from bulletin prices were

not slight. Almarin Phillips has noted that some actual prices for tanks and bowls may have varied as much as 40 per cent from the "official" bulletin prices. Clearly, then, the Trenton Potteries conspiracy was not able to fix "uniform, arbitrary and non-competitive" prices for vitreous pottery in the period under consideration. And in the "leading case on price fixing," prices were not being "fixed."

One can speculate as to why the "conspiracy" failed. Almarin Phillips suggests that the industry lacked "the leadership required to establish an effective market organization";[32] the markets were disorganized, the pottery firms had widely different objectives, and there was no "dominant firm" to whip the smaller firms into price line. With no assurance that *anybody* was following bulletin prices, *all* had to "cheat" to insure their proper share of new orders. And since there were no penalties associated with "shading" bulletin prices (outside of occasional admonishments), the financial benefits of competition apparently exceeded the costs of unsure price agreement. Under such conditions, a successful price collusion was extremely unlikely.

The 1918–1922 period was also high in other economic uncertainties. The disequilibriums of World War I must have been severe, especially in an industry as sensitive to construction spending and housing starts. At the same time, a major technological change had threatened to revolutionize the manufacturing process in the industry.[33] All these factors together must have placed intense competitive pressure on the existing market structure of independent pottery manufacturers, and made them extremely price conscious.

As already noted above, however, the Supreme Court regarded such contextual information as "immaterial," and reversed the Appeals Court decision that such economic evidence or analysis should have been part of the deliberations of the jury.

---

[30] *Records & Briefs, Brief for Respondents*, No. 27, pp. 10–11.

[31] *Ibid.*, p. 11.

[32] Phillips, *op. cit.*, pp. 173–176.

[33] *Ibid.*, pp. 175–176.

In 1927, and rather consistently since then,[34] any price agreement—or any sort of combination that "tampers with price structures"[35]—has been regarded as unlawful. Whether the prices have *actually* been fixed, or whether they have been fixed at unreasonable levels, has been immaterial to a determination of guilt or innocence. To presume automatically, therefore, that "price-fixing" antitrust cases demonstrate that successful price fixing is easy or common throughout the American business system—or would be without a protective Sherman Act—is not justifiable. In many cases, the information relevant to decide such an issue has been "immaterial" at court.

The Great Electrical Equipment Conspiracy

Undoubtedly the most celebrated price-fixing antitrust case of modern times is the electrical equipment manufacturers price conspiracy, decided in 1961.[36] Involved were some of the nation's largest and most prestigious firms, such as General Electric, Westinghouse, Allis-Chalmers, Federal Pacific, I-T-E Circuit Breaker, Carrier, and many others. The charges: that various employees of said firms had, between 1956 and 1959, combined and conspired to "raise, fix, and maintain" the prices of insulators, transformers, power switchgear, condensors, circuit breakers, and various other electrical equipment and apparatus involving an es-

timated $1.7 billion worth of business annually.[37]

A series of Philadelphia grand jury indictments were returned during 1960. After much discussion between the defendants and the Department of Justice, the firms were allowed to plead guilty to some of the more serious charges, and *nolo contendere* to the rest. On February 6, 1961, Judge Ganey sent seven executives off to jail, gave twenty-three others suspended jail sentences, and fined the firms involved nearly $2 million. Subsequent triple damage suits, brought against the equipment manufacturers by the TVA and private firms that had been "overcharged," increased the financial penalty many times. And so ended the most publicized price conspiracy in all business history.

The fact that there were price "meetings" among various electrical equipment producers between 1956 and 1959 was indisputable. The meetings were a "way of life" in the industry.[38] Some of the meetings were little more than hastily called "gripe" sessions where the various firm representatives complained about price discounting and foreign competition. But others were more sophisticated and, apparently, involved the determination and application of secret bidding formulas and the allocation of market business. Certainly the most incredible aspect of the conspiracy was not the price meetings but the absolute disclaimer by top General Electric and Westinghouse executives of any knowledge of any "conspiracy." The executives actually involved in the meetings bore the brunt of the financial and social penalties.

---

[34] *Appalachian Coals, Inc.* v. *United States,* 288 U.S. 344 (1933), is a strange exception to the *per se* approach in price fixing cases. See Stelzer, *op. cit.,* pp. 165–170.

[35] *United States* v. *Socony-Vacuum Oil Company,* 310 U.S. 150 (1940), quoted in Stelzer, *Ibid.,* p. 175.

[36] Background information can be obtained from Richard Austin Smith, "The Incredible Electrical Conspiracy," *Fortune,* LXIII (April and May, 1961); John Fuller, *The Gentlemen Conspirators* (New York: Grove Press, 1962); John Herling, *The Great Price Conspiracy: The Story of the Anti-trust Violations in the Electrical Industry* (Washington: Robert B. Luce, 1962).

---

[37] Clarence C. Walton and Frederick W. Cleveland, Jr., *Corporations on Trial: The Electric Cases* (Belmont, Calif.: Wadsworth Publishing Company, 1964), p. 12.

[38] *Ibid.,* p. 11. The best source of information about the conspiracy meetings is the Hearings on Administered Prices by the United States Senate Committee on the Judiciary, Subcommittee on Antitrust and Monopoly, *Price-Fixing and Bid-Rigging in the Electrical Manufacturing Industry,* Parts 27 and 28, 87th Congress, 1st session, April, May, and June 1961.

If an "agreement" to fix prices is price fixing, then the electrical manufacturers were certainly guilty of price fixing and the issue is a dead one. Or if "tampering with price structures" constitutes price fixing, then these meetings were illegal and in clear violation of the Sherman Act. But for the purposes of this discussion the important questions are not legal (or moral) but *economic*. Did the conspiracy in fact "raise fix and maintain" unreasonable prices as the twenty-odd indictments had charged? Did it "restrain, suppress and eliminate" price competition with respect to the selling of various kinds of electrical machinery or apparatus? Did the conspiracy work to "cheat" buyers of the benefits of free competition?

To comprehend correctly the issue of price conspiracy, one must understand the usual and normal pricing practices in this multiproduct, oligopolistic industry. General Electric, Westinghouse, and to a lesser extent, the smaller manufacturers, sell hundreds of thousands of electrical products that have been "standardized" to a high degree by the industry's trade association. The products are sold out of huge catalogues where potential customers may obtain a detailed description of the product and its suggested list price. Almost all the catalogue products are so-called "shelf" items that the huge manufacturers produce continuously and hold in inventory. When an order is received a computer fills the request and directs that the particular product be shipped from the closest warehouse to the customer.

Since the products produced by the electrical equipment manufacturers are almost identical, and all firms quote delivered prices, the selling prices for standardized shelf items are almost identical to all buyers.[39] Any price decrease by one seller—usually announced with a mimeographed price sheet to customers—is quickly matched by other sellers. On sealed bid business, the price cut is "announced" when the bids are opened. In any case, the pressure of the marketplace, i.e., the desire on the part of each manufacturer to keep or increase his customers, makes the new (lower) price the new catalogue price, which is, again, nearly identical for all firms that want to be "competitive." Although there may be recognized quality differences that eventually "sell" an order, it still appears that the price of the higher-quality product must nearly equal its lower-quality competitor. The testimony of John K. Hodnette, executive vice-president of Westinghouse, illustrates the pricing procedures with respect to such a shelf item, electric meters:[40]

> This is a standard item. It is the meter that goes on the outside of the house that measures the use of current, protects the customer, tells the utility how much electricity has been used so that they can render a bill. We have been manufacturing these meters for 75 years. The selling price is approximately $16 . . . About 60 days ago, I think it was, one of our competitors decreased the price of his watt-hour meter that corresponded to the one in question in Cleveland. When we learned of this, which we do very promptly, because they send out published catalogs, and our customers call them to our attention, so with the large number that are printed it is very easy matter to get a copy of a competitors' catalog and determine his prices, they reduced the price of the meter 30 cents per meter, when the new pricelist came out. We had just concluded the development of a meter which we thought was superior, better than any in the industry. We advised our field salespeople that we were not at that time planning to reduce our prices. We felt that we could sell a superior product at a higher price. We very soon learned that customers would not pay us the price, and many of them came to us and asked us to reduce our price to the same as those charged by competitors, so that they could continue to buy meters from us.[41]

Thus, Hodnette argued, competition pro-

---

[39] There was testimony to the effect that the Robinson-Patman Act made quantity discounts difficult. See *Price-Fixing and Bid-Rigging* . . . , p. 17619

[40] All the quoted testimony to follow in this chapter is taken from *Price-Fixing and Bid-Rigging in the Electrical Manufacturing Industry*, unless otherwise indicated.

[41] *Ibid.*, p. 17430.

duced identical prices. And the pricing procedure was no different with reference to "sealed bid" business. As he explained:

> The City of Cleveland and many other people recognize no brand preference or quality preference of one meter manufactured by one company as against another. In order to obtain business in any location, it is necessary that he be competitive with respect to price. This is total cost to the customer, whether he be the city of Cleveland or TVA, delivered to him at the site he wants it. He will not pay more . . . In order for a manufacturer to get an order, he must quote a competitive price. He must quote a price that is equal to that of any of his competitors, delivered to the customer, and without any qualifications.[42]

From these remarks, it is clear that the normal forces of competition tended to produce identically quoted list prices in the electrical equipment manufacturers industry. To regard such identical quotations as *per se* evidence of collusion or conspiracy would be naïve and wrong. A final note on this extremely important issue from Ralph Cordiner, president of General Electric during this period, will suffice:

> In the course of these hearings, considerable attention has been devoted to the frequent identity of prices charged by competitors. It has been suggested that this identity, where it occurs, indicates a lack of competition, or even continuing conspiracy, among competing manufacturers. In all candor, may I say that identity of prices on standard, mass-produced items normally indicates no such thing. On the contrary, such price identity is the inevitable and necessary result of the force of competition—a force that requires sellers of standardized items to meet the lowest price offered in the market. The manufacturer who makes a product on a mass-produced basis and where minimum performance or quality standards are a part of the customer specifications will not long be in business if he prices that product above the market. The customers will purchase elsewhere unless his product has demonstrable additional values accepted by a reasonably large number of customers. The manufacturer who prices his prod-

ucts below the market will quickly discover there is no advantage to him because his competitors drop their prices to the price level he establishes . . . It is simply not true that uniformity of prices is evidence of collusion. Nor is it true that uniformity of prices on sealed bids amounts to an elimination of price competition. The facts are that vigorous price competition continually takes place with one effect being a uniformity of catalog prices and, therefore, a uniformity of sealed bid quotations. Suppliers come to the conclusion—some possibly reluctantly —that if they want to continue to offer a particular product for sale that they will have to offer it at market prices equal to the lowest available from any supplier of any acceptable product.[43]

Even if the product being sold is *not* a standardized shelf item, firms desiring to be "competitive" tend to meet the already established price. This procedure will hold even if a firm has not as yet manufactured the specialized electrical apparatus; it will quote the price of its competitor to announce to its potential customers that it *can* and *will* be competitive if orders should appear. Thus the "costs" in the short run, or even before the product is actually made, are *irrelevant* to price determination. Again and again, the businessmen that testified before the Senate Subcommittee on Antitrust and Monopoly pointed out that market prices were determined by the firm willing to sell at the lowest price. But again and again, many of the Senators on the committee, particularly Kefauver, refused to accept that explanation. Like many economists, Senator Kefauver implied that competitive prices should have been determined by "costs"—completely ignoring the fact that buyers of electrical apparatus have no idea what producer "costs" are, and care less. Note the following exchange of views with respect to "costs" and competition:

> SENATOR KEFAUVER: How does it happen that each one of these other companies comes up with exactly the same cost figures and decides that should be their price?
>
> MR. HODNETTE: I have no idea what

---

[42] *Ibid.,* p. 17431.

[43] *Ibid.,* pp. 17672–17673.

their costs are. The prices are determined by competition in the market place, not by cost.[44]

Or note the discussion below between Senator Kefauver and Mark W. Cresap, Jr., president of Westinghouse, with respect to the nearly identical prices ($17,402,300) submitted by different companies on a 500,000 kilo-watt turbine:

SENATOR KEFAUVER: . . . did you arrive at that price independently?

MR. CRESAP: Yes, sir.

SENATOR KEFAUVER: You figured it yourself?

MR. CRESAP: We arrived at that particular one on the basis of the fact that General Electric Co. had lowered its costs for this type of machine, and we met it.

SENATOR KEFAUVER: You mean you copied it from G.E.?

MR. CRESAP: No, we met the price.

SENATOR KEFAUVER: Have you ever made one?

MR. CRESAP: Have we ever made—

SENATOR KEFAUVER: A 500,000 kilowatt turbine?

MR. CRESAP: We had not at that time, no sir.

SENATOR KEFAUVER: Have you made one yet?

MR. CRESAP: No.

SENATOR KEFAUVER: Has G.E. ever made one?

MR. CRESAP: Yes, they are making one.

SENATOR KEFAUVER: They have never made one, though?

MR. CRESAP: Well, this is the price that they established for this machine, and we met it.

SENATOR KEFAUVER: You mean you copied it?

MR. CRESAP: We didn't copy the machine. We met the price because it was the lowest price in the marketplace.

SENATOR KEFAUVER: In other words, you copied the figures exactly, $17,-402,300, from General Electric?

MR. CRESAP: Senator, we had a higher price on the machine on our former book, and when they reduced, we reduced to meet them, to meet competition.

SENATOR KEFAUVER: If you never made one, how would you know how much to lower or how much to raise?

MR. CRESAP: You would know by the basis of how much you needed the business, what the conditions of your backlog was, what your plant load was, what your employment was, and what you thought you had to do in order to get the business.

SENATOR KEFAUVER: In any event, you would not know whether you were making money or losing money on this bid, because you had never made one, and Mr. Eckert told us you had no figures on which to base this price. You just followed along with G.E. Is that the policy of your company?

MR. CRESAP: The policy of our company is to meet competitive prices, and this is the manner in which the book price on this particular machine was arrived at . . .

SENATOR KEFAUVER: Even if you lost money?

MR. CRESAP: Even if we lost money, if we needed the business to cover our overheads and to keep our people working . . .

SENATOR KEFAUVER: On something that you had never sold, had never made, and that you have not made yet, and they have not made one yet, their price is $17,-402,300, the same as yours.

MR. CRESAP: They would have to be, Mr. Chairman, if we are going to be competitive. We cannot have a higher price than our competition.

SENATOR KEFAUVER: How about a lower price?

MR. CRESAP: If we had a lower price, I am sure they would meet it, if they wanted to get the business very badly.[45]

The Effectiveness of Conspiracy: The Conspirators' View. The essential question to be answered in this section is: did the electrical equipment manufacturers successfully conspire to raise, fix and maintain prices? Did the meetings—which many executives admitted attending—actually fix the level of prices and price changes, or did competition? Was the driving force behind price identity collusion or competition?

The most acceptable generalization concerning the nature of the price conspiracy meetings must be that they were a failure or, as one executive rather disgustedly put it, "a waste of time." Without exception, every witness queried before the Senate Subcommittee on Antitrust and Monop-

---

[44] *Ibid.,* p. 17438.

[45] *Ibid.,* pp. 17628–17630.

oly stated that the meetings were *not* effective at all. (Why they attended will be discussed below.) Because this particular aspect of the conspiracy is so important—and so neglected—it must be documented thoroughly with direct testimony. The following exchange concerns "collusion" on *medium turbine* sales:

> SENATOR KEFAUVER: How would it work out? Just tell us how it worked.
> MR. JENKINS: It didn't work very good.
> SENATOR KEFAUVER: It looks as if it had the possibilities of working good.
> MR. JENKINS: The thing that is important, this is a dog-eat-dog business and everybody wanted it. There has never been enough business.[46]

And again, with Mr. Jenkins with respect to the end of the price meetings on *turbines*:

> SENATOR KEFAUVER: When did they break up?
> MR. JENKINS: In early 1959.
> SENATOR KEFAUVER: What happened then to cause this cessation?
> MR. JENKINS: It was a waste of time and effort. There was very little business. We were at the bottom of a buying cycle. Everybody wanted every job, and it was of no value.[47]

The following exchange concerns price "collusion" on *electrical condensers*:

> SENATOR BLAKLEY: If I understand, then, if your competitors were of the same mind as you, then it would be a general feeling that these meetings for the purpose of fixing prices would be in order; is that the way to interpret it?
> MR. BUNCH: An attempt may have been made to fix these prices, but, it was entirely unsuccessful.[48]

The following exchange concerns price "collusion" on *small turbine generators*:

> MR. FLURRY: What was decided at that meeting with respect to price level?

> MR. SELLERS: This meeting consisted of perhaps—I say "perhaps"—there were six manufacturers in this small turbine generator business represented. This was recognition of the fact that the prior bid price discussions which had been going on among the manufacturers *was so ineffective as to be rather useless*, and to try to determine whether or not people were serious in this endeavor or whether—well, it had become so useless that there was a question as to whether you should continue, and this was a meeting to discuss that. Also, an effort to stabilize the market at some place within a few percent of a published price, rather than 10 or 15 percent, where the market had drifted. Again, the meeting *was so ineffectual as far as I am concerned, because it promptly all fell apart*. This rugged individual type of business that we are in simply ignored—I will put it a different way. The forces that were coming about from lack of volume, and the pressure that was on a manufacturer to get volume, negated any price discussion. It just did not amount to anything.[49] (Emphasis added.)

The following exchange concerns meetings and alleged price collusion with respect to *medium voltage switchgear*:

> MR. FLURRY: I understood you to say that this broke off some time before 1959?
> MR. HENTSCHEL: That is right, sir.
> MR. FLURRY: What was the cause of that break-off?
> MR. HENTSCHEL: Basically the thing wasn't working. In other words, everybody would come to the meeting, the figures would be settled, and *they were only as good as the distance to the closest telephone before they were broken*. In other words, so the thing just wasn't working.[50] (Emphasis added.)

The following exchange concerns meetings that were designed to set and maintain the prices of *power transformers*:

> MR. FERRALL: What do you mean, Mr. Smith, when you say you did not know

---

[46] *Ibid.*, p. 16608. Jenkins was sales manager of medium turbine sales for Westinghouse.

[47] *Ibid.*, p. 16614.

[48] *Ibid.*, p. 16639. Bunch was manager of the condenser division of Ingersoll-Rand Company.

[49] *Ibid.*, p. 16669. Sellers was manager of the turbine generator division of the Carrier Corporation.

[50] *Ibid.*, p. 16884. Hentschel was general manager of the medium voltage switchgear department for General Electric.

whether any good would come of it or not?

MR. SMITH: Well, I meant by that, whether there was anything done at the meeting with competitors, which would in any way improve the price situation. Past meetings with competitors had been rather unfruitful in that respect.

MR. FERRALL: You mean you did not know whether they would abide by their agreements?

MR. SMITH: I don't know whether you can say that we had real agreement at any time . . . [51]

MR. SMITH: (continuing) My experience in meeting with competitors, as I have said before, indicated to me that it was a rather fruitless endeavor. It might be one day, it might be two days, after a meeting, before jobs would be bid all over the place, and there seemed to be no real continuity that came out of those meetings in the way of stabilizing prices at any level.[52]

And again with Smith of General Electric with respect to "price agreements" on *power transformers:*

SENATOR CARROLL: In other words, you reached agreement that there could be some stabilization?

MR. SMITH: There could be, but we agreed upon no stabilization.

SENATOR CARROLL: I understand that. I am not asking you to commit yourself, but there was this general agreement that you could stabilize?

MR. SMITH: General understandings that it would probably be best if it was possible.

SENATOR CARROLL: Did you remove the threat of price cutting?

MR. SMITH: No, sir.

SENATOR CARROLL: Was there any price cutting after that?

MR. SMITH: Surely, sir.

SENATOR CARROLL: Did it continue?

MR. SMITH: Yes, sir . . .

SENATOR CARROLL: (Continuing) I think I have asked this question, but I will ask it again. Do the records then reflect that you got some price stabilization after that time? I mean, not the records, but the practice, your profits.

MR. SMITH: The price curves which

were maintained by the power transformer department all the way through this whole period is one of this kind of picture, up and down all the time.

SENATOR CARROLL: Did it improve after your last conference, the conference in 1958? Did it improve in 1958 after the two presidents got together?

MR. SMITH: No, sir, not to amount to anything.

SENATOR CARROLL: Did it improve any in 1959?

MR. SMITH: It got worse in 1959.[53]

The following exchange again concerns price meetings with respect to fixing prices on *power transformers:*

SENATOR HRUSKA: By and large, Mr. Ginn, you have had considerable experience in the business of meetings with competitors. How effective were those meetings to get the job done that they purported to have as an objective?

MR. GINN: Senator, this is the way I will put it. *If people did not have the desire to make it work, it never worked. And if people had the desire to make it work, it wasn't necessary to have the meetings and violate the law.*

SENATOR HRUSKA: So that your preliminary discussions and meetings with competitors—

MR. GINN: *Were worthless.*

SENATOR HRUSKA: Were not necessarily controlling?

MR. GINN: *Were worthless . . . I think that the boys could resist everything but temptation.* No sir, I'll tell you frankly, Senator, I think if one thing I would pass on to posterity, that it wasn't worth it. *It didn't accomplish anything,* and all you end up with is by getting in trouble.[54] (Emphasis added.)

And a final exchange with respect to the effectiveness of "fixing" *transformer* prices:

MR. ROSENMAN: And you fixed prices, you participated in the fixing of prices?

MR. MCCOLLOM: That is right.

MR. ROSENMAN: Fixing of the book price—

MR. MCCOLLOM: We discussed those in meetings.

---

[51] *Ibid.,* p. 16961. Smith was the general manager of the transformer division for General Electric.

[52] *Ibid.,* p. 16962.

[53] *Ibid.,* pp. 17013, 17029.

[54] *Ibid.,* pp. 17069–17070. Ginn was vice president and general manager of the turbine division for General Electric.

MR. ROSENMAN: But you maintain that there was no agreement as to these?

MR. MCCOLLOM: We discussed these generally, and I say that there was no agreement, because *it didn't result in prices being quoted at those levels that were discussed*. There was just no evidence of any agreements in the actions that were taken by the parties in the meetings. There was no formal definite agreement in writing on this thing.

SENATOR KEFAUVER: None of it was in writing?

MR. MCCOLLOM: There was no verbal agreement, just a discussion.

SENATOR KEFAUVER: Just an understanding?

MR. MCCOLLOM: Just a discussion of it.

SENATOR KEFAUVER: Was there, or was there not, an understanding about what was going to be done?

MR. MCCOLLOM: Well, *I think the results indicate that there was no understanding*.

SENATOR KEFAUVER: *I am not talking about results*. I am asking whether at the meeting there was an understanding about what was going to be done?

MR. MCCOLLOM: Well there was a discussion of price levels 15 percent off book. I might have gone out of the meeting thinking the other people understood it; they might have gone out thinking I did; *but there was no action that supported any understanding of it*, that there was any understanding because it did not occur. It did not happen.[55] (Emphasis added.)

Summary and Conclusions. Through the entire period of the conspiracy, the firms could not suspend price competition. Although there had been repeated *attempts* to fix, raise, and maintain prices, the attempts rather monotonously failed. Price agreement might last a day or two, and "then somebody would break the line and there would be another meeting." [56] In most cases, the prime purpose of the meetings was an attempt to restore "agreements" that were being openly and regularly violated in the marketplace. In other instances, the meetings were an attempt by some firms

to "get the line on prices," i.e., to find out what a competitor might do with his price in the near future.[57] Such information would allow a firm to bid just under its competitor and secure the desired business. As Raymond Smith, former general manager of the transformer division at General Electric, put it:

> . . . my prime objective was to find out whether the Westinghouse people had received any instructions from their people, and failing to do so, I thought the meeting was worthless.[58]

The Ineffectiveness of Conspiracy. Hard and fast evidence on *actual* prices and price changes during the period of the conspiracy is extremely spotty. The Bureau of Labor Statistics (BLS) indexes of wholesale prices show substantial increases for various kinds of electrical apparatus. Switchgear prices, for example, increase from an index number of 112.7 in 1950 to 127.4 in 1952, to 135.1 in 1954, to 154.1 in 1956, to 172.8 in 1958, and to 176.6 in 1960.[59] Since there were "meetings" with respect to the prices of switchgear—at least during the latter part of the 1950s—the impression conveyed is that prices were rather routinely raised and maintained at "unreasonable" levels.

The impression conveyed by the BLS statistics is an altogether incorrect impression. The statistics are based on catalog prices, and they do not necessarily relate to the *actual* prices being charged in the marketplace. The fact remains that all during the "conspiracy" period, switchgear sold at particular percentages off of book or catalog price. This "discounting" was particularly pronounced during the infamous "white sale" of 1954 and 1955, when switchgear was selling for as much as 45 per cent to 50 per cent off of book.[60] This "sale" was repeated in late 1957 and early 1958 when

---

[55] *Ibid.*, pp. 17378–17379. McCollom was the manager of the power transformer department for Westinghouse.

[56] *Ibid.*, p. 17883.

[57] *Ibid.*, p. 17523.

[58] *Ibid.*, p. 17013.

[59] *Ibid.*, p. 17767.

[60] *Ibid.*, p. 16740.

market prices were as much as 60 per cent off of book.[61] Ironically, the entire purpose of the switchgear meetings was to "do something" with respect to the "unreasonably" *low* switchgear prices. The meetings ended in failure and were abandoned before the conspiracy was discovered by the Department of Justice. There was no effective price fixing in switchgear at all.[62]

The fact that there was no effective price fixing in switchgear, or in many other electrical products, might be substantiated by an examination of profit data for some of the firms involved during the period of conspiracy. Although a positive relationship between "periods of conspiracy" and "unreasonable profit" would not prove cause and effect, the complete *lack* of any such relationship might be indicative of ineffectual price collusion. Indeed, if price conspiracy cannot produce "unreasonable" profit levels—and, thus, generate the misallocation of resources that so concerns the economists—why it is important at all? If collusion does not generate substantial profits, economists—for at least a generation—have made mountains out of molehills.

The twenty separate indictments returned by the grand jury in 1960 charged that a price conspiracy had been in effect in the electrical equipment manufacturers industry between 1956 and 1959. A comparison of the rates of return on both capital and sales for that period, with some previous period, is reproduced below for four of the most important firms involved in that conspiracy.[63]

Table 1

General Electric		
Years	Profits on Capital (Percentage)	Profits on Sales (Percentage)
1950–1955	20.5	5.9
1956–1959	20.1	5.8

Table 2

Westinghouse		
Years	Profits on Capital (Percentage)	Profits on Sales (Percentage)
1950–1955	10.8	5.1
1956–1959	7.0	3.0

Table 3

Allis-Chalmers		
Years	Profits on Capital (Percentage)	Profits on Sales (Percentage)
1950–1955	11.3	5.1
1956–1959	6.6	3.7

Table 4

Carrier		
Years	Profits on Capital (Percentage)	Profits on Sales (Percentage)
1950–1955	12.9	4.4
1956–1959	7.9	3.5

It can be observed from these tables that in *all* cases, without exception, the rates of return on capital and on sales were actually *lower* during the period of alleged conspiracy than during the previous period.[64] If the conspiracy was successful, the price and profit behavior of the firms involved certainly does not reflect that "success." More than likely, the conspiracy was a sad failure from the start to finish.

To understand why the conspiracy failed, it is necessary to examine two cru-

---

[61] *Ibid.*, p. 17103.

[62] The same conclusion might be made with respect to the prices of "large circuit breakers." See George J. Stigler and James K. Kindahl, *The Behavior of Industrial Prices* (New York: National Bureau of Economic Research, 1970), p. 31. See also Jules Backman, *The Economics of the Electrical Machinery Industry* (New York: New York University Press, 1962), especially Chapters 5 and 6.

[63] The tables are based on figures taken from *Moody's Industrial Manual,* and from *Price-fixing and Bid-Rigging in the Electrical Manu-*

facturing Industry, Exhibits 54A, B, C, pp. 17960–17961.

[64] The profits may have been lower for a good many reasons, the 1957–1958 recession in the economy is the best candidate. The point here, however, is that the collusion did *not* generate monopoly profits.

cial elements of the electrical equipment manufacturers industry: the industry's cost structure, and the nature of the demand for electrical apparatus.

Although there are thousands of firms that produce and sell electrical apparatus and machinery—and although entry remains relatively easy[65]—the important parts of the industry are dominated by a relatively few, extremely capital intensive firms. As might be expected, these firms are rather sophisticated innovators, and all maintain substantial research and development facilities at great expense. More important for our purposes, however, is the fact that the extremely high capital intensity, and the resultant scale economies,[66] generate pressures for "selective" price cutting when demand is low to gain volume.

The demand for electrical equipment is derived almost equally from industrial firms and electric utility companies. Since a high proportion of the total demand for electrical equipment is associated with new construction, or new generating capacity on the part of utilities, it becomes extremely sensitive to money market conditions. In addition, since it is a demand for a (postponable) producer's durable good, it can be expected to display the violent instability commonly associated with the "feast or famine" capital goods industry. Both factors foretell an extremely cyclical demand for electrical apparatus.

Given the instability in the economy and in the money markets during the period 1955–1960, and given the cost structure of the equipment manufacturers, it is not at all surprising to discover that price competition was severe and that catalog prices were not being honored. Here were expensively equipped firms with huge overhead costs hungry for a volume of business that did not materialize at existing price levels; this volume simply had to be attracted. In

such circumstances price cutting was inevitable. Although there is numerous testimony to support this view,[67] the remarks of George E. Burens, former division general manager of switchgear at General Electric, are indicative of the real situation:

> Everybody has their plant in shape. They have the facility. They have the organization. But they have no business. So, they are out grabbing. I think that is the thing.[68]

It was, indeed, the thing.

Price fixing was also difficult because there were always competitors who did not compete on a national basis. When demand was flat or falling, electrical firms closer to potential customers might simply figure the cost of a particular job, and quote a price to cover that cost.[69] Hence, price could be significantly different from national catalog prices, and "could be anywhere over the lot." In addition, there were so-called "tin makers" (firms that made "inferior" electrical equipment) that would make it a practice to underbid national competition, especially on sealed bid jobs.[70] Rarely would the non-national firms or the "tin makers" abide by any price agreement.

Further, there was the "problem" of price competition from the foreign firms. They could not be controlled directly, and they were not a part of the price conspiracy; accordingly, their pricing practices made it difficult—if not impossible—to raise, fix and maintain prices on electrical equipment. For example, prices on certain turbogenerators were cut 20 per cent when foreign competition entered the market, and meetings to "fix" that particular situation were "unsuccessful . . . quite unneces-

[65] The *Census of Manufacturers* reports that there were 7,066 "establishments" in the electrical machinery industry in 1958, compared with 3,970 in 1947.

[66] Walton and Cleveland, *op. cit.*, p. 13.

[67] See, for example, *Price-Fixing and Bid-Rigging in the Electrical Manufacturing Industry*, p. 16614.

[68] *Ibid.*, p. 16876.

[69] *Ibid.*, pp. 16693–16694.

[70] *Ibid.*, p. 17472.

sary and very foolish." [71] The ability of such meetings to contain price competition under such circumstances was nil.

Price collusion was ineffective in the electrical equipment manufacturers industry, therefore, because demand was unstable, economies of scale were substantial, competitors had different price and profit objectives, honesty and trust were nonexistent, and foreign imports were (increasingly) important. Under such circumstances, a successful price conspiracy would have been nearly impossible. The Justice

---

[71] *Ibid.*, pp. 16945, 17061.

Department, it appears, with all its legal fuss, fines, and headlines, ended a nearly impotent arrangement.

The general meaning of this chapter should not be misunderstood. It is not being argued here that "price conspiracy" is impossible, or that such a successful conspiracy might not work an "injury" to the buyers. What is being argued is (1) that the inherent market forces in a free market make most price conspiracies completely unworkable, and (2) that a sampling of the most famous price-fixing antitrust cases in history has revealed that they involved just such unworkable conspiracies.

31. Preface to *The Economic Effects of Regulation*

PAUL W. MacAVOY

To avoid all suggestions of mislabeling the product—an important consideration given the price—an advertisement might be provided at the outset as to what this study includes, and what it does not.

It is an attempt at analysis of the effects of cartel agreements among the major railroads east of the Mississippi River and north of the Ohio River before 1900. The effects take the form of changes in the time pattern of rates, tonnage, and profits following from formation or dissolution of such agreements. These effects are identified by the economic theories of competition, oligopoly, or monopoly.

The cartel agreement of greatest interest is that in operation at the time of the introduction of Interstate Commerce Commission regulation in 1887. The new Commission, from an economic point of view, placed controls over the railroads' business conduct. Particularly, it sought to prevent rate discrimination, to require certain services to be offered to all shippers, and to re-quire that rates or services be offered as publicized. These rules had some effect upon the actual rates set by the railroads—an effect estimated from a comparison of prices and outputs under regulation with those before regulation.

The regulation of the structure of rates, it is argued, tended to make more effective the cartel's control of the level of long-distance rates. The rates on eastbound transport between the Mississippi River Valley and the East Coast, in the fifteen years preceding regulation in 1887, fluctuated in consequence of frequent changes in the extent of cartel control. After 1875, there seems to have been persistent "cheating" on the rates set in conference, so that the level of rates declined markedly as one agreement after another broke down (particularly during 1876 to 1879 and 1883 to 1887). The effect of regulation, as assessed by comparing this period with 1887 to 1893, seems to have been to establish the cartel rates as the actual rates. Rates were "stabilized," and "increased," for long-distance transport of bulk commodities. Rates were "desta-bilized" when regulation was weakened by the Supreme Court in the later 1890's.

32. Competition in the Domestic Trunk Airline Industry: Excessive or Insufficient?

GEORGE EADS

It is clear that if the carriers in a market can agree, either tacitly or overtly, to exercise restraint in scheduling, load factors can be raised and profits improved. Such agreements would seem to be most likely in situations in which the number of competitors is few, in which each is of approximately equal size and financial strength, and at times when conditions in the industry have been relatively stable. The introduction of a new competitor who is either unfamiliar with the rules of the game or unwilling to play by the rules is likely to lead to a general breakdown of any tacit agreement that exists. We would expect capacity competition to be particularly intensive after a major series of route awards as new carriers attempt to win places in markets and old carriers react to these incursions. During such periods it is conceivable that carriers might incur short-run operating losses as they seek to improve their long-run market position.[1]

Furthermore, the willingness of the CAB in the past to grant fare increases during periods of low industry profits, regardless of the evidence that in certain instances these low profits have resulted from scheduling rivalry, has put the Board in a position of making possible and actually encouraging such service rivalry. In terms of the gaming model mentioned above, the policy of the Board has had the effect of raising all elements of the payoff matrix. The penalties attached to the solution in which all firms adopt aggressive capacity strategies have been lessened relative to the payoff to successful unilateral capacity aggressiveness.[2]

From *Competition and Regulation of Industry,* edited by Almarin Phillips. Published by The Brookings Institute, in press.

[1] A possible example is provided by recent developments in the Hawaii-U.S. Mainland market. Prior to 1968, United and Pan American offered the only unrestricted service between Los Angeles, San Francisco, and Honolulu. In addition, United, but not Pan American, had the right to offer unrestricted domestic service to feed into these markets. In 1968 United had 60 percent of the market and claimed an operating profit of $22.4 million on the routes, 25 percent of the airline's total operating profit. Then the CAB allowed TWA, Continental, and Western into the Los Angeles-Honolulu market; and Western and Northwest into the San Francisco-Honolulu market. Braniff and American were allowed into Honolulu but were required to overfly these West Coast gateways. These awards set off a competitive scramble that saw the number of seats in the Hawaiian market rise by 19 percent between February 1970 and February 1971, in contrast to the 2.4 percent growth in total domestic available seat miles during 1970. Passengers in the Hawaiian-Mainland markets grew by only 5 percent, causing load factors to fall from 46.3 percent to 42.9 percent. United was particularly hard hit. By February 1971, its share of the U.S.-Hawaii market was down to 36 percent. United claimed that its operating loss on its Hawaiian routes during fiscal 1971 would be $4.6 million. "Can a Hotelman Run an Airline?" *Fortune,* February 1971, pp. 31–32; Harold D. Watkins, "Hawaii Market Tests Airline Policies," *Aviation Week,* April 6, 1970, pp. 31–34, "Mainland-Hawaii Market Participation, February 1970" (*Aviation Week,* May 11, 1970, p. 46), "February 1971" (*Aviation Week,* April 26, 1971, p. 30).

[2] For a discussion of the possible implications of Board Fare Policy in this regard see "Rebuttal Testimony of George W. Douglas," Exhibit DOT-RT-2, CAB Docket 21866-7. The Board's recent acceptance of the principle that load factors should be taken into consideration when setting fares designed to produce a "fair and reasonable rate of return" for the industry is a recognition of the validity of this principle. See the decision of the Board in Docket 21866-6B, Domestic Passenger Fare Investigation, Phase 6B—Load Factor, April 9, 1971.

The decline of load factors with distance—a phenomenon that appears to occur to a significantly greater degree in competitive than in non-competitive markets—is a direct result of the interaction of the fare structure policy pursued by the Board until very recently and the forces just discussed that make for frequency of service rivalry in competitive markets.

Since much of the cost associated with transporting a passenger between two points is independent of the distance traveled (e.g., the cost of ticketing, the cost of processing the passenger and his luggage at the terminal, and the cost of taking off and landing the aircraft) costs per mile will fall with trip distance. Operating costs also decline—at least to a point—as the number of passengers flying between two points—known as the "route density"—increases.

Figure 1 shows the relationship that existed between costs and fares as of 1965–66 as estimated by the CAB staff in its study of the domestic air fare structure. The curve labeled "fares" shows published jet day coach fares as a function of distance. The curve labeled "yields" shows the average revenue per revenue passenger mile received by carriers as a function of distance and diverges from the "fares" line because of the greater availability of discount fares for trips of longer distances.

The curve labeled "Costs at Observed Load Factors" shows the "total economic cost" per revenue passenger mile as a function of distance. This includes total operating costs, and provision for a 10.5 percent rate of return on investment and normal income taxes. Since costs are on a revenue passenger mile basis, they are sensitive to the load factor assumed. The Board's staff used load factors that were considered to be representative for various aircraft types and distances based upon 1965 experience.[3] The load factors are shown in Table 1.

[3] For an explanation of the methodology employed in deriving cost, fare, and yield curves, see CAB, *A Study of the Domestic Passenger Air Fare Structure*, pp. 78–99.

Table 1 • **Jet Day Coach Load Factors by Distance Employed in CAB Staff Study of the Domestic Air Fare Structure**

Mileage	Jet Day Coach Load Factor (percent)
100	56.0
200	58.5
300	60.5
400	62.0
500	63.0
600	63.5
800	64.5
1000	64.0
1300	61.5
1600	58.0
1900	55.5
2200	51.5
2500	46.0

Source: CAB, *A Study of the Domestic Passenger Air Fare Structure*, p. 94.

That both fares and yields exceeded costs as estimated by the CAB staff on long-haul routes and were less than costs on short-haul routes reflects the long-standing CAB policy of cross-subsidization, a policy that has been vigorously attacked as inefficient and inequitable by economists.[4] However, what is important to note for purposes of the current paper is that the decline in fares with distance, generally called the fare "taper," that existed in the mid-1960s not only permitted the carriers to engage in cross-subsidization and still earn what the Board considers to be a "fair and reasonable" return on their investment,[5] but it allowed them to do so while experiencing the load factors shown in Table 1. A fare structure more tapered would have produced losses of the low load

[4] See, for example, Richard E. Caves, *Air Transport and Its Regulators*, (Harvard University Press, 1962). Pp. 402–3, 435–36.

[5] In 1965 the trunklines earned a 12.2 percent rate of return on investment (total investment less equipment deposits and capitalized interest) and in 1966 they earned a 10.6 percent rate return. (Both figures exclude the influence of the investment tax credit.) The Board at that time considered 10.5 percent as a "fair and reasonable" rate of return. CAB, *Handbook of Airline Statistics*, 1969 ed., p. 371.

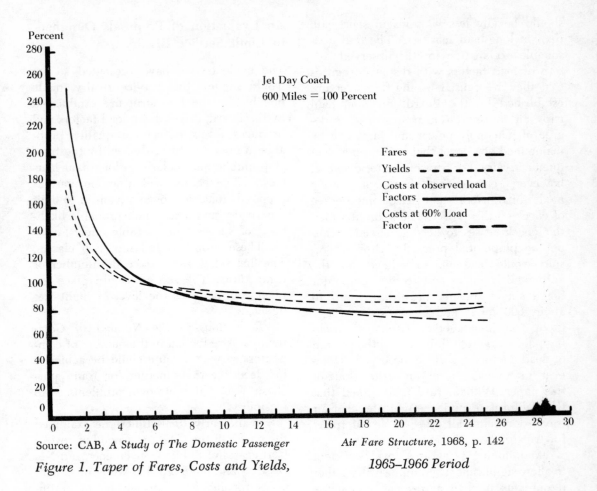

Jet Day Coach
600 Miles = 100 Percent

Fares
Yields
Costs at observed load
Factors
Costs at 60% Load
Factor

Source: CAB, *A Study of The Domestic Passenger*   *Air Fare Structure*, 1968, p. 142

Figure 1. Taper of Fares, Costs and Yields,   *1965–1966 Period*

factors experienced on longer-haul flights.

To illustrate this we constructed the curve labeled "Costs at 60% Load Factor." The points on this curve were derived using the same methodology employed by the CAB staff, but it was assumed that a 60 percent load factor, a figure roughly in the middle of Douglas' "optimal" range for longer distances, was achieved for trips of 900 miles or more.[6] The difference between the "cost" curve and the "cost at 60% Load Factor" curve at any given distance represents the cost to the passenger of maintaining the lower load factors em-

bodied in the former curve.[7] The Board, by establishing the fare and yield taper shown was validating this degree of frequency rivalry.

We find no basis for concluding that, holding the number of competitors and market density constant, frequency rivalry

---

[6] The basic cost data used in constructing this curve are contained in Tables 4–7, CAB, *A Study . . .* , pp. 84–91, column BBB in each case. The choice of which type aircraft to assign to a given distance was made according to Tables 11 and 12, pp. 98–99.

[7] An example may clarify this point. The load factor for trips of 2,500 miles, roughly the distance between New York and Los Angeles, was 46.0 percent in 1965. The total economic cost of providing a trip of this distance (jet coach) was $101.50 (CAB, *A Study of the Domestic Air Fare Structure*, p. 99). The total economic cost of providing the same trip at 60 percent load factor on the same type of aircraft (four engine turbo-fan) would have been $85.25 (p. 84 Column 34BBB: 3.41 cents per mile x 2.500 miles), or $16.25 less. This $16.25 went to provide the higher quality of service represented by a 46.0 percent rather than a 60.0 percent average load factor.

should be any less vigorous in short-haul than in long-haul markets.[8] The only reasonable explanation for the observed pattern of load factors with distance, then, is that they are caused by the fare structure established by the Board. For long-haul trips, air transportation possesses some degree of monopoly power and fares can be maintained at a level that will support frequency rivalry. For trips of shorter distance, however, competition from alternative modes of transportation place some degree of check on this power. The point at which this check ceases to become effective cannot be pinpointed precisely. Gronau's results would lead one to believe that the automobile remains an effective competitor for a single traveler at distances up to about 600 miles and even further for a group traveling together. Gronau's switching points would fit in well with the pattern of load factors we have observed. However, in commenting on an earlier draft of this paper, William Jordan remarked that the California experience indicates that air travel dominates all other modes of travel for trips of over 200 miles in length.[9]

Maintaining fares at a level sufficient to allow significant scheduling rivalry either requires an implicit agreement among the air carriers not to compete on price but instead to compete on the basis of service quality or, what is more likely, a regulatory agency willing, either tacitly or overtly, to enforce such an understanding.[10]

---

[8] Douglas' load factor regressions include the number of passengers in a city-pair market as an independent variable yet he still finds that load factors decline with distance. Douglas, "Excess Capacity: The Cost of Service Quality. . . ." Table 7.

[9] This observation obviously reflects the fact that air fares in the major California markets are approximately half what they are in similar markets elsewhere. If these fares were employed in Gronau's model, the switching points would shift inward substantially.

[10] This explanation is consistent with Jordan's conclusion that "CAB regulation has made it possible for the certified carriers to operate as a cartel, albeit an imperfect one." William Jordan, *Airline Regulation in America; Effects and Im-*

An Evaluation of Proposals Designed to Limit Service Rivalry

The evidence we have presented so far would suggest that service rivalry, made possible by the fare structure established by the Board, drives down load factors and produces levels of service quality probably in excess of those desired by the traveling public, particularly in long-haul markets. This section will examine various proposals that have been advanced to limit this rivalry and assess their probable likelihood of success and possible effects.

These proposals fall into two classes. The first set would reduce the number of competitors. The second would place explicit controls over the level of flight frequencies.

Reductions in the Number of Competitors. A reduction in the number of competitors serving a route could be achieved by decertification, merger, or route purchase. Each raises its own problems as to feasibility.

In the early 1950s Bluestone examined the power of the CAB to suspend or revoke Certificates of Public Convenience and Necessity[11] and observed that while precedent exists for indefinite suspension of certificates subject to the requirements of public convenience and necessity, outright revocation of a certificate can only occur if a carrier intentionally fails to carry out an order of the CAB and continues to fail to comply after the CAB issues another order directing compliance. Bluestone noted, however, that even the Board's suspension power had not been tested thoroughly in the courts.

In the early 1950s two suits were filed by trunk carriers against the CAB alleging that suspending their authority at points where they were permanently certificated and replacing them with local service carriers constituted a taking of property with-

---

perfections (John Hopkins Press, 1970), p. 227.

[11] Bluestone, "The Problem of Competition . . . Part II," pp. 70–72.

out due process of law. The courts found for the Board in both cases, but specifically refused to consider the question of the boundaries of the Board's suspension powers, contenting themselves with ruling that, in the cases before them, the Board had not exceeded its statutory authority.[12] We are unaware of any subsequent cases. However, there can be no doubt that should the Board undertake a policy of industry "restructuring" through its suspension powers, numerous legal challenges would arise. Amendment of the Federal Aviation Act by Congress to permit their broader use might well be required.

The authority of the Board to approve carrier-initiated mergers—even ones which would result in a substantial lessening of competition—is clear. The Board also has the power, obviously, to suggest mergers that it would like to see proposed. However, that the Board could force mergers upon unwilling carriers is open to question. When the trunk carriers were dependent upon the government for subsidies, the Board had a weapon that could have been used to "encourage" mergers. Today, the Board might be able to threaten to withhold fare increases at crucial times or to inundate a carrier with competition on important routes; however, should the Board resort to such action, legal challenges likely would result. Again congressional sanction might be necessary.

The CAB's power to approve purchases of one carrier's routes by another also seems to be well established. All that is required is the finding that such a transfer would be in the public interest. In 1947 United Air Lines was allowed to purchase Western Air Lines Route 68 from Denver to Los Angeles.[13] The only condition set down by the Board was that the transaction not result in any net increase in the asset base of the combined carriers since

this would have raised the total dollar profits United could have earned under a constant allowed rate of return. We are skeptical, however, that any major restructuring of routes that would likely involve the dismemberment of existing carriers, some of which might be quite unwilling victims, could be achieved by the method of route purchase.

Controls over Frequency Competition. In part because of a recognition of the above-mentioned problems, most proposals for reducing inter-carrier competition do not envision a reduction in the number of carriers competing on any one route but instead propose that direct controls over flight frequencies be established. Direct control by the Board over service frequency is forbidden by the Federal Aviation Act,[14] but other avenues are available to achieve the same result. Under the plans that have been advanced by the airlines, whenever load factors on any competitive route fall below a certain level (55 percent has been mentioned) the carriers flying the route would be authorized to meet and negotiate a program of mutual schedule cutbacks.[15] Presumably, enforcement would depend upon the recognition of mutual interest by the carriers involved, for no formal enforcement scheme has been proposed.

Experience with cartels leads us to believe that it would be extremely difficult to negotiate and even more difficult to enforce such voluntary agreements.[16] Recent experience bears this out. As mentioned above, in late 1970 TWA suggested that carriers be allowed to meet and negotiate schedule cutbacks on certain city-pairs. Formal requests for permission were filed early in the Spring of 1971.[17] The Board

---

[12] Western Air Lines vs. CAB, 196F. 2d 933; United Air Lines vs. CAB, 198F. 2d 100.

[13] United Air Lines, Inc.—Western Air Lines, Inc., Acquisition of Air Carrier Property, 8CAB 298 (1947).

[14] 49 U.S.C.A. 1371(e)(4).

[15] "TWA Asks the CAB for Talks on Problem of Excess Capacity," *Wall Street Journal*, December 22, 1970, p. 4.

[16] See, for example, F. M. Scherer, *Industrial Market Structure and Economic Performance* (Rand McNally, 1970), pp. 160–61.

[17] Permission of the CAB to hold such talks is necessary in order to avoid antitrust problems.

issued the necessary approval, and a meeting of carriers was held in which twenty-one "over-served" markets were identified.[18] However, in eight of the twenty-one markets, at least one carrier objected to even a discussion of limitations. Therefore, the Board approved discussions for only the thirteen markets for which no objections were raised.[19] Agreement could only be reached on a formula for capacity reduction on four of these routes. On the other nine the talks broke down over such things as the proper weight to allow wide-body jets in the reduction formula.[20] In the four markets where an agreement could be reached, the negotiated reductions were to average 29 per cent during the winter of 1971 and 14 per cent during the summer of 1972. The aim of the agreement was to raise load factors on the four routes to the 52 per cent level.

The only markets in which an agreement could be reached were markets in which the Big-Three transcontinental carriers (American, TWA, and United) were the only ones certificated to provide service.[21] The smaller carriers either were unwilling to engage in capacity limitation talks at all or mistrustful of the motives of the Big-Three.[22] In fact, not even the Big-Three could agree on a formula in three city pairs in which they were the only competitors.[23]

Such difficulties should not be unexpected. As we have seen, since carriers do not normally compete on the basis of price, frequency of service determines market share to a substantial degree. A carrier that has a relatively small share of a market condemns itself to a permanently inferior position in that market if it agrees to go along with a cut in schedules, though such a cut indeed may raise its profits. The carrier with the most to gain is the carrier with the largest market share. Its dominant market share remains secure and its profits increase. Suppose, furthermore, that an agreement is reached and load factors rise to above the triggering level. Carriers who find themselves in an inferior position in the number of flights they are allowed to offer under the terms of the agreement would have a strong incentive immediately to initiate a new scheduling war in hopes of improving their position in the next round of negotiations. To assure that such agreements were effective, they would have to be permanent (i.e., not initiated by any trigger mechanism), and they would have to be legally enforceable in court, even upon nonsigners. Congressional legislation

---

An earlier attempt to reach a general capacity cutback agreement was torpedoed when it was alleged that the carriers had met *prior* to receiving CAB permission. If true, this would have been a *per se* violation of Section 1 of the Sherman Act. "Eight Airlines Granted Permission to Discuss Joint Flight Cutbacks," *Wall Street Journal*, May 17, 1971, p. 10.

[18] Laurence Doty, "Opposition May Stall Agreement on Flight Cuts," *Aviation Week*, March 29, 1971, p. 28.

[19] "Eight Airlines Granted Permission . . . ," p. 10. These thirteen markets included the top twelve ranked by passenger-miles.

[20] "Reduction Impasse," *Aviation Week*, June 28, 1971, p. 15; "Airlines Sign Pact to Reduce Flights on 4 U.S. Routes," *Wall Street Journal*, June 22, 1971, p. 5.

[21] The markets where cutbacks are scheduled are New York/Newark–Los Angeles, New York/Newark–San Francisco, Chicago–San Francisco, and Baltimore–Los Angeles.

[22] Braniff, Northwest, and Delta opposed the idea of capacity limitations and refused to participate in discussions. Continental was reported as having only a "casual interest." (Laurence Doty, "Opposition May Stall . . ."), Northeast balked at the proposed formulae in the three Florida markets in which discussions were held ("Reduction Impasse"). See also, Laurence Doty, "CAB Control of Scheduling Feared," *Aviation Week*, August 30, 1971, pp. 19–20.

[23] Agreement was not reached in the following markets: New York–Newark–Chicago, Philadelphia–Los Angeles, and Boston–Los Angeles. This example suggests that a Board policy of merging trunkline carriers into two or three large systems which still competed with each other on most routes might be necessary in order to achieve the degree of recognition of mutual self interest required to make a policy of "voluntary" capacity agreements even a possibility.

would appear necessary to accomplish this, but precedent exists in the Resale Price Maintenance agreements authorized by the Miller-Tydings Act of 1937 and the McGuire Act of 1952.[24]

As an alternative to attempting to reach an agreement on flight schedules, revenue pooling might be tried. This practice is common among European carriers and, according to Bluestone, is legal under Section 412 of the Civil Aeronautics Act.[25] However, the CAB has never permitted domestic carriers to pool revenues and has forbidden U.S. international carriers from participating in international pooling agreements. Under pooling, each carrier bears the cost of operating his own schedules, but revenues are placed in a common pool and divided up on an agreed-upon basis. This removes any incentive to overschedule. Indeed, marginal carriers have a strong incentive to withdraw from the market provided they continue to receive a split of the pool.

The adoption of pooling would not solve the problem of negotiating an agreement among the participating carriers—it would merely shift the focus of the negotiations from schedules to the division of the revenue pool. As with any cartel agreement, the problems of maintaining a pooling arrangement over time are formidable, and success would likely require legal enforceability of the agreement upon both signers and nonsigners.[26] Even Bluestone advocates that pooling be tried only for "temporary" periods.[27]

Effects on Service Quality, Air Fares, and Carrier Profits. Reductions in the number of competitors would lead to a substantial reduction in the number of flights offered and to increases in load factors if the evidence presented in Section III is to be believed. Agreements among carriers, if they can be made effective, also would have this result. The increased spread between actual and break even load factors would mean increased industry profits which *could* be shared with consumers in the form of fare reductions.[28]

---

[24] 50 Stat. 693 (1937) and 66 Stat. 631 (1952). For an account of the conditions under which nonenforceable cartel agreements may be expected to be effective, see Daniel Orr and Paul MacAvoy, "Price Strategies to Promote Cartel Stability," *Economica*, May 1965, pp. 186–197. Presumably a similar sort of analysis could be performed in the present case in which price is set and the agreement concerns a cost-increasing promotional activity.

[25] Bluestone, "The Problem of Competition . . . Part II," p. 82.

---

[26] For an account of European problems, see Richard F. Cobern, "Pooling Runs into Cost, Revenue Share Snags," *Aviation Week*, October 20, 1969, pp. 204–209.

[27] Bluestone, "The Problem of Competition . . . Part II," p. 87.

[28] A reduction in fares would raise break-even load factors and narrow the gap between them and actual load factors.

33. Overt and Covert Agreements[*]

FREDERIC M. SCHERER

The electrical equipment case illustrates vividly the fragility of non-binding collusive agreements, for parties to the agreements of the 1950s 'cheated' repeatedly, touching off bitter price wars. As one General Electric executive explained his group's decision to go its own independent way in 1953, "No one was living up to the agreements and we . . . were being made suckers. On every job some one would cut our throat; we lost confidence in the group."[1]

Two problems underlie the tendency for informal price-fixing and output-restricting agreements to break down. First, the parties to the conspiracy may have divergent ideas about appropriate price levels and market shares, making it difficult to reach an understanding which all will respect. Second, when the group agrees to fix and abide by a price approaching monopoly levels, strong incentives are created for individual members to cheat—that is, to increase their profits by undercutting the fixed price slightly, gaining additional orders at a price which still exceeds marginal cost. These two problems often interact, for parties dissatisfied with the original agreement may be especially prone to cheat in its subsequent execution.

The first of these difficulties has already been raised in the previous chapter. Hard bargaining lubricated by hard liquor cannot eliminate differences in firms' price and output preferences due to cost and market share disparities; it can only provide a favorable environment for compromise, if compromise is possible at all. Because price-fixing negotiations are usually conducted in secrecy, we have little evidence on the amount of internal stress encountered in establishing agreements. But there are indications that it is considerable. In the electrical equipment conspiracy, for example, there were conflicts over pricing policy between the high- and low-cost producers, and over market shares between the bigger firms and two smaller firms—one a new entrant. Both disputes were resolved only when General Electric and Westinghouse made concessions to save the agreement. Some of the richest insights have been provided by Bjarke Fog from interviews with company officials involved in six price-fixing agreements legal under the Danish laws.[2] Fog found that agreements were not easily reached; that negotiations were characterized by "reciprocal suspicion and distrust" concerning others' prices and motives; and that in two cases negotiations broke down completely even though agreement would have been to the mutual benefit of all industry members. Disparities in cost were one source of disagreement, as the pure theory predicts. Fog observed in addition that differences over broad policy —i.e., whether to take a long-run or short-run approach—were an even more important hurdle. In the industries he studied, the smaller firms generally preferred to make the most of short-term possibilities, while larger firms advocated a longer-range pricing perspective.

Given the difficulty of agreeing, there is a propensity for changes to be avoided once agreements are reached. The International Air Transport Association, for example, has been continuously divided into two camps: members preferring low trans-

---

[*] An excerpt from this section of a chapter on "Conditions Facilitating Oligopolistic Coordination" in F. M. Scherer, *Industrial Market Structure and Economic Performance*. © 1970 by Rand McNally and Company, Chicago, pp. 160–62. Reprinted by permission of Rand McNally College Publishing Company.

[1] Smith, *op. cit.*, April 1961, p. 172, quoting Clarence Burke.

[2] "How Are Cartel Prices Determined?" *Journal of Industrial Economics*, November 1956, pp. 16–23.

atlantic fares to encourage high volume, and those favoring high fares. Since the Association by-laws require that fare changes be approved unanimously, the result—at least up to 1969—was a perpetuation of the status quo. Changes were for the most part confined to such peripheral matters as jet surcharges, motion picture fees, and the definition of a sandwich. In his study of Danish cartels, Fog uncovered an extreme case in which a key product's price was left unchanged for a decade, despite rising costs and disappearing profits. Parties to the agreement were reluctant to suggest a price increase for fear of appearing weak to their confederates.

Once agreement has been reached, a different set of problems arises. The very act of fixing the price at a monopolistic level creates incentives to expand output beyond that quantity which will sustain the agreed-upon price. If a firm sells only a modest fraction of the total output, it may consider the price to be truly parametric—that is, not perceptibly affected by its own output decisions. As a result, it may choose to break formally or informally with the agreement, quoting a slightly lower price and expanding output until its marginal cost rises almost to the level of the fixed price. Of course, if every firm were to behave in this manner, the price will descend from the agreed-upon monopoly value to the level of all producers' combined marginal cost, where no further incentive for output expansion remains.[3] However short-sighted such undercutting may be, it has been known to topple many a price-fixing scheme. An additional hazard is the lure a high price holds for new entrants. The added output contributed by such entrants either drives down the price

immediately, or it forces parties to the original agreement to restrict their own outputs in defending the price, and this in turn can evoke such dissatisfaction among the original producers that they choose to abandon the agreement. In his study of German cartels, Fritz Voigt found that a combination of cheating, bickering among insiders, and new entry from outsiders cause numerous price-fixing agreements to be short-lived, breaking down after periods of operation as short as a few months.[4]

Despite these difficulties faced by groups seeking to restrict competition, we cannot conclude that explicit collusion is necessarily ineffective or unsuccessful. An agreement successful over even a short period can yield monopoly profits sufficient to make the effort worth while. Furthermore, many businessmen are farsighted enough to recognize that their long-run interests are served best by maintaining industry discipline, and this may be enough to inhibit widespread price-shading. Finally, it is often possible (especially in nations with weak antitrust laws) to formalize restrictive agreements in such a way as to reduce greatly the incentives for cheating.

An approach particularly popular because of its effectiveness and compatibility with antitrust policies is the insertion of restrictive provisions into patent licenses. Several types of restriction are possible when one firm or (outside the United States) several firms jointly hold a strong patent position. First, the entry of new sellers can be blocked by refusal to grant licenses. Second, each licensee can be restricted to a specific geographic territory or segment of the market. Third, the price of the patented product can be specified as one of the license terms.[5] And fourth, direct or indirect output restrictions can

---

[3] For an ingenious mathematical analysis of pricing strategies by which a cartel can deter specific firms from cheating, see Daniel Orr and Paul W. MacAvoy, "Price Strategies to Promote Cartel Stability," *Economica*, May 1965, pp. 186–197. The main weakness in their analysis is that almost any firm may be a cheater, and if all recognize the symmetric incentive for cheating, deterministic solutions lose their compelling character.

[4] *Op. cit.*, pp. 169–208.

[5] Patent license restrictions, and particularly price restrictions, lie in a grey area of American antitrust law. See U.S. Attorney General, *Report of the Attorney General's National Committee to Study the Antitrust Laws* (Washington: 1955), pp. 231–246.

be incorporated in the licensing agreement. A potent way of damping licensees' incentive to expand output by shading prices is to combine quota restrictions with punitive royalty provisions. For example, during the 1930s Westinghouse's license to General Electric's incandescent lamp improvement patents stipulated a royalty of 2 per cent for sales by Westinghouse up to 25.4421 per cent of the two firms' combined sales, but the royalty rate increased to 30 per cent for sales exceeding this quota.[6] Similarly, du Pont's moistureproof cellophane patent license to Sylvania during the 1930s prescribed a punitive royalty rate of 30 per cent or more for sales exceeding some predetermined share of the total cellophane market.[7]

When patent protection is lacking, output restrictions may be enforced through various other formal cartel agreements. One approach is the so-called compulsory cartel, under which a government agency imposes binding production and marketing restrictions upon individual firms. The first true modern cartels (dating back to the late 18th century) were of this type, and governments (including that of the United States) have over the years continued to encourage output restriction in some in-dustries, particularly for raw materials such as petroleum, tobacco, coal, sugar, tin, tea, coffee, and rubber.[8] If national laws permit, industry members may enter voluntarily into formal cartel agreements prescribing penalty payments when output quotas are exceeded. Excess production penalties were a prominent feature of the European steel and aluminum cartels following World War I.[9] As a third possibility, work week limitations written into labor contracts through collective bargaining may be used as a means of restricting output. This approach was successful in the U.S. flat glass industry during the 1920s.[10] The United Mine Workers have been accused of similar attempts in the bituminous coal industry, although the evidence is disputed.[11]

---

[6] See G. W. Stocking and M. W. Watkins, *Cartels in Action*, pp. 304–362; and H. C. Passer, *The Electrical Manufacturers* (Cambridge: Harvard University Press, 1953), pp. 161–164.

[7] G. W. Stocking and W. F. Mueller, "The Cellophane Case and the New Competition," *American Economic Review*, March 1955, p. 43.

[8] G. W. Stocking and M. W. Watkins, *Cartels or Competition?* (New York: Twentieth Century Fund, 1948), Chapter 1.

[9] *Ibid.*, pp. 185–186; and R. F. Lanzillotti, "The Aluminum Industry," in Walter Adams, ed., *The Structure of American Industry* (Third ed.; New York: Macmillan, 1961), p. 192. For an analysis of the statics and dynamics of quota systems, see Fritz Machlup, *The Economics of Sellers' Competition* (Baltimore: Johns Hopkins Press, 1952), pp. 482–488.

[10] G. W. Stocking and M. W. Watkins, *Monopoly and Free Enterprise* (New York: Twentieth Century Fund, 1951), pp. 123–124.

[11] For conflicting views, see Almarin Phillips, *Market Structure, Organization and Performance* (Cambridge: Harvard University Press, 1962), p. 134; and Reed Moyer, *Competition in the Midwestern Coal Industry* (Cambridge: Harvard University Press, 1964), pp. 162–164.

34. Price Behavior in the Gulf Coast Refinery Market

DANIEL C. HAMILTON

The third instance of separate listings for domestic and export prices concerns the attempt at discrimination that failed. In January 1929, the Export Petroleum Association had been incorporated under the terms of the Webb Act to engage in the export trade of crude and products on behalf of its members. At the time of incorporation sixteen American oil companies executed membership agreements. One additional member joined in 1930, to make a total membership of seventeen companies, as follows: Atlantic Refining, Cities Service, Continental Oil, Gulf, Maryland Oil Company, Pure Oil, Richfield, Shell-Union, Sinclair, Standard of California, Standard of Indiana, Standard of New York, Standard Oil Export Corporation (a subsidiary of Standard of New Jersey), Texas, Tidewater, Union Oil, and Vacuum Oil Company.

The membership agreements provided that each member would abide by the association's export price committee with respect to prices, its quota committee with respect to quotas, and its general committee with respect to the other conditions and details of all offerings, sales, or deliveries in or for the export trade. However, this seemingly comprehensive control arrangement ran afoul of the usual snags of such coöperative attempts. On the one hand, internal disagreements hamstrung the Association from the outset—an outcome that was perhaps implicit in the necessity of establishing a unanimous consent rule on the part of its committee's decisions before the member companies were willing to join. On the other hand, even in its heyday the Association membership accounted for less than one half of the industry's total exports of crude and products, a circumstance that had a direct bearing on the organization's short and unsuccessful life.[1]

Apparently the Association's activities were never extended beyond kerosene and gasoline, and troubles were encountered from the start. The first reference to the organization in the trade press is found in the *National Petroleum News* for January 23, 1929. There, the organization of the Association is noted, with the observation that the overnight advance of 0.250–0.625¢ in the Gulf cargo market for gasoline and kerosene was believed to result from the Association's formation.[2]

From then until its collapse and the cancellation of its export price schedules on November 7, 1930, the Association functioned in a limited and increasingly ineffective manner. The trade press during this interval was full of rumors of internecine strife and reports of nonmember competition both in the Gulf and from foreign refiners. As early as February 20 the press reported great concern among Association members over a sale by one member which was below Association prices. A further straw in the wind was the simultaneous offering of U.S. Motor (regular-grade gasoline) by nonmembers at one-half cent under Association prices, and the reduction of mid-continent quotations of 64–66 gravity (which was more important in the export trade) to a point at which their delivered costs at the Gulf would also be under the Association quotation.[3] The next week foreign buyers were pictured as holding back, feeling that weaker domestic

[1] Federal Trade Commission, *The International Petroleum Cartel*, pp. 220–6.

[2] *National Petroleum News*, January 23, 1929, pp. 28, 112.

[3] *Ibid.*, February 20, 1929, p. 104.

markets would force an early cut in export prices, and early in March the sale of two cargoes of 61–63 gravity gasoline by non-members was reported as greatly concerning Association members.[4]

This set the tone. In April "for the second time recently" a commission broker purchased a large cargo of mid-continent gasoline for a foreign company, "understood to result from the elimination of much competitive bidding at the Gulf by the export Association." [5] In June, the competition of Dutch West Indies, Anglo-Persian, Romanian, and Russian refiners was reported as further hampering the efforts of the Association to advance Gulf export quotations.[6] In August, weakness in the mid-continent market further alarmed Association members by enabling foreign buyers to enter that market directly, and in September rumors were heard of an impending cut in Association prices as a result of such direct inquiries in the field.[7] This trend of events apparently continued through the fall months, and by December the Association was reported as buying heavily in the mid-continent for January and February shipment. Had such buying not occurred, the North Texas refiners would have had "to sell to independent exporters or foreign buyers direct," or else switch to the production of U.S. Motor for shipment into Group 3 territory.[8] Additional purchases were recorded in February and April, and in June there were further rumors of an Association price cut because mid-continent

supplies could again be delivered at the Gulf below Association postings.[9] In August, it was reported that Association sales had for some time been held back by its high quotations, but that two members had refused to approve a price reduction because the bulk of their shipments at that time were moving under contract at posted prices and they did not wish to cut the price on this business to protect their much smaller volume of spot sales.[10] On September 17 the *National Petroleum News* stated that the Association had denied permission for members to shade postings "where competition requires," but the next issue reported persisting rumors that cuts would be made "to meet foreign competition as well as nonmember competition," and on October 1, the Association cut its prices "to the levels of independent exporters." [11] In the first week of November, Gulf brokers were again one-half cent under Association prices, and on November 7 all postings were withdrawn, the Association having failed in its attempt to maintain export prices "which both foreign and independent United States companies undercut." Only when Association quotations were at domestic levels "would members get their usual business." [12]

This brought to an end the only known attempt at systematic and purposive price discrimination between domestic and export sales in the Gulf market. Although backed by the combined efforts of seventeen major refiners, competitive forces both within and without had brought it to an early and unsuccessful demise.

---

[4] *Ibid.*, February 27, 1929, p. 120; and March 13, 1929, p. 112.

[5] *Ibid.*, April 24, 1929, p. 125.

[6] *Ibid.*, June 26, 1929, p. 128.

[7] *Ibid.*, August 7, 1929, p. 136; and September 4, 1929, p. 120.

[8] *Ibid.*, October 9, 1929, p. 128; October 16, 1929, p. 112; October 30, 1929, p. 162; November 11, 1929, p. 112; December 18, 1929, p. 31.

[9] *Ibid.*, February 26, 1930, p. 112; April 2, 1930, p. 109; June 25, 1930, p. 119.

[10] *Ibid.*, August 6, 1930, p. 112.

[11] *Ibid.*, September 17, 1930, p. 88; September 24, 1930, p. 224; October 1, 1930, p. 95.

[12] *Ibid.*, November 5, 1930, p. 88; and November 12, 1930, p. 286.

35. The American Sugar Refinery Company, 1887-1914: The Story of a Monopoly*

RICHARD O. ZERBE

This paper examines the formation and aspects of the operation until 1914 of the American sugar monopoly. In so doing, it casts some doubts on what is more or less the standard interpretation[1] of this period, especially as it pertains to the concepts of excessive or ruinous competition, retail price maintenance, and predatory pricing. The paper, therefore, necessarily reflects on the viability of modern notions partially derived from this era. Specifically, this paper deals with the question of why and how the sugar monopoly was formed and with certain of its subsequent operations.

The Formation of the Trust

The sugar monopoly was formed for reasons both general and specific. Speaking generally, of obvious importance are the characteristics of the period such as its sweeping mergers and the rise of the corporation concomitant with the rise of large-scale financial markets and related phenomena. However, as far as the specifics with which this paper deals, the proximate reason for the sugar monopoly was that at that time its formation was both profitable and possible.

Patently, a low demand elasticity and low cross elasticity of demand indicate that sugar might be a desirable product over which to gain monopoly power.[2] But, of course, this was also true before 1887, the date of the sugar trust's incipiency. Why was a monopoly not formed before this time? The point is that the convenience, or more economically, the cost of formation was not always constant and it is from this standpoint that 1887 or thereabouts appears a logical date for monopoly formation. Increasing market and geographic concentration within the industry made formation significantly easier.

In a sense, the mergers forming the trust were merely a continuation of the concentration which had gone on before. Between 1867 and 1887, the twenty years prior to the trust's formation, there was a striking decline in the number of firms engaged in sugar refining from about 52 to 24, as well as in the number of plants from about 60 to 27.[3] Since the total production

* I wish to thank especially John S. McGee, and Dick Hamilton, and Prem Laumas for reading and commenting on earlier drafts of this paper. I would be happy for them to assume all blame and myself any credit.

Reprinted from 12 The Journal of Law and Economics, 339 (1969). Excerpt. Copyright 1969. By permission of the University of Chicago.

[1] Standard interpretation refers to the treatment of most histories and economic histories dealing with this period. See for example, the interpretation in the well-known text by Harold Underwood Faulkner, American Economic History (8th ed. 1960). Probably one of the reasons why this period seems subject to misinterpretation lies not as much in its absence of data as in its richness of life and change. This very richness makes it difficult to frame general hypotheses which will explain multifarious historical threads and attracts few who wish to plow through the material necessary to back up their hypotheses.

[2] See Henry Schultz, The Theory and Measurement of Demand 192 (1938).

[3] H.R. Rep. No. 3112, 50th Cong., 1st Sess. 73 (1887-88). H.R. Doc. No. 476, 56th Cong., 1st Sess. 109 (1899-1900). New York Investigation of Trusts 447 (1897) (Testimony of L. A. Fuller). Duns Industrial Directory (1867). John E. Searles, One Hundred Years of American Manufacturing 260 (Depew ed., 1900). The government census for 1890 gives the completely nonsensical figure of 393 for the number of refineries. This evidently was arrived at by counting plants also producing raw sugar. Between 1867 and 1887 about 30

of refined sugar rose from 0.54 million tons in 1869 to 1.00 million tons in 1886, the average plant size greatly increased.[4] From the above figures the increase would seem to be from about 200 to about 1,000 barrels per day.

Indeed, the reduced number of firms gave rise to an abortive cartel in 1882. Since its arrangements were to be carried out by voluntary agreements, the attempt proved futile.[5] The project was not a total loss, however, representing instead the purchase of knowledge. This experience of 1882 was undoubtedly one of the reasons why in 1887 the trust form of organization was used instead of a cartel form.

The structure of the sugar industry in 1886, the year before the trust's formation, was a result not only of industrial but also of geographic concentration and concentration in ownership as well. The refineries tended to locate in the great port cities which were centers of population and depots for the raw sugar. Of the twenty-three refineries in operation at the time of the formation of the trust, ten were in New York, four in Boston, three in Philadelphia, two each in New Orleans and San Francisco, one in Portland, Maine, and another in St. Louis.[6] At least six refineries, including three of the four largest, were in Kings County, New York.[7] These three and one small plant, totalling 55 per cent of the country's capacity and 70 per cent of the trust's potential capacity upon formation, were owned by one branch or another of the Havemeyer family.[8] The twenty-seven original stockholders comprised nearly all the original owners of the refineries who had acquired interest in the trust in the process of monopoly creation—at large gain to themselves—and the original eleven-member board of trustees or directors for Sugar Refineries Company included a good portion of all the important sugar men in the industry.[9]

It is the suggestion here that greater industrial and geographical concentration made monopoly formation cheaper. Certainly, if promoters' profits during this period were any indication of organizational costs, then these must have been of considerable importance.[10] Indeed, the costs of organization and negotiation were apparently important barriers to the success of the Spanish sugar monopoly.[11] Moreover, greater concentration is apt to be associated, *ceteris paribus,* with larger plants and therefore with greater capital requirements, and insofar as greater capital requirements are a barrier to entry, it would be easier to hold monopoly power where plants are large than where they are small. We conclude therefore that this growth of concentration within the sugar industry prior to the trust's formation was not coincidental and bore directly on the trust's formation.

Another relevant factor was the tariff. Henry Havemeyer, the first president of the trust, before a Congressional hearing in 1899 stated:

---

refineries went out of existence, according to the above sources.

[4] U.S. Bureau of the Census, Statistical Abstract of the United States 536 (1910). Hugh Camp, a former refiner, testified that the average plant, when he quit refining in 1870, had a capacity of about 200 barrels daily. H.R. Rep. No. 3112, *supra* note 3. Average plant size for 1869, obtained by dividing total consumption by number of plants, is 220 barrels.

[5] Searles, *supra* note 3, at 200.

[6] U.S. Supreme Court Briefs and Records at 164–171, United States v. E. C. Knight, 156 U.S. 1 (1894).

[7] *Id.*

[8] Hearings held before the Special Committee on the Investigation of the American Sugar Refining Company and Others, 62d Cong., 2d Sess., 181 (1911) [hereinafter cited as the Hardwick Committee].

[9] H.R. Rep. No. 3112, *supra* note 3, at 62; 2 Hardwick Committee, 2065.

[10] See for example, Eliot Jones, The Trust Problem in the United States, ch. 12 (1921). As will be seen, promoters' profits in the mergers of sugar refining companies were large and accrued to men within the industry, mainly to H. O. Havemeyer.

[11] John S. McGee, The Spanish Sugar Industry, 7 J. Law & Econ. 136 (1964).

The mother of all trusts is the customs tariff bill. The existing bill (tariff of 1897) and the preceding ones have been the occasion of the formation of all large trusts, inasmuch as they provide for an inordinate protection to all the interests of the country, sugar refining excepted.[12]

And, at another point, he maintained that:

Without the tariff I doubt if we should have dared to take the risk of forming the trust. It could have been done but I certainly should not have risked all I had, which was embarked in the sugar business, in a trust unless the business had been protected as it was by the tariff.[13]

The quotes are confusing and partially contradictory but suggest the tariff should be examined. This is also suggested by the wide press given to trusts and the tariffs around the turn of the century. Nearly all writers of the time who touched on the subject certainly agreed with Havemeyer about the tariff being the mother of trusts.[14] Unfortunately they seem more interested in repeating the statement than in resolving the question raised. Two persons, however, have attempted to show in more or less systematic manner that in general the tariff was the mother of trusts and both found sugar refining to be an egregious example

of this contention. Charles Beardsley, writing in 1900, found that "almost all the more important trusts are to be found in the protected industries" and that "the American Sugar Refining Company is the notorious example of the danger of overprotection."[15] Beardsley arrived at this conclusion by selecting a year, apparently arbitrarily, and calculating the tariff *ad valorem* of the price in European markets. For sugar under the Dingley Tariff of 1899 he finds a rate for 1899 of 71.23 per cent. Using approximately the same procedure, Byron Holt arrives at substantially the same results.[16]

This method is not adequate. A more satisfactory approach is pursued in Table 1 where the *ad valorem* tariff rate for the years surrounding the trust's formation has been calculated, as has the cost for various years of bringing sugar to the New York market. Apparently the tariff afforded protection to domestic refiners against their European rivals, although this does not mean the Europeans were more efficient since most received export subsidies.

Another piece of evidence that the tariff was important to the trust lies in its concern with the tariff bills. This is an area in which the trust received the worst kind of publicity. They lobbied heavily for the McKinley tariff[17] of 1890, which gave them free raw sugar, and also in connection with the Wilson Bill of 1894 and the 1897 Dingley Bill.[18] The trust's tariff activities were denounced by the muckrakers and others in strong and acerbic language.[19]

Another set of explanations of the trust's formation can be called a "hard times" theory of the trust.[20] These explanations

---

[12] H.R. Doc. No. 476, *supra* note 3, at 101. As far as I can tell, this is the origin of the cliche, "the tariff is the mother of trusts."

[13] *Id.* at 101.

[14] A special Senate committee ordered to investigate alleged attempts at bribery by the Sugar Trust and an investigation by General George Forsythe condemned the activities of the trust in connection with the 1894 tariff. See F. W. Taussig, Tariff History of the United States, 7 305–14 (5th ed., 1910); and 9 Political Science Quarterly 604–5 (1894); actually Taussig says that by the close of the nineteenth century, the sugar refining industry no longer needed protection. F. W. Taussig, Some Aspects of the Tariff Question 107 (1915). Muckrakers and others attack the trust on this score: Franklin Pierce, The Tariff and the Trusts 292–93 (1907); Henry Lloyd, Lords of Industry 217, 223 (1910); George Gunton, Trusts and the Public 205–08 (1899); New York Commercial Bulletin June 4, 1894 at 5; George Bolen, Plain Facts as to the Trusts and the Tariff (1902).

[15] Charles Beardsley, The Tariff and the Trusts, 15 Q.J. Econ. 379, 384 (1900–1901).

[16] Byron Holt, Review of Reviews (1899). In their overall argument, Beardsley and Holt confuse large size and monopoly.

[17] S. Doc. No. 378, 62d Cong., 2d Sess. (1912).

[18] *Id.*

[19] See *supra* note 14.

[20] 1 Hardwick Committee, 13–16; 2 *id.* at 2084–85. Paul Vogt, The Sugar Refining Industry in the

Table 1 • The Tariff and Sugar Prices

**Tariff on Refined Sugar as a percentage
of the Price in the London Market**

Year	Low	High
1869–1873	49	65
1874–1882	75	81
1883–1889	58	97
1890	12	120
1891	11	n.a.
1899	53	n.a.

Year	Export Price in London Market (Dollars/cwt)	Differential Allowance for Grade	Freight and Insurance	Total Cost of Shipping Sugar from Great Britain Excluding Tariff	Total Plus Tariff	United States Price
1885	$4.42	$.18	$.10	$4.70	$8.38	$6.44
1886	4.06	.18	.10	4.34	7.75	6.12
1887	3.81	.18	.10	4.09	7.38	6.01
1888	4.30	.18	.10	4.58	8.38	7.01
1889	4.79	.18	.12	5.09	8.18	7.64
1890	3.98	.18	.12	4.28	8.98	6.17

Source: The English prices come from 26 Encyclopedia Britannica 46 (11th ed. 1910–11); the United States prices are from Willet & Gray's Weekly Statistical Sugar Trade Journal, February 1900.
n.a. not available.

contend that the depressed state of the industry forced the refineries to join in an act of self-preservation; that excess competition necessitated the trust. As Edward Atkins, an early refiner and later president of the American Sugar Refining Company, stated: "Everybody wanted to run full time and the consequence was that nobody made any money." [21] Atkins was arguing that the industry was depressed, that this was a "sick" industry and that "sickness" caused the trust. This interpretation explains nothing. Nevertheless, this explanation is analogous to the one applied by historians to many industries of the period, including that of sugar refining. Faulkner in his popular textbook of American economic history makes sugar refining his illustration of excessive competition: "Competition was so excessive in the refining of

sugar, for example, that eighteen out of about forty refineries had failed before consolidation was begun." [22]

This view and important ramifications of it are, and were, fairly general and extend to more than the sugar refining industry. Much of the writing about this late nineteenth century period conveys the impression that the Industrial Revolution and unbridled laissez-faire working together gave rise to a perverted and self-destructive competition unforeseen by the proponents of laissez-faire. [23] This view of competition

[22] Harold Underwood Faulkner, *supra* note 1, at 422. Faulkner is used as an example not because he deserves particular castigation; on the contrary, he is cited because his is one of the outstanding texts.

[23] But a few examples are Faulkner, *supra* note 1, at 420–33; The Growth of the American Economy 605 (Harold F. Williamson, ed. 1944); Eliot Jones, *supra* note 10, at 66–67; 1, 2 Ida Tarbell, The History of the Standard Oil Company (1904); Henry Lloyd, *supra* note 14 and Wealth Against Commonwealth (1963); Paul Vogt, *supra* note 20, at 33.

United States 33 (1910). See, for example, the opinion of Professor Jeremiah Jenks, H.R. Doc. No. 476, *supra* note 3, at 45, 59–60, 109. Havemeyer subscribed to this theory, *id.* at 109.

[21] H.R. Doc. No. 476, *supra* note 3, at 59.

as warfare envisaged a number of instruments of this warfare, the more important being excessive competition, predatory pricing, retail price maintenance, unfair railroad rebates, and vertical integration.[24] Such a view has done great harm.

It is this author's contention that such a view is substantially wrong and stems firstly from the confusion of political evils and the evils of monopoly with competitive phenomena, and secondly from the misinterpretation of the above supposed instruments of competitive warfare. Probably, however, no better case for this view of competition as warfare could be found than in the sugar refining industry during the period covered here. Yet it will be seen that even here this view is found wanting.

Excessive competition is a misleading concept as a description of the situation in the sugar refining industry. Plants and firms have an optimum size or a range of optimum sizes. When the optimum size is greater than that of many of the plants or firms, or the optimum size is growing, those plants and firms smaller than the optimum must grow through internal growth or merger or be abandoned. When technical change is rapid, and the optimum size is significantly greater than the given plant or firm and/or is growing rapidly, the rational policy may well be to abandon the particular plant or firm. During the period in question technical change and innovation were manifestly rapid, and these changes affected a rapid change in the optimum plant and firm size for many, perhaps most, industries. This process naturally involved the abandonment of many of the old production units as well as forms of production.

As far as sugar refining was concerned not only were at least some of the refineries

patently profitable,[25] but most firms including Atkins',[26] were expanding capacity and also improving plants, a sign that their expected profitability was not too low. Perhaps more to the point, the industry's productive capacity had been rising steadily and rapidly in this period prior to the trust, and as Atkins pointed out, everybody was running full time. It does not seem useful to call such an industry sick.

Summary and Conclusions

The sugar trust originally arose out of the desire for profits concomitant with the greater ease of establishing a monopoly due both to increased industrial concentration and to the existence of a tariff. Neither excessive competition nor hard times in the industry furnish an explanation of the trust's origin.

In its beginnings and for quite some time thereafter the monopoly was dominated by one man, H. O. Havemeyer. In part this was probably due to the necessity of having Havemeyer's large refining capacity in the trust, his autocratic nature, the expediency of having one man decidedly at the helm in a new undertaking during a period of risks and rapidly changing conditions, and the promoter's profits which were open to Havemeyer as president. This is consistent with the fact that with Havemeyer's death the company was to a greater extent under the direction of a corporate board and management group, rather than a single individual.

The expansion of firms outside the monopoly and the entry of new firms into the business cut quickly into the monopoly's market position. Possible minor cartel arrangements aside, it was necessary for the monopoly to form and reform four times between 1887 and 1901. After each formation, it took between three and five years before sufficient competition arose to neces-

[24] See John S. McGee, Predatory Price Cutting: The Standard Oil (N.J.) Case, 1 J. Law & Econ. 137 (1958); Donald Dewey, The Shaky Case for Antitrust, Challenge 18–19 (Jan.–Feb., 1960); Ward Bowman, Prerequisites and Effects of Resale Price Maintenance, 22 U. Chi. L. Rev. 825 (1955); Robert Bork, Vertical Integration and The Sherman Act, 22 U. Chi. L. Rev. 157 (1954).

[25] H. R. Rep. No. 3112, *supra* note 3, at 49, 109. The large Havemeyer and Elder plant in New York, for example.

[26] H.R. Doc. No. 476, *supra* note 3, at 59.

sitate a reformation. The chief method of reformation was to buy out the competition. This was accompanied by large prices for the refineries being bought, substantial promoter's profits to those promoting the sale and increased profits to the monopoly.

Although it was suggested that under certain conditions price wars may arise, of three alleged predatory price wars conducted by American two were clearly not predatory but the inevitable result of increased capacity in lieu of an agreement controlling production. The data are insufficient for an explanation of the third, although if there was predatory pricing it does not seem to have been successful in the sense that the victims were bought out at depressed values or driven out of business.

As with the price wars, a retail price maintenance scheme generated adverse publicity for American. However, the initiative for the scheme came not from American but from the wholesale grocers. Likewise American received bad press for allegedly receiving unfair railroad rebates, while in fact testimony is directly conflicting on this score.

Under Havemeyer's leadership the monopoly attempted to control beet sugar production, but gave it up about 1905 possibly because such investments were proving unprofitable and because control was proving too difficult in the sense that entry was quite rapid.

Measured by a variety of criteria the monopoly seems to have been successful. Additional income was generated for at least promoters, the original owners of refineries going into the trust, and the owners of independent refineries. Contrary to suggestions there is no evidence that the original owners unloaded overvalued stock on to an unsuspecting public.

Not the least social cost of the monopoly has been the good use to which it put its early cartel experience. This experience probably enhanced the industry's ability to use the government in cartelizing the industry during World War I and especially since World War II. Former Agriculture Undersecretary Charles Murphy said of the 1963 sugar bill: "It was an ideal bill politically because it had something for everyone. Each sugar bill is a green pasture for some foreign sugar growers, domestic sugar growers, the sugar lobbyists, the sugar refiner, and the government because it gives each of them something."[27] Senator Paul Douglas estimated that our sugar legislation costs the American consumer about $400 million a year.[28]

The monopoly then would seem to have engendered a variety of social costs. There seems to have been the traditional misallocation due to monopoly with little justification from economies achieved. In addition it is suggested here that present misallocations due to government intervention in the sugar industry to some degree have a root in the early success of the sugar monopoly and in their experiences at cartel formation. Finally a not inconsequential cost lies in long standing misconceptions about predatory pricing, retail price maintenance, and railroad rebates which derived from the era covered here and towards which American's activities contributed significantly.

---

[27] The Charleston Gazette, Oct. 26, 1965, at 7.

[28] Id.

36. Oligopoly and the Antitrust Laws: A Suggested Approach

RICHARD C. POSNER [*]

This Article proposes for consideration a new approach[1] to a persistent and difficult problem of antitrust policy. The problem is: What rules and remedies are necessary to prevent supracompetitive prices in oligopolies, markets in which a few sellers account for most of the output? The heart of the suggested approach is a questioning of the prevailing view that monopoly pricing by oligopolists, when unaccompanied by any detectable acts of collusion, constitutes an economically and legally distinct problem requiring new doctrines and new remedies for its solution. The interdependence theory of oligopoly that underlies this view, in treating explicit and tacit collusion dichotomously, has obscured the similarities between the two kinds of anticompetitive behavior. I shall argue that both forms of collusion can be proceeded against under section 1 of the Sherman Act [2] as conspir-

acies in restraint of trade. The employment of section 1 against purely tacit collusion would do no violence to the statutory language or purpose; and while difficult problems of proof and of remedy would be involved, I am not convinced that they would be insuperable.

Part I of the Article summarizes the prevailing view in the economic and legal literature as to the distinctive character of the problem of oligopoly and notes the proposals to which this view has given rise; the focus is on the writings of Donald Turner, a distinguished scholar and former chief of the Antitrust Division. Part II explains my disagreement with Professor Turner's approach and suggests a reformulation of the problem of oligopoly that emphasizes the congruence between ordinary cartels, routinely dealt with under section 1 of the Sherman Act, and the special type of collusion that may arise under conditions of oligopoly. There are a number of serious problems in applying the statute to non-express collusion: the problems of establishing the requisite degree of agreement, of proving to the degree of certainty required by the courts that the defendants have tacity colluded, and of elimating violations once they have been proved; part III points out possible solutions to these problems. Part IV extends the analysis to some other approaches to the oligopoly problem, which differ from the section 1 approach in emphasizing the correction of market structure rather than behavior. Considered are proposed legislation that would authorize the dissolution of the leading firms in certain oligopolistic markets; a suggested interpretation of section 2 of the Sherman Act [3] to forbid "oligopolizing"; and the recent Department of Justice Merger Guide-

[*] A.B. 1959, Yale University; LL.B. 1962, Harvard University. Associate Professor of Law, Stanford University.

The suggested approach is a product of collaboration with Aaron Director, who, in addition, first suggested many of the ideas that are developed in it. I am also greatly indebted to George J. Stigler. I have drawn heavily not only on his published work in the field of industrial organization, but also on ideas suggested by him in conversation and on his helpful comments on an earlier draft. I also wish to thank the participants in the Industrial Organization Workshop of the University of Chicago, where an earlier version of the piece was given, for their helpful suggestions.

This article first appeared in the *Stanford Law Review*, volume 21, pp. 1562–1606. Copyright 1969 by the Board of Trustees of the Leland Stanford Junior University.

[1] For an older proposal having a family resemblance see Conant, *Consciously Parallel Action in Restraint of Trade*, 38 Minn. L. Rev. 797 (1954).

[2] 15 U.S.C. § 1 (1964).

[3] 15 U.S.C. § 2 (1964).

lines,[4] which strictly limit mergers that increase concentration.

I. Professor Turner on the Inapplicability of Section 1 of the Sherman Act to Oligopolistic Interdependence

The principal thesis of this Article is that section 1 of the Sherman Act, which prohibits "[e]very contract, combination in the form of trust or otherwise, or conspiracy, in restraint of trade," is an appropriate weapon to use against noncompetitive pricing in oligopolistic industries. That is not a popular view, partly because it is erroneously[5] thought to be foreclosed by the famous dictum in *Theatre Enterprises, Inc. v. Paramount Film Distributing Corp.* that "'conscious parallelism' has not yet read conspiracy out of the Sherman Act entirely," [6] and partly because it was forcefully denounced in an article written by Donald Turner in 1962.[7] That article is a good place to begin discussion, although a rounded conception of Professor Turner's approach will require reference to some of his other writings as well.

At the heart of Turner's analysis is the theory of oligopolistic interdependence.[8] The theory will be examined critically at a later point; for now, a brief summary will suffice. In a market of many sellers the individual seller is too small for his decisions on pricing and output to affect the market price. He can sell all that he can produce at the market price, and nothing above it. He can shade the price without fear of retaliation because the resulting expansion of his output at the expense of his rivals will divert an imperceptible amount of business from each. For example, in a market of 100 sellers of equal size, an expansion in output of 20 per cent by one will result in a fall of output of only about 0.2 per cent for each of the others. Under these conditions a seller will not worry about rivals' reactions in making his pricing decisions.

In contrast, in a market where sellers are few, a price reduction that produces a substantial expansion in the output of one will result in so substantial a contraction in the output of the others that they will quickly respond to the reduction. If, for example, there are three sellers of equal size in a market, a 20 per cent expansion in the output of one will cause the output of each of the others to fall not by 0.2 per cent but by 10 per cent, a contraction the victims can hardly overlook. Anticipating a prompt reaction by his rivals that will quickly nullify his gains, the seller in a concentrated market will be less likely to initiate a price reduction than his counterpart in the atomized market. Oligopolists are thus "interdependent" in their pricing. They base their pricing decisions in part on anticipated reactions to them. The result is a tendency to avoid vigorous price competition.

Professor Turner asks whether oligopolistic interdependence should be viewed as a form of agreement to fix prices that violates section 1 of the Sherman Act. The question has two parts: Is interdependence agreement? If so is it unlawful agreement? Turner is prepared to allow that, "[c]onsidered purely as a problem in linguistic definition," interdependent pricing could be deemed a type of collusion.[9] But to him a more important consideration is that "the rational oligopolist is behaving in exactly the same way as is the rational seller in a

---

[4] 1 TRADE REG. REP. ¶ 4430 (1968).

[5] *See* text accompanying notes 42–44 *infra.*

[6] 346 U.S. 537, 541 (1954).

[7] Turner, *The Definition of Agreement Under the Sherman Act: Conscious Parallelism and Refusals to Deal,* 75 HARV. L. REV. 655 (1962).

[8] *See id.* at 660–66. The economic literature expounding the interdependence theory is voluminous. Some places to begin are E. CHAMBERLIN, THE THEORY OF MONOPOLISTIC COMPETITION 30–55 (8th ed. 1962); W. FELLNER, COMPETITION AMONG THE FEW 3–50, 175–83 (1949); and Kaysen, *Collusion Under the Sherman Act,* 65 Q.J. ECON. 263 (1951). For a sense of the impression that the theory has made on judicial thinking in the antitrust field see United States v. Philadelphia Nat'l Bank, 374 U.S. 321, 363 (1963).

[9] Turner, *supra* note 7, at 665.

competitively structured industry; he is simply taking another factor into account" [10] (the reactions of his rivals to any price cut) "which he has to take into account because the situation in which he finds himself puts it there." [11] Since the oligopolist is behaving just like the seller in an atomized market, oligopoly pricing can be described as "rational individual decision in the light of relevant economic facts" as well as it can be described as collusion.[12]

Turner's decisive argument is that there is no effective remedy, fairly to be implied from section 1, against oligopolistic interdependence. An injuction that merely "prohibited each defendant from taking into account the probable price decisions of his competitors in determining his own price or output" would "demand such irrational behavior that full compliance would be virtually impossible." [13] To be effective, the injunction would have to require that the defendants reduce price to marginal cost, and the enforcement of such a decree would involve the courts in a public utility type of rate regulation for which they are ill equipped.[14] Dissolution of the guilty firms would be inappropirate in a section 1 context because

> to fall back on this remedy is virtually to concede that the finding of liability on the ground of conspiracy is dubious at best. If effective and workable relief requires a radical structural reformation of the industry, this indicates that it was the structural situation, not the behavior of the industry members, which was fundamentally responsible for the unsatisfactory results.[15]

---

[10] *Id.* at 665–66.

[11] *Id.* at 666.

[12] *Id.*

[13] *Id.* at 669.

[14] *Id.* at 670.

[15] *Id.* at 671. A conception of oligopoly quite similar to Turner's is basic to one of the recommendations (*see* note 83 *infra*) of the recently released *Report of the White House Task Force on Antitrust Policy* (July 5, 1968, mimeo.). As a succinct and lucid summary of the position that

Oligopolistic interdependence, in short, is inherent in the structure of certain markets. Only semantically can it be equated with collusive price-fixing, for it is unresponsive to the remedies appropriate in price-fixing cases. How, then, to deal with the phenomenon? Professor Turner had suggested an answer to the question in *Antitrust Policy*, a book written in 1959 in collaboration with the distinguished economist Carl Kaysen: enact legislation to condemn "unreasonable market power" and to authorize the dissolution of firms found to possess it.[16] If the earlier book is set along-

---

it is my main purpose in this Article to question, the relevant passage from the report deserves to be quoted in full: "[I]n markets with a very few firms effects equivalent to those of collusion may occur even in the absence of collusion. In a market with numerous firms, each having a small share, no single firm by its action alone can exert a significant influence over price and thus output will be carried to the point where each seller's marginal cost equals the market price. This level of output is optimal from the point of view of the economy as a whole.

"Under conditions of monopoly—with only a single seller in a market—the monopolist can increase his profits by restricting output and thus raising his price; accordingly, prices will tend to be above, and output correspondingly below, the optimum point. In an oligopoly market—one in which there is a small number of dominant sellers, each with a large market share—each must consider the effect of his output on the total market and the probable reactions of the other sellers to his decisions; the results of their combined decisions may approximate the profit-maximizing decisions of a monopolist. Not only does the small number of sellers facilitate agreement, but agreement in the ordinary sense may be unnecessary. Thus, phrases such as 'price leadership' or 'administered pricing' often do no more than describe behavior which is the inevitable result of structure. Under such conditions, it does not suffice for antitrust law to attempt to reach anticompetitive behavior; it cannot order the several firms to ignore each other's existence. The alternatives, other than accepting the undesirable economic consequences, are either regulation of price (and other decisions) or improving the competitive structure of the market." *Id.* at I–4 to I–5.

[16] *See* C. KAYSEN & D. TURNER, ANTITRUST POLICY 110–19, 266–72 (1959).

side the later article, however, the analysis is seen to be incomplete. *Antitrust Policy* correctly points out that the Supreme Court has never ruled that oligopolistic interdependence is a violation of antitrust law.[17] But it is a big step from this observation to the conclusion that new legislation is required to deal with the problem. It is always open to persuade the Supreme Court to revise its interpretation of existing law; and, to be realistic, it is much easier to sell novel doctrine in the antitrust field to the Court than to the Congress. (In fairness, it should be added that the Court's receptivity to novel antitrust doctrine is more apparent today than it was in 1959.) The Court would not even have to overrule a prior decision, for it has never been called upon to decide the legality of oligopolistic interdependence. The 1962 article explained why Turner believed that section 1 was not a suitable vehicle for an attack on oligopoly, but that left open the possibility of using section 2 of the Sherman Act (which forbids monopolization), as had been urged years before by Eugene Rostow.[18] In a very recent article Turner has endorsed that approach, arguing that section 2 can and should be interpreted to authorize the dissolution of leading firms in oligopolistic industries.[19]

In both *Antitrust Policy* and the Department of Justice Merger Guidelines, promulgated when he was chief of the Antitrust Division, Turner supported as a prophylactic against oligopoly a strict policy, founded on section 7 of the Clayton Act,[20]

of limiting horizontal mergers.[21] Since mergers historically have been an important source of concentration, a strong antimerger policy should do much to prevent new oligopolies from emerging and loosely oligopolistic industries from becoming tightly oligopolistic. The extraordinary stringency of the Guidelines may reflect in part Turner's earlier expressed view that once a market has become highly concentrated there is little than can be done under existing law to prevent noncompetitive, interdependent pricing.

II. Of Oligopoly, Cartels, and Tacit Collusion

A.

Professor Turner's analysis of the problem of oligopoly and his conclusion that section 1 of the Sherman Act is not an apt vehicle for its solution depend critically on a theory of oligopoly behavior that, although widely accepted, is unsatisfactory in important respects. The crux of the theory is that sellers in a concentrated market will be reluctant to initiate price reductions because they know that, unlike in an atomized market, a reduction by one will have so large an impact on the sales of the others as to force a prompt matching price reduction, wiping out the first seller's advantage and leaving everyone worse off than before.[22] Among other deficiencies, this formulation conceals some crucial factual assumptions. One is that there will be no appreciable time lag between the initial price cut and the response. But there will be

---

[17] *Id.* at 106–09.

[18] Rostow, *The New Sherman Act: A Positive Instrument of Progress*, 14 U. CHI. L. REV. 567 (1947). *See also* Rostow, *Monopoly Under the Sherman Act: Power or Purpose?*, 43 ILL. L. REV. 745 (1949); Levy, *Some Thoughts on "Antitrust Policy" and the Antitrust Community*, 45 MINN. L. REV. 963 (1961).

[19] Turner, *The Scope of Antitrust and Other Economic Regulatory Policies*, 82 HARV. L. REV. 1207, 1231 (1969).

[20] 15 U.S.C. § 18 (1964).

[21] *See* C. KAYSEN & D. TURNER, *supra* note 16, at 132–33; Department of Justice Merger Guidelines, 1 TRADE REG. REP. ¶ 4430, at 6683–85 (1968).

[22] I limit discussion of the effects of oligopoly in this Article to price competition. There are those who believe that oligopolists are prone to forgo other types of rivalry as well, but the evidentiary and theoretical underpinnings of this belief are as yet rudimentary. *Cf.* E. MANSFIELD, THE ECONOMICS OF TECHNOLOGICAL CHANGE 215–17 (1968).

a lag if the price cut can be concealed or if the other sellers are uncertain about the appropriate response and hesitate; and if a lag does occur, the price cut may pay even though it will eventually be matched. Similarly, if the other sellers cannot expand their output as rapidly as the first to meet the greater demand at the lower price, the first seller may improve his position even if the others meet his price reduction immediately. Lags in adjusting output to price changes must be quite common. Otherwise *any* price cut by a seller would, unless promptly matched, give him the whole market, regardless of the number of other sellers.

The interdependence theory also overstates the impact of one oligopolist's price reduction on the sales of the others. When a seller expands his output by lowering his price, only part of the additional output consists of sales diverted from his rivals. The rest consists of new sales to buyers who bought less or none of the product at the higher price. Depending on the elasticity of demand to price, then, much of the price cutter's new business may come from outside the market rather than from rivals. That will diminish the impact of the price cut upon them and so the likelihood of their responding immediately. The impact will also be diminished if the price cutter initially reduces price on only a portion of his output.

Moreover, the asserted distinction between atomized and concentrated markets with respect to price competition depends on a seemingly artificial convention. Different changes in output are compared, related only in that each represents the same percentage of each seller's previous output. It is true that if there are 100 sellers of equal size in a market having a total output of 1000 units and one increases his output by 2 units—20 per cent—the effect on the remaining sellers will be slight. But were there only three sellers in the market (each the same size) and one increased his output by 2 units, the effect on his rivals would also be negligible, a 0.33 per cent fall in output for each of them. To produce dramatic effects under oligopoly, a much larger expansion of output by the price cutter is required. Let the oligopolist in our example expand output by 20 per cent of his previous output (67 units) and, true enough, his rivals will be hit so hard that they will want to respond. But if, on the other hand, the same market were unconcentrated, and a seller (or several sellers) increased output by 67 units, the remaining sellers would equally want to respond. The theory must assume, then, both that an individual seller can expand output by only a fraction of his previous output and that individual sellers in an atomistic market, unlike their counterparts in concentrated markets, will lack the foresight to realize that a price cut by several of them may have an aggregate impact on the remaining sellers so large as to provoke a prompt matching response by those sellers. These may be broadly correct assumptions, but they are more properly matters to be studied empirically than to be tacitly assumed.

A further difficulty arises from the emphasis that the theory places on price *reductions*. The supposed reluctance of oligopolists to reduce prices is cause for concern only if there is reason to believe that their prices are supracompetitive. The interdependence theory does not explain, however, how oligopolistic sellers establish a supracompetitive price. To be sure, if costs or demand in a market decline, a failure to reduce price may have the effect of transforming a previously competitive price into a monopolistic one. But, given inflation, a supracompetitive price level normally could not be maintained without occasional market-wide price increases. How are these effected? The answer given by adherents of the interdependence theory is "price leadership." Consider an atomistic market in which price is equal to cost (including in cost an allowance for a fair return to the investors). As the result of a series of mergers, the market becomes oligopolistic. One of the leading firms then raises its price. It knows that it will be unable to maintain a supracompetitive price if its rivals do not match the increase; but it relies (so the argument goes) on their having the good sense to realize that all would be better off at the higher price, a price that approaches what a single firm would charge if it had a monopoly of the market.

This reasoning may be plausible; at the same time it undermines the proposition that oligopolists will be reluctant to reduce prices. That proposition depends on each oligopolist's reasoning that if his rivals match his price reduction, everyone, himself included, will end up worse than before, because they will be at a lower price level. But why will that unhappy result not be prevented on the way down by an appropriate exercise of price leadership? If, in consequence of the first seller's price reduction, the market price begins to crumble, one would expect either he or another seller to raise price and the others to follow, restoring the previous price level. Anticipating this sequence, oligopolists should not hesitate to undertake price experiments. Each should reason: "If I reduce my price, and the others do not follow, I will have increased my profits. If they match my reduction, any lower price will soon turn unprofitable, but when that happens I can restore my price to the original level confident that the others will follow." There is of course the danger that one of the others, reasoning similarly, will not follow him back up, but will say to himself: "If I raise my price more slowly than the others, I can increase my profits at their expense; should they come back down to my price, it will be time enough to raise my price then, and they will follow." If sellers reason thus, price reductions may be a dangerous tactic after all. But, then, if such reasoning is common, it will be difficult for oligopolists to reach noncompetitive price levels in the first place. Each will be reluctant to exercise price leadership knowing that the others will be tempted by the prospect of short-term gains at his expense to lag in following.

Further discussion is unnecessary to indicate my doubts that the interdependence theory of oligopoly provides an adequate explanation as to why prices in oligopolistic industries should exceed competitive levels. Nor need we pause to consider whether, by introducing the objections raised above as qualifications to the interdependence theory, it could be given a consistent and intelligible expression.[23] The relationship between the level of concentration in a market and the probability that pricing in that market will be noncompetitive can be elucidated in simpler and more fruitful terms than interdependence: in terms of the theory of cartels.[24]

B.

Let us return to our market of 100 sellers of equal size. Despite the large number of firms in the market, they would be better off if the market price were somewhere above their cost—ideally, at the level that a single-firm monopolist of the market would price. It does not follow that they will agree to fix prices or that if they do the price level will in fact be altered significantly. Collusion is a rational and effective business strategy only if its returns exceed its costs. One of the factors that affects the returns from collusion is the elasticity to price of the demand for the market's product. If the demand is highly elastic the monopoly price will lie close to the competitive price and collusion will yield only

---

[23] Competent expressions of the interdependence theory do qualify the simple view that I have been criticizing (see especially J. BAIN, INDUSTRIAL ORGANIZATION 304–48 (2d ed. 1968)), although not, in my opinion, adequately.

[24] For good discussions of cartel theory see J. BAIN, PRICE THEORY 283–97 (1952); D. DEWEY, MONOPOLY IN ECONOMICS AND LAW 7–24 (1959); G. STIGLER, THE THEORY OF PRICE 230–38 (3d ed. 1966); McGee, *Ocean Freight Rate Conferences and the American Merchant Marine*, 27 U. CHI. L. REV. 191 (1960); Patinkin, *Multiple-Plant Firms, Cartels, and Imperfect Competition*, 61 Q.J. ECON. 173 (1947). For some case studies see L. MARLIO, THE ALUMINUM CARTEL (1947); G. STOCKING, THE POTASH INDUSTRY (1931). The treatment of oligopolistic pricing as a form of cartelization is implicit in G. STIGLER, *supra* at 219–20, and in Stigler, *A Theory of Oligopoly*, 72 J. POL. ECON. 44 (1964), *reprinted in* G. STIGLER, THE ORGANIZATION OF INDUSTRY 39 (1968).

modest returns. Another important factor is the condition of entry. A supracompetitive price will attract new entrants. Unless there are barriers to entry, or at least an appreciable time lag before a new firm can enter, the cartel will be in jeopardy from the very start. If new entrants are not admitted to the cartel the maintenance of a supracompetitive price will be impossible. If they are admitted the monopoly profits will have to be spread more thinly. There is the additional risk to be considered that, should the cartel eventually break down, the market will find itself with too many firms, leading to ferocious competition and many failures. A third important factor (discussed below under the costs of enforcing collusive agreements) relevant to the returns from collusion is whether and how long widespread cheating can be prevented.

The costs of collusion have two main components: coordination costs and enforcement costs.[25] Like any agreement, a price-fixing agreement requires bargaining among the parties, and bargaining is not costless. Moreover, once the initial price is fixed there must be a mechanism for changing it to adapt to changed conditions of cost and demand. Coordination costs are affected by the number of sellers whose actions must be coordinated and by differences in costs, product, and judgment among the sellers.

Once the agreement is in force, the parties must have effective means of assuring adherence to it. A price-fixing agreement raises acute problems of enforcement because each seller, by shading the agreed price, can increase his share of the monopoly profits. One might wonder why any seller would be so foolish and short-sighted as to cheat when he must know that cheating will lead to the breakdown of the cartel. Without assuming that any sellers are stupid, one can suggest a number of plausible reasons for expecting cheating to occur.

A seller might cheat inadvertently, because of a mistake in computation or a failure of communication of the agreed price. He might have reason to believe that he could get away with cheating for quite a while and that his additional profits during that period would adequately compensate for the profits he would lose as a result of the eventual collapse of the agreement. He might cheat because he suspected that others were cheating. Or, a related point, he might cheat because he lacked confidence that the cartel would endure and saw no advantage in forgoing short-term gains for long-term gains unlikely to be realized. There is no a priori reason why sellers should yield to the various temptations to cheat, but there is abundant evidence that they commonly do.[26] To control cheating effectively, parties to price-fixing agreements may have to create elaborate machinery for the prevention, detection, and punishment of cheaters—joint sales agencies, systems for reporting transaction prices, penalties for cheating, and so forth. Such machinery is not costless, however, and in markets governed by the Sherman Act the most effective methods of achieving compliance with price-fixing agreements, such as joint sales agencies and legally enforced penalties for violations, are out of the question because they are illegal and cannot be concealed. The clandestine mehods of enforcing cartels are much less effective.

The point to be emphasized is that the attractiveness and feasibility of a price-fix-

---

[25] Another category, which will not be discussed, consists of the costs of negotiating with, or repelling, new entrants. These can be viewed as enforcement costs.

[26] *See, e.g.*, P. MacAvoy, The Economic Effects of Regulation: The Trunk-Line Railroad Cartels and the Interstate Commerce Commission Before 1900 (1965), recounting the constant cheating that plagued the railroad cartels at a time when the Sherman Act prohibition against cartels had not yet crystallized. On the instability even of fully enforceable cartel agreements see Voigt, *German Experience With Cartels and Their Control During the Pre-War and Post-War Periods,* in Competition, Cartels and Their Regulation 169 (J. Miller ed. 1962). And for a contemporary example of recurrent cheating by members of a price-fixing scheme see Smith, *The Incredible Electrical Conspiracy,* Fortune, Apr. 1961, at 132, 170.

ing scheme to the sellers in a market are limited by the costs of bargaining to agreement and of enforcing the agreement to prevent cheating. And one way to view the price-fixing prohibition of section 1 of the Sherman Act is as a device for increasing the costs involved in establishing and maintaining noncompetitive prices. It is in this light that the relevance of oligopoly to pricing behavior emerges most clearly.[27] The analysis of bargaining and enforcement costs in other contexts indicates that they tend to rise sharply with the number of parties whose actions must be coordinated for a desired arrangement to emerge.[28] This experience can be transferred to the price-fixing context. In a market of many sellers the problems of bargaining to a mutually agreeable price and of preventing cheating are formidable. Substantial unanimity is necessary to a successful price-fixing scheme, and the larger a group the more difficult and costly it will be to achieve. In a market of many sellers there will be many points of view, some extremely recalcitrant individuals, many potential cheaters, and a vast number of transactions in which cheating could occur. The problems of obtaining and enforcing agreement become magnified to a point where a formal and elaborate machinery of coordination and implementation is bound to be necessary. But section 1 of the Sherman Act limits the parties to clandestine methods. It seems unlikely, in these circumstances, that price-fixing agreements will flourish in markets that have very many sellers.[29]

Oligopoly thus emerges as a necessary condition (in most cases) of successful price-fixing where the Sherman Act is applicable; that is the first implication of the analysis. But, equally important, it is not a sufficient condition. Much more is necessary to the disappearance of competitive pricing than the bare fact that there are only a few sellers in the market. To begin with, just as in the atomistic market, each seller must make a deliberate choice not to expand output to the point where the cost of the last unit of output equals the market price, or, if he is at that point, to reduce output. There is a real choice here. It is not irrational for an oligopolist to decide to set a price that approximates marginal cost. It is not an unprofitable point at which to sell (so long as cost is defined to include a sufficient profit to make production attractive to investors), and it may have definite attractions: if the oligopolist finds speculation about the probable reactions of his rivals as inconclusive as suggested in the earlier discussion of interdependence; if he believes that new entry or the competition of substitute products will prevent him from obtaining appreciable monopoly profits; if he distrusts his competitors and fears that any higher price would quickly be eroded by cheaters, placing him at a temporary disadvantage if he did not cheat; or if restricting output would lay him open to heavy punishment (more on that later).[30]

If each oligopolist in a particular market should decide to go for the approximate joint maximizing price, the problems

---

[27] In addition, however, the barriers to entry in a market of many sellers are likely to be trivial; in an oligopolistic market that had formidable barriers to entry the attractiveness of collusion would, other things being equal, be much greater. Another relationship between oligopoly and pricing is discussed in text following note 37 *infra*.

[28] *See, e.g.,* Demsetz, *Toward a Theory of Property Rights*, 57 AM. ECON. REV. PAPERS & PROCEEDINGS 347 (1967).

[29] A recent study of criminal prosecutions under the antitrust laws (mostly price-fixing cases) found as much enforcement activity in rela-

tively unconcentrated as in highly concentrated industries. *See* J. CLABAULT & J. BURTON, SHERMAN ACT INDICTMENTS 1955–1965—A LEGAL AND ECONOMIC ANALYSIS 128–44 (1966). However, the industry classifications employed are crude and in many instances do not describe relevant markets; the study contains no data from which one could infer how successful the efforts at price-fixing in the unconcentrated industries were; and, most important, the study provides no basis for estimating the amount of effectively concealed price-fixing in highly concentrated industries, where concealment should be more practicable.

[30] *See* part III–C *infra*.

of coordination and enforcement must still be faced. The sellers must have some method of getting to the maximizing price and, once arrived, of altering price as conditions of cost and demand change. There are several possibilities: actually meet together and decide on a price; each publicly announce what he thinks the right price is and why, and gradually all converge on a mutually acceptable price; or by express or tacit understanding designate one seller as the price leader whose moves the others will follow, relying on his judgment of market conditions. If the oligopolists have different costs or different judgments about demand conditions (including the effect of a higher price on entry), finding a mutually agreeable price may be impossible without (or even with) actual negotiation. If, moreover, freight, extras, quality differences, or other factors that produce deviations from a single basic price are common, causing transaction prices to vary, the sellers must arrive at an understanding on how these items will be computed. Otherwise they will be unable to determine when the agreed price is actually being charged or precisely what prices they should charge on the basis of the observed transaction prices of the price leader. Alternatively, the parties can attempt to standardize the product, but that will often be a highly unprofitable course of action.[31] Further, there must be adequate dissemination of the agreed price and of any price change lest the followers be caught by surprise by the leader's pricing changes or fail altogether to match them. Even when sellers are few, then, coordination is not a simple or costless process.

Nor does the condition of fewness eliminate the problem of cheating. Each seller has the same temptation to cheat as in a market of many sellers. Because of the constraints of the Sherman Act, colluding sellers cannot punish cheaters (at least not without compounding their antitrust viola-

tions). Probably the best they can do in most cases is to try to make cheating difficult to conceal, in the hope that its incidence will be reduced if the gains are short-lived. But that is hard to do. The most efficacious means by which competitors can eliminate uncertainty as to each other's transaction prices, such as by an exchange of the terms of specific sales, have been condemned [32] and are difficult to implement covertly. Nor are these methods, even when practical, always effective. There is no assurance that the sellers will report their transaction prices accurately; the absence of any legal sanctions makes this an inviting area for fraud. Sellers may also find it possible, without fraud, to conceal price cutting through the practice of reciprocal buying. Critics of the practice tend to overlook the fact that it is an effective method of secret price cutting. Seller X sells product A to seller Y at list price, but then buys from Y product B on terms more favorable to Y than Y could command ordinarily. In effect, X is granting Y a discount on A, but in so roundabout a fashion that X's competitors are unlikely to learn what is going on.

Short of direct knowledge of competitors' transaction prices, the most reliable method of determining whether the competition is cheating is by consulting one's own sales experience.[33] The fact that a seller's market share is declining while he is maintaining the agreed price may indicate cheating by others. But in many cases it will be an ambiguous indication. If the product is not a standard one the loss of sales may be the result of nonprice rather than price rivalry. If there are large buyers in the market a substantial contraction of market share may be the result of the defection of a single buyer, and it will be difficult to determine whether his defection represents an isolated piece of bad luck or was the result of price cutting. (One can of course ask the buyer why he switched, but if he says that it was because of a discount he may very

---

[31] *See* Stigler, *A Theory of Oligopoly,* 72 J. Pol. Econ. 44 (1964), *reprinted in* G. Stigler, The Organization of Industry 39 (1968).

[32] Most recently in United States v. Container Corp. of America, 393 U.S. 333 (1969).

[33] *See* Stigler, *supra* note 31.

well be lying in order to induce a larger discount from the inquirer.) If demand is growing, so that many sales are to buyers new to the market, it will be difficult for a seller to infer cheating from the fact that he is not getting a proportionate share of the new buyers; he has less reason to expect to attract any particular proportion of new buyers than to retain his old customers. The dilemma for the seller who sees his market share declining is that if cheating is not the cause he will be even worse off if he cuts price and thereby jeopardizes the cartel.

In enumerating the problems of coordination and enforcement that oligopolists bent on charging supracompetitive prices must overcome, I do not mean to imply that they are never solved, although few price-fixing conspiracies have come to light in which cheating was not rife and the benefits to the conspirators were enduring.[34] What the discussion does imply is, first, that oligopolists cannot be presumed always or often to charge supracompetitive prices. Like atomistic sellers they must (with an exception shortly to be noted) collude in one fashion or another and the costs of collusion will frequently exceed the returns. Second, it seems improbable that prices could long be maintained above cost in a market, even a highly oligopolistic one, without *some* explicit acts of communication and implementation. One can, to be sure, specify an extreme case in which such acts might be unnecessary. No more than three sellers selling a completely standardized product to a multitude of buyers (none large) should be able to maintain the joint maximizing price without explicit collusion. However, not many industries resemble this model. More realistically, one might be concerned that purely tacit collu-

sion would be attempted sufficiently often in highly oligopolistic industries to raise the long-run average price in those industries above the competitive level, even if collusion was highly imperfect and the average price substantially below the joint maximizing price. It is also possible that such formal machinery as is used by oligopolists to fix prices is often difficult to detect, at least with the certainty required in a legal proceeding and especially in a criminal one.

This is speculation. The theory of oligopoly advanced here, although useful in identifying relevant criteria, is not refined to the point where one can predict the markets in which price-fixing, with or without explicit (but covert) acts of collusion, is likely to be found. We need to know much more about the costs and returns of cartelizing than we do. Although a number of cross-sectional statistical studies have found a correlation between profitability and concentration,[35] the findings contain perplexing features[36] and in many studies the correlation is weak.[37] More to the point, assuming

---

[34] Admittedly, this is a biased sample. By definition, completely successful price-fixing conspiracies never come to light. Still, the repeated breakdown of the electrical conspiracy, *see* Smith, *supra* note 26, is a significant illustration of the difficulty of fixing prices even when the market is oligopolistic and the sellers establish elaborate collusive arrangements.

[35] *See* Telser, *Some Determinants of the Returns to Manufacturing Industries* (Apr. 1969, mimeo.); N. COLLINS & L. PRESTON, CONCENTRATION AND PRICE-COST MARGINS IN MANUFACTURING INDUSTRIES (1968). The latter work contains a summary of earlier studies. *Id.* at 18–50.

[36] *See id.* at 109; G. STIGLER, *supra* note 31, at 145–46. For example, the findings show a stronger correlation between concentration and profitability when gross census industry classifications are used than when more refined industry classifications are used, even though the latter are likelier to approximate relevant markets rather than purely arbitrary groupings.

[37] *See* G. STIGLER, *supra* note 31, at 145 n.5. As Professor Stigler notes, "not more than one-half, and often less than one-fifth, of the variance of rates of return among industries is accounted for by differences in concentration." *Id.* at 145. It would be interesting to find out how much of the variation in profitability between concentrated and nonconcentrated industries is accounted for by the single most profitable firm in each of the concentrated industries. It is possible that the abnormal profits of such industries are to a significant degree a result not of collusion or interdependence but of the unusual efficiency—or, as explored in the next paragraph of text, market power—of one firm.

that the correlation is meaningful, we do not know whether or in what proportions it reflects purely tacit collusion, or explicit collusion successfully concealed, or perhaps other factors altogether.

One of the other factors that deserve specific mention is single-firm monopoly. It would be an error to suppose that a firm must control its market completely in order to have monopoly power. If a firm has a very large market share and its competitors cannot expand their output very rapidly, it may pay the firm to charge a supracompetitive price; its market share will erode, but only gradually. Nor is it always necessary that the firm have an overwhelming share of the market. Consider a market of two firms, each with a 50 per cent market share. If marginal cost in that market rises with output, one firm can raise its price above its marginal cost secure in the knowledge that the competitor cannot take away its business by remaining at the former price; the competitor cannot supply additional output at that price. Although this is a case where price can rise above marginal cost without any element of cooperation between the sellers in a market, it can be viewed as a subcategory of the single-firm monopoly situation. Monopoly signifies the power to increase price above the competitive level without immediately losing one's entire trade to rivals; the two-firm example given above fits that definition. If the case has any counterparts in the real world they would be governed by the discussion later in this Article of appropriate antitrust policies toward single-firm monopolies.[38]

III. Section I and Tacit Collusion

To summarize the discussion at this point, the conventional formulation of the oligopoly problem, which holds that oligopolists are interdependent as to price and output, is inadequate. With the exception

just noted, voluntary actions by the sellers are necessary to translate the bare condition of an oligopoly market into a situation of noncompetitive pricing. Perhaps in an extreme case no explicit acts of collusion or enforcement are necessary for this translation, only a tacit understanding on restricting output, and perhaps in a larger number of cases explicit acts are necessary but completely concealable. There is no need to distinguish these categories. Both can be considered forms of tacit collusion (or, synonymously, noncompetitive pricing by oligopolists), since that is how they would appear to a trier of fact. The essential point, in any event, is that tacit collusion thus defined is very like express collusion.

The major implication of viewing noncompetitive pricing by oligopolists as a form of collusion is that section 1 of the Sherman Act emerges as prima facie the appropriate remedy. There is, as we have seen, no vital difference between formal cartels and tacit collusive arrangements; the latter are simply easier to conceal. The purpose of section 1 is to deter collusion by increasing its costs; this suggests that the tacit colluder should be punished like the express colluder. And tacit collusion is voluntary behavior, which should be deterrable by appropriate punishment.

These propositions will now be tested through an examination of the three major problems that the proposed employment of section 1 raises: an interpretive problem, of satisfying the jurisdictional requirement of section 1 that there be concerted action; an evidentiary problem, of proving collusion to the satisfaction of a court in a case where acts of collusion cannot be shown; and a remedial problem, of preventing violations of the suggested new rule.

A. *The Problem of Concerted Action.* Since section 1 reaches only concerted activity—activity arising from a "contract, combination . . . , or conspiracy"—we must decide whether noncompetitive pricing by oligopolists can fairly be so classified when there is no proof that the oligopolists directly communicated with one another or took steps to enforce an understanding. **The**

[38] *See* text accompanying notes 93–95 *infra.* The example given in the text is one version of the Edgeworth duopoly model. *See* F. MACHLUP, THE ECONOMICS OF SELLERS' COMPETITION 382 n.13 (1952).

question will be considered at three levels: the level of semantics, the level of judicial precedent, and the level of statutory purpose.

The dictionary is no longer a fashionable aid to statutory interpretation, and for good reason: Context is vitally important. Nonetheless, an attempt to torture statutory language very far from accepted meanings does place the burden of explanation on the proponent of the interpretation. There is no distortion of accepted meanings, however, in viewing what I have termed tacit collusion as a form of concerted rather than unilateral activity. If seller A restricts his output in the expectation that B will do likewise, and B restricts his output in a like expectation, there is quite literally a meeting of the minds or mutual understanding even if there is no overt communication. In forbearing to seek short-term gains at each other's expense in order to reap monopoly benefits that only such mutual forbearance will allow, they are much like the parties to a "unilateral contract," which is treated by the law as a contract rather than as individual behavior. If someone advertises in a newspaper that he will pay $10 to the person who finds and returns his dog, anyone who meets the condition has an enforceable claim against him for the promised reward. The finder's action in complying with the specified condition is all the indication of assent that the law requires for a binding contract. Tacit collusion by oligopolists is at least analogous. A seller communicates his "offer" by restricting output, and the offer is "accepted" by the actions of his rivals in restricting their outputs as well.[39]

This analysis might well commend itself to the Supreme Court, which has frequently declared that section 1 does not require proof of express collusion.[40] None of the cases containing such declarations, to be sure, is quite like what is suggested here. In *Interstate Circuit, Inc. v. United States*,[41] a motion-picture exhibitor sent an identical letter to competing distributors asking them to maintain a certain minimum admission price on subsequent runs of their pictures. There was no evidence that the distributors ever communicated with one another with reference to this letter. Nonetheless, the Court upheld the finding that in observing the minimum price specified in the letter the distributors had engaged in a price-fixing conspiracy. Despite the absence of any overt communication, there had been a meeting of minds on the price to be charged and mutual forbearance to under-

---

may play a strategic role, there is some essential need for the signaling of intentions and the meeting of minds. . . .

". . . .

". . . Whenever the communication structure [or the legal structure, one might add] does not permit players to divide the task ahead of time according to an explicit plan, it may not be easy to coordinate behavior in the course of the game. Players have to understand each other, to discover patterns of individual behavior that make each player's actions predictable to the other; they have to test each other for a shared sense of pattern or regularity. . . . They must communicate by hint and by suggestive behavior. Two vehicles trying to avoid collision, two people dancing together to unfamiliar music, or members of a guerrilla force that become separated in combat have to concert their intentions in this fashion, as do the applauding members of a concert audience, who must at some point 'agree' on whether to press for an encore or taper off together." T. SCHELLING, THE STRATEGY OF CONFLICT 83–85 (1960).

[40] *See, e.g.,* United States v. Paramount Pictures, Inc., 334 U.S. 131, 142 (1948); United States v. Masonite Corp., 316 U.S. 265, 275–76 (1942); Interstate Circuit, Inc. v. United States, 306 U.S. 208, 226–27 (1939); Eastern States Retail Lumber Dealers' Ass'n v. United States, 234 U.S. 600, 612 (1914).

[41] 306 U.S. 208 (1939).

---

[39] The proposition that a belief in mental telepathy is not necessary to allow one to conclude that there may be a "meeting of the minds" without verbal interchanges has been illuminated by game theorists. The oligopoly "game" is an example of games "in which, though the element of conflict provides the dramatic interest, mutual dependence is part of the logical structure and demands some kind of collaboration or mutual accommodation—tacit, if not explicit—even if only in the avoidance of mutual disaster. These are also games in which, though secrecy

cut the price; and this was deemed sufficient agreement or concert of action to satisfy the requirement of the statute. Unlike a pure case of tacit collusion, an agreement involving some actual communication among the distributors could in fact have been inferred from the evidence. But the Court's formulation of the elements of a section 1 conspiracy is easily broad enough to encompass oligopolists who are able without any overt communication to raise price and restrict output in anticipation that each will perceive the advantage of that course of action and adhere to it.

Nor was this formulation superseded by the dictum in the *Theatre Enterprises* opinion, quoted earlier, that " 'conscious parallelism' has not yet read conspiracy out of the Sherman Act entirely." [42] As Professor Turner has pointed out, that was a case where the behavior of the rival firms was found to be consistent with an inference of perfectly independent pricing.[43] For reasons to appear shortly,[44] I prefer to illustrate the principle by a different set of facts. Suppose that there is a rise in the price of a raw material used in fabricating widgets. It would not be surprising if this led to a rise in the market price of widgets. If so, not only would every producer have raised his price, but each would know that the others had raised their price. In this sense, their collective action in raising the price of widgets would be "consciously parallel." But no inference that the price rise was the result of an understanding to move from a competitive to a monopolistic price by contracting output could be drawn. One might, if he liked, say that the widget producers had acted in concert or even by agreement. But there was no agreement in restraint of trade, no interference with market forces. That is the essential teaching of *Theatre Enterprises*.

The suggested approach, finally, is consistent with the purposes of section 1. The statute is addressed to concerted activity because the evil against which the framers were legislating was the banding together of rivals, as in cartels or trusts, to extract monopoly profits by agreeing to end competition and charge the joint maximizing price.[45] Tacit collusion by oligopolists has the same character. It is a concert of firms for the purpose of charging monopoly prices and extracting monopoly profits.

Professor Rahl has argued that the requirement of proving actual agreement must be retained because the Sherman Act is a penal statute.[46] His argument is not that its penal character precludes a flexible interpretation—it is much too late in the day to make that argument about the Sherman Act—but that to dispense with the requirement of proving actual agreement would be "to imply criminality generally as to large enterprise in America." [47] This assumes, however, that noncompetitive pricing follows automatically from the condition of being an oligopolist, an assumption I reject. As explained earlier, tacit collusion or noncompetitive pricing is not inherent in an oligopolistic market structure but, like conventional cartelizing, requires additional, voluntary behavior by the sellers.

B. *The Problem of Proof.* The biggest problem in applying section 1 of the Sherman Act to tacit collusion is that of proof: How can the existence of noncompetitive pricing be established without any proof of acts of agreement, implementation, or enforcement? Without denying that these will be extremely difficult cases, one can point to several types of evidence that should convince the trier of fact that sellers are guilty of tacit collusion as that term is used here.

---

[42] *See* note 6 *supra.*

[43] Turner, *supra* note 7, at 658.

[44] *See* text following note 57 *infra.*

[45] Any doubt that one of the major evils against which section 1 was aimed was the loose-knit combination or cartel is dispelled by Bork, *Legislative Intent and the Policy of the Sherman Act,* 9 J. Law & Econ. 7, 21–24 (1966).

[46] *See* Rahl, *Price Competition and the Price Fixing Rule—Preface and Perspective,* 57 Nw. U.L. Rev. 137, 147 (1962).

[47] *Id.*

The first is evidence that they practice systematic price discrimination. By price discrimination I mean a pattern of selling in which the ratio of price to marginal cost is not the same for all sales of a commodity.[48] Discrimination in this sense cannot be systematically and persistently employed in a competitive market; competition will prevent sellers from extracting disproportionate returns in some transactions for long. Monopoly power is necessary for persistent discrimination, and in a market that has more than one major seller the usual source of such power is collusion, tacit or express. If the Government can prove systematic price discrimination, an inference of noncompetitive pricing should be drawn. One can object that such proof is an unsatisfactory ground on which to establish tacit collusion because it leaves the defendants free to continue colluding, save that they must fix a single monopoly price rather than discriminate. This point is valid to the extent that it implies that the decree in such a case should not be limited to abating the discrimination. The decree should forbid tacit collusion by any means, thus laying a predicate for prompt and severe punishment[49] should defendants comply only by ceasing to discriminate. But even if the decree had no effect beyond termination of discrimination, the proceeding would not have been wholly in vain. Discrimination enables a monopolist (or joint monopolists, in our case) to increase the profits from monopoly. To prevent discrimination by tacit colluders, therefore, is to reduce the returns to collusion and hence the incentive to engage in it.

One form of discrimination deserves separate attention. Because the costs and difficulty of coordination and enforcement are increased if transaction prices in the market vary considerably at every moment as a result of differences in freight, custom features, or other extras, colluding sellers may find it advantageous to agree on a highly simplified pricing system. Under such a system, prices will be discriminatorily uniform because they will fail to reflect fully the different costs associated with different sales; this will be additional evidence of collusion.

I do not suggest that proof of discrimination will present no problems. There will frequently be problems of characterization. Consider the practice of resort hotels in charging different rates for the same accommodations, depending on the time of year. That may seem a discriminatory practice, but it is not, at least in the sense used here. It is an example of peak-load pricing, which is fully consistent with competition.[50] Another problem in proving discrimination is that such proof requires a comparison of the marginal costs of the different sales, and cost determinations are fraught with practical and conceptual difficulties. But there is this saving grace: There should be no need actually to determine the marginal cost of any sale. It should be enough to determine the difference in marginal costs attributable to the different circumstances of the sales that are compared, and that should be a much easier task.

Another indication of noncompetitive pricing is a prolonged excess of capacity over demand. A movement from a competitive to a monopolistic price involves a contraction of output. A single-firm monopolist will reduce its capacity to a level appropriate to the reduced level of output. But because of the fragility of cartels, the members of a price-fixing conspiracy—tacitly colluding oligopolists in our case—may not reduce their capacity as their output contracts. They have no assurance that the reduced level of output will persist. Each must be prepared, if the cartel breaks

---

[48] This is the economic definition of discrimination. It should be carefully distinguished from the usual legal definition, *i.e.,* any price difference. *See* Clayton Act § 2(a), *as amended,* 15 U.S.C. § 13(a) (1964); FTC v. Anheuser-Busch, Inc., 363 U.S. 536, 549 (1960).

[49] *See* notes 76–77 *infra* and accompanying text.

[50] *See* Hirshleifer, *Peak Loads and Efficient Pricing: Comment,* 72 Q.J. ECON. 451 (1958).

down, to expand output promptly or lose position to its rivals.

Evidence of excess capacity is unlikely, however, to play a large role in cases under the new standard. Proof of the condition is very difficult. Moreover, if a cartel does function successfully, the parties should eventually be able to bring capacity into phase with their monopolistic level of output, perhaps by agreeing on the rate at which they will change capacity. In such a case there will be no evidence that present capacity is excess; any evidence will relate to a much earlier period. Furthermore, there are other causes of excess capacity besides noncompetitive pricing. The Government should be required, therefore, to prove a prolonged, rather than merely transient, condition of excess capacity, and defendants should be permitted to rebut by showing that the condition had an innocent cause.

A potentially important class of evidence relates to changes in the market price. In general, the prices of noncompeting sellers should change less frequently than the prices of competing firms. The difficulty involved in arriving at a mutually agreeable price counsels for infrequent redeterminations; in addition, the opportunities to cheat are increased by frequent market-price changes. One would also expect cost changes to affect the market price proportionately less in a noncompetitive than in a competitive market. To illustrate, if a widget costs 10 cents to produce (regardless of quantity), under competition the price will be 10 cents. But suppose that, by colluding, the sellers are able to raise the price to 16 cents. If the cost of producing a widget now declines by 2 cents, the price will fall by 12.5 per cent even if the sellers pass the entire cost reduction to the purchaser, whereas if the market were at the competitive price the same cost reduction would lead to a 20 per cent price reduction. Moreover, colluding sellers will in some cases be able to appropriate the greater part of any cost savings as additional profit and pass less of the savings to the pur-

chaser—reduce price less—than would competing firms.[51]

I am not suggesting that a direct comparison of costs between a competitive market and one suspected of being noncompetitive be attempted, but only that in some cases it may be possible, by a comparison with pricing behavior in other markets, to infer collusive behavior from the lesser frequency and smaller amplitude of price changes in the market under scrutiny. Some words of caution are necessary here, however. First, a technical point but an important one, the effect under discussion is certain to occur only if the cost and demand functions of the firms are linear, and they may not be. Second, the effect may be offset by the tendency under monopoly to alter price more when demand shifts than would competitive firms.[52] Third, meaningful inferences can be drawn only from the actual transaction prices in the market, which may be different from the list prices. Rigid list prices do not prove collusion if transaction prices depart substantially from

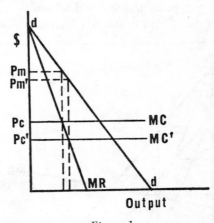

Figure 1

[51] This point may be illustrated graphically. In Figure 1, a reduction in cost from *MC* to *MC′* will lead to a reduction of the competitive price from *Pc* to *Pc′* and of the monopoly price from *Pm* to *Pm′*; as is evident, the monopoly price falls less, not only as a percentage of the former price but absolutely.

[52] Figure 2 illustrates this point. When demand shifts from *dd* to *dd′*, the monopoly price falls from *Pm* to *Pm′*, a greater distance than from

list. The Government should be able to obtain representative transaction prices from buyers. If this seems too onerous a burden to place on the Government, the rule might be to permit the Government to base inferences on list prices, while allowing defendants to rebut by showing that many sales were not at list.

Two other kinds of evidence of tacit collusion that will require delicate handling are abnormal profits and price leadership. It would be a mistake for courts to emulate public-utility commissions and attempt to determine the reasonable or competitive price in a market where tacit collusion was alleged. All other considerations aside, it would extend section 1 proceedings inordinately to undertake a valuation of the defendants' assets and a thorough review of their costs—two fearfully complicated and laborious steps in the determination of reasonable price. But there may be some cases where price is so out of line with any reasonable estimate of capital and operating costs that persistent abnormal profits can be demonstrated without a full public-utility type of inquiry and where no inference other than collusion (such as persistent

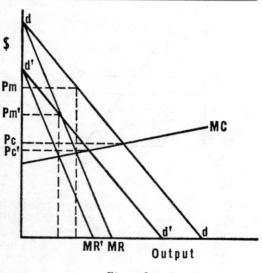

Figure 2

Pc to Pc'. I have assumed in the example that marginal costs rise with output; if they are constant, as of course they may be in an actual case, price will not fall at all under competition, although it will fall under monopoly.

success at innovation) is possible. Evidence relating to profits should therefore not be ruled out entirely. A nice question is whether defendants should be allowed to rebut a showing of tacit collusion based on other evidence by proof that they did not enjoy any monopoly profits. Since it is quite possible that the members of a cartel, due to entry of new firms into the market, will not have substantial monopoly profits at the monopoly price, the answer should be no.

The problem with price leadership is not that it is difficult to establish but that its significance is equivocal. It is true that colluding sellers may find it necessary to agree on a price leader. On the other hand, price leadership may emerge in a market simply because one of the firms is thought to have good judgment of market conditions and the others regularly defer to it. Still, there may be some cases where price leadership is so uniform and long-continued as to warrant an inference of tacit collusion.

Some of the more traditional methods of proving collusion circumstantially should also be useful in proving tacit collusion. One such method is by showing that the defendants have had fixed market shares for a substantial period of time; another, that they filed identical sealed bids on nonstandard items. Among other indicia of tacit collusion, I shall mention in closing just three: refusal to offer discounts in the face of substantial excess capacity; the announcement of price increases far in advance, without legitimate business justification for so doing; and public statements as to what a seller considers the right price for the industry to maintain. When a seller has substantial excess capacity, the pressure to cut prices is strong, because the cost of utilizing idle capacity will be only a fraction of the usual cost of production. For sellers in these circumstances to refuse to reduce price suggests collusion. The practices of announcing price increases long in advance, and of discussing publicly what is the right price for the industry (not the individual firm), are methods of indirect communication by which sellers iron out possible differences among them and arrive at the mutually agreeable price. Evidence relating to public discussion or announcements of price increases will usually not be sufficient by itself, but together with evidence of the actual pricing of the industry members could provide convincing support for an inference of tacit collusion.

Clearly, the kinds of evidence that would be admissible in a tacit-collusion case cover a wide spectrum. These would inevitably be "big" cases. But the scope of permissible inquiry would not be unlimited, and should not be unmanageable. Unlike proceedings under Kaysen and Turner's "unreasonable market power" standard, in which the Government would be required to adduce a variety of evidence concerning the structural features (for example, market shares and condition of entry) and performance characteristics (for example, technical efficiency) of the market in question,[53] I would limit inquiry by and large to conduct—how the firms behave—and more narrowly still to conduct from which an absence of effective competition can be inferred: cartel-like conduct. The more serious problem is whether it will be possible, given the limitations of economic science and of judicial fact-finding processes, to prove, by the kinds of evidence enumerated above, that firms have been guilty of noncompetitive pricing. While it is true that such evidence is not entirely alien to Sher-

man Act proceedings,[54] the record of the courts, as we are about to see, has not been one to inspire confidence in their ability to handle economic evidence. Before elaborating this point, may I point out that the workability of the proposed standard could be improved if a substantial research effort in the area of cartel and oligopoly behavior were undertaken. Despite decades of intense concern with pricing under oligopoly, we know little about which industries in fact exhibit noncompetitive pricing and what patterns of price leadership, price rigidity, market-share stability, and other market phenomena connote collusion. This deficiency should be remediable, although it will require not only scholarly attention but also the cooperation of the government agencies that have the necessary fact-gathering powers and functions, such as the Bureau of the Census and the Federal Trade Commission.

Pending this improvement in knowledge, courts will have to exercise extreme care in drawing inferences of tacit collusion from market conduct. The pitfalls that abound in this area are illustrated by Professor Turner's discussion of the *Theatre Enterprises* and *American Tobacco* cases in his 1962 article. In the former case,[55] the owner of a suburban theater tried to purchase rights to first-run movies from several producer-distributors and was turned down by each. Professor Turner notes that "there was . . . a great deal of testimony by defendants to the effect that the decision of each was an independent one, based on purely individual considerations," [56] and concludes that the case "was one in which it would have been absurd to direct a verdict on the ground that consciously parallel action clearly showed agreement." [57] I am more troubled by the case. The practice of selling the right to exhibit a film at two prices, a higher price for immediate exhibition ("first runs") and a lower price for

---

[53] See C. KAYSEN & D. TURNER, *supra* note 16, at 112–13. *But cf. id.* at 267–68.

[54] See, *e.g.*, American Tobacco Co. v. United States, 328 U.S. 781 (1946) (discussed in text following note 58 *infra*); C-O-Two Fire Equip. Co. v. United States, 197 F.2d 489 (9th Cir.), *cert. denied*, 344 U.S. 892 (1952); United States v. Aluminum Co. of America, 148 F.2d 416 (2d Cir. 1945). For an example of how an economic study can shed light on whether a market is behaving competitively see 2 J. BAIN, THE ECONOMICS OF THE PACIFIC COAST PETROLEUM INDUSTRY 330–60 (1945). For an excellent recent case study of how sophisticated economic evidence can be used in antitrust litigation see Lozowick, Steiner & Miller, *Law and Quantitative Multivariate Analysis: An Encounter*, 66 MICH. L. REV. 1641 (1968).

[55] Theatre Enterprises, Inc. v. Paramount Film Distrib. Corp., 346 U.S. 537 (1954).

[56] Turner, *supra* note 7, at 657.

[57] *Id.* at 658.

later exhibition, would appear to be a form of price discrimination. The cost to the distributor is the same regardless of when the film is to be exhibited, but a two-price system enables him to exploit the willingness of some moviegoers to pay a premium to see a film when it is first released. As noted earlier, systematic price discrimination cannot persist for long under competition. If, therefore, one assumes, as has the Court in all of the movie cases, that the distributors are in competition with each other—are selling close substitutes even though their films are copyrighted and in that sense unique—the refusal of any distributor to sell first runs to the plaintiff in *Theatre Enterprises* is difficult to understand other than in a context of collusive behavior.

The distributors, it is true, expressed concern that the plaintiff would be in competition with their existing first-run theaters; but this only underscores their reluctance to spoil the higher-priced market by freely granting first-run rights. And, although they expressed skepticism as to the plaintiff's ability to pay first-run prices, there was no suggestion that any distributor would not have made money doing business with plaintiff. The distributors testified that their films would receive greater "exposure" by being shown in downtown theaters first, but one would think that maximum exposure would be promoted rather than impaired by licensing additional first-run theaters; it is especially difficult to understand how a two-*price* system fosters exposure. The inference that the refusal was motivated by fear that an expansion in the number of first-run theaters would endanger the defendants' discriminatory system of film distribution seems, in the circumstances, the most plausible, although I do not consider the evidence for this interpretation conclusive. Here, incidentally, is a case where purely tacit collusion was quite feasible. A distributor could not have concealed the grant of first-run status to the plaintiff. Competing distributors would have found out what had happened as soon as they read the theater page.

American Tobacco Co. v. United States[58] is a case that Turner views as a classic example of noncompetitive behavior under oligopoly:

> [T]he Government charged that the three leading cigarette manufacturers had, among other things, conspired to fix prices in the sale of their cigarettes. The Government's evidence on this aspect of the case consisted chiefly of economic facts, including the following. All three companies charged identical prices for their cigarettes from 1928 to 1940. In this period, there were only seven price changes. A price change initiated by one company would be almost immediately followed by the other two, who refused to make further sales to dealers until their corresponding price changes were made effective. The three companies substantially raised their prices in 1931, though their costs were declining and there was a general depression. This led to a substantial increase in their profits for a period of time, even though their total sales declined as some consumers switched to the cheap "ten cent" brands. In 1931, at the time of the price increase, the three large companies together accounted for ninety per cent of all cigarette sales.
>
> Any economist worthy of the name would immediately brand this price behavior as noncompetitive. One can hardly find clearer evidence of an absence of effective competition than an increase of prices in the face of declining costs and weakening demand.[59]

I consider the evidence recited by Turner more equivocal. The fact that the three leading cigarette manufacturers charged identical prices for 12 years would indicate a suspicious rigidity and uniformity of prices if these were transaction prices. But they were list prices, and identity of list prices in an industry with only three major sellers, selling a standard product, is unsurprising, as are the facts that list prices were changed infrequently and that a change in list price by one was matched promptly by the others. The vital question is how much shading of the list prices there was; we know there was some.[60]

---

[58] 328 U.S. 781 (1946).

[59] Turner, *supra* note 7, at 660–61.

[60] *See* W. NICHOLLS, PRICE POLICIES IN THE CIGA-

The most curious aspect of the evidence relates to the 1931 price increase. For a monopolist (or a cartel) to raise price in the face of declining costs and demand is evidence not of noncompetitive conduct but of irrationality. A profit-maximizing monopolist or cartel will reduce price when either costs or demand—or both—decline.[61] The only exceptions would be if the monopoly or cartel were first formed in a period of declining cost or demand, or if it had

previously been unable to establish the joint maximizing price; but if there was tacit collusion among the leading cigarette manufacturers it was apparently fully operative well before the 1931 price increase.[62]

There is another version of what happened in 1931, which runs as follows.[63] Reynolds was the first cigarette manufacturer to wrap cigarette packages in cellophane and its rivals were not immediately able to adopt the technique. Thinking that consumers would pay more for "humidor-wrapped" cigarettes, especially if the innovation was well advertised, Reynolds raised its price by about 6 per cent and at the same time substantially increased its advertising. Its major competitors could have remained at the previous price, but they decided to match Reynolds' price increase and to counter its advertising campaign with stepped-up efforts of their own. They were convinced that the consumer was insensitive to small price differences. After all, cigarette revenues had held up well during the depression without any price cut, indicating no weakening in demand despite the general economic condition. The consumer might even infer that their product was inferior to Reynolds' if sold at a lower price. Tobacco costs were declining, but, as mentioned, increased advertising outlays were contemplated. This pattern of conduct—successful product differentiation leading to a higher price and higher advertising outlays—could occur under competitive conditions.

The companies' estimate of market conditions was poor. Within 18 months the market share of the economy brands had increased more than 70-fold, from 0.3 to 22.8 per cent,[64] and the major sellers had

---

RETTE INDUSTRY—A STUDY OF "CONCERTED ACTION" AND ITS SOCIAL CONTROL 1911–50, at 78, 89 (1951).

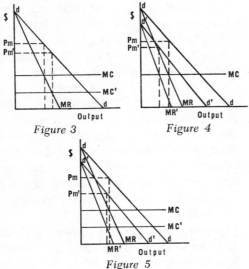

Figure 3   *Figure 4*

Figure 5

[61] In Figure 3, costs have fallen from *MC* to *MC'*; the new profit-maximizing price, *Pm'*, is lower than the old. In Figure 4, demand has declined from *dd* to *dd'*; again, the new profit-maximizing price is lower than the old. In Figure 5, both costs and demand have declined, resulting in an even sharper drop in price by the profit-maximizing monopolist.

It might well be rational for a monopolist or cartel to raise price if demand were not declining but rather becoming more inelastic; and there are some who believe that demand curves do tend to become more inelastic in times of depression (and some who believe the opposite). *See* Ruggles, *The Nature of Price Flexibility and the Determinants of Relative Price Changes in the Economy,* in BUSINESS CONCENTRATION AND PRICE POLICY 441, 461–62 (Nat'l Bureau Econ. Research 1955). There is no evidence, however, that the cigarette manufacturers believed that the depression had made the demand for cigarettes less elastic.

---

[62] *See* W. NICHOLLS, *supra* note 60, at 78, 88–89.

[63] The following description is based on *id.* at 83–88. Nicholls himself, it should be noted, concludes that "the fact that all saw fit to follow Reynolds' increase in 1931 suggests a strong element of cartel-like behavior." *Id.* at 89. The facts that he recites, however, support the alternative explanation given in text.

[64] *Id.* at 92.

rescinded the price increase, their position permanently impaired.[65] The rapid erosion of the majors' market share indicates how limited their power over price actually was; but what is more important to the present discussion is that their pricing behavior can be plausibly explained without hypothesizing tacit collusion. Not to labor the point unduly, price behavior is often equivocal evidence of collusion. That should not lead one to despair entirely of the workability of the suggested rule. If sellers engage in tacit collusion with any success they will generate some of the kinds of evidence discussed,[66] and I do not assume that courts are congenitally incapable of handling such evidence intelligently. If colluding sellers generate no such evidence, their collusive efforts will not have amounted to much. Economically significant collusion should leave some visible traces in the pricing behavior of the market, even granting fully the interpretive difficulties that such behavior presents.

C. *The Problem of Remedy.* It remains to consider whether an interpretation of section 1 forbidding tacit collusion would be effective in altering the conduct of sellers in the desired way; whether, in other words, the sanctions for violation of the rule would be adequate. I shall address, first, the general adequacy of the sanctions for illegal

price-fixing, and then the special problems that might be involved in fashioning remedies against tacit collusion.

It will be convenient to distinguish two types of sanction: the remedial and the punitive. The line between the two categories is not hard and fast, but in general the remedial sanction seeks merely to redress or head off injury—simple damages and an injunction are examples—while the punitive sanction seeks to deter violations by an exaction that may be greater than either the profit to the wrongdoer or the injury to his victims. Price-fixing provides an excellent example of why punitive sanctions are sometimes necessary to ensure reasonable compliance with the law. In deciding whether to comply with a legal rule, a rational individual will discount the gravity of the possible sanction by the probability of escaping detection.[67] Price-fixing can be concealed. The probability of escaping detection is greater than zero, probably far greater. If the only sanction for illegal price-fixing were simple damages or injunction, firms would have an inadequate incentive to comply with the law. If caught, they would simply be forced to disgorge past profits from price-fixing or to forgo future opportunities to fix prices; and since they would often not be caught, it would in general be worth their while to fix prices, assuming, of course, that the costs of collusion in the particular circumstances were less than the anticipated returns.

I have overstated the case slightly. Damages, were they correctly computed in price-fixing cases, would normally exceed the monopoly profits of the colluders,[68] and a broadly worded injunction might inhibit a defendant's freedom of action beyond simply preventing it from engaging in illegal price-fixing. Even remedial sanctions against price-fixing, therefore, would inescapably contain punitive features in the sense I am using the term. Still, there is little doubt that punitive sanctions are a

---

[65] *See* Tennant, *The Cigarette Industry,* in The Structure of American Industry 357, 367 (3d ed. W. Adams 1961).

[66] For a persuasive argument that the behavior of the steel industry in the 1950's indicated tacit collusion see Adelman, *Steel, Administered Prices and Inflation,* 75 Q.J. Econ. 16 (1961). The type of evidence that Professor Adelman was able to obtain from public documents—evidence relating to the manner and timing of price increases and to the pricing behavior of the industry in the face of very substantial excess capacity—might not be sufficient to persuade a court that the firms had in fact tacitly colluded; but the circumstances he relates are exceedingly suspicious, and a diligent inquiry by the Department of Justice might well have developed sufficient economic evidence to justify a finding of guilt under the standard proposed in this Article. Only an actual attempt to apply the standard will reveal whether it is workable.

[67] *Cf.* Becker, *Crime and Punishment: An Economic Approach,* 78 J. Pol. Econ. 169 (1968).

[68] *See* note 103 *infra.*

necessary element of an effective rule against price-fixing.

There is reason to question whether the punitive sanctions that can be imposed against price fixers under existing law are adequate. Violation of the Sherman Act is a misdemeanor; violators can be fined up to $50,000 and (if individuals) imprisoned for up to one year.[69] Prison terms, however, are rarely imposed and when imposed are usually nominal in length,[70] and the maximum fine is too small to have a significant deterrent effect on a large corporation. To be sure, a corporation must act through individuals, and the fine, together with the stigma of criminal conviction, may be quite enough to deter most corporate officers and employees from attempting to fix prices even when no prison sentence is likely to be imposed. Still, the absence of effective penalties on the corporation is troubling.

The threat of a private treble-damage suit[71] provides an additional, and probably quite important, element of deterrence; but its deterrent value is limited. The penalty component in the award, being limited to twice the actual damages, may not be adequate in all cases. Moreover, since damages are extremely difficult to prove in a price-fixing case—what is involved is a determination of what the competitive price would have been had the defendants not colluded—tying the penalty to the provable damages may frequently result in judgments that are too small. Perhaps the most serious deficiency of the treble-damage suit is that the usual victims of illegal price-fixing are in no position to invoke it. In general, a price-fixing conspiracy, if effective, will inflict harm (1) on a large number of nonbusiness (mostly individual) consumers and (2), if the members of the conspiracy sell to other business firms rather than directly to the ultimate consumer, possibly on the owners of certain

factors of production used by those firms, who need not be the firms' shareholders.[72] The injury to an individual consumer or factor owner, however, will ordinarily be too small to warrant incurring the expense of a lawsuit.

The courts in recent years have sought to get around this problem by permitting business customers to sue for thrice the difference between what they paid the conspirators and what they would have paid under competition, regardless of whether the higher price in fact caused *them* any injury, and by sanctioning class actions in

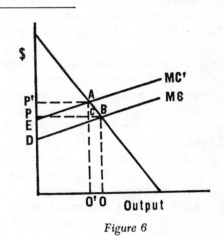

Figure 6

[69] Sherman Antitrust Act § 1, 15 U.S.C. § 1 (1964).

[70] *See* J. CLABAULT & J. BURTON, *supra* note 29, at 11, 55.

[71] *See* Clayton Act § 4, 15 U.S.C. § 15 (1964).

[72] This point is illustrated in Figure 6. Suppose that the purchasers of the product whose price is fixed are themselves business firms, and the effect of the conspiracy is to raise their costs from MC to MC′. The firms will raise their price from P to P′ and reduce their output from O to O′. Customers of the firms will suffer. They will pay P′ACP more, and will also be forced to turn to substitute products that are inferior for their purposes, a loss in value to them measured by the area ABC. Owners of certain durable instruments of production (such as land) will also be hurt, although to a much lesser extent; their returns (or "quasi-rents") will be reduced from PBD to P′AE. The firms' shareholders will not be harmed, however, unless the firms are themselves the owners of the rent-receiving factors or were previously receiving monopoly profits. Furthermore, there will be no loss of quasi-rents if costs are constant rather than increasing or if the rent-receiving factors are nonspecialized and can earn equivalent rents in other employments. In general, then, it would appear that consumers are the principal victims of price-fixing conspiracies.

which the class consists of consumers injured by the conspiracy.[73] Both devices are
unsatisfactory. It is anomalous to permit
suits for damages by firms that have not
been injured; moreover, a firm may hesitate to jeopardize its good relations with
suppliers merely to bring a suit for windfall profits. The class action, save for large
institutional purchasers, is a delusion. There
is no feasible method of locating and reim-
bursing the consumer who several years
ago may have paid too much for a toothbrush (or substituted another product) as
the result of a price-fixing conspiracy among
toothbrush manufacturers. In these circumstances the class action becomes a device
by which enterprising lawyers obtain large
fees.

Both the remedial and punitive sanctions for illegal price-fixing would be
strengthened by amending the Sherman
Act to authorize suits by the United States
for both the total damages attributable to
an alleged conspiracy and an appropriate
civil monetary penalty. (At present the
Government can sue for damages only when
it has been a victim of the unlawful conspiracy and can recover only its actual damages plus the cost of suit.)[74] Determination
of the amount of the penalty should be left
to the judge's discretion, to be exercised in
light of the gravity of the offense, the size
of the corporation, and its previous record
of antitrust violations. (One might wish to
retain double the actual damages as the
minimum penalty, but there should be no
maximum.) The entire judgment, both actual damages and penalty, would be paid

into the Treasury. The procedure would
displace the private suit in any case where
the Government sued, since it would be
inappropriate to permit the same damages
to be recovered in successive suits.

Pending such a reform, one is compelled to acknowledge a deficiency in the
penalty structure of the price-fixing prohibition. This deficiency would be especially serious in the context of tacit collusion. Being more difficult to detect than
express collusion, it should be punished, if
anything, more severely.[75] In a case of tacit
collusion, moreover, a court might be reluctant to impose any criminal penalties,
at least until the rule forbidding it had become well established and clearly defined.
I am not prepared to admit, however, that
the deficiency in the penalty structure, serious as it is, would be fatal to a rule forbidding tacit collusion under section 1. The
threat of private treble-damage actions
would provide some deterrence. In addition, when a violation was discovered and
enjoined,[76] there would then be an effective deterrent against a repetition of the
offense by the convicted firms. The penalty
for violating the injunction would depend
entirely upon the discretion of the judge;
there is no fixed maximum.[77] Violation of
an injunction against tacit collusion may be
difficult to prove, but no more so than the
original violation of law that gave rise to
the injunction.

Moreover, there may be extreme cases
where dissolution is the appropriate remedy
for convicted tacit colluders because repe-

[73] See Hanover Shoe, Inc. v. United Shoe Mach.
Corp., 392 U.S. 481 (1968); City of Philadelphia v. Morton Salt Co., 385 F.2d 122 (3d Cir.
1967), cert. denied sub nom. New York v. Morton Salt Co., 390 U.S. 995 (1968). I know of
no antitrust class action in which individual
(as opposed to institutional) consumers have
been permitted to recover, although such recovery would be permitted under a recent settlement proposal made by a group of drug manufacturers who are defendants in a private price-
fixing suit. Wall Street Journal, Feb. 6, 1969,
at 2, col. 2.

[74] See Clayton Act § 4A, 15 U.S.C. § 15a (1964).

[75] This assumes, but I think reasonably, that tacit
price-fixing is no less morally opprobrious than
express price-fixing.

[76] I have in mind a relatively simple and general
injunction against express or tacit price-fixing,
the principal purpose of which would be to
supply a predicate, as discussed in the text, for
the imposition of very severe penalties in the
event of a subsequent episode of price-fixing by
the defendants. I do not suggest that the injunction attempt to regulate the details of the
defendants' pricing.

[77] See United States v. United Mine Workers, 330
U.S. 258, 302–06 (1947).

tition of the offense is difficult to prevent by other means. Ordinarily the conventional remedies should be adequate, but courts should not shrink from employing dissolution in an exceptional case.[78] It is no objection that dissolution is addressed to market structure rather than behavior. As noted earlier, noncompetitive pricing is very much a function of the structure of the market; even express collusion is rarely practicable in markets that are not oligopolistic in structure. The possibility of dissolution should provide an additional deterrent to tacit collusion.

Assuming that the oligopolist can be given a strong incentive to comply with a legal rule forbidding tacit collusion, will it be possible for him to comply? Or would compliance involve such irrational behavior, as Professor Turner argues, that it could not realistically be expected? [79] I observed earlier that it is quite rational for an oligopolist to decide not to collude. What is involved is a decision to expand output until the return to investors is roughly equal to what they could earn in other activities, a course routinely followed by sellers in competitive markets. There are, as we saw, quite good reasons why even in the absence of legal penalty an oligopolist might decide not to restrict output: inability to predict his rivals' reactions and fear that they would cheat. Punishing tacit colluders would provide an additional and potent reason to abjure noncompetitive pricing.[80] This should

be true even in the example that Turner offers as the clinching argument for his view: where demand is declining and competitive prices would entail losses to the industry.[81] Express collusion may often be the only expedient that will enable an industry to avoid losses in a period of declining demand, yet one assumes that the prohibition against such collusion retains a considerable deterrent effect even in those circumstances. Firms faced with losses will not collude if they anticipate that the cost of collusion, as a result of punishment, will exceed its benefit in averting business losses. Oligopolists would reason the same way were tacit collusion illegal under section 1.

Businessmen should have no difficulty, moreover, in determining when they are behaving noncompetitively. Tacit collusion is not an unconscious state. If the sales division of a company recommends that it offer a wider variety of products in order to exploit consumer demand more effectively, and the financial division recommends against that course on the ground that it will make it more difficult for the industry to maintain "healthy" prices, top management can be in no doubt of the significance of its action if it adopts the financial division's recommendation. More generally, given the tension between sales and financial executives that characterizes most corporations, the question whether to collude tacitly will be thrust upon management constantly. The sales people will argue for offering discounts to lure away rivals' customers, for varying prices promptly as conditions of demand and cost change, for reducing prices to utilize idle capacity or to exploit locational advantages, and for other competitive, sales-increasing tactics; and, whenever they do, management will have to balance their

---

[78] In some cases a conditional decree of dissolution might be the appropriate remedy. The defendants would know that a resumption of noncompetitive pricing would result in actual dissolution. *Cf.* United States v. American Optical Co., 1966 Trade Cas. 82,610 (E.D. Wis. 1966). The courts clearly have power to order dissolution in any price-fixing case in which that is the appropriate remedy. Dissolution has, of course, been ordered in a number of monopolization cases, and the remedial provisions for sections 1 and 2 of the Sherman Act are identical. *See* Sherman Antitrust Act § 4, 15 U.S.C. § 4 (1964).

[79] *See* Turner, *supra* note 7, at 669.

[80] I emphasize that I am not proposing that equiv-

alence of price and marginal cost be the test of compliance with section 1. All I am arguing is that a deliberate restriction of output by competitors is conduct that rational men can avoid —and will avoid if it is made sufficiently costly to them to engage in it.

[81] *See* Turner, *supra* note 7, at 670.

claims against the advantages of securing or maintaining an understanding with the company's rivals to limit price competition. This calculus will be affected by threat of punishment.

The oligopolist who does refrain from restricting output runs no appreciable risk of being penalized for collusion nonetheless. If he is a leading seller—and a rule against tacit collusion would be invoked only against the leading sellers in a market —his refusal to accede to an understanding on prices will make it impossible for the other firms to maintain noncompetitive prices, and there will be no systematic price discrimination, no persistent excess capacity attributable to restriction of output, no monopolistic pattern of reaction of price to cost changes—in short, none of the symptoms of collusion.

In closing, might I suggest that if there is a good case to be made against the proposed employment of section 1 of the Sherman Act, it will be built on the practical difficulties of proving tacit collusion. That, rather than the doctrinal or remedial questions, is the heart of the problem and should be the focus of the debate.

IV. Structural Solutions to the Oligopoly Problem

I turn now to other remedies, alternative or supplemental, that have been suggested for dealing with the problem of noncompetitive pricing by oligopolists: new legislation dealing specifically with oligopolies; a reinterpretation of section 2 of the Sherman Act (the monopolization provision) to reach oligopolies; and strict enforcement of section 7 of the Clayton Act against horizontal mergers, to prevent the emergence of new or the aggravation of existing oligopolies. These remedies have in common the fact that they regulate the structure of markets rather than the pricing or other behavior of the sellers in them. Among structural remedies, one can distinguish between those that change existing market structures through dissolution of large firms and prophylactic remedies that attack the

causes of concentration, as by forbidding mergers.

A. *Restructuring Oligopoly Markets.* 1. *The legislative route.*— In *Antitrust Policy*, Professors Kaysen and Turner proposed the enactment of a statute condemning "unreasonable market power" and authorizing the dissolution of firms found to possess it.[82] The premise of this approach is that the existing antitrust laws cannot deal effectively with noncompetitive pricing by oligopolists. If that premise is rejected, the proposal is unattractive. To prevail under the unreasonable-market-power standard, the Government would have to establish the existence of a variety of structural, behavioral, and performance characteristics. The scope of inquiry contemplated is broader than in a section 1 proceeding, and indeed so broad as to raise serious questions of practicability.

A variation of this approach, which Kaysen and Turner also discuss and endorse, would equate unreasonable market power with the possession by the leading firms of a particular aggregate share of the market.[83] This approach is much like that employed in the administration of the antimerger law against horizontal mergers, where market-share percentages are the

---

[82] *See* text accompanying note 16 *supra.*

[83] They propose the following statutory provision: "Market power . . . shall be conclusively presumed where, for five years or more, one company has accounted for 50 per cent or more of annual sales in the market, or four or fewer companies have accounted for 80 per cent of sales." C. KAYSEN & D. TURNER, *supra* note 16, at 267. Unless the defendants could show that their market power was justified (as by economies of scale), it would be deemed unreasonable. *See id.* at 268. It is interesting to note that elsewhere in *Antitrust Policy* the authors express considerable skepticism as to the appropriateness of their market-share test of market power. *See id.* at 98–99. President Johnson's antitrust task force (*see* note 15 *supra*) proposed a similar statute. *See Report of the White House Task Force on Antitrust Policy*, Part II and App. A (July 5, 1968, mimeo.). The differences of detail between the Kaysen-Turner and task-force proposals do not affect the discussion in text.

basic touchstone of illegality. Its principal appeal lies in dispensing with the requirement of proof that pricing is in fact noncompetitive in the highly concentrated industries subject to the legislation. But that is a questionable advantage, unless one is quite confident, contrary to our conclusion in part II–B, that high concentration is by itself a sufficient condition for noncompetitive pricing. It is an advantage of my proposal that, by requiring the Government to prove noncompetitive pricing, it will force inquiry as to whether and in what circumstances oligopoly in fact leads to such pricing. One might reply that the best way to learn about the economic characteristics of an industry is by patient academic study, not litigation. In principle that may be correct, but in fact most industry studies by economists have been based on the records of antitrust cases.

The approach has other troublesome aspects. One is its coverage. Not only is it unclear whether tacit collusion is rife in the limited number of industries embraced by any proposal that defines the area of illegality solely in terms of market shares, but tacit collusion may be a serious problem in many of the remaining industries.[84] Furthermore, dissolution, which Kaysen and Turner propose as the normal remedy in unreasonable market-power cases,[85] is neither the only possible remedy for noncompetitive pricing by oligopolists, as we have seen, nor generally the best remedy. It is likely to involve appreciable social cost. At the least, the reconstitution of a major industry will involve substantial administrative expenses; and if the firms are dissolved into units smaller than the efficient scale of operation in the industry, much larger social costs may be incurred. One can attempt to avoid the second result

by allowing in defense proof that economies of scale would be lost by the reduction of firm size. But having to litigate that issue will increase the expenses of the proceeding; and the difficulty of determining efficient scale is such that erroneous results can be anticipated in many cases,[86] so that economies of scale may be sacrificed inadvertently. The threat of dissolution may also have a serious disincentive effect. Firms might hold back from expanding sales to the point at which they would become subject to dissolution under the statute, even if they were more efficient than their competitors. Kaysen and Turner would, to be sure, allow defendants to show in defense that their market power was attributable to completely laudable circumstances, notably their "extraordinary efficiency," [87] but such a concept is, in my opinion, too nebulous to serve as a criterion of legality. Nor would such a defense, even if feasible, entirely solve the problem of dis-

---

[84] Kaysen and Turner get around this problem by proposing the market-share test as a supplement, rather than as an alternative, to their basic standard of unreasonable market power. *See* C. KAYSEN & D. TURNER, *supra* note 16, at 267. The task-force proposal (*see* note 83 *supra*) lacks this feature.

[85] C. KAYSEN & D. TURNER, *supra* note 16, at 269.

[86] There are two methods of determining efficient scale. One is by means of engineering and cost studies that attempt to determine efficiency directly. The extraordinary, and indeed disabling, difficulties involved in that method are discussed in Smith, *Survey of the Empirical Evidence on Economies of Scale*, in BUSINESS CONCENTRATION AND PRICE POLICY 213 (Nat'l Bureau Econ. Research 1955); Friedman, *Comment*, in *id.* at 230. The other, and more promising, method is the survivor method. *See* Stigler, *The Economies of Scale*, 1 J. LAW & ECON. 54 (1958), *reprinted in* G. STIGLER, *supra* note 31, at 71. Under that method, a scale of operation is deemed efficient if the total output of firms having that scale is stable or growing in relation to the other firms in the industry, and inefficient if it is declining. The survivor method is not, however, free from substantial difficulties of application; these are discussed by Professor Stigler in his *Addendum: Drawing Inferences from Firm Size on the Economies of Scale*, in G. STIGLER, *supra* at 89. An important problem in the immediate context is that application of the survivor method may require charting the fortunes of various size classes of firms over a substantial period of time during which efficient size in the industry may be changing as a result of changes in demand or technology.

[87] C. KAYSEN & D. TURNER, *supra* note 16, at 268.

incentive effects. As leading sellers approached the point at which their aggregate market share would be so large as to trigger dissolution proceedings, they might decide to raise price as a means of preventing further growth and forestalling dissolution. That would aggravate the very problem, monopoly pricing, to which the proposed legislation is principally addressed.

2. *Joint monopolization.*— Under current interpretations of section 2 of the Sherman Act,[88] a single firm that has had a monopoly of a relevant market for a substantial period of time will probably be adjudged guilty of monopolization unless the market is a natural monopoly (that is, can efficiently accommodate only a single firm) or unless its monopoly is the result of a patent still in force.[89] It has been urged that this principle should be extended to oligopoly.[90] Oligopoly (under this view) is simply shared or joint monopoly, and oligopolists should be dissolved so as to dissipate their monopoly power. The attraction of this approach to its proponents is that it leads to the same result as special oligopoly legislation without having to persuade Congress to amend the law. I could rest, therefore, with a reference back to my objections to the legislative route. But the judicial approach has problems of its own that merit discussion.

It seems fairly clear that the original purpose of section 2 was to reach practices by which firms achieved monopoly power or sought to maintain it against potential entrants.[91] Many such practices, to be sure,

could readily have been attacked as conspiracies in restraint of trade (for example, the series of acquisitions that resulted in the formation of the Standard Oil Trust),[92] but not all: Monopolizing practices of a single firm could not be reached under the first section. Construed along the forgoing lines, section 2 might still have some application to oligopolists; for there may be cases where firms seek to obtain or retain an oligopoly position as a basis for exercising monopoly power through express or tacit collusion, and I would have no difficulty in viewing these as monopolization cases. But this would provide no general answer to the oligopoly problem.

Learned Hand's *Alcoa* opinion[93] seems to have broken decisively with the interpretation of section 2 suggested above by holding (or at least implying) that the condition of being a monopolist for a substantial period of time is a violation, regardless of whether improper tactics were used to obtain or maintain the monopoly, unless the defendant can show that the monopoly was the product purely of economies of scale or of superior technical excellence (for example, as embodied in patents). Even in its original context of single-firm monopoly, the *Alcoa* doctrine seems open to serious question. There are three plausible explanations as to why a nonregulated monopoly has continued for a long time. The monopolist may have charged a low price, which made entry unattractive. He may have charged monopoly prices, but still not attracted new entry, either because the economies of scale were such as to allow room for only one firm in the market or because the monopolist, due to superior efficiency, had lower costs than a new entrant would have had. Finally, the monop-

---

[88] 15 U.S.C. § 2 (1964).

[89] This is Professor Turner's conclusion in his most recent article, *supra* note 19, at 1219; I am inclined to agree.

[90] *See id.* at 1231. *See also* references cited in note 18 *supra*. Professor Turner implies, however, that something more than merely an oligopoly market share would be required to trigger the application of section 2 in this context; evidence of noncompetitive pricing would apparently be required. *See* Turner, *supra* note 19, at 1225–26.

[91] *See, e.g.,* United States v. American Tobacco

Co., 221 U.S. 106, 181–83 (1911); Bork, *supra* note 45, at 28–30.

[92] *See* McGee, *Predatory Price Cutting: The Standard Oil (N.J.) Case,* 1 J. LAW & ECON. 137 (1958).

[93] United States v. Aluminum Co. of America, 148 F.2d 416 (2d Cir. 1945).

olist may have employed bad practices such as patent abuse or area price discrimination to keep out entrants (for reasons that would carry us too far afield to consider here, this last hypothesis is perhaps the least likely). In none of these cases would elaborate structural reformation of the industry—whose costs have already been discussed—be warranted. In the first, the usual objections to monopoly lack force. In the second, the *Alcoa* court itself would exonerate the defendant. One could argue that exceptional technical or managerial efficiency should not be a defense because dissolution of the firm would not necessarily entail the sacrifice of efficiencies unrelated to scale. But of course the parceling out of the firm's assets and personnel among the successor firms might well destroy whatever happy combination of resources had been responsible for the firm's exceptional efficiency. Judge Hand was also on sound ground in worrying about the disincentive effects of visiting dissolution upon a firm whose monopoly is the product of such efficiency. In the third case, an injunction against the bad practices should normally provide adequate relief. Perhaps there are instances where a monopolist, although not unusually efficient or aggressive, or favored by overwhelming economies of scale, can nonetheless persist over a substantial period of time in charging monopoly prices without attracting new entry; but this is a matter for inquiry, not assumption.

If the *Alcoa* doctrine seems inappropriate as a solution to the problems raised by single-firm monopoly, it seems doubly inappropriate as applied to oligopoly. The basis for inferring undesirable performance is much stronger in the monopoly than in the oligopoly context. There are also exquisite difficulties in defining the scope of the rule in the latter context. It may not be entirely easy to decide what market share justifies classifying a single firm as a monopolist, but it would be far more difficult to decide when a firm was an oligopolist for the purpose of triggering an extended *Alcoa* doctrine. In this respect, a

legislative cut-off point has much to recommend it.

My reservations concerning structural reformation, whether by new or under existing legislation, as a solution to the oligopoly problem can be restated as follows: With a few exceptions, such as where monopoly is conferred or protected by governmental franchise, a monopolist (or group of jointly acting oligopolists) can maintain its position in the market for a long time only (1) by forgoing monopoly gains, (2) by superior skill, (3) by predatory practices directed against prospective entrants, or (4) because the market is a natural monopoly. For the reasons noted earlier, none of these conditions warrants a restructuring of the firms in the market. Monopolies that lack the support of these conditions will usually be short-lived,[94] and radical structural remedies, which are themselves costly and protracted, seem inappropriate to cure transitory market imperfections. It follows that antitrust policy should emphasize the prevention of practices by which market power is obtained or exploited,[95] but steer generally clear of radical structural remedies.

I should make explicit two assumptions in the foregoing discussion. The first is that the behavioral and prophylactic antitrust remedies such as penalties and injunction are swift and relatively costless compared to dissolution proceedings. I suspect that careful empirical study would bear this out,

---

[94] There is, of course, the possibility of recurrence, which may be especially great where the source of the monopoly power is collusion. A collusive arrangement may be short-lived, but be revived again and again.

[95] One form of monopoly exploitation that I do not think the antitrust laws should attempt to prevent is monopoly pricing by the single-firm monopolist. Where monopoly pricing is the result of collusive activity, tacit or express, it is possible to eliminate it by eliminating the collusive activity. But monopoly pricing by a single-firm monopolist can be eliminated only by fixing the prices it charges. I have discussed elsewhere the acute problems involved in the direct regulation of monopoly prices and profits. *See* Posner, *Natural Monopoly and Its Regulation,* 21 STAN. L. REV. 548 (1969).

although no such study has, to my knowledge, ever been made. But a proceeding against tacit collusion would doubtless be more costly and protracted than most price-fixing—or even merger—cases. The second assumption is that market processes will usually eliminate a monopoly position not supported by one of the four mentioned conditions as quickly as would a dissolution proceeding: more precisely, that the difference between the costs imposed on society by a monopoly that is permitted to fall of its own weight and the costs imposed by one that is eventually dissolved by governmental action will usually not exceed the various direct and indirect costs attributable to the dissolution proceeding. Unable to prove that this is a correct assumption, I fall back on the proposition that the Government ought not intervene in private affairs unless its intervention can be expected to have a positive net social product. It follows that if my proposal to employ section 1 of the Sherman Act against tacit collusion is rejected as unfeasible, the alternative of applying radical structural remedies in highly concentrated markets should, on the basis of present knowledge, also be rejected.[96]

B. *The Merger Guidelines.* Section 7 of the Clayton Act, as amended in 1950, forbids mergers or acquisitions whose effect may be substantially to lessen competition or tend to create a monopoly in any line of commerce in any section of the country.[97] The statute has been applied with extraordinary rigor to mergers between direct competitors.[98] The primary justification for so strict a policy is that it is necessary to prevent oligopoly pricing. This subpart will attempt an evaluation of that policy, drawing on the general analysis of oligopoly presented earlier in this Article. Our text will be the Department of Justice Merger Guidelines,[99] a recent, authoritative, and reasoned exposition of the strict approach, and one premised explicitly on the concept of oligopoly questioned here—the concept that a probability of noncompetitive pricing can be inferred from the number and size distribution alone of the firms in the relevant market.[100]

1. *The definition of market.*— I begin with a necessary digression on the principles for defining the relevant market in which to appraise a merger. A merger between a firm that sells 25 per cent of the canned apricots sold in Tacoma and one that sells 20 per cent cannot injure competition unless the sellers of canned apricots in Tacoma could, by colluding, raise price above its previous level without immediately losing the trade to other sellers. That will be impossible either if canned apricots have a close substitute (or many less-close substitutes) or if other sellers of canned apricots would, despite transportation costs or other barriers, find it profitable to sell in Tacoma should the market price there rise by even a small amount. Only if neither of these conditions is present can the merger affect price.

The Guidelines' handling of the concept of market leaves much to be desired.

---

[96] It has been argued that forced deconcentration of highly concentrated industries is warranted by the extensive econometric evidence correlating concentration with profitability and the lack of comparable evidence correlating concentration with economies of scale. *Report of the White House Task Force on Antitrust Policy,* separate statement of Paul W. MacAvoy, 1–B to 2–B (July 5, 1968, mimeo.). Apart from questions as to the adequacy of the econometric evidence (*see* notes 36–37 *supra* and accompanying text), the analysis has two major weaknesses: (1) Given the acute difficulties involved in measuring economies of scale (*see* note 86 *supra*), no inference concerning their importance in concentrated industries can fairly be drawn from the absence of a substantial body of econometric studies; (2) as mentioned earlier, forced deconcentration would involve other costs besides the possible sacrifice of economies of scale.

---

[97] Clayton Act § 7, *as amended,* 15 U.S.C. § 18 (1964).

[98] *See, e.g.,* United States v. Pabst Brewing Co., 384 U.S. 546 (1966); United States v. Von's Grocery Co., 384 U.S. 270 (1966).

[99] 1 TRADE REG. REP. ¶ 4430 (1968).

[100] *See id.* at 6681–82.

A seller will not be deemed a part of the market if the included sellers enjoy "some advantage" [101] over him (an advantage that "need not be great . . . so long as it is significant").[102] However, if the cost spread between the included and excluded sellers (holding quality constant) was only a few per cent—not great, but significant, since it would be enough to prevent the excluded sellers from diverting any business from the included sellers so long as the latter did not raise their price—one would not be greatly concerned even if all the included sellers merged. Such a merger could not result in a price rise greater than the cost spread between excluded and included sellers, and the actual cost to society of the higher price would probably be much less.[103] In the more common case of a merger that did not create a monopoly, the impact on price would be still smaller.

The specific provisions of the Guide-

lines relating to the geographical dimension of the market are especially troublesome. Any geographical area may be deemed a relevant market unless it clearly appears that there are no transportation costs or other barriers to outsiders.[104] This is too sweeping. The existence of economic barriers confronting sellers not active in a particular local area does not make that area a market. To illustrate, if tin cans sell for 25 cents in Kansas City and 20 cents in Pittsburgh, and the cost of transporting cans from Pittsburgh to Kansas City is 5 cents, the Pittsburgh sellers may very well sell no cans in Kansas City. But a slight price rise in the Kansas City market would draw the Pittsburgh sellers in. They are a part of the Kansas City market so far as predicting the possible price consequences of a merger is concerned.[105]

The Guidelines should be revised to dispel the unfortunate impression (perhaps unintended) that it is proper to exclude from the relevant market sellers who are barred by transportation or other costs from selling there *at the existing price* but who would not be barred if that price were to rise, even slightly, as a result of price-fixing. It would also be an improvement if the Guidelines were more specific on market definition. I would suggest two new

---

[101] *Id.* at 6682.

[102] *Id.*

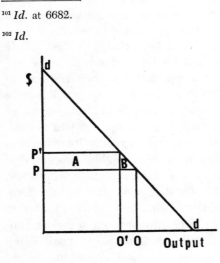

Figure 7

[103] Figure 7 illustrates this point. When the market price rises from *P* to *P'*, those purchasers who continue to buy the product pay a total of *A* more than they paid at the lower price. While a private cost to the purchasers, this amount is not a cost to society but merely a transfer to the sellers: The reduction in consumers' surplus is exactly matched by the increase in producers' surplus. The social cost of the higher price is the smaller area *B*, the additional consumers' surplus that was generated at the greater output.

---

[104] Department of Justice Merger Guidelines, .1 TRADE REG. REP. ¶ 4430, at 6683 (1968).

[105] The qualifying clause in this sentence—"so far as predicting the effects of a merger is concerned"—deserves emphasis. In a monopolization, rather than a merger, case it might be quite appropriate to exclude the Pittsburgh sellers. Suppose only one company sold tin cans in Kansas City, and the question was whether it had a monopoly of a relevant market. It would not be enough to find that substitution would occur if the Kansas City seller raised his price further; the 25-cent price might be the monopoly price. The relevant inquiry would be whether Pittsburgh sellers could sell in Kansas City if the price there rose slightly above competitive levels; if not, Kansas City is a relevant market so far as determining the existence of market power is concerned. When the question is what further effect on price a merger might have, however, it is unnecessary to inquire whether existing prices are competitive.

rules for this purpose. The first is that *all* sales of plants that have (or at some time during the recent past had) *some* (nontrivial) sales in the relevant market be included in the market. Such a plant should be able quite easily to shift additional output to the area should a differential price rise make such a shift attractive. Since this assumption will not always be correct, the rule should allow for an exception. For example, where sales from distant plants had been made only in periods of shortage when prices in the local area were very high, the rule would not apply.

The second rule is that other sellers—that is, those who do not sell and have not recently sold any part of their output in the area in question—should be excluded from the relevant market if (1) the price (or prices) they charge in their own market (or markets), plus the common-carrier charges for shipping the product from their markets to the one in question, appreciably exceed (say, by 5 or more per cent, depending on the absolute size of the market in question) the market price in the latter market; or (2) they are forbidden by law to sell in that market. This is an easily applied test for excluding from the relevant market firms that would be barred by transportation costs or legal restrictions even if the market price rose appreciably. Again, an exception is necessary. Sometimes it may be possible for outside sellers quite inexpensively to overcome apparently formidable transport problems by establishing a local production or distribution point.

A considerable gray area will remain: (1) cases where an exception to one of the rules is argued; (2) cases in which transportation charges are not readily determinable by inspection of filed common-carrier tariffs or where additional costs (transportation costs in the broadest sense but not freight costs) peculiar to the local market in question may prevent outsiders from selling there unless the market price rises by a considerable amount. These exceptional situations will have to be treated on a case-by-case basis; guidelines cannot be particularly helpful.

2. *The criteria of illegality for horizontal mergers.*— The Guidelines provide that if a market is "highly concentrated" (defined as where the four largest firms account for at least 75 per cent of the sales in the market), a merger between two firms each with a 4 per cent market share will be challenged; but if the acquiring firm has a 15 per cent share the acquired firm need have only 1 per cent for the merger to be challenged.[106] If the market is "less highly concentrated," the operative percentages are higher, although not by much: 5 per cent for the acquiring firm if the firms are the same size, 25 per cent if the acquired firm has only a 1 per cent market share.[107] If there is a "significant trend toward increased concentration" (defined as where the market share of any grouping of firms between the two and the eight largest has increased by 7 per cent in the previous 5–10 years), any acquisition by a firm in that grouping of any other firm having a market share of 2 per cent or more will be challenged unless the market is "wholly unconcentrated," [108] a term that, like "less highly concentrated," is not defined.

I am sympathetic in two respects to the Guidelines' emphasis on market-share percentages as the primary touchstone of legality. First, it seems appropriate to challenge mergers that markedly increase concentration in already highly concentrated markets or that create high concentration in an industry that previously had an atomistic structure. Since oligopoly appears to be a necessary although not sufficient condition of collusive behavior that will often escape detection (tacit collusion, in my term), a proper office of the merger law is to prevent the emergence of highly concentrated markets. Second, tacit collusion is rarely a problem when a market is not highly concentrated. It follows that we need have little concern with mergers that

---

[106] Department of Justice Merger Guidelines, 1 TRADE REG. REP. ¶ 4430, at 6683 (1968).

[107] *Id.* at 6684.

[108] *Id.*

do not create (or aggravate) a high level of concentration.[109] Nevertheless the present Guidelines forbid a variety of mergers, some quite small, in markets that are not highly concentrated.

A better approach would be to begin by identifying some threshold below which the danger of effective tacit collusion is slight. One could then ignore any merger in a market that had not reached the threshold unless the merger pushed the market across it. An initial question is how to measure concentration. It is customary to describe the level of concentration in a market in terms of the aggregate market share of the four or eight largest firms. This takes no account, however, of the distribution of market shares within the top group or of the number and size of the firms outside that group, although the likelihood of noncompetitive pricing is diminished if there is a fringe of small firms and enhanced if one or two firms are clearly dominant. Compare a market of eight firms in which the leading firm has a 65 per cent market share and the other seven each have 5 per cent with a market of 100 sellers in which the four largest firms have 20 per cent each, with the rest divided about equally among the remaining firms. The first market is more likely than the second to behave noncompetitively, but the four-firm concentration ratios are the same (80 per cent).

A more discriminating index of concentration is provided by the Herfindahl measure, which expresses the level of concentration in terms of the sum of the squares of each firm's market share.[110] In our ex-

ample, the first market would have a Herfindahl measure of 0.44, and the second a much lower Herfindahl measure: a shade over 0.16. One can complain that the Herfindahl measure is also arbitrary. But too little is known about the precise relationship of concentration to collusion to devise a measure of concentration that will accurately gauge the probable effect of different concentration patterns on pricing, and the Herfindahl measure, in addition to the virtues already mentioned, correlates well with a factor that is crucial to behavior in oligopolies: the ease of detecting cheating.[111]

The advantages of the Herfindahl measure can be further illustrated by considering specific thresholds. If one were to use four- or eight-firm concentration ratios as the basis for determining the threshold below which mergers would not be challenged, a plausible rule would be not to challenge a merger if the eight largest firms in the market had less than 50 per cent of the sales, unless the merger put the market across the threshold. But that would mean that in a market composed of two very large firms, each with a market share of 20 per cent, and a scattering of much smaller firms, a merger of the two leaders would be insulated from challenge. In contrast, if the threshold were 0.1 Herfindahl, small mergers in such a market would escape scrutiny but not a merger of the two leading firms, since it would raise the Herfindahl index to above 0.16.

I am less concerned with proposing exact figures than with asserting two principles: first, that the Herfindahl measure seems more appropriate than four- or eight-firm concentration ratios as a measure of concentration, and second, that one function of merger guidelines should be to delineate as clearly as possible the class of

---

[109] One could argue that small horizontal mergers should be forbidden lest a series of such mergers, each innocuous in itself, result in transforming an unconcentrated into a highly concentrated market. But that danger should be adequately taken care of by the threshold device discussed in the following paragraph of text.

[110] *See* G. STIGLER, *supra* note 31, at 31–36; Adelman, *Comment on the "H" Concentration Measure as a Numbers-Equivalent*, 51 REV. ECON. & STAT. 99 (1969). In contrast, the rather

similar "entropy" measure of concentration, *see* Finkelstein & Friedberg, *The Application of an Entropy Theory of Concentration to the Clayton Act*, 76 YALE L.J. 677 (1967), lacks a theoretical rationale. G. STIGLER, *supra* at 33; Stigler, *Comment*, 76 YALE L.J. 718 (1967).

[111] *See* G. STIGLER, *supra* note 31, at 55.

horizontal mergers that will *not* be challenged. The second principle can be extended to define a class of mergers that will automatically be challenged. For example, the Guidelines might provide that in any market in which the Herfindahl measure exceeded 0.2 any merger that increased the measure by at least 0.04 Herfindahl would be challenged. An example of the operation of this rule is given in the margin.[112]

This approach again leaves a middle area where uncertainty is unavoidable, unless one prefers to be extremely arbitrary. In this middle area it is appropriate to go beyond market-share percentages and consider several other dimensions of market structure that bear on the likelihood of successful price-fixing. One is the absolute number of sellers. Collusion is more difficult in a market that has a large number of sellers than in one with relatively few, even if the additional sellers are too small to have much effect on concentration ratios or the Herfindahl measure. This is because it will normally be impractical to include the many small sellers in the cartel, and they will be tempted to expand their market positions at the expense of the major sellers if the latter, through collusion, raise their prices above the competitive level. Another pertinent factor is the level of concentration on the buying side of the market. The more concentrated the buying side is, the less likely is successful collusion by the sellers. A third factor is the homogeneity of the product. Cheating is hard to detect in the case of a nonstandardized product. A fourth is the history of collusion in the market. If a market has a history of section 1 violations, concern with further increases

in concentration becomes more than theoretical.[113]

One could enumerate other considerations that are relevant to the feasibility of collusion, but a desire to keep enforcement of section 7 as simple as possible prompts me to exclude factors that may be difficult to measure (such as the condition of entry or the economies of scale) or whose significance is unclear (such as a previous trend toward concentration, or a shift in rank among the leading firms). The included factors are both clearly material to the likelihood of successful collusion and relatively easy to measure. The number of sellers in the relevant market can easily be counted; it should be possible to estimate the concentration on the buying side; it should not be too difficult to classify products along a spectrum between the highly customized and the completely standardized (even as to credit, delivery, and other terms of sale); and the record of previous section 1 violations in an industry can be compiled very easily. The weight to be given these factors in comparison to various levels of concentration between the lower and upper thresholds will require an exercise of judgment in each case, but the gain in discriminating enforcement should outweigh the slight loss in certainty.[114]

---

[113] These factors are discussed in G. STIGLER, *supra* note 31, at 39–62, 300.

[114] Other provisions of the Guidelines are relevant to the control of oligopoly, in particular those relating to potential competition. *See* Department of Justice Merger Guidelines, 1 TRADE REG. REP. ¶ 4430, at 6687–88 (1968). One who accepts that a highly concentrated market structure fosters collusion will desire to preserve potential competition both as a limitation on anticompetitive behavior by the firms in such markets and as a source of new competitors who by entering such markets would reduce concentration in them. The Guidelines accordingly provide that a merger between a leading firm in a concentrated market and "one of the most likely entrants" into the market is forbidden, with the class of "most likely entrants" to be delineated in each case by reference to the natural expansion patterns of firms, their financial resources, and so forth. *Id.* I have no objection in principle to this approach, but am troubled

---

[112] Suppose a market consisting of five firms with the following market shares: $s_1 = 40\%$, $s_2 = 30\%$, $s_3 = 20\%$, $s_4 = 8\%$, and $s_5 = 2\%$. Then $H = s_1^2 + s_2^2 + s_3^2 + s_4^2 + s_5^2$, or 0.2968. Now suppose that the second and fourth firms merge. Now $H = s_1^2 + (s_2 + s_4)^2 + s_3^2 + s_5^2$, and $(s_2 + s_4)^2 = s_2^2 + 2s_2s_4 + s_4^2$. Thus, the increase in the Herfindahl measure as the result of a merger is twice the product of the market shares of the merging firms, or in our example 0.0480. The new Herfindahl measure is 0.2968 + 0.0480, or 0.3448.

A word, in closing, on the defense of efficiencies in a section 7 proceeding. The Guidelines reject any such defense,[115] and I am broadly sympathetic to this approach.[116] A merger may, to be sure, enable the merging firms to achieve economies of scale, or facilitate the replacement of inferior by superior management, although, since there are a number of other possible motivations for mergers, no general presumption that mergers promote efficiency can be indulged. The difficulty, one discussed earlier in a slightly different context,[117] is in measuring efficiency. That difficulty is aggravated in the present context

by two features of it. First, the Department has failed to confine its attention to those markets sufficiently concentrated to create a plausible danger of tacit collusion. I have discussed that point in the horizontal context and will not pursue it here. Second, if the class of most likely entrants contains more than a few firms, the elimination of one is unlikely to affect materially the effectiveness of potential competition or the likelihood of actual entry. This qualification is absent from the Guidelines.

[115] Department of Justice Merger Guidelines, 1 TRADE REG. REP. ¶ 4430, at 6684–85 (1968).

[116] As I have argued elsewhere, however, there should be an exception (perhaps it is implicit in the Guidelines' reference to "exceptional circumstances" in which a defense of efficiencies may be accepted) for the situation in which a market is a natural monopoly, that is, incapable of efficiently supporting more than one firm. *See* Posner, *supra* note 95, at 586–87 (1969). If, the merger route blocked, the firms in such a market compete vigorously, all but one—by definition—will fail. Competition is so dangerous a strategy in these circumstances for most of the participants that they will be strongly motivated to collude rather than compete; and since there are unlikely to be more than a very few firms in a market that is a natural monopoly, conditions may be highly favorable for collusion in a form difficult to detect. These unusual circumstances warrant, in my judgment, an exception to the general policy of refusing to entertain defenses based on the alleged efficiencies that a merger will confer.

[117] *See* note 86 *supra*. The discussion in that note concerns the difficulty of determining efficient scale. I have discussed elsewhere some of the difficulties involved in determining managerial efficiency. *See* Posner, *supra* note 95, at 628–30.

by the fact that, since firms can grow and change other than by merger, the effect of blocking a merger that would increase efficiency is ordinarily at most to postpone rather than to preclude altogether the achievement of the efficiencies in question. To determine the cost of blocking the merger would require, therefore, a determination not only of the magnitude of the efficiencies that it would produce but also the probable interval of time before they would be realized in any event. Until there is better evidence that these are tractable inquiries, there is much to be said for excluding them from section 7 proceedings.[118] That is not an optimum solution, for its consequence is that section 7 enforcement may involve social costs of unknown dimensions. Perhaps the best that can be done, in the present state of our understanding, is to disallow the defense[119] but at the same time reduce the prohibitory scope of the statute to realistic limits and thereby minimize the occasions on which enforcement may impede the achievement of efficiencies. That is the course advocated here.

Conclusion

The supposed inadequacy of section 1 of the Sherman Act to deal effectively with noncompetitive pricing by oligopolists has been a persistent theme in discussions of antitrust policy and a fertile source of proposals for new legislation and new applications of other antitrust provisions. This view of section 1 is rooted in the theory that noncompetitive pricing is virtually inevitable in a market having an oligopolistic market structure and hence not amenable to rules and remedies concerned with altering behavior without changing structure, and perhaps also in a lawyers' habit in ap-

[118] And, a fortiori, for not attempting to balance the efficiency gains of a merger against its welfare losses (*see* note 103 *supra*)—another factor normally impossible to quantify—as proposed in Williamson, *Economies as an Antitrust Defense: The Welfare Tradeoffs*, 58 AM. ECON. REV. 18 (1968).

[119] With the exception noted in note 116 *supra*.

plying section 1 of looking for evidence of actual agreement rather than for evidence of effects on competition. I have argued that noncompetitive pricing by oligopolists is not compelled, although it is facilitated, by the structure of the market. It is a variant of conventional cartel behavior, and there is a good chance that it can be controlled effectively by proceedings under section 1. Revision of section 1 to improve the penalties for violation, and improvements in economic knowledge to facilitate the drawing of inferences of collusion from observed firm behavior, would greatly assist but do not seem absolutely essential to this employment of section 1.

Analysis of the basic question—the applicability of the traditional remedies against cartelization to noncompetitive pricing by oligopolists—led to a critical examination of other proposals for dealing with the problem. In general, these proposals, which involve the dismemberment of existing oligopolies and extremely stringent prohibitions against horizontal mergers, were found to be unduly severe. I ventured the suggestion that restructuring markets by breaking up existing firms can rarely be justified as sound antitrust policy. In the matter of prophylactic remedies, the approach in the Department of Justice Merger Guidelines of making market-share percentages the primary test of when to challenge a horizontal merger seems basically sound. However, the definition of market requires revision; the Guidelines should delineate a class of mergers that the Department will *not* challenge; a different measure of concentration should be employed; and the test of whether to challenge a merger should be broadened, in a middle range of cases, to include a few readily determinable factors in addition to market shares that analysis of oligopoly indicates to be relevant to predicting noncompetitive pricing. These factors are the absolute number of sellers in the market, the concentration on the buying side, the degree of standardization of the product, and the history of collusive activities in the market.

IV · UNFAIR COMPETITION

Part IV · *Unfair Competition*

In the opening reading of this section, Professor John McGee tells us the Standard Oil case of 1911 created a legend. Standard "became the archetype of predatory monopoly." More than any other antitrust legend, this is the one usually cited by the average citizen as proof of the need for antitrust laws. The fear that predatory competition would enable a dominant firm to prevent entry, maintain its dominance, and charge supracompetitive prices was also shared by prominent economists early in the century. This led them to support the passage of legislation creating the Federal Trade Commission whose special charge was to prevent "unfair methods of competition."

McGee finds predatory price-cutting by a dominant firm to be irrational and, for that reason, unlikely. Exploring the record of the Standard Oil case, he concludes that "Standard Oil did not use predatory price discrimination to drive out competing refiners, nor did its pricing practice have that effect." Some of the most telling evidence that Standard did not engage in predatory pricing or, if it did, that it was not effective in frightening off potential competitors, consists of the fact that ex-Standard employees "entered the oil business when they left Standard."

In the following selection, Professor Kenneth Elzinga examines another instance of alleged predatory pricing—a practice which the Circuit Court and most of the literature discussing the history of the Gunpowder Trust agree occurred. Yet, a careful analysis of the record concerning each of the alleged instances turns up what appears to be simple competitive behavior. Perhaps one of the alleged instances was predatory. If so, it was irrational and ineffective. Where price cutting occurred, it was usually the supposed victim who initiated it. The fact that powder mills were often founded for the express purpose of selling out to DuPont (as sugar mills were often started for the express purpose of selling out to American Sugar Refining) indicates that predatory pricing did not occur on the part of the would-be monopolizer or, if it did, was ineffective in stopping entry, driving out competitors, or making them willing to sell out at low prices. As Elzinga points out, "If predatory pricing has the effect often attributed to it, one would certainly not expect to find independent firms being sold at a profit or the former owners anxious to reenter the business."

Since a major argument against allowing conglomerates to be formed is the presumption that a conglomerate will subsidize economic warfare intended to obtain a monopoly in one market with the profits made in another, the findings of Professors McGee and Elzinga bear on this issue. The survey of predatory pricing by Professor Roland Koller in the next selection concludes that, if any public policy action is taken concerning conglomerates, it should be to encourage them. "The logical conclusion . . . is that if one wants to confine industrial predation to its present status of popular myth and not to encourage its emergence as an economic reality, an indiscriminate prohibition of all conglomerate mergers would not really be the optimum policy."

Selection 40 deals with the attempt to stop some varieties of alleged price discrimination by the Robinson-Patman Act. Of all our antitrust laws, this one appears to do more to stop competition than any other. It forces price discrimination on the market where it would otherwise tend to disappear. It prevents the sporadic price discrimination that moves a market toward a new long-run competitive equilibrium. As Professor McGee observes, ". . . there will normally be a certain amount of real price discrimination amongst sellers. Some of it, at least, will result from rivalrous seller behavior; and stopping that may remove such price competition as can normally be expected."

In the following selection, Professor Ward Bowman, examining the Supreme Court's Utah Pie decision, tells us that ". . . the Supreme Court has used section 2(a) of the Robinson-Patman Act to strike directly at price competition itself." The story of Pet, Carnation, and Continental's competition with the Utah Pie Co. is a classic description of sporadic price discrimination in the process of moving a market to a new, long-run, competitive equilibrium. The Court's view of the matter, however, was as Kafkaeque as Professor Elzinga's description of the proceedings in the Gunpowder Case where he observes that ". . . the government lawyers believed they had scored points when they cajoled a witness into testifying that the GTA [Gunpowder Trade Association] charged low prices; the defendants then attempting to prove that the trust kept its prices up! With only a couple of possible exceptions, the Powder Trust was a combination trying to maintain a monopolistic price structure."

In Utah Pie, the Court's ruling implies that major companies must not respond to the competition of a local company but, instead, hold a price umbrella which would result in their own elimination from the market. As it was, the three defendants' share of the market had declined markedly. But to hold their Salt Lake City market, the Court, in effect, ruled that any price cuts by the defendants should have been simultaneous in their major markets with price cuts in Salt Lake City rather than lagging. Such a requirement would slow the price decline, since a local price cut would become far more expensive if it would have to be matched in major markets. In such circumstances, major sellers would tend to be slower in making price cuts and the long run competitive equilibrium would be reached less rapidly.

In the final selection, Professor Basil Yamey agrees that predatory competition is rare, but argues that it does occur occasionally. He describes what appears to be a successful instance.[1] In addition, he suggests that predatory pricing may also be used to discipline a price cutting rival and not just to kill a rival.

---

[1] For another view, see John McGee, *Ocean Freight Rate Conferences and the American Merchant Marine,* 27 University of Chicago Law Review (1960) note 98 at 234.

37. Predatory Price Cutting: The Standard Oil (N.J.) Case

JOHN S. McGEE

He [Rockefeller] applied underselling for destroying his rivals' markets with the same deliberation and persistency that characterized all his efforts, and in the long run he always won.—IDA TARBELL.

I. Introduction

The purpose of this paper is to determine whether the pre-dissolution Standard Oil Company actually used predatory price cutting to achieve or maintain its monopoly. This issue is of much more than antiquarian or theoretic interest. Settling it is of direct importance to present anti-trust policy. At the very least, finding the facts should aid in defining certain hazy notions that now figure in discussions of monopoly and its control.

The *Standard Oil* case of 1911 [1] is a landmark in the development of anti-trust law. But it is more than a famous law case: it created a legend. The firm whose history it relates became the archetype of predatory monopoly.

It is sometimes said that *Standard Oil* was influential because it revealed deadly and reprehensible techniques by which Monopoly on a heroic scale could be achieved and, probably more important, perpetuated. Historians tell us that the facts revealed in *Standard Oil* were in good part responsible for the emphasis that the anti-trust laws came to place upon unfair and monopolizing business practices.

Perhaps the most famous of all of the monopolizing techniques that Standard is supposed to have used is local price cutting. Given the bad repute in which monopoly has long been officially held in this country,

and the prominence of predatory pricing in *Standard Oil*, it is not surprising that the practice received special attention in the law. Monopoly was not new in 1911, but a predatory giant may have seemed novel. The vision of a giant firm that used a brutally scientific, and completely effective, technique for acquiring and maintaining monopoly must have aroused uncommon concern. Standard was invincible. Anything economists could say about the transience of monopoly must have seemed hopelessly unrealistic in view of the vigor and success with which Standard was said to have prevented entry.

In any case, by 1914, in the Clayton Act, predatory price discrimination was included among a select group of business practices the character or effect of which called for explicit statutory prohibition. The Robinson-Patman amendment of 1936 lengthened the list, but certainly did not weaken the hostility toward local price cutting. Indeed, its legislative history and subsequent interpretation reveal a continuing dread of the device.

Predatory discrimination thus occupies a special and almost unquestioned place in law and economics. This has led to a certain amount of difficulty, especially in connection with the Robinson-Patman Act. Some critics claim that this statute unnecessarily restricts rivalry, thereby softening competition. Yet even the critics apparently fear that if we permit the helpful kind of discrimination we will encourage the lethal kind. Most are obliged to rely on the tenuous standard of intent to distinguish one kind from the other.

Reprinted from 1 *Journal of Law and Economics* 137 (1958). Copyright 1958, the University of Chicago.

[1] Standard Oil Co. of New Jersey v. United States, 221 U.S. 1 (1911).

This fearful ambivalence, in which the spectre of *Standard Oil* figures prominently, may be responsible for the continuing, and somewhat fruitless, arguments about the proper role of a "good faith" defense under Section 2(B) of the Robinson-Patman Act. It may also account for the popular view that disciplinary price cutting makes car-telization easier and its benefits more lasting. It surely has influenced thinking about small firms that face large rivals.

For these reasons, a re-examination of *Standard Oil* may be worthwhile.

II. Predatory Price Cutting: Some Hypotheses

According to most accounts, the Standard Oil Co. of New Jersey established an oil refining monopoly in the United States, in large part through the systematic use of predatory price discrimination. Standard struck down its competitors, in one market at a time, until it enjoyed a monopoly position everywhere. Similarly, it preserved its monopoly by cutting prices selectively wherever competitors dared enter. Price discrimination, so the story goes, was both the technique by which it obtained its dominance and the device with which it maintained it.

The main trouble with this "history" is that it is logically deficient, and I can find little or no evidence to support it.[2]

A brief examination of the logic of predatory price discrimination is helpful in interpreting the facts. In the beginning, oil refining in the United States apparently was competitive. Necessary capital was relatively slight, because of the modest quality demands imposed by consumer preferences and the primitive technological character of the refining process itself. The number of refiners was evidently large, since the Standard interests bought out more than a hundred of them. Standard Oil was not born with monopoly power: as late as 1870 it had only 10 per cent of the refining business.

The usual argument that local price cutting is a monopolizing technique *begins* by assuming that the predator has important monopoly power, which is his "war chest" for supporting the unprofitable raids and forays. Evidently the technique could not be used until the Standard interests achieved the necessary monopoly power. Similarly, advantages from monopsonistic bargaining[3] would not be available until the buyer attained considerable stature.

A simpler technique did exist, and Standard used it. Unless there are legal restraints, anyone can monopolize an industry through mergers and acquisitions, paying for the acquisitions by permitting participation of the former owners in the expected monopoly gains. Since profits are thus expanded, all of the participants can be better off even after paying an innovator's share to the enterpriser who got the idea in the first place.

Under either competition or monopoly, the value of a firm is the present worth of its future income stream. Competitive firms can be purchased for competitive asset values or, at worst, for only a little more. Even in the case of important recalcitrants, anything up to the present value of the future monopoly profits from the property will be a worthwhile exchange to the buyer, and a bountiful windfall to the seller.

It is conceivable that Standard did not merge to the full size it wanted, but did

---

[2] I am profoundly indebted to Aaron Director, of the University of Chicago Law School, who in 1953 suggested that this study be undertaken. Professor Director, without investigating the facts, developed a logical framework by which he predicted that Standard Oil had not gotten or maintained its monopoly position by using predatory price cutting. In truth, he predicted, on purely logical grounds, that they never systematically used the technique at all. I was astounded by these hypotheses, and doubtful of their validity, but was also impressed by the logic which produced them. As a consequence, I resolved to investigate the matter, admittedly against my better judgment; for, like everyone else, I knew full well what Standard had really done.

[3] Example: railroad rebates. Although this subject lies outside the present inquiry, I am convinced that the significance of railroad rebates has also been misunderstood.

achieve whatever size was necessary to use predatory techniques to grow the rest of the way. How would it go about using them? Assume that Standard had an absolute monopoly in some important markets, and was earning substantial profits there. Assume that in another market there are several competitors, all of whom Standard wants to get out of the way. Standard cuts the price below cost. Everyone suffers losses. Standard would, of course, suffer losses even though it has other profitable markets: it could have been earning at least competitive returns and is not. The war could go on until average variable costs are not covered and are not expected to be covered; and the competitors drop out. In the meanwhile, the predator would have been pouring money in to crush them. If, instead of fighting, the would-be monopolist bought out his competitors directly, he could afford to pay them up to the discounted value of the expected monopoly profits to be gotten as a result of their extinction. Anything above the competitive value of their firms should be enough to buy them. In the purchase case, monopoly profits could begin at once; in the predatory case, large losses would first have to be incurred. Losses would have to be set off against the prospective monopoly profits, discounted appropriately. Even supposing that the competitors would not sell for competitive value, it is difficult to see why the predator would be unwilling to take the amount that he would otherwise spend in price wars and pay it as a bonus.

Since the revenues to be gotten during the predatory price war will always be less than those that could be gotten immediately through purchase, and will not be higher after the war is concluded, present worth will be higher in the purchase case. For a predatory campaign to make sense the direct costs of the price war must be less than for purchase. It is necessary to determine whether that is possible.

Assume that the monopolizer's costs are equal to those of his competitors. The market has enough independent sellers to be competitive. Otherwise the problem of monopolizing it ceases to concern us. This im-

plies that the monopolist does not now sell enough in the market to control it. If he seeks to depress the price below the competitive level he must be prepared to sell increasing quantities, since the mechanism of forcing a lower price compels him to lure customers away from his rivals, making them meet his price or go without customers. To lure customers away from somebody, he must be prepared to serve them himself. The monopolizer thus finds himself in the position of selling more—and therefore losing more—than his competitors. Standard's market share was often 75 per cent or more. In the 75 per cent case the monopolizer would sell three times as much as all competitors taken together, and, on the assumption of equal unit costs, would lose roughly three times as much as all of them taken together.[4]

Losses incurred in this way are losses judged even by the standard of competitive returns. Since the alternative of outright purchase of rivals would have produced immediate monopoly returns, the loss in view of the alternatives can be very great indeed.[5] Furthermore, at some stage of the game the competitors may simply shut down operations temporarily, letting the monopolist take all the business (and all the losses), then simply resume operations when he raises prices again. At prices above average variable costs, but below total unit costs, the "war" might go on for years.

Purchase has an additional marked advantage over the predatory technique. It is rare for an industrial plant to wear out all at once. If price does not cover average variable costs, the operation is suspended. This will often leave the plant wholly intact. In the longer run, it may simply be the failure of some key unit, the replacement of which

---

[4] Any assumption that the monopolizer's size gives him sufficient cost advantages rapidly takes us away from a predatory price cutting example and into the realm of so-called natural monopolies.

[5] It must not be supposed that, just because he enjoys profits elsewhere, anyone will be so stupid as to assume that it is costless to use them for anything but the best alternatives.

is uneconomic at the present price level, that precipitates shut-down. In either case, physical capacity remains, and will be brought back into play by some opportunist once the monopolizer raises prices to enjoy the fruits of the battle he has spent so much in winning.

All in all, then, purchase would not be more expensive than war without quarter, and should be both cheaper and more permanent. It may at first be thought that predatory pricing more than makes up for its expense by depressing the purchase price of the properties to be absorbed. In effect, this requires that large losses reduce asset values less than smaller losses. This is not at all likely. Furthermore, assuming that the properties in question are economic,[6] it is unlikely that their long-run market value will be much reduced by an artificially low price that clearly will not be permanent. The owners can shut down temporarily, allowing the monopolist to carry all of the very unprofitable business, or simply wait for him to see the error of his ways and purchase. Even if there is widespread bankruptcy, wise men will see the value to the monopolist of bringing the facilities under his control, and find it profitable to purchase them at some price below what the monopolist can be expected to pay if he must. Since the monopolist is presumably interested in profits, and has a notion of the effect of discount factors upon future income, he cannot afford to wait forever. Properties that a would-be monopolist needs to control can be an attractive investment.

Predation would thus be profitable only when the process produces purchase prices that are so far below competitive asset figures that they more than offset the large losses necessary to produce them. One empirical test, for those who suspect the logic, would be to examine prices paid for properties in cases where predatory pricing is alleged to have been practiced.

Some of the most strategic factors to be monopolized may be the skilled managerial and technical personnel of competitors. Reproducing them can be a much more formidable and longer job than the construction of physical facilities. But short of murder, the cost of which can also be expected to be high if undertaken in any quantity, the only feasible way of preventing their embarrassing and costly reappearance is to hire, retire, or share with them. None of these things can be accomplished well or permanently if these people are too much badgered in the process.[7]

There are two other crucial issues that must be examined, the first dealing with the extent to which monopolization is profitable; the second, with the necessary conditions for its success. Monopolization as such will be carried only so far as is necessary to maximize profits, since it inevitably involves certain expenses of planning, purchase, and rationalization. In the case of a vertically integrated industry the would-be monopolist will choose to monopolize the level that will produce the largest net profit. This requires choosing that one which is both cheapest to control and over which control is likely to endure. If a monopoly can be achieved at the refining level, for example, there is little sense trying to achieve one at the crude oil producing level, or marketing. Standard Oil of New Jersey achieved a refinery monopoly; anything more would have been redundant.[8]

---

[6] If they are not, they need not concern us, since their extinction might be expected or welcomed under competition.

[7] "[A]s Mr. Rockefeller and Mr. Archbold testified, most of the concerns which were brought together continued to be operated and managed by the former owners." Brief for the U.S., Vol. 1, at 19.

Further, "There are only a few cases in which the Standard interests, during this period [1872–80], acquired stock in concerns without taking the former owners in as stockholders of the Standard, or bringing them into the combination by leaving them a minority interest in the original concern." Id., at 32.

[8] This abstracts from any cost reductions that integration may make possible. These have nothing to do with the problem at hand.

See Bork, Vertical Integration and the Sherman Act, 22 U. of Chi. L. Rev. 157 (1954). Standard began producing crude oil in 1889,

This should not be taken to mean that the monopolist will not care what happens to the other levels; for he has every interest in seeing to it that the other levels are not monopolized by someone else. In marketing, for example, he would prefer that the product be distributed as cheaply as possible, since he can then extract full monopoly revenues from the level in his control. This point is important in interpreting the facts of the *Standard Oil* case.

Obstacles to entry are necessary conditions for success. Entry is the nemesis of monopoly. It is foolish to monopolize an area or market into which entry is quick and easy. Moreover, monopolization that produces a firm of greater than optimum size is in for trouble if entry can occur even over a longer period. In general, monopolization will not pay if there is no special qualification for entry, or no relatively long gestation period for the facilities that must be committed for successful entry.

Finally, it is necessary to examine certain data that are often taken to be symptomatic of predatory price cutting, when in fact they may be nothing of the sort. Assume that a monopolist sells in two markets, separated effectively by transport costs or other impediments to free interchange, and that he has a complete monopoly in both. Elasticity of demand is assumed to be the same in both markets, and monopoly prices are identical. Assume that, for some unknown reason, entry occurs in one market but not in the other. Supplies are increased in the first and price falls; price in the second remains unchanged. There are now two different prices in the two markets, reflecting the existence of alternative supplies in the first. The theory of the dominant firm, maximizing by taking into account the outputs of his lesser rivals at various prices, appears to fit the case. An objective fact-finder discovers that the monopolist is discriminating in price between the two markets. A bad theorist then concludes that he is preying on somebody. In truth, the principle established is only that greater supplies bring lower prices.

Compare this example with another. Assume that we have two separate markets, and that each is in short-run competitive equilibrium with firms earning super-normal returns. Assume that, for some reason, entry takes place in one market but not in the other. Supply increases and price falls in one but not in the other. From this evidence of price changes in both the monopoly and competition examples, the inference is simply that greater supplies lower prices. We should not infer from the price data that either case has anything to do with predatory price-cutting.

To sum up: (1) Predatory price cutting does not explain how a seller acquires the monopoly power that he must have before he could practice it. (2) Whereas it is *conceivable* that someone might embark on a predatory program, I cannot see that it would pay him to do so, since outright purchase is both cheaper and more reliable. (3) Because monopolization by any technique always involves some expense, a firm *qua* monopolizer will carry it to the one securest level in an integrated industry, not to all. (4) Actual variations in prices among markets may be accounted for in terms of variations in demand elasticities, but do not imply or establish that anybody is preying on anybody else.

III. Testing the Hypotheses

The voluminous Record in the Standard Oil of N.J. dissolution suit furnishes a test of these propositions.[9]

The Record shows that Standard estab-

---

and by 1898 produced 33 per cent of the total. By 1906, its share declined to 11.11 per cent. Transcript of Record Vol., 19, at 626 (Def. Exh. 266).

[9] The Transcript of Record consists of over 11,000 printed pages of exhibits and testimony; Appellants' briefs and oral argument covers more than 900 pages; Appellee's briefs and arguments almost 1300 pages. The full record is thus more than 13,500 pages long. Unless otherwise noted, volume references are to the Transcript of Record.

lished a refining monopoly.[10] Collusion among 100 to 200 different sellers was unstable. Standard achieved its monopoly position through merger and acquisition.[11] Although the Government alleged that Standard employed other techniques as well, it concluded that:

> Unquestionably the principal means used by the defendants to monopolize and restrain trade and commerce in petroleum has been the combination of previously independent concerns. . . .[12]
>
> . . . Standard acquired 123 refineries (many of which also did a marketing business), 11 lubricating oil works, 24 pipeline concerns, and 64 exclusively marketing concerns; a total number of 223.
>
> Neither did these acquisitions all occur at an early date, about half of them, in number, occurred since 1879, and

---

[10] In 1879, Standard and those concerns "in harmony" with it, apparently refined from 90 to 95 per cent of the U.S. output. See Vol. 6, at 3303. It is not clear just what these data mean. Mr. Archbold testified that in 1870 Standard did about 10 per cent of the refining business in the United States; and that for 1888 Standard's share was probably 75 per cent. Id., at 3246–68. I think that much work remains to be done to determine how Standard's market position really changed over time. See e.g., Vol. 2, at 783–784.

In any case, Standard's position in crude oil production was relatively small; it did very little retailing and did not perform all of its own wholesaling; several major railroads and the pipeline systems of Pure, Tidewater, Texas Co., Gulf, and others competed in the transportation of crude oil. Its strongest position was evidently in refining.

[11] "Q. Had you difficulty before you entered into relations with the Standard Oil Company to make money out of the business? A. The competition was always very sharp, and there was always some one that was willing to sell goods for less than they cost, and that made the market price for everything; we got up an association, and took in all the refiners until some of them went back on us, and that would break up the association; we tried that two or three times." Vol. 6, at 3303.

See also Mr. Rockefeller's interesting testimony on the difficulty of effecting stable conspiracies. Vol. 16, especially at 3074–75.

[12] Brief for the United States, Vol. 1, at 169.

many important ones between 1890 and 1902. . . .[13]

Of the refineries it acquired, Standard dismantled at least 75, and ultimately produced a greatly increased volume in only 20 separate installations.[14]

1. Price Cutting Against Competing Refiners. Standard's monopoly was in refining. Is there any evidence that predatory price cutting helped to achieve it? [15] To discover whether local price cutting played any part in the many refinery acquisitions made by the Standard interests, I checked the whole Record for testimony about every refinery known to have been bought.[16] Furthermore, I have tried to check every alleged case of local price cutting involving competitive refiners that Standard did *not* buy. I can find few specific references to refiners in connection with allegations that Standard cut prices to drive out competitors. The following are the principal examples, including cases in which the marketing subsidiaries or branches of Standard's integrated competitors were involved. They are certainly the most significant ones.

a) "Suspect" Cases Involving Acquisitions

The Cleveland acquisitions.— During 1871–72 the Rockefeller interests purchased at least 17 Cleveland refineries.[17] I can find no real evidence that predatory price cutting or any other type of coercion figured

---

[13] Reply Brief for the United States, at 62. See Appendix C, Sheets 1–11.

[14] Id., at 63–64.

[15] The first problem is to discover which companies were really refiners. Oddly enough, many of the firms mentioned in the record have "Refining Company" as part of their names, but were apparently not refiners at all. One example is Mr. Castle's Columbia Refining Co., wholly a marketing concern. Possibly the owners concluded that customers are better disposed towards marketers who make the products they sell.

[16] Brief for the United States, Vol. 1, Appendices C & D; Vol. 19, at 662–63; Vol. 17, at 3290.

[17] Reply Brief for the United States, Appendix C, Sheet 1.

in the acquisitions. According to Mr. Rockefeller, the consolidation of the Cleveland refineries was a blessing to all concerned, and arose

> In a most natural way. . . . We were; [sic] neighbors, acquaintances, friends, having had our prosperity there together in the business in the good days; and beginning generally to recognize the changes that were coming, and the lessening of the chance of good returns from the refining business on account of the overproduction of refined oil, or the overproduction of the refinery construction.[18]

On the other hand, Mr. Lewis Emery, Jr., a long-time crude oil producer and refiner from Bradford, Pennsylvania, offered the following hearsay on the subject: "I talked with quite a number of them afterwards, and they said they thought the case was hopeless and they had arranged with the combination." [19]

Predatory price cutting had nothing to do with the acquisitions, according even to Mr. Emery's version. There is some question about Mr. Emery's testimony in any case: Emery was testifying, in 1908, about events that occurred 36 years earlier. Furthermore, he had evidently not been in Cleveland at this time and had no first-hand knowledge of the affair.[20]

There are very good reasons to suppose

that no kind of coercion figured in the Cleveland purchases. The stock records and a great deal of testimony confirm that Standard's usual practice during this time was to employ the managers and owners of the firms they absorbed, and often to make them shareholders as well. Victimized ex-rivals might be expected to make poor employees and dissident or unwilling shareholders.

Mr. Emery's own experience.— Lewis Emery entered the industry as a crude oil producer in 1865. By 1870 he became interested in the Octave Oil Company and Refinery. In 1875, Emery closed down the Octave, and in 1876 sold it to the Standard interests for $45,000.[21] Emery claimed that the railroad pool agreement of 1874 had squeezed him out along with other small Western Pennsylvania refiners. Predatory price cutting clearly had nothing to do with it.[22]

Whatever his reasons for selling the Octave, Mr. Emery was apparently not discouraged. For, in 1879, Emery and two partners formed Logan, Emery & Weaver, and started a new refinery at Philadelphia.[23] By 1880 the refinery was completed.[24] Nevertheless, he testified, his firm soon had

---

[18] Vol. 16, at 3065.

[19] Vol. 6, at 2625. According to Emery, the refiners were pushed into consolidation because of the rail rate "preferences" given to Standard in the South Improvement Company program and the succeeding pool agreement of 1874. The South Improvement program apparently never became effective; and the contract of 1874, which Emery said sealed the doom of Pennsylvania independent refiners, simply *equalized* rail freight from Cleveland and Western Pennsylvania refineries. Id., at 2724, 2732. See testimony of Archbold, id., at 3244–45.

[20] Though it does not really prove anything, it is interesting that Emery was first of all a crude producer and like any raw materials supplier had little affection for the monopsony that faced him. He was also a successful politician during a period in which anti-trust had great popular appeal. Id., at 2642.

[21] Id., at 2610, 2640. It was small, and must have been relatively high cost, since Standard dismantled it forthwith.

[22] See Note 19, supra. Apparently even the railroad rebates, which Emery claimed built Standard, were also available to the small refiner:
"[I]n the very early history of the Octave Oil Company, when we were shut down, we went to the railroads and they said they would give us 25 cents rebate. . . . [p]er barrel on oil." Id., at 2772–73.
See also the testimony of Archbold, id., at 3244–45; and Josiah Lombard, an independent: "They gave . . . all shippers over that road a rebate of ten per cent, which we got with others." Vol. 1, at 265. See also note 37, infra.

[23] Mr. Emery was by this time a member of the Pennsylvania Legislature and remained in office for 10 years thereafter. Vol. 6, at 2642.

[24] Interestingly enough, Mr. Emery had borrowed $25,000 from—of all people—the Standard Oil Company. Id., at 2643.

trouble getting empty railroad cars.[25] Seven years later, Logan, Emery & Weaver sold out to Standard.[26] According to Emery, the original cost of the refinery, lands and wharves was $350,000. Standard bought the refinery for $275,000 and promptly dismantled it, though Emery claimed that the plant was "[f]irst class in every sense." [27] He did admit that refinery depreciation was commonly 10 to 15 per cent per annum.[28] Emery said he sold because he could not get crude oil. The problem was, according to Emery, that Standard and the crude oil producers had agreed to reduce crude output after the excessive production of 1887.[29]

Mr. Emery had also been interested in the Equitable Company, which built a crude oil pipeline in 1878, and sold it to the Tidewater interests for $178,000 in 1879. In 1889 Mr. Emery bought a small Bradford refinery for $5,000, commencing business with 250-barrel stills.[30] By 1908, output was 1,500 barrels per day. The Emery Manu-

facturing Company at Bradford, Pennsylvania thus had a much-enlarged refinery worth $250,000 to $400,000 and gathering lines worth $200,000. Sales had expanded from about $20,000 per year to between $480,000 and $600,000 per year. Standard's "predatory" tactics, if there were any, had apparently neither discouraged nor ruined Mr. Emery's own business.[31]

Furthermore, Emery became president of the United States Pipeline Company, which, in 1891, constructed a crude oil pipeline. The United States Pipeline Company later sold out to the Pure Oil Company.[32] When Emery sold the company, he took about $100,000 in Pure Oil Company stock, and retained a $15,000 interest in U.S. Pipeline. By 1893, Standard had bought a four-tenths interest in the United States Pipeline, but Emery and his colleagues frustrated their efforts to vote the stock.[33] In 1908, Emery's Philadelphia refinery had a capacity of 2,000 barrels per day, and his other oil interests were extensive. Emery clearly had a successful career, an important part of which consisted of selling companies to Standard and others. However rough the competitive storm may have been, Emery certainly weathered it well.

Emery's sole allegation of local price cutting concerns his Philadelphia marketing business, which he ultimately leased to Pure Oil Co. He admits he did not know who really started the Philadelphia price war.[34]

Holdship & Irwin.— In 1878 this Allegheny, Pennsylvania firm, with an output of 1,000 barrels of products per day, leased

---

[25] Id. General rail car shortages were not infrequent during this period. Some oldtimers indicated that certain rail centers attracted refiners because they typically provided plenty of empty freight cars.

[26] Id., at 2645.

[27] Id., at 2646. Emery asked $750,000 for the refinery, but accepted $275,000. Id., at 2768. Emery thought the plant was worth the money, "[b]ecause we had a large export trade, what independent refineries there were, and a very good opportunity to make a margin on our oils if we could get them there at the same price the Standard Oil Company did." Id.

It is not clear whether Standard bought only the refinery for $275,000 or refinery, wharves, and real estate.

[28] Id., at 2738.

[29] Id., at 2646. It seems strange that Standard, a large net purchaser of crude oil, would acquiesce in any scheme to increase the price of its principal raw material. In any case, abortive crude oil producers' cartels attempted, from time to time, to monopolize and shut in wells. See testimony of Rockefeller on the 1872–74 shut down. Vol. 16 at 3073 et seq.; also testimony of Tarbell, Vol. 3, at 1430.

[30] With a probable daily output of 90 to 150 barrels.

[31] Vol. 6, at 2769–70.

[32] Emery summed up Pure Oil's business by saying that "Their money has been principally made in the production of crude oil." Id., at 2718. According to Emery, Pure Oil's sales rose at least 15 per cent to 20 per cent between 1900 and 1908; dividends were 8 per cent per annum.

[33] Id., at 2659–60.

[34] Id., at 2668–69. Emery did admit that he had cut Standard's prices, at 2785 ff.

their refinery to Standard for 5 years.[35] Under the lease, the partners continued to run the refinery for Standard on a salary basis till 1883, when the lease expired and Holdship & Irwin resumed operation on their own account.[36] In 1886, they sold the refinery to Standard, with the understanding that they would not go back into the oil refining business. Mr. Irwin's testimony does not indicate that Standard used coercion of any kind.[37]

The Empire Oil Works, and the Globe Refining Co.— In 1875 or 1876, Mr. David P. Reighard started the Empire Oil works in Pittsburgh. When Holdship & Irwin sold in 1886, Reighard also sold out to Standard.[38] Reighard stayed out of the oil business till 1887, when he built the Globe Refining Company at Pittsburgh.[39] He ran the Globe for 18 to 20 months, then sold out to Standard again. At the same time, Mr. Reighard sold a large Philadelphia refinery, which he was in the process of building.[40] The sale was no occasion for sadness, for as Mr. Reighard put it:

> Well, the reason I sold out was I found that the bonus that I asked those people (the Standard Oil) was as much as I could actually make on the profits for 15 or 20 years to come.[41]

Reighard sold for $1,224,800 in trust certificates and $50,000 cash.[42] Each of the last two refineries that Reighard sold to Standard had cost between $200,000 and $250,000. Thus it was that Mr. Reighard managed to build and sell three refineries to Standard, all on excellent terms.

Woodland Oil Company (Mr. C. J. Castle).— Mr. Castle was an important government witness on predatory price cutting and other unfair competition. He had been an oil refiner, and was still a marketer of petroleum products when he testified. At this point we will deal only with Mr. Castle's early role as a refiner who sold out to the Rockefeller group.

In 1883, Mr. Castle and a partner started the Woodland Oil Company, a small Cleveland refinery.[43] They began with $8,000 to $10,000 capital. By 1886, book capital was $14,000, and Woodland sold to the Rockefeller interests for the same amount. Castle implied that one reason he sold was inability to get crude oil from the Standard Oil pipeline. But he did not allege that predatory price cutting played any part in the sale, and did not feel aggrieved at the price Standard paid for his property.[44] Indeed, after selling the refinery, he went to work for Standard and remained in their employ for about 14 years.

Castle told several other stories about Standard's predatory price cutting during the period in which he worked for them.[44a] Nevertheless, I think it is significant that when he left Standard in 1900 he was

---

[35] Id., at 3013—Testimony of Lewis Irwin.

[36] Id., at 3014.

[37] Id. Irwin's testimony is also interesting on other grounds. (1) He claims that Standard accomplished considerable economies of scale. Id., at 3022. (2) In the period 1872–74, when both the railroad and oil industries were overbuilt and "demoralized," everyone in the oil business was getting rail freight rebates ("drawbacks"). In Irwin's words, "There were drawbacks and drawbacks within drawbacks. . . . Everybody got drawbacks in those days." Id., at 3026–27.

[38] The Empire and Holdship & Irwin were co-owners of a pipeline system. Id., at 3131.

[39] It had 12 crude stills, each of 600 barrels capacity, and some pipelines. Id., at 3134.

[40] Id., at 3136.

[41] Id., at 3135.

[42] "Well, they didn't want us to take any certificates at all. . . . I forced them, or went after them several times till I got them to give me some certificates." Ibid. The value given for the trust certificates was par value. Market value was higher. Vol. 17, at 3332. The Government gives the "competitive value" of the two Reighard properties as $823,000. Reply Brief for the United States, Appendix C, Sheet 8.

[43] Capacity: 200 barrels per day. Vol. 6, at 3060. By 1908, capacity of Standard's Whiting, Indiana refinery was 25,000–30,000 barrels per day.

[44] Id., at 3029.

[44a] The relevant anecdotes are analyzed in the Marketing section of this paper.

clearly unafraid: he immediately started a rival oil marketing firm.

The Rocky Mountain Oil Company.—Mr. E. M. Wilhoit's brief but pointed version of this affair clearly implies intent and ability to crush out competition. Wilhoit was employed by Standard at the time this incident took place, and claimed to know something about it. In his words,

> Before the Refinery got in operation, the Standard Oil made our fight on the Rocky Mountain Company and the Union Pacific went into the hands of a receiver and the Refinery was afterwards dismantled—went broke of course.[45]

On the surface, this incident is the nearest thing to predatory price cutting that I found in the Record. But there are reasons to suppose that there was something more here than meets the eye.

First, it is interesting that no complaint from the Rocky Mountain interests appears in the Record. Second, Continental—the Standard Company in the area—had entered into an agreement with the Florence Oil and Refinery Company and the United Oil Company, both located at Florence, Colorado.[46] Under the agreement, the two refiners sold their whole output of refined products to Continental. Prices were presumably attractive to the refiners, though, in view of the almost complete marketing monopoly of Standard in the area, quantities taken must have been limited.[47]

The United commenced refining oil about 1887 or 1888.[48] Sometime after Florence and United entered into the exclusive arrangement with Continental, shareholders of United and Florence started the Rocky Mountain Company at Pueblo, Colorado. A price war with Continental ensued. About 1894, after some two years of conflict, Rocky Mountain sold its crude oil properties to Western Oil Company, a producing subsidiary of United and Rocky Mountain. It is not clear what happened to the refinery itself, except that Rocky Mountain no longer ran it.[49]

What does this episode mean? Although the facts are not as ample as we would like, there is one hypothesis that is both logical and wholly consistent with what facts we do have: Standard had marketing facilities in the area, but no local supplies. Standard's refined products had to be brought in from Whiting, Indiana. The United-Florence interests had crude oil and refinery capacity. There may have been other competing refiners in the market as well.

Standard agreed to take certain quantities of refined products from United-Florence, at specified prices, in return for which the refiners agreed not to sell to anyone else. A restricted refinery output could be better for all concerned. But to get it, Standard would have to share monopoly gains with the refiners. In that way duplication of marketing facilities and refining capacity could be avoided.

In this case, as in other such sales arrangements, there must have been a temptation for the producers to sneak out a little more output on the side, in violation of the agreement, and thereby make supernormal returns on a larger output. That would be the best of all possible worlds: the monopoly price could be gotten from Standard on a limited quantity; in addition, a larger amount could be disposed of, on the side, at higher than competitive prices. Since United and Florence had an agreement with Standard for limited quantities, one way to

---

[45] Vol. 3, at 1216. The Government's position runs less to intent and causes, and more to a history of events. For, in Volume 2 of Brief for the United States, at 157, the Government says: "parties connected with the United Company undertook to establish another refinery known as the Rocky Mountain . . . a violent price-cutting competition started in between the Standard's marketing company, the Continental, and this company . . . the Rocky Mountain Company failed and went out of business."

[46] Standard later came to own 17 per cent of the stock of the United. Ibid. This may raise certain questions of minority shareholders' interests.

[47] The government claimed that a little over 1 per cent of the market was supplied by independents and "the marketing of oil in this territory is extremely profitable." Ibid.

[48] Vol. 1, at 155.

[49] Id., at 181.

chisel or to work their way into a larger share of the cartel profits would be to start a new firm. This they did in the form of the Rocky Mountain Company. Mr. Wesley H. Tilford, Treasurer of the Standard Oil Company of New Jersey, explained the purpose of Rocky Mountain in these words:

> They were not satisfied with the interest in the United and they built another refinery to take part of their own business.[50]

Mr. Henry M. Tilford, President of Continental since 1893, confirmed and elaborated Wesley Tilford's recollection of the incident:

> Early in 1891 or 1892 Mr. Daniel Eells came to our office, and had an interview with W. H. Tilford and myself in which he stated that he and some friends proposed to build a refinery in Colorado, and asked if the Continental Oil Company would take their output. He was told the Continental Oil Company was getting from the Florence Oil and Refining Company and the United Oil Company all the oil they could market in that vicinity. Some little time afterwards he came back to the office and said that the refinery had been built, and asked again if the Continental Oil Company could take the output, and he was advised that they could not, that the situation was the same as it was before. . . . They commenced business and they commenced cutting prices.[51]

What happened after the reabsorption of Rocky Mountain is also consistent with the cartel hypothesis: The refiners *raised* the prices of refined products to Continental. Whatever their object, then, the net result was that United and Florence apparently emerged from the conflict with more favorable contract terms *vis à vis* Standard.[52] Tilford did not regard Rocky

Mountain as having failed, but simply as having been reabsorbed by those who started it.[53]

With the passage of time, more refineries were built in the Rockies. By 1907, when Mr. Henry Tilford testified, refineries had been built in Sugar Creek and Evanston, Wyoming; Spring Valley, and Boulder, Colorado. At least two, those at Spring Valley and Boulder, were independent, and built between 1905 and 1906.[54] This suggests either that memories are short; or that those who were familiar with the episode did not regard the Rocky Mountain incident as a case of predatory price cutting.

The 1895 purchases.— James W. Lee, Vice President and Director of Pure Oil, testified that in the 1890's a group of Pennsylvania refiners sent emissaries to Standard to moderate the "destructive competition" that plagued them.[55] Standard offered to purchase their pipelines and facilities, for cost plus 12 per cent. Whether for those terms or not, some of the group sold out, including Mr. Ramage.[56] It is interesting that none of those who sold out came forward to testify that they had been abused in any way.

Most did not sell, but banded together and formed the Pure Oil Company in 1895.[57] Pure Oil thus became the largest independent oil company in the United States. It was also a profitable one.[58]

Although Lee did not allege local price cutting, he claimed that Standard had squeezed the independent refiners by bid-

---

[50] Id., at 156.

[51] Vol. 2, at 730–31.

[52] It may be that the cartel had more refiner members than United and Florence, for Tilford said "there were other people in the oil business selling oil to the Continental, and indirectly it affected them, of course." Vol. 1, at 177, and see also 180.

[53] Id., at 181.

[54] Vol. 2, at 731–32.

[55] Vol. 6, at 3169–70. Lee did not refer to local price-cutting as a factor.

[56] Ramage evidently took some Standard stock, for he appears on the Standard stockholder lists. Messrs. Fertig and Burwell also sold.

[57] Consistent with logic, but not with a theory of predation, are Standard's persistent efforts to buy stock control in Pure Oil Company affiliates. Vol. 6, at 3176–79.

[58] Id., at 3191.

ding up the price of crude oil in 1895.[59] As it turns out, however, since Standard was actually buying 90 per cent of the crude oil in question, such a maneuver would have cost Standard a great deal more than those it was seeking to punish.[60]

The Argand Refining Company.— In spite of having "the regular severe competition of the Standard all the way through," [61] this refinery was a profitable business. It earned "a little over $35,000" a year, net, with 600 barrel still capacity and $50,000 beginning capital.[62] Dividends were paid regularly at the rate of 2½ per cent per quarter.

Argand included among its stockholders several railroad officials.[63] According to Cram,

> There were no threats as to what they [Standard] would do if we didn't sell out. Our railroad stockholders became convinced that we would lose our railroad business, from which we derived half of our net profit.[64]

The refinery was finally disposed of [to Standard] on a lease basis for $20,000 a year, for a period of ten years. It was afterwards adjusted on a cash basis on

which our stockholders, on which the company, got $180,000.[65]

Predatory price cutting obviously had nothing to do with the sale.[66]

Scofield, Shurmer and Teagle.— This firm was one of the last large refiners purchased by Standard before its dissolution. SS&T had a refinery at Cleveland,[67] and sold about 200,000 barrels of refined products a year in Michigan, Illinois, Indiana, Iowa, Nebraska, Kansas and Missouri.[68] SS&T and Standard were old rivals, and had several clashes over the years. In 1876 Standard and SS&T ended one competitive struggle by signing a market-sharing contract. Under its terms Standard guaranteed a minimum profit to SS&T, in exchange for output limitation; and shared additional profits in specified proportions.[69] But in 1880, SS&T broke the contract, and, when Standard sought to enforce it, denounced the instrument as a tool of an unlawful monopoly.[70]

Nevertheless, when SS&T sold out, Wal-

---

[59] Id., at 3192–93.

[60] Id., at 3192–3194. Apart from this elementary fact, quite acceptable and logical alternative explanations were given.

[61] Testimony of Cram, Volume 3, at 1349. Earlier he had said: "Not anything more than ordinary competition in their business, I should judge. . . . Well, I cannot say they cut on us particularly; they were a larger concern than we were and we followed their prices." Vol. 5, at 2422.

[62] Vol. 3, at 1351. At that time, a still would be "run off" about once every two or three days at best. This would have made a 200 barrel per day output, or 73,000 barrels per year without allowance for down time and "turnarounds." Actual output was probably lower. See Vol. 5, at 2419–20.

[63] Vol. 3, at 1349.

[64] Id., at 1350. About half of the $200,000 capital stock was held by officials of the B&OSW and the Marietta & Columbus Northern Railroads. These railroads bought about one-fourth or one-fifth of Argand's output.

[65] Id., at 1352. The sale apparently was consummated in 1897. Cram agreed to stay out of the oil business, as did some others. Vol. 5, at 2424.

[66] It is curious that in his much earlier testimony Cram did not mention the possible loss of railroad business as a factor in the sale. Whereas in his later testimony he is not really hostile to Standard, and certainly does not claim local price cutting, Cram seems less happy with the sale. Perhaps he came to regret it. One possibility is that Cram felt aggrieved when the ample "stand-by" salaries Standard paid the managers under the original settlement gave way to a cash settlement to stockholders.

[67] According to Teagle, "We had a refinery at Cleveland, but the refinery at Cleveland was old and out of date, and the capacity of it was limited as compared with the sales end of our business. I don't suppose we refined, during the years immediately previous to our sale, over 35 to 40 per cent of the refined oil products that we sold. Cleveland had ceased to be a refining center." Vol. 3, at 1467.

[68] Id., at 1468.

[69] Vol. 16, at 3204.

[70] Id., at 3205.

ter Teagle joined Standard, as did the old staff. According to Walter C. Teagle, son of the head of SS&T, Standard continued to employ all but three SS&T employees after the acquisition.[71] Standard operated the SS&T facilities under the style of Republic Oil Company till about 1905.[72] Claims that Standard operated SS&T as a "bogus independent" only strengthen the hypothesis that there was no coercion surrounding the sale. For it is impossible to keep a secret when those who must be relied on to keep it can injure their enemies by betraying it.

In any case, there is no evidence that predatory price cutting had anything to do with the SS&T acquisition, or with the terms on which Standard purchased it.[73]

Summary.— The record does not indicate that predatory price cutting forced any refiner to sell out. The only doubtful case is that of the Rocky Mountain Company and, in my opinion, this incident is no exception to the rule. Furthermore, there is no evidence that predatory price cutting was used to depress asset value of any of the more than one hundred-twenty competitive refineries that Standard bought.[74] So far as I can make out, Standard's purchase terms were generally very good, and sometimes lavish. Abstracting from purchases, the mortality rate in refining was evidently low after Standard achieved a monopoly position.

---

[71] Vol. 3, at 1150. SS&T sold out in 1901. Id., at 1153. After the dissolution Mr. Teagle became president of Standard Oil of New Jersey.

[72] Id., at 1153 ff.

[73] One independent oil man made the following observation about SS&T: "They had a plant that they maintained and they maintained it until they *succeeded* in selling out to the Standard." Vol. 2, at 987. (Italics supplied.)

There is no real evidence that the "bogus" Republic waged predatory price cutting campaigns, either. See testimony of Crenshaw, for example, on the amicable settlement of one price cutting flurry in 1902: Vol. 3, at 1173–74.

[74] See Mr. Lombard's testimony on the "very fair" prices Standard paid the refiners it bought out. Vol. 1, at 250.

b) "Suspect" Cases That Did Not Result in Merger or Purchase

There remains the possibility that Standard used local price cutting to drive rival refiners to the wall without purchasing them. Perhaps Standard, without having to buy them out, simply exterminated them.

The following integrated refining firms at one time or another had local, or general, clashes with Standard. Standard did not buy, or merge with, any of these firms. Testimony about these incidents was often vague, which is not too surprising in view of the very long period covered.[75] There is also a large amount of pure hearsay, and many facts were hotly controverted.

Fehsenfeld (the Red C interests).—Mr. W. H. Fehsenfeld was president of the Red C Oil Manufacturing Co. of Baltimore.[76] Red C was a marketing company, but Fehsenfeld was also president of Island Petroleum, a refiner.[77]

Fehsenfeld testified that up to about 1897, Red C and Standard competed in the South in the sale of barreled refined products. After 1897, Standard relied increasingly upon the tank wagon method of distribution. Red C continued to emphasize barrel distribution.[78] According to Fehsenfeld, Standard systematically offered price inducements to merchants to prevent Red C from making up carload shipments of 60 barrels, and sometimes induced Red C customers to countermand their orders.[79]

At one time or another, Red C faced competition from five different "bogus in-

---

[75] Testimony covered the period 1865 through 1908.

[76] Vol. 5, at 2302.

[77] Id., at 2330. Fehsenfeld was also President of the Columbia Oil Co., and Vice-President of both the Georgia Oil Co. and the Richmond Oil Co. All but Island were marketing companies. Island owned stock in the various marketing companies.

[78] Red C did sell by tank wagons in and around Baltimore, and had various commission agents and jobbers over the country.

[79] Id., at 2303.

dependents" operated by Standard.[80] According to Fehsenfeld, "[T]hey sold regardless of price, in order to secure our business. . . ." [81] On some occasions, at least, Red C clearly started the price cutting. Indeed, Red C evidently employed price cutting whenever it served their interests. As Fehsenfeld explained:

> I did certainly cut the price in order to get the business. . . . As occasion was necessary; that is to say, *in going into a territory we would have to offer some inducement.* . . . Sometimes I would sell— it would depend entirely upon the quality of the oil—at prices lower than the Standard or sell at prices higher than the Standard.[82]

According to C. T. Collings, Second Vice-President of the Standard Oil Company of Kentucky, Red C had always been a price cutter. Standard, on the other hand, found price cutting an unattractive policy. In Collings' words,

> Red C . . . had a way every once in a while of sending out one or two men, rushing them around over the South Carolina Field, and making up carload orders by cutting our prices from a half to one and a half cent a gallon. . . . we had lost quite a good deal of business in years gone by by this system. . . . As you will see here in every one of those letters where their prices are mentioned, they are from half a cent to a cent and a half below our price. . . . We didn't go down to their very low prices, except, I believe, in one case, and that was at Union, South Carolina. . . . We do not initiate the cut. We rely on our having been the pioneers in establishing the business, serving the trade with good oil in the most-up-to-date manner, and that if a competitor comes in there to get our business he must necessarily cut the price or offer some inducement in order to wean the trade away from us. Therefore, it is not necessary for us to cut prices.[83]

Although he said that thirty years of competing with Standard were hard, Fehsenfeld acknowledged that the Red C interests had grown steadily and prosperous since their modest beginning in 1878.[84] Before 1903, Standard twice tried to purchase the Red C group but failed.[85]

Cornplanter Refining Company.— Founded about 1888, Cornplanter was an old rival of Standard. Although there was a good deal of hearsay about Standard "attacking" Cornplanter over the years, it is clear that from time to time Standard and Cornplanter entered into agreements to avoid competition.[86] Mr. Todd, Cornplanter's Manager, testified that Standard had threatened Cornplanter with extinction, but that it never materialized.[87] Cornplanter was a Warren, Pennsylvania refiner, but, among other places, also sold in the St. Paul area.[88] The Manager of Standard's Whiting refinery told Todd that Cornplanter was selling too much kerosene in the St. Paul territory, and that if they did not agree to reduce output and regulate sales, Standard would run them out of business. Mr. Todd understood well the economics of local price cutting, for, as he testified:

> Well, I says, "Mr. Moffett, I am very glad you put it that way, because if it is

See, for example, Vol. 13, at 1306 et seq., 1322 et seq., 1362 et seq., 1364–65, 1440. The Record is liberally sprinkled with evidence, and anecdotes of competition between Red C and Standard. For example, see Vol. 5, at 2303, 2307, 2310, 2313, 2316, 2406–9, 2476; Vol. 10, at 1747–58, 1760–1775; Vol. 12, p. 913; Vol. 13, at 1110–13, 1139–44, 1158 et seq., 1167, 1239, 1250, 1305–07; Vol. 15, at 2443–44; Vol. 20 at 100–101, 146–48, 152–3, 156–68, 212 et seq. In fact, much of Volumes 13 and 20 concerns this rivalry.

[84] Vol. 5, at 2333. Island was organized in 1901, when Red C integrated "backwards" into refining. Id., at 2337. Island owned the controlling interest in the Richmond Oil Co.

[85] Id., at 2329.

[86] See, e.g., Vol. 6, at 3209 et seq.

[87] Id., at 3212.

[88] Id., at 3213.

[80] Id., at 2311.

[81] Id., at 2319.

[82] Id., at 2341. (Italics supplied).

[83] Vol. 12, at 895–96. See also Vol. 13, at 1536–37. There is a great deal of corroborating testimony.

up to you the only way you can get it [the business] is to cut the market, and if you cut the market I will cut you for 200 miles around, and I will make you sell the stuff," and I says, "I don't want a bigger picnic than that; sell it if you want to," and I bid him good day and left.[89]

The Standard threat never materialized.

Todd also testified that about 1898 a Standard Oil executive told him Standard's policy was to put all independents out of business.[90] Standard then launched a price-cutting war against Cornplanter in New York. Todd said Standard started it, but acknowledged that Cornplanter had started a price-cutting campaign around Boston.[91] The "war" was costly to both sides, and they entered into a market-sharing agreement for the Boston territory. Prices rose "from 6½ to 10 cents in a very few days, and they remained there for a long time." [92] The agreement, first for three years and later renewed for five, remained in effect until about 1906. At that time, Cornplanter sold its Boston distribution facilities to the Gulf Refining Company, an aggressive independent concern.

Todd testified to other conflicts,[93] and still other agreements,[94] with Standard. In spite of their difficulties with Standard, Cornplanter's capital had grown, in the twenty years of its existence, from $10,000 to $450,000. Todd admitted that they were still alive and, indeed, very healthy.[95]

Crew-Levick.— Crew-Levick had several refineries.[96] George J. Wolff, Baltimore manager, testified that a Standard "bogus" concern had waged war on them. Wolff admitted that he sometimes cut Standard's prices in Baltimore,[97] and acknowledged that Standard, whatever its motives, hadn't been able to kill Crew-Levick:

> Q. You don't think you need any guardian for carrying on business against the Standard Oil Company, do you?
> A. No, by gosh! I don't.[98]

Crew-Levick had apparently done well in Baltimore, for as Wolff testified:

> Q. From 1904 until recently you had a pretty steady increase, haven't you?
> A. Yes, sir. The day I took charge I only sold 400 gallons, and that was all my own.
> Q. And that would be about 2,000 gallons a week?
> A. Yes.
> Q. And now you sell about 20,000 gallons a week?
> A. Yes, Sir.[99]

Some other refining companies.— Defendant's Exhibit 277 [100] indicates that in 1908 there were 123 independent refineries in the United States. Some were undoubtedly very small; some were not. The list includes firms which are major companies today and which were substantial even then. Pure Oil, Tidewater, Gulf, The Texas Company, Sun Oil Company, and Union Oil are perhaps the outstanding examples. By 1908,

---

[89] Id., at 3214, and also at 3227.

[90] Id., at 3215–16.

[91] Id., at 3216. Cornplanter's gallonage trebled in Boston. Id., at 3231.

[92] Id., at 3217. Cornplanter had acquired the Boston facilities when it bought out the New England Oil Company about 1897. Id., at 3228, 3230.

[93] Id., at 3220–21. See also testimony of Hopkins, Vol. 3, at 1030 about cutting Standard's prices.

[94] Vol. 6, at 3207–8, 3220, 3223–28.

[95] Id., at 3221. Cornplanter had numerous other oil interests as well. Id., at 3232 et seq. They marketed under several names, including Tiona Oil.

There are many references to the competition of Cornplanter and Standard. See, e.g., Vol. 20, at 45, 61–62, 114; Vol. 6, at 3213–18; Vol. 15, at 2383–87; Pet. Exh. 635.

[96] See Vol. 20, at 105–106. Interestingly enough, they were operated under different names: Crew-Levick, The Glade Oil Works, The Muir Works, The Seaboard Oil Works.

[97] See, e.g., Vol. 20, at 118 et seq., 122, 126, 131. See also Vol. 16, at 2612 et seq.

[98] Vol. 20, at 126.

[99] Id., at 109.

[100] Vol. 19, at 662–63.

the Texas Company had a refinery of 12,000 barrels per day capacity; Gulf had two: one of 10,800, another of 41,600 barrels per day.[101] Pure, Tidewater, Gulf, and Texas each had large crude oil pipeline systems.

Standard owned about 31 per cent of Tidewater's common stock, and had various agreements with that firm.[102] It also owned a substantial interest in the Pure Oil pipeline affiliate, but never achieved control.

There always had been some competing refiners.[103] At least 10 independent refineries which were built before 1890 were in continuous operation through 1908.[104] By 1895, there were 38 competing refineries.[105] By 1906, the figure had grown to 123.[106]

The Pure Oil Company, formed in 1895, is only one example of the growth and prosperity of independent refiners.[107]

Refining: Summary.— I can not find a single instance in which Standard used predatory price cutting to force a rival refiner to sell out, to reduce asset values for purchase, or to drive a competitor out of business. I do not believe that Standard even tried to do it; if it tried, it did not work.

Standard bought many firms, and paid well to get them. Its purchases continued pretty much up till dissolution, and were apparently necessary to preserve the monopoly position it had built. In addition to purchasing many competitors, Standard entered into market-sharing and price-fixing agreements with still others.[108]

From the beginning of Standard's power, and throughout the period of its greatest strength, new firms sprang up and prospered; old firms survived and grew.

2. Price Cutting Involving Jobbers and Retailers. It is significant that far and away the largest amount of testimony about price cutting concerns the jobbing and retail levels. Most of the firms alleged to have been involved in price cutting by Standard were non-integrated marketers; the bulk of them were retail merchants and peddlers. Marketing affiliates of competing refiners have already been discussed.

Oil marketing, though different from what we know today, was changing. Before about 1890, refiners sold most of their products in barrels to jobbers, who then distributed the product locally.[109] About that time Standard began "tank wagon" delivery to grocers and other retailers. Under that system, Standard set up bulk stations to which it shipped barrels or tank cars of products, and from which it sent out tank-wagons to serve retailers directly. A tank wagon was just what the name implies: a horse-drawn wagon with a wooden or iron tank mounted on it. Each tank wagon served 30 to 50 specified retail customers. Tank wagon drivers poured or pumped gasoline and kerosene into store-keepers' tanks, taking cash on delivery. Standard ultimately sold most of its products through the tank wagon channel.[110] Collings, of the Standard

---

[101] A 40,000 barrel per day refinery is of quite respectable size even today, and very large for its time. Testimony of Emery, Vol. 6 at 2704, 2710–12.

[102] See e.g., Archbold's testimony, Vol. 17, at 3321.

[103] Vol. 1, at 243–44; Vol. 3, at 1467; Vol. 5, at 2542; Vol. 6, at 2626, 2642, 2705, 3015, 3131, 3132; Vol. 16, at 3139; Vol. 17, at 3446; Vol. 20, at 31.

[104] Vol. 5, at 2542; Vol. 6, at 2651, 2705, 2840, 3015, 3061, 3207; Vol. 20, at 106–107.

[105] Vol. 6, at 2690–2712.

[106] Vol. 2, at 651; Vol. 5, at 2543–45; Vol. 6, at 2691, 2700, 2704, 2710, 2711–12; Vol. 8, at 1002 (Pet. Exh. 396); Vol. 17, at 3290; Vol. 19, at 627 (Def. Exh. 269), 662; Brief For Appellants, Vol. 1, Appendix III, at 266.

For the more rapid growth of competition in the export trade, see Vol. 8, at 904 (Pet. Exh. 377). Competitors' greatest growth was in products other than kerosene. Brief for Appellants, Vol. 2, at 102–03.

[107] Pure's crude oil receipts more than doubled between 1900 and 1906. Vol. 3, at 1443, 1451. Another interesting example is the New York Lubricating Co. Vol. 2, at 532–33, 766–67, 773.

[108] For some of the agreements, see Vol. 1, at 175–76, 214–23; Vol. 2, at 734, 738, 946, 950; Vol. 3, at 1130; Vol. 17, at 3321; Vol. 12, at 955.

[109] Testimony of Archbold, Vol. 17, at 3467–68.

[110] The proportion varied among the different terri-

Oil of Kentucky, testified that as much as 90 per cent of his sales were made in that way.[111] The remainder continued to go to jobbers and peddlers.

Peddlers usually called at a tank station and filled their own wagons. To reflect the savings on delivery, and their larger average purchase, peddlers usually paid ½ to 1 cent per gallon less than the tank wagon price.[112] Retail peddling wagons made 150 or more selling stops per day.

Jobbers were thus being displaced by an integrated marketing apparatus pioneered by Standard and imitated quickly by its competitors. Peddlers too, faced sweeping changes. Gas and electricity had begun to challenge the household kerosene market on which peddlers depended. The rise of the automobile was just beginning. These forces would ultimately make kerosene, then the principal product, a fourth-rate fuel.

At the same time these changes were taking place, refiners were groping for more efficient ways to market their products. Even as it was developing tank wagon delivery, Standard also experienced with its own peddling operations. It tried to keep its ownership of them secret. These constituted most of the "bogus independents" about which we have heard so often. Almost all the rest were jobbing concerns, generally small ones. They were never of great importance quantitatively.[113] And, for

whatever it is worth, Standard was not the only company with "bogus" peddlers and jobbers.[114]

Standard gave several reasons for not advertising its connection with these firms. First, persistent public attacks on its monopoly and high profits had prejudiced some of the trade against buying Standard products.[115] Second, some of the marketing concerns that it bought had substantial good will and better local market acceptance than Standard could economically create. Third, to break local retailer and peddler cartels and to meet the competition of other peddlers, from time to time Standard found it useful to run in a retail outfit selling at competitive prices. But to do these things without antagonizing its tank wagon customers, secrecy was useful.[116] Fourth, this approach permitted Standard to experiment with new personnel and marketing methods without abandoning the old, and without committing large resources.

As tank wagon distribution largely displaced barrel delivery to jobbers, Standard

---

tories. Barrel, jobber, and commission-agent distribution were more important in very small communities, and in certain mountainous areas. As late as 1904, for example, Standard was still extending tank wagon service to small New York communities. In all areas, tank wagon delivery was coming to be the dominant method.

[111] Vol. 12, at 896.

[112] Standard's competitors also granted these terms.

[113] More than half of the "bogus" concerns were strictly retail peddling outfits. Most were very small; they averaged, perhaps, two or three peddling wagons. In addition, most did not last very long. "They were an experiment in selling oil directly to the consumer, which largely on account of the necessity of giving credit, proved

a failure." Brief for Appellants, Vol. 2, at 192. See also Vol. 13, at 1523–25. Most were gradually withdrawn as the equipment wore out. Those few that continued became "Can Departments" of the various Standard companies.

Furthermore, there is some question about just how secret these firms were supposed to be, and grave doubts about how secret they in fact were. Finally, the government, and witnesses for it, erroneously accused Standard of owning and operating firms that it did not really have anything to do with. For example, see Vol. 5, at 2412, Vol. 12, at 779–80, 790–91; Vol. 13, at 1218–20, 1279–83, 1307, 1533–35.

[114] There are many examples, including the firms operated by Mr. Castle, National Refining Co., Red C, Crew-Levick, et al.

[115] It is impossible to know how important this prejudice was, but it is clear that it existed. One possible symptom is the flavor of names adopted by some competitors: Antitrust Oil Co.; Freedom Oil; Uncle Sam Oil Co.; etc.

[116] Collings: "We would much prefer selling to the dealer. That was the business that we were especially engaged in and prepared to take care of." Vol. 12, at 887.

sought to extend integration further. As Mr. Squires put it:

> [W]e reached a point where it was felt that possibly another step nearer the consumer might be taken and save him money. It was learned that the retailer was making from 50 to 100 percent profit, and it was believed that we could save one-half of this to the consumer. To make this move required a great deal of care and caution, so that the trade which we were supplying might not be antagonized; also for the purpose of developing any impracticable features which in the end might prove it was not the proper course to pursue. Therefore a few towns were selected to make the experiment, and the towns quoted above were used for the purpose. . . .

But a very serious obstacle soon developed itself, namely, the giving of credit. The storekeeper gave credit to his customers, whereas with us they paid cash. This became such a factor as to make it almost impossible to sell the large quantity which was sought through this medium. Various ways were tried to see if it could not be overcome—like the sale of tickets by milkmen—but it did not work. Then credit was given, but our loss by bad debts was in itself sufficient to practically kill the enterprise. In addition to this we discovered that the expense due to wear and tear of the equipment was great. On account of loaning the cans to the consumer, being our property and not theirs, they did not take the proper care of them. More or less were damaged by carelessness and some were lost entirely. Therefore it was decided, after a very careful canvass of the experience of the different towns, to abandon the idea. Gradually from point to point the equipment was withdrawn, with the exception of two, namely, Youngstown and Cleveland, which have always been known by refiners as peddling points, due to the fact that a number of peddlers had been in existence there for years and the consumer had become familiarized with that means of delivery.[117]

Whether these were really Standard's motives, or merely clever rationalizations, is both imponderable and irrelevant. Suffice it to say that such a course of action is reasonable in light of the evolution of the industry. This evolution in fact accelerated after the 1911 dissolution when competition increased. It was not a creature of monopoly. After all, where are the kerosene peddlers today? The alternative explanation, that Standard sought to monopolize wholesale and retail distribution, is certainly less logical and is less consistent with the facts that we have.

In retailing, numbers were often very large, and entry was cheap and quick. Standard Oil never had, or apparently sought, a monopoly of retailing. It would have been pointless to try, and probably impossible to achieve. With a refining monopoly, Standard's interest in marketing should logically have been to keep it efficient and highly competitive.[118]

Of all the "levels" in the oil business, retailing would have been the most difficult for Standard to monopolize, and a monopoly there would have been the most transient of all. The reasons are simple. Kerosene retailers were of two sorts: grocers and other retail merchants, who kept tanks or barrels from which they filled customers' oil cans; and peddlers, who operated one or more wagons which went house-to-house on regular routes, much like the milkman of today and the iceman of old.

The skills and resources devoted to refined oil peddling were neither expensive, scarce, nor specific. A wagon, horse, driver, and some cans or a tank made a peddler.[119]

---

[117] Vol. 13, at 1523–24. Mr. Squire was not exaggerating retail margins, as the Record amply confirms. Whether margins were high because of retailer cartels or high costs does not matter. What does matter is that Standard, like any refiner, had every interest in reducing them. See also, Vol. 2, pp. 757–58; Vol. 3, p. 1109; Vol. 5, pp. 2583, 2602, 2584.

[118] A monopolist in manufacturing would prefer that marketing have zero costs and be competitive. In that way, the maximum monopoly returns could be extracted from manufacturing.

[119] Shea testified that he entered the peddling business in 1892 with $25.00 of his own money, $25.00 borrowed capital, and a borrowed horse. He grew rapidly, and branched off into jobbing as well as retailing. "I would imagine that we are doing about 30 times as much business as we were in 1892 when we first started." Vol. 5, at 2493.

A large peddling concern might have two or three wagons. The resources could, and did, move quickly out of oil peddling and back again, lured by the prospects for gain.

Similarly, entry into grocery retailing and general merchandising has never been difficult. Very early in the game, Mr. Rockefeller realized that a private monopoly of crude oil was impossible.[120] He must have realized that a retailing monopoly was even more hopeless. Only governments succeed for very long in monopolizing activities of that kind. Furthermore, Standard evidently concluded that its interests could usually best be served by letting someone else perform the retailing function.

Thus it was that before the dissolution jobbers and retailers were exposed to evolutionary forces at work in the industry at large. These changes persisted, indeed probably accelerated, after the dissolution.[121] In addition, jobbers and retailers were subject to all the ills and quarrels that characterize petty trade, where size was small and numbers large. It is not surprising, therefore, that most complaints about price cutting involved non-integrated marketers.[122]

It is clearly impossible to review here all of the incidents involving jobbers and retailers. The record is filled with many very similar examples, and commenting on each of them is an unnecessary and uneconomic task.[123] For present purposes, it is enough to review some of the more important and representative cases. The incidents can conveniently be divided into three categories: (a) alleged price cutting which involved competing marketers, but which had no particular outcome; (b) alleged price cutting accompanied by purchase of competing marketers; (c) alleged price cutting accompanied by the disappearance of competing marketers. Alleged incidents of the first class are numerous, but do not support a theory of predatory monopolization. Examples of the second and third class would be more useful for such a theory, but are very scarce.[124]

Only a few representative incidents will be discussed in detail; others will be cited.

a) Price Cutting with No Specified Outcome

The bulk of evidence, and assertion, established only that Standard sold at different prices within the same community or

---

[120] Rockefeller's description of the ill-fated crude producers' agreement of 1872 is classic:

"I could not state how long it was in existence or said to be operative, but the high price for the crude oil resulted, as it had always done before and will always do so long as oil comes out of the ground, in increasing the production, and they got too much oil. We could not find a market for it.

"[O]f course any who were not in this association were undertaking to produce all they possibly could; and as to those who were in the association, many of them men of honor and high standing, the temptation was very great to get a little more oil than they had promised their associates or us would come. It seemed very difficult to prevent the oil coming at that price. . . . There was a limitation beyond which we, as refiners and merchandizers in the oil, could not go. We were their servants in passing on to the consumer the refined product, and the limitation was there in what we could at that time sell." Vol. 16, at 3074.

[121] In 1911, for the first time, gasoline sales passed kerosene.

[122] Standard claimed that its tank wagons served

37,000 towns in the United States. The number of jobbers and peddlers must also have been large.

[123] To a remarkable degree, the record is freighted with casual hearsay, petty complaints of small traders, and countless unimportant charges and countercharges. This is probably attributable to the nature of the proceedings under which testimony was taken. Witnesses appeared before an Examiner, not a judge, who felt that he had no power to rule on the admissibility of evidence. A large amount of the Government's testimony came from ex-employees of Standard, most of whom had been discharged or resigned under pressure. Several admitted grudges against Standard management. Some of these witnesses were testifying about Standard operations of which they had no direct knowledge. E.g., Vol. 5, at 2347, 2364, 2381; Vol. 15, at 2472.

[124] Because firms often were both jobbers and peddlers, and testimony about them was often scant, it is impossible to segregate the incidents into those involving jobbers or peddlers. Such a distinction would have little value in any case.

among communities; and that the lower prices often resulted from greater competition.[125]

Hisgen Brothers.— A typical example of a marketing firm that complained about local price cutting is Hisgen Brothers. The type of evidence presented is also representative of this whole class of incidents.

Hisgen started selling axle grease in 1889.[126] In 1900, they began retailing and wholesaling kerosene, which they purchased from independent refiners. They complained that in 1901, when they started selling kerosene in various small towns along the Hudson River, Standard cut prices to run them out. Prices elsewhere were said to have remained high. Standard's records indicated that their kerosene prices actually rose during the time Hisgen said Standard was cutting in the six towns involved.[127] Six grocers testified that it was Hisgen, not Standard, who started price-cutting.[128] In any case, Hisgen admitted that he sometimes did cut Standard's prices,[129] and was very vague about Standard's cuts against him.[130] Later episodes around Springfield, Massachusetts show

that, at least part of the time, Hisgen initiated price cuts against Standard.[131]

Quite apart from the question of who started the price wars, Hisgen apparently did well. During 1904, for example, Hisgen Brothers did 21 per cent of the oil business at Springfield, and increased their share to 30 per cent in 1905.[132] After 1900, they greatly enlarged their territory and business and apparently prospered in the process.[133]

---

[131] In 1904 Hisgen began selling at 10½¢ per gallon, undercutting Standard by ½¢. Part of the following decline was attributed to a general price reduction over a wide territory; part to further cutting by Hisgen. In 1905, Hisgen stopped cutting, and Standard's prices rose. Vol. 10, at 1636.

[132] Brief for Appellants, Vol. II, p. 177. See also Vol. 12, at 782–85, 809–810; Vol. 10, at 1636.

[133] Vol. 4, at 1836–44.

There are numerous other examples of this class of incidents. See, for example:

H. C. Boardman. In 1904, when Standard fired him, Boardman opened a marketing business in Augusta. Vol. 5, at 2189. Prices fell. Id., at 2169–71. Boardman captured and held one-third of the trade. In his words:

"If I could get a third of the trade, I was satisfied. I recognized the fact that the Standard had to live, too, and needed the money, and so I thought I would let them live. So I kept it at 11 cents." Id., at 2171.

In 1906 Boardman opened up a tank station in Denmark, South Carolina. While he was erecting tanks, Standard cut prices. Id., at 2175. But, cut as they would, Boardman got about 40 per cent of the business. Although he was largely confined to one territory, and therefore should, so we are told, have been particularly vulnerable to "discriminatory sharp-shooting," Boardman prospered. His trade was profitable from the start; by 1908 he had 75 per cent of the Augusta lubricating oil business, and one third of the refined oils trade. Id., at 2171, 2181. Boardman started business with a capital of $3,000, including tanks and a wagon. The first year his sales were $40,000, the second year, $50,000, and the third year $60,000. "I have never had a month yet that I haven't made a nice profit, even from the first month." Id., at 2181.

C. J. Castle. Vol. 6, at 3040, 3044–46, 3055–57, 3067–68, 3088; Vol. 13, at 1483, 1517–18.

St. Louis Oil Co. Vol. 2, at 891, 894, 896, 899, 900. For a similar case, see Vol. 15, pp. 2411–2415, 2425; Vol. 20, pp. 229–33.

---

[125] See, for example, Vol. 8, at 905–1011 (Petitioner's Exhibit 379–96); Vol. 10, at 1624–1659 (Pet. Exh. 628–635). But compare Vol. 8, at 664; Vol. 10, at 1624; Vol. 21, at 133 (Pet. Exh. 962). See also, Vol. 2, at 937; Vol. 3, at 1046; Vol. 5, at 2484, 2490–91; Vol. 17, at 3620–2, 3628; Vol. 20, at 229–31, 233.

[126] Vol. 4, at 1795. By the second year business trebled, and kept on increasing. By 1900 sales were $80,000 to $100,000. Hisgen twice ran for Governor of Massachusetts on an anti-trust (anti-Standard Oil) platform. Vol. 4, at 1800, 1841, 1848–49, 1852.

[127] Vol. 12, at 713, 813–15. At one time prices did decline, allegedly because of price cutting by Tiona, marketing subsidiary of Cornplanter Refining Co. Id., at 716.

[128] Vol. 12, at 780–82, 812–13, 818–19, 822–24, 826–27, 830–31, 833–35; Vol. 4, at 1894–95, 1963–66.

[129] Vol. 4, at 1813–15, 1856 et seq., 1888–89, 1898, 1977–78. See also id., at 1932–37, 1952, 1964–72; Vol. 12, 729–37, 782–88, 810–17, 822–37.

[130] Vol. 4, at 1861, 1874.

b) Price Cutting and Purchasing

There were several allegations that Standard used local price cutting to force independent marketers to sell out. For the most part, the evidence was simply that there was price cutting and someone affected by it sold out to Standard. In a few cases, the testimony was somewhat more pointed. The following are the most important and relevant examples.

G. T. Wofford.— From 1898–1902, Mr. Wofford was chief clerk and assistant to the Manager in the Birmingham headquarters of the Standard Oil Company of Kentucky.[134] He testified that Standard gave rebates to induce countermands or requirements contracts. Collings denied these allegations.[135] About the end of 1902, Wofford and some associates started the Southeastern Oil Company—a marketing firm—in Birmingham. According to Wofford, Kerosene prices fell steadily from 14 cents to 11 cents per gallon. Southeastern lost money, and sold out to Standard about 1904. There are several convincing reasons why this is *not* a case of successful predation: First, Wofford admitted that it was not Standard's price-cutting on kerosene that made the business unprofitable: "We made a reasonable profit on that particular grade of oil, but we lost money on the general business." [136] Second, Standard claimed, and there is some evidence to support it, that Southeastern solicited the sale to Standard.[137] Third, there was even some testimony that Standard did not ac-

tually cut prices before Southeastern sold out.[138]

Fourth, the Government claimed that Standard's Birmingham business was profitable during 1903.[139]

People's Oil Company.— E. N. Wooten, an ex-Standard employee, testified that from 1892 to 1898 Standard cut prices severely at Atlanta to kill off the People's and the Commercial, and that both were forced to sell out to the Standard.[140] Collings denied that Standard started a price war or tried to drive them out.[141] There is both indirect and direct evidence that they were not *forced* out: First, Wooten said the sales were secret, and secrets cannot usually be kept when parties are aggrieved. Second, People's was a *customer* of Standard. Third, the former owner of People's explicitly denied that she was forced out or underpaid.[142] Fourth, Wooten acknowledged that the value of People's and the Commercial had not been higher at any time than when they sold out.[143]

---

[138] Id., at 847–48, 908.

[139] Brief for the United States, Vol. 2, at 486. After the sale, Wofford went on to establish another successful oil marketing firm.

[140] Vol. 5, at 2096–2103. Commercial was owned by the Peerless Refining Company of Cleveland. Standard claimed to have fired Wooten because of his alleged "drug habit." Vol. 12, at 906.

[141] Id., at 897–901.

[142] Vol. 18, at 253 (Def. Exh. 92½).

[143] Vol. 5, at 2149. Another example is the purchase of two wholesale marketing organizations started by a Mr. Joseph. According to Cooke, a Government witness,

"[T]he Standard was anxious to get a location . . . and they realized there was hardly room for two companies (it was not a large town), and they went to Joseph and offered to buy him out; and I must say for the Standard Oil Company, they were very fair and equitable with him because they gave him a darned sight more than the old trap was worth." Id., at 2531.

Joseph agreed to stay out of the oil business, but soon came back, put up another bulk plant, and started cutting prices.

"Q. And the Standard met his cut?

"A. Well, you wouldn't expect them to take

E. M. Wilhoit. Vol. 3, at 1037–38 et seq., 1269–70. "In going into a new territory I cut usually the Standard price." Id., at p. 1227.

Cooper Brothers. Vol. 5, at 2358–59, 2392–2400; Vol. 15, at 2434, 2453, 2472–73, 2542–46.

Testimony of Maxon and Kercher. Vol. 5, at 2459–70; Vol. 6, at 2811–13, 2815–33. But see Vol. 12, at 922–23, 969.

[134] Vol. 5, at 2150.

[135] Id., at 2155–56; Vol. 12, at 908.

[136] Vol. 5, at 2156.

[137] Vol. 12, at 848.

Testimony of Mr. Castle.— Castle testified that while employed by Standard, he forced an independent Port Huron, Michigan dealer—Mr. Campfield—to sell out to Standard sometime after 1889.[144] Correspondence indicated that Castle was supposed to rebate to dealers to keep the Port Huron kerosene price depressed to 6 cents per gallon to combat Campfield.[145] It is not clear who started the price cutting, and I can find no further evidence about the incident. There is no doubt that Castle employed rebates extensively in the Ohio territory;[146] that is why Standard claimed they fired him. Castle also testified that he forced a Cuyahoga Falls peddler named Blackburn to sell out.[147] For one who claimed to have waged war so long and widely, even the results that Castle claimed appear slender, indeed.[148]

c) Price Cutting and Business Extinction

There remains the possibility that marketers were exterminated rather than purchased. The evidence is scanty and unconvincing.

Decline of Cleveland peddlers.— According to Castle, in 1903, when Standard sent peddling wagons into Cleveland, the independent peddlers were doomed.[149] Whereas before that time independent peddlers flourished, their numbers declined drastically:

> [A]t that time peddlers were getting a pretty good rebate and the retail prices hadn't been brought down. They were doing pretty well there for a start. . . . After they brought these wagons on. . . . [I]t made the margin very small, and it had the effect that up to this time there are very few peddlers in the business, at the present time. Out of probably two hundred and fifty at that time, I don't think you could find fifty now.[150]

Squire, of Standard, offered a different and more sensible explanation:

> [I]n 1902 there were 115 peddlers, with no natural-gas meters in use. In 1903 there were 90 peddlers, with 16,194 natural-gas meters in use. In 1904 there were 80 peddlers, with 30,165 natural-gas meters in use. In 1905, there were 78 peddlers, with 46,819 natural-gas meters in use. In 1906 there were 61 peddlers, with 66,743 natural-gas meters in use. In 1907 there were 43 peddlers, with 77,646 natural-gas meters in use. In 1908 there were 40 peddlers, with 83,976 natural-gas meters in use.[151]

Natural gas, of course, was used both for heating and lighting.

The Mahle testimony.— Mahle gave a great deal of hearsay testimony. For example, he said that three oil dealers in the Baltimore territory had been run out of business by Standard: Tough-Rutherford, McNeil, and the Purse family at Seaford, Delaware. I cannot find any evidence on the first two, but the allegation with respect to Purse is erroneous. The Seaford Company was a Crew-Levick concern, not a Standard "bogus" company,[152] and the

---

bank shots all the time, would you?" Ibid. Joseph sold out again.

[144] Vol. 6, at 3059–60.

[145] Vol. 10, at 1894–95 (Pet. Exh. 836, 837).

[146] Vol. 3, at 1362–3; Vol. 6, at 3030, 3037–38, 3039–45, 3071; Vol. 10, at 1886 (Pet. Exh. 829); Vol. 13, at 1511–15; 1576.

[147] Vol. 6, at 3044. At 3041, he says an unnamed peddler at Columbiana, Ohio also was forced to sell. The Columbiana affair arose out of price-cutting by Freedom Oil, Vol. 13, at 1511–15, as did many incidents in Ohio. Vol. 6, at 3040, 3044.

[148] Mahle, a former Standard stenographer, claimed that Blaustein tried to run Fivel, a peddler, out of Norfolk. Vol. 5, pp. 2211–12, 2360–62. Blaustein denied that, but admitted buying Fivel's wagon and supplies. Vol. 15, at 2434–39. Farquaharson said Blaustein ultimately bought Fivel out for $50 more than the "excessive" figure at which he first offered to sell. Vol. 5, at 2211. See also Vol. 2, at 725–27; Vol. 5, 2100–2, 2107, 2279; Vol. 12, at 902–05; Vol. 15, at 2445–7; 2549–52, 2544.

[149] Vol. 6, at 3054–56, 3108–19, 3124, 3201, 3206; see also Vol. 3, at 1507–10.

[150] Vol. 6, at 3056.

[151] Vol. 13, 1532.

[152] Vol. 13, at 1218, 1278–79, 1281, 1283, 1307. Cf. Vol. 5, at 2412; Vol. 13, at 1219–20.

Purse family said it was Red C price-cutting that drove them out.

Other incidents.— H. C. Boardman worked for Standard in Augusta, Georgia from 1886–1904, and testified that during that period Standard cut prices to drive out competitors.[153] Boardman said that one marketer, J. T. Thornhill, "finally abandoned business"; and that other major integrated competitors of Standard withdrew from the territory. These allegations were controverted.[154] Even Boardman admitted that Standard cut prices only "as last resort." [155]

Maywood Maxon, once a Standard employee, testified that in 1899 an unnamed independent oil dealer at Paris, Illinois was forced out of business after a year of rebating and price war.[156] Collings denied the whole affair.[157] In another instance, Kercher claimed that a peddler named Wagner left the business.[158]

C. M. Lines testified that he ran a string of bogus peddling wagons for Standard between 1900 and 1903.[159] He said he thought that these concerns lost money.[160] George Lane, who had worked for Lines, said that in Youngstown Lines made a "drive" on another peddler's business, and drove everybody out of business except the

man he was after.[161] On the other hand, Vahey, the peddler who was alleged to be the object of Lines' warfare, testified that he did a land office business when the Standard group attacked him.[162] Far from going out of business, he apparently flourished.

Marketing: Summary.— This testimony is voluminous, controverted, and confusing. Many exhibits were ambiguous, and some are of dubious authenticity. Several conclusions stand out, however:

1. If Standard's object was to monopolize marketing—and that would have been irrational to begin with—they failed. For, if we abstract from the decline of kerosene peddling that followed the growth of natural gas in Cleveland, I can find less than 10 small oil dealers whose sale or disappearance appears to have anything to do with local-price cutting. And that is a liberal estimate of the evidence. Some of the firms were nameless; allegations were often vague; most claims were disproved; some, while not controverted, were never really proved. In many cases, probably most of them, the independents clearly initiated price cuts.

The "possible" cases are, therefore, really unexplained cases. Most of them involved peddlers, among whom I would expect failures to be relatively numerous in the absence of predatory practices.

"Fatalities," from all causes, were apparently not very numerous in petroleum retailing and wholesaling, which is surprising in the light of the usual experience in petty trade. There were a fair number of purchases, but fewer than one might have expected.

2. Standard's correspondence and directives to salesmen show that they were

---

[153] Vol. 5, at 2163–67.

[154] See e.g., Vol. 12, at 910; Vol. 5, 2163. Boardman himself was a little vague: "I don't know whether they sold out, but the impression was that they sold out to the Standard." Vol. 5, at 2166. Boardman claimed that Tidewater; Crew-Levick; and Blodgett, Moore & Co., all withdrew.

[155] Id., at 2164.

[156] Vol. 3, at 1291, 1293, 1294, 1313. Maxon obviously wanted revenge on Standard; id., at 1294.

[157] Vol. 12, at 890. See also Vol. 5, at 2466–69.

[158] Vol. 6, at 2832–3. But see Vol. 10 at 1846 (Pet. Exh. 798). Kercher was an admitted perjurer. He also had a grudge against Standard, and apparently tried to blackmail them. Vol. 6, at 2949 et seq., 2969 et seq., 2990.

[159] Vol. 6, at 3201 et seq.

[160] Ibid., at 3205.

[161] Vol. 3, at 1356–61.

[162] Vol. 3, pp. 1366–67. Though just a peddler, Vahey was no fool. He claimed that when a Standard employee threatened to put him out of business, he replied that ". . . I was positive it would take him at least two years to put me out of business and maybe he couldn't do it then. . . ." Id., at 1367. For another alleged instance see Nicolai Brothers, Vol. 13, at 1196.

intent on getting business that paid, but were not going to give away anything to get it.[163] Salesmen were cautioned to "be as economical in getting this business as possible";[164] were denounced for cutting prices when it was not necessary[165] and for selling too much oil at special prices.[166]

3. It is interesting that most of the ex-Standard employees who testified about Standard's deadly predatory tactics entered the oil business when they left the Standard. They also prospered.

4. Standard apparently had a shrewd and hard marketing organization. It had

every interest in distributing as cheaply as possible, and tried to achieve that result.[167]

IV. Conclusions

Judging from the Record, Standard Oil did not use predatory price discrimination to drive out competing refiners, nor did its pricing practice have that effect. Whereas there may be a very few cases in which retail kerosene peddlers or dealers went out of business after or during price cutting, there is no real proof that Standard's pricing policies were responsible. I am convinced that Standard did not systematically, if ever, use local price cutting in retailing, or anywhere else, to reduce competition. To do so would have been foolish; and, whatever else has been said about them, the old Standard organization was seldom criticized for making less money when it could readily have made more.

In some respects it is too bad that Standard did not employ predatory price cutting to achieve its monopoly position. In doing so it would surely have gotten no

---

[163] Standard's salesmen and agents had to fill in "Form 29" requesting permission to cut prices. E.g., Vol. 3, at 1021–22; Vol. 12, at 962. Permission was often withheld. Vol. 10, at 1758–59 (Pet. Exh. 690). See Vol. 12, at 688, 845, 907. Standard's employees by and large appear to have learned what they were told. As one Waters-Pierce man put it:

"Our goods was [sic] just as good or [a] little better than our competitors and I thought we should get as much for them as possible. [Cutting price] might increase the gallonage, but I figured we would lose money." Vol. 3, at 1170.

Wilmer also testified that Standard expected its salesmen to get the business at remunerative prices, for "[a]nyone could give goods away." Vol. 13, at 1250. Metzell, a competitor's salesman, agreed that "[t]hey are getting all they can." Vol. 5, at 2418. Wilhoit knew that Standard's profitability rested on high prices, not low ones. As he put it,

"[I]f I could market my goods at such prices as the Standard Oil Company get for them regularly, I would not want but one year's business at their regular prices, if I got twenty-five per cent of the business. One year would be all I want to retire on at their regular price. We don't get their regular price." Vol. 3, at 1038.

[164] Vol. 10 at 1840 (Pet. Exh. 790).

[165] "I have also corresponded with our agents in the South Carolina field and they fully understand we want to retain our business and would reduce our market ½ cent per gallon rather than see the business go to the other oil companies, but I have impressed upon their minds that we do not want to put this reduction into effect unless it is absolutely necessary." Vol. 10, at 1758–59. (Pet. Exh. 690).

[166] Vol. 12, at 1019.

[167] Collings said that the incidents in Standard of Kentucky territory were in large part caused by excessively high dealer prices that Standard was in the process of breaking down. Vol. 5, at 2462; Vol. 12, at 886–89, 923–927. According to Collings, a peddler working on a 4¢ per gallon margin can do well: As he put it,

"So that at 4 cents a gallon it will be about, at 150 gallons a day, $6 a day. A man with one horse and wagon that can make $6 a day is doing very well. . . . [W]e figure that from 2 to 3 cents over the tank-wagon price was a fair price for the peddler. They could make a good living out of that. . . . And where they tried to hold up the customer to a fancy profit above that we used our efforts in one way or another to get them to bring it down, the object being, of course, to increase the consumption of oil. We felt, of course, that if they held the price up to 15 or 20 cents a gallon for oil, people would be more economical in the use of it."

Id., at 890. See also id. at 917–18. Cooke, a Government witness, testified that the effect of Standard's Capital City Wagons was to force peddlers to charge reasonable prices to consumers.

greater monopoly power than it achieved in other ways, and during the process consumers could have bought petroleum products for a great deal less money. Standard would thereby not only have given some of its own capital away, but would also have compelled competitors to donate a smaller amount.[168]

It is correct that Standard discriminated in price, but it did so to maximize profits given the elasticities of demand of markets in which it sold. It did not use price discrimination to change those elasticities. Anyone who has relied upon price discrimination to explain Standard's dominance would do well to start looking for something else.[169] The place to start is merger.

It should be quite clear that this is not a verdict of acquittal for the Standard Oil Company; the issue of monopoly remains. What this study says is that Standard did not achieve or maintain a monopoly position through price discrimination. The issue of whether the monopoly should have been dissolved is quite separate.

I think one further observation can tentatively be made. If the popular interpretation of the *Standard Oil* case is at all responsible for the emphasis that anti-trust policy places on "unfair" and "monopolizing" business practices, that emphasis is misplaced.[170] This limited study suggests that what businessmen do *to* one another is much less significant to monopoly than what they find it useful to do together to serve their common interest.

---

[168] This, of course, ignores certain moral issues. Economics is not a particularly useful tool for dealing with them.

[169] In arguing against the Defendant's motion for adjournment to prepare its case, Government Counsel may have admitted what I have concluded:

"What is there, then, to prepare for in this case? Simply the question of unfair competition. The Examiner can see from the testimony that has already been taken that that is not a great task; that it won't take any particular time for

them to prepare to meet that testimony." Vol. 6, at 3333.

[170] The Standard Legend may also be responsible for the strained analogy often drawn between business and war. Analogies to chess strike me as being equally weak. Chess is a competitive game which one player wins, while the other loses. Successful quasi-monopoly seeks to avoid the competitive game, since all players lose as soon as they begin playing it.

38. Predatory Pricing: The Case of the Gunpowder Trust*

KENNETH G. ELZINGA

Introduction

Few articles appearing in this Journal have been cited and reprinted as often as McGee's "Predatory Price Cutting: The Standard Oil (N.J.) Case." [1] McGee investigated the common allegation that Standard Oil of New Jersey used predatory price cuts in selected geographic markets to drive out rivals and bar new entry, thereby securing and maintaining a monopoly position in petroleum refining. McGee's study led him to conclude, on the basis of both logic and empirical evidence, that Standard Oil did not engage in this pricing practice, indeed for it to do so would have been irrational. A few others, notably Telser, have further examined this pricing method but to my knowledge no one has ever examined in detail, as McGee did, other alleged incidents of predatory pricing.[2] What follows is an examination of such pricing in the so-called Gunpowder Trust, or hereafter, simply the Powder Trust.

Reprinted from the *Journal of Law & Economics*, Vol. 13, 1970. The University of Chicago.

* I would like to thank John McGee and Lester Telser for their comments on this paper and the Wilson Gee Institute for its financial support.

[1] John S. McGee, Predatory Price Cutting: The Standard Oil (N.J.) Case, 1 J. Law & Econ. 137 (1958).

[2] L. G. Telser, Cutthroat Competition and the Long Purse, 9 J. Law & Econ. 259 (1966). Telser argues that predatory pricing may be used as a *threat* by business rivals and if so would be important in setting the terms of an eventual merger. He also indicates the advantage and importance of holding sizable funds by both would-be monopolists and potential entrants.

The Powder Trust

In 1907 the Department of Justice filed suit under the Sherman Act against 43 corporations and individuals in the explosives industry. The case, won by the government, never received the attention of certain other government antitrust suits of that era, partly because the decision contained no important precedents, mostly because the defendants did not appeal the adverse decision of the Circuit Court.[3] Nevertheless the government's victory over the Powder Trust was a major one, for this was a combination of considerable duration involving substantial commerce.

The term Powder Trust refers to a combination in the explosives industry spanning almost 40 years. The trust originated in 1872 when it consisted of a loose-knit combination of seven powder manufacturers known as the Gunpowder Trade Association of the United States (hereafter the GTA).[4] The GTA established various committees to oversee the workings of the cartel, to set prices, allot sales, and discipline those guilty of infractions of the agreement. The cartel suffered the usual problems of cartelization, that is, alleged cheating by the members, new entrants, periods of deterioration during business declines, etc., but still displayed remarkable durability. The synonymity between the GTA and E. I. DuPont de Nemours & Company (hereafter DuPont) stems from DuPont's eventual acquisition of the stock of several members of the GTA, including the two most promi-

[3] United States v. E. I. DuPont, 188 F. 127 (C.C.D. Del. 1911).

[4] The cartel is misnamed in that it sought to rationalize sales of not only gunpowder but also blasting powder and later dynamite.

nent members, The Hazard Powder Company and the Laflin & Rand Company. The GTA began as a loose-knit combination. After the turn of the century, it was much more tight-knit, with DuPont being the binding agent.

What is of interest here is not the history of the GTA or its subsequent amalgamation by DuPont. All this has been recorded elsewhere.[5] What is of interest is the common allegation that the trust had made extensive use of predatory pricing tactics; moreover that the trust used this practice systematically to ruin new entrants, forcing them to sell out, thereby effectuating their absorption into the combination. Allegations of this practice are an accepted part of the writings on the Powder Trust, being found in the economics literature, various histories of the DuPonts, indeed, in the Circuit Court's decision.[6] Stevens, in his *Unfair Competition,* cites the oil and powder trusts as "the best examples of the operation and effects of local price-cutting. . . ."[7] In Winkler's history of the DuPonts he states: "Explosives were sold below cost in the territories of the independents until the latter were either forced out of business or to sell out to the Association."[8] The Circuit Court referred to the GTA as ". . . waging a disastrous warfare against competitors until they were coerced into terms

satisfactory to the association or brought into the association."[9]

Predatory Pricing in the Explosives Industry

The purpose of this study is to investigate the alleged predatory pricing by the Powder Trust. My definition of predatory pricing is this: knowingly pricing below marginal cost in certain geographic markets for the purpose of disciplining or removing particular rivals and, as an ancillary effect, discouraging new entrants. I am not investigating whether the GTA or DuPont secured market power in the explosives industry. It is my impression that they possessed such power and that the court's finding of a Sherman Act violation was an appropriate one. I am not investigating whether the Powder Trust ever engaged in geographic (or primary line) price discrimination. Clearly this was a common practice. Finally, there is a mixed bag of business strategies often called "predatory tactics" or "cutthroat competition" which includes such activities as bribing rival employees, misrepresentation of one's own or rival products, even arson. Whether or not the GTA or DuPont engaged in any tactics of this sort is also not at issue here. My concern is narrow: whether the Powder Trust used predatory pricing and if so whether this served to effectuate or enhance its market power.

In the Powder Trust, the machinery for predatory pricing seemed ominously apparent. The Fundamental Agreement of 1899 provided that the Board of Trade of the GTA shall have

> . . . power to fix prices and to vary or change the same at any time and for any place, to meet contingencies and for protection of the common interests. It shall have power to . . . take any measures . . . which may in its judgment be necessary.

[5] *Cf.* W. S. Stevens, The Powder Trust, 1872–1912, 26 Q. J. Econ. 444 (1912), or Edward Proctor, Antitrust Policy and the Industrial Explosives Industry (unpublished doctoral dissertation, Harvard University, 1951), or Willard Mueller, DuPont: A Study in Firm Growth (unpublished doctoral dissertation, Vanderbilt University, chs. 3 & 4, 1955).

[6] *Cf.* Edward Proctor, *supra* note 5, at 14–46, 106–107; W. S. Stevens, *supra* note 5, at 447–461; Henry R. Seager & Charles A. Gulick, Trust and Corporation Problems, 406–408 (1929); William H. A. Carr, The Du Ponts of Delaware, 191–192 (1964).

[7] William S. Stevens, Unfair Competition, 11 (1917).

[8] John K. Winkler, The DuPont Dynasty, 144 (1935).

[9] United States v. DuPont, 188 F. 127, 140 (C.C.D. Del. 1911).

The Agreement also stipulated:

> That any party hereto who shall suffer excessive loss by an overt act of the Board of Trade—as for instance the reduction of a price at a place, in the treatment of a local disturbance of trade,—shall receive compensation for the damage it shall sustain by payment of money . . . on the recommendation of the Board of Trade.[10]

This seems to be *prima facie* evidence that predatory pricing was to be part of the trust's arsenal.

More specifically the government's case included the charge that at least 14 companies were subjected to this pricing strategy.[11] Following McGee's procedure I have examined all of the trial records, as well as other data, to ascertain the validity of these charges.[12] The 14 companies, in the order in which they were allegedly preyed upon, are:

1. The California Powder Works

2. Sycamore Manufacturing Co. (formerly Sycamore Powder Co.)

3. Lake Superior Powder Co.

4. King's Great Western Powder Co. (or King Powder Co.)

5. Marcellus Powder Co.

6. Ohio Powder Co.

7. Chattanooga Powder Co.

8. Phoenix Powder Manufacturing Co.

9. Southern Powder Co.

10. Indiana Powder Co.

11. Birmingham Powder Co.

12. Northwestern Powder Co.

13. Buckeye Powder Co.

14. Rockdale Powder Co.

I shall take them up in order.

(1) The government's Amended Petition states that the GTA began a price war against the California Powder Works in 1875 which culminated in California's joining the GTA and DuPont's acquiring 43 per cent of the capital stock. But the government presents no evidence of predatory pricing against this firm and the available evidence does not support the allegation. DuPont actually began buying stock in California in 1871, well before the alleged predatory pricing began. In addition, J. Haggin, one of the principal stockholders in the firm, stated that the sale of his stock to DuPont was voluntary, that at the time his firm was prosperous, and that it did not sell powder below cost out of compulsion.[13] VanGelder and Schlatter, in their history of the explosives industry, confirm Haggin's testimony that California was prosperous and well established, when it entered the GTA.[14]

W. Colvin, president of Hazard, a major member of the GTA, testified that DuPont and Hazard began selling blasting powder

---

[10] Government Exhibit (GX) 6, pars. 17 & 22; Record, United States v. DuPont, 188 F. 127 (C.C.D. Del. 1911).

[11] I have included the 12 companies specifically singled out in the government's Amended Petition. The government also alleges that 24 explosives companies in operation at the time of the Petition were subjected to predatory pricing. Only two of these, however, are considered in the Record and these two, along with the dozen, constitute my sample.

[12] I have examined both DuPont's copy of the records, now at the University of Delaware Library, and the original court records, now at the Philadelphia Federal Records Center. The official court records are numbered consecutively by page numbers. The DuPont records, however,

consist of: Petitioner's record testimony (pet. test.), defendant's record testimony (def. test.), petitioner's record exhibits, defendant's record exhibits, rebuttal record, and pleadings, each of which have separate pagination. Hereinafter the official court records are cited "Record." The DuPont records are cited "DuPont Record, pet. test." or "DuPont Record, def. test.," etc., depending upon the section of the DuPont records in which the testimony is recorded.

[13] Record at 2896, United States v. DuPont, 188 F. 127 (C.C.D. Del. 1911).

[14] Arthur P. VanGelder & Hugo Schlatter, History of the Explosives Industry in America, 286–90 (1927).

on the West Coast in competition with California. In response, California threatened to sell in the Eastern markets of DuPont and Hazard. This threat prompted the GTA to enter into a market sharing agreement. The agreement resulted in a distribution of trade on the Pacific Coast giving California a "practical monopoly," a five state neutral belt subject to GTA regulation, and the stipulation that California not send any powder to Atlantic Coast Markets.[15]

(2) In the case of the Sycamore Powder Company, what evidence there is hinges on the testimony of E. Lewis, a former salesman, later president of Sycamore. Lewis was no longer in the powder business at the time of the trial. He testified that coercion was not the reason for the sale of Sycamore to DuPont. The majority of the company's stock was family owned and the death of the major shareholder, Watson, and family debt, led the Watson family to approach the DuPonts. The DuPonts, who held almost half of the company's stock as early as 1873, purchased the majority share from the Watsons in "very satisfactory" negotiations, according to Lewis. Lewis also indicated that, far from being driven to the wall, Sycamore was doing very well due to its favorable location and that there was no warfare from or with the Powder Trust. Moreover the DuPonts invited W. Watson, the son of the deceased Watson, to stay on in the business, which he did, contributing some of his own funds, along with DuPont monies, to enlarge the plant.[16] While this last item is a minor point, McGee correctly points out that "Victimized ex-rivals might be expected to make poor employees . . ." [17] The government presented no evidence to support its charge regarding Sycamore.

(3) There is no evidence in the record supporting the charge of predatory pricing against the Lake Superior Powder Company, either before it elected to join the GTA or before DuPont and Laflin & Rand

purchased stock interests in the company. J. Reynolds, superintendent of the company and a shareholder who sold out to DuPont, testified that the GTA had not engaged in any predatory pricing prior to his selling out or prior to the company joining the GTA, that he sold out voluntarily, and the company was prospering prior to joining the GTA.[18]

(4) R. S. Waddell, a very important government witness in this case, testified that while an employee of the Hazard Powder Company he had instructions to cut the price of powder in Cincinnati such that it would be 10¢/keg lower than any price offered by the King's Great Western Powder Company.[19] While this does not necessarily entail pricing below cost, the government's Amended Petition states that prices fell as low as 80¢/keg and that this was "less than the cost of manufacture. . . ." The defendants however introduced witnesses who testified contrary to Waddell. Colvin, the president of Hazard, had no recollection of warfare with King's.[20] And E. Rice, the general agent for DuPont and Hazard in Chicago, claimed King's had only a small share of the market in his territory, that he never had made an offer to match, much less beat King's prices, since he had trouble getting enough powder to sell as it was.[21] The testimony regarding this company seems contradictory.

In spite of the inconsistent testimony above, I think the testimony of G. Peters, president of King's, is revealing. First, King's never actually sold out to GTA interests, instead turning down their purchase offer, and agreeing only to join the cartel.[22] Peters also testified that the company, which began in 1878, faced no concerted price war prior to joining the GTA in 1886, that the GTA "never manifested any such disposition." What prompted King's joining the

[15] Record at 47–48; Arthur P. VanGelder & Hugo Schlatter, *supra* note 14, at 131–32, 290.

[16] Record at 2513–2527.

[17] John S. McGee, *supra* note 1, at 145.

[18] Record at 2771–2774.

[19] DuPont Record, pet. test. 100–107.

[20] Record at 55.

[21] *Id.* at 2380.

[22] *Id.* at 142–143.

GTA, according to Peters, was the sorry powder market of 1884–1885. He stated that during these years there was a "general scramble" for business, that sales were beginning to go below cost, that "there was no money being made."[23] Indeed it was apparently this general demoralization in prices that stimulated the GTA to renew its efforts in 1886, add to its membership, and produce a new agreement, much more detailed in its coverage.

In addition to denying any systematic efforts against his firm, Peters displayed considerable independence for a man allegedly subject to "ruinous and destructive competition." Refusing to sell out to GTA firms, he joined the GTA in 1886, withdrew later, then joined again. King's was the only member of the 1886 agreement to get a larger allotment in the 1889 Fundamental Agreement, making good a threat to drop out if this was not granted.[24] In 1901 King's agreed to sell DuPont all its output.[25] Later, prior to the filing of the antitrust suit, King's was able to obtain $100,000 from DuPont to reestablish its marketing organization when DuPont wanted out of the above contract.[26]

GTA prices did drop, relative to other areas, in the territory served by King's. Blasting powder was selling for $3.00/keg in both Cincinnati and Buffalo in May 1878. By April 1879, the price was $2.00/keg in Cincinnati, unchanged in Buffalo. At the October 1879 meeting of the GTA, the association agreed to hold blasting powder at $2.00/keg with each member pledging not to drop below this regardless of prices charged by King's.[27] While it is true that prices did then go below $2.00, as seen by the GTA trials of the violators, this hardly seems to be systematic, premeditated predatory pricing by the powder combination but rather a case of cheating by members who saw opportunities for a quick profit.

One other point is of interest: not only did Peters turn down the opportunity to confirm the alleged price war against his firm, strange behavior if there was in fact such a war, but he also indicated that J. King, the founder of King's, was for many years with the Miami Powder Company (an original member of the GTA) until he founded his own company in 1878.[28] While this is only a minor point, it does seem unlikely that someone who had viewed effective predatory campaigns against independents would be apt to open his own mill.

G. Rood, formerly with Hazard before starting one of the independent powder mills allegedly preyed upon, also testified about King's. He stated that King's, and even more so the Northwestern Powder Company, were price cutters and that the GTA price cuts were instituted only to protect trade, not to put King's out of business.[29] I can see no way that Rood's testimony is self-serving and should, I think, carry more weight than the similar statements by Colvin and Rice.

(5) There is no evidence in the record to support or rebut the allegation that the Marcellus Powder Company sold out as a result of predatory pricing. All I can find is that J. Griswald was the owner, that Hazard and Laflin & Rand bought shares in 1885 and 1886, and that by 1886 Marcellus was in the GTA.

(6) As in the case of King's Great Western, R. S. Waddell testified that he had a part in the price warfare against the Ohio Powder Company, stating that prices went as low as 80¢/keg, this being purportedly below cost. Ohio began in business in 1882 and became a member of the GTA in 1886, with the majority of its stock held by Hazard and Laflin & Rand.[30]

P. Laughlin, for 23 years a general agent

[23] DuPont Record, def. test. 690–693.

[24] Edward Proctor, *supra* note 5, at 29–32.

[25] DuPont Record, def. test. 709.

[26] Record at 2660.

[27] Edward Proctor, *supra* note 5, at 23–25.

[28] Record at 2916–2917.

[29] DuPont Record, def. test. 421–422.

[30] DuPont Record, pet. test. 105–106.

of Ohio, who became employed by DuPont after Ohio was bought out, testified that the GTA initiated the price cuts against Ohio. On the other hand, G. Weightman, secretary of Hazard, and E. Rice, the DuPont-Hazard agent for Chicago, both testified that Ohio, not the GTA, was the initiator of these price cuts which resulted in the demoralization of prices prior to Ohio's joining of the GTA.

This is an appropriate time to indicate that the vast amount of (often contradictory) testimony in this case relating to exactly which firm, the independent or the GTA member, first cut the price is mostly, if not totally, without value in attempting to determine the existence of predatory pricing. Lawyers on both sides attempted to wring testimony on the timing of price cuts, with the respondent lawyers seeming to feel they had proved the lack of predatory pricing if a witness claimed the independent cut prices first, the government lawyers believing they had made their case by securing testimony that the Powder Trust had initiated the price cuts. At first I put stock in this testimony; but in a market with literally hundreds of customers, finding that "first price cut" is like finding a will-o'-the wisp. Moreover, once found it is not clear what it proves.

At any rate, the record regarding the Ohio Powder Company seems to relate to finding the initiator of the price cutting which began sometime around 1882. There is no proof presented that the declining prices became less than cost, only that the companies were engaged in price competition with the initiator being uncertain, and Ohio surviving for four years before joining the trust.

(7) R. S. Waddell testified that the Powder Trust preyed upon the Chattanooga Powder Company and that ". . . we sold powder at cost, or below it" during the battle lasting from 1892 to 1896.[31] F. J. Waddell, his brother who also was one time employed by the trust, testified that Eugene DuPont had given him instructions to drive

Chattanooga out of business; in his words he had "carte blanche to name any prices I choosed." [32] R. S. Waddell claimed that the price of blasting powder dropped to around 80¢/keg, that the cost of producing a keg was 70–80¢/keg, and with an approximate shipping charge of 28¢/keg from Hazard's plant in Connecticut to the Birmingham powder market, the trust was losing around 20¢/keg on blasting powder.[33]

Given the lack of rebuttal evidence on the part of respondents, I tend to believe that prices dropped below costs for the trust. The trust wanted this mill since they had no capacity in that area. However, the evidence is not at all clear that the trust was wise in using this tactic. Contrary to F. J. Waddell's allegation that Chattanooga was in financial straits and that its owners grudgingly sold out, F. Connable, a former director of Chattanooga during the price war, claims that Chattanooga was a successful and profitable mill at the time it sold out to DuPont and Laflin & Rand interests.[34] The testimony of F. J. Waddell indicates quite clearly that Chattanooga was capable of underbidding the GTA as much as three years after the price cutting began.[35]

(8) R. S. Waddell stated that the contest against the Phoenix Powder Manufacturing Company involved "a very great reduction in the price of powder . . ." with the price competition lasting from 1892–1896 and prices on blasting powder going down to $1.00/keg. It ended when all the Phoenix stock was purchased by GTA interests.[36] There is a paucity of other data on this alleged price war. The cost data, such as it is, is not conclusive since, with the cost of powder being somewhere around 70¢/

---

[31] Id. at 123.

[32] Id. at 258. He stated that prices "decidedly" went below cost. Record at 363.

[33] Record at 169.

[34] DuPont Record, pet. test. 306; Answer to Chattanooga Powder Company at 4, United States v. DuPont, 188 F. 127 (C.C.D. Del. 1911).

[35] DuPont Record, pet. .est. 324.

[36] Id. at 126.

keg, it is not clear that a price of $100/keg would be below costs in this area. It is clear that the GTA was not making as large a margin at a dollar a keg as it was making in other markets. But simple price discrimination is not the same as predatory pricing.

In addition, F. Kellogg, who organized Phoenix, had ample opportunity to witness the fate of independents. He had been general sales agent for Laflin & Rand, then became manager of a powder firm that sold out to Laflin & Rand shortly after beginning operations. These experiences apparently did not discourage him from starting the Phoenix Company.[37]

(9) There is no evidence that predatory pricing was used against the Southern Powder Company, in spite of R. S. Waddell's testimony that we tried to "shut it out of the market as quickly as we could." [38] Indeed, F. J. Waddell admitted that in all but one instance, the GTA at best only met the price reduction of Southern, that prior to its absorption by GTA members, Southern was known as a price-cutter.[39]

Moreover there is rather clear evidence that this mill was built for the express purpose of selling out to DuPont. This was F. J. Waddell's opinion and is supported by the fact that the owners of this mill, after its sale, built another mill (the Birmingham Powder Company) and once again began cutting powder prices.[40] G. Hamlin of the Dittmar Powder Company later testified that the two owners of Southern asked him to join them in their second venture, indicating at the time that they "unloaded that [Southern] at a profit." [41] Needless to say, behavior of this sort does not support the position that predatory pricing is a

viable pro-monopoly tool. If predatory pricing has the effect often attributed to it, one would certainly not expect to find independent firms being sold at a profit or the former owners anxious to reenter the business.

(10) The evidence is not convincing that the Indiana Powder Company faced predatory pricing. Moreover it is apparent that if it did, the strategy also did not have the effect so often attributed to it. R. S. Waddell testified that while with Hazard, he approached Indiana with a purchase offer before it began operations; he indicated to Indiana at the time that the alternative to selling out was a price war. He then portrayed the strategy devised to bring about the demise of Indiana. This strategy included cutting prices, setting up a new selling corporation located near the mines and supplied by the GTA, designating a particular man to oversee the rivalry with Indiana, selling powder direct to the miners instead of to the mine operators (who normally then sold to the miners), and also attending miners' union meetings and hawking GTA power there.[42] To many academics, this portrayal would sound ominous. To those who have been in business it will probably be recognized as a rather commonplace portrayal of active business rivalry.

At any rate, Waddell's description of the events is rebutted by G. Rood, a former employee of Waddell's at Hazard, who started Indiana. Rood testified that all the negotiations with the GTA were friendly and that there was no predatory pricing.[43] It is important to note that Rood was an employee of Hazard from 1882–1897, knew the operations of the GTA well, and still elected to enter the powder business. As in the previous case, there is evidence that Rood entered the powder business for the sole purpose of selling out to the trust. E. Rice testified to this effect and R. S. Waddell admitted learning from his former employee that "he had sold out and did pretty

---

[37] Arthur P. VanGelder & Hugo Schlatter, *supra* note 14, at 141.

[38] DuPont Record, pet. test. 131.

[39] *Id.* at 342.

[40] *Id.*

[41] DuPont Record, def. test. 1291; John S. McGee also found examples of this behavior, *supra* note 1, at 146–147.

[42] DuPont Record, pet. test. 151–156.

[43] Record at 2547–2548.

well . . ." [44] Waddell testified that the price of blasting powder went as low as 80¢/keg before Indiana sold out. But the record is not at all clear on this. H. Barksdale, a director of DuPont, and C. Alward, a salesman under Waddell at the time of the alleged price war (at trial date an employee of a rival powder firm), both testified that DuPont sold at around $1.25/keg against Indiana, with Indiana selling at around $1.10/keg.[45] Rood also said that Indiana never sold below $1.10/keg.[46] Since even Waddell himself admitted that Indiana powder could not compete with DuPont powder at equal prices, the available evidence seems to point to DuPont not undercutting Indiana. In addition, Indiana hardly seemed pressed by the alleged price war. It was a very prosperous mill paying stockholders $1.89 on the dollar until it sold out to GTA interests in 1902.[47] To prevent Rood from again re-entering, the sales contract called for him to stay out of the powder business for 20 years. If he had actually been drubbed in a price war, such a stipulation would seem unnecessary. The contract apparently did not include Rood's son who, outdoing his father, began two independent explosives companies and later became vice-president of the Hercules Powder Company.

(11) The Birmingham Powder Company is the outfit started by the two former owners of the Southern. G. Hamlin was told by its two owners that their object was "to build a small plant for the manufacture of blasting powder. Their principal argument was that after this was established it would be purchased at a profit, by what was then known as the Powder Combination." [48] The fact that they promptly re-entered with this mill indicates that the alleged price war

against them did not succeed the first time. Unfortunately the record is not clear for the second alleged war faced by these two men though one remained as superintendent of the mill after the GTA takeover.

The GTA did set up a Special Committee of its Advisory Board to deal with lower prices in various areas and, on the Meeting of February 2, 1889, two members were specifically authorized to "consult together and make prices wherever necessary to meet prices made by the Birmingham Mills . . ." [49] However this Special Committee was directed never to undercut Birmingham prices. F. J. Waddell stated that Birmingham had a reputation as a price-cutter, with their prices going to 99¢/keg; he was only authorized to go as low as $1.10/keg. My judgment is that this price, given the freight charges, could not leave a large margin for DuPont. Whether such a price would be below cost is just not clear. R. S. Waddell testified that GTA affiliates set a price in the Birmingham market which they believed to be "pretty close to their [Birmingham's] cost." [50] But there is no conclusive evidence to support a position that the price charge by the GTA was above or below its marginal costs.

(12) The record contains no evidence to support or rebut the government's charge that Northwestern Powder Company, purchased by GTA interests in 1902, was a victim of predatory pricing.

(13) To appreciate the charge of predatory price cuts against the Buckeye Company, some further information on its owner R. S. Waddell is appropriate. While with the GTA, Waddell complained of the independent powder companies, after they were bought out, being allocated large shares of his business, for example he grumbled that ". . . trade that we built up and supplied has been turned over to competitors." [51] He was obviously a man of great independence, a salesman, and a price-cutter, who did not fit in a world of cartel

---

[44] DuPont Record, def. test. 311–312; pet. test. 902.

[45] DuPont Record, def. test. 638; Alward, Record at 3350.

[46] Record at 2550.

[47] Id. at 2557; Arthur P. VanGelder & Hugo Schlatter, supra note 14, at 152–153.

[48] DuPont Record, def. test. 1290.

[49] Record, GX 124-D.

[50] DuPont Record, pet. test. 158.

[51] Record, GX 27.

quotas and price rigidity. So he left the GTA to build his own mill, declining their offer of financial assistance.

Around 1905 Waddell began a one-man campaign to arouse congressional and public indignation over the Powder Trust. His *coup de grace* was presenting the Department of Justice with an armload of correspondence, pertaining to the GTA, which he had conveniently saved from his employment with the GTA affiliates.

Waddell claimed that as soon as he opened his own mill until he sold out, ". . . there was one continuous warfare made by [the GTA]." [52] P. Laughlin, a former DuPont employee who joined Buckeye, testified that when he was with DuPont he was involved in a "contest" with Buckeye.[53] However, there is no evidence that prices, though they did decline, actually went below cost; and, though no details are available, one cannot help but wonder what would prompt Laughlin to join Buckeye if the "contest" were actually predatory in nature. Dutton, in his history of DuPont, found that Waddell's mill actually prospered for two years until the depression of 1907, implying that this was the real source of his financial problems.[54]

The respondents seemed to spare no effort in trying to rebut the Waddell-Laughlin testimony regarding this company. Several DuPont employees who had responsibilities for trade in the Buckeye area testified that there was no predatory price cutting directed against Buckeye.[55] In addition, a parade of 13 buyers of explosives testified that they did not get lower prices from DuPont, that Buckeye was generally the price-cutter, that Buckeye powder was of low quality, and several willingly paid the higher price for DuPont powder due to its superior quality.[56] Waddell, in rebuttal to this latter parade, argued that many of these were not his regular customers, some having been solicited only once; he added that subtracting 2 of the 13 left a group of "customers" who accounted for only 1/5 to 1/10 of 1 per cent of his business.[57]

Since their testimony might be only self-serving, one would naturally view with caution the testimony of trust officials. It appears however that in the case of Waddell, former writers on the Powder Trust have taken what he has said at its face value. I think it is only fair that his testimony be viewed with the same healthy skepticism. It is curious that a man who had witnessed first hand the supposedly rapacious pricing tactics of the GTA would enter the industry as an independent. This casts some doubt on the alleged predatory behavior against the previous independents though it tells us nothing about whether he experienced such tactics himself. But it was important to him that the existence of such tactics be established. For in a private suit right after the Circuit Court decision, Waddell sued the Powder Trust for treble damages amounting to over $1.2 million. Ironically while the government won its suit, Waddell lost his.[58]

(14) W. Koller, the owner of Rockdale Powder Company, testified that DuPont engaged in a price war with his firm, employing H. G. Nicoll specifically to "put the Rockdale Powder Company out of business." [59] Nicoll, no longer with DuPont, confirmed this when he stated he had received

[52] DuPont Record, pet. test. 239.

[53] *Id.* at 949.

[54] William S. Dutton, DuPont; One Hundred and Forty Years, 193 (1949).

[55] *See* Dooley, DuPont Record, def. test. 873; Haskell, *id.* at 1055; Donnely, *id.* at 1253–1255; Macklem, Record at 1903; Mathews, *id.* at 1911.

[56] Record at 3617–3693; the last witness, C. Keeler, seems to contradict himself. *See* Record, GX 443–445.

[57] Record at 3865–3882.

[58] Buckeye Powder Co. v. DuPont, 196 F. 514 (1912), 223 F. 881 (1916), 248 U.S. 55 (1918). Since this suit was prior to 1914, Waddell was not able to rely on the government case. In a jury trial, it was held that Buckeye folded due to its own weaknesses, not due to the practices of the trust, *id.*

[59] DuPont Record, pet. test. 809.

instructions to "get the business" of Rockdale and, while he was "not to cut the price unless it was absolutely necessary," he was to "go the limit to get the business." [60] But apparently, though the record is not clear, the "limit" was cost.[61]

There are several items that cause me to doubt the allegation of predatory pricing in this case, aside from the denials by three DuPont employees. There is a record of Nicoll calling on approximately 30 Rockdale customers, all formerly in the DuPont fold, and getting the business of only two of them —which seems strange if he were offering prices below cost.[62] Eight explosives customers of Rockdale all testified that none had ever received a price offer from DuPont at less than Rockdale prices, though some switched back to DuPont in spite of the higher prices.[63] All of these customers were listed by Koller as those he lost due to DuPont cutting.[64] Finally, in spite of the alleged war, Rockdale did not go under.

Summary for the 14 Independents

Of the 14 companies allegedly preyed upon, the evidence is quite clear that six of these [1, 2, 3, 9, 10, 14] suffered no such fate, it is my impression that another [4] was not subjected to this pricing strategy, the evidence does not allow any conclusion as to five of the companies [5, 6, 8, 11, 12], and possibly two [7, 13] were in fact subjected to the practice, though even here the evidence is hardly conclusive. These are admittedly rather impressionistic findings but not so impressionistic to vitiate the conclusion that predatory pricing, if it existed, was not nearly as widespread as a casual reading of many writings on the Powder

Trust would suggest. This study, coupled with McGee's, indicates that two trusts, both supposedly using predatory pricing with great skill, actually relied upon mergers and loose-knit agreements for the positions of market dominance achieved.

The testimony of numerous GTA executives as well as other witnesses is a portrayal of an association trying to maintain prices, not lower them—that the public policy problem was not one of low prices in some markets, but rather one of high (monopoly) prices in others. Indeed someone naive to the vagaries of antitrust would find the trial almost Kafkasque, with the government lawyers believing they had scored points when they cajoled a witness into testifying that the GTA charged low prices, the defendants then attempting to prove that the trust kept its prices up! With only a couple of possible exceptions, the Powder Trust was a combination trying to maintain a monopolistic price structure. The trust lowered prices with considerable reluctance when faced by competition from independents, for this threatened the price structure, and it was anxious to bring the independents into the combination. My impression is that the meetings of the GTA were not occupied with discussions of where to lower prices, but often with how to prevent clandestine price lowering, that is, cheating. Proctor reports that from 1881–1883 the GTA tried 230 cases of price infractions by association members.[65] Apparently keeping salesmen in line, that is, preventing them from offering discounts and rebates, was a big problem for the GTA.[66] Due to the inability to effectively bar entry, the combination faced the usual problems of cartel instability—hence the incentive for DuPont to weld a tighter organization. A more plausible explanation for the price differentials between different regions is the response by the GTA to differing demand elasticities for explosives, or perhaps a limit pricing strat-

---

[60] Record at 1075–1078.

[61] Id. at 1085.

[62] Hamlin, Record at 2130–2133 and GX 80 & 81.

[63] Jemison, Aubrey, Henderson, Ireland, Record at 2299–2317; Weast, Dobling, Shirk, id. at 2479–2495; Barrick, id. at 2599.

[64] See Record, GX 415.

[65] Edward Proctor, supra note 5, at 13.

[66] Cf. Record at 1976–2117, 2135–2297, 2352–2371, 2377–2980.

egy by the GTA to discourage output expansion by independent firms.

The Issue of Predatory Pricing

The rationality of pricing in a predatory manner is a contested issue. On the one hand, there is what I shall call the conventional wisdom, that is, that predatory pricing makes sense and is consequently a public policy problem in the maintenance of free markets. The conventional wisdom is exemplified in a quotation from a document in this case:

> [The predatory pricing tactics of the Powder Trust] . . . had become generally known among powder manufacturers and dealers . . . and . . . had long been . . . employed against other manufacturers and vendors of powder who had attempted to operate independently . . . and that generally independent operators had been unable to survive . . . and for this reason there was no market for such property except among the defendants and their co-conspirators.[67]

In other words, the independent cannot last long in a price war against a trust that can "make up" its losses with profits from other markets; when finally subdued, the independent must sell out to the trust for a song since potential purchasers of his properties, having observed his fate, naturally elect not to bid.

Opposing the conventional wisdom is what can be called the McGee hypothesis (or position): namely that predatory pricing is irrational and one should not expect to find it used to secure or maintain a monopoly position. McGee sums it up this way:

> If, instead of fighting, the would-be monopolist bought out his competitors directly, he could afford to pay them up to the discounted value of the expected mo-

nopoly profits to be gotten as a result of their extinction. Anything above the competitive value of their firms should be enough to buy them. In the purchase case, monopoly profits could begin at once; in the predatory case large losses would first have to be incurred.[68]

While the dispute can be outlined rather briefly, the appropriate test for proving or disproving the rationality of predatory pricing is not readily apparent. The historical approach of McGee and myself, needless to say, is fraught with difficulties, especially for economists, since it relies so much on what people say—which in this case was at times contradictory and quite possibly self-serving. This approach is valid only when the testimony can be supplemented by what people do, in addition to what they say.

Since the issue is whether explosives (or some other product) were ever sold below marginal cost, one apparent approach would be to compare prices charged with the appropriate costs. Unfortunately, while the evidence on prices is fairly abundant in the trial records of this case, data on powder costs are very sketchy and unreliable. This problem, along with the usual ones economists have with accounting data, make this an unworkable approach. And as Bowman has pointed out, it is not clear why accounting costs, even if properly reworked, have any relevance to either a firm's pricing strategy or public policy.[69]

Perhaps the most satisfactory test is observing whether or not new firms enter the industry in the face of alleged predatory pricing. One would not predict new entrants if the conventional wisdom is the better theory; on the other hand, new entry is perfectly consistent with the McGee hypothesis, indeed one would predict it, provided the monopoly is profitable as the Powder

---

[67] Amended Declaration of Buckeye Powder Company against Court's Relief Decree (Oct. 6, 1911), Record, vol. 1, at 29, Buckeye Powder Co. v. DuPont, 248 U.S. 55 (1918).

[68] John S. McGee, *supra* note 1, at 139.

[69] Ward S. Bowman, Restraint of Trade by the Supreme Court: The Utah Pie Case, 77 Yale L.J. 70, 76 (1967).

Trust was. The difficult question is: how much new entry makes a case for either position?

As mentioned above, both McGee and myself found examples of owners, allegedly driven out, reentering the industry anew. Unfortunately additional evidence on entry rates in the explosives industry is somewhat sketchy, though what is available shows that there were *more* new entrants during the trust's activities than after the relief decree which broke up DuPont and ordered the end of all loose-knit agreements in the industry. There were approximately 53 independent explosives manufacturers at the time of the government's suit in 1907, 27 in 1913, and only 19 in 1921.[70] From 1903, the time of DuPont's incorporation, until 1907, the time of the suit, 14 new high explosives companies entered; during the same period 11 independent black powder producers opened for business.[71]

Of course even finding examples of predatory pricing does not conclusively rebut the McGee position. For example, I believe DuPont may have used predatory pricing against R. S. Waddell's mill. This does not mean such pricing strategy is rational (profit maximizing) behavior. Two other possible explanations exist, both plausible, both consistent with McGee. First, the DuPont management may have made a mistake. If economists cannot easily ascertain whether predatory pricing might be rational, management, at least some management, also might not know! That DuPont management tried predatory pricing and discovered that this was not a profitable strategy might explain why, with the demise of blasting powder, its efforts to rationalize the burgeoning dynamite industry was a pattern of mergers and agreements.[72] Second, DuPont might have had non-pecuniary motives for pricing below cost against Waddell, if in fact it did. He had left their employ, refused to join the GTA, wrote nasty

things about them to newspapers, all of which could have induced DuPont management to pay a cost to eliminate him.

There is precedent for this non-pecuniary motivation to drive a rival out of business in this manner. Anyone who is familiar with the well-documented case of predatory pricing in the chicory duopoly probably has the impression that McMorran's price cutting efforts were not rational, in a profit maximizing sense, but based rather on motives more properly in the domain of a psychologist than an economist.[73]

The resolution of this issue (along with not a few others in economics) rests on finding the degree of imperfection in the capital market as Stigler has pointed out.[74] With a perfect capital market, a defender of the conventional wisdom would be hard pressed to explain why the preyed upon independent would not ride out the price war since he could absorb losses on a par with the dominant firm. Nor could he explain how the dominant firm would be able to buy the vanquished firm's assets for some price approaching their scrap value, that is why the auction block will be, in Stigler's terms, so "poorly attended." [75]

Related to this issue of the capital market, and equally difficult to test, is the importance of what might be termed the "demonstration effect" of predatory pricing. McGee's logic showing the irrationality of predatory pricing is impeccable where there is one dominant firm faced with only a few independents and no potential entrants. Barring a significant imperfection in the capital market, one would not predict predatory pricing in such a situation. But what

---

[70] Edward Proctor, *supra* note 5, at 341–348.

[71] Barksdale, DuPont Record, def. test. 634–636.

[72] Edward Proctor, *supra* note 5, at 48–58, 74–76.

[73] E. B. Muller v. F.T.C. 142 F.2d 511 (6th Cir., 1944).

[74] George J. Stigler, Imperfections in the Capital Market, 75 J. Pol. Econ. 287 (1967), *see also* L. G. Telser, *supra* note 2, at 270–276.

[75] George J. Stigler, *supra* note 74, at 287. The only evidence I encountered on this point *was* a poorly attended auction. R. S. Waddell, in spite of his efforts to sell elsewhere, could find only one bidder for his mill—the Powder Trust. Amended Declaration of Buckeye Powder Company, *supra* note 67, at 29.

if there are potential entrants who can, at little cost, observe the fate of the independents? Seeing the independents bought out at remunerative prices, these potential entrants might enter in such numbers as to extinguish all monopoly rents. But if they observe the existing independents driven out by the dominant firm, then their response is not easily predicted. They (some) may realize the inability of the dominant firm to continue such a costly practice and promptly enter. Or the demonstration effect may deter them (some) from entering, in which case the cost of the price war may be a rational expenditure by the dominant firm no different from the expenditure to secure a government license or tariff. All it would take for successful entry deterrence is for each potential entrant to think *he* is the one who would be preyed upon. If all the potential entrants and existing independents could band together, the dominant firm would be forced into either a coalition or at best competitive behavior.

But the costs of coalition for potential entrants is probably high.[76]

Conclusion

While this study neither conclusively supports the McGee position nor rebuts the conventional wisdom, it does indicate that predatory pricing by the Power Trust, if it existed at all, was not nearly as prevalent as numerous writings have indicated. What should be apparent, even to those who still believe predatory pricing might be rational monopolizing behavior under certain conditions, is that mergers and cartels provide a much greater threat to free markets than predatory pricing. Predatory price cutting, given its unlikely occurrence and visual similarity to healthy business rivalry, should be well down the priority list of the antitrust authorities.

---

[76] I am indebted to Tom Borcherding for pointing out the importance of coalition costs.

39. The Myth of Predatory Pricing: An Empirical Study

ROLAND H. KOLLER II [*]

The Popular Versus the Professional View of Predation

The predatory price-cutter is one of the oldest and most familiar villains in our economic folklore. Defined as the financially-powerful competitor who monopolizes his industry by cutting prices below cost and holding them there until his weaker rivals have gone into bankruptcy, he is a significant figure in the public's perception of economic affairs and undoubtedly exerts a very considerable influence on its attitude toward economic matters in the large, particularly its view of the government's proper role in economic policy. Supporting the layman's view here, popular economic history is filled with the price-cutter's exploits. The economic literature, on the other hand, accords this ubiquitous character no such front-and-center role on the economic stage. Indeed, the standard theoretical analysis in this area treats predation as a form of non-maximizing (irrational) behavior and thus as an unlikely occurrence in the real world.[1] Given this wide disparity between the popular and the professional view of the subject, and assuming that any phenomenon exerting such a broad influence on the public mind is an appropriate subject for economic analysis, a detailed study of predatory pricing has recently been completed.[2]

Definitions—Sales Below 'Cost'

For the purpose of this study, predatory pricing is divided into two general broad categories. In one of them (Type 1), the objective of the predator is to *eliminate* a competitor. In the other (Type 2), predatory pricing is undertaken for the purpose of persuading the victim to either (a) *merge* with the predator or (b) join a *price-fixing* ring (cartel) or other collusive arrangement with the predator. Employing both the popular and the professional view of the problem, we define predation itself here in terms of three criteria, namely, (1) the sale of a product at a loss, (2) with what can reasonably be described as a predatory intent, and (3) the achievement of the result intended, i.e., the elimination of the rival or a bending of him to the predator's will. Each of these criteria is important to the definition. The first, use

* Dr. Koller is assistant professor of economics at Brigham Young University, Provo, Utah. The instant paper is based on his doctoral dissertation, *Predatory Pricing in a Market Economy* (University of Wisconsin, 1969).

[1] See, e.g., Morris A. Adelman, "Geographical Price Differentials: An Economic Commentary," 48 *Illinois Bar Journal* (March 1960), p. 514; Robert C. Brooks, Jr., "Price Cutting and Monopoly Power," 25 *Journal of Marketing* (July 1961); Donald Dewey, "Competitive Policy and National Goals: The Doubtful Relevance of Antitrust," in Almarin Phillips (ed.), *Perspectives in Antitrust Policy* (Princeton, 1965); Kenneth G. Elzinga, "Predatory Pricing: The Case of the Gunpowder Trust," 13 *Journal of Law & Economics* (April 1970), p. 223; W. A. Leeman, "The Limitations of Local Price-Cutting as a Barrier to Entry," 64 *Journal of Political Economy* (August 1956), p. 329; Samuel M. Loescher, "Geographical Pricing Policies and the Law," 27 *Journal of Business* (July 1954), p. 211; John S. McGee, "Predatory Price-Cutting: The Standard Oil (N.J.) Case," 1 *Journal of Law & Economics* (October 1958), p. 137; Lester G. Telser, "Cutthroat Competition and the Long Purse," 9 *Journal of Law & Economics* (October 1966), p. 259; and Donald F. Turner, "Conglomerate Mergers and Section 7 of the Clayton Act," 78 *Harvard Law Review* (May 1965), p. 1313.

[2] Roland H. Koller II, *Predatory Pricing in a Market Economy* (University of Wisconsin, 1969) (doctoral dissertation).

of a below-cost price,[3] focuses the inquiry on the precise phenomena to be explored —the incurring of short-term losses that are to be recovered from *future* excess profits —and distinguishes this kind of activity from pricing practices that are in fact *profitable at the time they are employed*.[4] The second criterion, some sort of subjective predatory "intent" on the part of the aggressor firm, is an essential counterpart to the first one, since a firm's prices can fall below its short-run average total cost for a variety of reasons having nothing to do with predation, e.g., product obsolescence, insufficient demand, and so forth. The third criterion here, the success of the practice, is essential if one is to evaluate its real economic significance, particularly its effects on competition.[5]

Predatory Pricing in Economic Theory

The standard theoretical analysis of predatory pricing[6] can be readily illustrated by way of the following hypothetical. Firm A, realizing that in order to acquire monopolistic control of a market it shares with B it must eliminate that latter firm as an independent decision-maker, plots a predatory pricing campaign against B. To de-

stroy B's pricing independence, A has three possible avenues of attack. It must either (a) drive B out of the market, (b) merge with it, or (c) induce it to cooperate with A's plans to monopolize the market.

Economic analysis postulates that the first alternative, an attempt to drive B out of the market, will not be undertaken simply because it is the *least profitable* route for A to follow. Unlike the situation in real physical "wars," one does not simply "drive out" a rival business firm. Should B become bankrupt, its fixed assets will revert to its creditors, who will normally either operate them or dispose of them to the highest bidder, thus replacing the old competitor with a new one. Firm B can be made to vanish in a physical sense only if (1) fixed costs represent an insignificant fraction of this particular industry's total costs; (2) firm A's fixed assets are sufficiently obsolete to be economically valueless; or (3) these assets can be readily shifted into other industries. In cases (1) and (3) here, however, the industry involved will possess entry barriers sufficiently low to prevent firm A's subsequent exploitation of its monopoly position and, in case (2), the competition represented by firm B must by definition have been very tenuous to begin with. We thus conclude that predation to "drive out" a competitor is an extremely unlikely occurrence and that, should it actually occur (through, for example, a misunderstanding on the part of A), it will not be harmful to competition in any meaningful sense.

Mergers and Predatory Pricing

If predation is to be undertaken by A, then, it will almost certainly have as its objective the inducement of B to "cooperate" with or accommodate A by either selling out to it, merging with it, or colluding (formally or tacitly) with it. Will predation be employed to attain any of these ends? Consider first the possibility of a merger. We assume that the *monopoly power* B's assets will confer upon A are valued by the latter at X dollars and that these assets are worth Y dollars to firm B

---

[3] Selling at a "loss" refers to the use of a price that fails to cover short-run average *total* cost (as reflected in accounting data), a definition that of course produces a much higher figure than either short-run *marginal* cost or average variable cost (both of which would be preferable on theoretical grounds).

[4] A further factor here is the rather high probability that, if predatory pricing is really involved, the price will in fact be plunged below cost. The lower the price, the quicker the victim can be expected to capitulate. And the quicker the victim is brought to his knees, the more profitable the practice will be for the predator. See Koller, note 2, supra, pp. 18–20, 30–31.

[5] For a more detailed justification of the criteria used here in defining the practice at issue, see Koller, note 2, supra.

[6] See particularly Telser, Leeman, and McGee, note 1, supra.

itself or to any third firm C that might acquire them. Under these conditions, the price at which A could purchase them from B would necessarily lie somewhere *between* X and Y, since it will pay no more than X and B can sell them to C for Y. Should we expect A to undertake a price war against B? A knows that the price cannot be reduced below Y and that, if C turns out to be a well-financed firm, it (A) may end up in the position of having paid the cost of a price war for the opportunity of bargaining later on with a more powerful opponent for the assets initially controlled by B. It would therefore be rational for A to offer B *at least* Y dollars for its assets, a price that will reflect the capitalized value of any monopoly profit either B or C could have obtained through collusion with A. At the same time, B, having the alternative of either accepting an amount of at least Y from A or suffering the anticipated price war losses and *then* having to accept Y from C, should rationally choose the former. As Telser has concluded, then,[7] firms A and B should be expected to come to a mutually-acceptable agreement among themselves without the occurrence of a price war. A similar analysis applies to the predation-for-collusion situation, both tacit and formal, and carries the implication that *predation will occur only through some misunderstanding of their available alternatives on the part of A or B, that is, by mistake.*

Profit-Maximization and Market Knowledge

In more formal terms, predation will never occur in any form if one assumes *both* (a) profit-maximizing motivations on the part of the firms involved and (b) perfect knowledge of the market factors involved. If one relaxes the first assumption—that the firms are motivated by a desire to maximize their respective profits—the result here (as in other areas of economic theory) is of course to introduce general uncertainty into

the equation. There is no reliable evidence as to either the propensity of corporate executives to engage in purely vindictive (non-profit maximizing) price wars nor the willingness of their directors and stockholders to allow such a dissipation of the assets of their organizations in pricing adventures that promise long-run (rather than merely short-run) losses.

A relaxation of the second assumption, the existence of perfect market knowledge, introduces, as noted, the possibility of price war through miscalculation. In this situation, however, again as noted, no social harm will result: If its purpose is to drive out a competitor, competition will not in fact be impaired; and if the object is to precipitate a merger or collusion, the outcome will be no worse than it would have been had A and B possessed greater sagacity and proceeded directly to these alternatives in the first place.

The Empirical Investigation

Is there a flaw somewhere in this tidy theoretical analysis of the predatory pricing phenomenon, some unsupported assumption or hypothesis that causes it to miss what the layman and the antitrust agencies apparently have no difficulty finding in the "real" world? Do financially powerful entrepreneurs, with the same disregard for economic theory that the bumblebee is said to hold for the laws of aerodynamics, nonetheless use predatory pricing in the everyday business world to convert workably competitive industries into effectively monopolistic ones? The instant study was designed to probe the allegedly predatory pricing examples of the past 100 years in American history with an eye to determining whether the evidence can fairly be said to support the charge, i.e., whether it is really likely that the three criteria mentioned above—sales below cost, a predatory intent, and success in eliminating the rival or bending him to the predator's will —were in fact present in those historical examples that underlie the popular view of the phenomenon.

---

[7] Note 1, supra.

The Case Data

Unfortunately for the comprehensiveness of the study, a complete list of history's instances of past predation is not available. And even if such a list had been available, the necessary data on the individual examples would almost certainly have been lacking. Fortunately, however, at least some of the more important instances could be examined in some detail, including most of those we would have preferred to examine had we been allowed to select our sample, that is, the more serious instances of alleged predatory pricing, those that were considered serious enough by those involved, and by the authorities, to justify formal complaints and legal action.

The leading antitrust reporting service, the CCH *Trade Regulation Reporter* (Commerce Clearing House, Chicago), lists approximately 123 federal antitrust cases since the passage of the Sherman Act in 1890 in which it was alleged that behavior generally resembling predation had played a significant role in the matter complained of. In 28 of these cases, the defendant was acquitted (on other than procedural grounds), leaving a total of 95 instances in which individuals or corporations were legally adjudged to have engaged in what the tribunal in question found to have been predatory pricing behavior. While the variety of forms under which cases are brought and the sheer volume of the relevant case material makes it less than certain that this is in fact a complete population of all such cases, there can be little doubt that it includes all of the more important ones, that is, those that are repeatedly cited in the court decisions and that have created the contemporary image of predation.

The Sample Studied—26 Cases

Of the 95 "convictions" for predatory pricing, however, only 26 of them both involved a substantive trial and produced a factual record adequate for the kind of analysis employed here.[8] The findings reported below are thus based on a study of these 26 cases, including the court records, the briefs of the parties, and the published decisions. (It should be emphasized that this data, gathered from the files of the various federal trial and appellate courts across the country, and from the Federal Records Centers, is a great deal more comprehensive than the fragmentary factual material contained in the published decisions themselves.)

The Study Criteria—Predation and Competitive Injury

The evidence in each of these 26 cases was analyzed to determine, as noted, (1) whether the accused predator had reduced his price to less than his short-run average total cost; (2) whether this seemed to have been done with a predatory intent; and (3) whether the activity was successful in either eliminating a competitor, precipitating a merger, or improving market "discipline." (If all three elements were present, the case was considered an exam-

---

[8] 18 of the others went to trial but on procedural issues that produced no substantive information for analysis. And while another 19 also went to trial (before FTC hearing examiners), the official "findings of fact" were not sufficiently complete to permit a meaningful analysis. And a third group, one involving 32 cases in which "consent decrees" had been entered by either the federal courts or the FTC, was similarly excluded because of insufficient data in the records. (In proceedings of this kind, the defendant neither admits nor denies the charges and the tribunal is not required to determine the facts of the matter.) It should be added, however, that, on the basis of such data as *was* available on these three groups of excluded cases (69 altogether), the findings and analysis would probably be much the same here as they were for the group actually studied in detail, the 26 cases emphasized below. The barriers to entry around the industries involved in these excluded cases, for example, are quite similar to those around the 26 industries included in the sample that was analyzed—and barriers are of course a good indicator of the profitability of predation and of its potential harm to resource allocation (competition).

ple of "successful" predation. If the first two were present but not the third, it was considered a case of "attempted" predation.) In addition, the examples of successful predation were further analyzed to determine (a) whether the predator found the activity in question to be profitable and (b) whether that predatory pricing caused significant harm to "resource allocation," the latter term being defined as the making of the market in question significantly more imperfect than it was prior to the challenged activity.

The Findings—Predation 'Successful' in 5 Cases

The individual case studies are summarized in Table 1, below. Our conclusions are these:

1. In 16 of the 26 cases, predation does not seem to have actually taken place. And in another three of them, the data was insufficient to determine whether predation had been present or not.

2. In the remaining seven cases, predation seems to have been at least attempted, i.e., below-cost pricing was in fact undertaken with what appears to have been a predatory intent.

3. These seven cases of predation were almost evenly divided—four to three —between our Type 1 (predatory pricing to eliminate a rival) and Type 2 (predatory pricing to precipitate a merger or collusion) varieties of the practice.

4. Four of these seven cases of predation were *successful,* i.e., either the rival was eliminated or the merger or market discipline the predator had in mind was achieved. Three of them involved Type 2 predation (to precipitate a merger or collusion), the other being a Type 1 (to eliminate a rival) example. Had the three indeterminate cases mentioned in 1, above, been classified as actual predation cases,

another example of Type 1 predation would have been added.

Only 'Collusive' Predation Harmful to Competition

5. Of the five examples of successful predation found here, significant harm to resource allocation (competition) seems to have been a reasonable probability in three of them, *all of which involved Type 2 predation, predatory pricing to effect a merger or collusion.*

6. Predation of the Type 1 variety, that is, to drive out one's competitors and establish a monopoly, does not seem to have been much of a problem during the period studied. Of the 22 cases that involved this allegation, the alleged predator was successful in eliminating *a* competitor in two instances (in no case were all of the competitors eliminated) but there was no reasonable probability of significant harm to resource allocation or effective competition in either of them.

7. Type 2 predation, on the other hand, seems to have been a more significant phenomenon. Of the four such cases studied, real predation was probably present in three of them (the issue was uncertain in the fourth) and all seem to have involved significant harm to resource allocation in the industries in question.

Role of Government in Predatory Pricing

8. A particularly interesting finding here is that, of the seven cases in which predation seems clearly to have been attempted, four of them involved *governmental activity* which seems to have helped precipitate the objectionable private behavior. Tariff policies triggered the predation in two instances (the *E. B. Muller* and *Forster Mfg.* cases), another involved a clumsily-executed excise tax measure which virtually compelled the predation in

question (the *Porto Rican American Tobacco* case), and a fourth involved a local licensing ordinance, the repeal of which seems to have created unusually severe competitive conditions in the affected market (the *National Dairy Products* case). The single instance of successful Type 1 predation is, interestingly enough, included here.

The Tobacco Case (1944)

A brief example will illustrate the kind of analysis involved here. In the *American Tobacco* case of 1944,[9] the three major cigarette companies, American Tobacco, R. J. Reynolds, and Liggett & Myers, were charged with collusively and predatorily selling below cost to eliminate a group of smaller cigarette manufacturers that had successfully invaded the market with a lower-priced product (the so-called "10-cent brands"). In October 1929, the three alleged predators had increased their wholesale prices from $6.00 to $6.40 per 1000 cigarettes and in June 1931, despite the fact that (thanks to a widespread economic depression) production costs had been declining for years, they raised them again, from $6.40 to $6.85 per 1000 cigarettes. The result was that 1931, a year that was not a particularly good one for most industries, was the most profitable year in the history of the cigarette industry.

The Price Cut of 1933

This increased prosperity of the big-three cigarette firms was short-lived, however. Their higher wholesale prices quickly resulted in higher *retail* prices on their own cigarettes (the "standard brands"); the depression had made the smoking public increasingly price-conscious; and a number of previously unimportant companies soon began producing cigarettes designed to retail at 10 cents per package, or 5 cents less

---

[9] *United States v. American Tobacco Company et al.,* 147 F 2d 93 (6th Cir., 1944).

than the retail price of the big-three's own "standard brands." The result was that the 10-cent brands, whose market share had been less than 1% during the first six months of 1931, saw this figure rise steadily to 22.78% in November 1932.

In January 1933, the big three reduced their wholesale list prices from $6.85 to $6.00 (versus a $4.75 price for the 10-cent brands at wholesale) and, in February 1933, to $5.50. They also made a vigorous effort to get the retailers to narrow the *retail* differential between theirs and the 10-cent brands, an effort that apparently enjoyed some success in view of the fact that the average price for *all* cigarettes, including the 10-cent brands, was, according to a Department of Labor study at the time, down to 11.5 cents in 32 leading cities in June 1933. The result was that the average monthly market share of the 10-cent brands fell from 20.67% in the last four months of 1932 to 9.62% in 1933. In January 1934, the big three raised their wholesale list prices to $6.10 per 1000 and kept them there for three years, to January 1937, when they were raised to $6.25. The average monthly market shares of the 10-cent brands were 11.32% in 1934 and 11.95% in 1935.

Temporary Losses by 'Big Three'

Were the lowest prices charged by the big-three cigarette firms, the $5.50 wholesale price that prevailed from February 1933 to January 1934, below their short-run average total costs? Apparently not. True, two of them, Reynolds and American, incurred a loss during the last three months of 1933. They all operated in the black for the year as a whole, however, and they would have made a profit even during the last quarter had it not been for a new processing tax (i.e., a tax on tobacco processed out of inventory) levied under the newly-enacted Agricultural Adjustment Act in October 1933 *after* the $5.50 price had been put into effect. In other words, their losses during that period were traceable not to the lower prices themselves but to a later—

Table 1 • Findings of the Case Studies[i]

Case Name	Industry	Was Price Cut Below Cost?	Was There a Predatory Intent?	Was the Price War Successful?	Was the Activity Profitable?	Was the Activity Harmful?
United States v. Standard Oil Company of New Jersey (1907)	Petroleum	Probable	No	No	—[ii]	—
United States v. American Tobacco Company (1908)	Tobacco Products	Yes	Yes[iii]	Yes	Yes[iii]	Yes[iii]
Nash v. United States (1910)	Naval Stores	—	—	No	No	No
United States v. E. I. DuPont de Nemours and Company, Inc. (1911)[iv]	Explosives	Probable	Yes[iii]	Yes	Yes[iii]	Yes[iii]
United States v. Hamburgh-American S. S. Line, et al. (1911)	Ocean Shipping	Unknown	Unknown[iii]	Unknown	Unknown	No
Porto Rican American Tobacco Co. v. American Tobacco Co. (1929)	Cigarettes	Yes	Unknown	Unknown	Unknown	Unknown
E. B. Muller and Company et al. v. Federal Trade Commission (1941)	Chicory	Yes	Probable	No	No	No
United States v. American Tobacco Company et al. (1944)	Cigarettes	Yes	No	No	—	—
Samuel H. Moss, Inc. v. Federal Trade Commission (1945)	Rubber Stamps	Unknown	No	Yes	No	No
United States v. New York Great Atlantic and Pacific Tea Company (1946)	Grocery Retailing	Unknown	No	No	—	—
Gordon, Wolf, Cohen Company, Inc. v. Independent Halvah and Candies, Inc. (1949)	Halvah	No	No	Yes	No	No
Atlantic Company v. Citizen's Ice and Cold Storage Company et al. (1949)	Ice	Yes	Unknown	No	Unknown	Not Likely
A. J. Goodman and Son, Inc. v. United Lacquer Manufacturing Company (1949)	Highway Lacquer	No	No	No	—	No
Moore v. Mead Service Co. et al. (1950)	Bread	Yes	No	Yes	Not Likely	No

Table 1 (*Continued*)

Case Name	Industry	Was Price Cut Below Cost?	Was There a Predatory Intent?	Was the Price War Successful?	Was the Activity Profitable?	Was the Activity Harmful?
Herschel California Fruit Products Co., Inc. et al. v. Hunt's Foods, Inc. (1953)	Tomato Paste	Yes	Unknown	No	No	No
Vance v. Safeway Stores, Inc. (1956)	Grocery Retailing	Yes	Unknown	Yes	No	No
Maryland Baking Company, Inc. v. Federal Trade Commission (1957)	Ice-Cream Cones	No	Unknown	No	No	No
Atlas Building Products Co. v. Diamond Block and Gravel Company (1958)	Concrete Block	No	Unknown	No	No	No
H. J. Heinz Company v. Beech-Nut Life Savers, Inc. (1958)	Baby Food	Yes	No	No	—	—
Anheuser Busch, Inc. v. Federal Trade Commission (1957)	Beer	No	No	No	—	—
General Gas Corporation v. National Utilities of Gainesville, Inc. (1959)	LP Gas	No	No	Unknown	No	No
Union Leader Corp. v. Newspapers of New England, Inc. (1960)	Newspapers	Probable	Yes	No	No	No
United States v. National Dairy Products Corp. et al. (1961)	Fluid Milk	Yes	Yes[iii]	Yes	Yes[iii]	Yes[iii]
Reynolds Metals Company v. Federal Trade Commission (1962)	Florist Foil	Yes	No	No	No	No
Forster Manufacturing Co., Inc. v. Federal Trade Commission (1964)	Wooden Meat Skewers	Yes	Probable	Yes	No	No
Utah Pie Company v. Continental Baking Company et al. (1965)	Frozen Pies	Yes	No	No	No	No

[i] Roland H. Koller II, *Predatory Pricing in a Market Economy* (University of Wisconsin, 1969), pp. 336–337.
[ii] Information not appropriate in the case involved.
[iii] Type II predation was involved in this case.
[iv] For a recent and somewhat contrary view, see Elzinga, note 1, supra.

and externally imposed—increase in their costs. It was never alleged by the government, interestingly enough, that the third member of the big-three, Liggett & Myers, ever sold below cost. And as soon as the losses became apparent to the other two firms, the price was increased to the profitable $6.10 per 1000 figure.

No Predatory 'Intent'

Was there a predatory "intent" here? If so, it was inconsistent with, as noted, both the shallowness of the price cuts allegedly used to implement it and with the further fact that it was rather plainly unsuccessful. The share of the 10-cent brands rose from, as noted, 9.62% in 1933, to 10.4% in 1936, and to 14.2% in 1939. They thrived until July 1940, when a tax increase prompted them to raise their wholesale prices from $4.75 per 1000 cigarettes to $5.05. They began to fade from the American scene shortly thereafter. The big-three defendants, beginning in 1929 with 83.6% of the market, saw their share fall to 76.4% in 1932, to 74.9% in 1934, and to 63.2% in 1939.

Perhaps the most intriguing piece of evidence in this case, however, had to do with the subject of profits. During the most intense period of the alleged "price war," from 1932 to 1933, the profits of the big-three defendants had declined by $45 million. But in approximately 13,000 pages of testimony, exhibits, and briefs, the author was *unable to find one sentence concerning the profits of the 10-cent firms.*

Price Increases and Market Power

We conclude that what happened in this case was the very *opposite* of predatory pricing as defined in this study. *It was the price increase of 1931*—one effected, as noted, in the face of a national depression and declining costs in the industry—*that represented the willful exercise of market power, not the price cut of 1933.* That latter event reflected a quite ordinary (nonpredatory) response to an unexpected situation, namely, a realization by the big-

three defendants that they had previously underestimated the elasticity of the demand for their particular "brands" of cigarettes. As collusive oligopolists pushing up their prices to exploit the assumed inelasticity of the demand for their products (consumer insensitivity to price increases), they discovered that the public was in fact quite willing to shift to lower-priced substitute products and that, if they were to prevent a still further erosion of their market shares, they were going to have to compete on a *price* basis. And even in the face of those large market-share losses, these big-three defendants were still unwilling to pay the price (in terms of lost revenues) that would have been required to either eliminate those firms altogether or even to push their market share back to the less than 1% figure they had held before they had been given a "break" by the big-three's improvident price increase of 1931.

Monopoly Power and Tariff Policy

One further observation might be made here. If the government had in fact been concerned in this case with the exploitation of market power and with the putting of effective limits on its exercise, it might have addressed itself to the *tariff protection* enjoyed by the industry. At the time of the 1933 price cuts that formed the basis for this case of alleged predatory pricing, cigarettes enjoyed a tariff barrier of $4.50 per pound or roughly $10.50 per 1000 cigarettes *plus* a 25% ad valorem tax.[10]

---

[10] There was another charge involved in the case, the contention that the big-three defendants had also attempted to destroy the 10-cent brands by bidding up the price of the low-grade tobacco used by the latter and forcing down the price of the high-grade varieties used by themselves. The evidence here, however, was, if anything, even more ambiguous than that offered on the predatory pricing charge. The price spread between the high- and the low-grade tobacco, for example, was only slightly smaller at the end of the relevant period than at the beginning and actually seems to have *increased* during the middle part of the period, i.e., during the time when the defendants were allegedly closing it.

Qualifications—Availability of Complainants

A number of qualifications should be mentioned here. First, since predation designed to precipitate a merger or collusion is likely to leave both parties relatively satisfied and hence lacking in an incentive to complain, a study confined to court cases might well understate the frequency of the phenomenon in question. It would not understate, however, its *severity* in those instances in which there was in fact an unsatisfied party and in which a complaint had actually been filed. And of course there is no lack of an injured party with an incentive to make his grievance known in those instances where this kind of predation is unsuccessful (e.g., where no merger or collusion resulted) nor in those cases, both successful and otherwise, where predation of the Type 1 variety (to eliminate a competitor) is involved.

A second qualification centers around the argument that the relative infrequency of predation as reported here is explained simply by the fact that it is against the law. The major thrust of our findings, however, is not simply that predatory pricing does not occur very often but that, when it *does* occur, it produces little or no harm to competition. And if, as we maintain, the activity itself is for the most part harmless, it makes no real difference whether or not it has been deterred by the law's critical attitude toward it. Nothing in our analysis suggests that a worse form of such behavior would have been found in the absence of these anti-predation laws.

Non-Predatory 'Price Wars'

A third criticism of such a study is the argument that its results fail to take into account those instances where smaller firms, though not actually subjected to industrial predation, have nonetheless *feared* a predatory attack and thus refrained from entering certain industries or from expanding their operations in them. Given an institutional setting in which any firm able to demonstrate that it has been a victim of such a practice is rewarded with three times the amount of its actual damages, it seems difficult to believe that anyone is actually deterred from otherwise profitable behavior by a fear of this kind.

A fourth and final qualification might be noted here, one centering around the argument that, by defining predation so as to exclude the more *moderate* kinds of price wars that presumably occur with some frequency in the economy, we have again understated the actual effects of the basic phenomenon in issue, particularly its effects in maintaining price discipline in oligopolistic markets. A limitation of that kind, however, is inherent in all studies. One has to have a cut-off point somewhere and, because our primary interest here was in that variety of the phenomenon that is basic to the popular notion of predation— the use of prices that produce short-term losses but long-term monopoly gains—the boundaries of the instant study were drawn at that particular conceptual line.

Policy Implications

Predatory pricing of the kind designed to eliminate a competitor being, in our study, an infrequent occurrence of fairly insignificant competitive effects, it follows that our concern with predation, if any, should be focused on the other variety of the phenomenon, predatory pricing designed to precipitate either merger or collusion. Here, however, we are met with the fact that anticompetitive mergers and cartels *are themselves already illegal*, leaving us to wonder how frequently one can really expect a firm to sell at a loss to discipline a rival when it knows that the anti-merger laws will not permit it to buy that rival out in the end and that, unless the latter's plant and equipment are of no value to anyone else, it will ultimately have to face a new rival who may or may not be more cooperative than the first one. The net result, then, is that the anti-predation laws forbid a practice that is either not likely to occur (predatory pricing to eliminate a rival) and/or one that, if it occurs, is likely to produce an effect that is itself unlawful under other statutes (predation to induce merger or collusion).

Predatory Pricing and Conglomerate Mergers

A second implication here has to do with the phenomenon of the conglomerate merger. One of the major factors in the prevention of predatory pricing of the Type 1 variety analyzed in this study, predation to eliminate a rival, is the assumed opportu-

nity of the victim to sell out to a *third-party* buyer (firm C in the example used above). And it is of course precisely the merger-minded conglomerate firm that constitutes the major source of merger partners for such beleaguered small firms, those that feel themselves threatened by more powerful rivals in their respective markets. The logical conclusion, then, is that if one wants to confine industrial predation to its present status of popular myth and not to encourage its emergence as an economic reality, an indiscriminate prohibition of all conglomerate mergers would not really be the optimum policy.

40. Some Economic Issues in Robinson-Patman Land

JOHN S. McGEE [*]

Introduction

We are in the thirtieth year of something called the Robinson-Patman Act.[1] In the study of obscure poetry and lost cities, as with Robinson-Patman, there have been many efforts to discover the intentions of authors and builders both for the sport of quest and to learn what and where things are and what they mean. Archaeology, geology, and case-watching are not useless. For holy men and technicians versed in them can earn their fees. It is worth something to neutralize curses for drilling into sacred tombs. It will pay to avoid (or prepare for) the pains of blundering into minefields and cutting into geyser sources, even if no high social purpose is served by their being there in the first place. The task of the antitrust bar is harder, and the fees higher, in some part, I suppose, because the law may move.

There is some evidence that Robinson-Patman standards may now be shifting, even for eternals like brokerage, costs, and competitive "injury." Nevertheless, in this paper I have wholly avoided the temptation to review cases and to point out shocking or pleasing ways in which the law appears recently to have changed, or failed to change. I have done so for several reasons. Given the instability of legal trajectories and the character of case reports, the law reviews and other professional sources have handled the case-to-case accumulation about as well as can be; and voluminous treatises have added further to our sense of history and prospect.[2] Although recent changes can raise false hopes and obscure larger and more abiding issues, times of change are good ones for rethinking old and new goals. For reason may channel movement. Further, to be somewhat less hopeful, the reports may serve well enough as symbols for long-run legal classifications; but I am leery about using them as empirical evidence for policy evaluation. Finally, as an economist I think a different job needs to be attempted with Robinson-Patman. Although for a long time good and bad economics has been filtering into antitrust, in recent years scholars have begun systematically to take the law apart, using the machinery of economic theory together with empirical observation. The process has now gone far in academic circles; and I think we are on the threshold of a much more open intellectual debate about antitrust policy.[3]

Aaron Director of the University of Chicago has been a powerful participant and influence in completely re-analyzing the law, theory, and facts of monopolizing practices, for example.[4] The work of Morris

Reprinted, with permission, from a symposium, on The Antitrust Laws and Single-Firm conduct, appearing in *Law and Contemporary Problems* (Vol. 30, No. 3, Summer, 1965), published by the Duke University School of Law, Durham, North Carolina. Copyright, 1965, by Duke University.

[*] A.B. 1947, University of Texas; Ph.D. 1952, Vanderbilt University. Professor of Economics, Duke University.

[1] 49 Stat. 1526 (1936), 15 U.S.C. §§ 13–13b, 21a (1964).

[2] See, *e.g.*, CORWIN D. EDWARDS, THE PRICE DISCRIMINATION LAW (1959); FREDERICK C. ROWE, PRICE DISCRIMINATION UNDER THE ROBINSON-PATMAN ACT (1962) and SUPPLEMENT (1964).

[3] What is relatively novel is not contention but that opposing academics, many of whom share the same economic objectives, are digging to the roots of rival theories and visions of reality. What is going on is not business apology but academic radicalism in the best sense.

[4] See his classic article with Edward H. Levi, *Law*

Adelman, particularly with respect to Robinson-Patman, has become classic.[5] Both have shown the merits, and surprises, of going to transcripts of record rather than to the reports. A recent spirited exchange in a leading law review is more evidence.[6] Old assumptions and assertions are being ventilated. The antitrust field will never be the same again.

It would be presumptuous both to announce a new wave and to claim to be riding on it. But what I will try here is to comment on a few Robinson-Patman problems in a spirit that I hope will not only be consistent with that of the new debate but will contribute in small ways to it. I do not proceed section by section to analyze the meaning or effect of the statute; and I ignore completely sections 2(c) through 2(f). This essay may not help anybody win a case. I hope it will persuade or shock some practitioners, academics, and jurists into revisiting their logic, transcripts, and the real world.

I

Priorities in Antitrust

If there is anything that economics can teach us it is that we cannot do as much of everything as we would like at the same time. Knowingly or not, we all proceed under some system of priorities. It may be random, rational, or perverse. Antitrust is also subject to principles of scarce resources. Whether antitrust is or should be motivated by purely economic considerations is perhaps debatable. Nevertheless, as an economist I will concentrate on economic values, leaving others aside. This is more convenient and useful than purely narrow-minded, for it would be helpful to everyone to know what it costs to pursue noneconomic goals.

---

and the Future: Trade Regulation, 51 Nw. U.L. Rev. 281 (1956).

[5] For a bibliography through 1961, see PACKER, THE STATE OF RESEARCH IN ANTITRUST LAW 154–55, n.16 (1963).

[6] Bork & Bowman *versus* Blake & Jones, *The Goals of Antitrust: A Dialogue on Policy,* 65 COLUM. L. REV. 363 (1965).

In addition, the discussion will prove useful for a later section. To establish priorities requires standards of importance.

Economic priorities are based on alternative costs and benefits. Classical economics furnishes some guidelines. A key concept is full competitive equilibrium, one important conceptual benchmark for judging economic performance. In full equilibrium no firm would have any incentive to alter its output rate or to leave the industry of which it is a part. The firm's total proceeds would precisely equal its total costs, including competitive returns on owners' capital and sweat. No one outside the industry could improve his position by entering it. The industry would be of equilibrium size. For each firm, marginal cost—the change in total cost accompanying a unit change in output—would equal price. In a competitive world, costs would reflect returns to resources in alternative uses. Hence, marginal costs would approximate the worth of what is being given up to produce the good in question.

Similarly, in equilibrium, consumers would have no incentive to alter their consumption patterns. Given tastes, income distribution, and the prices of all goods and services, the traditional theory argues that this equilibrium pattern maximizes consumer satisfaction. Consumers' satisfaction is the god; the competitive process and market mechanism—together with firms and factors of production—are judged by how well they serve it.

Of course, even competitive equilibrium need not always be "full" in that sense. Though prices everywhere equaled each existing firm's marginal cost, in the short run revenues could exceed or fall short of total costs. Profits indicate areas in which goods are "worth" more than they cost to produce, and new firms will spring up until equilibrium is achieved. Losses shrink an industry.

Monopoly is something else again. If it does anything relevant, monopoly raises price above marginal cost, *i.e.,* makes price higher than the worth of resources necessary to do the job. As a consequence, consumers buy less of a monopolized good, and more of other goods, than would otherwise be the case. According to traditional theory, consumer satisfaction is thereby reduced. It is this allocative and real income effect—too little production of monopolized goods and too much of competitive goods—that is really at issue, and not whether a monopolist is rich. In theory, at least, it would be possible to measure the loss in consumer welfare—roughly one-half of the product of quantity reduction and price increase—because of monopoly, and there have been some attempts to do so.[7]

The purely economic rationale for antitrust or monopoly regulation must be that it increases consumer welfare both by more than it costs and by more than the same volume of resources could accomplish in other ways.[8] Nevertheless, I will uncritically accept the total antitrust budget as given. However its amount is determined, the antitrust budget should be allocated to maximize the satisfaction of consumers and not that of agency staffs, businessmen, or other special interests. If it is legitimate to ignore possible net values of antitrust as entertainment, the goal is to attack (or avoid) the most important monopolies or monopolizing practices within the reach of law.

Subtle questions arise with respect to "importance." If a potential antitrust case could yield general, unambiguous, and self-diffusing rules, its proper priority position would have little to do with the importance of the industry or monopoly with which it specifically deals. Agencies might properly try to generate as much (and hopefully as valid) principle as possible—even if developed from trivial industries—for the budget they have.[9] There are several possible reasons to distrust this procedure in the real world. Case-by-case economics and law often lack explicit and coherent theoretic underpinning. As a consequence, the whole procedure has an *ad hoc* flavor, which is often emphasized by emptily formalistic distinctions between fact situations that often differ in economically irrelevant ways. However desirable or inevitable this may be in law, it defers or bars rules of general application. Even if this were not so, whatever general rules do emerge are not self-diffusing. Out of millions of firms and billions of transactions very few are chosen for antitrust action. Even if it is expensive to be chosen, odds are long. It is not surprising that many businessmen claim they pay absolutely no attention to the Robinson-Patman Act. In any case, it is not proved that statutes like Robinson-Patman have large effects on business conduct generally.[10]

---

[7] See Harberger, *Monopoly and Resource Allocation*, 44 AM. ECON. REV. 77 (1954), and three articles by Schwartzman: *The Effect of Monopoly on Price*, 67 J. POL. ECON. 352 (1959); *The Burden of Monopoly*, 68 *id.* 627 (1960); *The Effect of Monopoly: A Correction*, 69 *id.* 494 (1961). *But see* Stigler, *The Statistics of Monopoly and Merger*, 64 J. POL. ECON. 33 (1956); Lancaster & Lipsey, *The General Theory of Second Best*, 24 REV. ECON. STUDIES 11 (1957); E. J. MISHAN, WELFARE ECONOMICS: FIVE INTRODUCTORY ESSAYS, esp. xii–xv, 24–27, 28–30, 79–80, 155–83 (1964).

[8] Costs of fear, avoidance, and litigation are additional taxes on business subject to the law. Their full allocation and income distribution effects are, in practice, somewhat obscure.

One neglected implication of monopoly theory should be noted at this point. Traditional analysis has it that the gain to monopolists is less than the loss to consumers—*i.e.*, that there is a "dead-weight" loss from monopoly. For a simple introduction to the point, see PAUL A. SAMUELSON, ECONOMICS, AN INTRODUCTORY ANALYSIS, 496–97 (6th ed. 1964). It therefore appears that consumers could buy out monopolies (for prices that would satisfy their owners) and still be better off. On this simplified level, however, there could still be a rationale for antitrust. In the first place, it may be prohibitively expensive or administratively impossible to form the necessary syndicate of large numbers of consumers. Second, it is possible that government can break (or avoid) the monopoly for less than it would take to buy out the monopoly.

[9] If results of policy are perverse, priorities might profitably be reversed. Application of perverse rules might then be made as expensive as possible and confined to as few and as trivial areas as possible.

[10] Nor, to digress, is it clear to me that present procedures against mislabeling, inflammable sweaters, and so forth are more effective (or efficient) than simply publicizing quality findings à la

Some of the foregoing argument sounds as though antitrust enforcement is random. Apparently it is not, which may be a mixed blessing. There are several reasons to suppose nonrandomness in actual antitrust enforcement. For example, it is conceivable that the criteria by which agency performance is judged and differences in emphasis in the statutes may encourage the selection of many relatively sure, but economically trivial, cases. The historic preponderance of section 2(c) cases, for example, and the apparent increase in other *per se* types of Robinson-Patman proceedings may not be fortuitous.

Of course, there is nothing inherently evil in nonrandomness; but bias should make sense.[11] For, even if all that traditional static theory says is taken whole, all existing or threatened monopolies are not equally important. And, if legal rules are both ambiguous and applied case-by-case, it makes sense to emphasize the probable direct consequences of each case. From the standpoint of economic efficiency, what should be opposed are those monopolies that would or actually do most reduce output and raise price for the longest time. For this appraisal the absolute quantities are highly relevant. A small increase in price on a very large volume has the same economic importance as a large increase in price on a small volume. Each individual case of small price effects on small volumes is simply trivial unless such effects last correspondingly longer. Rational priorities for the antimonopoly laws seem at least to require estimates of (1) the industry and/or monopolizing firm's (*a*) costs and (*b*) demand elasticities over a range of prices and (2) the probable

duration of the existing or prospective monopoly under consideration.

These look like modest requirements;[12] but perhaps we can be content, or at least better off than we now are, with even less. The Robinson-Patman Act and the Clayton Act[13] deal importantly with incipient monopoly. A marked change in the pattern of litigation might occur even if the Federal Trade Commission ranked potential cases by simply asking (and honestly answering) the following questions with respect to each: (1) if the most pessimistic view of this industry's development is correct, approximately how much will consumers suffer? (2) What is the most probable consumer loss? (3) How long is it reasonable to suppose that either resulting distortion would persist? Perhaps price discrimination cases would still be brought against firms making rubber stamps, flax rugs, garments, or numbering machines and against atomistic fish and food packers, brokers, and other market intermediaries; but one could hope not.[14]

Survival characteristics of antitrust administrators and lawyers, as well as those of college professors, are substantially influenced by the rules of the games they play. If the budget of an agency and the salaries, fame, and prestige of its employees are directly related to the number of cases it brings, or wins, the result is unambiguously

---

Consumer Reports. Similarly, it is conceivable that substantial rewards to informers—geared to value-added or, even, sales—might prove more worthwhile in combating cartels than less direct approaches.

[11] The drift of this argument is especially likely to infuriate those who think in terms of common criminal offenses. Is one murder (and murder-victim) more important than another? So far as economics is concerned, the answer is, clearly, "yes."

[12] Observers have long noted impressive evidence of blind theologies in antitrust. Here is some more, if more is needed: confronted by even slender demands for data showing the importance of any or all monopoly power, some economists, at least, instantaneously complain that the data are unobtainable or that search for them would slacken the pace of antitrust; yet the same economists who plead lack of information see no inconsistency in their perennial assertions that the monopoly problem *in toto* is great and that this or that monopoly should be dissolved forthwith.

[13] 38 Stat. 730 (1914), as amended, 15 U.S.C. §§ 12–27 (1964).

[14] For a plausible explanation of the historic pattern of Robinson-Patman Act enforcement by section, see CORWIN D. EDWARDS, THE PRICE DISCRIMINATION LAW, esp. 69–72 (1959).

predicted by economic theory. They will bring large numbers of cheap and easy cases, emphasizing *per se* sections and those whose rules of thumb are satisfied with minimum toil. In some instances, a good deal of the toil can even be provided by special interests. Since there is no direct bonus or other mechanism permitting agency employees to share in any economic benefits they provide to consumers by avoiding or breaking important monopolies, they are not to be blamed if they emphasize different things than the broader social interest. The principal amelioration, if any, would arise either from irrational zeal or the possibility of later employment outside government in jobs requiring skills revealed in nontrivial litigation and research.

Lamentation about the "disproportionate" emphasis upon trivial research by college faculties is also somewhat misdirected. Students pay tuition to universities, not to individual teachers. If salary, promotions, and prestige depend upon producing large numbers of articles, that is what society will get, even if this means trivial articles and total inattention to teaching. The principal amelioration, if any, would arise from irrational zeal or the possibility of later and better employment in other universities or in nonacademic jobs requiring skills revealed in nontrivial research or good teaching.

I would welcome, and society should demand, a detailed statement showing how Federal Trade Commission priorities are actually established and pointing out what legal (and even political) constraints influence the process.

Presumably some operational priority standards could be developed by using industry (or market) size and, perhaps, bracket estimates of demand elasticity. For example, suppose we observe an industry in which price discrimination of one kind or another allegedly threatens competition. If the industry has been small under competition—as measured by value added, income generated, and so forth—it would be even smaller under monopoly. Unless there are good reasons to think that the industry price elasticity is extraordinarily low over wide ranges—betraying poor total substitution from all other industries—it simply does not very much matter what happens to competition in that industry. Of course, if there are no other kinds of industries in which bad things may happen and this kind is very numerous, aggregate effects could be serious. But so long as there are more important problems, economic analysis seems to suggest that they be looked into first, leaving fallen sparrows to heaven.

Of those who will agree with the truth of the preceding argument, some cynics—or realists, if there is a difference—will no doubt pronounce it naïve. For they have long pointed out that statutes like Robinson-Patman have little or nothing to do with economics and were not intended to. Some argue that such law is crassly political. Others will say that it cultivates among the masses a warm sense that no one is too trivial to be protected by his government and will contend that, to the benefit of all, this prevents far-reaching and dangerous radicalism.

I am aware that improved priorities could leave us worse off if the legal rules applied are anti-economic: it is better to bungle trivial things than those that matter. As a consequence, I will later have to comment upon the sense of the rules.

II
Science and Pedagogy

This brings me to a point over which—like most teachers—I am liable to make too much. It is the scientific and educative contribution of antitrust in general and Robinson-Patman in particular. The narrow problem arises partly because the statute and opinions incorporate various economic terms but leave behind the analytic framework from which they were wrenched. In addition, the cases often do not clearly point out either what has actually happened or the special or multiple senses in which certain economic terms are being used. Such a procedure could conceivably produce good policy and justice, but it surely sets low scientific standards. A good deal of what economists think they know about real-world pricing practices and markets has been learned from congressional hearings and the law cases as reported. And a good deal of that turns out to be surprisingly theoretical and inferential.

Long ago Aaron Director suggested to me what seemed at the time a strange experiment: take five or six FTC or court decisions, and for each summarize only what is definitely known to have happened; omit inferred motive and hypotheses about prospective effect. He made his point, for I tried it. It is truly remarkable what and how little often remains. A refinement can be added to the game: rewrite the summaries of facts in several styles, ranging from the colorless recitation found in clinical studies to a more readable one that shimmers with words like *dominance, power, exclusion,* and so forth. Whatever they may have learned from it, lawyers have played formally similar games for years. But they are concerned with somewhat different matters and forms, and are differently concerned with them. Economists are concerned with prediction and the general allocative significance of market definition, structure, and performance.

From pedagogical and informational standpoints, many FTC and court decisions are a bust. At a bare minimum, the opinions should point out which of the possible statutory injuries has been established and where, in the record, specific evidence of it is to be found. Lawyers are a scholarly lot, and this is a minimum standard for scholarship. For example, it is now fashionable for Robinson-Patman commentators to distinguish between general or "broad" reductions in competition (as in a tendency to monopoly) and "narrow" injuries to competitors (as in simple diversion of trade from one seller to another). Yet quite often it is impossible to discover from findings or opinions which type of injury has been inferred.[15]

There are two closely related reasons to decry this state of affairs. The first has to do with information and propaganda; the second, which I will later examine in detail, with the substance of social policy itself. Even if Robinson-Patman did not make policy but were simply pure rhetoric, many people would be interested in understanding it. Intellectual curiosity is hard to satisfy as things stand. Furthermore, everything the Commission and courts write is news and is published, often at public expense. Arms of government command respect. A nonnegligible amount of what citizens (even students) learn about competition and monopoly derives from such utterances. They should therefore be really intelligible and make sense. Note the different informational content of these two (altogether hypothetical) summary statements about the same (altogether hypothetical) facts:

1. The Tillen Company, the third largest U.S. manufacturer of golf balls, discriminated in price in the sale of such golf balls to competing resellers, where the effect of such discrimination may be substantially to lessen competition or tend to create a monopoly, or to injure, destroy, or prevent competition.

2. In August, 1963, the Tillen Company, the third largest U.S. manufacturer of golf balls, sold nineteen dozen golf balls to Benny's Sporting Goods for $4 per dozen and six dozen identical balls to Piltz's Sports Store for $4.50 per dozen. Both stores are in New York City. At least 200 stores sell golf balls

---

Robinson-Patman cases to discover which type of injury has actually been inferred: John S. McGee, The Robinson-Patman Act and Effective Competition (unpublished Ph.D. dissertation, Vanderbilt University, 1952); Robert C. Brooks, Jr., The Meaning and Determination of "Injury to Competition" Under the Robinson-Patman Act (unpublished Ph.D. dissertation, University of Chicago, 1959); CORWIN D. EDWARDS, THE PRICE DISCRIMINATION LAW (1959). In various ways, each of these studies reveals the difficulty of finding what type of injury was inferred. See EDWARDS, *op. cit. supra,* at 521, 541.

---

[15] I am personally familiar with three studies that, among other things, analyze large numbers of

in New York City. Piltz testified that he lost at least two customers to Benny because of the lower resale price charged by the latter. (Piltz, pp. 117–136.) There is no evidence that a monopoly of golf ball manufacturers or retailers has been created by respondent's discrimination, that concentration is increasing in either field, or that either development is likely. Nevertheless, the statute also provides narrower standards of injury. They are met in this case. Because of Tillen's discrimination, Piltz lost some business, and that is enough.

I am not asserting that most, or even much, Robinson-Patman law rests on such narrow grounds. I am suggesting that it is very difficult to find out which and how much of it has. This is in principle quite serious, for biases favor all statutes. Not since heads of state appointed favorite horses to high office could one expect to find laws the avowed object of which is to do evil or spread ruin. All law is, by definition, well-intentioned.

It is important that the FTC adopt for its own utterances the same rules with respect to false and misleading advertising that it would impose upon business concerns. It may be that recent and current FTC practice in this respect is better than it used to be; but there would still be merit in explicitly recognizing a permanent obligation.

It is hard to say whether harm has been caused by congressional phrasemakers who have called resale price maintenance "fair trade" and trade diversion "injury to competition." It is acceptable to call "up" "down"; but perhaps we should be told about it each time. It would cost the FTC and courts much less to spell out what they think they are doing than it costs for outsiders to go to the transcripts to find what they did, with what, and to spread the word. There are very few economists who have read as many as three whole antitrust records. Not everyone who votes has been to college; not everyone in college studies Robinson-Patman or, even,

economics; and it takes a while to explain even to bright economics students what may be going on in spite of what the statute itself seems to say. If there is value in knowledge, it might be diffused more cheaply if the FTC and the courts became less ritualistic and more reportorial in their summaries. Then, at least, outside analysts would better be able to choose which transcripts need to be looked into first. Probably the most reliable index has historically been the occasional full dissent that is based on data or economic inference. Ex-Commissioner Lowell Mason, for example, merits high praise in this role.

The foregoing criticisms and suggestions might turn out to be fairly trivial, as, for example, if economically valid conclusions consistently emerged for the wrong reasons or from the use of irrelevant or anti-economic standards. I have read just enough antitrust transcripts to be leery of Commission and court opinions and of scholarly analyses that do not go deeply into the transcripts behind them.

But apart from how well the Commission discharges its roles as reporter and as maker and enforcer of law, it is subject to another serious criticism. The FTC has much greater powers to inquire and to discover than does any academic researcher. Yet, I believe an impartial appraisal would show, during the last twenty years, each of several academic economists has produced more, more objective, and more important research on industrial organization and monopoly than has emerged from the FTC altogether. For an expert agency one of whose functions was to be inquiry and revelation, that is truly a remarkable record.

III

Some Selected Aspects of Costs

It is often asserted that all alleged cost differences that are based on marginal or incremental costs[16] are economically illegitimate,

---

[16] Marginal cost at a given output rate is, in essence, the change in total cost resulting from the

whatever their status at law. This general denial rests upon particular parables, all of which incorporate special assumptions. Among the most important suppositions are that all customers are sold precisely identical goods that are produced, stored, and marketed continuously in ways and quantities and at times that are in all respects identical. Two major possibilities are now apparent.

First, marginal cost may decline as output increases. Charging one purchaser less than others might then be defended because marginal cost is lower with his business than it would be without it. Such a *cost* justification is economically invalid, since it is the *total* output rate that lowers marginal cost. Under present rarified assumptions, one buyer contributes as much to total output, and thus to lower marginal cost, as does any other. Much more complicated and important is the broader question: does the resulting discrimination—for by economic standards that is what it is—increase consumer welfare? An example will illustrate the problem. If an unreformable monopoly produces with marginal costs that decline rapidly with output, welfare may be increased by price discrimination even though the monopoly industry would be viable without it. For if discrimination increases output, the resultant reduction of marginal cost could lower prices to *all* customers below what they would otherwise have been. Some assertions made with respect to discriminatory pricing of medical services rest, implicitly, on this theoretic argument.

A second possibility is that marginal costs may remain constant or rise with increased output but be below average cost. Consider now an arrangement that gives a marginal cost price to one group of buyers and prices at or above average costs to the others. In

defense, it is said that the "marginal buyer" adds little (*i.e.*, "less than average") to total cost and that the marginal cost price is therefore appropriate. So far as *costs* go, the defense is economically invalid, for the same reasons given before. But, as before, a welfare problem presents itself, even though marginal cost rises or is constant with increased output. Given a single-firm monopoly, permitting price discrimination may make some output possible when, without price discrimination, none would be produced. This could occur if no nondiscriminatory price that consumers will pay would cover the relevant costs of providing the service. Discrimination may collect enough revenue to cover costs, in which case the industry would survive. Consumers of the service are better off with it than without it. Less clear, perhaps, is whether discrimination would improve the general welfare as well, since resources used by the monopoly may be more expensive to other industries if the monopoly is permitted to operate by discriminating in sales prices. Even so, it is difficult to argue that consumers paying the higher prices for the service are hurt because others obtain it for less. Indeed, the contrary is true.

To this point, I have given little analytic support for *cost* distinctions that are based on marginal costs. In important instances, however, such distinctions *are* economically valid. Among other reasons, they now arise because of differences in the timing of purchases. When there are substantial peaks and troughs in the time-pattern of demand, cost distinctions *should* be made on a marginal cost basis if they are to be economically meaningful. It is wholly inappropriate to allocate to off-peak buyers any charges for fixed facilities required to meet the demands of peak buyers, no increase in which is necessary to serve the others. Many regulatory commissions, accountants, and even economists are unlikely even to see, let alone appreciate, the point; but it is correct.[17]

---

smallest possible change in output. Incremental cost has been used in various senses. The meaning here adopted is the change in total cost resulting from a finite—and possibly large—change in output. The latter concept, at least, is often operational and has been used, for example, in the computation of sealed bids.

---

[17] See, *e.g.*, WILLIAM S. VICKREY, MICROSTATICS, esp. 225–36, 242–44, 256–58, 388 (1964); RALPH K. DAVIDSON, PRICE DISCRIMINATION IN

However equitable it may appear to allocate fixed costs to such off-peak buyers, it is both altogether arbitrary and probably hurtful in terms of resource allocation. Indeed, in the economic sense, prices that impute such fixed charges to off-peak purchasers are themselves *discriminatory* beyond redemption.[18] It is one thing grudgingly to tolerate such discrimination on grounds that the price flexibility required to avoid it is too expensive or that the relevant cost data are too hard to extract. It is quite another thing to *require* price discrimination of this type by rejecting marginal cost approximations out of hand. That is apparently what we tend to do. Basic functions of prices, after all, are to ration existing goods amongst competing uses and buyers and to signal desired changes in capacity and future outputs.

If the price discrimination law is intolerant of sensible pricing rules, there are various possible ways out. First, an attempt can be made to emphasize that the law calls for "real" rather than "estimated" or "calculated" costs. Nothing could be less real than allocating costs of providing capacity used fully in one period and little in another. Second, it may be possible to convince commissions and courts that, so far as seller and buyers are concerned, the "same" goods bought at peak and off-peak periods are simply different goods,[19] and, as such, may fall outside the price discrimination definition.

An even more subtle problem arises because of risk. It exists whether cost defenses

SELLING GAS AND ELECTRICITY (1955); Wellisz, *Regulation of Natural Gas Pipeline Companies: An Economic Analysis*, 71 J. POL. ECON. 30 (1963).

[18] This point is made most convincingly by DAVIDSON, *op. cit. supra* note 17.

[19] This is true even if off-peak buyers did not incur offsetting storage or other costs. This point is made to avoid confusion with the increasingly popular plea that no competitive injuries arise when buyers' additional costs offset their price-savings or that such favorable prices are analogous to functional discounts given to defray distributors' differential expenses.

rest on average or marginal cost concepts. It is a highly important commonplace that risk costs something. In many—perhaps all—production and marketing processes, less expensive ways of doing things will be adopted if odds are good that certain minimum sales will be enjoyed. Risks of low sales are a barrier to employing techniques and processes that could be efficient at higher rates of output. Put in another way, processes and techniques adopted, and therefore costs, will be influenced by expected output and sales. *Even if*, under certainty and other unrealistic conditions, real costs of service did not vary among customers, risk changes the picture. A much simplified example shows how. Suppose that for the relevant future a producer expects sales to be somewhere between 1,000 and 6,000 units, with his own probability "weights" attached as follows:

(1) *Sales, physical units*	*(2)* *Probability*	*(3)* *(1)* × *(2)*
1,000	.20	200
2,000	.20	400
3,000	.20	600
4,000	.30	1,200
5,000	.05	250
6,000	.05	300
	1.00	2,950

Although it is true that 4,000 units is the most likely single quantity, all things considered, the expected value of sales is 2,950. What output our producer actually decides to tool up to produce, and how he does it, will of course also depend upon costs under different plans and the costliness of being wrong once any production plan is adopted. Tooling to produce, say, 4,000 units could be disastrously expensive if only 2,000 are sold. Similarly, apparatus planned for 2,000 units may be highly inefficient if 4,000 are actually sold.

What happens to sales prospects and costs if firm contracts could be made in advance for a total of, say, 2,001 units? The probability of selling 1,000 or 2,000 units is now zero. Assuming that the *other* sales possibilities (and their *relative* probability) are not changed by the contracts,[20] two highly unfavorable possibilities have been eliminated, raising average prospects. One plausible result is the following:

(1) Sales, physical units	(2) Probability	(3) (1) × (2)
3,000	.333 . . .	1,000
4,000	.500	2,000
5,000	.083 . . .	417
6,000	.083 . . .	500
	1.000	3,917

The expected value of sales has now risen to 3,917 units, an increase of about one-third. It is entirely reasonable that the producer alter his production and sales apparatus as a consequence. It also seems likely, if not absolutely inevitable, that this will lower costs. Such cost reductions are directly attributable to a reduced risk of small volumes. In this simple example, those who contracted in advance permitted or "caused" the cost savings.

Note, now, a peculiar and important aspect of this whole affair. On entirely plausible assumptions, reduced risk permitted cheaper ways of doing things for *all* customers. A *post-hoc* cost analysis, even if it could be made *perfectly* by exemplary accountants, might reveal that (marginal or average) costs of serving all customers are absolutely identical.[21] Presumably no cost defense would lie. It would be fruitless for the producer to argue that those who contracted made costs for everyone lower than they otherwise would have been. And this is a serious flaw. For it is naïve to suppose that those buyers who contract, thereby increasing *their* risks, will do so for nothing. If there is nothing in it for them, because law does not permit them to get discounts, they will stop contracting. Costs then would

be higher for everybody, a development that all but the perverse should lament.

An additional point needs development. When a firm's customers are numerous (and each relatively small), it might appear that it would not pay to discount for advance contracts. The conclusion is based on the fact that no such single contract would be worth much. The conclusion is incorrect. For experience will reveal, if vision does not, that each given discount for contracts will induce so many customers to contract and that this number will rise with the discount offered. Of course, a seller will want to discount as little as possible for a given volume of contracts, but competition would force him to discount up to the full cost savings that the contracts permit. Relax assumptions somewhat, so that buyers do not all take the same quantities per unit of time. In some ways matters are now more complicated: there are two possible sources of cost savings rather than only one. First, volume discounts or firm contracts may reduce risks, making it possible to adopt generally cheaper ways of doing things; and, second, once more efficient processes *are* adopted, it may be less expensive to fill larger orders, and so on. In principle, at least, the law permits prices to reflect the latter type of savings but apparently makes no room for the former.

Even if the law were sympathetic, which evidently it is not, it would be difficult to cost-justify such schemes. Doubtless some will argue that rules sufficiently relaxed to permit cost-justification in cases like this would permit anything. The law would then become difficult to enforce. There are several answers. First, it is altogether clear that the quality of law is not to be judged solely by how easy it makes life for those who administer it. Second, recognition of new types of socially—if not legally—justifiable cost-savings demands more meaningful standards of adverse competitive effects. It makes it even harder, in classrooms if not in court and hearing rooms, to argue that overly sensitive indexes of competition don't matter so much because a cost-defense escape is provided. Re-emphasis on competition

---

[20] Strengthened demand might underlie the increased willingness to contract. This would presumably alter the producer's prospects and probability weights.

[21] As, for example, when the quantities bought, the timing of purchases, and so forth, turn out to be identical for all. This need not be the case; and, indeed, other cost aspects of the transactions could be either reinforcing or opposed.

standards, even if forced, could be wholesome.

IV

Volume Discounts

The FTC has often concluded that volume discounts may injure or lessen competition.[22] Such a finding could rest upon the different prices accorded competing purchases who buy different volumes or upon the effect of volume discounts in barring entry or "access" to the primary line in which the seller is engaged. I will ignore the problem of "injury" in the secondary line, since no unique problem arises with respect to it.

Long ago the Commission specifically emphasized that volume discounts inhibit new entry and expansion by relatively smaller firms.[23] More recently, Robert C. Brooks, Jr., in strengthening the logical core of the old FTC argument, has sharply narrowed the area of its potential application.[24] We are in his debt.

The bold FTC-style argument can be analyzed first by stripping it down to a simple form. Assume that a (relatively) large firm sells one product at net prices that decline as a buyer purchases larger volumes. Any buyer whose purchases are at or near the minimum volume necessary to qualify for all but the lowest discount bracket is allegedly insulated from blandishments of other sellers. This is said to be so because transferring some, but not all, of his business will require that the price on units bought from the new supplier be low enough to compensate the buyer for the

higher discount lost on all the other business.[25] Of course, as Brooks recognizes, this clog on access will be absent or mitigated if a buyer's volume is substantially above a volume discount breaking point, if the volume brackets are simply not enforced, or if, no matter where a buyer is located in the volume scale, there are enough or large enough outside suppliers to satisfy his total requirements.

As I interpret his article, Brooks still claims too much. Examine the one-product case.[26] In the first place, before enconomists should have any interest in the question, there should be some evidence that prices substantially exceed marginal cost—*i.e.*, that there is a monopoly problem. Second, as will become abundantly clear later on, we should be reasonably sure that the monopoly does not rest on size economies before attributing monopoly or no entry to volume discounts. Third, even if there is such a problem, economic appraisal of it presumably requires knowing whether the discounts are broadly based on cost savings.[27]

A new firm would face no unique "access" problem if the optimum size of seller is equal to or smaller than the sum of the following: (1) volumes of business done in the lowest discount bracket; (2) all business in excess of the lower volume limit in those brackets in which buyers now find themselves, and (3) other business that will result in lower discounts but that still yields prices equal to or greater than marginal

---

[22] In pure form, volume discounts apply to quantities purchased over a substantial interval of time rather than to quantities bought at or delivered at one time. Volume and quantity discounts are sometimes joined.

[23] See, *e.g.*, American Optical Co., 28 F.T.C. 169, 181–82 (1939); Simmons Co., 29 F.T.C. 727, 740–42 (1939).

[24] Brooks, *Volume Discounts as Barriers to Entry and Access*, 69 J. POL. ECON. 63 (1961).

[25] This alleged compound leverage would be greater the smaller the volume of business transferred to the newcomer, assuming a buyer's volume is reduced below a discount-bracket breaking point. All, or any part, of the business of any buyer whose volume of purchases qualifies him only for the smallest discount is in any sense quite "accessible" to competing sellers.

[26] He often commingles diversified and one-product lines, absolute and relative size, and patent and *de facto* monopoly.

[27] I do not mean that a cost defense must satisfy any given FTC accountant to be meaningful economically. See the discussion of costs *supra*.

cost.[28] Even this may be too restrictive. For, if newcomers can offer equivalent goods,[29] it is enough for access by existing sellers that in sum they are or can become big enough to satisfy all of the requirements of one or more even of those sellers whose volumes are close to a volume discount breaking point of the "dominant firm." [30]

Of course, competition is more important than "access" to business by specific firms. It may be that every existing firm has "access" to business (in the sense outlined above) and is prosperous but that when all this "accessible" business has been acquired there are still not enough firms to produce a roughly competitive outcome. What, then, about entry? Suppose, for example, that several buyers who together make a large percentage of the total purchases are attached to the dominant firm and that the volume of each (identical or not) is just above a volume discount breaking-point. What would prevent the entry of new firms? If the volume of each of these large buyers is smaller than or equal to the optimum size of selling firm, volume discounts are not a barrier to entry. It is conceivable, I suppose, that any such buyer's volume is still so large relative to the total market—i.e., that total demand for the product becomes highly inelastic below present prices—that there is no room for one more optimum-size firm—i.e., that there is natural monopoly (or natural oligopoly, if you prefer).[31] But this fact appears to have nothing to do with volume discounts, since it would operate without them.

What if the volume of each of the relatively large buyers is larger than the minimum optimum size of seller? Several firms could enter.[32] It may be argued that no single seller will enter until he is sure that there will be enough newcomers to furnish the total requirements of at least one of the larger buyers. Perhaps, then, none will enter. Apart from the implicit assumption that information is frightfully poor and expensive, this argument suffers another defect. Any such larger buyer will have a real incentive to encourage entry of enough firms to break his present attachment.[33] One can certainly imagine his offering firm contracts, or at least prices, to potential entrants, integrating vertically, or informing the business community (probably the world) of his present plight.

Though volume discounts now look somewhat tattered as an entry and "access" barrier raised by a single-product firm,[34] there remains the issue of the "dominant" seller with a diversified line, all items of which are included in a single volume discount plan. Though Brooks does not ask them, two additional questions should be

---

[28] This is apparently sufficient for the entry of at least one firm, but not necessary, for the volume of purchases now made will be increased at lower prices. I say "apparently" sufficient because it may turn out that the optimum size of firm is so large relative to the total market that there is not room for two firms. That is natural monopoly.

[29] If they cannot, it is at least premature to say that volume discounts are the real barrier.

[30] Some may argue that if they are not already big enough they cannot grow enough. This seems somewhat strange. For if monopoly rates of return are available they will have the best incentive to grow. Critics should point out precisely what would keep them from growing and what evidence of it exists. Vague complaints about "capital requirements" are certainly not sufficient.

[31] A subtle and misleading geometric game could be commenced at this point. It might be argued that the available business of one of these relatively large buyers is too small for optimum operation, but the business of two is so large as to produce diseconomies of large size to the entrant. How, then, do we explain why the "dominant" firm is even larger (and that some other sellers may be so much smaller)?

[32] This could be expected if there is a unique optimum size. But, again, why is the "dominant" seller so much larger?

[33] This assumes he is paying higher than competitive prices. If not, there is no rationale for entry into this segment of the market—or any other, since larger buyers get lowest prices. In any case, the other segments—composed of smaller buyers—would pose no such problem.

[34] It is not really a question of the total number of different products sold but of the number lumped into one volume discount scale.

answered:[35] (1) Are these different products produced or sold together because doing so reduces costs?[36] (2) Are they substitutes or complements or are they unrelated in demand?[37]

Now the objection to this type of volume discount has been that "it automatically makes *any* part of . . . [the seller's] line that a potential competitor might consider entering the lowest profit part."[38] As a consequence, so the theory goes, he enters none. If it turns out that there are not effective patent or other artificial impediments to entry into any of the dominant firm's diversified product line, we can largely apply the economics previously developed for the single-product case. An exception apparently arises if present or potential competitors are incompetent to make one or more products in the line but are quite capable, if given a chance, of effectively producing the others. If there are economies of producing or selling all together, the dominant firm would then have an advantage that most would characterize as "natural." Mechanically, the results appear to be closely similar to the situation where one of the products is patented, and I will discuss them together.

The question then becomes whether volume discounts can be used to extend the monopoly of one product to products that otherwise would be produced competitively. Note that there is little reason to brood about monopoly in the first product, for it is largely irremediable. Assume that there are no economies of joint production or sale and that the products in the line are unrelated through price.[39] Only a part of the business available in the one-product case is "accessible," since we assume one product is irremediably monopolized. That leaves such business in the other products that is done in the lowest discount brackets plus whatever volumes will not place buyers in lower discount brackets plus that which would place buyers in lower discount brackets but which can be attracted at prices equal to or greater than marginal cost.[40] As before, if this volume is greater than or equal to the optimum size of selling firm, there is room for one or more firms. There may even be room for enough firms to establish competitive prices for all but the irremediably monopolized good.

But there may not be room for enough firms; and here Brooks may have a point. For some, perhaps small, part of the potentially competitive goods market a shelter might have been erected. I have, of course, strengthened Brooks' case by assuming an iron-clad and important monopoly on one good.[41] Yet, in such a case, it remains a fair and troublesome question why the monopolist simply does not extract all of the monopoly profit by charging higher prices explicitly for the primary monopoly good itself.[42]

---

[35] Others previously asked remain relevant: (1) Is there a significant monopoly problem? (2) May it rest on economies of size? (3) Are the volume discounts plausibly related to obvious cost savings?

[36] Such goods are called complements in production or sale.

[37] Cutting the price of one substitute reduces the demand for the others. Cutting the price of one complement increases demand for the others. See Bowman, *Tying Arrangements and the Leverage Problem*, 67 YALE L.J. 19 (1957).

[38] Brooks, *supra* note 24, at 69.

[39] That is, a change in the price of one product does not change the demand for the others. I doubt that this case is very much encountered in the real world, since it is not clear why some or all buyers would then purchase the products together.

[40] Whether Brooks' arithmetic examples are atypically severe, the direction of their effects is correct. What he does not explicitly recognize is that having to recompense customers for lost discounts may still leave the challenging seller(s) with higher than competitive prices.

[41] This means more than, say, that one good is merely patented. It implies that the restraint bestows important monopoly power over a wide range of prices, *i.e.*, demand elasticities substantially less than infinite.

[42] We should include the possibility of all-or-none perfect discrimination that charges, for given volumes, almost as much as would induce the buyer to do without the good altogether. Compare Director & Levi, *supra* note 4, at 290–91, with Bowman, *supra* note 37.

For that is where its power really inheres, and no one would cherish another illusion.

In any case, it appears that the old FTC theory with respect to volume discounts must be narrowed substantially even according to Brooks and still more according to my argument. If Brooks is correct, two types of situation that bear watching are those in which (1) the largest buyers are too large to be served by one seller of minimum optimum size and/or (2) there is a diversified line. In my view, the real problem—if any—is more likely to arise when (1) the minimum optimum size of seller is large relative to the market and/or (2) there is strong monopoly in some part of a diversified line.

To be cautious, then, the FTC could investigate volume discounts used in these rather narrow fact situations. Proceeding much more broadly against them is probably to tilt at windmills, which is not necessarily innocuous since windmills produce flour if left alone.

V

Predatory Practices

Monopolizing techniques tend to increase the spread between marginal cost and price. Cartels and horizontal mergers are classic forms, the theory and practice with respect to which are reasonably well settled. Arson, mayhem, and assassination are also plausible candidates in principle, since they tend to be both more expensive to victim than to predator and less expensive to predator than the benefits they make it possible for him to reap. Deferred rebates[43] and, possibly, volume discounts may also be practicable exclusionary techniques under some conditions.

---

[43] For an analytic history of collusive loyalty ties in ocean transport, see McGee, *Ocean Freight Rate Conferences and the American Merchant Marine*, 27 U. CHI. L. REV. 191, esp. 213–38 (1960), and A. R. FERGUSON, E. M. LERNER, J. S. MCGEE, W. Y. OI, L. A. RAPPING & S. P. SABOTKA. THE ECONOMIC VALUE OF THE UNITED STATES MERCHANT MARINE, esp. 376–404 (1961).

Much less plausible, in my opinion—if, indeed, plausible at all—are general [44] or discriminatory price cuts to drive out present, or keep out potential, rivals. I have explained elsewhere why I doubt that discriminatory price cutting is a very sensible monopolizing technique.[45] Furthermore, theoretically sensible or not, there have been surprisingly few cases (even as reported) that so much as look at first glance to be predatory price discrimination. Nevertheless, many people are still concerned about predatory price discrimination, and I admit that the questions of theory and fact that it poses are less frivolous than cold-trailing bubble gum and baseball trading-card "monopolies." [46]

Even those who fear predatory price discrimination should be careful in framing legal rules to avoid it. First, it should now be clear that at worst there have not been very many instances of attempted, let alone successful, predatory pricing, even in periods and places with no antitrust laws. This suggests that necessary conditions for successful predation are not ubiquitous, and that narrow rules can be developed. Second, ordinary spatial competition may often look like what is called "predatory" pricing. En-

---

[44] Modigliani, *New Developments on the Oligopoly Front*, 66 J. POL. ECON. 215, 217 (1958), and sources cited therein. A key, and doubtful, assumption is "that potential entrants behave as though they expected existing firms to adopt the policy most unfavorable to them, namely, the policy of maintaining output while reducing the price. . . ." Even on purely theoretic grounds, the assumption seems strange. For any entrant knows that, once he is actually there, the "dominant" firms can probably do better by adjusting to his existence. In any case, the theory suffers when it is tested by the history of early American "trusts" and more recent experience. For example, see GEORGE J. STIGLER, FIVE LECTURES ON ECONOMIC PROBLEMS, 46–65, esp. 63–65 (1949), and Osborne, *The Role of Entry in Oligopoly Theory*, 72 J. POL. ECON. 396 (1964).

[45] McGee, *Predatory Price Cutting: The Standard Oil (N.J.) Case*, 1 J. LAW & ECON. 137 (1958).

[46] This particular trail has just been abandoned: Topps Chewing Gum, Inc., 3 TRADE REG. REP. ¶ 17251 (FTC 1965).

forcing sweeping rules against these common symptoms could be like feeding a fine bird dog powerful poisons to avoid a kind of parasite that is rare, if it exists at all.

Most would probably agree that predatory price cutting is unappealing, if not ludicrous, when the minimum efficient size of firm is small relative to the market and the skills necessary to enter are not rare. This, I should think, rules out most if not all trade and agriculture. Predatory price cutting would require large relative size—*i.e.*, monopoly power—which raises the possibility of proceeding against the monopoly directly. It also rules out firms with minority market shares, I should think. Indeed, even a firm with high regional but low national share is not a very good candidate, since other national firms are a menace to advancing prices (and profit) afterwards. A firm which has a very high national market share but which faces numbers of rivals in most or all regions is not a prime candidate for predator either. Not only is this situation symptomatic of potential entry everywhere, but it would be more than slightly expensive to kill off present rivals. Long-lived and large capital investment is not too favorable, since prices below average total costs (but above average variable cost) would take a long time to kill. Holding prices below average variable costs would be frightfully expensive. Furthermore, even if predatory pricing were undertaken and worked, rivals' plants would probably have to be bought.[47] Enforcing laws against monopolizing by merger would make the whole procedure still more unattractive.

For those who want to exercise against "predatory" price cutters, where are they least unlikely to be found? Look for a prosperous and liquid firm with high national share of the sales of a distinct product, with no rivals most places and with very few elsewhere. Rivals should be operating in absolutely small markets. There should be powerful impediments to entry—as, for example, when very scarce and specialized talents are necessary to engage in the business and all of them are now engaged in it. Rivals should be poor, illiquid, and—for some reason—incapable of borrowing. Average variable cost should be close to price before price cutting begins. These conditions do not explain why the dominant firm would engage in more expensive predatory activities rather than merging or colluding with its rivals, but they do afford some chance for cutthroat activities to work mechanically.[48]

One of the troubles with the "predation" complex is that it focuses policy against "predator" and in favor of "prey," rather than toward competitive allocation goals. In one sense, competition is a process thought to be more probable within some industrial structures than others. In another sense, it is a set of allocative performance standards. But in no useful sense is competition a cast of characters. If one or many farmers fail or die of plague, competition is not reduced. If one pure monopolist totally displaces another, competition is not reduced. If one of only two sellers buys or assassinates the other, competition is reduced, at least for a time. If a large proportion—just how large a share is necessary no one can say in advance for all cases—of the capacity of the industry is merged into one dominant firm, competition is reduced. Similarly for effective collusion. In principle, the issue is whether there is a widened gap between price and marginal cost.

Assume that a monopolist sells in two or more markets and that significant entry ocurs for the moment in only one of them. Traditional nonpredatory theory predicts that price will fall in one market but, depending on the slope of marginal cost, perhaps not in the other. Entrants would prefer, of course, that the monopolist never be permitted to cut prices anywhere, but that would serve consumers poorly by deferring convergence of price and marginal cost.[49]

---

[47] Otherwise, they would be reopened by the old staff or picked up very cheaply by adventurers and operated when prices rose.

[48] They also mean that the maximum increase in monopoly power to be gained is relatively small.

[49] The danger of rules whose function is simply to

So long as the same prices that cover the monopolist's variable costs would not cover an entrant's total costs, entry will not occur. Rules that force the monopolist to retire from that market,[50] or that otherwise raise prices in it, are questionable on allocative grounds. No doubt discriminatory price cutting has been used by new firms on entering an industry and by established firms in markets into which they are entering for the first time. At least the immediate effect of such price cutting is to press prices towards marginal cost. Perhaps we should be reasonably sure, then, that greater movements in the other direction are likely to follow before intervening.

Hopefully without encouraging further congestion in the courts and subsidy to the accounting profession, perhaps the bar and economists should consider the following possibility. Marginal cost is often difficult to estimate. Average variable cost and "direct" or "prime" cost are much easier to ascertain from existing records. If there were solid grounds to suspect predatory pricing, perhaps it would be feasible to discover whether prices are being held below the suspected predator's average variable cost for periods "unreasonably" long to be purely promotional. Such investigations could open the door further to the difficulties and frustrations now encountered with section 2(a) cost defenses.[51] On the other hand, the notion may be broadly appealing and may not be worse than either excursions into "intent" and other shadow lands or overly broad rules that tax all geographic price differences.

---

increase the number and comfort of sellers can well be seen in the theory and practice of resale price maintenance. Probable effects of legally enforced, and high, retail margins are decreased "concentration" in retailing—and high prices.

[50] Possible examples are ouster and prohibitions against freight absorption and other discrimination.

[51] For a monumental study of those problems, see HERBERT F. TAGGART, COST JUSTIFICATION (1959). As one who has read a mere thousand pages of cost defense testimony, I can only marvel at Taggart's tenacity.

Yet, when all is said and done, the present Clayton Act law of horizontal mergers and the Sherman Law[52] are more than sufficiently powerful to attack the whole problem, if there is one.[53]

VI

Secondary and Nth-Level "Injury"

Though there is not space here fully to analyse the problem of injury to or lessening of competition at secondary and lower levels, I would apply most of the foregoing argument to it with slight change. Indeed, consumer hurt through damage to competition is probably less likely on secondary and lower levels than at the primary level. Numbers of firms are often higher, scale economies generally not massive, and entry is often quick and easy. It is useful, however, to pose a few additional questions that must be answered in each case if Robinson-Patman is ever to be as successful a policy in the economic sense as it has apparently been in the political sense.

Imagine a single-firm manufacturing monopoly whose many identical customers compete in reselling to identical final consumers. Note that the allocative effect of monopoly at the manufacturing level is transmitted to the consumer level, even when competition amongst resellers is perfect.[54] Apart from entry into manufacturing

---

[52] 26 Stat. 209 (1890), as amended, 15 U.S.C. §§ 1–7 (1964).

[53] As Bork & Bowman put it, "Has anybody ever seen a firm gain a monopoly or anything like one through . . . price discrimination?" Bork & Bowman, *supra* note 6, at 367. See also Bowman, *supra* note 6, at 421.

[54] That is, if from the beginning the manufacturing monopoly had integrated completely from mill through retail shop at the same marketing costs as would have prevailed for independent resellers, output at manufacturing and retail levels would be the same as when there is explicit monopoly only in manufacturing. This does *not* argue that consumers would be unaffected if a strong cartel of independent resellers were created to confront the manufacturing monopoly. Consumers could hardly be helped by this de-

—which involves the problems of "primary" competition discussed above—what changes in assumptions could produce price discrimination and "injury" at the secondary level? They are basically of two sorts.[55] First, for various reasons costs might differ systematically amongst resellers. Naturally the manufacturer would prefer to deal only with efficient intermediaries, but the output he wants may require using outlets amongst which costs vary widely. If he is able to discriminate and consumers are all alike, he would charge higher prices to low-cost resellers and lower prices to high-cost ones. Ideally, all resellers would charge the same prices to consumers, and all would earn only competitive returns. In general, consumers would not be hurt, apart from the usual monopoly effects, and could easily be benefited by such discrimination. If non-discrimination had been succeeded by discrimination, the sales of one group of resellers would have been reduced and those of the other increased. This "trade diversion" has nothing to do with lessening of competition. There *is* a monopoly problem, but secondary-line injuries have little or nothing to do with it.

Second, resellers might all be alike, but consumers could have different demands for the product. If the consumer markets are separable, the monopoly may obtain the desired prices at the consumer level by discrimination amongst resellers. Much the same conclusions about "injury" apply in this case as before. The plight of the ultimate consumer is less clear. Output effects of discrimination would have to be evaluated with others: consumers as a whole would pay more for each total quantity sold.

In cases of dominant-firm monopoly,

oligopoly, and imperfect competition, matters are somewhat more complex. Apart from price differences that reflect cost savings of all kinds, there will normally be a certain amount of real price discrimination amongst resellers. Some of it, at least, will result from rivalrous seller behavior; and stopping that may remove such price competition as can normally be expected.

As before, the "injury" focus should not be on participants but upon estimated changes in the price-marginal cost relationships that consumers face. Injury at primary levels has already been discussed. A few additional remarks about secondary-line effects are probably necessary. In evaluating discrimination, several logical presumptions should be kept in view: No seller will cavalierly scuttle the resellers he depends upon for survival, create monopsony power in resellers with whom he deals, or undertake to increase reseller margins unnecessarily. Add to this a question: Would disadvantaged resellers or consumers be better off if the primary seller refused to deal with some resellers instead of discriminating against them? So far as I can see, there are two not wholly impossible sets of circumstances that bear open-minded investigation, though theory and fact with respect to both are in a most untidy condition. Both would apparently require certain critical relationships between market size and most efficient size of firm—of the sorts previously alluded to in connection with volume discounts—and perhaps institutional entry barriers as well. The first is bilateral monopoly, with very high single firm shares on both sides of the market, and the *possibility of quid pro quos* that might conceivably—given critical assumptions about entry, economies of size, and market size—influence primary-line and secondary-line competition together.[56] The second, and closely related, case might conceivably occur if an

---

velopment, called "bilateral monopoly," and could be hurt. See GEORGE J. STIGLER, THE THEORY OF PRICE 240–41 (1952).

[55] Both require wholly or partly separable markets. If market overlaps are complete, there is but one market, and higher prices in one part would drive all custom to the others. This requires, for the first example, no resale amongst resellers; in the second, no resale amongst consumers as well.

---

[56] See the rather puzzling case of the "BAPS" ring and the general discussion of abstract possibilities in McGee, *Ocean Freight Rate Conferences and the American Merchant Marine*, 27 U. CHI. L. REV. 191, 238–42, 269–70 (1960).

almost pure monopsonist is also an almost pure monopolist. Both of these situations require so many and such restrictive assumptions as surely to be quite rare, at worst, but are sufficiently interesting to merit further theoretic and empirical investigation. In addition, both require such a degree of actual monopoly power as more properly to fall within the province of the Sherman Law than within Robinson-Patman concepts.

Conclusions

Using standards of allocative efficiency, with consumer benefit the goal, I have argued that the Robinson-Patman Act has suffered both from inadequate economic theory and explicit anti-economic biases; has been enforced with no socially rational system of priority; and has produced a core of scientific information that is relatively meager and sometimes wrong and implicit definitions of competition and efficiency that are confusing to the body politic. Competition is not handicap trapshooting, and I do not think it pays to force the better performers to stand farther from the targets.

But, unlike some critics of the law, I am also concerned over the achievable and desirable limits in reforming a congenitally flawed statute by shifts in Commission and court sentiment. This kind of concern is a continuing one in our society, and can be summed up in the words of Edward H. Levi:

> In many controversial situations, legislative revision cannot be expected. It often appears that the only hope lies with the courts. Yet the democratic process seems to require that controversial changes should be made by the legislative body. This is not only because there is a mechanism for holding legislators responsible. It is also because courts are normally timid. . . . The difficulties which administrative agencies have in the face of sustained pressure serve as a warning. When courts enter the area of great controversy, they require unusual protection. They must be ready to appeal to the constitution.[57]

---

[57] Edward H. Levi, An Introduction to Legal Reasoning 23 (1959).

41. Restraint of Trade by the Supreme Court: The Utah Pie Case

WARD S. BOWMAN †

The Supreme Court shows a growing determination in its antitrust decisions to convert laws designed to promote competition into laws which regulate or hamper the competitive process.[1] Succeeding interpretations of the Clayton[2] and Robinson-Patman[3] Acts—and, by infectious contamination, the Sherman Act[4]—demonstrate an increasingly apparent disregard for the central purpose of antitrust, the promotion of consumer welfare through the promotion of a competitive market process. Now, in *Utah Pie Co. v. Continental Baking Co.*,[5] the Supreme Court has used section 2(a) of the Robinson-Patman Act[6] to strike directly at price competition itself.

For more than 30 years there has been, except to a small but increasing number of skeptics, an ambiguity whether the Robinson-Patman Act is a law in favor of or opposed to competition. The statute, although phrased in terms of a "lessening of competition" or "tendency toward monopoly," also includes, and in the alternative, a more ambiguous clause: "or to injure, destroy, or prevent competition with any

person who either grants or knowingly receives the benefit of such discrimination. . . ."[7] All of these phrases, but especially the last, have been interpreted to protect competitors at the expense of the competitive process.

Such restrictive interpretations have eliminated in some measure the ambiguity of the Robinson-Patman Act, although the clarity produced is scarcely a happy one. But the residue of confusion which remains continues to trouble practitioners, commentators and lower courts, if not the present majorities of the Federal Trade Commission and the Supreme Court. Does, or should, the first clause of section 2(a), which refers to anticompetitive effect in general—language which the Robinson-Patman Act shares with sections 3 and 7 of the Clayton Act[8]—complement or conflict with the language referring to the more specific competition "with any person"?

The Supreme Court decision in *Utah Pie* resolves the competitor-competition dilemma, and with a vengeance, against competition. The case arose from a claim for treble damages by the Utah Pie Company against three respondents—the Pet Milk Company, the Carnation Milk Company and the Continental Baking Company—which had allegedly injured the plaintiff's competitive position by selling frozen fruit pies at discriminatory prices in the Salt Lake City market, thereby violating section 2(a). The facts showed that the Utah Pie Company, a local baker, entered the frozen-pie business in late 1957 and built a new plant in 1958. The Salt Lake City

---

Reprinted by permission of The Yale Law Journal Company and Fred B. Rothman and Company from *The Yale Law Journal*, Vol. 77, pp. 70–85.

† Professor of Law and Economics, Yale University, A.B. Washington University, M.A. Yale University.

[1] *See generally* Bork & Bowman, *The Crisis in Antitrust*, FORTUNE, Dec. 1963, at 138, expanded and revised in 65 COLUM. L. REV. 363 (1965).

[2] 15 U.S.C. §§ 12–27, 44 (1964).

[3] *Id.* §§ 13, 13a–b, 21a.

[4] *Id.* §§ 1–7.

[5] 386 U.S. 685 (1967).

[6] 15 U.S.C. § 13a (1964).

[7] *Id.*

[8] *Id.* §§ 14, 18.

frozen-pie market was a rapidly expanding one, growing from about 57,000 dozen pies in 1958 to almost 267,000 dozen pies in 1961. Before the entry of Utah Pie, it was served principally by branches of national food companies with plants outside Utah. The Utah Pie Company, with local production advantages, adopted an aggressive market campaign based on low prices. During its first full year of business, 1958, Utah Pie was thereby able to garner two-thirds of the frozen fruit pie market in Salt Lake City. The three respondents, faced with new and vigorous price competition, chose not to watch idly while their customers were being lost. Instead they sought to retain or expand their sales by lowering their prices in Utah. As a consequence, although Utah Pie's sales and profits continued to expand, its share of the market dropped from 66.5 per cent in 1958 to 34.3 per cent in 1959, then rose to 45.5 and 45.3 per cent in 1960 and 1961. (See chart 1.)

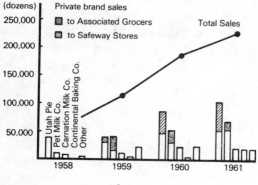

Chart 1

Frozen Pie Sales in Salt Lake City Market

The response by Pet, Carnation and Consolidated to the price reductions by Utah Pie on occasion made their prices in Salt Lake City lower than in other markets. And at times, depending upon relative price conditions in the various markets, higher prices prevailed near the respondents' bakeries than in the more distant Utah market. Although the jury rejected the allegation of a conspiracy, it found that the respond-

ents had individually violated section 2(a) by this "area price discrimination."

The court of appeals overturned the verdict.[9] In its view the central issue was whether the evidence against the allegedly price-discriminating competitors was sufficient to support a finding of probable injury to competition. The court held that there was not such evidence of an adverse effect on competition.

The Supreme Court in reversing spoke of this "single issue" to which the court of appeals addressed itself and then went on to decide that the lower court's finding of no probable adverse effect on *competition* was overcome by the decline in the share of the market held by the plaintiff, Utah Pie. Thus, an adverse effect on a *competitor*, even on one in a quasi-monopoly position, whose sales and profits continue to expand, and whose only injury is the loss of market dominance as a result of price competition which he himself engenders, is enough for the Supreme Court.

But that is not all. The Court found evidence that the Robinson-Patman Act was violated in the working of the competitive process itself, since the price level in Utah was eroded as a result [10]—and eroded to the benefit of consumers without evidence that either the purpose or

---

[9] Continental Baking Co. v. Utah Pie Co., 349 F.2d 122 (10th Cir. 1965).

[10] Respondents had relied upon Anheuser-Busch, Inc. v. FTC, 289 F.2d 835 (7th Cir. 1961), and Borden Co. v. FTC, 339 F.2d 953 (7th Cir. 1964), in arguing in support of the opinion of Judge Phillips in the court of appeals, namely, that "no primary line injury to competition was found." 386 U.S. at 703 n.15. Mr. Justice White finds these cases "readily distinguishable" because in these cases, unlike *Utah Pie*, "there was no general decline in the price structure attributable to defendant's price discrimination. . . ." *Id.* at 704 n.15. Instead, White cites with approval an FTC decision in Maryland Baking Co., 52 F.T.C. 1679 (1956), *aff'd*, 243 F.2d 716 (4th Cir. 1957), which held that creating competition in an almost completely monopolized local market could not nullify a finding of price discrimination.

the effect of the competition was to further an eventual monopoly.

Mr. Justice White, as clearly and unambiguously as anyone could, used the very evidence of competition which convinced the court of appeals that no violation existed to decide that there was an antitrust violation. The core of the Supreme Court holding is contained in the following sentences of the opinion:

> The major competitive weapon in the Utah market was price. The location of petitioner's plant gave it natural advantages in the Salt Lake City marketing area and it entered the market at a price below the then going prices for the respondents' comparable pies. For most of the period involved here [1958–1961] its prices were the lowest in the Salt Lake City market. It was, however, challenged by each of the respondents at one time or another and for varying periods. There was ample evidence to show that *each of the respondents contributed to what proved to be a deteriorating price structure over the period covered by this suit,* and each of the respondents *in the course of the ongoing price competition* sold frozen pies in the Salt Lake market at prices lower than it sold pies of like grade and quality in other markets considerably closer to their plants.[11]

The case involved injury to "competition" in the sellers' market. The court of appeals, as Mr. Justice White acknowledged, had "placed heavy emphasis on the fact that Utah Pie constantly increased its sales volume and continued to make a profit." [12] But White views the Robinson-Patman Act as more concerned with "ground rules of the game" [13] than with probable competitive effects. He finds no need for a showing that discriminatory prices for pies of like grade and quality "consistently undercut" [14] other competi-

---

[11] 386 U.S. at 690 (emphasis added).

[12] *Id.* at 702.

[13] *Id.*

[14] *Id.* The record shows that only occasionally were respondents' prices lower than in markets nearer their California plants. *See* charts 2 & 3, for lowest prices by months.

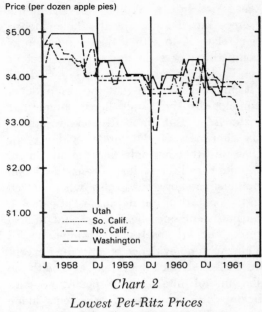

Price (per dozen apple pies)

Utah
So. Calif.
No. Calif.
Washington

J 1958 DJ 1959 DJ 1960 DJ 1961 D

Chart 2
Lowest Pet-Ritz Prices
In Selected Western Market Areas

tors. Nor is there a need for a showing of "blatant [or non-blatant] predatory price discriminations employed with the hope of immediate [or eventual] destruction of a particular competitor." [15] The court of appeals found no evidence of predatory in-

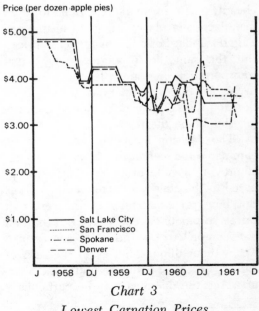

Price (per dozen apple pies)

Salt Lake City
San Francisco
Spokane
Denver

J 1958 DJ 1959 DJ 1960 DJ 1961 D

Chart 3
Lowest Carnation Prices
In Selected Western Market Areas

---

[15] *Id.*

tent. Mr. Justice White said there was "some" but did not specify the evidence, nor relate it to either the elimination of competition or even its possible effect on the Utah Pie Company. He acknowledged, "It might be argued that the respondents' conduct displayed only fierce competitive instincts." [16] But, implicitly acknowledging the flimsiness of the intent evidence, he then said that not only does "actual intent to injure" call for exclusion from this "competitive" category, but so also "when viewed in the context of the Robinson-Patman Act, do persistent sales below cost and radical price cuts themselves discriminatory." [17] Thus, with no evidence of any effect except an increase in competition, and with no showing of intent or of persistent sales below cost, non-uniform price cuts alone must create the violation. What there is about nonuniform price cuts that is more injurious to competition—or for that matter even to competitors—than across-the-board price cuts the opinion never explains.

Neither does it establish any rational guidelines for acceptable competitive behavior. The White opinion, by so belaboring the fact that the respondents occasionally sold their pies in Salt Lake City more cheaply than in markets closer to their manufacturing plants, seems to insist upon a rigid standard of uniform delivered prices. But the same logic might suggest that transportation costs must be fully reflected in higher prices in markets farther from the factory—i.e., that uniform mill net pricing should be the test.

The decision itself has not, of course, eliminated the technically available defense of proving a good faith "meeting" (as opposed to "beating") of a competitor's price. But now price-matching of the sort that cartels promote is encouraged if not all but compelled by the Robinson-Patman Act without diminishing at all the risks of a charge of price collusion under the Sherman Act; the dilemma may be particularly

acute where the competing sellers in a market are few, as in *Utah Pie*.[18]

Neither does this decision provide any predictable "cost justification" escape for competitors caught in the Act's net. Private-label sales were made by respondent Pet Milk Company and by petitioner Utah Pie Company to Safeway Stores at prices below those of equivalent frozen pies sold to others under regular brands. Utah Pie also sold even larger quantities of private-label pies (Frost 'N' Flame) at special prices to another account in 1960 and 1961.[19] In its sale to Safeway, Pet Milk made a contract in accordance with Safeway's established practice of requiring its suppliers to cost-justify their sales. The Supreme Court indicated little sympathy for anything but detailed and complete cost justification. Pet admitted that its cost justification figures were drawn from past performances. "[E]ven crediting the data accompanying the 1960 contract regarding cost differences," wrote Mr. Justice White, "Pet's additional evidence would bring under the justification umbrella only 1959 sales. Thus, at the least, the jury was free to consider the 1960 Safeway sales as inadequately cost justified. These sales accounted for 12.3 per cent of the entire Salt Lake City market in that year." [20] The next sentence of the opinion then restresses the dominant theme of the whole case: "In the context of this case, the sales to Safeway are particularly relevant since there was evidence that private-label sales influenced the general market, in this case *depressing overall market prices*." [21] Perhaps the Pet Milk Company was not as meticulous as it

[18] Chart 1, which was compiled from the court of appeals opinion, indicates that in the Utah market four firms sold over 90 per cent of the frozen pies in 1961. The petitioner, Utah Pie Co., sold 45.3 per cent, and the three respondents, Pet Milk, Carnation, and Continental Baking, sold respectively 29.4, 8.8 and 8.3 per cent.

[19] See chart 1.

[20] 386 U.S. at 695 n.10.

[21] *Id*. (emphasis added).

[16] *Id*. at 702 n.14.

[17] *Id*.

should have been in detailing a cost defense since the absence of competitive injury to Utah Pie seemed so apparent. In any event, the *Utah Pie* decision provides no clarification of the cost justification defense. Confusion still reigns. As Professor Adelman has stressed, "[T]he lengthy and confusing rigmarole prescribed by Robinson-Patman has nothing to do with costs as they exist in the real world and influence business conduct." [22] The operative costs as far as producers are concerned, under competition or under monopoly, are the incremental costs of making particular sales. And these costs, properly conceived, are opportunity costs—that is, the income foregone from the next best alternative use of the resources committed to the enterprise to produce the goods in question. Under this analysis, historical costs in the conventional sense have no rational relevancy to pricing policy. In the *Utah Pie* case the respondents incurred transportation costs on Utah sales. The magnitude of the cost advantage this afforded Utah Pie as a local producer is not revealed. But Pet, Carnation and Consolidated did lower prices in Utah rather than withdraw from the market. In economic terms this simply demonstrates that the companies decided their returns in Salt Lake City after this pricing action would still be higher than the alternative of not selling in Utah or selling more elsewhere. Since the Robinson-Patman Act ignores this economic reality, it should not be surprising that the "cost justification" defense turns out to be a mirage.

"In no field of the law is the danger of petrified opinion and casuistic reasoning greater than in antitrust." [23] And nowhere, it might be added, has this danger been substantiated more clearly than by the havoc wrought on the competitive process in Robinson-Patman cases. Regardless of the motives or intentions of the framers of the Act to make life more secure for inde-

pendent business units competing with the chains, the Act itself has as its stated aim the preservation of competition and the prevention of monopoly. Whether or not it was seriously urged in the legislature that the Act should have as its ultimate purpose the protection of particular competitors at the expense of competition, the legislature found it expedient to phrase the statute in terms of competition.

This is not to say that this Act, or indeed the Clayton Act which it was designed to shore up, was not concerned with the fate of competitors, the elimination of whom would create a market structure inimical to a competitive system. But in measuring the concern of the Robinson-Patman Act for competitors, the Act should be read as a statutory embodiment of an economic hypothesis about the means by which competition might be restricted or monopoly created through acts of aggression against particular competitors to drive them out or keep them out of markets—markets which, it must be emphasized, could be expected in the absence of such long-run effects to provide consumers more of what they wanted at lower costs.

The Robinson-Patman Act rests upon a presumption that price discrimination can or might be used as a monopolizing technique. This, as more recent economic literature confirms, is at best a highly dubious presumption. But even if it were not, the fact that price discrimination *may* tend toward monopoly scarcely deserves ballooning into the proposition that, absent positive evidence to the contrary, it can be *expected* to have the result of eliminating competition by killing off or disciplining rivals.

A "kill-the-rival" theory of price discrimination is only one of three competing theories of why price discrimination might be practiced. [24] The other two, unlike the

---

[22] Adelman, Book Review, 30 U. Chi. L. Rev. 791, 792 (1963).

[23] Elman, *"Petrified Opinions" and Competitive Realities*, 66 Colum. L. Rev. 625 (1966).

[24] *See generally* Machlup, *Characteristics and Types of Price Discrimination*, in Business Concentration and Price Policy 397 (Nat'l Bureau of Econ. Research 1955). For comments on the "kill-the-rival" theory, see *id.* 423–27. But for critical analysis of this latter concept, see Mc-

first, are theoretically plausible and have empirical support. In addition to (1) the incipient monopoly achieved by killing rivals (or barring them from the market) are (2) price discrimination for the purpose of maximizing revenue from a monopoly position already held,[25] and (3) price discrimination practiced for the purpose and with the effect of *creating* rather than eliminating competition, either defensively to protect or build market acceptance, or offensively as a means of eroding an existing monopoly, quasi-monopoly or cartel.[26]

The second of the three price-discrimination theories—maximizing the revenue from a monopoly position by segregating noncompeting customers and charging them different prices related to their differing elasticities of demand—was not at issue in the *Utah Pie* case. Large buyers, particularly Safeway and Associated Grocers, did receive lower prices for their private-brand pies, the former from Pet, the latter from Utah Pie. But no adverse effect on competing customers was alleged in this case. Here the question presented to the Court involved the alleged use of price discrimination by Pet, Carnation and Consolidated as a device by which the plaintiff Utah Pie was or might be foreclosed from the Utah frozen-fruit-pie market in such manner as to violate section 2(a) of the Act.

The issue, then, as the court of appeals saw it, involved deciding whether the "kill-the-rival" face of price discrimination was either intended or foreseeable. Was there any evidence that the Utah Pie Company would be eliminated, or even cowed into following the price leadership of the national firms that had entered the Salt Lake City market? If so, was it likely that competition would be lessened in the mar-

ket, in the short or long run? Conceptually, the questions could be considered discretely. If competition was in fact to be considered the ultimate aim of the Robinson-Patman Act, the court of appeals could have considered the death or disciplining of the Utah Pie Company irrelevant to the purposes of the Act if it concluded that the remaining firms would among themselves provide a competitive market. But even if the preservation of the Utah Pie Company as an active competitor was considered the final goal, the court of appeals might well have found from the robust good health and continued price competition of that firm that the Act was not violated. The court of appeals in overturning the jury verdict and holding for the respondents did not clearly indicate whether its decision was based on the health of competition in the market or the health of Utah Pie as a competitor. The Supreme Court opinion, because of its slight of hand in submerging the "effect-on-competition" issue, did not answer either question.

The White opinion could slide by the crucial question—whether competitive effect is irrelevant, since only competitors count, or conclusively presume to follow from the adverse effect of price discrimination on rivals—only because the majority completely rejects the third theory of price discrimination: use to promote competition by undermining local cartels or monopolies.

This procompetitive use of price discrimination has been widely recognized in the economic literature, even by strong believers in the "kill-the-rival" theory. Careful assessment is correspondingly acknowledged to be a prerequisite to a determination whether competition is, proximately and ultimately, promoted or inhibited by discrimination. This approach, unlike the Supreme Court opinion in *Utah Pie*, focuses on the central purpose of antitrust law, competitive market effect. Friends as well as foes of an anti-price-discrimination law, for example, have expressed grave doubts about the appropriateness of an automatic rule regarding sporadic or selective area price discrimination of the type involved

---

Gee, *Predatory Price Cutting: The Standard Oil (N.J.) Case,* 1 J. LAW & ECON. 137 (1958).

[25] *See, e.g.,* G. STIGLER, THE THEORY OF PRICE 210–18 (3d ed. 1966).

[26] *See* Elman, *The Robinson-Patman Act and Antitrust Policy: A Time for Reappraisal,* 42 U. WASH. L. REV. 1, 13 (1966).

in *Utah Pie*. Commissioner Elman, for example, has commented in a recent article:

> In a local market dominated by few firms, the entry of a national seller prepared to lower its price in order to secure a foothold in a market may be the only cure for a rigid price structure characteristic of oligopoly. Such a national seller may be unwilling to lower its price in such a local market if it is required to make the same price reduction in all the markets in which it does business. Selective price cutting may also be the necessary first step in a general lowering of prices. . . . In general, a lack of uniformity in the prices of a national seller, competing in many geographic markets, may simply reflect the seller's flexibility in adjusting price to meet different competitive conditions in different markets. Insistence on price uniformity in such situations could lead to high rigid prices and thereby hurt competition seriously.[27]

The Commissioner might have had the facts of the *Utah Pie* case before him as he wrote this, as charts 1 through 4[28] clearly indicate. Chart 1 shows the oligopolistic nature of the Salt Lake City market and, in addition, indicates the importance of two large customers—Safeway Stores and Associated Grocers. The prime factor in Pet's mushrooming sales in 1959 was its contract for Safeway's private-brand business. The emergence of Associated Grocers as an even larger account for Utah Pie in 1960 allowed the latter to increase its sales and partially recoup the market share lost to Pet in 1959. Notable also in chart 1 is the decline in Pet's private-brand sales to Safeway in 1960 and 1961 while Utah Pie's business with Associated Grocers continued to rise. It is also apparent that except for 1961 Continental was a minor factor in the market. One conclusion is eminently clear: if any rival was being killed, it was not Utah Pie.

Charts 2 and 3 compare the lowest prices charged by Pet and Carnation month

[27] *Id.*

[28] The charts are compiled from data contained in the Supreme Court and appellate court opinions.

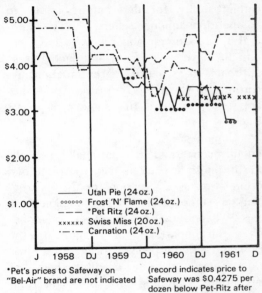

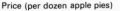

Price (per dozen apple pies)

—— Utah Pie (24 oz.)
ooooooo Frost 'N' Flame (24 oz.)
– – – *Pet Ritz (24 oz.)
xxxxxx Swiss Miss (20 oz.)
·—·— Carnation (24 oz.)

J 1958 DJ 1959 DJ 1960 DJ 1961 D

*Pet's prices to Safeway on "Bel-Air" brand are not indicated

(record indicates price to Safeway was $0.4275 per dozen below Pet-Ritz after Dec. '59, but individual data by area not shown)

Chart 4

Lowest Prices in Salt Lake City Market by Brand

by month in several Western markets. There was clearly no consistent pattern; indeed, prices were lower in Utah than in other areas for either company only in several exceptional months of the 44 months reported. This sort of sporadic, unsystematic hodgepodge of price differences is precisely what Elman has described as "seller's flexibility in adjusting price to meet different competitive conditions in different markets."

Chart 4 depicts the lowest price offers month by month of the three major competitors in the Salt Lake City market. The downward trend of prices is apparent. The generally lower prices of the Utah Pie Company indicate the market conditions faced by its competitors. The comparison of prices surely does not show Pet or Carnation as price aggressors, much less potential "rival killers."

A reappraisal of standards for competitive injury is urgently needed, as Elman argues. "It should be clear," he wrote, "that a simple test of whether a price reduction results in a diversion of business cannot suffice for determining injury to competition among sellers." [29] The Federal Trade Commission seems to have begun to move away from any such per se approach to area price discrimination, according to Elman.[30] Mr. Justice White has apparently stopped this movement in its tracks.

Commissioner Elman is, however, equally concerned that national firms selling in multiple markets may use price discrimination as a "weapon for the destruction of competition." [31] The weakness of this "weapon theory," however, reemphasizes the importance of recognizing the procompetitive aspects of price discrimination. There just is no credible theory of predation explaining how price discrimination can be an effective "weapon" in killing rivals. Such a theory would expose how the predator could use price discrimination as a means of imposing higher costs upon his victim than himself. Instead this condemnation of price discrimination relies upon what may be called a "deep-pocket" mythology. If a deep pocket filled with loot from selling "goods of the same quality" in another market is to be viewed as providing funds for waging warfare, why do not gains from unrelated sales do the job as well? And what about a windfall from a wealthy relative? Indeed, why is not any departure from dead-level equality of wealth an equally good weapon with which to kill rivals? Could it not be argued as plausibly that all price competition should be banned because substantial equality of financial resources is beyond reach?

Outlawing price discrimination because it might transfer funds to kill or harass competitors deserves about as much support as outlawing income itself because it might be spent on burglars' tools. The procompetitive aspects of price discrimination, in contrast, are manifest. But one need not con-

clude that price discrimination is no more anticompetitive than other forms of aggressive prices, financed from unrelated sources, to deplore the *Utah Pie* decision. In the first place, the evidence that respondents Continental and Pet did in fact transfer funds earned elsewhere to finance price discrimination in the Salt Lake City market is at best shaky. Pet was sustaining accounting losses in its frozen-pie operations during the greater part of the period in question. To suggest, as Mr. Justice White seems to have, that the greater losses in the Salt Lake City market were in some sense made possible by smaller losses elsewhere defies logic. Respondent Continental sold below average total cost, but not below marginal cost. To claim that an entrepreneur meeting marginal costs and making some contribution toward overhead is not behaving in good businesslike fashion ignores elementary economics. And if entrepreneurs do in fact set prices by the sort of opportunity-cost analysis discussed earlier in conjunction with the "cost justification" defense, the very concept of sales "below (historical) cost" becomes irrelevant.

In the second place, the task is not completed even if it can be concluded that (1) the respondents in *Utah Pie* transferred funds to the Salt Lake City market in some conceptualistic sense, and (2) the antitrust law should regard such "loot" earned by a firm bent on expanding its empire, and with the marketing savvy to do so, as more "dangerous" than an untainted windfall to an untutored heir. A theory of predatory pricing, discriminatory or nondiscriminatory, must assume that the aggressor expects his temporary losses to be overbalanced by higher prices after his "victim" has been eliminated. This in turn requires the further assumption that neither the victim nor anyone else will reenter the market and eliminate the new monopoly when prices are raised. For this to be true there must be an effective barrier to entry or reentry. Much has been written—most of it more confusing than clarifying— about entry barriers arising from the unequal availability of funds to large and

---

[29] Elman, *supra* note 26, at 13–14.

[30] *Id.* 14.

[31] *Id.* 8.

small firms, or from the advantages of internal profits as contrasted with the financial markets as a source of funds. But the actual existence of such barriers remains a conundrum. In any event, these problems were never reached in *Utah Pie* because the plaintiff-petitioner was prospering.

The Supreme Court ignored these basic issues properly raised by a charge that price discrimination has or is likely to injure primary-line competition. In doing so it ignored its role of providing reasoned decision. The result is not very serious to pie-eaters in Utah. They can eat cake. But it is indeed serious that the antitrust law has been turned into a law against price competition. *Utah Pie* must rank as the most anticompetitive antitrust decision of the decade. This is no mean achievement

in view of strong competition from such decisions as *Brown Shoe*,[32] *Von's Grocery*,[33] *Clorox*[34] and *Consolidated Foods*.[35] The protection of competitors is characteristic of each of these cases. The decisions there, however, although muddled in their economic analysis and blind to important consumer-benefitting efficiencies, did not strike direct blows at competitive pricing. Prior to *Utah Pie* the Supreme Court never unequivocally required a restraint of trade.

---

[32] Brown Shoe Co. v. United States, 370 U.S. 294 (1962).

[33] United States v. Von's Grocery Co., 384 U.S. 270 (1966).

[34] FTC v. Procter & Gamble Co., 386 U.S. 568 (1967).

[35] FTC v. Consolidated Foods Corp., 380 U.S. 592 (1965).

42. Predatory Price Cutting: Notes and Comments[*]

BASIL S. YAMEY

I

In various post-war contributions to the analysis and empirical study of predatory price cutting, the practice has been defined as temporary selling, at prices below its costs, by a firm (or concerted group of firms) to drive out or crush a competitor. For convenience, the two firms will be called aggressor and rival, or predator and victim.

An early contribution, by John S. McGee, broke new ground by arguing that price cutting of this kind is not a sensible or profitable strategy for an aggressor to adopt since a better alternative is at hand.[1] He concluded: "Whereas it is *conceivable* that some one might embark on a predatory program, I cannot see that it would pay him to do so, since outright purchase [of the rival firm] is both cheaper and more reliable."[2] McGee did not consider specifically a close substitute for acquisition, namely the formation of a cartel between the two firms jointly to exploit the monopoly. In the earlier of two papers on predatory pricing Lester Telser noted this alternative, and concluded on lines similar to McGee's: "Either some form of collusion or a merger of the competitors would seem preferable to any possible outcome of economic predation."[3]

The key element in McGee's analysis is that predatory price cutting involves both firms, the predator and its victim, in unnecessary and avoidable loss of profits. In McGee's words: "Since the revenues to be gotten during the predatory price war will always be less than those that could be gotten immediately through purchase, and will not be higher after the war is concluded [as compared with the revenues after the merger], present worth [of the aggressor] will be higher in the purchase case."[4] Telser's more striking formulation is similar: "Price warfare between the two [firms] is equivalent to forming a coalition between each firm and the consumers, such that the consumers gain from the conflict between the firms. Since both firms can benefit by agreeing on a merger price, and both stand to lose by sales below cost, one would think that rational men would prefer merger."[5]

McGee's strong conclusion that monopoly achieved by the acquisition of the rival is cheaper than monopoly achieved by the elimination of the rival in economic war was modified by later contributors, including Telser.[6] Considerations omitted or

---

[*] I am grateful to R. H. Coase and G. R. J. Richardson for valuable comments and suggestions. Reprinted from 15 *Journal of Law and Economics* 129 (1972). Copyright 1972, The University of Chicago.

[1] John S. McGee, Predatory Price Cutting: The Standard Oil (N.J.) Case, 1 J. Law & Econ. 137, 138–43 (1958). See also Lester G. Telser, Abusive Trade Practices: An Economic Analysis, 30 Law & Contemp. Prob. 488, 494–96 (1965).

[2] John S. McGee, *supra* note 1, at 143; see also 168. The inclusion of the word "conceivable" seems to have been made to cover cases of error. The word "reliable" refers to the advantage of purchase of assets over their competitive elimination, since the latter course does not sterilise them from further use.

[3] Lester G. Telser, *supra* note 1, at 495.

[4] John S. McGee, *supra* note 1, at 140.

[5] Lester G. Telser, Cutthroat Competition and the Long Purse, 9 J. Law & Econ. 259, 265 (1966).

[6] For the relevant contributions, see Lester G. Telser, *supra* note 5, at 259–70; Richard Zerbe, The American Sugar Refinery Company, 1887–1914: The Story of a Monopoly, 12 J. Law & Econ. 339, 363 n.120 (1969); Donald Dewey, The Theory of Imperfect Competition: A Radical Reconstruction, ch. 7 (1969); Kenneth G.

dismissed in McGee's study have been brought into the analysis; and their inclusion serves to mitigate the conclusion that predatory pricing necessarily is economic folly. These considerations concern, *inter alia,* the elements of strategical and tactical manoeuvre which may affect the outcomes, including the long-term implications, of the alternative courses of action open to the aggressor. Some elaboration of these considerations follows.

The price to be agreed upon in the purchase of the rival is not a matter of indifference to the aggressor, can affect its choice of a strategy for dealing with the problem created by the presence of the rival, and may itself be capable of being affected by predatory pricing. Initially it is unlikely that the aggressor and its rival will make the same assessment and valuation of the latter's prospects of profits in the given situation. Two possibilities can be distinguished. First, initially the rival's minimum asking price may exceed the aggressor's maximum offer price (and, *mutatis mutandis,* a similar deadlock may exist when the formation of a cartel is at issue). A bout of price warfare initiated by the aggressor, or a threat of such activity, might serve to cause the rival to revise its expectations, and hence to alter its terms of sale to an acceptable level.[7] Second, initially the minimum asking price of the rival may be less than the maximum price the aggressor is willing to pay, so that a mutually satisfactory transaction would be possible. Nevertheless, the use, or the threat, of predatory pricing may be a useful

component in the course of bargaining in which the aggressor tries to beat down the actual price to be paid towards the minimum asking price, as well as to induce the rival to reduce the minimum price.[8]

The aggressor will, moreover, be looking beyond the immediate problem of dealing with its present rival. Alternative strategies for dealing with that rival may have different effects on the flow of future rivals. A policy of preserving monopoly by buying-up rivals may possibly be inferred from the purchase of a particular rival; and the purchase may then have the unfortunate effect of encouraging potential entrants to enter and to offer themselves as willing sellers, thereby progressively diluting the original owners' share of the monopoly profits. A policy of using predatory pricing, either regularly or occasionally, is likely to have a more discouraging effect.[9] It may be noted, in passing, that the effect of predatory pricing on the calculations of potential entrants makes it yet more difficult for the empirical investigator to determine whether or not a particular attempt

---

Elzinga, Predatory Pricing: The Case of the Gunpowder Trust, 13 J. Law & Econ. 223 (1970).

[7] It is conceivable that even where both the aggressor and the rival have identical expectations about the future profits of the latter, no acquisition price may be acceptable to both parties. This could be the case, for example, where the owners of the independent firm place a high value on their independence and on the ownership and control of their own enterprise. A period of losses induced by predatory pricing may change their attitude.

[8] It is not only the dominant firm or group which can initiate temporary price cutting in an attempt to achieve its anti-competitive ends. The analysis applies symmetrically to a dominant firm and to the independent rival. Provided that the rival has, or can expand its output to secure, a sufficient share of business in that sector of the market in which it wishes to concentrate its pressure—the sector could be a separate region, a particular class of customer, or selected qualities or varieties of the product—it can initiate price cutting with the intention of inducing the dominant firm to agree to a more favourable settlement (that is, a bigger share of the cartel or a higher acquisition price) than it otherwise would have been prepared to grant.

[9] Elzinga has suggested that the response of potential entrants to the driving-out of established independents by predatory pricing "is not easily predicted." The "demonstration effect" may deter some. On the other hand, others "may realize the inability of the dominant firm to continue such a costly practice and promptly enter." Kenneth G. Elzinga, supra note 6, at 240. The latter possibility cannot be denied. But a policy of buying up new entrants without a fight is bound to attract new entrants.

at predation succeeded in achieving its purpose.

The preceding considerations apply independently of any assumption that the rival has less easy access to capital than the aggressor. Where access is more restricted for the former, perhaps because it is the smaller firm in the relevant market, the relative advantages of predatory pricing may be increased. However, in assessing the impact of the relative ease of access to capital, it should be recognised that the drain on resources would be larger for the firm with the larger share of the affected market (assuming the costs of the two firms to be the same). The aggressor may ordinarily be expected to be the larger of the two firms.

The modification of McGee's strong proposition about the folly of predatory pricing makes it difficult to predict the frequency with which the practice is likely to be used and the types of circumstances in which it may be expected to be relatively more or less common. Nevertheless, the opinion has been expressed that predatory pricing will be rare. Thus Telser has written: "Although it does not seem possible a priori to predict the frequency of price warfare, these will be rare if entrepreneurs are reasonable and intelligent." [10] Zerbe's view is "that predatory price wars might occur but would be unlikely." [11] One imagines that these views are not only influenced by the appeal of McGee's analysis but also that they are coloured to some extent by the fact that systematic and searching examinations of the historical record have shown, in a number of cases, that supposed instances of price predation were nothing of the kind, or that the available evidence is incomplete or consistent with different explanations.[12]

It is not suggested in this paper that predatory pricing in the McGee sense has been frequent or is likely to be frequent even in the absence of hostile legislation. Indeed, because reasonably documented examples of the use of the practice are rare —a dearth intensified by the results of the thorough researches of McGee and others —there is some interest in presenting, in section III, a short account of one reasonably clear-cut example of predatory pricing, to augment by one the exiguous stock of recorded cases. Before coming to that section, however, the argument in the next section will suggest that predatory pricing, as it is currently defined, should be considered not as constituting a distinct analytical category but rather as being an extreme variant of a broader class of temporary price cutting practices designed to drive out or crush an independent competitor so that the aggressor can achieve or restore a monopoly position. Although their identification is beset with difficulties, examples of this broader class may not be so hard to find as are examples of predatory pricing in the strict McGee sense.

II

The crucial point in McGee's analysis of predatory pricing is that the practice involves predator and victim in unnecessary loss of profits. Such loss or sacrifice of profits is independent, however, of whether the deliberate price cutting by the predator takes the price below cost (say, below its long-run marginal cost or average cost): all that is necessary is that the price is taken to a level lower than that which would otherwise prevail. Any deliberate price cut to achieve some ulterior aim involves a sacrifice of profits of this kind. The only special

---

[10] Lester G. Telser, *supra* note 5, at 268.

[11] Richard Zerbe, *supra* note 6, at 363 n.120. See also Kenneth G. Elzinga, *supra* note 6, at 240.

[12] For studies of real or alleged instances of predation, see John S. McGee, *supra* note 1; Richard Zerbe, *supra* note 6; Kenneth G. Elzinga, *supra* note 6; P. T. Bauer, West African Trade

121–24 (1954); M. A. Adelman, A & P: A Study in Price-Cost Behavior and Public Policy 372–79 (1959); and Gt. Brit., Monopolies Comm'n, Electrical Wiring, Harnesses for Motor Vehicles: A Report on Whether Uneconomic Prices are Quoted (1966). See also F. M. Scherer, Industrial Market Structure and Economic Performance 273–78 (1970).

feature of price cutting below cost is that the loss of profits includes some loss in the absolute sense, that is, that the firm is "losing money." But nothing either in McGee's original analysis or in subsequent elaborations depends upon this feature, which cannot have any distinctive analytical significance.

It is true that in their expositions both McGee and Telser seem to assume that the price ruling before predatory pricing is instigated (or the merger concluded) is at the competitive level,[13] so that any deliberate price cut must be a cut below cost. But this restrictive assumption is not required for their analyses. In the duopolistic market situation which is postulated the initial price could be at any level, from the competitive price at one extreme to the monopoly price at the other. The considerations included in McGee's analysis would be relevant regardless of the level of the initial price,[14] and of the extent of the reduction from the price.

Again, the considerations which have led to the withdrawal from McGee's strong proposition do not depend for their relevance on the fact that sales are being made at a price below cost during the period of predatory pricing. The aggressor may be able to achieve its objective of eliminating or disciplining the rival and of discouraging potential entrants by means of price cutting falling short of predatory pricing as this is defined currently. The aggressor has an obvious interest in minimizing the extent of its price cutting to achieve a particular result, and has a choice of tactics. A smaller cut may in some circumstances be as effective as a larger cut, especially where the rival has reason to suppose that the aggressor will go further if necessary. On the other hand, a sharp initial cut may sometimes convey the intended message more emphatically and achieve the intended result more quickly.[15]

In so far as the aggressor's pricing behaviour may have the desired effect, this will stem from the rival's assessment of the aggressor's determination to frustrate its expectations, for example, as to the rate of growth of its sales and its attainable profit margins. It is improbable that the fact that the aggressor has taken price below its own cost rather than, say, to a level somewhat above it, would make any difference. It should be remembered, furthermore, that the rival at which the price cutting is being directed cannot know, save in extreme cases, whether prices are in fact being cut below the aggressor's costs, of which it cannot be fully informed. Moreover, in so far as it is the fact that sales are being made at prices below the cutter's costs that is considered to be the crucial element in predatory pricing, the message of the strategy may fail to get through to the victim who may not know which of the various possible concepts of cost—marginal or average, short-run or long-run—it should apply when trying to interpret what course the aggressor is following.[16]

---

[13] John S. McGee, *supra* note 1, at 140; Lester G. Telser, *supra* note 5, at 263.

[14] This is seen to be so even where the initial price is the monopoly price. The aggressor has an incentive to remove or neutralise the rival if the prevailing situation does not maximise joint profits because costs are higher than they need be.

[15] Thus one member of a shipping conference expressed the following view in the course of a rate-cutting war with outsiders in the 1890's: "We still think here . . . that it would be better to go at once to an irreducible minimum to show Hendersons [one of the outsiders] that we are really in earnest. The extra cost would not matter if it shortened the struggle." Quoted in Francis E. Hyde, Shipping Enterprise and Management 1830–1939: Harrisons of Liverpool 76 (1967).

[16] It might seem more relevant to define predatory pricing as pricing below the costs of the rival to be eliminated rather than to regard the predator's costs as the standard by which to appraise the character of the price cutting. But this alternative definition would carry no greater analytical significance. And, save in extreme cases, the predator would not know for certain whether the price he set was below the level of his rival's costs in their relevant specification.

In the recent Bolton Committee Report on Small Firms it is noted that the published ac-

It follows from the foregoing that there can be predatory intent in price cutting whether or not the aggressor sets its prices above or below its costs (in one or other meaning of the latter term). Apart from intent, the common characteristic of predatory price cutting in the broad sense is that it is temporary and that it is in the predator's interest to confine, where possible, the temporary sacrifice of profits to those parts of the market (regions, product varieties, classes of customer) in which the victim is trading.

It follows, further, that an outside observer may often have considerable difficulty in deciding whether predatory pricing has been practised, even when the category is widened by the removal of the condition that the price must be below cost for the action to qualify as predatory. This is so because a firm may reduce its prices for a variety of reasons and need not change them equally in all sub-markets or for all products. It may reduce prices because a new firm has entered the market or an established firm has increased its output, so adding to total supply. It may reduce its prices because of an actual or expected change in costs or in demand, or in an attempt to induce non-users of its products to become users. The predatory nature of temporary price cutting, where it is present, is a reflection of the aggressor's intention, which is to eliminate its rival as an independent competitor, not through the

exercise of greater efficiency in the usual sense but through a pricing manoeuvre containing an undertone of threat. Such an intention is obviously difficult to establish conclusively, and can be inferred with reasonable confidence only when the observer, be he judge or academic, has been able to gain a detailed and thorough understanding of the surrounding circumstances in all their complexity. It would certainly be incorrect to describe an established firm as a predator simply on the basis of a record that it had reduced the price of its product and then raised it when a rival withdrew or came to terms with it. Any attempt to define predation in this way and to brand it as illegal would make it virtually impossible for an established firm with a large share of the market to compete effectively with smaller firms or new entrants. (One may note, parenthetically, that, according to McGee's analysis it would be economic folly for such a firm to compete on prices either in a predatory or a non-predatory way—unless mergers by such firms were ruled out by law.) On the other hand, any attempt to narrow the definition by inserting in it the requirement that the reduced price be lower than cost (in some sense) would be inappropriate, since it has been shown here that selling at reduced prices above cost can serve the same purpose in the context of predatory intent. Moreover, the difficulties of identifying predatory pricing in the McGee sense are certainly no smaller than those noted above.

It is perhaps not surprising that it has been hard to find clear-cut historical examples of the extreme McGee variant of predatory price cutting, even when one is not unduly fussy about the appropriate definition of cost which should be used. But if it is correct to infer from the McGee analysis and its elaboration that predatory pricing (involving sales below cost) is likely to be rare or exceptional, it would also be correct to infer that predatory price cutting activities of a less extreme kind should also be rare or exceptional.

Temporary price cutting by dominant firms or groups has, of course, been prac-

---

counts of small, typically specialised, companies "may give a complete picture of the company's turnover and therefore the profitability of its limited range of products." (The disclosure provisions of companies legislation do not require diversified companies to give comparable information for each of their activities.) Fears were frequently expressed to the Committee that the large diversified company "having learned the profit margins of a competitor from his accounts," "could undercut his prices for a period and thus force his closure." The Committee reported that while this practice was "certainly conceivable," "no single case of this kind has been brought to our notice." Small Firms: Report of the Committee of Inquiry on Small Firms, Cmnd. No. 4811, at 307 (1971).

tised quite frequently. And although, as has been suggested above, there are severe difficulties in distinguishing between temporary price cutting which is predatory in intent and that which is not, it appears that the predatory variety may not have been uncommon. If this were the case, it would seem to follow that the weight to be given to the factors which weaken McGee's strong conclusion concerning the folly of economic warfare should be greater than that suggested in several of the contributions on the subject which have appeared since McGee's paper was published.

On the information available several of the bouts of price cutting rejected in the recent literature as instances of predatory pricing seem to be eligible as instances of temporary, localised price cutting designed to deal predatorily with an independent competitor. Further examples can be suggested. The use of "fighting ships" by shipping cartels (conferences) is well documented, the Mogul case discussed in the next section being one example. The essence of the practice is for ships belonging to the conference to be used to cut freight rates when and where independent rivals are active so as to deny them business and profits. The special rates are not offered at other times and places. Both the majority and the minority groups of the Royal Commission on Shipping Rings reported in 1909 in terms suggesting that such temporary price cutting was a standard weapon in the armoury of shipping conferences for dealing with interlopers. The majority reported that the practice (together with other practices) was used "until the opposition line is either driven off or admitted to the Conference," and the minority that "undercutting their competitors" continued "until they have driven them away." [17]

Other examples of temporary price cutting which may be predatory are provided by the use of "fighting brands" by a monopolist to meet the competition of a new entrant in those parts of the market where it is trying to become established or to extend its operations. A special brand is introduced for the purpose. Its sale is confined to the affected areas; the quantities offered are controlled so as not to make unnecessary sacrifices of profit; and it is withdrawn as soon as the objective has been attained, namely the acquisition of the independent by the monopolist, or the withdrawal of the independent, or its abandonment of plans for enlarging its share of the market. Good examples of the use of fighting brands are provided by the activities of the match monopoly in Canada from its creation, by merger, in 1927 to the outbreak of the Second World War. The dominant firm used the device at various times, and this suggests that the firm was convinced of its efficacy.[18]

The use of temporary localised price cuts probably with predatory intent can

---

[17] Report of the Royal Comm'n on Shipping Rings, Cd. No. 4668, at 35, 96 (1909).

"Perhaps the most spectacular instance of this practice [the use of fighting ships] was the Syndikats-Rhederi, a 'fighting corporation' established in 1905 by six important German lines trading out of Hamburg. The corporation pur-

chased four small and comparatively inexpensive vessels which, with others chartered from time to time, were hired out to the six owners of the syndicate to throttle competition. In time of 'peace' the syndicate's ships engaged in regular trade on time charters." Daniel Marx, Jr., International Shipping Cartels, A Study of Industrial Self-Regulation by Shipping Conferences 55 (1953). See also Alfred Marshall, Industry and Trade 434 n.2, 533 (1919: references to 1932 ed.).

[18] Can., Dep't of Justice, Combines Investigation Comm'r, Matches, Investigation into an Alleged Combine in the Manufacture, Distribution & Sales of Matches, *passim* (1949). For description and discussion of the use of fighting brands in the match industry in the United Kingdom, see Gt. Brit., Monopolies & Restrictive Practices Comm'n, Report on the Supply and Export of Matches and the Supply of Match-making Machinery, 59, 62, 85 (1953). For fighting companies, successful and unsuccessful, see Gt. Brit., Monopolies & Restrictive Practices Comm'n, Report on the Supply of Cast Iron Rainwater Goods, 23, 26–28 (1951); Report on the Supply of Electric Lamps, 43, 44, 90 (1951); Report on the Supply of Certain Industrial and Medical Gases, 21, 92 (1965).

also be illustrated from the workings of the basing point system in some industries. The normal operation of the system itself discouraged independent pricing because other sellers, regardless of their location, would match a reduction in a base price initiated by one of their number. The use of punitive basing points and punitive base prices went further. A small seller who was not adhering strictly to the rules of the system could be punished, and brought back into line, by the expedient of the cartel introducing a deliberately low base price in his principal production centre: all (or most of) his sales would have to be made at this low price because of his competitors' willingness to supply at that price in the affected area. This practice of localised price cutting was used, for example, with some effect in the United States cement industry in the inter-war years.[19]

It has sometimes been suggested that alleged examples of predatory pricing in a particular sub-market may be nothing other than manifestations of profit-maximising price discrimination. However, the various examples touched upon here cannot reasonably be regarded as instances of the exploitation by a monopolist of a perceived opportunity to discriminate in his prices between sub-markets in which demand intrinsically is of materially different price elasticities. The price differentiation is removed as soon as the rival comes to heel. The long arm of coincidence would have had to be in frequent operation for the successful neutralisation of the rival in such cases to have been coincident with changes in underlying demand elasticities.

However, while the explanation of the phenomena as instances of price discrimination may be rejected, it must be stressed that it is not possible, on the information available, to decide unambiguously whether all our examples of temporary price cutting should be classified as predatory or not. The distinction turns not on form but on intent; and on the latter the available information is incomplete.

III

This section presents an account of what seems to be as clear-cut an example of predatory pricing in the McGee sense (that is, involving selling deliberately below cost) as one is likely to find, bearing in mind the difficulties of tracking down all the relevant information, including data on the predator's costs.

In December 1891 the law lords in the House of Lords pronounced upon the activities of a conference of shipowners in the China-England trade designed to exclude competitors so as to maintain a monopoly. This important decision, *Mogul Steamship Co. v. McGregor, Gow and Co. et al.*, terminated litigation which had been started in 1885 and concerned events of that year.[20]

Shipowners regularly engaged in the China trade had formed a conference in 1879 to regulate freight rates and the sailings of the ships of each member. The object was to improve the profitability of the trade by removing competition among members, especially at the height of the tea harvest (May and June) when large

---

[19] Samuel M. Loescher, Imperfect Collusion in the Cement Industry, esp. 22–25, 125–29 (1959).

[20] Mogul Steamship Co. v. McGregor, Gow & Co., *et al.*, 54 L.J.Q.B. 540 (1884/5); 57 L.J.Q.B. 541 (1887/8); 23 Q.B.D. 598 (C.A.) (1889); [1892] A.C. 25. For contemporary views on the importance of the decision, see Notes, 8 Law Q. Rev. 101 (1892); and Leading Article, The (London) Times, Dec. 25, 1891, at 7. For recent comment on the decision and its influence on the development of the law in the United States, see William Letwin, Law and Economic Policy in America: the Evolution of the Sherman Antitrust Act 49–51, 148, 149, 176 (1965). The various successive judgments in the case were each the subject of a leading article in The (London) Times, Aug. 14, 1888; July 15, 1889; and Dec. 19, 1891. Some account of the background and course of the dispute is to be found in Francis E. Hyde & J. R. Harris, Blue Funnel: A History of Alfred Holt & Co. of Liverpool from 1865 to 1914, at chs 3 & 4 (1956); and Sheila Marriner & Francis E. Hyde, The Senior, John Samuel Swire 1825–98, chs 8 & 9 (1967).

quantities of tea were shipped from Han-kow and elsewhere down the Yang-tse-Kiang river to Shanghai, and thence to London. At some time before 1884 the conference introduced a 5 per cent rebate payable to such shippers as gave all their business to conference companies during the particular year. This was designed to discourage shippers from giving business to interlopers who might be attracted into the trade, particularly at the height of the tea season when demand for shipping space was high and, presumably, also relatively inelastic.

The plaintiff company, Mogul, was formed in 1883, with ships engaged pri-marily in the Australia trade. It had an interest in picking up freights in China at the time of the year when homeward freight was plentiful in China but hard to come by in Australia. In the 1884 season the conference allowed two sailings to Mo-gul ships,[21] although the company was not admitted as a full member. In the next year Mogul asked to be admitted as a full mem-ber of the conference, and threatened to cut rates if its request was not granted.[22] The conference refused the request, and decided to treat Mogul as an outsider which had to be excluded from the trade.[23] The reason for the refusal is not clear. There is a contemporary reference to a "dis-pute";[24] and The Times (London) believed that the exclusion of Mogul was decided upon "probably because the shipowners . . . believed that their own vessels and resources were sufficient to supply all the

demands of the trade."[25] Presumably Mo-gul had asked for an unacceptably large share of the trade, and the conference thought it more profitable to adopt tactics to exclude Mogul and to discourage others.

The methods of exclusion were the ap-plication of the loyalty rebate system to the disadvantage of Mogul and others, induce-ment of shipping agents in China to shun dealings with non-conference shipping lines, and the undercutting of freight rates when and where interloping vessels were active. In the first phase of the litigation only the rebate system was complained of; in the second phase, the other two methods were also at issue.

It is not necessary to give here an anal-ysis of the reasons for the decision of the House of Lords adverse to Mogul—a de-cision which was unanimous, which con-firmed a 2-1 decision in the Court of Ap-peal and which in turn had confirmed the decision in the Queen's Bench. It is suffi-cient to note, in broad terms, that the at-tempts of the conference to exclude com-petitors and to monopolize the trade were held not to be in unlawful restraint of trade; that the methods used by the con-ference were not unlawful *per se* (in that, for example, they did not involve violence, molestation or intimidation); and that the methods used did not become unlawful by virtue of the fact that they were used by a concerted group of firms rather than by a single firm. Present concern is to see whether the price cutting component in the conference strategy should qualify as an example of successful predatory pricing in the strict McGee sense.

The facts referred to in the law re-ports do not appear to have been in dis-pute. In 1885 the conference decided "that if any non-Conference steamer should pro-ceed to Hankow to load independently any necessary number of Conference steamers should be sent at the same time to Han-kow, in order to underbid the freight which the independent shipowners might offer, without any regard to whether the freight

---

[21] Sheila Marriner & Francis E. Hyde, *supra* note 20, at 148.

[22] *Id.* at 148.

[23] According to a trade paper, Mogul was "amongst the most inveterate ring men in London," and they instituted the action "because they were unable to participate in that which they subse-quently denounced as wrong and an evil." 17 Fairplay 1372 (London, 1891). See also 13 Fairplay 110–11 (London, 1889).

[24] The (London) Times, Aug. 14, 1888, at 9.

[25] The (London) Times, Dec. 19, 1891, at 9.

they should bid would be remunerative or not." [26] Three independent ships were sent to Hankow, two of them being Mogul ships; and the agents for the conference lines responded by sending such ships as they thought necessary. Freight rates fell dramatically. It was accepted in the Court of Appeal and in the House of Lords that they fell to a level unremunerative alike to independent and to conference shipowners. According to Lord Esher, Master of the Rolls, rates were "so low that if they [defendants] continued it they themselves could not carry on trade." [27] Several of the law lords made similar statements. Thus Lord Halsbury, L.C.: "The sending up of ships to Hankow, which in itself and to the knowledge of the associated traders, would be unprofitable, but was done for the purpose of influencing other traders against coming there. . . ." [28] Apparently in the event the losses of the conference were larger than those of the outsiders, since some conference ships sailed empty from Hankow, while all the outsiders' vessels were able to load up with some cargo and did not have to sail in ballast.[29]

It is reasonably clear that the intentions of the conference were those of predatory pricing, that the conference contemplated pricing below cost, and that in the event its members did cut prices below their costs (in the sense that the voyages in question were unremunerative at the prices charged).

It is more difficult to establish the even-

tual outcome of the predatory pricing practised in conjunction with the other restrictive arrangements of the conference. The more immediate consequences of the events of 1885 are blurred by the occurrence of other developments. In 1882 a shipping company, The China Shippers Mutual Steam Navigation Company, financed largely by shippers, had been formed primarily so that the co-operating firms could avoid the terms and restrictions imposed by shipping conferences.[30] Quite soon, however, the Mutual was working with the China conferences.[31] But in 1887 it withdrew from the conference arrangements and entered into an alliance with Mogul in terms of which the ships were to run under the Mutual flag as one line both outwards to China and homewards.[32] (It was this step which probably emboldened Mogul to continue with its expensive litigation.[33]) By 1891 the situation had

---

[26] Mogul Steamship Co. v. McGregor, Gow & Co. et al., 23 Q.B.D. 598 (C.A.) (1889), at 602.

[27] Id. at 610. Bowen, L. J., expressed the view that "All commercial men with capital are acquainted with the ordinary expedient of sowing one year a crop of apparently unfruitful prices, in order by driving competition away to reap a fuller harvest of profit in future. . . ." Id. at 615.

[28] Mogul Steamship Co. v. McGregor, Gow & Co. et al., [1892] A.C. 25, at 37. See also id. at 43 (Lord Watson); at 44 (Lord Bramwell); and at 56 (Lord Field).

[29] Id. at 56.

[30] Sheila Marriner & Francis E. Hyde, supra note 20, at 154–56. The formation of the first shipping conferences in the China trade naturally aroused the suspicions and opposition of some shippers. As early as December 1879 several shippers "decided on united action against the shipowners," and formed the China and Japan Shippers Association. The main bones of contention were the alleged elimination of competition in the supply of shipping services, the deferment of the payment to shippers of the loyalty rebates, and the treatment for rebate purposes of forwarding charges. The Association chartered some ships so as to become independent of the conferences. There were difficulties in securing such charters. In 1882 shippers took a more positive step in forming the Mutual to continue the fight against the conferences on a better organised basis. Id. at 150–56.

[31] Id. at 138–39, 156. But see Francis E. Hyde & J. R. Harris, supra note 20, at 71, where it is said that because of the hostile reactions and concerted actions of the conference companies "the China Mutual could do nothing but comply and between 1884 and 1887 the Company was forced to instruct its agents to agree to the Conference terms."

[32] Francis E. Hyde & J. R. Harris, supra note 20, at 72–73.

[33] Sheila Marriner & Francis E. Hyde, supra note 20, at 149.

changed once more. The rate war which had begun in 1887 had "continued with unabated ferocity," and Mutual "was finally forced to agree to Conference terms and became a member of a new Homeward Conference in 1891." [34]

Mogul was not admitted to membership of this conference then or later.[35] It is not included among the members of the Far East Homeward Conference listed in the Report of the Royal Commission on Shipping Rings of 1909.[36] The exclusion of Mogul from the homeward conference after 1885 is all the more noticeable and remarkable in that, after the events of the 1880's, the company was included as a member of other shipping conferences, including the conference on the outward trade to China and the Far East in which its main adversaries were engaged. In this capacity Mogul is listed in the Report of 1909 referred to above.

Thus the actions, including the predatory pricing, taken against Mogul in the 1880's appear to have succeeded in achieving the intended goal of excluding Mogul. The only minor qualification to be made

is that Mogul, after negotiations, was given "certain rights of loading on its own berth" in a Yang-tse port.[37]

It is obviously not possible to determine whether the predatory pricing was unprofitable in the sense that the conference might have achieved its objective at lower cost to itself without involving itself in selling its services below cost. The fact that shipping companies continued to use fighting ships after the Mogul affair suggests that predatory pricing and the standing threat of such action were considered efficacious. Price cutting by fighting ships did not, of course, necessarily involve prices below cost, but only temporary low prices. But it is the burden of the argument in section II that the *size* of the temporary price reductions is not to be regarded as the determining characteristic of predatory pricing.

The point is frequently made in the literature on predatory pricing that the practice makes little sense where entry into the industry or trade in question is easy. However, the Mogul story serves to illustrate a general point, namely, that predatory pricing, or the threat of its use, *may* itself operate as an effective hindrance to new entry even in situations where the conventional barriers to entry are weak or absent. In this respect predatory pricing, like certain other pricing practices, should be given a place in the analysis of barriers to entry.

[34] Francis E. Hyde & J. R. Harris, *supra* note 20, at 73. According to Sheila Marriner & Francis E. Hyde, *supra* note 20, at 166, the first new homeward agreement after the completion of the Mogul litigation took effect in January 1893.

[35] For the revision of the agreement in 1894, see Francis E. Hyde & J. R. Harris, *supra* note 20, at 82.

[36] Report of the Royal Comm'n on Shipping Rings, *supra* note 17.

[37] George Blake, Gellatly's 1862–1962: A Short History of the Firm 78 (1962).

Index

Texts of selected readings reprinted in this volume are indicated by boldface type.

M